PUBLIC

POLICY

PUBLIC

POLICY

Investing for a Better World

MICHAEL MINTROM
Monash University

NEW YORK   OXFORD
OXFORD UNIVERSITY PRESS

Oxford University Press is a department of the University of Oxford. It furthers
the University's objective of excellence in research, scholarship, and education
by publishing worldwide. Oxford is a registered trade mark of Oxford University
Press in the UK and certain other countries.

Published in the United States of America by Oxford University Press
198 Madison Avenue, New York, NY 10016, United States of America.

Library of Congress Cataloging-in-Publication Data
Names: Mintrom, Michael, 1963– author.
Title: Public policy : investing for a better world / Michael Mintrom.
Description: New York : Oxford University Press, [2019]
Identifiers: LCCN 2017035299 | ISBN 9780199975976 (softcover : alk. paper)
Subjects: LCSH: Policy sciences. | Political planning. | Policy
 Sciences—United States. | United States—Politics and government.
Classification: LCC H97 .M565 2019 | DDC 320.6—dc23
LC record available at https://lccn.loc.gov/2017035299

9 8 7 6 5 4 3 2 1
Printed by LSC Communications, United States of America

With love, to Jacqui True

There is another world—and it is this one

BRIEF CONTENTS

CONTENTS

PART I   FRAMEWORKS

CHAPTER 2   **THE POLICY-MAKING PROCESS   38**

CHAPTER 3 ## PUBLIC POLICIES AS INVESTMENTS   72

PART II   APPLICATIONS

CHAPTER 5

DEFENSE AND HOMELAND SECURITY   136

CHAPTER 10   SCIENCE FUNDING   324

PART III   An Agenda for Change

PREFACE

I believe we are here on earth to live, grow, and do what we can to

make this world a better place for all people to enjoy freedom.

—Rosa Parks

We live in a world exhibiting wide material differences among people, where the wealth and life prospects of those in some countries are phenomenal, while others elsewhere live in extreme poverty with little prospect of change. In this world, having a sound understanding of public policy is of great value, because the public policy choices that governments make can have huge consequences for their citizens, both in present times and well into the future.

This text offers a snapshot of current thinking about public policy. The evidence is grounded in public policy experiences in the United States, but the lessons for policy practice are universally applicable. The distinguishing contribution of this text is that it argues throughout that public policies should be treated as investments. Often in the past they were not, but today, investment models are starting to be used more systematically to guide government decision making. An opportunity exists to extend the logic of investment decision making to most government spending choices.

Since its inception, public policy education in the academy has lacked conceptual coherence in how it has introduced students to various substantive public policy issues. This shortcoming reinforces the view that it is entirely reasonable for policy making in specific areas to occur without reference to the broader portfolio of governmental interests and activities. Meanwhile, over recent decades, advisors in government have more commonly construed government expenditures as investments. Reports produced in the United States, the United Kingdom, New Zealand, Canada, and Australia often now explicitly portray and discuss a range of public policies as investments.

Treating public policies as investments is implicit in cost-benefit analysis, which government advisors now use routinely as they seek to clarify the impacts of policy choices. A key aspect of cost-benefit analysis involves calculating expected returns on investments. However, although all public finance textbooks and most public policy textbooks discuss how cost-benefit analysis can be performed, they rarely include any sustained discussion of public policies as investments.

It would be easy for an exploration of public policies that treats them as investments to become a narrow, technical exercise. I have avoided that here. While indicating the tools for treating policies as financial investments and measuring their return on investment, I seek to emphasize the importance of broadening the investment metaphor. Thus, among other things, I make clear—both in the ongoing text and in numerous case studies—how well-designed public policies can serve as effective platforms for the further development of programs and practices that, over time, add high value to citizens' lives.

In writing this book, I have been well aware of the scholarly tradition to which I am contributing. Milton Friedman's *Capitalism and Freedom* (1962) is recognized as one of the most important books on public policy published in the 20th century. Ideas in it subsequently influenced reform of public policy in many countries. Writing from the position of classical liberalism, Friedman put forward three central propositions:

- First, individual freedom is essential to human creativity and experimentation.
- Second, economic freedom is the basis of all other forms of individual freedom, including political freedom.
- Third, limited, decentralized government is the key to preserving individual freedoms.

Working from these propositions, Friedman contended that government had a fundamental role to play in society: "Government is essential both as a forum for determining the 'rules of the game' and as an umpire to interpret and enforce the rules decided on."[1] According to Friedman, in a free-market, capitalist economy, government is necessary for defining property rights, maintaining law and order, and ensuring a stable monetary system. Beyond these mandates, on a case-by-case basis, government may be necessary for two other reasons:

- First, government may need to exert control when goods or services are most effectively supplied by one producer.
- Second, government action may be required when the behavior of one individual can have implications for another, and where a voluntarily negotiated resolution is difficult to attain.

Friedman's propositions remain valid. Nothing in this book contradicts them. In the decades since he wrote *Capitalism and Freedom,* there has been a burgeoning of research concerning the impacts of public policies, and how differences in policy settings can produce different economic, social, and environmental outcomes. That research has been produced by scholars around the world, and studies have explored policy impacts in many jurisdictions.

Looking back 50 years or so, it is noteworthy that many political leaders in the United States and elsewhere have been motivated by the desire to limit the role of government in society. Frequently that motivation has come from worries over how to balance government budgets, rather than by any strict adherence to a specific ideology. That said, most of these efforts to limit the role of government in society have not succeeded, or have succeeded for only a short time.

If we consider the ratio of government spending to Gross Domestic Product, the picture becomes clear. In rich countries—those with membership in the Paris-based Organisation for Economic Co-operation and Development (OECD)—the size of government relative to the economy as a whole has been growing. When Milton Friedman was writing *Capitalism and Freedom,* government activity in the United States accounted for less than a quarter of all economic activity; today, it accounts for more than a third. The argument for limited government might have informed a range of battles over the appropriate role of government in society. But taken on the evidence, the argument for limited government has not succeeded.

My claim that public policies are investments has a strong normative aspect. By implication, the claim suggests public policies should yield benefits that continue through time and outweigh their costs. Public policies that do not perform in this fashion typically amount to poor, even inappropriate, uses of collective resources. In itself, this is not an argument for limited government. However, it does raise the threshold of acceptability for what constitutes good public policy.

If requiring that public policies should be treated as investments were to inhibit wasteful public spending, the investment perspective would be consistent with an argument for limited government. The differences matter, though, between the call for limited government and the call for public policies to be treated as investments. Those who promote limited government have often been content with shabby public-service provision. Indeed, some political leaders appear to have deliberately sought to limit government through offering services of such inferior quality that any remaining public support is rapidly eroded. Evidence is everywhere to support that view. In the drive for limited government and fiscal austerity, too often sight has been lost of how we might do more with less, and how we might continuously improve the quality of government services while improving efficiency.

The investment perspective is based on the view that all public policies should be treated as investments whereby current expenditures serve to promote better social outcomes for the future. The approach deserves careful scrutiny, because the normative implications—especially when public policy investments are construed narrowly—can be unpleasant. In a relevant commentary published in *The Guardian Weekly,* Madeleine Bunting noted that "caring for others cannot be toted up according to a calculus of costs and returns." Bunting went on to state:

> Care for children fits into a marketized understanding of relationships: we talk of "investing" in our children. The state sees children as important because of their future worth to the economy as labor. But in this marketized mindset, the elderly have no economic value; they are perceived as a burden. The only values ascribed to the elderly are found . . . in silver-haired celebrities still working. . . .[2]

Bunting's critique is not of the investment perspective so much as of the narrowness with which people apply it when discussing policy choices of governments or the day-to-day choices of citizens and family members.

In contrast, I take the view that good public policy analysis should begin by considering what goals governments wish to promote through public policy. Start with the goal of promoting public value. The analysis should then indicate an effective strategy—a model of investment—for increasing the likelihood that public value will be enhanced, rather than inadvertently displaced or ignored. Indeed, an assumption underlying this approach is that explicit and thorough analysis of government choices is the best way to move society in the direction of generating the greatest good for the greatest number of people.

The investment perspective can be applied in a manner that is consistent with the deeply compassionate goal of maximizing individual human well-being over the life-course. That is the approach taken here.

Through this text, I hope to encourage new generations of young professionals to take great interest in public policy and the workings of government. More people displaying sharp intelligence and public spirit are sorely needed to contribute powerfully to public policy debates in the United States and elsewhere. Grounded in the tradition of theoretically driven, evidence-based analysis, this text offers exactly the tools such people need to articulately discuss, debate, and chart future directions for government. That is how the best value-creating public policy legacies begin.

SPECIAL FEATURES OF THE TEXT

This text has been designed to illustrate the merits of using theory consistently and applying it in a similar fashion across very dissimilar policy areas. This approach represents an important point of difference with earlier textbook treatments of public policy.

Among the other key features of the book are the following:

GENERAL ORGANIZATION

- The text begins with a chapter that carefully summarizes the nature and purpose of public policy. Here, students will find explanations of common goals of government, along with descriptions of common policy instruments.
- Two framework chapters then provide overviews, respectively, of the policymaking process and the investment perspective. The investment perspective chapter introduces a new tool for policy analysis—the Policy Investment Checklist.
- With these theoretical building blocks in place, the book then covers eight major areas of contemporary public policy. Taken together, the topics of these chapters cover much of the range of contemporary government activity.
- The investment perspective is introduced in every chapter covering substantive policy topics. Throughout, a consistent approach to treating policies as

investments summarizes the cases under discussion. The Policy Investment Checklist is applied in every instance. This consistency of approach will help students see how the investment perspective can be effectively applied across a variety of policy contexts—and well beyond those covered in this text.

- Each chapter opens with a brief explanatory list of its content and ends with a summary, a list of key terms, questions for discussion, suggestions for further readings, and a list of useful websites.
- Each chapter also contains a discussion of policy making in the federal system of government.

COVERAGE OF CIVIL RIGHTS

Given the central importance of civil rights both in the history of the United States and to contemporary policy discussions, every chapter includes a section relating the policy focus of that chapter to the pursuit of civil rights. In this way, the text makes explicit the connections between every major area of contemporary public policy and aspects of civil rights. Indeed, the investment perspective on public policies is shown to be entirely consistent with the promotion of civil rights.

USE OF CASE STUDIES

- To make it highly accessible to students, the book contains many brief case studies highlighting broader theoretical points being made in the text. Each case is accompanied by critical thinking questions.
- Additional In Focus boxes provide further insight into specific topics or government programs discussed in the text.

ACKNOWLEDGMENTS

I have long had an interest in public policy. That interest was nurtured in my undergraduate years at the University of Canterbury, in New Zealand (1982–1985), where I was fortunate to be taught and encouraged by Jonathan Boston. I am grateful to Jonathan for indicating a career path for me in this area. He has supported me at every step in my career, and has talked at length with me about the focus of this book. I extend to him my sincere thanks.

My years as a policy analyst in the New Zealand Treasury (1987–1990) confirmed that working and studying in the field of public policy was the right vocation for me. I am grateful to colleagues from those days, including Edith Brashares, Brent McClintock, Mark Prebble, and Timothy Sinclair, who encouraged me to develop my analytical skills through further study.

As a doctoral student in political science at the State University of New York at Stony Brook (1990–1994), I learned much about public policy and policy research from the members of my dissertation committee: Mark Schneider, John Scholz, and Paul Teske.

In my first academic position, in the Department of Political Science at Michigan State University (1994–2002), I benefitted greatly from the mentoring and encouragement of senior colleagues, especially Jack Knott, Charles Ostrom, and Carol Weissert.

This book had its genesis in August 2010 in Washington, DC, during a discussion with my editor at Oxford University Press, Jennifer Carpenter. After I had just completed the manuscript of *Contemporary Policy Analysis,* Jennifer encouraged me to write another book covering a range of substantive areas of public policy, applying a coherent theoretical perspective throughout. Around the same time, I was invited by Bill English, then New Zealand's deputy prime minister and minister of finance, to chair a Taskforce on Early Childhood Education. I subsequently spent several months guiding and contributing to a wide-ranging policy project that resulted in *An Agenda for Amazing Children* (2011). I am indebted to Richard Walley who, as a senior manager in the New Zealand Ministry of Education, was a close colleague working with me on that project. It was during those months that I realized just how important it is to view public policies as investments.

In 2012, having spent almost a decade based in New Zealand, my family and I moved to Melbourne, where I took up a joint position as professor of public management at Monash University and the Australia and New Zealand School of Government. The position provided me with the time, resources, and perfect intellectual community for researching and writing on public policy. I laid out the plan for this book in my inaugural lecture, "Public Policies as Investments," given in the Old Treasury Building in Melbourne on February 20, 2012. I am grateful to Monica Pfeffer, of the Australia and New Zealand School of Government, for organizing the event. I subsequently elaborated on the ideas presented there in Occasional Paper No. 24, "Public Policies as Investments," published jointly by the Australia and New Zealand School of Government and the State Services Authority of Victoria in February 2013. Early research assistance was provided by Alix Jansen (at the University of Auckland), and Victoria Musgrove and Jane Hosking (at the Australia and New Zealand School of Government).

I am indebted to Joannah Luetjens, who, starting in 2013, undertook extensive research support for the project, and who continued to support completion of the book throughout the writing and publication process. I could not have had a better colleague in this regard. Barbara Conover came on board as development editor after the initial draft was completed. Barbara's many suggestions transformed the book, and I owe her deeply for her extensive advice and continuous encouragement. Thanks are also due to Madeline Thomas, who helped with preparation of the final manuscript.

I wish to thank Jennifer Carpenter at Oxford University Press for her enthusiasm and patience as the book progressed. I could not have asked for a better editor. I am also grateful to the many reviewers who provided excellent suggestions for improvement at every step in the book's evolution: Brenda Bushouse (University of Massachusetts), Kenneth Fernandez (University of Nevada, Las Vegas), Daniel Gitterman (University of North Carolina, Chapel Hill), David Konisky (Georgetown University), Greg McAvoy (University of North Carolina, Greensboro), Keith

Revell (Florida International University), Greg Streib (Georgia State University), William Wallis (California State University, Northridge), Karen M. Kedrowski (Winthrop University), Sherri L. Wallace (University of Louisville), Dylan Bennett (University of Wisconsin, Waukesha), Christopher Ellis (Bucknell University), Matthew Eshbaugh-Soha (University of North Texas), Kerri Milita (Illinois State University), Saundra K. Schneider (Michigan State University), Neal Woods (University of South Carolina), Richard Michael Yawn (Sam Houston State University), Dorothy Dillard (Delaware State University), Rosalie Schofield (Temple University College of Public Health), Andrea Mayo Jacks (Arizona State University), Richardson Dilworth (Drexel University), Patricia A. Jaramillo (University of Texas, San Antonio), Michael New (Ave Maria University), Mordu Serry-Kamal (Winston-Salem State University), Hugh Bartling (DePaul University), Michelle Belco (University of Houston), Aubrey Jewett (University of Central Florida), Craig Ortsey (Indiana University–Purdue University Fort Wayne), Derek Reiners (Florida Gulf Coast University), and Ronald G. Shaiko (Dartmouth University). I am also indebted to Andrew Blitzer, Keith Faivre, and James Fraleigh of Oxford University Press for their terrific work on production of the book.

Writing a book takes time and attention. I am grateful to my colleagues at the Australia and New Zealand School of Government for their understanding and support as I worked on this book. I wish especially to acknowledge John Alford, George Argyrous, and Michael DiFrancesco for our conversations. Anne Tiernan, at Griffith University, talked at length with me about issues in public policy development, as we co-taught a graduate course on policy design and worked together as consultants on an education reform project. I am grateful to Anne for her enthusiasm toward the investment perspective on public policy. Andrew Gunn, at the University of Leeds, worked with me in recent years exploring how the investment perspective can be applied to government funding and monitoring of university research. I benefitted from our many conversations. Thanks go to David Greig, another former colleague from the New Zealand Treasury, who introduced me to the literature on real options and investment under uncertainty. Jane Durlacher, a colleague at the Australia and New Zealand School of Government, provided initial designs for the book's cover and was continuously encouraging as the project evolved.

My greatest thanks are reserved for my family—for Jacqui True, my wife and Monash University colleague, and for our schoolboy sons, Seamus and Hugo. Jacqui and I talked extensively over several years about the approach and content of this book. She was especially helpful in directing me to literature on US defense policy. She also reported the value of the investment perspective after using it to assess provision of government social services in postconflict countries.

I appreciate the concessions my family made during weekends and vacation time that allowed me to keep this book progressing. Our shared lives continually reinforce the lesson that strong, early investments can yield incredible payoffs. Jacqui, Hugo, and Seamus also remind me that great fun can be had in the present, even as we carefully prepare for the years ahead.

ABOUT THE AUTHOR

Michael Mintrom is a professor of public sector management at Monash University. He holds a joint appointment at the Australia and New Zealand School of Government as academic director of its Executive Master of Public Administration degree, offered in collaboration with the organization's eleven university partners. Michael is past president of the Public Policy Section of the American Political Science Association. He is a globally respected expert on policy analysis and policy entrepreneurship. His books include *Contemporary Policy Analysis* (Oxford University Press, 2012), *People Skills for Policy Analysts* (Georgetown University Press, 2003), and *Policy Entrepreneurs and School Choice* (Georgetown University Press, 2000). Michael holds a PhD from the State University of New York at Stony Brook. He has taught public policy at Michigan State University, Monash University, the University of Auckland, and the University of Southern California. He lives with his family in Melbourne, Australia.

PUBLIC

POLICY

CHAPTER 1

THE PURPOSE AND NATURE
OF PUBLIC POLICY

Public policies comprise the rules governments enforce and the actions they take in society. Public policies are essential to establish orderly and productive communities. Systems of government both develop and implement public policies. Complications arise in federal systems of government because of questions over where policy-making authority should lie. Throughout this text, we will treat public policies as investments. Sound investments can generate ongoing good outcomes for societies.

After establishing the broader context for government and policy making, this chapter introduces the investment approach. It also explains common goals of public policy, including the promotion of civil rights. It then discusses the work of policy analysts and enumerates policy instruments used by governments. The chapter concludes by reviewing several indicators of well-being that clearly show how public policy choices influence the quality of people's lives.

This chapter introduces you to:

- The meaning of the term "public policy"
- The importance of collective action
- The purpose and nature of institutions in society
- Government structures for policy making
- Public policy formation in a federal system
- The treatment of public policies as investments
- The goals of public policy
- Public policy and the promotion of civil rights
- The work of policy analysts
- Policy instruments used by governments
- Indicators of well-being

Facing page: The United States Congress is a major forum for making public policy.

(Joshua Roberts/Alamy Stock Photo)

WHAT IS PUBLIC POLICY?

Public policy is a form of collective action intended to make the world a better place. This collective action is coordinated by governments on behalf of their citizens. **Collective action** calls for individuals to coordinate their intentions with others and accept that whatever outcomes emerge may differ from those they, individually, would have desired. In their interactions in the market and in other social arenas, individuals face freedoms concerning whether to opt in, stay, accept, or opt out of collective efforts. In contrast, when governments coordinate collective action, involvement is no longer optional. Once governments establish rules, all individuals within their jurisdictions must either follow those rules or confront the police powers of those governments. We will discuss collective action in more depth at the beginning of Chapter 2, which reviews the policy-making process.

Public policy consists of rules governments enforce and the actions they take in society. Good public policy facilitates human achievement. Consider the evidence. Compared with earlier generations, our lives are rich in many ways. Most of us have enough food to eat, enjoy good health, can read, and can do things that bring benefits and joy to others. Most importantly, we experience many freedoms. Actions that governments take create those freedoms. Through provision of public infrastructure, laws, security systems, public schooling, health care, and many other things, governments open new opportunities and choices for everyone. When we abide by rules defining socially appropriate behavior, we are free to think and act as we wish. We are free to apply our talents as we see fit.

This text explores how specific public policy settings can make a better world. When governments direct collective action effectively, they raise the odds that all people within their jurisdictions will be better off. Improved social and economic conditions encourage people to invent, create, and contribute in ways that advance human well-being. In this sense, well-designed and well-implemented public policies are investments. They guide people to act in ways that do not harm their fellow citizens and—more positively—make the world a better place for themselves and others.

This **investment perspective** on public policy guides the discussion in this chapter and the overall structure of this text. An investment occurs when an item or asset is bought with the hope that, in the future, it will generate income or appreciate in value. Investment always involves making a trade-off between present consumption and hoped-for future consumption. We must recognize the investment perspective for what it is—a powerful *idea*. And that idea is open to contention. Critics might argue the investment perspective is only marginally relevant to policy making, because politics and power drive policy choices. Of course politics and power matter, but ideas matter, too. Although this text makes clear the multiple forces shaping public policies, the idea that public policies are investments will guide our discussions of contemporary areas of public policy in later chapters. This reveals a distinguishing characteristic of the text: although it continuously acknowledges the power of institutions, interest groups, and political and ethical pressures, it accentuates the power of ideas. A discussion of public policy and its impact on the 2014 Ebola crisis (Case Study 1.1) illustrates the approach of treating public policies as investments.

case study 1.1 Fighting Ebola

Ebola is a deadly viral disease. Containing it requires effective public policy. Historically, infectious diseases like Ebola, HIV, influenza, and tuberculosis have devastated countries. A similar concern has emerged with the spread of the Zika virus.

Reported Ebola epidemics have occurred in Africa since the 1970s. Once contracted by humans, the virus can rapidly spread. In 2014, the worst-ever Ebola epidemic occurred in several countries—the highest number of reported cases being in Guinea, Liberia, and Sierra Leone. This outbreak led to around 25,000 reported cases and 10,000 reported deaths.[1]

The World Bank estimated the economic impact of this outbreak and concluded that funding swift action to contain the disease would be money well spent.[2] The Bank warned that significant economic harm occurs when people engage in **aversion behavior**—where people avoid work or school, or abandon travel plans, through fear of a catastrophic event. In this case, the fear concerned contracting Ebola. Governments need to manage a disease and simultaneously engender trust in citizens, so that people who are not at risk of contracting the disease remain socially and economically engaged.

Of course, there are good reasons for people to worry. People infected with Ebola face the threat of dying. Ebola spreads through contact with the blood or body fluids of people with the symptoms or through contact with the bodies of victims. So, when an outbreak occurs, victims' bodies must be safely handled to avoid spreading the disease. Such actions occur most successfully in societies with good sanitation systems, reliable sources of clean water, and hygienic, uncrowded housing.

Infectious diseases create classic collective action problems. Since infected individuals can transmit disease to others, it is risky to assume that everyone will voluntarily do the

A doctor wearing protective clothing treats a person with Ebola.

(Tommy Trenchard/Alamy Stock Photo)

right thing. Well-designed public policies become critical to stopping the spread of disease. Only governments have the authority and resources to coordinate actions to combat viral diseases. Even so, governments differ in their capabilities, and international responses are often necessary. Deadly epidemics highlight how much the good health of individuals depends on a well-functioning society, and this comes through enforcement of sensible rules, adequate infrastructure, administrative systems, high levels of general education, and appropriate training of health professionals.

In the United States, the **Centers for Disease Control and Prevention (CDC)** is the national public health institute. It operates within the Department of Health and Human Services. The CDC has long known that managing an epidemic means containing it at its source, and therefore has established procedures to arrest deadly diseases before they spread within the United States.

When the Ebola epidemic began in early 2014, the CDC worked with the United States Agency for International Development (USAID) to determine appropriate interventions to contain the disease in Guinea, Liberia, and Sierra Leone. With almost one billion dollars of funding made available, the CDC, USAID, and the Department of Defense sent over 3,000 aid workers to those countries. The U.S. government also worked with the United Nations to contain the disease. Because it has better resources than the governments of the nations where the epidemic was spreading, the U.S. government took the lead in several ways. It established 15 Ebola treatment units in West Africa, provided personal protective equipment and other medical supplies, trained health care workers, operated burial teams, identified chains of transmission of the disease, and worked with others to identify travelers who may have had Ebola before they left the region.

Subsequently, the U.S. Congress and President Obama approved a further $5.4 billion to fight Ebola. This involved preparing the U.S. health care system for Ebola cases, developing Ebola vaccines and treatments, continuing work in West Africa, and improving means of detecting the virus and preventing its spread. Also, the CDC and personnel from the Department of Homeland Security began in early October 2014 to conduct entry screening at five major U.S. airports to detect signs of Ebola or potential exposure among all passengers arriving directly from countries affected by the epidemic. A group of hospitals across the country made physical alterations to be able to effectively isolate large numbers of people should the disease spread within the United States.

In fighting Ebola in 2014 and beyond, the U.S. government led international collective action and engaged in well-orchestrated domestic precautions. Despite these efforts, in October 2014 a traveler from Liberia died in Texas from Ebola and, in the process, infected two nurses. One nurse later died. These fatalities led "Ebola alarmists"—mostly politicians and media figures—to question the government's preparedness for responding to a domestic outbreak.[3] However, the swift and comprehensive actions the government took greatly reduced the risk of an epidemic.

CRITICAL THINKING QUESTIONS

1. What aspects of the U.S. government's response to Ebola would you expect to be used to address the outbreak of other viral diseases?
2. How does the Ebola case illustrate government coordination of collective action?

The fight against Ebola illustrates several themes of this text:

1. There are many instances in contemporary society where carefully coordinated, collective action is required. Often, governments are most able to take the lead, given the resources and powers at their disposal.
2. Citizens can benefit greatly from the public policies that earlier generations establish. Good public policies function like good investments. They yield positive gains for society that it can realize over many years.
3. Many rationales can justify specific policy choices. Showing leadership, showing respect for the dignity of all human life, and exhibiting other laudable goals are often consistent with economic reasons for taking specific actions. The perspective of this text—that public policies are investments—is compatible with many other policy goals.
4. Making public policy is controversial. Although the U.S. government took actions to fight Ebola that were supported by expert judgment and received international respect, some commentators still criticized the government.

INSTITUTIONS IN SOCIETY

Governments can contribute to economic development and the overall well-being of citizens. But governments are not responsible for every aspect of social organization. People interested in public policy need a way to conceptualize broader social organization and the role of government within it. An institutional perspective is helpful. **Institutions** are sets of rules that structure how we interact in various social settings. Institutions help groups overcome collective action problems because they guide our behavior in given situations. Institutions reward actions consistent with desired social outcomes and punish undesirable actions. Institutions show themselves through organizations and the behavior of individuals and groups within those organizations. Long-standing examples of institutions include families, schools, professions, businesses, and sports.

Institutions and the people they guide typically develop efficient ways to impart relevant rules. Rules come in three distinct forms:

1. Formal statements of acceptable and unacceptable behavior.
2. Informal norms of behavior, passed on to new members through actions, examples, and lessons.
3. Internalized, unspoken, taken-for-granted notions that individuals hold concerning "how we do things around here."[4]

Rules can seem arbitrary. Consider driving. In the United States and Europe, everyone drives on the right-hand side of the road. In the United Kingdom and Japan everyone drives on the left-hand side. Once these rules are established we must follow them to avoid trouble. Other road rules make it explicit how we are to operate an automobile in a given jurisdiction. After taking exams to get a license, we are able to internalize the rules of the road. Soon, we are driving along the highway, doing everything right and hardly thinking about it. Following the rules keeps us safe, keeps other drivers safe, and allows us to focus on other things—like our plans upon reaching our destination. Driving rules facilitate well-coordinated collective action. Ultimately, that is the goal of all institutions.

By structuring actions and reinforcing acceptable behavior, institutions support human development, freedom of action, and creativity. Institutions also establish stability. In various social settings, rules typically place certain behaviors off limits. Yet this inhibition of freedoms opens space for people to get along, work together, and improve the quality of their lives.

The literature on institutions explains that well-functioning structures of government are required to support and shape other institutions in society.[5] Elinor Ostrom's influential studies of voluntary efforts to establish institutions highlighted the importance of shared interests, monitoring, and credible sanctions in the management of common resources among small groups.[6] However, this work also made clear that voluntary collective action becomes hard to maintain with growing numbers of people. Government involvement becomes necessary. With their powers to control resources and structure individual actions, governments enable massive scaling up of mutually beneficial, coordinated action.

GOVERNMENTS AS INSTITUTIONS

Governments themselves are institutions that set the terms upon which other institutions in society operate. They do not usurp other institutions. Rather, they establish rules about the nature and scope of the decisions that nongovernmental entities might make. When governments serve in this role, disputes become inevitable. For example, when governments make rules about employment conditions, tensions arise between representatives of governments and representatives of businesses. We might ask: Why should governments decide who can and cannot work, how long people can work at a stretch, and what kind of minimum wages should be paid? Aren't these private matters?

One thing is clear. Governments are needed to establish common ground and stability in society. Beyond the commune or small village, it is impossible to achieve wide-scale collective action without the presence of government. However, because government actions tend to limit and structure the powers of others, few actions taken by governments occur without controversy.

The observation was once made that it is better to have a police officer in everyone's head than one on every corner. Societies need well-functioning governments to set and enforce the rules as necessary. With one entity playing this role, it becomes easier for disagreements and tensions to be peacefully managed. At the same time, governments cannot act alone. Governments rely greatly on individuals and groups in society—on other institutions—to contribute to stable and productive social relations.

If governments were required to stand vigilant at all times to enforce all rules and correct any wrongdoing, soon all social resources would be devoted to those efforts. There would be no surplus capacity left for creative actions. Indeed, this "police state" system would rapidly collapse. The only way out of the conundrum is that individuals and groups in society actively contribute to the development of social order. That is why adherence to informal norms of behavior and the development of self-disciplining habits of mind serve as essential pillars that, along with the pillar of formal rules, ensure we can all get along together. Governments set rules and take actions that create new opportunities for human creativity, collective action, and social and economic development. These rules and actions comprise the essence of public policy. But all government rules and actions are predicated on general cooperation from nongovernmental entities.

The institutional perspective makes us mindful of the limits of public policy. As long as a high degree of goodwill is present between government and society in a given jurisdiction, there exists a fair chance that government actions will be met with expected actions from others. Most governments can introduce policy changes only when those changes have broad public support. This assumption suggests that stable, functional government is dependent on political leadership that is fully in tune with public sentiments.

GOVERNMENT STRUCTURES AND POLICY MAKING

When studying governments and policy making, we should begin by considering the **jurisdiction**. A jurisdiction can be a nation, state, city, or school district. Through history, many jurisdictions have established forms of government that serve to develop, adopt, and enforce public policies. We are most familiar with democratic forms of government. Here, the basic arrangements are the same across jurisdictions. However, differences in details can produce major differences in how democracies operate.

Within a jurisdiction, two questions arise. First, who are its citizens? Second, which citizens have the right to vote? Eligible voters are often called *constituents*, or simply, the *electorate*. Under forms of **direct democracy**, eligible voters get to deliberate and vote on each policy issue. Yet direct democracy can typically work only when the constituency is small. Thus, **representative democracy** is the most common form of democracy in mass societies and the form most commonly practiced in the United States. Citizens vote periodically for candidates who will represent them in deliberative bodies—such as committees, boards, councils, or legislatures.

POLITICAL PARTIES

Under representative democracy, roles emerge for political parties. Political party loyalties influence legislators' positions on particular policy proposals, just as they shape candidates' positions during election campaigns. Political parties have historically served the function of summarizing and signaling basic information about a candidate for office. If a candidate is a member of the Democratic Party rather than the Republican Party, this membership is assumed to convey the candidate's positions with respect to, among other things, the role of government in society, the level of taxation that is reasonable, and tolerance of income inequality. The role of political pressure on public policy making will be discussed in greater depth in both Chapter 2 and the Applications chapters.

THE LEGISLATURE

Public policy is generally formulated, debated, and approved in the legislative arm of government. Relevant **legislatures** are given names like the US Congress, the Wisconsin State Assembly, the California State Legislature, and the UK Parliament. Proposals for policy change are presented to the legislative body for consideration. If the jurisdiction is large, it is likely to have a legislature with a large number of representatives. It is impossible for all members of large legislatures to be fully briefed on all policy issues. Therefore, many legislatures have elaborate committee systems. These allow committee members with specific knowledge to efficiently consider policy proposals. They can then recommend to the main legislative body proposals they deem appropriate.

THE JUDICIARY

The **judiciary** is the branch of government that interprets legislation and tests its correspondence with the broader body of established law within a jurisdiction. Often, these responsibilities entail testing new laws against the provisions of the relevant constitution, to determine their fidelity to constitutional intent. The judiciary has been viewed as a policy-making body in its own right. Certainly, state supreme courts in the United States and the U.S. Supreme Court are powerful and influential bodies. However, judges do not write law. They can confirm laws, they can develop commentaries on interpretations of laws, and they can strike down laws—or parts of them—that they deem unconstitutional. Since the courts are the last resort for legislative interpretation, all judicial systems have elaborate appeals processes built into them. The presence of the judiciary places a powerful brake on the "adventurism" of legislatures when they are devising new public policies. If they are to make laws having any permanence, they must draft them in consultation with legal experts, so that they are likely to survive judicial scrutiny once they have been adopted by the executive.

THE EXECUTIVE

The **executive** of any government tends to comprise the leading political figure in the jurisdiction and his or her cabinet colleagues. In the United States, the executive is the president, supported by the vice president and various appointed cabinet secretaries. The cabinet secretaries preside over specific U.S. government departments. At the state level in the United States, the executive is the governor. At the city level, the executive is the mayor.

Across all democratic jurisdictions, the executive guides and controls the **bureaucracy**—the major "doing" part of government. Proposals for new public policies or for policy change often come from the executive. Policy proposals the executive sends to the legislature tend to be backed by evidence gathered, analyzed, and presented from units within the bureaucracy. Given its size and importance to making public policy happen, the bureaucracy is often portrayed as a separate branch of government, reporting to the executive.

INTEREST GROUPS, LOBBYISTS, AND THINK TANKS

Within representative systems, lobbying of representatives is commonplace. This involves different interest groups and lobbyists offering advice to representatives. **Interest groups** embody organized efforts of people who share common goals. Examples include groups representing banks, manufacturers, farmers, teachers, and medical specialists. Given the nature of mass politics, interest groups frequently lobby during policy making and also make financial contributions to electoral candidates. Although there should be a degree of independence between campaign funding by interest groups and their lobbying efforts, representatives often form policy views that are closely aligned with the interests of powerful allies.

Lobbyists comprise any people seeking to influence the policy preferences of law makers. However, the most powerful lobbyists are either those who represent significant interest groups, or lobbying professionals who act on behalf of paying clients. For example, when businesses or interest groups do not have the capacity or desire to employ full-time lobbyists, they may periodically use the services of lobbying firms.

Think tanks tend to be nonprofit organizations that gather evidence and make arguments with the intention of influencing the policy-making process. Like interest groups and lobbyists, think tanks have become increasingly important in shaping political discussions and debates as societies have grown in size and the issues that governments must wrestle with have become more complex.

PUBLIC POLICY FORMATION IN A FEDERAL SYSTEM

Federalism is a system of government in which multiple governments hold power over specific jurisdictions. Federalism exists in many countries around the world, especially those that are geographically large, with dispersed and diverse populations. In the United States, federalism refers to the coexistence of the U.S. government as the national government, along with the 50 state governments. Each state establishes laws that are solely enforceable in their own territories. Since all states in the United States contain multiple forms of local government, there are many levels of government and a lot of jurisdictional overlap. Effective management of intergovernmental relationships is vital within such complex structures.

The ideals of federalism historically have been tied to the ideals of democracy and freedom. In the United States, the War of Independence with Great Britain (1775–1783) was fought over issues of representation and taxation. Revolutionaries in the 13 colonies claimed Britain had no basis for imposing the **rule of law**— the notion that individuals should submit to rules made by a specific government. The Revolutionaries rejected imposition of taxes on people with no voting rights, and the colonies declared themselves independent states. Subsequently, at the Second Continental Congress, state delegates adopted the Articles of Confederation (1777), an early constitution that established the United States of America and that stayed in place until the drafting of the U.S. Constitution (1787) and its subsequent ratification (1788).

During the Revolutionary period, the national war effort and aspects of diplomacy were fully funded by contributions from the member states. This arrangement made the national government a creature of the member states, fully reliant upon them for authority and revenues. With limited resources, the confederation sometimes found it difficult to finance the war effort. This major weakness threatened the viability of the whole independence movement. When the U.S. Constitution was drafted, the Founding Fathers ensured that the new national government would have powers to independently establish its own revenue base by imposing taxes. To this day, federalism in the context of the United States sees the fifty states and the national government as independent entities, each with independent taxing authority and powers to govern. Within each state, local governments tend to be creations of the state governments. However, high levels of local delegation are commonplace, and it is usual for local governments to have their own tax bases (usually in the form of property taxes, levies, and fees).

The overlay of the U.S. government on the one hand, and the presence of fifty independent state governments and myriad local governments on the other, has created rich conditions for policy divergence and the diffusion of policy innovations. The system opens possibilities for local citizens to shape how they live together and solve problems of collective action. As we shall see in the Application chapters that follow, the price of such autonomy is that policy making at the state level frequently becomes fraught, with people differing sharply over what kinds of public policies are in the collective interest. Recognition of difference, and the need to respect it, also accounts for the seeming intractability of many policy disputes at the national level.

TREATING PUBLIC POLICIES AS INVESTMENTS

The central theme of this text is that public policies should be treated as investments. Here and in Chapter 2 we discuss key features of the approach. Then, in Chapter 3 we consider the investment approach in more detail. This introductory coverage sets the scene for discussing specific policies as investments throughout all of the Applications chapters.

The stance that public policies are investments implies that public policies should yield benefits that continue through time and that outweigh their costs. Public policies that do not perform in this fashion typically amount to poor, even inappropriate, uses of collective resources. Their purpose is hard to justify, and good grounds exist for abandoning them.

In itself, the investment stance is not an argument for limited government. However, it raises the threshold for what constitutes good public policy. If requiring that public policies be treated as investments were to inhibit wasteful public spending, then the investment perspective would be consistent with an argument for limited government. The differences matter, though, between the call for limited government and the call for public policies to be treated as investments. In the drive for limited government, sight has too often been lost of how we might do more with less, and how we might continuously improve the quality of government services while improving efficiency.

If we start from the position that public policies are investments, then shabby public service provision cannot play a part. The crux of the investment approach is to promote public value. Government revenues are to be used to make the world a better place. Available resources are allocated in a manner that yields the highest possible benefits. When public policies affecting various human activities are all treated as investments and they deliver on those investments, significant leverage is attained. Dollars spent to ensure good roads, schools, and health care systems contribute to economic growth. These investments can then enhance Gross Domestic Product (GDP) in the years ahead. Under such conditions (and assuming other factors are not promoting greater government activity), the size of government would be expected to decrease over time as a proportion of GDP. When governments maintain their commitment to funding sound public policies that operate as investments, the size of government relative to GDP should incrementally shrink from year to year. The result is an entirely reasonable form of limited government.

Treating public policies as investments can indeed lead to longer-term reductions in the relative size of government in the economy. For example:

- When individuals receive good schooling, the odds are raised that they will go on to be productively employed, taxpaying citizens who make limited demands on government services.
- Health care policies that encourage preventive care are known to reduce the risks that individuals' health will decline and require expensive, publicly subsidized medical interventions later in life.
- Effective systems of criminal justice can reduce the risk that juvenile deviants will fall into lives of crime punctuated by prison time. Keeping people out of prison can save a lot of taxpayer money.

These are just three examples of how treating public policies as investments can reduce subsequent demands on government spending. This focus on investing today to make savings tomorrow represents only the most direct claim for why an investment perspective matters. More importantly, people who benefit from a good education, who experience good health, and who live within the law have high-quality lives. Their education, good health, and good citizenship allow them freedoms and opportunities they would otherwise miss. The experience of living a good life is impossible to quantify in any simple fashion. Still, everyone benefits when as many people as possible are enabled to live well. Good public policy can produce that result, as the discussion of the value of higher education in Case Study 1.2 illustrates.

The discussion in Case Study 1.2 shows how we can use the investment perspective to assess specific public policies. The example exhibits the five major steps to treating public policies as investments, which we will discuss in detail in Chapter 3.

case study 1.2 Applying the Investment Perspective: The Value of Higher Education

The world's wealthiest countries have long-established systems of higher education. Students attending colleges and universities there generally benefit from government subsidies that support their studies. The United States makes subsidized and nonsubsidized student loans available to students, and the federal government guarantees their repayment. This guarantee has recently sparked contentious debate, because delinquent federally underwritten loans create major long-term government debt. Additional financial support for students from low-income families is provided through the U.S. government's Pell Grants. The federal and state governments also provide direct financial support to universities. All these programs reduce barriers to higher education.

Government support for individual students, and for universities as a whole, is based on the assumption that higher education produces public benefits. Policy makers have anticipated that whenever a student attends a university or college and earns a degree, both the individual graduate and the whole of society are made better off.

A public policy question arises: *What value does society derive from citizens holding university and college degrees?* Analyses of global production processes reveal that the highest rewards for producers now go to those firms whose primary contribution is knowledge.[7] Awareness of the gains from such activities as industrial research and development, product and service design, market analysis, process management, and effective maintenance of customer relations has fueled calls for improving society's overall level of education.[8]

For individuals considering higher education, or currently enrolled in a degree program, it makes sense to ask: What will be the payoff from all this study? Evidence from the Organisation for Economic Co-operation and Development (OECD), a Paris-based think tank, shows individuals who have pursued higher education benefit greatly through higher lifetime wages compared to those who with no education beyond high school.[9] In the United States, many studies confirm there is a large payoff for obtaining a university or college degree, even when accounting for the costs of study and foregone income. Anthony P. Carnevale and colleagues estimated that returns increase even further as people acquire traditional master's, doctoral, and professional degrees such as MBAs (see Table 1.1).

The evidence in Table 1.1 suggests that, over their lifetimes, holders of bachelor's degrees can expect to earn around 1.7 times the income of non–degree holders. Other studies indicate these wage differentials tend to increase as people spend more years in the labor force. Also, people with degrees are less susceptible to job losses during economic downturns. These gains by individual degree holders confirm the estimates of overall societal benefits of higher education.

Most importantly, people with higher education generate more social value through their work than those without, one of the reasons why employers are prepared to pay them higher wages. Further, people earning higher wages tend to pay more per year in taxes than those earning lower wages. Those taxes contribute in many ways to improved social outcomes for all.

TABLE 1.1 Estimates of Lifetime Earnings by Education Level Attained

EDUCATION LEVEL ATTAINED	MEDIAN LIFETIME EARNINGS (U.S. DOLLARS, 2016)
High School Diploma	$1,439,855
Bachelor's Degree	$2,414,624
Master's Degree	$2,847,855
Professional Degree	$3,673,966
Doctoral Degree	$2,809,629

Source: The methodology underlying the figures presented here is reported by Anthony P. Carnevale, Stephen J. Rose, and Ban Cheah, The College Payoff: Education, Occupations, Lifetime Earnings *(Washington, DC: Georgetown University Center on Education and the Workforce, 2011), p. 3, Figure 1.*[10]

CRITICAL THINKING QUESTIONS

1. Why do people with degrees tend to earn more than people without them?
2. Do the findings on the benefits of higher education suggest that all young people should strive to earn degrees? When might this not be a good investment?

1. We focused on existing policies and programs.
2. Because those policies and programs have existed for a long time, we were able to gather relevant policy evidence.
3. We sought to measure the desired effect—looking for evidence that higher education provides benefits for individuals holding university or college degrees and for society as a whole.
4. We assessed the costs and benefits of pursuing a particular action and, from there, determined the return on investment.
5. Our final step in the investment perspective is to offer robust advice—that is, we need to explain how the analysis was performed and note the benefits and limitations of that analysis.

These five steps form the core of the Policy Investment Checklist, a unique tool for policy analysis introduced in Chapter 3 and consistently applied throughout the Applications chapters.

GOALS OF PUBLIC POLICY

Governments bring order and stability to society. These give people opportunities to create and achieve, and thus contribute to a better world. As societies develop and become more complex, governments also assume greater responsibilities. The actions that governments take to promote good outcomes become more varied. Here, we review seven goals of governments and the public policies they establish and implement: (1) defending people and property and maintaining public order, (2) promoting human flourishing, (3) supporting effective nongovernmental institutions, (4) promoting efficiency, (5) promoting sustainability, (6) promoting social equity, and (7) advancing human rights. This list is not exhaustive. Nor are these policy goals mutually exclusive. Together, however, the goals help explain why governments do what they do.[11]

DEFENDING PEOPLE AND PROPERTY AND MAINTAINING PUBLIC ORDER

Assurance of our survival is fundamental to our pursuit of any other activities. In peaceful, orderly societies, it is easy to take for granted this essential point. However, threat of violence against us—initiated by fellow citizens, outsiders engaging in acts of terrorism, or other nations at war with our own—can rapidly curtail many aspects of "normal life." Feeding ourselves, raising children, and performing paid work all become more difficult when the risk of harm increases.

From a public policy perspective, the goal of defending people and property and maintaining public order is expensive. All governments must provide national defense and homeland security, activities we will discuss in detail in Chapter 5. We can broadly define this goal as keeping the peace in all forms, so citizens can confidently engage in social and economic activities that enrich their lives and the lives of others, without being threatened by other people or adverse natural events.

Defending a nation requires the establishment of military power sufficient to protect it from outsiders engaging in acts of war. The doctrine of the balance of power suggests that nations must be adequately armed to deter acts of aggression; that is, they must have the capabilities both to maintain the integrity of national borders and to take credible retaliatory action if a threat is imminent.

The United States has long spent more money on national defense than any other country in the world. However, the amount it has spent at any given time has fluctuated greatly. U.S. military spending generally peaks at times of war or heightened external threat. For a time during World War II, the United States devoted more than 40 percent of its GDP to military spending; recently that total has hovered around 4 percent.[12] This proportion remains high by world standards, although it has been eclipsed by proportions spent on the military in nations experiencing conflict and significant threats, like Israel, Pakistan, Afghanistan, Iraq, and Syria. As forms of warfare have shifted, and terrorism has become a greater risk in the United States and elsewhere, spending on homeland security has risen.

The expenditures noted here do not take into account another form of spending relating to defense and security. Most nations spend large amounts of money on diplomacy and other "soft power" efforts intended to build good external relations with other nations. Such efforts reduce the likelihood that hostilities will arise. For example, peace treaties and formation of military alliances all help to reduce international tensions.

PROMOTING HUMAN FLOURISHING

Humans appear to have an inherent desire to advance themselves. In families, that desire for advancement is manifest in how adults nurture children and young people. Humans often defer present gratification so they can invest in their own development or in that of others around them. This same desire for advancement occurs in the realm of business. The drive to achieve monetary success serves as a powerful motivator for business leaders to deliver products and services that customers like. The monetary motives of business leaders contribute to broader social outcomes. Once again, we can equate striving to advance ourselves and others with the desire to promote human flourishing.

Efforts to promote human flourishing are not solely geared toward individuals. Governments also take many actions intended to promote a sense of community. These can include adopting local planning rules, supporting education, creating social welfare systems, and advancing democracy.

SUPPORTING EFFECTIVE NONGOVERNMENTAL INSTITUTIONS

Through the rules and structures they develop and maintain, governments do a lot to support nongovernmental institutions in society, such as the family and the marketplace. Given the powerful role that governments can play in supporting institutions, it is often government that people turn to when they seek to promote institutional change. Indeed, many public policies are governmental efforts to reform and improve the workings of the broader set of societal institutions. For example, governments frequently use regulations to promote desirable actions by businesses and individuals—a topic we return to later in this chapter.

PROMOTING EFFICIENCY

Most people agree that we live in a world of scarce resources. However, because of human discovery and innovation, over time we have been able to improve the use we make of the resources we have. For example, advances in medical knowledge have extended life expectancies—allowing people both to enjoy more years of good health and contribute more to the lives of those around them. Discoveries that have allowed the development of metals, plastics, and semiconductors have contributed greatly to the quality of human life. Historically, efforts to transform public property into private property—such as grazing space for cattle and land for planting crops—likewise resulted in more efficient use of resources.

Governments can do a lot to promote economic advance and, hence, the over-all advance of human society. On this score, governmental efforts to support the development and expansion of markets have been vital. As market-based systems of commercial activity evolve, governments are often called upon to develop policies that promote more efficient outcomes. For example, when the costs of a transac-tion are not fully covered by those who pay for a product, there is a tendency for people to consume more of it than they would if they were responsible for all the costs. A case in point involves coal-fired electricity plants producing pollution, the costs of which have not always been reflected in electricity prices that consumers pay. Situations like these are often remedied by policy actions, which serve to pro-mote economic efficiency.

PROMOTING SUSTAINABILITY

The environmental movement, manifest in the actions of various interest groups across many countries, has changed how people think about human activity and its broader impacts. Increased knowledge of how atmospheric emissions contribute to global warming and of how consumer and industrial waste pose ongoing hazards has prompted governments to encourage sustainable development. **Sustainability**, or the ability to endure indefinitely, has become a significant consideration across a range of commercial, environmental, governmental, and household activities. Gov-ernments have tended to spearhead actions on the part of others by introducing new regulations, taxes, fees, subsidies, and other incentive schemes. In promoting sustainability, governments commit to related goals, including encouraging envi-ronmental protection and the use of renewable energy sources.

PROMOTING SOCIAL EQUITY

Everyone wants to be treated fairly. Most people also like to see others treated fairly. In addition, we might say that, just as we judge people by how they treat others who are weaker than they are, so we judge whole societies by how well they treat their weakest members.

A starting point for our thinking about social equity is the realization that we come into the world with different endowments of physical and intellectual capability. These affect our life chances. Further, the environments we are born into also influence how well we will be able to grow, develop, and ultimately take care of ourselves. Stark differences in our starting positions in life can have major implica-tions for the distribution of resources in society.

A commitment to respecting the human dignity of all people and the sanctity of life must include efforts to help those with limited abilities to help themselves.

When we show respect for the human dignity of others, we affirm our own humanity and our own sense of self-respect. Beyond such appeals to our humanity, two instrumental reasons exist for respecting the human dignity of all people and the sanctity of life.

The first is clear from the many stories about incredibly gifted and talented individuals who started life in difficult circumstances but who benefited from the benevolence of others. As a society, we gain immeasurably from the fully developed actions, creativity, discoveries, and tenacity of other human beings.

The second is a concern for maintaining the legitimacy of the social order. If people develop a broadly shared view that the governing structures are unfair, they can express high levels of social unrest. This in turn can hamper prospects for social harmony and for economic and social advance. Therefore, in the interests of preserving current institutional structures, it is expedient to ensure a degree of social redistribution that reduces wealth disparities. This legitimacy argument can also support government provision of benefits that extend to many groups in society, even when an income test would suggest that many recipients need no such benefits.

ADVANCING HUMAN RIGHTS

Efforts to protect and advance human rights represent a significant way that governments can promote human flourishing. Since it was adopted in 1791, the Bill of Rights that comprises the first 10 amendments to the U.S. Constitution has been a vitally important document for advancing and protecting human rights in the United States. Successive U.S. governments have sought to act in ways that are consistent with the spirit and letter of the Bill of Rights. It has been instrumental in protecting the freedom of citizens to worship as they see fit, to exercise freedom of speech, to be treated respectfully by government agents, to be fairly tried in courts of law, and to be protected from cruel and unusual punishments.

The Universal Declaration of Human Rights, adopted by the United Nations General Assembly in 1948, has promoted human rights around the world. Its 30 articles enumerate the rights that individuals should enjoy throughout their lives. The document recognizes the inherent dignity of all people and their equal and inalienable rights. It argues that no distinctions should be made among people on the basis of race, color, sex, language, religion, political or other opinion, national or social origin, property, birth, or other status. The Universal Declaration urges education to be made available freely to all and to be compulsory, at least at the elementary level. In addition, all people are to have the right to work, to free choice of employment, to just and favorable conditions of work, and to protection against unemployment.

As globalization has accelerated, flows of immigrants and refugees across borders have greatly increased. Now, more than ever, it is common to find many people living and working in countries that are far different from their countries of birth. Into these new contexts people bring their prior cultural assumptions, customs, and beliefs. Although many adapt to their new cultures, others seek to protect and pass on their cultural heritage. The multiculturalism that emerges from these processes introduces many opportunities to advance human flourishing, and for individuals to be exposed to different and exciting approaches to living a good life. Yet multiculturalism can also generate clashing views about appropriate social practices and how we should engage with one another. As part of their efforts to advance human rights, governments everywhere must find effective ways to mediate among the competing claims that different groups make for the recognition of the cultures and practices that are integral to them. The treatment of immigrants will be discussed further in Chapter 8, "Poverty Alleviation."

PUBLIC POLICY AND THE PROMOTION OF CIVIL RIGHTS

In the history of the United States, many political movements have worked to improve the civil rights of specific groups in society. Clear historical examples include efforts to eliminate slavery, obtain voting rights for women, and eliminate barriers to African Americans' full and equal participation in American society. Many struggles continue today, not only for African Americans and women, but also for a range of groups in society, such as people with disabilities and of diverse sexual orientations.

If we consider a variety of indicators of well-being and equality, it is clear that even today, on average, African Americans face many structural challenges in American society that make it difficult for them to enjoy the same social and economic privileges enjoyed by many white people. Likewise, despite having made major advances in their overall education levels, women in American society, especially those in the workforce, often feel they are held back from promotion or from some of the best work due to invisible "glass ceilings."

As other historically disadvantaged groups in society have observed various struggles for civil rights, they too have sought to remove barriers to their full participation as equals in society and the economy. The Americans with Disabilities Act of 1990 was a landmark effort to reduce a class of discrimination. Efforts to secure rights for the LGBTQ (lesbian, gay, bisexual, transgender, and queer) community—such as legalization of same-sex marriage and workplace equality— are ongoing. In many respects, the public policy goals in the United States of promoting social equity and advancing human rights have been subsumed within the promotion of civil rights.

Public policies can do many things to improve people's sense of security, their inclusion into society, and their capacity to be economically independent. The perspective that public policies are investments is fully consistent with the promotion of civil rights. To the extent that a society unjustly excludes or limits people from enjoying life as others do, it reduces its own potential to realize greater outcomes. Therefore, the current set of policy choices does not produce the return on investment that could be achieved through policy reform. The disproportionate incarceration rates of African American men in U.S. state and federal prisons serves as one kind of indicator that current policy settings are faulty. We discuss this matter further in Chapter 9, "Criminal Justice." The biases experienced by other groups when they seek promotions at work or nominations for political office suggest that more work is needed to make all groups in society feel welcomed for what they have to offer, and not judged or excluded because of specific differences.

Public policy, construed as investing for a better world, is never static. The struggles and gains of the past continuously open opportunities for us to explore how we can do things better. The promotion of civil rights, the making of "a more perfect union," should never cease. This objective does not negate the incredible improvements in civil rights that the United States has achieved in the past. It just reminds us that those who worked so hard before us to make the world a better place would expect nothing less of us than to follow their example. Yes, we should celebrate historic achievements. But we must also remember: the effort never ends. The world will indeed become a better place because people believe this—and then get to work.

In each of the Application chapters of this text, we return to the theme of pursuing civil rights. In this way, the text makes an explicit effort to show how treating public policies as investments is consistent with the advancement of civil rights.

THE WORK OF POLICY ANALYSTS

Policy analysts work in many organizations both inside and outside government. Government decision makers such as presidents, governors, prime ministers, cabinet members, and legislators have for centuries required advisors to assist them in considering the consequences of specific actions. As advisors began to rely on the careful analysis and interpretation of statistics, financial accounts, and other forms of evidence, the analysts producing this work often came from specialized backgrounds in economics, applied mathematics, and operations research.[13]

In the United States, the presidential administrations of John Kennedy (1961–1963) and Lyndon Johnson (1963–1969) employed a cadre of "whiz kids"—exemplified by Defense Secretary Robert S. McNamara—to develop highly detailed analytical work to support policy recommendations. The effect on Washington, DC, was galvanizing. Soon, members of Congress called for improvements in their own analytical resources. These included the establishment of the Congressional Budget Office (CBO) in 1975. Those outside government also saw the need to boost their analytical firepower, and soon many interest groups, lobbyists, and think tanks around the nation's capital were employing policy analysts to improve the quality of their advisory and lobbying efforts.[14]

This analytical arms race was replicated in state capitals across the United States during the 1970s and 1980s. A similar phenomenon occurred in national and regional capitals around the world. In an era when government systems had become large and complex, it was widely understood that people with sharp intellectual and communication skills were sorely needed to ensure that policy making was well informed. Since those early years marking the rise of policy analysis as a feature of modern government, the employment of analysts has continued to expand.[15]

Policy analysts make many contributions to policy making. As advisors, their most important work involves appropriately defining policy problems, identifying possible policy options to address those problems, and then weighing the positives and negatives of each option. Inevitably, this work involves identifying tradeoffs across different policy options. Good policy analysts do not simply look at a given problem and propose a satisfactory response. Concerned that solving one problem might cause another, they assess what the long-term effects of a policy change might be. To assist them in their work, policy analysts make use of various analytical frameworks. These include cost-benefit analysis and comparative institutional analysis, approaches we will define and apply throughout this text. Policy analysts also need to consider how policies can affect diverse groups differently. In so doing, they often draw upon other analytical approaches, such as gender and race analyses.

Last, policy analysts need to exhibit political astuteness.[16] Knowledge of the politics of an issue can help them determine what policy goals to emphasize in their analysis. Likewise, knowledge of the government's current fiscal situation—whether it is flush with cash or in serious debt—can help them develop the best financial advice for decision makers. We will discuss the work of policy analysts further as we proceed through the following chapters.

POLICY INSTRUMENTS THAT GOVERNMENTS USE

Over centuries, governments have developed increasingly sophisticated means of structuring interactions in society and promoting continuous social and economic advancement. Here, we review contemporary policy instruments falling into seven categories: (1) market making, (2) taxes, (3) subsidies, (4) regulation, (5) direct service supply, (6) funding and contracting, and (7) information provision and social marketing.[17] Governments often devise policy responses to specific problems that combine two or more of these instruments. This approach makes sense since all policy instruments have strengths and weaknesses. Given any specific context, combining complementary instruments can generate better overall outcomes than relying on a single instrument would.

MARKET MAKING

Markets operate through individuals and organizations pursuing actions they consider to be in their own interests. Prices in markets provide signals to producers and consumers. Producers generate more goods and services when they can do so while generating a profit. Consumers buy goods and services when they consider that they are getting a good deal. Because markets do not require central coordination and authority figures telling people what to do, they operate in a distinctive way from systems of government, where control and direction are central modes of activity. However, governments can create policy settings that enhance market performance. It is this facet of government that we refer to as **market making**. It has three aspects.

1. Establishing Property Rights   To operate efficiently, markets depend on clearly specified property rights and a system of rules and procedures that allow for their effective enforcement. These create a need for a legal system and a police force to uphold the rule of law. Markets also need a monetary system so that people can use cash as a medium of exchange. Stability of this monetary system is crucial. Inflationary pressures must be limited so that people can make accurate predictions about the future value of goods and services. This necessity calls for creation of government infrastructure, in the form of a central bank. It also requires systems of banking regulation that ensure people have peace of mind when engaging in transactions or planning for future ones.

2. Improving Market Performance   The second way that governments make markets concerns efforts to facilitate or improve the functioning of specific markets. Often, they achieve these by removing impediments to market activity. For example, if some parties to transactions routinely have more information than others and tend to use this information to their advantage, it is possible that the market will collapse. The market for used cars offers a classic case. It is helpful to know the history of a car—how many owners it has had, where it has been used, and if it has been involved in major accidents. Incentives often exist for associations of sellers or buyers or even nontrading third parties to provide information or establish other market conditions that allow the market to function. But if those remedial private-party actions do not transpire, government action may be called for. This could take the form of requirements for traders to reveal information or the creation of rules concerning fair trade practices.

3. Creating Market-Like Systems or Quasi-markets   A third sense in which governments act as market makers has become more common in the past few decades. As knowledge of market processes has deepened, governments have sought ways to create market-like systems or quasi-markets to allocate goods, services, and rights that otherwise would have been allocated by centralized government action. For example, governments now offer many services on a fee-for-service or user-pays basis. Toll roads provide an obvious case. Indeed, governments have increasingly considered ways to balance traffic flow on toll roads by charging more to use them when demand is highest. Governments also use vouchers as a method of subsidizing citizens' use of services while creating competitive dynamics in service supply. When citizens receive a voucher from the government, they are enabled to purchase specified services from suppliers of their choice. For example, families may be granted the right to purchase government-subsidized childcare services. Given that right, they can then shop around to find a childcare service that is most appropriate for their needs. Instances of voucher use have created new markets in education, training, and health care.

TAXES

All governments impose taxes; nobody enjoys paying them. By doing so, we give up spending and consumption options. Governments know that imposing taxes will make them unpopular. They also know that citizens will look for ways to avoid paying taxes. Thus, governments must take great care when imposing taxes, so that they attain their anticipated goals without creating other distortions in society.

There are two main reasons why governments impose taxes: raising revenues and influencing behavior.

1. Raising Revenues   Governments use taxes to raise revenues that fund all their other activities. Taxes make it possible for governments to develop policies and manage their organizational structures. Taxes come in many forms, including taxes on income, businesses, sales, and property, and fees for services. The most important aspect of revenue-raising taxes is that they need to have limited impact on the behavior of citizens. If income taxes were to reduce work incentives, or to lead people to hide their true amount of income, it would be difficult for governments to achieve stable, predictable revenues. The general insight that emerges here is that governments should try to avoid imposing taxes at levels that most citizens perceive as unfair or onerous.

2. Influencing Behavior   Governments also impose taxes—often called **excise taxes**—to influence behavior. Classic examples include taxes on cigarettes and alcohol and fines for traffic infringements or other illegal behavior. These taxes are not intended primarily to raise revenues, although sometimes governments do generate a lot of income from sources such as traffic fines.

SUBSIDIES

Governments provide subsidies, or cash transfers, to citizens, nonprofit organizations, and businesses. A **subsidy** occurs whenever an individual or entity receives cash from the government that is not a payment for service. Subsidies can also come in the form of service provision. For example, people may receive a service at zero or greatly reduced cost. In such cases, no cash payments go from the government to the recipients, but the recipients do experience a benefit equivalent to a deposit of cash into their bank accounts.

As with a tax, the intentions behind any given subsidy greatly influence how it is designed and administered. Because subsidies are funded from taxes, it is common for taxpayers who do not expect to gain from a subsidy to resist it. For example, elderly property owners on fixed incomes often resist local government efforts to raise property taxes for the funding of local public schools. Arguments about how to limit specific subsidies are motivated primarily by the desire to limit taxes and perceptions of too much government control of people's lives. Discussion and debate concerning the Affordable Care Act of 2010 provide a classic example in which people have argued against a subsidy—in this case, of health insurance—because they have wanted to limit taxes and the reach of government in society. (See Chapter 7 for a detailed discussion of the act.) Governments typically use subsidies for two reasons: helping those in need or influencing behaviors.

1. Helping Those in Need   Some subsidies are designed as social cushions, to help people or organizations during difficult or transitional times. In the first instance, they are not intended to change behavior. For example, people who have been in full-time employment but who lose their jobs and are required to search for new employment might reasonably be expected to live on any savings they have while looking for a new job. However, they might be entitled to a government benefit. In some countries, such as the United States, this is referred to as **unemployment insurance**; in others, it is called the **unemployment benefit**. In both cases, it is a subsidy in the form of a cash payment.

Most importantly, this unemployment subsidy is designed to help a person cover the costs of living with dignity during temporary unemployment—not to change behavior. It would be a policy failure, for example, if those deemed eligible for the subsidy were to claim it and promptly abandon their job search in favor of taking a holiday at taxpayer expense. To guard against such abuses, most subsidies of this kind come with caveats—typically a period of time between when a person leaves a job and when he or she becomes eligible for a benefit. There are usually also limits on how long a benefit will be paid, as well as requirements of proof that the person is actively seeking work or is enrolled in some kind of training. (Such matters are discussed further in Chapter 8.)

2. Influencing Behavior   Many subsidies are designed to encourage behavioral changes on the part of individuals and organizations. These payment "carrots" operate as mirror images of excise tax "sticks." Vast arrays of examples exist of government use of subsidies as incentives to promote desired behaviors. Many subsidies are almost invisible to most people. For example, they might come in the form of copayments from the government to general medical practitioners so that patients rarely need to cover the full cost of seeing doctors when they are ill. The reasoning behind subsidies of this sort is that it is better to have patients establish contact with the healthcare system shortly after the onset of illness, than to put off seeking help until the illness requires the more costly options of emergency treatment or hospitalization.

REGULATION

Governments can improve the well-being of all members of society by guiding the behaviors of individuals, families, nonprofit organizations, and firms. They often impose sets of rules, referred to as **regulations**, defining what is considered appropriate behavior. Government regulation comes in three main forms.

1. Technical Regulations   Governments use procedural and technical regulations to achieve greater safety and higher standards of professional practice in society. In all cases, the purpose of such regulations is to reduce the possibility of negative social consequences or harm arising from specific activities. Licensing represents a classic form of regulation. Individuals associated with the building industry, such as plumbers, electricians, and engineers, must all have up-to-date operating licenses and are usually required to hold specific forms of insurance to cover catastrophic events that might arise out of malpractice. For instance, to operate a crane on a construction site, people must obtain a license. Obviously, if crane operators were not held to specific standards of practice and knowledge, they could easily be a danger to themselves and others around them.

2. Economic Regulations   Governments use economic regulations to guide and constrain the activities of businesses in sectors where, for technical reasons, it is most feasible for just one or a small number of suppliers to operate. During phases of their development, large infrastructural industries such as electricity, railroads, and airlines have been subjected to significant regulation with regard to pricing arrangements and other aspects of their relations with consumers. Often, as industries mature and more knowledge emerges of how they operate, fewer government regulations are necessary.

   Deregulation, which involves reducing the amount of regulation currently in place, demands careful handling, however. By significantly altering the general operating contexts for industries, deregulation typically ushers in periods of **structural reforms**. These can have unintended consequences, such as the jeopardizing of continuous service, even when the longer-term results of a deregulatory move might be highly positive for consumers. Airline deregulation, introduced in the United States in the 1970s, created more opportunities for competition on airline routes. While the results have been generally positive, heightened cost pressures placed on airlines have sometimes led commentators to speculate that deregulation has raised safety issues by leading some carriers to cut corners on aircraft maintenance.[18]

3. Social Regulations

Social regulations cover yet another broad field of human endeavor. They can include rules concerning appropriate disposal and recycling of household waste, the amount of noise people can make in their neighborhoods, censorship of films and literature, the eligibility of two people for marriage, and appropriate ways to discipline children, among many other things.

A significant concern that arises whenever governments impose regulations is that they might reduce the potential for innovation to occur within the regulated area of activity—sometimes referred to as **technical lock-in**. Critics of heavy-handed or "command and control" regulation have proposed the use of alternative mechanisms to promote behaviors that will yield desired social and economic outcomes. For example, recent efforts to reduce greenhouse gas emissions have tended to make use of both regulation and tax-based incentive programs.

DIRECT SERVICE SUPPLY

Governments often take responsibility for providing services for public use. This **direct service supply** is most appropriate where the existence of adequate, consistent service provision would be unlikely if left to nongovernment entities. Most of the responsibilities for service provision that fall to governments do so because they have ended up in society's "too hard" basket. Examples of direct service supply include most local government services, such as water supply, sewage systems, roads, and parks. They also include national defense, the legal system, and police services.

It is useful for us to think of government involvement in direct service supply as consisting of two broad functions: funding and service provision.

1. Funding Services

Governments raise taxes to fund services such as public schools, roads, and sewage systems. In some instances, some part of the costs associated with service supply might have to be paid for by service recipients. For example, the basic infrastructure of water supply is usually funded by government. However, individual households usually pay for water supply based on how much they use. Sometimes this funding function of government is also referred to as "service provision"—that is, governments, through funding, make service provision possible.

2. Delivering Services

The second broad function of government in direct service supply is **service delivery**, in which governments employ the service providers and coordinate the creation and maintenance of the facilities that allow for service delivery. In the water supply example, governments often manage the reservoirs, pumps, and pipelines that supply water to households. They also employ the workers who maintain these systems and interact with consumers.

In all cases of direct government supply, governments take responsibility for both service funding and service delivery. However, considering these to be separate functions has led to a range of cases where governments have moved toward using other parties to engage in service delivery. In the case of public schooling, it remains commonplace around the world for governments both to fund and to supply schooling. Most teachers are paid as government employees, and school buildings and grounds are treated as government property. However, examples also exist in which funding and supply are separate. School voucher programs introduce the possibility of public funding of schools with private supply. As noted, when citizens receive a voucher from the government, they are enabled to purchase specified services from suppliers of their choice. In the case of schooling, companies or nonprofit organizations establish schools and employ the teachers. The ongoing viability of the schools depends on their ability to attract revenue, which is directly related to their ability to attract and keep students.

FUNDING AND CONTRACTING

The conceptual distinction between funding for service provision and actual service delivery introduces a significant question: When should governments do things for themselves and when should they purchase services from others? We can also think of this quandary as the "make or buy" decision. Many examples exist where governments act as the funders of services but contract service supply to third parties. Those third parties, which can be either corporations or nonprofit organization, serve as intermediaries between the government and the service recipients.

Funding and contracting have been attractive to many governments—both national and local—because they are a useful way to reduce the costs of service supply. For example, a local government might fund garbage collection but contract private companies to do the actual work of regularly collecting and disposing of domestic waste. Those contract agreements might last for a period of several years before a new call is made for private companies to bid for the contract for the next time period. The likelihood that there will be competition for the service contract increases the pressure placed on each company bidding for the contract to offer the best cost and package of proposed services.

INFORMATION PROVISION AND SOCIAL MARKETING

The quality of human decision making is influenced both by the information that people have to base their decisions on, and by their abilities to effectively process that information. To a significant degree, efforts to carefully present information to people compensate for lack of understanding. Therefore, the quality of information and the effectiveness of its presentation are vital keys to promoting good social outcomes. Governments engage in a variety of efforts to support improved decision-making on the part of citizens.

It is common for producers to have more information about their products than average consumers. This informational difference need not be a problem unless the producers are tempted to use it to their advantage. Producers often recognize the value in sharing product information with consumers. But to help consumers make well-informed purchases, governments frequently apply regulations requiring producers to reveal specific product details. For example, packaging for most food products now includes a table or list setting out the main ingredients, energy content, and any ingredients that could harm people's health.

Governments can use other instruments to improve citizen decision making. For example, the increased uses of organizational report cards help citizens compare service provision on a variety of attributes. Many government websites provide detailed comparative information on the quality of schools, health care services, and other public services. Of course, nongovernment entities also produce report cards. College guides are a classic example, as are guides to the differing qualities and attributes of automobiles.

Thus, in many cases it is possible to access appropriate information without government efforts. But sometimes, because governments tend to amass high-quality information as part of routine monitoring and their efforts to ensure spending accountability, they may be better able than nongovernment actors to collate and present this information.

At a minimum, organizational report cards present comparative information and leave it to consumer-citizens to draw their own conclusions. However, we can also find report cards that contain advice-giving narratives. For example, many governments either fund or actually produce websites and supporting literature and activities designed to give advice on how to establish and run businesses and how to address common business problems or concerns. Government-supported websites offering advice on how to stay healthy are also prevalent, as are those that offer guidance to parents on child-rearing or raising happy, energetic, community-minded teenagers.

A further variation on the advice-giving efforts of government involves the use of public information campaigns, sometimes called social marketing. Here, governments make use of various media formats with the explicit goal of shaping citizen attitudes in the hopes that these will promote positive behavioral changes. An example is a marketing campaign to promote safe driving. At any given time, the package of activities for such a campaign might include graphic television advertisements, pamphlet drops in schools and workplaces, and use of billboards along highways. Other examples of social marketing include efforts to change people's consumption of alcohol and to encourage people to quit smoking. Often these marketing efforts reinforce the goals of other policy instruments, such as fines for driving infringements, taxes on alcohol and tobacco, restrictions on who can buy certain goods, and regulations prohibiting consumption of particular products in specific places.

INDICATORS OF WELL-BEING

The public policy choices that governments make can significantly affect the well-being of their citizens. When people feel safe, are protected from ill health, are well educated, and have good access to transport systems, they are better able to contribute to social activities and make economic contributions through paid work.

One way to assess well-being is through measuring annual economic output per person. Countries whose governments have established public policy settings that promote economic development have tended to perform comparatively well on measures of **Gross Domestic Product (GDP)** per capita. Some of those countries have effectively parlayed their relatively high per-capita GDP into even better rankings on social progress.

Economic growth typically drives improvements in human well-being. Since appropriate public policy settings can greatly facilitate economic growth, the annual measure of GDP per capita has long been treated as a useful indicator of how well governments have performed in contributing to the well-being of their citizens. Table 1.2 reports the GDP per capita in twenty-five selected countries, as of 2015. The differences among them are stark. For example, an average citizen in Norway had 20 times the purchasing power of an average citizen in Kenya. However, although improvements over time in GDP per capita tell us about how things might be for average citizens of a given country, they tell us nothing about the distribution of income within it. A country might be extremely wealthy, relative to other countries, and yet have very uneven distribution of wealth, leaving some people well off and others relatively poor. That observation has led various organizations to explore other ways of measuring and comparing the overall well-being of people living in different countries.

A number of alternatives to GDP per capita are now used to measure how well people live across the world. For example, the **Human Development Index** (HDI) is calculated and reported by the United Nations. Developed during the 1980s, it combines the measure of GDP per capita with measures of access to education and life expectancy. Table 1.2 also reports the HDI scores and world rankings for 25 selected countries. By comparing the rankings of these countries on the HDI with their rankings on GDP per capita, it is clear that the two are highly correlated.

The United States performs very well on both GDP per capita and the HDI. Indeed, because the United States ensures that all children have access to education, and life expectancies in the United States are relatively high by world standards, it ranks higher on the HDI than it does on the ranking by GDP per capita. A similar pattern exists for Australia, Germany, Japan, and New Zealand. In contrast, Iraq is ranked around the middle of all countries in the world for GDP per capita. But Iraq's ranking falls much lower on the HDI, given that the country operated under a dictatorship for many years and continues to be plagued by conflict. Egypt, India, Pakistan, and Sudan likewise drop further down in world ranking when we compare their relatively low GDP per capita against their HDI rankings. These countries have patchy records on access to education and do not perform well on life expectancies. We can conclude that the HDI offers more insight into the well-being of citizens in countries than does GDP per capita.

The Social Progress Index (SPI) first appeared in 2014. The SPI is calculated and reported by the Social Progress Imperative, a U.S.-based nonprofit organization dedicated to promoting broader discussion of factors shaping the quality of life for citizens. According to the Social Progress Imperative, "economic growth without social progress results in lack of inclusion, discontent, and social unrest."[19]

Measures captured in the SPI include, among other things, access to basic medical care, quality of water supply, personal safety, health and well-being, access to information and communications, access to basic and advanced knowledge, personal rights, and tolerance and inclusion. Table 1.2 also presents SPI scores and world rankings for 25 selected countries, alongside the values, scores, and world rankings on GDP per capita and HDI. As with the HDI, it is immediately apparent that a high correlation exists between the SPI and GDP per capita. However, some deviations are noteworthy.

The evidence in Table 1.2 shows some countries have effectively leveraged their relatively high ranking by GDP per capita into even better rankings on social progress. Canada, ranked 20th on GDP per capita, comes out 2nd on the Social Progress Index. A similar pattern exists for Australia, Denmark, New Zealand, Sweden, and several other countries. In contrast, the United States goes from a ranking of 10th for GDP per capita to 19th on the Social Progress Index. That pattern is unusual, and authors of the SPI interpret this gap as being driven by wide income disparities in the United States. These leave substantial sections of the population in fear for their personal safety and lacking adequate access to good nutrition, shelter, and medical care.[20] The United States ranks strongly, however, on measures that capture the opportunities it gives its citizens for success through attainment of basic and higher education.

The relationship between public policy and the development of advanced societies and economies is complicated. Good governments, through public policy settings, create conditions that allow for peaceful social relations, orderly trade, and economic growth. Yet changing social and economic conditions tend to generate new collective action problems, and these frequently call for development of new public policies. For example, historically, as national frontiers expanded and commerce developed, demand also expanded for governments to establish and enforce property rights, regulate trade, and provide suitable infrastructure to support economic activity in frontier communities.

Today, new frontiers are continually emerging. The provision of excellent transportation systems in the form of highways, airports, and shipping container ports can open new trading frontiers, easing the ability of domestic businesses to participate in international trade. New frontiers have also opened through advances in information technology and the Internet. This process has led to calls for governments to establish appropriate means of protecting intellectual property rights, ensuring the security of data shared on the Internet, and so on.

A further example of new frontiers is developments in biomedical research. As we learn more about the human body and ways of improving human health care, a variety of ethical, privacy, and funding issues have arisen, and many of these have

TABLE 1.2 Three Indicators of Well-Being for 25 Selected Countries

COUNTRY	INDICATOR					
	GDP PER CAPITA, 2015 (PPP[a] ADJUSTED)		HUMAN DEVELOPMENT INDEX, 2015		SOCIAL PROGRESS INDEX, 2016	
	VALUE	WORLD RANKING[b]	SCORE[c]	WORLD RANKING	SCORE[c]	WORLD RANKING
Australia	$46,270	19	0.935	2	89.13	4
Brazil	$15,390	77	0.755	75	71.70	46
Canada	$44,197	20	0.913	9	89.49	2
China	$14,450	80	0.727	90	62.10	84
Denmark	$48,009	16	0.923	4	89.39	3
Egypt	$10,913	99	0.690	108	60.74	89
France	$41,016	25	0.888	22	84.79	18
Germany	$48,041	14	0.916	6	86.42	15
India	$6,100	123	0.609	130	53.92	98
Indonesia	$11,057	96	0.684	110	62.27	82
Iraq	$15,394	76	0.654	121	52.28	104
Israel	$36,575	30	0.894	18	75.32	37
Japan	$40,763	27	0.891	20	86.54	14
Kenya	$3,088	149	0.548	145	53.72	99
Malaysia	$26,950	43	0.779	62	70.08	50
Mexico	$16,988	68	0.776	74	70.02	51
New Zealand	$37,575	28	0.913	9	88.45	10
Norway	$62,083	8	0.944	1	88.70	7
Pakistan	$5,010	134	0.538	147	49.13	113
Russia	$24,451	49	0.798	50	64.19	75
Sudan	$4,387	135	0.479	167	38.45	128
Sweden	$47,855	15	0.907	14	88.80	6
Switzerland	$62,557	9	0.930	3	88.87	5
United Kingdom	$41,755	22	0.907	14	88.58	9
United States	$56,115	10	0.915	8	84.62	19

Sources: GDP per capita: The World Bank Data, 2015, http://data.worldbank.org/indicator/NY.GDP.PCAP.PP.CD; Human Development Index, 2015: United Nations Development Programs, Human Development Report, 2015; Social Progress Index, 2016: Social Progress Index Report, 2016.

Note: The GDP values reported in the table have been adjusted to take account of differences in living costs across countries.

[a]PPP = purchasing power parity. [b]Calculated by the author. [c]Max = 1.000.

fallen to governments to address. These examples of expanding frontiers suggest that—even in well-structured, wealthy, and high-functioning jurisdictions—the relationships among governments, economic activities, and social processes are subject to continuous adjustment.

Knowledge of what public policies work well elsewhere is a vital starting point for local discussion concerning approaches to policy design. Still, as we will see in the chapters to come, many barriers can stand in the way of countries trying to adjust established policy settings, even when powerful evidence suggests policy changes could lead to overall better outcomes.

CHAPTER SUMMARY

This chapter has introduced the purpose and nature of public policy. Public policies are defined as the rules governments enforce and the actions they take in society. They are forms of collective action that establish an orderly and productive society. The separation of powers among the legislature, the judiciary, and the executive often makes it difficult for policy makers to introduce policy changes. Long-standing ways of doing things and particular political conditions also serve to inhibit policy change. Further complications to policy development arise in federal systems of government because of questions over where authority should lie in making public policy.

Although governments can do a lot to improve the well-being of their citizens, they must work effectively with other institutions in society. Families, businesses, and community organizations all play vital roles in a good society. When governments do not adequately align actions among these different institutions, they may not realize their policy goals.

This chapter has also introduced the key theme of this book—*that public policies are investments.* Well-designed public policies contribute to the good functioning of society and the economy. They establish the foundations upon which individuals and whole societies can flourish. In contrast, poorly designed and implemented policies can create a drag on society, holding everyone back.

After establishing the broader context for government and policy making, the chapter reviewed common goals of public policy, including the promotion of civil rights. Discussion included the work of policy analysts, and the policy instruments that governments use. As people interested in public policy, it is crucial that we understand why governments do what they do, and recognize the tools they use to change institutional arrangements and human behavior.

The chapter ended with a review of several indicators of well-being. The public policy choices that governments make affect their citizens' quality of life. The massive variation in indicators of well-being across countries suggests there is great potential for governments to productively apply existing knowledge of what works in the development of sound public policies in the future.

CONNECTIONS TO OTHER CHAPTERS

This opening chapter has presented the basic argument of the text—that is, public policies are investments intended to make the world a better place. Those public policies are the product of collective action. When effective public policies are established in a jurisdiction, the odds are raised that all people living there will be made better off.

In the following chapters, we initially consider frameworks for making sense of public policy settings. The first framework, presented in Chapter 2, is a characterization of the policy-making process. Chapter 2 also discusses program evaluation, a vital activity for improving our knowledge of how well implemented policies perform. The second framework, discussed in Chapter 3, treats public policies as investments, and explains how consistent use of evidence and application of cost-benefit analyses can do this. The eight chapters that follow apply knowledge of collective action, policy goals, policy instruments, the policy-making process, and the investment perspective to the assessment of specific areas of public policy: public infrastructure, defense and homeland security, public schooling, health care, poverty alleviation, criminal justice, science funding, and environmental protection. In the final chapter, we consider key lessons drawn from this survey and how they might shape future public policy.

KEY TERMS

Aversion behavior
Centers for Disease Control and
    Prevention (CDC)
Public policy
Investment perspective
Collective action
Institutions
Jurisdiction
Direct democracy
Representative democracy
Legislature
Judiciary
Executive
Bureaucracy
Interest groups
Lobbyists
Think tanks

Federalism
Rule of law
Sustainability
Market making
Excise taxes
Subsidy
Unemployment insurance
Unemployment benefit
Regulation
Deregulation
Structural reform
Technical lock-in
Direct service supply
Service delivery
Gross Domestic Product (GDP)
Human Development Index (HDI)
Social Progress Index (SPI)

SUGGESTIONS FOR FURTHER READING

Balla, Steven J., Martin Lodge, and Edward C. Page. *The Oxford Handbook of Classics in Public Policy and Administration.* New York: Oxford University Press, 2015. This book reflects on the ongoing influence of a large number of classic contributions to the study of both public policy and public administration.

Kernell, Samuel, and Steven S. Smith. *Principles and Practice of American Politics: Classic and Contemporary Readings,* 5th ed. Washington, DC: CQ Press, 2012. This volume brings together classic writings on many topics in American politics. The selected readings on collective action, institutional design, the branches of government, federalism, and civil rights are relevant to those interested in public policy.

Mintrom, Michael. *Contemporary Policy Analysis.* New York: Oxford University Press, 2012. This book offers an easily accessible, comprehensive introduction to concepts and analytical strategies used by policy analysts.

Moran, Michael, Martin Rein, and Robert E. Goodin, eds. *The Oxford Handbook of Public Policy.* New York: Oxford University Press, 2006. This book offers a set of literature reviews covering all major aspects of public policy. It is especially strong in discussions of institutional settings, policy-making processes, and policy instruments.

Theodoulou, Stella Z., and Matthew A. Cahn, eds. *Public Policy: The Essential Readings.* Boston: Pearson, 2013. This volume brings together many original articles and book chapters that have contributed to the development of the study of public policy.

WEBSITES

- The Organization for Economic Co-operation and Development is a Paris-based think tank, funded by 35 countries committed to democracy and the market economy. The organization collects a vast array of statistical and substantive policy information from its members, and offers useful information on many policy issues. http://www.oecd.org
- The World Bank was established by the United Nations as a source of financial and technical assistance to developing countries. Its primary goal is to reduce poverty through development. The Bank collects statistics and produces reports of high relevance to people with public policy interests. http://www.worldbank.org
- The Congressional Budget Office produces independent analyses of budgetary and economic issues to support the U.S. congressional budget process. This nonpartisan agency produces dozens of reports and hundreds of cost estimates for proposed legislation each year. https://www.cbo.gov/
- The California Legislative Analyst's Office is an independent source of policy advice to the California Legislature. It is known for its fiscal and

programmatic expertise and nonpartisan analyses. It produces reports on a variety of policy issues. Most other states in America have similar offices. http://www.lao.ca.gov

- The Brookings Institution is a privately funded, centrist think tank located in Washington, DC. Its website offers information relating to many contemporary policy issues. www.brookings.edu
- *The Economist* is a weekly news magazine headquartered in London. Its consistent position is that of classical and economic liberalism. It supports free trade, globalization, and the general expansion of markets and is opposed to intrusive government regulation of individual lives and individual choices. The magazine and its archive are a rich source of information for people with public policy interests. http://www.economist.com
- The *New York Times* is a high-profile American daily newspaper, considered by many to be the country's leading newspaper of record. The newspaper reports on leading public policy topics at the national and state level in the United States. Its archives can be helpful in building knowledge on specific public policy issues. http://www.nytimes.com

FOR DISCUSSION

1. The separation of powers among the U.S. Congress, the president, and the judiciary was a deliberate design choice of the Founding Fathers, which they embodied in the U.S. Constitution. Yet this separation greatly complicates the making of public policies. How does the separation of powers serve to promote discussion of policy ideas?

2. Specific policy problems often can be addressed by using one of several policy instruments. For example, smoking cigarettes has been discouraged for many years through a combination of taxes, regulations, and information provision. Discuss how each of these policy instruments has reduced the prevalence of smoking. Then list other examples where governments have combined policy instruments to pursue specific public policy goals.

3. People sharply disagree on the role of government in society. The Affordable Care Act (ACA) of 2010 prompted ongoing discussions about the role of government in American society. Why do people disagree on the merits of government-supported health insurance coverage?

CHAPTER 2

THE POLICY-MAKING PROCESS

To appreciate why public policies are designed in specific ways, we need to understand the nature of the policy-making process. This chapter introduces a framework for thinking about the world of public policy making. It highlights key considerations arising in contemporary discussions of the policy-making process. Over the past few decades, policy experts have devised several theories of policy making. The intent of these theories is to explain policy making in general; they do not restrict themselves to the level of telling us "how a bill becomes a law" in a specific jurisdiction. By presenting and explaining a framework concerning the policy-making process, this chapter sets the scene for interpreting major theories of policy making.

This chapter introduces you to:

- Government and collective action
- A policy-process framework
- Influences on policy making
- The five stages of policy making
- Policy making and the promotion of civil rights
- Policy innovation in a federal system
- Prevailing theories of policy making

Facing page: Chicago teachers protest expansion of charter schools in March 2013. In the policy-making process, it is common to find powerful, established interests who benefit from current policy settings taking actions that block proposals for change.

(Kenneth Ilio/Contributor/Getty Images)

GOVERNMENT AND COLLECTIVE ACTION

As we noted in Chapter 1, **collective action** calls on individuals to coordinate their intentions with others. When governments serve to coordinate collective action, voluntary involvement is no longer an option. Once governments establish rules, all individuals within their jurisdictions must either follow those rules or confront the police powers of those governments. Viewed in this way, collective action coordinated by governments inevitably comes with "a sting in its tail." The move from a world of voluntary participation to a world of directives and controls brings many improvements in the quality of our lives together. Yet we forfeit some freedoms toward that end.

Americans, like citizens of other countries, do not welcome restrictions on their freedoms. Indeed, most of us probably have believed at times we could devise better ways of doing things than the governments that have power over certain aspects of our lives. As much as we appreciate what governments do for us, we usually feel a pang of resentment when we see how much of our income we forfeit in taxes. Paying our taxes restricts our freedom in a salient way—our freedom to do what we like with all our income. At the same time, paying our taxes contributes to funding government actions that greatly extend our freedoms. Yet those extensions of our freedoms can be easy for us both to take for granted and to forget. This observation explains why we frequently contest government actions. It also hints at why public policy making is often a noisy, argumentative business. Politicians and those around them are a hard-nosed bunch. Nonetheless, most also tend to be deeply committed to improving society and to the creation of public value.

Otto von Bismarck (1815–1898), the first chancellor of Germany, famously observed that "laws are like sausages—it is better not to see them being made." Bismarck was masterful at diplomacy and coalition building. Aside from establishing Germany as a unified nation, Bismarck is also credited with initiating the first modern **welfare state**, where government provides a social safety net for citizens, to keep them from falling into long-term poverty. Bismarck did this through introducing accident and health insurance programs that kept the working poor fed, clothed, and housed. Legislators around the world often repeat Bismarck's laws-and-sausages observation.

Stanley A. Feder, president of Simply Sausage in Landover, Maryland, is a political scientist who took up sausage making after a career that included working for the U.S. Central Intelligence Agency. According to Mr. Feder, Bismarck's observation is an insult to sausage makers. In a sausage plant, everybody is on the same team. By contrast, when people make laws, there is a lot of contestation. If they were actually making sausages, legislators would be arguing over the recipe, and quite a few would probably prefer that no sausages be made at all.

"In sausage making, you generally have one person . . . who runs the business and makes the decisions," says Feder. "With legislation, you can have hundreds of cooks—members of Congress, lobbyists, federal agency officials, state officials."[1] That's the business. Blood, guts, good meat, bad meat, other stuff too, recipes old and new, and plenty of wannabe cooks crowding the vats. The miracle is, at its best, that this enterprise improves the human condition, and makes the world a better place.

A POLICY-MAKING PROCESS FRAMEWORK

To understand the policy-making process, we need a model that breaks it into logical parts. In this chapter, we will consider the policy-making process as a set of stages, each of which is subject to broad influences.

There are many forms of influence on policy-making. Politics is a central influence, as are various aspects of contemporary culture. Here, we distill all these various influences on policy making into three broad forms:

- institutions
- interests
- knowledge

These three broad forms of influence, which we will discuss in detail, are present at every stage in policy making. By shaping and constraining the actions of people engaging with the policy-making process, these influences provide the motivation that takes us from stage to stage. How institutions, interests, and knowledge influence the process depends, however, upon the specific process stage. The process framework developed here will help explain why specific policy proposals tend to be transformed during the policy-making process. It also offers insights as to why the nature of policy implementation can determine the ultimate effectiveness of public policies.

We can think of policy making as occurring in five stages:

1. Problem definition
2. Agenda setting
3. Policy adoption
4. Policy implementation
5. Program evaluation

After an initial discussion of the influences on the policy-making process, we will consider these stages in detail, noting especially the influence of institutions, interests, and knowledge at each stage.

Too often in the past, program evaluation has not been accorded the importance it deserves in discussions of the policy-making process. Because this text makes treating public policies as investments its central theme, we will avoid that omission. Indeed, Chapter 3 shows how evidence gathered through evaluations informs the estimation of returns from investments in public policies. Evaluation evidence has also heavily informed the discussions in subsequent chapters about public policies and their effects in specific policy areas. This approach offers another justification for incorporating the stages perspective into the policy-process framework.

The framework developed in this chapter is applicable to a range of policy-making venues—federal government, state government, and local government. It is also broad enough to make clear the ways that jurisdictional layers and the dynamics of intergovernmental relations might influence policy choices in specific policy-making venues.

INFLUENCES ON POLICY MAKING

Formal policy making occurs among people in positions of authority in government. These people represent the inner circle of policy makers. However, all policy makers are susceptible to influence from broader forces, and not just from those who immediately surround them. Although it is impossible to identify all the factors shaping and constraining policy making, we can sort most, as mentioned, into three major categories: institutions, interests, and knowledge.

Institutions include all structures and systems of rules in society—both formal and informal, governmental and nongovernmental. Institutions shape the actions of people in predictable ways. By studying relevant institutional arrangements, we can usually anticipate how they will affect specific aspects of policy making. **Interests** include all the ways that organizations and people believe their well-being can be enhanced or diminished by taking specific actions. We can usually identify material interests quickly and, from there, make predictions about the likely behaviors of individuals and groups.

Taken together, the study of institutions and interests gives us insights into how structures and actions interact. **Knowledge** is the third major influence we consider here. As human knowledge of natural and social phenomena grows, as our conceptions of the world broaden, and as technology develops, our perceptions of possibilities and limits of human endeavors change. As such, the expansion of knowledge, and how that knowledge is shared, can have profound effects on the policy-making process.

INSTITUTIONS

The current state of institutions influences the development and implementation of public policies and programs in any jurisdiction. We can see this influence when we compare the size, reach, and sophistication of government structures across countries. In those where there have been long periods of peaceful settlement, good social relations, and economic growth, concerted efforts have led to improved social and economic outcomes through government activities. It is no coincidence that effective infrastructure, well-performing schools, and good systems of government-subsidized health care and other public services exist in societies where the nongovernmental institutions are also highly effective. In contrast, some less developed societies with historically familial or tribally based systems of property rights seem stuck in situations of mass deprivation, with limited internal capacity for social and economic improvement.

These institutional differences and differences in governmental arrangements also have significant implications for human rights and individual freedoms. Even within highly advanced societies, such as the United States, there are stark differences at the state and local levels in the size, reach, and sophistication of government structures. Again, these generate meaningful differences in outcomes for individuals, their life chances, and their freedoms.

At a more focused level, current institutional settings can affect the types of social conditions that advocates of change might compellingly portray as public problems. For example, in societies with strong religious traditions and related philanthropic systems for supporting the needy and homeless, it may be more difficult to advocate for new government-funded social programs, such as subsidized visits to general practitioners, than it would be in societies where there has long been a well-established welfare state.

INTERESTS

Much of the blood and guts of politics associated with the policy-making process emerge from the clash of material interests inherent in any actions that produce rule changes. Individuals and groups get used to settled ways of doing things, and their different interests often drive political disputes. Those who are comfortable with the status quo often fight any change they perceive as a threat to their well-being. Interests can also reflect identities and people's desires for fair treatment, recognition, and respect. Since we sometimes perceive as selfish people who pursue or block policy changes based on self-interest, individuals and groups seeking either to promote or to block change will often make arguments that mask these basic interests. Thus, it is common for journalists and political scientists "to follow the money" when investigating the alignment of interest groups around specific policy issues. That is, they look carefully to uncover the financial benefits that specific groups derive—directly or indirectly—from the public policy positions that they most vocally support.

Interests play out in agenda setting and policy adoption, and it is here that they are most visible. However, people familiar with policy processes know that how problems get defined—the very first step in the policy-making process—can have major implications for what solutions get canvassed. Therefore, interested parties will often go to great lengths to influence the definition of problems.

Interests also play out during implementation, the fourth step in the policy-making process. Those who support a policy change are most likely to contribute to the implementation effort. In contrast, people who did not support the policy change might look for ways to block it during implementation. In the United States, federal government policy changes that have relied on state support for their implementation have often been embraced by states where there is strong political support for the president. However, they have been shunned in states where the president is less popular.

Interests can also be significant in promoting or blocking evaluations, the fifth and final step in the policy-making process. In this instance, the alignment of interests may be different from the alignments in earlier stages of the policy process. For example, program creation can establish new interests, in the form of program staff and recipients of program benefits. Such groups may be reluctant to see an evaluation completed because they fear it might prompt program changes that, from their perspective, would limit their interests.

KNOWLEDGE

The state of knowledge in a jurisdiction greatly affects each step of the policy-making process. As human knowledge expands, it is common for policy analysts to treat social conditions as public problems. For instance, establishment of a scientifically proven link between inhalation of tobacco smoke and the likelihood of contracting lung cancer has prompted many policy changes around the world. Likewise, with the amassing of scientific knowledge about the link between atmospheric pollution from burning fossil fuels and evidence of climate change, governments throughout the world have introduced policies to reduce the negative environmental impacts of human development. Just a few decades ago, only a handful of environmental scientists and activists took these matters seriously. Despite the naysayers, attitudes about the environment have changed, and the improving knowledge base has been central to that. So, when presented appropriately, knowledge can influence problem definition, agenda setting, and policy adoption.

Knowledge can also affect policy implementation. Knowledge from other jurisdictions about how to devise effective programs to achieve desired policy goals can strongly affect program design. In addition, knowledge can have profound implications for evaluation. For example, changes in knowledge may lead people to ask new questions about the effectiveness of certain policies and programs. At a more subtle level, new understandings of the merits of different analytic techniques can influence the ways that evaluations are conducted, information is collected, and implications are drawn from data analysis.

Federal systems of government offer many opportunities for the spread of knowledge, both horizontally across jurisdictions (i.e., from state to state) and vertically between jurisdictions (i.e., from national or local governments to states, and vice versa).

THE FIVE STAGES OF POLICY MAKING

Having noted major influences on policy making, we will now consider in more depth how those influences play out at each stage of the policy-making process.[2] Figure 2.1 presents a policy-making process framework that sets out these five stages, the influences on policy making discussed earlier, and key considerations that influence actions taken within each of these stages.

STAGE 1: PROBLEM DEFINITION

All public policies emerge from efforts to address specific problems through government action. Unless the public perceives them as having public relevance, those problems are unlikely to receive serious attention in the policy-making community. Whenever policy scholars and practitioners examine public policies, it is useful for them to consider what the public problem might be; that is, to come up with a **problem definition**. Over time they have developed a set of "market failures" that they know are the source of problems for which government responses are often

FIGURE 2.1   A Policy-Making Process Framework

STAGES	INFLUENCES	KEY CONSIDERATIONS
1. Problem Definition	Institutions ⇨ Interests ⇨ Knowledge ⇨	• Current policy settings • Identity of parties affected by problem • Energy, strength, and resources of advocates, those opposing change, and other interested parties • Salience of the problem • Quality of evidence concerning the problem and possible solutions • Beliefs about existence of a workable solution
2. Agenda Setting	Institutions ⇨ Interests ⇨ Knowledge ⇨	• Government priorities • Fiscal situation • Relative strengths of advocacy groups • Commitment of advocates • Issue salience and appeal • Effectiveness of problem definition and "softening up" activities • Strength of policy arguments • Evidence of workability of policy options
3. Policy Adoption	Institutions ⇨ Interests ⇨ Knowledge ⇨	• Government support • The electoral cycle • Effectiveness of agenda-setting activities • Energy and political astuteness of key advocates • Public mood • Fiscal situation • Strength of opposing forces • History of the issue • Quality of evidence concerning costs and risks • Scope of measures to be taken • Anticipated impacts
4. Policy Implementation	Institutions ⇨ Interests ⇨ Knowledge ⇨	• Strength of the legislative mandate • Absence of judicial challenges • Current organizational arrangements • Interest group opposition or support • Intergovernmental relations • Political savvy of policy champions • Breadth of political support • Workability of policy • Available resources
5. Program Evaluation	Institutions ⇨ Interests ⇨ Knowledge ⇨	• Maturity of the policy • Salience of policy and related programs • Strength of associated organizations • Stakeholder demand for evaluation • Public support for policy • Fiscal situation • Availability of appropriate evidence • Resources for evaluation

required. These include problems in markets caused by lack of well-specified property rights. As a result of such problems, people often benefit or suffer from transactions between others. For example, because a nearby car plant generates noxious fumes from its painting operations, citizens breathe polluted air. Other market failures can arise when parties to transactions hold different levels of information and those with the largest amount of information exploit the situation.

Of course, it is not simply problems with market processes that present grounds for government action. Often, problems arise because of failures of social institutions. Violence in the community, the rise of terrorism, or lack of resources for the elderly or poor can prompt calls for government actions. Public policy experts increasingly have come to view forms of government activity—or the efforts of people and organizations to exploit government funding—as sources of problems; these they refer to as "government failures."

The existence of a problem judged to be of broad public concern is not, in itself, enough reason to develop public policies to address it. Policy makers do not want to waste their time considering problems that do not have feasible solutions, as such efforts draw their attention away from solvable problems. They also raise the risk that the public will see policy makers as having tried and failed to address a problem. To maintain legitimacy, it is vital that policy makers carefully choose the problems they will tackle. Thus, those engaged in problem definition need to think carefully about how they can define a problem in such a way that policy makers can address it with a feasible—and politically acceptable—policy solution.

Various issues arise during the problem-definition stage. Current policy settings tend to shape discussions for two reasons:

1. Policies that are in place and are relevant to a given problem serve as anchors. They become the points against which all other policy ideas are judged during assessments of what is working and what is not.
2. Established policies tend to be supported by organizational structures. Those who work in and benefit from those programs will have specific views about where current problems lie and how they might be addressed.

In policy making, time and established practices matter.[3] Once a specific policy direction is in place, deviation from it becomes hard. This is a result of risk aversion on the part of decision makers, as well as the uniting of interests around existing systems.

Although current institutional arrangements and interests usually limit how problems are defined, knowledge can be crucial in prompting new definitions of problems. Various factors based on the provision of new knowledge about current arrangements and how they might be improved can shape the definition of problems.[4] For example, collection of information, summarized in indicators, can be a powerful way of demonstrating that a problem exists. Indicators can track changes over time within a jurisdiction. They can also allow comparisons to be drawn across jurisdictions. In this way, it becomes easy for policy makers to talk about deficits or excesses and explain how they might be tackled.

The Organisation for Economic Co-operation and Development (OECD) is a unique forum where the governments of 35 democracies with market economies work with each other, as well as with more than 70 nonmember economies, to promote economic growth, prosperity, and sustainable development. Every few years, the OECD, in its Programme for International Student Assessment (PISA), reports the aptitude of an international sample of 15-year-old high school students across a range of academic subjects. The reported results have prompted governments in many countries to conclude that their systems of public schooling are inferior to those of others. This assumption has subsequently triggered efforts to initiate significant educational reforms.

Table 2.1 presents results of the 2015 PISA tests. It allows for ready comparison between the average results for American students in mathematics, reading, and science, compared with the OECD average and results for other selected countries. This evidence suggests a pattern that has existed across all PISA studies since they were first conducted in 2000. That is, although average student results in the United States are close to the OECD average, they are significantly below those of other notable wealthy countries. For comparison, the table presents the results of a range of other countries.

Data collected as part of the administration of current programs can be the basis for discussion of system performance and arguments for the definition of problems in specific ways. **Focusing events** can also draw attention to problems. For example, the outbreak of a disease like measles among people in a specific region of the United States has triggered discussions of why immunizations have not been sought when they were available and what might be done to encourage their use.

Fifteen-year-old American students taking tests as part of the OECD's Programme for International Student Assessment. Its reports summarizing international differences in student achievement on these tests have promoted many discussions concerning the reform of public education systems around the world.

(Press Association via AP Images)

TABLE 2.1 Results of the OECD's Programme for International Student Assessment for the United States and Selected Other Countries: Average Scores, 2015

COUNTRY	MATHEMATICS	READING	SCIENCE
Brazil	377	407	401
Canada	516	527	528
Finland	511	526	531
Germany	506	509	509
Japan	532	516	538
Korea	524	517	516
Mexico	408	423	416
OECD average	**490**	**493**	**493**
Peru	387	398	397
Russian Federation	494	495	487
United States	**470**	**497**	**496**

Source: Table produced by author based on data reported in OECD, "PISA 2015 Results in Focus," Country Note: United States (2016), p. 5.

STAGE 2: AGENDA SETTING

Agenda setting is a catch-all term that describes how advocates, interest groups, and others concerned about specific public problems work to draw attention to those problems and their proposed policy solutions. Whether a problem or issue will receive much attention beyond the problem-definition stage will depend on the relative energy and skill of those seeking policy change, compared with those who are comfortable with the status quo. In thinking about agenda setting, it is useful for us to consider the ways that advocates make arguments, how they reach out to others in the hope of building strong coalitions for policy change, and how they shape their policy recommendations to take account of prevailing political conditions. Those political conditions include the ideological stances of parties in power, the overall economic situation, and the health of the government budget.

Public opinion can have a powerful impact on the issues that policy makers choose to engage. Politicians are well known to keep their eyes on the results of public opinion surveys, and to take many of their leadership cues from them. That said, many experts as well as media pundits believe that public opinion is malleable and can be shaped through the agenda-setting efforts of opinion leaders. In recent decades, political scientists have come to talk about the public mood.[5] **Public mood,** defined as a widely shared emotional state, can serve to condition the degree to which communities and individuals will support specific government actions. For example, a mood that exhibits suspicion for politicians and for government in general can place a brake on any efforts to introduce new government programs.

The initially lackluster and sometimes hostile public response to the Affordable Care Act of 2010 (ACA; also called Obamacare) offers a classic example of how mistrust of government can limit policy actions—even those expected to create generally positive results. We discuss this further in Case Study 2.3 later in this chapter, as well as in Chapter 7.

In the process of agenda setting, strategic policy action needs to take place on multiple fronts. However, agenda setting will generally have three key components:

1. Efforts to build a coalition among people and groups who are highly interested in the issue and who have information and resources that could prove critical for promoting policy change.
2. Efforts to expand the scope of interest, by using various publicity methods, discussion forums, meetings, and media campaigns to draw interested members of the public into the discussion.
3. Efforts to raise the issue onto the government's legislative agenda.

Within the agenda-setting process, knowledge use and interests become joined. Advocates draw on available knowledge and use it to make their arguments for policy change. Opponents likewise use available knowledge to make their arguments. Thus, various parties seek to be viewed as "voices of reason" or "neutral umpires" or "information brokers." Everyone wants to claim the truth. It is here that well-trained policy analysts and advisors with strong communication skills can make a big difference in the quality of the policy debate and, ultimately, in what ideas for policy change go forward.

Economist and Nobel Prize winner Paul Krugman observed that bad ideas are "like cockroaches," in the sense that no matter how powerful the efforts to get rid of them, they will inevitably return.[6] The problem for any of us, including Paul Krugman, is that nobody has a monopoly on the truth—an explanation for why there is the need for so much discussion and debate.

The goal of democratic politics—which facilitates the ongoing contestation of ideas, arguments, and knowledge claims—is that eventually some form of consensus will emerge. We will come to agreement on what the evidence is telling us. Given this goal, it is entirely reasonable to find that the public can ultimately view a specific public policy adopted to address a specific problem at a given moment as outmoded and in need of reform or removal. At the same time, since policies become programs and those programs serve to create supportive constituents, it becomes difficult to remove them. Thus, there are many reasons why most ideas for policy change never make it to the agenda-setting stage. Among those that do, just a handful eventually receive policy makers' serious attention.

STAGE 3: POLICY ADOPTION

For advocates of policy change, the primary objective of agenda setting activities is to have the policy issue find a place on the government's legislative agenda. This is when elected officials give issues the most attention. However, there are limits to how much legislation the government can consider in any given year. Therefore, various filtering processes determine which issues it will consider and which it will leave for another year. Judgments about the likelihood that an issue will receive serious legislative attention are crucial for determining what resources decision makers will devote to advocating policy change. In the best-case scenario, government agencies will devote their resources to careful exploration of the policy problem, the most relevant options for addressing it, the feasibility of implementing those options, and the costs and benefits associated with a policy change.

Politics plays a major role when it comes to considering a policy for adoption, just as in the agenda-setting stage. Various elements of the political environment powerfully affect the degree of traction specific policy issues get. Policy makers tend to consider more controversial policy changes shortly after an election. In contrast, heading into an election, policy makers rarely show interest in pursuing any legislative changes that could provoke an electoral backlash. Once again, consideration of the public mood matters, as does the fiscal situation. At a time when many people think government is too large or the economy is weak and there is a drive to rein in government spending, it is unlikely that policy makers will contemplate any policy changes that would come with a big price tag. Policy changes promising to generate cost savings would meet with more interest.

The history of a policy issue can also influence how much attention it will receive from legislators. For example, if a policy change were to build on current policy settings, policy makers would view it as less controversial and, hence, less politically risky than one that would move the government into new territory. As with agenda setting, the political astuteness of advocates matters for policy change. By making compelling arguments, advocates can create opportunities for themselves. The challenge is to transform perceptions of proposals from risky to safe. Sometimes, this move involves efforts to link newer, riskier policy issues to safer ones. In this way, it becomes possible for a new policy to be adopted on the back of a range of other, less controversial, incremental policy changes.[7]

Policy adoption is affected by current relations among branches of government and by historical precedent. Local institutional arrangements—formal and informal—that have established how legislative change happens in a specific jurisdiction can shape the issues to be considered. Thus, coalitions of supporters for policy change tend to work hard to acquire the support of key policy makers who are extremely well skilled at handling the complex systems of rules and procedures that govern local policy making. Of course, interest group lobbyists have extensive knowledge of these rules and procedures as well, and they know the policy makers who are likely to do their bidding during committee hearings and legislative sessions. Without support from a well-formed group of insiders, any proposal for change will likely die a rapid death in the legislature.

Even if all the political forces for support of a policy change are in order, the quality of the proposal and the knowledge supporting it will play a crucial role in determining its fate. The well-made argument, supported with well-presented evidence, is never enough in itself. But when those advocates for policy change have taken care to expertly manage the legislative processes, have worked hard to explain the proposed change to all key interests, and have presented a powerful case based on strong evidence, they can significantly raise the odds that the proposed change will be adopted.

STAGE 4: POLICY IMPLEMENTATION

A naïve view of the policy-making process sees politicians as the people who set the direction for government actions and government bureaucrats as those who implement the government's wishes. In this view, once a policy is adopted by government, it is seamlessly translated into on-the-ground practices that are entirely consistent with the intentions of the guiding legislation. This view is not realistic.

Because of the combative nature of legislative politics, often legislators authorizing new policy initiatives leave many design details to those who will plan and coordinate the policy implementation. With the best of intentions, people charged with implementing public policies frequently do not discharge their duties as those designing the policies expected. For example, public managers working at the front end of service delivery must routinely innovate and compromise to find effective resolutions to dilemmas that might never have crossed the minds of the original policy designers.

Michael Fullan, noting how school administrators seek to comply with new policies, suggested that policies do not change schools. Rather, schools change policies.[8] When we consider, for a moment, the world of school principals and all the pressures they face in their roles, it is highly unlikely that they will give extensive attention to transforming school processes to comply with each new policy directive. The much more common scenario is that the principals look for ways to shape and work around policies so that they can be accommodated with the least disruptions to standard operating procedures in their schools. Schools change policies simply because those who lead them need to balance a range of considerations. More generally, we might say that those who implement policies might sometimes inadvertently undermine them. This can be the case especially when the implementers are not given sufficient guidance and resources to implement them as the policy designers intended.

Aside from sources of difficulty for implementation that arise within governmental systems, those outside government who have strong interests in government policies can make implementation challenging. Interests opposed to legislation, upon losing in the policy adoption stage, might subsequently work to disrupt implementation. A common strategy involves challenging the constitutionality of the relevant legislation. By invoking the legal process, opponents of new laws can effectively block policy changes for months or years, while lawyers and judges—even the Supreme

Court—decide on the merits of the legislation under consideration. For example, implementation of the ACA was delayed multiple times because of legal challenges, some of which went to the U.S. Supreme Court. Similarly, the Civil Rights Act of 1964 was often undermined at the state and local level; we discuss this case later in this chapter.

Since a lot of public policies will achieve their intended purposes only if specific individuals or groups change their behaviors, implementation can also be undermined by various forms of passive and active resistance from opponents. Unintended consequences often emerge because people adjust their practices to meet the requirements of new laws, while still seeking to maximize their own benefits. Stories are told, for example, of rent controls being undermined in seemingly bizarre ways. Governments have often introduced rent controls to keep housing affordable when specific jurisdictions experience large increases in the population due to immigration. In an episode in Hong Kong, because of an unforeseen loophole in the relevant law in which new properties were exempt from rent controls, many landlords evicted current tenants, demolished perfectly good apartment buildings, and built new ones just to get around rent controls.[9]

These observations on the perils of implementation make clear that good intentions can often be upended even after new policies have been enacted. The risk of this outcome can be reduced, however. Policies that are viewed as compatible with current ways of doing things, that do not impose heavy costs or compliance responsibilities on specific groups, and that enjoy a strong political mandate and broad public support are much more likely to survive implementation. Since governments must worry that their legitimacy will be challenged through implementation failures, we would expect that politicians will take a lot of care to avoid introducing possible policy disasters.

STAGE 5: PROGRAM EVALUATION

Government programs and initiatives, whether they are new or long established, often evoke commentary as to their purpose, effectiveness, and value. That commentary can be informal and based on limited knowledge, or it can be based on more solid facts. Such evaluation generally takes three forms: political, judicial, and administrative.[10]

Political evaluations describe a range of primarily impressionistic reactions to specific government programs. Journalists drawing attention to public concerns about a program, politicians claiming a program is a success, or votes in a general election being construed as giving a mandate for keeping a program are all forms of political evaluation. Because of the contentious nature of politics and the policy-making process, evaluations of this form are never in short supply.

Judicial evaluations are based on more formal processes. They involve court cases concerning specific government programs. Usually these cases are prompted by concerns about the constitutional legitimacy of whole programs or—more commonly—of specific elements of programs, about how policies have been interpreted during the implementation stage, and so on. Political and judicial evaluations can hold major implications for programs. When judged favorably, programs no doubt will stay in operation. They may rapidly earn a permanent place within the broader structures of government in their jurisdiction. It is also possible that support and funding for them will continue, virtually without challenge, well into the future.

Administrative evaluations involve systematic efforts to explore the impacts of policies and associated programs and form judgments about how well they are achieving their intended goals. These formal evaluations also consider what programs could do better, and whether they constitute a worthwhile use of government money. Generally speaking, formal reviews of this kind are what policy scholars, evaluation specialists, and social scientists mean when they speak of "evaluation."[11]

Whereas informal "commentaries" on implemented policies provide a frequent form of evaluation, formal evaluations involving systematic collection and analysis of evidence occur less often. Formal evaluations take time, depend upon high-quality information systematically gathered by program staff and others, and are resource intensive. Strong motivations must exist for their use.

It is rare for new legislation authorizing a program to specify that evaluations should be conducted regularly. That said, evidence generated through formal evaluations can have a variety of uses. It can inform the development of program improvements. It can open new policy debates and prompt new policy-design work. It can generate knowledge for people in other jurisdictions with interests in this area of government activity. However, although formal evaluations have the potential to generate a lot of evidence that might be useful to many people for many reasons, the impetus for such efforts is always likely to be political.

Formal, systematic evaluations tend to be motivated by concerns over the effectiveness of programs, concerns over their costs, or the belief that knowledge found through evaluation might prove useful for supporting future policy agendas. These concerns hold true whether the evaluation work is funded by governments or by other sources, such as private foundations. Policy and program evaluations never just happen. The likelihood that a program will be subjected to systematic evaluation increases when it is highly visible, is considered expensive, or is seen as benefiting a few people at the expense of many; or when a well-resourced interest is able to make funding available for an evaluation.

The conduct of evaluation is inevitably influenced by relevant institutional structures, the power of interest groups that the program affects, and the state of knowledge concerning the specific program context. Consider, for example, an evaluation of the impact of teacher qualifications on the quality of learning of children in K-12 within a given state. As a starting point, even asking questions about the effects of teacher qualifications suggests that theories and knowledge generated elsewhere have raised concerns about what the relationship looks like in this jurisdiction. Knowledge about the increasing importance of education to ensuring a highly skilled, productive workforce is also likely to have informed some of the discussions leading to an evaluation. The institutional context matters in the sense that a formal evaluation is more likely to be conducted in a state where there is a professionalized legislature supported by well-trained policy advisors located both in the capitol and in relevant state or federal government agencies, such as the Office of Management and Budget and the Department of Education. Finally, if there is a powerful teachers' union in the state and its representatives have concerns about an evaluation of this kind, it is likely that the union will lobby to block an evaluation. Failing that, it might lobby to have a voice on any committee appointed to govern the evaluation process.

For their part, business interests are also likely to take a keen interest in such an evaluation. After all, the findings could hold implications for future state spending on teachers and teacher salaries (and hence tax rates). They could also have a bearing on the quality of education in the state, which would have implications for the quality of the future workforce.

Viewing policy making in stages has sometimes been seen as descriptively inaccurate, because policies rarely move through all five stages in a clean, linear fashion. But the absence of such linear moves does not render our framework descriptively inaccurate. Indeed, backward mapping from evaluation to problem definition suggests that a reasonable degree of descriptive accuracy is present. Evaluation can occur only for a program that has been implemented. A policy obviously cannot be implemented if there has been no policy adoption. Policy adoption is simply not going to happen without prior agenda setting. And agenda setting needs a purpose; hence the significance of problem definition

THE POLICY-MAKING PROCESS AND THE PROMOTION OF CIVIL RIGHTS: THE CIVIL RIGHTS ACT OF 1964

The Civil Rights Act of 1964 stands as a landmark piece of legislation in the United States. It addressed many egregious forms of discrimination in American society. It also opened up many opportunities for people who had previously been marginalized in educational systems, electoral systems, and the labor market. Here, we will use passage of the act to illustrate the five stages of the policy-making process.

STAGE 1: PROBLEM DEFINITION

Beginning in the late 1950s, many protests involving civil disobedience were launched in southern states to draw attention to the institutional barriers and informal practices that stood in the way of African Americans participating in society as equals with white people. These efforts were intended to show that there was a fundamental problem in the unequal treatment of people. Protesters promoting improvements in civil rights often invoked the language of the Declaration of Independence, the Constitution, and the Bible. They were seeking to illuminate contradictions in embedded institutional arrangements on the one hand, and popular perceptions of America as a land of opportunity for all on the other. The actions of civil rights activists during this period—exemplified by Martin Luther King Jr.'s speeches at public rallies—illustrate the importance of the public mood in shaping the views of political elites. During these formative years, efforts were made to shift how specific groups perceived their interests. Protest and strife—sometimes even leading to deaths—made many people feel uneasy with the status quo.

STAGE 2: AGENDA SETTING

When John F. Kennedy assumed the presidency in 1961, he intended to take a moderate, incremental approach to advancing civil rights. His views changed after he witnessed the growing strength of the civil rights movement. Although the president introduced a bill to the Congress in June 1963, the bill was subjected to extensive strategic delays by various House and Senate committees. In August 1963, more than 250,000 people crowded into the Mall in Washington, DC, to support civil and economic rights for African Americans. It was here that Martin Luther King Jr. made his famous "I Have a Dream" speech from the steps of the Lincoln Memorial. Following the march, President Kennedy redoubled his efforts to get his bill through Congress. It continued to face strong challenges from Republicans and Democrats alike. During this agenda-setting stage, strong pressure was put on the president and Congress to promote civil rights.

STAGE 3: POLICY ADOPTION

Effective policy making often requires high levels of cooperative action from many players in and around the legislature. This was certainly the case with development of the Civil Rights Act. Without the powerful persuasive efforts of Lyndon Johnson to have the House and Senate agree on and jointly approve a law, it is likely that its passage would have been delayed for years. After the assassination of President Kennedy, President Johnson, in his first address to a joint session of Congress on November 27, 1963, declared: "No memorial oration or eulogy could more eloquently honor President Kennedy's memory than the earliest possible passage of the civil rights bill for which he fought so long." In the months that followed, considerable energy went into both promoting the bill and stymieing it. Indeed, Senator Richard Russell of Georgia launched a seven-week filibuster to prevent passage of the bill. At this point, President Johnson used all of his famous skill, acquired through his years in the Senate, to lobby and cajole lawmakers to achieve a workable compromise and pass a strong bill. (See the photo on p. 56 capturing him in conversation with Richard Russell.)

Debate concerning the Civil Rights Act tended to pitch lawmakers from southern states against lawmakers from elsewhere in the country. Differences did not fall cleanly along party lines. Those who opposed the act sought to protect a society and a set of institutional arrangements that served the interests of white people from affluent or comfortable backgrounds. Those who supported the act

President Johnson confronts Senator Richard Russell, the leader of the filibuster against the civil rights bill. Johnson's knowledge of legislative processes and his ability to persuade were crucial in passing the Civil Rights Act of 1964.

(Yoichi Okamoto/National Archives)

were challenging prevailing interests. They tended to use arguments concerning equality, inequality, and justice to advance legislative change.

STAGE 4: POLICY IMPLEMENTATION

The Civil Rights Act was implemented through a variety of government programs and actions. Prior to passage of this new law, many long-established employment practices and everyday actions had institutionalized racism and other forms of discrimination. For the law to have any impact, it had to contain tough measures forcing compliance. One such measure required all organizations receiving government contracts to document how they were actively seeking to eliminate discrimination in their employment practices. To reduce discrimination in public schooling, the federal government funded initiatives such as the busing of children from schools in poor African American neighborhoods to public schools in wealthier, white suburbs. However, these actions on the part of the federal government often met powerful resistance from those who had gained from previous arrangements. Sometimes this resistance delayed local compliance with the Act for many years.

STAGE 5: PROGRAM EVALUATION

The Civil Rights Act of 1964 has had profound influence in the United States. Notably, it has reduced many forms of discrimination in society. It has also allowed African Americans and other minority groups to pursue higher education and professional careers in ways that would have seemed unattainable in the middle of the 20th century. Many issues remain on the civil rights agenda in the United States—as in all countries. However, the Civil Rights Act opened the way for people who had once experienced significant discrimination to begin taking their rightful place in society.

Viewed as an investment, the Civil Rights Act generated many positive outcomes for American society. It is now acknowledged as a precursor to subsequent civil rights legislation that has had implications for other marginalized groups. Economic analysis points to major economic transformations in America's southern states beginning in the late 1960s and 1970s. These positive changes have been credited in large part to the emancipatory effects of the Civil Rights Act of 1964.[12] The struggle for civil rights continues, and is likely to do so.

Later in this chapter, Case Study 2.2 discusses the more recent matter of state policy making and the recognition of same-sex marriage.

case study 2.1 Allegations of Racial Bias in Policing Practices in Ferguson, Missouri, and the Public Policy Response

In August 2014, a white police officer named Darren Wilson fatally shot an unarmed black teenager named Michael Brown in Ferguson, Missouri. Ferguson is a poor, mostly black community with a population of 21,000 nestled among the suburbs north of St. Louis. At the time of the shooting, the Ferguson Police Department consisted of 53 officers, only three of whom were black.

Following the shooting, local residents staged a series of protests to highlight this instance of what they considered systematic racial bias on the part of the Ferguson Police Department. Some of these protests evolved into major confrontations with the local police. The clashes were widely reported by the national news media. In November 2015, Wilson was found not guilty of any wrongdoing. This ruling sparked further protests in Ferguson.

In the aftermath of this episode, a lot of evidence came to light concerning the ways that local policing tactics and the local court unreasonably impinged on the lives of Ferguson residents. Residents often had to pay hefty traffic fines for minor misdemeanors or spend time in jail for failing to produce identification upon request. It was clear the city administrators had used the questionable fines to raise revenues.

A range of public policy initiatives were canvassed to reduce the risk of more incidents of the sort that triggered the Ferguson protests. Among other things, the Missouri state legislature considered more than 20 bills to change law enforcement policies in the state. A state-appointed Ferguson Commission explored ideas to address police bias. The U.S. Justice Department's Civil Rights Division worked with city officials for months to produce a consent decree setting out required reforms for Ferguson to address problems with its police department and courts. The resulting changes in Ferguson were mostly minor.

The Ferguson episode quickly sparked increased awareness across the United States of ongoing problems of oppression for African American communities. Much evidence emerged suggesting serious bias in policing practices across many jurisdictions.

The public policy discussions and initiatives that happened after the shooting generated few immediate and powerful changes on the streets of Ferguson. Yet they certainly indicated that race issues in America are taken seriously. The episode also showed that it is becoming increasingly difficult for police departments to perpetuate systematic racial bias with impunity.

Greater use of cameras in policing situations and the sharing of video on social media offer examples of changes that serve to curb the abuses of the past.

Unfortunately, situations like that in Ferguson are likely to recur. The ray of hope here is that as more evidence of systemic racial bias is collected and made public, those seeking serious reform will gain more influence.

CRITICAL THINKING QUESTIONS

1. What kind of information would authorities and the public need to accurately determine if racial bias were an actual problem, and not just a perceived problem, in policing practices in places like Ferguson?
2. Why is it often difficult for lawmakers and officials at the state and federal levels to drive significant changes in local contexts like Ferguson?

POLICY INNOVATION IN A FEDERAL SYSTEM

Federal systems of government allow the independent states within them plenty of scope to forge their own paths in public policy design. In the United States, there is a tradition of state policy innovation and subsequent diffusion of innovations from state to state. In a famous opinion written in 1932, Supreme Court Justice Louis Brandeis observed: "It is one of the happy incidents of the federal system that a single courageous state may, if its citizens choose, serve as a laboratory; and try novel social and economic experiments without risk to the rest of the country."[13] Even in cases where individual state legislatures might make apparently unwise policy choices, Brandeis considered it better to let their unwise policies stand than to deny the right to experiment.

Policy innovation can happen as a result of specific demands in local circumstances or as a result of political pressures for certain policy options to be adopted. For example, states differ in the choices that they make about the organization and funding of public schooling. Over the past 50 years, most states have taken measures to reduce inequality in the funding of public schools. By providing more state funds to schools, they have reduced the extent to which resources in schools differ depending on whether they are located in districts with high or low property values. However, the ratio of state to local funding still differs significantly by state.

Likewise, state legislatures have exhibited distinctive preferences concerning the degree of autonomy publicly funded schools face regarding school policies. Over the past two decades, many states have encouraged the growth of **charter schools**, publicly funded schools that have a lot of independence in how they operate. Although the creation of charter schools represents a classic case of policy-innovation diffusion, charter school laws differ significantly in the details. Following Minnesota's adoption of the first charter school law in 1993, other states have adopted similar laws. However, they have differed significantly in the number of charter schools they allow in their states and the amount of autonomy granted to those schools. We discuss charter schools further in Chapter 6.

Many political scientists have studied policy-innovation diffusion in the United States. In a classic contribution, Jack L. Walker studied the adoption by state legislatures of a range of different policies.[14] By so doing, Walker deduced that some states are more likely than others to be policy "leaders" and some are more likely to be policy "laggards." He suggested that states that tended to be early adopters of novel policies were generally wealthier and had greater urban populations. However, subsequent studies by others suggest that motivation to change, lack of obstacles to change, and quality of the information provided to legislatures can strongly influence the adoption of new policies.

In an interesting side note, Walker reported that the California fair trade law of 1931 was followed either exactly, or with minor variations, by 20 other states. Indeed, 10 state legislatures, in passing "their" version of the law, even copied several typing mistakes that made their way into the original California law.

case study 2.2 State Policy Making and the Recognition of Same-Sex Marriage

Same-sex marriage has been legal everywhere in the United States since 2015. This outcome results from a U.S. Supreme Court ruling, *Obergefell v. Hodges.* This ruling declared that same-sex married couples were to be constitutionally accorded the same recognition as opposite-sex couples at the state level, as well as at the federal level. The *Obergefell* ruling represents another instance of the ongoing expansion of civil rights in the United States. The lead-up to *Obergefell* offers interesting insights into the making of public policy in the U.S. federal system of government.

For much of the history of the United States, it was the preserve of state governments to determine the eligibility of individuals to become married. This situation changed in 1996 when the U.S. Congress passed the Defense of Marriage Act (DOMA). This act emphasized that no state need recognize the validity of a same-sex relationship even if it was recognized as marriage by another state. At that time, no state in the United States had made provision for same-sex marriage to be recognized within its jurisdiction. A lot of changes happened after this.

Between 1996 and 2015, a majority of states established that same-sex marriage was permitted within their jurisdiction. They also recognized those who had been married to a person of the same sex in another jurisdiction. Massachusetts was the first state to move in this direction by issuing marriage licenses to same-sex couples starting in 2004, after the state's Supreme Court ruled that the denial of marriage licenses to same-sex couples violated provisions of the state constitution guaranteeing individual liberty and equality. Following this, equivalent state court rulings led to permission of same-sex marriage in Connecticut in 2008 and Iowa in 2009. In subsequent years, more states legalized same-sex marriage through passage of new legislation. In the cases of California, Maryland, and Washington, the law change was made through popular referendums. In the cases of New Jersey and New Mexico, state court rulings opened the way for same-sex marriage.

Meanwhile, many states, taking their cue from DOMA, used legislative action to ban same-sex marriage. Such bans, primarily based on religious beliefs, were introduced in over half the states in the years leading up to 2015. During that span of time, many states granted permission for same-sex marriage, often following state court rulings that upheld challenges to those very same bans. It turns out that a lot of legislative bans were followed by state or federal court rulings that overturned them. The flip-flops did not go in one direction. For example, California legalized same-sex marriage in May 2008 and banned it a few months later in November 2008.

While these actions were occurring at the state level, change was also happening in the federal court system, where decisions were beginning to overturn provisions of DOMA. Meanwhile the states also began relaxing their own restrictions, often through court action, including appeals heard in U.S. district courts. The *Obergefell* ruling emerged when one U.S. district court—the Sixth Circuit—ruled in 2014 that bans on same-sex marriage were constitutional. The ruling affected the law in Kentucky, Michigan, Ohio, and Tennessee. *Obergefell v. Hodges* was one of the appeals to the U.S. Supreme Court that emerged from this ruling.

Obergefell removed all doubt surrounding this issue, and removed state-level discretion concerning same-sex marriage. A range of studies have indicated that granting same-sex marriage equal status as opposite-sex marriage has generated benefits ranging from improvements in the financial status of same-sex couples to reduced discrimination against gays and lesbians in the workplace.

CRITICAL THINKING QUESTIONS

1. If we consider social institutions and their evolution, why has same-sex marriage created significant public policy controversy?
2. What is another example of a contemporary civil rights issue where states have been taking distinct public policy positions?

PREVAILING THEORIES OF POLICY MAKING

Despite the obvious advantages of treating the policy-making process as a series of stages, some scholars have criticized it as being descriptively inaccurate and conveying no sense of what causal mechanisms link the various stages.[15] These criticisms hold some validity. After all, it is entirely possible that problem definition, for example, is not confined to the start of the policy-making process. Some crucial aspects of problem definition might need bureaucrats to address them during policy implementation. Since any effort to achieve conceptual focus necessarily involves making exclusions, all efforts to conceptualize the policy-making process are potentially open to challenge.

Drawing somewhat artificial boundaries around problem definition, agenda setting, policy adoption, policy implementation, and program evaluation has its costs. That said, the stages approach to discussing the policy-making process has a fair degree of validity. Working backward, we can confidently claim program evaluation does not occur unless a policy has been implemented. Implementation only occurs if policy adoption has occurred. Adoption of a policy would be unlikely without agenda setting. And agenda setting tends only to occur when sufficient numbers of people and groups perceive a policy problem that requires a solution.

Here, we consider several prevailing theories of the policy-making process, noting where possible how they complement each other. Taken together, these theories deepen our appreciation of the linkages between stages of the policy-making process and the influences of institutions, interests, and knowledge on policy development.

ELITE THEORY

Political scientists have often disagreed on the sources of influence on policy making. There are several areas of contention. It is often said that interest groups have a lot of influence on policy choices. In this view, the most powerful interest groups—judged especially in terms of financial strength—are likely to have the most influence on the policy choices of elected decision makers. However, raw power is not sufficient to drive change. Those interest groups with major resources must use them in ways that shape popular ideas. A common view is that the most influential interest groups make persuasive policy arguments and back them up with careful financial support of political candidates during elections.

Elite theory represents an important variant of interest group theories. Associated most closely with Thomas R. Dye, elite theory posits that American democracy has long been dominated by powerful elites.[16] The theory divides society into the powerful few and the powerless, apathetic masses. Under this theory, those who are elected to legislatures or as political executives tend to come from, or be strongly supported by, the wealthiest groups in society. There is room within elite theory for individuals from non-elite backgrounds to get ahead and have influence. However, to do so, such people must generally show strong support for the values of the elites. This ability for non-elites to join the elites is considered essential to the stability of American society and the avoidance of civil unrest.

Elite theory holds several important implications for how we interpret the making of public policy:

1. Specific areas of public policy are likely to be dominated by specific elites, reflecting their interests. For example, agricultural policy is likely to heavily reflect the interests of farmers, large agribusinesses, and related industries. Likewise, health care policy is likely to be influenced by the interests of medical specialists, medical-equipment suppliers, and pharmaceutical companies, to name some of the key players.
2. Elite theory is consistent with the view that policies change slowly. This is called *incrementalism,* and we discuss this theory of policy making in that section. Elites have established the system to work for them. They will support changes only when they are helpful for maintaining the system that confers them their power and influence.
3. Elite theory suggests that the masses pay little attention to public policy making and that they have little influence in it.
4. Last, elite theory posits that the ruling elites hold a broad consensus in their views on how American society and politics should operate. This view again supports limited change over time, and that change happens only when it is clearly in the interests of elites.

Proponents of elite theory have used it to guide their analyses of specific decision-making processes in American history. A classic debate along these lines concerns the degree to which the Constitution was influenced by the financial interests of those who attended the Constitutional Convention in Philadelphia.[17] More recently, various studies have explored how many years of elite influence have shaped key institutions in American society.[18]

NEW INSTITUTIONALISM

Institutional accounts of government processes historically have been highly descriptive in nature and have not explained the actions of people within them. More recent work on institutions has emphasized the motives behind their design and the incentives they create to motivate human action. The literature comprising the **new institutionalism** has developed in a number of distinctive ways.[19] Yet despite the differences, contributions to this perspective on politics and society all share a deep interest in the interplay between structures and the effectiveness of people operating within or across them. Institutionalist accounts of the policy process and policy change identify considerable leeway for the actions of motivated individuals and groups to make a difference. However, these accounts are also useful for explaining the limits of such activism.

The new institutionalism highlights several attributes of actors that can significantly increase their ability to instigate change. These include having deep knowledge of relevant procedures and the local norms that serve to define acceptable behavior. Thus, an implication of the new institutionalism is that insider sensibilities must inform efforts to secure major change. That understanding helps us appreciate why the efforts of "outsiders" to make change often come to nothing.[20]

INCREMENTALISM

Charles Lindblom rejected the notion that policy makers follow a **rational choice strategy**, in the sense of defining the problem, laying out alternative solutions, predicting the consequences, valuing the outcomes, and making a choice. Lindblom's famous characterization of policy making as "muddling through" offered the first presentation of this argument.[21]

Even if a single actor were required to make policy in response to a given problem, complexity would soon make the exercise of rational choice impossible. The potential for rational choice is further stymied because reasonable people can be expected to disagree about many aspects of a policy issue. Both complexity and disagreement greatly reduce the odds that bold policy responses will ever be adopted with unanimity. The result is **incrementalism**, or the making of policy changes through small steps.

Even though making policy change in small steps may seem frustrating, Lindblom (1968) characterized it as a "shrewd, resourceful" way of wrestling with complex problems. In his conception of the policy-making process, he argued that we should devote most of our attention to the behavior of **proximate policy makers**. These include legislators, political executives, appointed bureaucrats, and some party officials; that is, anyone with some decision-making authority. Proximate policy makers operate within a "play of power" governed by institutional structures, or the rules of the game, that include the provisions of relevant constitutions, legislative acts, administrative rulings, executive orders, and judicial decisions.

Policy choices constitute products of the structured interactions among proximate policy makers. But no deterministic linkages exist between the preferences and actions of any given participants and specific policy choices. Prior to making formal decisions, the proximate policy makers are subject to influence both from one another and from outsiders, such as interest group leaders and people with ideas to push.

The nature of democratic government and the separation of powers together force participants in the policy-making process to cooperate in order to achieve policy change. Lindblom characterized formal procedures, like committee decision making in legislatures, as "islands of formal organization in a sea of informal mutual adjustment."[22] Often, participants consider their policy proposals from the perspective of those they seek to persuade, and they make adjustments to ensure that their proposals are attractive to others. Mutual adjustments are the means through which cooperation occurs, and policy makers are always interacting with each other in the hope of maximizing the chances that their particular policy preferences will prevail.

This process of mutual adjustment often results in new policies that do not reflect anyone's original views. When persuasion does not alter the views of others, coercion can sometimes do the job—but this requires one party to have authority over another. Since not all can work power to their advantage, informal opportunities for seeking cooperation among policy makers are always more numerous than those based on coercion.

In the years since Lindblom developed the incrementalism theory, many scholars have incorporated his key insights into their work. Notably, Aaron Wildavsky used incrementalism as a concept for understanding the politics of the budgetary process.[23] The typically accepted view is that policy making is predominantly incremental in nature. The question of who has the greatest influence on policy making is less settled. However, rarely contested is the view that policy makers have a significant amount of power when deciding what policy issues to consider and what proposed solutions to adopt.

THE PROBLEM STREAM, THE POLICY STREAM, THE POLITICAL STREAM, AND WINDOWS OF OPPORTUNITY

John Kingdon's conception of the policy-making process emphasizes how specific policy problems and solutions attain prominence at certain times.[24] Little if anything of what Kingdon says contradicts Lindblom's model of incremental policy making. Kingdon argues that agenda setting and policy change emerge through a combination of actions by participants and the operations of formal and informal social processes. Many individuals can call increasing attention through their various actions to specific policy issues. But it is primarily elected officials who decide which issues will become agenda items and hence set the scene for discussion of new policies or policy change. Kingdon emphasizes the important role that informal communication channels play in supporting the rise of policy issues to prominence. A range of individuals collectively serve to make up specialized policy communities or networks: elected officials, bureaucrats, interest group representatives, researchers, and engaged citizens.

Kingdon argues that policy issues emerge on government decision-making agendas as the result of developments in three separate process streams: the problem stream, the policy stream, and the political stream. He claims that advocates of policy change, who he terms "policy entrepreneurs," often serve to join the three independent streams through their efforts to bring specific problems and policy innovations to prominence. In this way, they significantly raise the likelihood that specific policy issues will stimulate policy change.

In the **problem stream**, efforts are made to draw attention to certain issues and to encourage a public policy response. Much is at stake when it comes to problem definition. Those benefiting from the status quo face incentives to convince others that no problem worthy of government attention exists. Those seeking to highlight a problem, aside from demonstrating the problem's significance, must show that policy solutions are available. Thus, policy makers often undertake problem definition with specific policy solutions in mind. Further, solutions sometimes chase problems. Those who think they have found a clever policy solution will look for ways to "hook" it to a specific problem. Contracting government services to private and not-for-profit organizations is a common example; distributing vouchers for services is another. To ensure problems are recognized, people use press releases, speeches, messages or visits to decision makers, and expert testimony.

The second process Kingdon highlights is the **policy stream**. In this stream, communities of policy specialists generate and debate numerous ideas for policy solutions or viable policy alternatives. Occasionally, members of the community come up with new ideas for policy solutions, but mostly they work with old ideas, thinking about ways to reformulate them or combine them with others. Even though ideas often sweep policy communities like fads, governments typically react quite slowly in response. To survive in the policy community, ideas must be perceived as workable and feasible, and must be compatible with the values of a majority of specialists in the relevant policy community.

The third independent process that Kingdon identifies is the **political stream**, composed of things like election results, changes in administrations, changes in the partisan or ideological distribution of legislatures, interest-group pressure campaigns, and changes in public opinion or the national mood. Changes in the political stream and occasional changes in the problem stream, like focusing events, provide the major opportunities for agenda changes in government. Agenda change can come rapidly at times, but organized political forces can serve as a brake. And, indeed, rapid change in the policy agenda might not produce rapid change in actual policy. For even the possibility of major policy change to arise, serious amounts of bargaining and coalition building in the political stream typically must occur.

In Kingdon's telling, agenda change emerges when the three process streams are joined. At critical times, dubbed **windows of opportunity**, the conditions in all three streams favor a joining of problems, solutions, and political momentum. To join the three streams, policy entrepreneurs must judge that the time is right. They "lie in wait in and around government with their solutions at hand, waiting for problems to float by to which they can attach their solutions, waiting for developments in the political stream they can use to their advantage."[25]

PUNCTUATED EQUILIBRIUM

A discrepancy exists between incrementalist accounts of policy change and those that discuss instances of dramatic policy shifts. In seeking to reconcile these different accounts, Frank R. Baumgartner and Bryan D. Jones developed their theory of the policy process as **punctuated equilibrium**, characterized by long periods of stability interrupted by moments of abrupt, significant change.[26] As in Lindblom's account, Baumgartner and Jones suggest that stability is the product of the limited ability for legislators to deal with more than a few issues at a time. Stability is further supported by the development of policy monopolies, controlled by people who go to considerable lengths to promote positive images of current policy settings and deflect calls for change. In this interpretation of policy making, the task for advocates of policy change is to bring the policy issues out into the public arena and invoke a groundswell of change-forcing interest. Even within stable systems, the potential for change exists. The challenge for those seeking such change is to undermine the present policy images and create new ones that emphasize major problems and why the status quo is not sustainable.

Under stable policy monopolies, members of the broader policy domain and interested citizens defer to the judgment of experts who have specialized knowledge of their specific policy area. This knowledge might include a full understanding of the scope and limits of the relevant laws, the organization and allocation of power within the supporting bureaucratic structures, and relevant technical issues. Deference of this sort ensures that policy monopolies are immune from interference by outsiders. But this system of deference and noninterference is largely contingent on the public's continuing to receive positive images regarding activities in the specific policy area. Negative images can serve as cues to alert politicians that policy reform may be needed. Such reform is expected to manifest itself through non-incremental policy change, and this can bring an established way of doing things to an end.

Baumgartner and Jones note that it is possible for policy changes to occur in multiple venues. When policy change appears blocked at one level (e.g., the federal government level), it might be effectively pursued elsewhere (e.g., at the state level). The insight here is that any efforts to establish new ways of doing things open the possibility of creating momentum for change across a whole system. For example, many state-level leaders in the United States have introduced major changes that other states subsequently adopted. Further, these state-level changes can serve to change conversations at the federal level. An obvious case in point is the efforts made in Massachusetts to introduce a form of universal health care coverage for its citizens. The Massachusetts model became a touchstone that significantly informed policy design work leading to the Affordable Care Act (see Case Study 2.3, and Chapter 7).

ADVOCACY COALITIONS

Paul A. Sabatier's theorization of policy change generated the advocacy coalition framework and ongoing refinements.[27] **Advocacy coalitions** are portrayed as "people from a variety of positions (e.g., elected and agency officials, interest group leaders, researchers) who share a specific belief system—i.e., a set of basic values, causal assumptions, and problem perceptions—and who show a nontrivial degree of coordinated activity over time."[28] Coalition participants seek to ensure the maintenance and evolution of policy in specific areas, such as public schooling, health care, and environmental protection.

The advocacy coalition framework tells us how ideas for change emerge from dedicated people who coalesce around an issue. Within the advocacy coalition framework, change comes from both internal and external sources. But, to have political effect, those catalysts for change need to be appropriately interpreted and translated. This process of translation takes, for example, objective social, economic, and environmental conditions and portrays them in ways designed to increase the likelihood that they will receive the decision makers' attention.

The value of the advocacy coalition framework lies in its emphasis on policy making involving a large number of actors and organizations. Policy change emerges out of conversations that take place among these entities. Shared meanings and new interpretations operate as mechanisms for making sense of specific new developments—which can emerge from changes in the natural environment, technical innovation, or political realignments. The quality of the collective interactions in the coalition and the coordination ability of those seeking to promote policy change greatly affect the likelihood that change will occur.

Case Study 2.3 discusses the application of the various theories we have just reviewed to the adoption in 2010 of the Affordable Care Act.

case study 2.3 Theories of Policy Making and the Affordable Care Act (2010)

The Patient Protection and Affordable Care Act (2010) was President Barack Obama's signature domestic policy initiative. It was designed mainly to address limitations in the existing health insurance system. Previous presidents had sought to reform health care policy in the United States, with limited impact. The ACA broadened health insurance coverage, while building on many features of the existing health insurance system. Here, we apply theories of policy making to interpret adoption of the act.

The Influence of Elites   Wealthy people have always enjoyed exceptional health care in the United States. The medical establishment, comprising medical specialists and health facility operators, were not lobbying for change. Elite resistance was high. In some instances, elites gave their support grudgingly, in acknowledgment that democratic politics sometimes requires compromise to maintain broader system legitimacy and stability.

Institutional Effects   Institutions played a big role in the development of the ACA. Outside government, long-standing institutional arrangements, embodied in the medical establishment and the insurance industry, framed and limited the terms of discussion and debate surrounding

possible policy changes. Change was strongly opposed by the Republican Party, but supported by the Democratic Party. With respect to government institutions, the president, who initiated it, had to work closely with Congressional committees in the House and Senate to gain majority support for a compromise law. The threat of legal challenge by the judiciary also influenced policy design.

Incremental Policy Change   For the majority of Americans, the ACA made no changes to their health care provision. They were not experiencing problems with their health insurance coverage and access to care. By avoiding unnecessary changes, President Obama and his allies were able to focus attention on the change that was most important to them—extending coverage to those without it.

Process Streams and Windows of Opportunity   A window of opportunity opened. A newly elected Democratic president was keen to capitalize on a strong electoral mandate. Lack of health insurance for many and the escalating costs of health care presented significant problems needing solutions. The expansion of health insurance coverage in Massachusetts offered a salient and workable solution that could be adapted for the national stage. Many supporters associated with the president and operating in the health policy space had learned lessons in policy design and coalition building from failed reform efforts of the past.

Punctuated Equilibrium Incremental changes in health policy had been happening for years. However, the problems of escalating costs on the one hand, and no health insurance for many on the other, created conditions ripe for change. The changes in Massachusetts indicated that government-supported expansion of health coverage could occur without breaking the system. These efforts to challenge the policy monopoly and use alternative venues to showcase a new policy model opened the way for major change. Once the act had been adopted, the appetite for further big changes eroded fast. Indeed, efforts continued to undermine the law, remove it, and partially replace it. Incremental policy making returned to the health care arena.

Advocacy Coalitions The ACA includes provisions that were not limited to expanding health insurance coverage. Those other provisions—such as efforts to contain health care costs and encourage innovation in medical technology—were instrumental in building a strong advocacy coalition to support adoption of the ACA.

CRITICAL THINKING QUESTIONS

1. If you were to choose one prevailing theory of policy making to further analyze adoption of the Affordable Care Act and subsequent actions to repeal it, which one would you choose? Why?
2. How would you use the five steps of the policy process framework detailed in this chapter (see Figure 2.1) to further analyze the adoption of the act?

CHAPTER SUMMARY

This chapter has given us a way to make sense of the policy-making process by developing a two-part framework. The first part considered influences on policy making. A range of arguments exist concerning the influential roles played by governmental and nongovernmental institutions, interests, and knowledge in affecting policy-making processes. Although it is inevitable that different pressures and processes will be at work in different policy-making situations, we can gain many insights into the nature of policy making by paying attention to how institutions, interests, and knowledge inform actions at different stages of the process.

The second part of the framework discussed the five stages of policy making: problem definition, agenda setting, policy adoption, policy implementation, and evaluation. We have seen throughout the chapter that there is no guarantee that any proposal for a new policy or for policy change will move cleanly through the problem definition, agenda setting, and policy adoption stages. Further, once a policy is adopted, there is no guarantee that it will be implemented in the anticipated time frames or that implementation will be funded at sufficiently high levels to ensure that the policy has its intended real-world impacts. In addition, those who make public policies seldom insist that the established programs be subjected to appropriate evaluation at a suitable time after implementation. In short, a straightforward move through the five stages of policy making is rare.

After introducing and discussing the two-part framework for examining the policy-making process, the chapter introduced several major theories of policy change. These theories are valuable for helping us interpret the political activities that accompany policy change. Most scholars of the policy process agree that policy change tends to occur incrementally—that is, in small steps. However, the structure of institutions around government can influence the speed and nature of policy change. The actions of advocacy groups can also significantly influence change processes. Explanations of more dynamic, significant change have focused on two processes:

1. There are times when political factors and others align to create windows of opportunity for policy advocates.
2. The accumulation of challenges to the status quo can result in dramatic shifts from a long period of stability in a given policy area to a period of dynamic change, followed by another longer period of relative stability.

Policy-making processes are inevitably complicated, with many components and many actors seeking to have influence. That is why scholars have spent so much effort developing alternative theories to account for actions in these processes and the policy outcomes. The framework presented here offers a way of drawing together insights from those theories.

CONNECTIONS TO OTHER CHAPTERS

This framework chapter on the policy-making process has presented various ways of understanding how interests, institutions, and knowledge shape public policy choices. It has set the scene for Chapter 3, where we will consider in detail what it means to treat public policies as investments, the overarching premise of the text. There, we consider both the evidence that is required to make sound policy investments and how that evidence can be translated into useful advice for decision makers.

Chapters 4 through 11 each assess a specific area of public policy. They discuss why governments have become involved in these areas, how public policy in them has evolved, and the key features of contemporary policy settings. Those discussions continuously draw upon general insights regarding the nature of public policy making to explain developments in specific policy areas. Observations made in this chapter, and the theories of policy making introduced here, will repeatedly show their relevance in the Applications chapters. For example, in each chapter we will discuss the pursuit of civil rights through policy design, and the influence of federalism on the evolution of different areas of public policy. Also, we will often discuss aspects of policy innovation and influences on policy making in specific time periods.

KEY TERMS

Collective action
Welfare state
Institutions
Interests
Knowledge
Problem definition
Focusing events
Agenda setting
Public opinion
Public mood
Policy adoption
Policy implementation
Political evaluation
Judicial evaluation

Administrative evaluation
Charter schools
Elite theory
New institutionalism
Rational choice strategy
Incrementalism
Proximate policy makers
Problem stream
Policy stream
Political stream
Windows of opportunity
Punctuated equilibrium
Advocacy coalitions

SUGGESTIONS FOR FURTHER READING

Birkland, Thomas A. *An Introduction to the Policy Process: Theories, Concepts, and Models of Public Policy Making,* 3rd ed. New York: Routledge, 2011. This book presents a comprehensive introduction to all aspects of the policy-making process and reviews major theories of policy making.

Kingdon, John W. *Agendas, Alternatives, and Public Policies,* updated 2nd ed. Boston: Longman, 2011. This book presents a classic and highly influential portrayal of the policy-making process. It treats politics, problems, and policies as operating in independent streams that become linked during "windows of opportunity."

Mintrom, Michael, and Phillipa Norman. "Policy Entrepreneurship and Policy Change," *Policy Studies Journal* 37, no. 4 (2009), pp. 649–67. This article offers an overview of how energetic individuals work with others to promote policy change.

Sabatier, Paul A., and Christopher M. Weible, eds. *Theories of the Policy Process,* 2nd ed. Boulder, CO: Westview Press, 2016. This volume introduces eight contemporary theories of policy-making processes. The authors compare the theories and indicate future directions for theory-building.

Weible, Christopher M., Paul A. Sabatier, and Kelly McQueen. "Themes and Variations: Taking Stock of the Advocacy Coalition Framework," *Policy Studies Journal* 37, no. 1 (2009): 121–40. This article systematically reviews recent applications of the highly influential advocacy coalition framework.

WEBSITES

- The House of Representatives in the U.S. Congress has a highly informative website: http://www.house.gov. Among other things, it provides background on the legislative process, profiles current members, and summarizes issues under legislative consideration. See also the U.S. Senate at http://www.senate.gov/
- The National Conference of State Legislatures, an organization based in Denver, Colorado, was established to improve the quality and effectiveness of U.S. state legislatures and to encourage policy innovation at the state level. Its website contains information on a variety of contemporary policy issues of high relevance to U.S. states and other jurisdictions. http://www.ncsl.org/
- The Pew Charitable Trusts is an organization committed to improving public policy, informing the public, and invigorating civic life. Its website provides background information on a range of contemporary policy issues. http://www.pewtrusts.org/
- The Inter-Parliamentary Union, based in Geneva, Switzerland, promotes better knowledge of the workings of representative institutions around the world. Its website provides links to the parliaments of many countries and contains extensive resources for use by those with interests in policy development. http://www.ipu.org/

FOR DISCUSSION

1. The media plays a vital role in conveying information between citizens and their governments. Most people find out about legislative decisions by tuning into TV and radio news, looking at their tablets or phones, and reading newspapers. Given that many details are involved in making public policies, should we worry that citizens often do not know much about policies that are apparently being made in their interests? What might be the result of their lack of knowledge?

2. Even though many elections are hotly contested and candidates draw big distinctions between themselves and their opponents, when it comes to policy making, most changes are small, representing "incremental departures" from what was done before. Why do politicians often talk about making significant changes when it seems that most changes they will make while in office will be small and incremental?

3. In the immortal words of President Abraham Lincoln (1863), democracy promises us "government of the people, by the people, for the people." However, as in many other countries in the world, underrepresented and minority groups in American society continue to struggle significantly to attain the same freedoms and quality of life as more privileged groups. What factors might explain why the promotion of civil liberties and rights is often a struggle? What do your answers tell us about the nature of policy making?

CHAPTER 3

PUBLIC POLICIES AS INVESTMENTS

In this text, public policy is consistently described as investing for a better world. Governments require citizens to forfeit some of their current consumption through the collection of income taxes, sales taxes, and so on, then devote these revenues to funding specific policies and programs, all with the goal of improving outcomes over what would have been experienced in the absence of such government action. The degree to which governments succeed in making the world a better place depends entirely on the quality of the policies and programs they establish. Poor choices can generate poor outcomes for society; good choices can generate good ones. By presenting and discussing a framework for assessing public policies as investments, this chapter establishes the primary analytical perspective of this text, which we will use in all the chapters that follow.

This chapter introduces you to:

- The work of policy analysts
- Why it makes sense to treat public policies as investments
- A general framework for assessing public policies as investments
- The Policy Investment Checklist
- Examples of public policies that have been treated as investments
- An example of an organization that routinely generates advice by treating public policies as investments
- Federalism and the assessment of public policies as investments
- The investment perspective and the promotion of civil rights
- Ways to think beyond financial concerns when treating public polices as investments

Facing page: Treating public policies as investments involves gathering and analyzing relevant evidence to assist politicians in making well-informed policy choices. In the best cases, policy choices generate more public value than any other available option.

(© Zadorozhnyi Viktor/Shutterstock.com)

THE WORK OF POLICY ANALYSTS

If the goal of government-led collective action is to make a better world, then policy advice must be well informed, rigorous, and persuasive. Here we focus on treating public policies as investments. This focus does not capture everything that is important and interesting about public policies; it is foundational, however, for effective policy advising. If the investment advice is poor, what follows will surely fail.

Investing is a common practice for all individuals and organizations in society. An **investment** is an item or asset that is bought with the hope that, in the future, it will generate income or appreciate in value. Investment always involves making a trade-off between present consumption and hoped-for future consumption. When an investment is made, resources that could have been consumed immediately are instead used to create conditions intended to produce better future outcomes. For example, people make investments when they buy items like an automobile or a house. Likewise, they invest when they decide to attend university to gain a degree. In all instances of investing, people devote resources (especially time and money) to an activity or purchase intended to generate future benefits, not just immediate gains. Various financial models can help people predict the stream of future benefits they are likely to realize over a period of years as the result of specific investment choices.

When it comes to making public policy, investment thinking is highly relevant.[1] As members of society, we rely on politicians to make decisions in our collective interests. Thus, politicians are often required to make investment decisions; for example, funding the development of roads, schools, prisons, and large science projects. Well-informed investment decisions are guided by knowledge of how much an element of government activity will cost and what benefits are likely to result from it. Sound investment thinking always considers alternative uses of money and the relative merits of pursuing each alternative.

No matter where policy analysts are located in and around the policy-making process, their central function is to improve the knowledge of others concerning policy choices. Given this goal, policy analysts amass information on current issues or challenges, identify policy alternatives that could address them, and indicate which potential policy changes would likely generate improvements compared with the current situation.

Immediate political considerations, including interest group pressures, can lead politicians to discount the advice that policy analysts provide. Policy choices are often biased because of the interplay of different interests. Biases also result from a tendency for people to show partiality toward what has worked in the past. Beyond these barriers to acceptance of their policy advice, policy analysts are often hindered in their work by the limitations of relevant information and of human capabilities to effectively use it. In combination, information problems and the risk aversion of politicians reduce the acceptance of many policy choices representing good investments. Also, just because policy choices made in the past come to be viewed as poor investments, we should not expect rapid policy corrections.

As Charles Lindblom observed, "Democracies change their policies almost entirely through incremental adjustments. Policy does not move in leaps and bounds."[2]

In Chapter 2, we noted that policy making is a process in which elected decision makers—and those who seek to influence them—formulate, establish, and evaluate government action with the intention of making the world a better place. This pursuit of collective well-being prompts the focusing of attention on discrete areas of social activity. For example, specific decision makers, administrators, interest groups, and policy analysts develop expertise in, say, criminal justice issues, and the relevant policy goals and policy instruments related to them. Advocacy coalitions, networks of policy specialists, and other parties interested in this specific area of public policy continuously engage in policy discussions. They talk about current policy concerns, evidence about them, and ideas about how those concerns might be addressed. Insights from prior policy-making efforts, war stories about legislative victories and failures, and evaluation results circulate within these professional specialist communities. Thus, at any given moment, many parallel efforts will be working to promote well-being in each distinct area of criminal justice.

At their best, policy analysts clarify the nature of public problems and contribute new knowledge about how they might effectively address them. Decision makers worry about the consequences of their choices. For the obvious reason of self-preservation, elected decision makers do not want to introduce new policies that are unpopular or that create negative unintended consequences—doing so raises the odds of losing power. For their part, appointed decision makers also seek to avoid unsettling people and, hence, making things difficult for those who appointed them. Clearly, policy analysts need to be aware of the preoccupations and sensitivities of those they advise.

Without paying attention to the preferences of decision makers, policy analysts can quickly acquire reputations for being unhelpful. When they lose the trust of those they advise, policy analysts lose all chances of influencing policy development. It is not sufficient, however, for policy analysts to pander. To increase the likelihood that policy changes will help those within a given jurisdiction, policy analysts must at least try to explore the broader implications of specific policy changes. As far as possible, they need to indicate how well such changes would meet intended goals, and what trade-offs might be necessary.

Interest in finding ways to improve the quality of evidence used to support government policy choices is growing. At various points in this chapter, we will encounter efforts of this kind. Case Study 3.1 describes one of the most salient of these efforts, the *Moneyball for Government* movement.

Although policy analysts can contribute valuable information to policy discussions, the task of raising overall levels of policy knowledge takes time. Observers of how information is used in policy making have noted that change rarely occurs as the result of one or a few well-developed policy reports.[3] Policy makers tend to interpret

case study 3.1 The *Moneyball for Government* Movement

The *Moneyball for Government* movement is a bipartisan effort to change how policy making works in the United States. The vision of its founders was to have policy makers routinely base decisions on solid evidence of what works, not simply on politics or expedience. The title of the movement is a deliberate reference to the title of the book **Moneyball,** by business writer Michael Lewis. There, Lewis documented how Billy Beane, general manager of Major League Baseball's Oakland A's, used player statistics to inform team-member selection. The strategy of basing decisions on systematically collected evidence of past player performance led the relatively low-budget team to national prominence and significant success. Under Beane's management, the team became highly cost effective. Lewis's book became the basis of the 2011 film *Moneyball,* starring Brad Pitt as Beane.

The *Moneyball* message is clear: use careful analysis of evidence as the basis for your investment decisions. The *Moneyball for Government* movement takes this idea seriously. The 2014 book *Moneyball for Government,* edited by Jim Nussle and Peter Orszag, is a manifesto for treating public policies as investments. Jim Nussle was director of the U.S. Office of Management and Budget under Republican president George W. Bush. Peter Orszag held the same position under Democratic president Barack Obama. Contributors to the volume all contended that basing policy choices on evidence of effectiveness is something of interest to politicians of any ideological persuasion.

What do those who advocate *Moneyball for Government* want? They list three goals:

1. Build evidence about the practices, policies, and programs that will achieve the most effective and efficient results.
2. Invest taxpayer dollars in practices, policies, and programs that use evidence and evaluation to demonstrate that they work.
3. Direct funds away from practices, policies, and programs that consistently fail to achieve measurable outcomes.[4]

Aren't these practices already happening? The answer is surprising. Nussle and Orszag claim that, by their estimates, very little federal government spending is currently backed by even the most basic evidence of effectiveness.[5] Clearly, a lot of latitude exists for governments to begin systematically treating public policies as investments. This chapter shows how to do it.

CRITICAL THINKING QUESTIONS

1. What might explain the apparent limited use of evidence of "what works" by policy makers when they are designing public policies?
2. What actions might be taken to increase investment thinking on the part of policy makers?

new information added to policy discussions in the light of existing policy understandings. It takes focus, persistence, and coordinated effort for new ways of thinking to pervade policy communities. The impact of new information also depends on the existing knowledge base in specific policy communities, and the willingness of those communities to consider theory, evidence, policy ideas, and insights from research.[6]

When political parties are deeply divided on the role of government in society, all new information presented by representatives of one party will probably meet with skepticism from their political opponents. Such division does not rule out the possibility for new policy ideas to gain broad support. However, it might take years before a majority of representatives are convinced by the evidence and arguments based on it.

Given how long it can take for new policy ideas to catch on, it is useful to recall cases where the slow, persistent accumulation of relevant evidence paid off. The story of how economist Alfred Kahn came to influence the process of airline deregulation and other forms of transportation deregulation in the 1970s is exemplary. During the 1960s, Kahn, along with others, worked carefully to create a strong base of evidence indicating that regulation of specific industries was serving the interests of those industries at the expense of consumers. After years of Kahn's making these arguments and presenting the best available evidence, change came, and came rapidly.[7] Some observers even claim that these early efforts to secure the deregulation of key industries set the scene for the more sweeping years of economic reform that occurred in the United States during the presidency of Ronald Reagan (1981–1989) and in the United Kingdom under Prime Minister Margaret Thatcher (1979–1990).[8] Those reform movements led to greater reliance on markets in society, and skepticism of the effectiveness of government. They influenced the development and execution of major reform agendas in other parts of the world, including Australia, Canada, and New Zealand.[9]

TREATING PUBLIC POLICIES AS INVESTMENTS

The notion of treating public policies as investments has often been implicit within literature on public policy and policy analysis. Yet until now, there has been no consideration as to how this focus might be consistently applied. The framework presented in this chapter fills that gap. It also sets the scene for its subsequent application to specific areas of public policy in the chapters that follow.

Over the past half century, policy analysts have developed various analytical tools to improve the production of good-quality advice. These include cost-benefit analysis, comparative institutional analysis, and policy and program evaluation techniques. They have been supported by other techniques of social science research that allow development of evidence-based policy. We review these analytical tools here, within the framework of public policies as investments.

Immediately we must realize that more work needs to be done to direct policy analysis capabilities toward the treatment of public policies as investments. Many limits in available evidence reduce the feasibility of measuring the returns realized from specific public policy investments. Although advances in the collection and analysis of evidence have eased the assessment of public policies as investments, challenges remain. Nonetheless, consistently viewing public policies as investments holds the possibility of changing popular narratives concerning the role of government in society. It can also change the terms of political debates. And, to the extent that such change occurs, conditions will improve for those seeking to effectively assess returns on public policy investments.

Cost-benefit analysis plays a central role in treating public policies as investments. This tool involves taking account of all the costs associated with a program, and all the benefits expected to come from it, over an appropriate period of time. Those policies that generate a high ratio of benefits to costs—also called the return on investment (ROI)—are viewed most favorably. We will discuss both cost-benefit analysis and ROI in detail in Step 4 of Policy Investment Checklist 3.1.

Advisors in government now use cost-benefit analysis routinely as they seek to clarify the impacts of policy choices. Although all public finance textbooks and most public policy textbooks discuss how to perform cost-benefit analysis, they rarely include any sustained discussion of public policies as investments.[10] In the realm of actual policy practice, the investment approach to public policy is starting to appear in discussion papers produced by policy advisors in and around government. For example, recent reports produced in the United States, Australia, Canada, New Zealand, and the United Kingdom have explicitly portrayed and discussed a range of public policies as investments (see Table 3.1).

TABLE 3.1 Recent Reports Portraying Public Policies as Investments

Aos, Steve, and Elizabeth Drake. *Prison, Police, and Programs: Evidence-Based Options that Reduce Crime and Save Money* (Doc. No. 13–11–1901). Olympia: Washington State Institute for Public Policy, 2013.

Ben-Shalom, Yonatan, and Hannah Burak. *The Case for Public Investment in Stay-At-Work/Return-to-Work Programs.* Princeton: Mathematica Policy Research, 2016.

Bivens, Josh, Emma Garcia, Elise Gould, Elaine Weiss, and Valerie Wilson. *It's time for an ambitious national investment in American's children.* Washington, D.C: Economic Policy Institute, 2016.

Gladkikh, Olga. *International Investment Models for Tertiary Education.* Wellington, New Zealand: Tertiary Education Commission, 2009.

House of Commons Committee of Public Accounts. *Big Science: Public Investment in Large Scientific Facilities.* Sixtieth Report of Session 2006–07. London, United Kingdom: The Stationery Office, 2007.

Karoly, Lynn A., and Francisco Perez-Arce. *A Cost-Benefit Framework for Analyzing the Economic and Fiscal Impacts of State-Level Immigration Policies.* Santa Monica, CA: RAND Corporation, 2016.

Lucius, Irene, et al. Green Infrastructure: *Sustainable Investments for the Benefit of Both People and Nature.* Brussels: European Union, 2011.

Steuerle, Eugene, and Leigh Miles Jackson. *Advancing the Power of Economic Evidence to Inform Investments in Children, Youth and Families.* Washington, D.C: The National Academies Press, 2016.

When using an investment approach, we should explore how well-designed public policies can serve as effective platforms for the ongoing development of programs and practices that, over time, add high value to citizens' lives. In so doing, we can avoid becoming technically narrow and intellectually and politically blinkered. Our goal should be to apply the investment perspective in a manner that is consistent with the deeply compassionate goal of maximizing human flourishing throughout the life course.

PUBLIC POLICIES AS INVESTMENTS: A FRAMEWORK

Here we will consider a five-step approach to treating public policies as investments. This is termed the Policy Investment Checklist. The intention is to indicate how both formal (or technical) approaches to treating public policies as investments and informal (or metaphorical) approaches hold the hope of bringing more rationality to the making of public policy. Policy Investment Checklist 3.1 sets out the steps in treating public policies as investments. In the checklist, each step is accompanied by key questions analysts should ask. These steps are discussed in detail in the sections that follow. Then, the basic approach shown in Policy Investment Checklist 3.1 is replicated in each of the Application chapters. This confirms that the investment

POLICY INVESTMENT CHECKLIST 3.1

Analyzing Public Policies as Investments

STEPS	KEY QUESTIONS
1. Focus on Existing Policies and Programs	Ask: Where are existing programs we can learn from? Policy analysts might need to show how lessons for policy design can be drawn from across distinctly different policy areas.
2. Gather Policy Evidence	Ask: What is the best evidence we can work with? The "gold standard" in evidence-based policy development is the randomized controlled trial. But other statistical evidence can also produce valid insights.
3. Measure Desired Effects	Ask: How much difference do policies of this kind tend to make? The more precise the answer, the greater the accuracy of the remaining analysis.
4. Assess Costs and Benefits	Ask two questions: First, how much is it likely to cost to produce the desired policy effect? Second, how much value—in dollar terms—is the desired effect likely to produce? Return on investment from a policy is estimated by dividing the sum of estimated policy benefits by the sum of estimated policy costs.
5. Offer Robust Advice	Ask: How much do our conclusions about this policy depend on how we have interpreted the evidence? Good policy advice is honest about how much confidence can be placed in the conclusions drawn from the evidence.

approach can be usefully and uniformly applied across a variety of substantive areas of public policy.

If we are destined to "muddle through" incrementally with policy making, as seems to be the case, we can at least work to improve the quality of the decisions being made. Consistently viewing public policies as investments holds the prospect that government-led collective action will create a continuously improving world. That is an outcome worth pursuing.

STEP 1: FOCUS ON EXISTING POLICIES AND PROGRAMS

Politicians touting their ideas for policy change often present them as novel and cast themselves as policy innovators. In popular culture, we accord a lot of value to novelty. However, consistent with the conception of policy making as incremental in nature, much policy and program design involves exploring how to make relatively minor adjustments to existing policy settings. As John Kingdon observed, "Nothing is new . . . everything has its antecedents . . . alternatives change not by mutation but by recombination."[11] Indeed, especially at the state level in the United States, there is a strong tendency for legislatures to adopt policy innovations that have already been developed and adopted elsewhere.

There is a lot of merit in devising proposals for policy change that take advantage of existing knowledge. It is a risk-reducing strategy. In his argument in favor of conducting comparative institutional analysis, Harold Demsetz observed that too often, advocates of policy change present the relevant choice as one between an ideal norm and an existing "imperfect" institutional arrangement. He called this a "nirvana approach" to policy design—an approach that assumes that what works well in theory will always represent an improvement over current arrangements. Demsetz proposed that policy analysts should conduct comparative institutional analysis, where "the relevant choice is between alternative real institutional arrangements."[12]

When we consider public policies as investments, focusing on existing policies and programs makes a lot of sense. Evidence generated by those policies and programs can offer important insights into how much they cost to operate, their actual outcomes, and how well those outcomes match originally intended goals. Then, we can readily assess the benefits of the policies or programs. The major difficulty with this approach is that it is explicitly conservative in nature. It cautions against doing anything novel. We might well ask: How, then, can innovations ever start? The key, as Kingdon observed, is to think in terms of **recombination**.

For example, suppose a local government is considering ways to encourage the emergence of a strong private or not-for-profit sector for the provision of high-quality early childhood education in its jurisdiction. Although this might be a new policy direction for that jurisdiction, its policy analysts could assess how well it might work by investigating the organizational arrangements and supply-and-demand dynamics associated with the introduction of K-12 charter schools in many American states, or the success or failure of some private educational voucher arrangements. (See Table 3.2 for further explanation of recombination and other key investment terms used in Steps 1 through 5 of the Policy Investment Checklist.)

TABLE 3.2 An Explanation of Technical Terms

Step 1: **Focus on Existing Policies and Programs**	**Recombination:** The concept of recombination relies on the assumption that some elements are similar and others are different from one another. Recombination results when different elements are brought together to inspire social, economic, and technological breakthroughs.
Step 2: Gather Policy Evidence	**Randomized Controlled Trial:** A study design that randomly assigns similar participants into either an experimental or a control group. The only expected difference between the two is the outcome of the study. **Quasi-experimental assessments:** A type of evaluation that aims to determine whether a program or intervention has the intended effect on a study's participants. These assessments lack one or more of the design elements that make up a true experiment; generally, the missing element is random assignment of participants to research conditions. **Regression Analysis:** A statistical measure that attempts to determine the strength of the relationship between one dependent variable and a series of other independent variables. Regression takes a group of variables, thought to be influencing the dependent variable, and tries to find a mathematical relationship between them.
Step 3: Measure Desired Effects	**Statistical Modeling:** A process in which mathematics and data are used to construct an equation that represents a given real-life phenomenon. Statistical modeling is a powerful tool for developing and testing theories by way of causal explanation, prediction, and description. **Meta-analysis:** A statistical technique for combining the findings from independent studies. This method can combine qualitative and quantitative study data from several selected studies to develop a single conclusion that has greater statistical power than that from a single study.
Step 4: Assess Costs and Benefits	**Net Present Value:** Net present value is used to calculate the total of all cash flows (in and out) that can be directly linked to a project. A positive value is good. Otherwise, the investment might be reconsidered. **Discount Rate:** Determining the value of a project is challenging because there are different ways to measure the value of future cash flows. Because of the time value of money, a dollar earned in the future will not be worth as much as one earned today. The discount rate is essentially the interest rate it will take to turn today's money into tomorrow's value. **Interest Rate:** Interest, or the cost of borrowing money, is normally expressed in terms of a percentage of the overall loan. With every loan, there is a risk that the borrower will not be able to pay it back. The higher the risk that the borrower will fail to repay the loan, the higher the interest rate.
Step 5: Offer Robust Advice	**Sensitivity Analysis:** A technique used to examine how a study's results would be affected by changes in the values of specific variables. Cost-benefit studies must make assumptions and use estimates to calculate the expected costs and benefits of a policy or program. Sensitivity analysis is used to determine what could happen if those assumptions and estimates were altered.

Many experiments have been conducted with private vouchers funded by philanthropic organizations, and those experiments have been rigorously evaluated.[13] Concentrating on already existing policies and programs gives policy analysts access to a great deal of rich evidence that can inform future policy making. Coupling this focus with the notion of recombination opens up plenty of opportunities for policy design work to be highly creative while building on existing program knowledge.

STEP 2: GATHER POLICY EVIDENCE

A lot of evidence has been generated about the workings of policies and programs, how they were adopted, how they were implemented, how different groups of people make sense of them, and so on. All of this evidence can be extremely helpful for informing policy design work. Indeed, routine reports on programs in the field often supply rich details that can enjoy a lot of relevance beyond meeting the needs of the intended audience. Policy analysts always must find ways to build their expert knowledge of policy issues—and they can use a range of useful strategies.[14] Assessing the likely ROI that a jurisdiction would obtain by adopting a policy already in place elsewhere demands both specific and high-quality information. Fortunately, the evidence-based policy movement has raised awareness among policy analysts and others about the issues they must consider when gathering policy evidence.

The "gold standard" often evoked in discussions of evidence-based policy is the **randomized controlled experiment**—an approach to trying out policy approaches that is informed by scientific methods. (See In Focus 3.1 for further discussion of randomized controlled experiments.) In such experiments, researchers take care during program implementation to ensure that they will be able to isolate and measure the effects of a program on the outcomes of interest to them. They can then use this approach to generate evidence to determine the impact of many policies and programs. For example, they might assess the impact of specific changes in teaching methods on students' standardized test scores. Or they might evaluate the health impacts of work-based preventive health programs on employee behavior in specific organizations. Such experimental work has the potential to generate high-quality evidence. However, it is also subject to critiques. The best of these critiques note that the technique has many virtues, but that it does not categorically answer the questions of, "If a policy worked well there, will it work well here?"[15]

Lacking evidence derived from such randomized controlled experiments, researchers can seek evidence from statistical studies where other methods such as **regression analysis** are used to conduct **quasi-experimental assessments** of policy impacts. As subsequent chapters of this text make clear, such studies can provide important insights into the ROI of policy changes in many areas, including the governance of infrastructure, efforts to commercialize scientific knowledge, and efforts to reduce pollution by promoting green energy-generation systems. Whether or not good quality policy evidence exists is highly dependent on the

in focus 3.1

PERSONAL SAFETY IN A COMMUNITY: AN EXAMPLE OF A RANDOMIZED CONTROLLED EXPERIMENT

Suppose researchers want to test the effect on citizens' perceptions of personal safety by increasing the visibility of police officers in communities. The effect can be tested through use of a randomized controlled experiment. Such experiments are conducted in natural social settings to test the impact of policy changes. All randomized controlled trials are set up following steps like those listed here:

1. The visibility of police officers in communities is treated as an independent variable, which researchers can manipulate.
2. Citizens' perceptions of personal safety is assumed to be affected by other things, including the visibility of police officers in the community. Citizens' perceptions of personal safety is treated as a dependent variable.
3. A number of communities would be selected for inclusion in the experiment. Suppose 20 were selected. Then traditional policing could continue in 10 of them, and police officers could be made more visible to the community in the remaining 10.
4. Next, before changes were made in the policing practices, a survey would be conducted across the 20 communities to determine citizens' current perceptions of personal safety. Those perceptions would provide the baseline for the study. Future outcomes could be compared with them.
5. Other factors in communities most likely influence perceptions of personal safety, not just the visibility of police officers. If some of these are well known, they can be assessed in the study. For example, the 20 communities might be divided into

10 matched pairs based on the level of reported crime rates.
6. Next, the new policing efforts intended to raise visibility of police officers would be introduced in 10 communities. To avoid the possibility that other factors influence experimental outcomes, the new program would be introduced randomly. For example, for each matched pair of communities, a coin flip could decide which community is to host the new program to enhance police visibility and which will continue with policing as usual.
7. After a period of time—say, six months or a year—another survey would be conducted across the 20 communities to measure citizens' perceptions of personal safety. The observations gained from this second survey would be compared with the baseline for the study. By comparing these "before" and "after" measures of citizens' perceptions of personal safety, researchers can assess if the program to enhance police visibility appears to have any effect—positive or negative—on citizen perceptions of personal safety.

The carefully controlled and monitored nature of this experiment would increase the confidence that any differences in perception of personal safety between the 10 communities where the program was introduced and the 10 where it was not were indeed caused by the program to enhance police visibility.

The randomized controlled trial approach described here exemplifies the policy research methods that generated evidence for many of the examples presented and discussed throughout this book.

development of good systems for data collection and the use of well-trained analysts to extract useful insights from those data.[16]

At a minimum, the production of good-quality evidence requires that those involved adhere to the principles of transparency and accountability. That is, researchers must make explicit their methods of collecting evidence, and they should be able to assess the validity of the data generated in the studies.[17]

The significance of good-quality evidence for assessing the ROI of policies reminds us of how important program evaluation is to the implementation and maintenance of public policies. The feasibility of conducting evidence-based policy work in general—and of calculating ROI specifically—depends on the existence of high-quality data.

STEP 3: MEASURE DESIRED EFFECTS

When public policies are treated as investments, the fundamental purpose of gathering policy evidence is its use to measure whether the policy—or programs associated with it—generated the desired effects. In randomized controlled experiments, program effects are isolated by comparing before-and-after changes in valued outcomes between those entities (e.g., people, organizations) that, through randomization, experienced the program, and those in the experiment that, again because of randomization, did not experience the program. In quasi-experimental research designs, analysts work with what evidence is available and seek to gain control over that evidence through application of different kinds of **statistical modeling**.[18]

One approach involves **meta-analysis** of policy and program impacts—that is, evaluating multiple high-quality studies of the programs of interest and determining the average "effect size" of the programs, found across the various studies. For example, John Hattie has employed meta-analytic data methods to measure the effects of a variety of activities in schools that have been expected to improve student performance.[19] By using this approach, Hattie claimed that most data indicate a hierarchy of educational interventions, from those that appear to make a big difference to student learning, to those that make no apparent difference. To cite one instance, he found that the quality of feedback that teachers provide to students can have strong effects on learning outcomes compared with efforts to reduce class sizes. This kind of finding matters. After all, it is much less expensive to train teachers to offer students useful feedback than it is to reduce the number of students in every classroom. This suggests that the ROI from training teachers to provide effective feedback is higher than the ROI from cutting class sizes. (We return to this topic in Chapter 6.)

A significant research issue arises when we consider the measurement of desired policy and program effects. That is, the paucity of high-quality quantitative research on policy outcomes greatly limits the extent to which researchers can perform meaningful statistical modeling work. Although meta-analyses are feasible in the fields of education and health and some areas of criminal justice, there remain many areas of policy interest for which quantitative studies exploring outcomes are limited. More such studies will hopefully emerge in the future. Indeed, if public policies are to be routinely assessed as investments, far more effort will need to go into funding high-quality program evaluations. The best of these will include randomized controlled experiments.

STEP 4: ASSESS COSTS AND BENEFITS

As an essential tool for conducting policy analysis, **cost-benefit analysis** lies at the heart of efforts to treat public policies as investments. Conceptually, the approach is straightforward. Here, we will analyze each step of the approach.

1. *We must define the scope of a study.* Should we consider costs and benefits over a short period of time—say, three years? Or should we consider them over a longer period, such as 10 years or even more? In addition, the question of scope can involve thinking about the extent of impacts of a policy or program. Take, for example, the provision of early childhood education. A range of studies have demonstrated a high ROI in this area. That means the benefits of early childhood education programs, especially for children from low-income families, appear to far outweigh the costs. However, most of those benefits become obvious only after many years.

Having selected a time period and initial scope, we need to refine the scope of the study even further. Should the assessment of benefits be confined to considering the outcomes for the individual children involved? Or should we consider the immediate benefits for families of having children attend early childhood education programs? When a child attends such a program, the adult who would otherwise be at home with the child is freed up. That adult might then choose to spend the child-free time engaging in paid work, voluntary work, or further study. Should such benefits for other family members be factored into the benefits deemed to flow from provision of early childhood education?

These questions indicate that defining the scope of a study is not easy. It can greatly affect the results of the cost-benefit analysis. The point of doing such an analysis, of course, is to assess whether the valued effects of a policy or program do, in fact, make it worth pursuing.

2. *We need to identify all the effects of the policy or program, both negative and positive.* Once we have established an inventory, we need to assign dollar values to the negative impacts (which become dollarized costs) and the positive impacts (which become dollarized benefits). We also need to take into account the actual costs of running the program of interest. Here, our previous experience can prove extremely helpful as we perform measurement work.

3. *We must allocate these costs and benefits to each year included in the analysis.* For example, if the model explores costs and benefits of a program over a 10-year period, we must compute estimates of costs and benefits in each of those years

separately. We should also account for the opportunity costs associated with funding the program in each of these periods—that is, we should consider the best alternative use of the money spent on this program and account for it in our modeling work. Usually, the best alternative use of the money is placing it into a portfolio of low-risk investments.

4. *We must compute the net present value of the program.* In effect, this calculation involves collapsing the series of years in the model into one time period. The chosen **discount rate** is usually the inverse of a **prevailing interest rate**. Therefore, the **net present value** is the total amount that comes from summing up discounted benefits minus costs over the assumed life of the policy or program. By dividing the sum of estimated policy benefits by the sum of estimated policy costs, we then calculate **return on investment (ROI)**. This is the expected return, in dollars, that would be realized for every dollar spent on the program. Only if the ROI is positive and well above zero should we believe that the policy or program under assessment represents a good use of public money.[20]

STEP 5: OFFER ROBUST ADVICE

Any advice treating public policies as investments must contain evidence that the estimated returns from adopting specific policies are trustworthy. Even in our brief discussion, we can see various instances where choices made during the development of the estimation methods can affect the results obtained. In light of this, we must take care to show how changes in the modeling assumptions would change the estimated returns on investment.

Such work, typically called **sensitivity analysis**, involves running a number of alternative scenarios using different modeling assumptions to test the extent to which the results are robust or, alternately, how much they are being driven by the choices we incorporated into the model. Offering a range of estimates of ROI is possible when we perform this kind of sensitivity analysis.

We might use additional practices to improve the quality of the advice being given about policies and their likely effects. For example, taking the kind of approach used by John Hattie in his assessments of educational interventions can be very instructive in policy design discussions. Suppose we report the estimated ROI of a policy option, such as reducing class sizes in every public school across a specific jurisdiction. We might augment that estimated ROI with evidence showing what alternative policy packages could be adopted at the same cost. Such a comparison would create an opportunity to explain how those alternative packages might improve student outcomes to a greater extent than the pursuit of smaller class sizes.

Advice presented in this way can still acknowledge the policy preferences of decision makers. Crucially, however, it also encourages a different discussion about the pursuit of smart policy and ways to enhance the expected returns on costly policy investments.

PUBLIC POLICIES AS INVESTMENTS: TWO CASES

Having explored the basic approach to treating public policies as investments, we now consider two cases that illustrate the merits of the approach. Case Study 3.2 considers government funding for **early childhood education**—that is, the care and education of children aged from a few months to 4 or 5 years. Even among the most developed countries in the world, big differences exist in the levels of commitment that their governments make to support this area of education. An investment perspective suggests that it should be a high priority for government funding.

case study 3.2 Early Childhood Education

Each of us benefits from education. In addition, we all benefit from having educated people around us. Thus, education is often considered a good that has both private benefits for the individuals receiving it and public benefits for all. Education is also a good that we often do not fully appreciate until long after we have completed our diplomas or degrees. When we are young, we need other people to act in our best interests. Within the field, early childhood education continues to be commonly viewed as less important than education at school or in higher education. Although attending school is compulsory in many countries, in contrast, no country requires children to attend early childhood education services. Sound evidence, however, shows that high-quality early childhood education services can have major and sustained benefits for individuals, especially those coming from families with less-educated parents and lower household incomes.

This evidence is based on **longitudinal studies** (those tracking individuals over many years), mostly conducted in the United States. These studies have involved random

assignment of individuals: some were directed into early childhood education programs and others were not. The process of **random assignment** allows researchers analyzing subsequent student outcomes to more easily identify the importance of the early childhood education programs in affecting people's life outcomes. They can also compare the impacts of the programs with other possible influences, such as parental educations of children in the program, or whether those children grew up in poor or more comfortable circumstances. Analysis of data collected in these longitudinal studies has shown major gains for people who have received good-quality early childhood education. Further, society in general has also benefited.

The measured ROI fluctuates across studies and is sensitive to how narrowly or broadly benefits are defined.[21] However, researchers have summarized the pattern of findings as follows. They all depend on a comparison of outcomes for individuals from poor families who attended high-quality early childhood education services with outcomes for individuals from poor families who did not attend. Those who attended were more likely to perform better at school, stay longer in school, attend universities, obtain and remain in steady employment, stay out of criminal behavior, get married and stay married, and form families. They were also found to experience better physical and mental health later in their lives.[22] Table 3.3 summarizes the ROI estimated from studies of three prominent programs. Brief descriptions of each program are provided here.

The High/Scope Perry Preschool Study examined the lives of 123 African Americans born in poverty and at high risk of failing in school. At ages 3 and 4, the individuals were randomly assigned to the experiment group, which received a high-quality preschool program, and the control group, which received no preschool program. The program was undertaken at Perry Elementary Public school in Ypsilanti, Michigan, between 1962 and 1965.

The Abecedarian Project, initiated in 1972 in Chapel Hill, North Carolina, provided full-time educational child care and high-quality preschool to children aged 0 to 5 from very disadvantaged backgrounds. The intervention was evaluated in a randomized controlled experiment involving 120 families; virtually all sample children were African American.

The Chicago Child–Parent Center Study was a longitudinal study that followed the progress of 989 children enrolled in 24 public preschools in low-income areas of Chicago between 1983 and 1986. It involved extensive family-support services as well as comprehensive educational services, health care, and free meals to each enrolled student. Their results were compared to 550 same-aged peers from similar socioeconomic backgrounds enrolled in other preschool programs throughout the area.

TABLE 3.3 Estimated ROI of Three Preschool Programs

PROGRAM	COST PER ENROLLEE, C	BENEFIT PER ENROLLEE, B[a]	ESTIMATED ROI = B/C
Perry Preschool	$20,591	$332,381	16.1
Abecedarian	$82,715	$206,252	2.5
Chicago	$9,622	$97,708	10.2

Sources: W. S. Barnett and L. N. Masse, "Early Childhood Program Design and Economic Returns: Comparative Benefit-Cost Analysis of the Abecedarian Program and Policy Implications," Economics of Education Review 26 (2007): 113–25; C. Belfield et al., "The High/Scope Perry Preschool Program," Journal of Human Resources 41, no. 1 (2006): 162–90; J. A. Temple and A. J. Reynolds, "Benefits and Costs of Investments in Preschool Education: Evidence from the Child-Parent Centers and Related Programs," Economics of Education Review 26, no. 1 (2007): 126–44.

Note: Values in 2015 dollars, converted by author from original published estimates.

[a]Benefit per enrollee refers to the dollar value of the gains from actually participating in one of these three programs.

Given this evidence, targeted subsidization of poor children into high-quality early childhood education services appears to be a very good use of government funding. Children from better-off families also benefit from early childhood education, but the long-term effects are less pronounced. It is also the case that better-off families are more likely than poor families to choose to place their children in early childhood education regardless of the amount of government subsidy.

Currently, most state governments in the United States provide at least some funding for early childhood education, usually for children from low-income households. Through the Head Start Program, discussed hereafter, the federal government offers similar support. Florida, Georgia, Oklahoma, and West Virginia offer universal preschool for all students. Significant advocacy efforts have taken place in some other states to encourage adoption of universal preschool education.[23]

CRITICAL THINKING QUESTIONS

1. Results from studies of early childhood education programs and their long-term impacts have not always suggested these programs have powerful, positive results. What factors might explain differences in these study findings?
2. What could policy makers learn from comparing evidence of long-term impacts across a variety of early childhood education programs?

Case Study 3.3 considers efforts to assist the **long-term unemployed** to return to paid employment. Long-term unemployment is typically defined as being without work for more than six months. It remains common for governments everywhere to offer meager income support to young people who are unemployed, and to impose make-work requirements as part of benefit payments. The investment perspective, however, encourages an alternative view. By making up-front efforts to support unemployed people and nurture their job skills, it is possible to transform them from facing a long period of benefit dependency to more rapidly becoming actively employed. As a result, they go from needing public support to being self-sufficient. They can become taxpayers, giving back to society. Such outcomes improve the well-being not only of the targeted individuals but also of society as a whole. The up-front expenditures needed to turn these lives around are ultimately minor, compared with the stream of benefits that can flow from this approach.

case study 3.3 Assisting the Long-Term Unemployed in Their Return to the Workforce

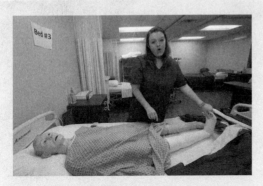

Trainees from a community college in California participate in a seven-day Summer Job Training Program that includes worksite visits and classes in interpersonal skills. Through such programs, job-seekers can gain greater self-confidence and insights into how to effectively add value as employees.

(AP Photo/Rogelio V. Solis)

For adolescents and young adults, spending too much time away from training or paid employment can have negative long-term effects. Economists refer to this situation as **scarring**.[24] Scarring can take several forms. Those who have been inactive as adolescents and young adults are more likely than others to experience future bouts of unemployment. Often, there is a mismatch between their skills or their work preferences and the jobs they are able to acquire. These people tend to have lower streams of income throughout their lives than do others who enjoy stable employment. There is also a greater likelihood that they will suffer psychological problems and the breakdown of the family in cases where one or more of the adults in the family is unemployed.[25]

In addition, people who take extensive spells outside the paid workforce to perform care duties in their families can have difficulties returning to paid employment. This situation is experienced primarily by women. The jobs that women enter after spells of full-time caregiving often seem poorly matched to their skills and are unsatisfying to them. Evidence shows a tendency for such women to retire from the labor force earlier than men and earlier than other women who did not lose touch with the workforce during their careers.[26]

Should policy makers care about these things? From an investment perspective, the answer is "yes." Studies have shown that appropriate support, guidance, or mentoring for people at critical decision points in their lives would likely have three kinds of positive benefit:

1. Such efforts can allow participants to have more satisfying, productive, higher-income, and socially engaged lives.
2. Through their support for participants, they can reduce future government spending by decreasing or eliminating benefit payments and the delivery of other individual and family support services.
3. They can increase the likelihood that participants will pay more taxes over the course of their lives.[27]

Governments in several countries are beginning to take an investment approach to working with people who are vulnerable to scarring effects. The United Kingdom is leading the way. For example, the Department for Work and Pensions conducted a multiyear randomized controlled experiment to test the effects of policies that helped long-term unemployed people return to and remain in permanent employment. The study findings showed strong positive returns on investments made in individuals.[28] Those who participated in the program were

TABLE 3.4 Estimated ROI for Assisting the Long-Term Unemployed in Their Return to the Workforce

PROGRAM	COST PER PARTICIPANT, C	BENEFIT PER PARTICIPANT, B[a]	ESTIMATED ROI = B/C
New Deal 25 Plus	$2,604	$6,162	2.4
New Deal for Lone Parents	$2,770	$3,889	1.4

Source: Richard Hendra et al., Breaking the Low-Pay, No-Pay Cycle: Final Evidence from the UK Employment Retention and Advancement (ERA) Demonstration, *Department for Work and Pensions Research Report No. 765 (London, UK: Department for Work and Pensions, 2011).*

Note: Values in 2015 dollars, converted by author from original published estimates.

[a] Benefit per enrollee refers to the dollar value of the gains from actually participating in one of these programs.

assisted to find employment. They were then supported by Advancement Support Advisers for up to two years. The advisers were expected to help the participants avoid some of the early pitfalls that sometimes cause new jobs to be short-lived. They were trained to help participants advance to positions of greater job security and better pay and working conditions, at either their current employers or new ones.

Special cash incentives were also given to encourage participants to remain in work, along with support to complete training while employed, and emergency payments were available to help participants overcome short-term barriers to staying in work. A cost-benefit analysis suggested that the ROI from one part of this program was equivalent to $2.40 for every $1.00 spent—a result well worth the expenditures. However, a variant program generated less promising results, suggesting that details of program design are critical. Table 3.4 summarizes the results of the analysis for two programs. **New Deal 25 Plus** was a mandatory program for longer-term unemployed people who were claiming a Jobseeker's Allowance for 18 or more months. **New Deal for Lone Parents** was a voluntary program that aimed to help and encourage single parents to improve their job readiness and employment opportunities and gain independence through working.[29]

CRITICAL THINKING QUESTIONS

1. What factors do you think would be critical for increasing the likelihood of long-term unemployed people successfully returning to paid work?
2. Some unemployed people will find it easier to return to work than others. Should governments treat all unemployed people similarly or differently in supporting their return to paid work? Explain your answer.

BROADER IMPLICATIONS FROM THE SPECIFIC CASES

These two cases highlight the possible gains when governments take care in choosing how to invest scarce program resources. The kind of knowledge that supports effective policy choices in early childhood education and in assisting job seekers can guide both government spending and cutting expenditures. Just as it would be foolish for governments to spend money poorly when they have large budgets, it is equally foolish—but commonly practiced—for governments to cut expenditures indiscriminately when belt-tightening is necessary.

If policy makers undertake serious, evidence-based efforts to determine the likely return from each additional dollar of expenditure in specific program areas, informed discussions can then take place as to where to prioritize the spending of new money and where to reduce current spending. Of course, governments will balance such decisions against their political calculations. Given their desire to remain in power, governments often make spending decisions in the hope of keeping the support of specific voters. That is the nature of democratic politics. Yet improving the evidence that guides government spending choices is highly desirable. It is likely to promote better overall social outcomes than have been achieved in the past. The approach of treating public policies as investments does not imply that all governments everywhere must suddenly start rushing to collect and analyze vast amounts of new data. Well-designed studies of specific programs can generate insights that transcend their limited origins. Toward this end, studies should exhibit several features:

- The studies should track program participants over time.
- Participants should be assigned randomly to the program being studied, and they should be matched with a control group of similar individuals who do not participate in the program. Such randomized controlled experiments that run over a period of years can generate rich evidence about program strengths and weaknesses.
- When matched with financial estimates of program costs and benefits, this information can tell us the estimated return to society of government investments in these public policies.

In many instances, jurisdictions can learn relevant and important lessons from observing the outcomes of policy studies performed elsewhere. Creative use of evidence-based investment analysis holds the promise of offering many insights for decision makers in jurisdictions where efforts to collect and analyze relevant data have not occurred. Thus, lack of evidence in a specific jurisdiction is no excuse for its political leaders to continue to make poorly informed policy choices.

THE INVESTMENT PERSPECTIVE AND THE FEDERAL SYSTEM OF GOVERNMENT

In federal systems of government, public policy choices made in one jurisdiction can influence citizens, organizations, and businesses in nearby jurisdictions. Sometimes such outcomes are anticipated. For example, policy makers and political pundits have long made arguments that American states should avoid becoming "welfare magnets" by offering income subsidies for poor people that are significantly higher than such subsidies in other states.[30] As another example, states often compete with one another to attract businesses by keeping corporate taxes low or by providing specific subsidies that support business development.[31] Sometimes changes in state-level policies generate unintended consequences in other states. Calculating policy impacts becomes more difficult whenever these interjurisdictional spillover effects occur.

The development of state transportation infrastructure offers a good example of state policy choices that can have major implications for neighboring states. When a state government contributes to the development of a new airport or expands an existing one, impacts beyond the state's border can occur. For example, the addition of a new runway at an airport can greatly enhance the capacity of that airport to support more aircraft takeoffs and landings. Assuming that the highways connecting to that airport can carry the additional traffic, this development can ease the ability of companies within a wide area—including in neighboring states—to ship their products to market more quickly.

To cite another example, of the top fifty busiest container ports in the world, six are located in the United States. Three are located in California (Los Angeles, Long Beach, and Oakland); the other three are in Newark, New Jersey, Tacoma, Washington, and Norfolk, Virginia. In recent times, the amount of freight these ports handle has doubled every decade. Analysis of port development and its impacts indicate that spending on infrastructure of this kind generally produces a major benefit for the state where the port is located. As anticipated, port expansion also tends to reduce transportation costs for businesses both within the home state and well beyond its borders.[32]

Analysis also suggests that port expansion can have a magnetic effect for business location. Businesses often crowd into the region close to the expanded port. This tendency draws employees from neighboring states and beyond into closer proximity to the port. The reduction in available employees in the neighboring states and beyond forces business located there to pay more for labor.

This discussion of port expansion and the broader, interstate consequences highlights one of the complications of federalism: public policies and programs established in one state can have positive or negative implications for

Container ports like this one at Long Beach, California, are essential to the functioning of the modern, globalized economy. Greater economic integration places more pressure on key points in the logistical chain. In federal systems of government, infrastructural investment decisions made by one state government can have significant implications for business growth in many other states.

(REUTERS/Alamy Stock Photo)

other states. Although national-level government policies sometimes reduce such impacts, they are ultimately a fixed characteristic of federalism. When we discuss public policies as investments, it is always worthwhile to consider how those policies might have either complementary or adverse effects on other nearby jurisdictions.[33]

LOOKING BEYOND FINANCIAL CONSIDERATIONS

Treating public policies as investments has numerous advantages, and we have encountered many of these at various points in this chapter. However, it is also important that we consider valid criticisms of this framework. We will consider two here.

The first concern is that talk of "investing" could lead policy makers to allocate resources mainly toward young people anticipated to make significant social contributions in the future. In the process, resources might be allocated away from the elderly and the seriously disadvantaged in society.[34] This legitimate concern suggests that we should always subsume discussions of public policies as investments within broader understandings about what values we ascribe to as a society—that is, the investment perspective should force more open discussion of values. In particular, the approach should encourage discussion of trade-offs among government spending choices. This can be useful for leading decision makers to discuss what matters in society, and how effectively different policy approaches contribute to desired social outcomes.

A second concern reflects a criticism directed long ago at cost-benefit analysis. That is, the approach assumes that the effects of public policies fall evenly across all groups in society. This assumption is patently false. Hence, gender analysis and race analysis have been advanced as alternative approaches to conducting policy analysis. These approaches force explicit consideration of how policy choices affect different groups of people differently.[35]

It is important for us to view the investment approach as a tool that gives a big picture assessment of the merits or disadvantages of specific public policy choices. At the same time, it is entirely reasonable to use this approach in combination with approaches that take into account such matters as gender and racial differences in policy impacts. In the future, we should consider developing more sophisticated models for assessing returns of investment, and determining if the returns differ markedly across different groups.

Consideration of these two critiques raises a third reservation about treating public policies as investments. That is, we should not stretch the use of the concept to the point that it becomes meaningless. For example, an investment perspective would never justify spending large amounts of money keeping very sick, very old people alive indefinitely on life-support systems. This view does not imply that the investment perspective should be used to promote euthanasia of those unable to contribute to society, as judged in merely material ways. Rather, it suggests that there are going to be times when acknowledging other values must accompany treating public policies as investments.

What remains important about the investment perspective is that it allows us to think hard about government spending and to avoid the possibility that scarce resources are being wasted. If we can find ways of promoting better economic outcomes while conserving government expenditures, we should always have some potential in society to allocate resources to the truly disadvantaged. We would do this because it is the right thing to do—not because it makes sense on narrow investment terms.

Other criticisms of the investment approach deserve our consideration. For example, we know that a lot of policies in society often end up providing assistance to middle-class families that could probably afford to purchase subsidized services at full cost. Examples include provision of early education programs and public schooling. However, many policy makers view these provisions for the middle classes as politically expedient in that they avoid the prospect that the middle classes will remove all support for programs that help people in serious need. Again, the investment perspective cannot really help sort out important policy issues like this one. However, discussing public policies as investments might increase the likelihood that politicians will talk more openly about such considerations.

THE INVESTMENT PERSPECTIVE AND THE PROMOTION OF CIVIL RIGHTS

The investment approach gives a big picture assessment of the strengths or weaknesses of specific public policy choices. It is entirely reasonable to use this approach in combination with approaches that take into account such matters as gender and racial differences in policy impacts. In the future, we should consider developing more sophisticated models for assessing returns of investment, and determine if the returns differ markedly across different groups. James Heckman's analyses of outcomes from early childhood education take us in that direction.[36] In that work, he compared the ROI for children from low-income households with that for children from middle- and high-income houses. Case Study 3.4 discusses the Head Start program and the investment perspective.

case study 3.4 The Head Start Program and the Pursuit of Civil Rights

Head Start programs like the one depicted here are now common across the United States.

(Marjorie Kamys Cotera/Bob Daemmrich Photography/Alamy Stock Photo)

The Head Start program, funded by the U.S. government, has been delivering early childhood education, health, and welfare services to children from impoverished families for over five decades. The program was established in 1964 as part of President Lyndon Johnson's Great Society agenda. At its core, Head Start aims to help children from impoverished backgrounds gain a better start in life than they otherwise would have. It was also designed to advance civil rights. Indeed, historians of the program have pointed to the direct link between economic advancement law and the Civil Rights Act of 1964.

Many programs funded by the federal government involve allocating money to the states, which in turn fund local activities. When Head Start was designed, attention was focused on the tendency for some state politicians to perpetuate racial inequality through their funding decisions. As one response to that, the Johnson administration deliberately sought to fund local Head Start programs directly. This action would help prevent state governments from undermining Head Start's address of racial inequality in the United States. In 1990, Congress passed the Head Start Expansion and Quality Improvement Act. In 1994, Congress authorized creation of Early Head Start, a companion program for low-income families with children aged 0 to 3.

Is investment in Head Start worthwhile? For several reasons, that question has been hotly debated over the years.

- First, for ideological reasons, some people oppose policies and programs to assist the poor. They believe it is better to have people find ways to support themselves or to receive voluntary support from those who are better off.
- Second, Head Start is a service for the truly disadvantaged, and often those who are disadvantaged come from minority groups in society. Racism and other forms of prejudice can drive the criticism of programs of this kind. When ideology and prejudice drive critique of programs, evidence of their impacts tends to be of little interest to the critics.

Evidence on the impact of Head Start has sometimes fueled opposition. From the outset, Head Start has been subjected to extensive evaluation, and these evaluations continue. Some critics have suggested that the evaluation evidence does not support the claim that Head Start makes a difference in the lives of the targeted children. Nevertheless, the current state of evaluation results and cost-benefit analyses suggest that the program serves as an important form of investment that yields sound ROI.[37] Further, over recent years, efforts have been made to significantly improve the quality of the evidence used to judge short- and long-term program effects. The expectation is that this better evidence will greatly improve future assessments of the ROI realized from Head Start programs.

Today, the Head Start program is thriving. Indeed, with the influx of immigrants to the United States from many countries in recent years, Head Start is now seen as more vital than ever as a policy that assists young children to participate effectively in schooling and more generally in society. Overall, Head Start is a well-established example of government treatment of a public policy as an investment while simultaneously using that policy to advance civil rights.

CRITICAL THINKING QUESTIONS

1. In what sense is the investment perspective consistent with the pursuit of civil rights?
2. What are some examples of instances where the investment perspective could potentially be inconsistent with the pursuit of civil rights?

TOWARD SYSTEMATIC APPLICATION OF THE INVESTMENT APPROACH

Treating public policies as investments is an important way to ensure that choices affecting specific policy areas are fully consistent with broader policy goals. The approach to public policy advocated here contrasts sharply with other policies that produce poorly functioning public services that are underfunded, populated by demoralized staff, and constantly criticized by citizens. When governments prioritize their activities and determine the most appropriate ways to meet specific policy goals, they open the possibility of delivering high-value public services by top-notch professionals, whose efforts are fully appreciated by citizens. That goal is attainable. But getting there takes resolve and calls for a way of approaching public policy making that is more focused and deliberate than ways in the past.

Applied consistently, the investment perspective on public policies holds the prospect of allowing governments to make evidence-based judgments concerning the policies and programs most worthy of additional spending and those for which spending could be reduced without major losses. Of course, such a comment suggests that politicians are ready and waiting for advice that will guide them to make economically rational decisions. In the cut and thrust of policy making, many other considerations, including interest group politics, public support for programs, perceptions of fairness, and concerns about winning the next election all lead to deviations from any kind of strict adherence to a calculus of costs, benefits, and estimated ROI. However, economic rationality cannot prevail if sound evidence to support it is not presented during policy discussions. Further, to the extent that the investment perspective is given appropriate emphasis in all policy discussions, the odds are higher that this way of thinking about public policies will become part of all policy discussions. When this goal is reached, the odds that investment thinking will inform popular discussions, media commentary, and electoral debates also will rise.

In 1983, the Washington state legislature created the Washington State Institute for Public Policy (WSIPP). The institute's mission is "to carry out practical, nonpartisan research at the direction of the legislature or board of directors."[38] For many years, the institute has led the way in treating public policies as investments. More recently, the Pew Charitable Trusts and the MacArthur Foundation have been collaborating with other states to establish similar institutes to deliver evidence-based advice to guide policy investments.

The WSIPP works closely with legislators, legislative and state agency staff, and subject matter experts to ensure its studies effectively answer policy questions. In many respects, WSIPP is like other nonpartisan policy research organizations, such as the Legislative Analyst's Office, which services the California State Legislature; the Congressional Budget Office in Washington, DC; and the RAND Corporation, a consultancy headquartered in Santa Monica, California, with offices around the United States.

What makes WSIPP distinctive is that for decades it has focused on producing comprehensive, evidence-based reviews of policy strategies that follow a common methodology. The overall purpose of the institute's work is to identify ideas for policies and programs that can deliver better outcomes per dollar of taxpayer spending. Toward this end, the Institute has developed a general research approach that combines amassing evidence from evaluation studies with the conduct of cost-benefit analysis. By consistently applying this approach, the Institute has developed a solid reputation for providing policy makers with trustworthy "bottom-line" estimates of the likely returns of investing in specific policies and programs. In the Institute's words: "We identify a number of evidence-based options that can help policy makers achieve desired outcomes as well as offer taxpayers a good return on investment, with low risk of failure."[39]

WSIPP's analytical approach offers an excellent example of how to treat public policies as investments, and how carefully and consistently to estimate return on those investments. The idea of grouping policies and programs into portfolios for consideration by policy makers takes the investment language to a logical conclusion. The calculation of risks associated with policies and programs also helps to address a key concern of elected decision makers: they do not want to adopt policies that subsequently blow up in their faces. As such, the risk calculations can also raise the chances that policy making will not be as timid and path dependent as the incremental view of policy making would predict. Case Study 3.5 presents an overview of the Institute's work, relating it to the general framework we have discussed so far.

case study 3.5 The Investment Approach, from Theory to Practice

The Washington State Institute for Public Policy has adopted a general approach to developing and offering advice on policy investments.[40] First, institute staff members ask: What works? They seek to answer this question through systematically assessing evidence concerning particular programs and their social outcomes—for example, programs designed to improve child welfare. One such program, the **Triple-P Positive Parenting Program**, was pioneered by Matt Sanders of the University of Queensland, Australia, and has been used in 25 countries around the world. It assists parents in creating more affirming relationships with their children, thus improving family life and reducing the risks of violence and instability in their families.

When beginning a new study, WSIPP staff members look for research studies produced in the United States and elsewhere concerning specific program interventions of this sort. They look for studies with strong, credible evaluation designs and ignore those employing weak research methods. In this way, Institute staff members systematically assess the extent to which given programs achieved their intended effects. Notice that this part of the approach combines

Step 1 (focus on existing policies and programs) and Step 2 (gather policy evidence) of the Policy Investment Checklist introduced earlier.

Next, WSIPP staff members ask: What makes economic sense? To answer this question, they conduct cost-benefit analysis. They determine what activities were undertaken to produce the program effects they have noted, and they calculate how much it would cost to replicate these activities in the context of Washington State. They then calculate how much the outcomes of the program would be worth to the state's population. This work is consistent with Step 3 (measure desired effects) and Step 4 (assess costs and benefits) of the Policy Investment Checklist.

Institute staff members have developed a continuously improving economic model that is designed to provide consistent valuations of program costs and benefits so that they can make fair comparisons across alternate policy options. For example, in considering programs to improve child welfare, they compared the Triple-P Positive Parenting Program with other interventions, such as the use of **Intensive Family Preservation Services**. These are short-term, home-based crisis intervention services intended to keep children in their biological home—rather than moving them to foster homes—by improving family functioning. This program emphasizes contact with the family within 24 hours of a crisis, staff accessibility around the clock, small caseload sizes, service duration of four to six weeks, and provision of intensive, concrete services and counseling for the involved families. When considering comparative program costs and benefits, WSIPP staff members routinely calculate and report the net present value of programs and their rates of ROI.

Next, institute staff members ask: What is the risk that a program, if adopted, would not yield a positive ROI? To answer this question, they explore the sensitivity of the results of a cost-benefit analysis. For example, the institute estimated positive returns from a range of child welfare programs. Through this work, they determined that the returns on both the Triple-P Positive Parenting Program and Intensive Family Preservation Services were positive. Further, they determined that, even if some of their cost and benefit estimates were wrong, the likelihood that program costs would outweigh program benefits was low in both cases. In contrast, they found some other programs they examined at the same time to be much less likely to generate benefits that outweighed their costs. These conclusions are consistent with Step 5 (offer robust advice) of the Policy Investment Checklist.

As their final analytical action (again, consistent with Step 5), WSIPP staff members ask: How would policy influence statewide outcomes? Here, they make an estimate of how a "portfolio" of programs and policies—introduced and implemented as a group—would affect valued outcomes in Washington State. This portfolio analysis was first applied in 2006, when the Institute estimated how a group of adult corrections programs, juvenile justice programs, and programs designed to assist at-risk young people through mentoring, guidance, and support strategies (placed in the catch-all category of "prevention programs") could affect valued outcomes in the state. Those outcomes included reducing Washington's crime rate, preventing the need to build more prisons, and reducing overall state and local criminal justice spending. The state legislature then used this portfolio information in subsequent sessions to guide budget choices and policy-making decisions. The Institute takes the view that portfolio analysis of this kind could be expanded and applied across a range of substantive policy areas.

CRITICAL THINKING QUESTIONS

1. What are some benefits of establishing an institute to routinely study the merits of public policy investments?
2. How could a systematic approach to studying policy investments be combined with systematic assessment of the contribution of policies to the pursuit of civil rights?

Of course, there is always more to policy and program design than what is achieved through the careful calculation of costs and benefits. In Chapter 1, seven general policy goals were introduced: (1) defending people and property and maintaining public order; (2) promoting human flourishing, (3) supporting effective nongovernmental institutions, (4) promoting efficiency, (5) promoting sustainability, (6) promoting social equity, and (7) advancing human rights. Construed narrowly, the investment perspective has the most to tell us about the goal of promoting efficiency. However, as the discussion in Case Study 3.5 has shown, it is possible to pay careful attention to a range of policies that, effectively implemented, could contribute to the development of young people, the strengthening of families, and less reliance on incarceration in the criminal justice system.

One way or another, then, efforts like those taken by WSIPP can increase the odds of achieving most of the general policy goals listed here. This is the greatest promise of an approach to policy analysis, policy advising, and policy making that treats public policies as investments.

CHAPTER SUMMARY

This chapter has introduced the core focus of this text: treating public policies as investments. All the chapters that follow apply this approach to assessing public policy choices in a broad variety of policy areas.

In setting the scene for treating public policies as investments, we first reviewed the function of policy analysis in the policy-making process. Policy analysts provide information with the intention of helping decision makers choose wisely when adopting public policies. They gather information on current issues or challenges, identify policy alternatives that could address them, and indicate policy approaches that would likely generate improvements over the current situation.

The framework for treating public policies as investments is captured in the Policy Investment Checklist, which has five steps:

1. Focus on existing policies and programs.
2. Gather policy evidence.
3. Measure desired effects.
4. Assess costs and benefits.
5. Offer robust advice.

Although there is far more to policy analysis than calculating the expected financial return to society of spending for specific policy options, it is fundamental to making informed choices that advice of this nature be offered to decision makers. The *Moneyball for Government* movement offers evidence of how the investment approach is beginning to gain attention among policy makers. Two case studies provided examples showing how public policies are analyzed as investments. The first considered the value to society of early childhood education programs. The second considered the value of helping the long-term unemployed return to the workforce.

After introducing a framework for treating public policies as investments, and examples of this treatment, we considered how federalism can produce state-to-state spillover effects from the policy choices made by individual states. Those effects can be positive or negative. We also considered the merits of broadening analysis beyond financial concerns. This topic led to a discussion of how viewing public policies as investments is compatible with the pursuit of civil rights. A major example is the long-standing Head Start program, designed to deliver early childhood education, health, and welfare services to children from impoverished families. The investment perspective on public policies is compatible with the pursuit of many nonmonetary values in society, such as human flourishing.

A final case study, of the Washington State Institute for Public Policy, showed how the Institute's analytical procedures are consistent with the Policy Investment Checklist. Their approach to treating public policies as investments is increasingly being applied elsewhere in the United States, especially at the state level.

CONNECTIONS TO OTHER CHAPTERS

Chapters 4 to 11 consistently apply the investment perspective to a broad variety of public policy areas. Throughout these chapters, the Policy Investment Checklist is used to assess specific public policy initiatives. Were the investment perspective and the Policy Investment Checklist to be routinely applied in government, smart policy choices would ultimately serve to limit the overall size of government, relative to economic activity. This argument assumes a situation where social preferences do not change over time, which is in fact highly debatable. But committing consistently to funding policies that yield positive ROI would grow the size of the economy in the specific jurisdiction.

When public policies generate good ROI, they improve the quality of people's lives and their capabilities to contribute to their own well-being and that of others. Good infrastructure, good defense and homeland security, good schooling, good health care, a social safety net, effective systems of criminal justice, smart investments in science, and concern for environmental protection are policy choices that hold the prospect of increasing overall social well-being. And this list is not exhaustive.

Smart investing today holds the prospect of promoting human flourishing and—crucially—of expanding the overall economy. If individuals can live more productive and richer lives, society as a whole will improve. Indeed, opportunities will open up for those societies to become even more compassionate and caring than societies with fewer economic resources. Treating public policies as investments can produce such outcomes. In the chapters to follow, we see how.

KEY TERMS

Investment

Recombination

Regression analysis

Quasi-experimental assessments

Statistical modeling

Meta-analysis

Cost-benefit analysis

Discount rate

Prevailing interest rate

Net present value

Return on investment (ROI)

Randomized controlled experiment

Sensitivity analysis

Early childhood education

Longitudinal studies

Random assignment

Long-term unemployed

New Deal 25 Plus

New Deal for Lone Parents

Scarring

Triple-P Positive Parenting Program

Intensive Family Preservation Services

SUGGESTIONS FOR FURTHER READING

Aos, Steve, and Elizabeth Drake. *Prison, Police, and Programs: Evidence-Based Options That Reduce Crime and Save Money* (Doc. No. 13–11–1901). Olympia: Washington State Institute for Public Policy, 2013. This report offers an excellent example of how the findings of investment analyses can be clearly summarized for policy makers.

Boardman, Anthony E., David Greenberg, Aidan Vining, and David Weimer. *Cost-Benefit Analysis: Concepts and Practice,* 4th ed. Boston: Prentice Hall, 2011. This book is recognized as an authoritative and comprehensive overview of cost-benefit analysis, which underpins the assessment of public policies as investments.

House of Commons Committee of Public Accounts. *Big Science: Public Investment in Large Scientific Facilities.* Sixtieth Report of Session 2006–07. London, UK: The Stationery Office, 2007. This report shows how the investment perspective can be used to organize a detailed discussion of a major policy issue.

Lucius, Irene, et al. *Green Infrastructure: Sustainable Investments for the Benefit of Both People and Nature.* Brussels: European Union, 2011. This report offers another example of how the investment perspective can be used to organize a detailed discussion of a major policy issue.

Mintrom, Michael. "Cost-Benefit Analysis," in *Contemporary Policy Analysis,* chap. 13. New York: Oxford University Press, 2012. This chapter offers an overview of cost-benefit analysis and how it might be applied to calculate the ROIs of public policies.

Mintrom, Michael, et al. *An Agenda for Amazing Children: Report of the Taskforce on Early Childhood Education.* Wellington, New Zealand: Ministry of Education, 2012. This report treats spending on early childhood education as an investment, but also discusses a range of issues that go well beyond the financial consequences of investing in this policy area.

Nussle, Jim, and Peter Orszag, eds. *Moneyball for Government.* San Bernardino, CA: Disruption Books, 2014. A collection of essays arguing for evidence-based policy making, placing central focus on ROI in public policies. It takes an explicitly bipartisan approach.

Weimer, David L., and Aidan R. Vining, eds. *Investing in the Disadvantaged: Assessing the Benefits and Costs of Social Programs.* Washington, DC: Georgetown University Press, 2009. This book offers a sustained exploration of how cost-benefit analysis can support policy investment decisions, edited by leading contributors to training in cost-benefit analysis.

WEBSITES

- The Washington State Institute for Public Policy provides Washington policy makers with lists of well-researched public policies expected to lead to better statewide outcomes. It is at the forefront of organizations that treat public policies as investments. http://www.wsipp.wa.gov/

- The Pew–MacArthur Results First Initiative has taken its cue from the work of the WSIPP. A project of the Pew Charitable Trusts and the John D. and Catherine T. MacArthur Foundation, it involves working with states "to implement an innovative cost-benefit analysis approach that helps them invest in policies and programs that are proven to work." http://www.pewtrusts.org/en/projects/pew-macarthur-results-first-initiative

- Results for America seeks to bring about broader systems change so that "investing in what works" becomes the new norm for allocating public dollars. http://results4america.org/

- Moneyball for Government is the website accompanying the book of the same name edited by Jim Nussle and Peter Orszag. The site includes a link to a 2014 *PBS News Hour* video segment in which Gwen Ifill interviewed John Bridgeland and Gene Sperling on why an investment approach may be the answer to solving political gridlock. http://moneyballforgov.com/using-a-numbers-based-approach-to-end-political-gridlock-in-moneyball-for-government/

FOR DISCUSSION

1. Many different groups of people and organizations seek to influence the public policy choices elected politicians make. What unique role do policy analysts play in the policy-making process?

2. Throughout this chapter, we have encountered a variety of examples of how the investment approach to public policies has been applied. Think about a public policy issue of high interest to you. How might you use an investment approach to assess the merits of public policy choices in this issue area? Beyond wanting to know if a policy approach would produce a worthwhile ROI, what other questions would you ask to assess the merits of that policy option?

3. Several times in this chapter, we have noted that lack of good information has often frustrated efforts to treat public policies as investments. How optimistic should we be that better policy evidence will be available in the future? If a specific state or country makes limited efforts to evaluate its existing policies and programs, does its limited efforts mean that it will have difficulty estimating the returns to be gained from future policy investments? Explain your answer by using specific present-day examples.

CHAPTER 4

PUBLIC INFRASTRUCTURE

Public infrastructure consists of all the collectively used structures and systems that support human activities in an economically advanced, sophisticated society. Specialists involved with public infrastructure tend to agree on the core set of structures and systems the term encompasses. It is a big set that includes roads, bridges, tunnels, mass transit systems, railroads, ports, canals, airports, and other transport facilities; water supply systems, reservoirs, drainage systems, and sewage systems and treatment plants; power generation plants, electricity transmission and distribution networks, oil and gas pipelines, refineries, and storage facilities; and telecommunications, television, and cable networks.

This list is not exhaustive.[1] With time, more structures and systems will join the list as part of the infrastructure of contemporary society. For example, wireless and satellite networks and cloud-computing platforms are now fully integrated into the telecommunications infrastructure. It is difficult to imagine life without them. Therefore, as technological experts develop and incorporate innovations into everyday life, the broader systems that support them can legitimately be classified as part of the public infrastructure. Beyond the items listed here, some infrastructure specialists also include government buildings and public recreation facilities in their inventory. Thus, we quite reasonably might extend the list to incorporate courthouses, jails, firehouses, police stations, school buildings, post offices, stadiums, and other arenas.

This chapter provides an introduction to policy making as it relates to the provision and control of public infrastructure. We will consider why public infrastructure matters, with special focus on the ways that aspects of public policy design can serve either to promote or to hinder efficient and effective asset management. Since private sector businesses conduct a lot of infrastructural activities, a history exists in which decision makers view public infrastructure development and maintenance from an investment perspective.

Facing page: Development of the Interstate Highway System in the United States began during the 1950s. Today, that system is integral to social and economic activities. Funded by federal and state governments, the system is a vital piece of contemporary public infrastructure.

(Harrison Shull/Aurora/Getty Images)

Although this chapter is of necessity introductory and general in its treatment of public infrastructure, it explores several major themes in contemporary discussions of public policy. Those themes include the origins of public value, the effective allocation of scarce resources, systems governance, ownership and control, and the calculation of return on investment (ROI).

This chapter introduces you to:

- Reasons why governments get involved in the provision of public infrastructure
- Traditional approaches to funding infrastructure
- Infrastructure investments in a federal system of government
- Contemporary policy issues
- Public infrastructure provision and the investment perspective
- How changing control and ownership of assets can potentially improve their value to the public
- Infrastructure and the promotion of civil rights
- Lessons for public policy emerging from this review of public infrastructure

AN INTRODUCTION TO PUBLIC INFRASTRUCTURE

For public policy specialists, public infrastructure represents an important area for consideration and analysis. When jurisdictions have an abundance of well-functioning public infrastructure, opportunities exist for people to thrive in countless ways. Water, sewage, and electrical systems ensure that people can live cleanly, comfortably, and at less risk of contracting communicable diseases. Their ability to be productive greatly increases. Accessible transport and telecommunications systems allow people to readily meet up, talk, and interact in all kinds of ways. These big systems supporting our lives allow us to be creative and to engage in meaningful work, paid or unpaid. Therefore, well-functioning public infrastructure extends the potential for people to flourish socially and economically. Given that access to this infrastructure is frequently open to all, it serves to create opportunities for everyone, whether rich, middle class, or poor. In this sense, public infrastructure can facilitate greater individual engagement in collective pursuits and also extend individual freedoms.

Government funding built and maintains a lot of the assets that make up the public infrastructure. In addition, governments frequently control operations of systems comprising parts of the public infrastructure—either through ownership and management or through **regulation**. Regulation of services—such as transport, electrical, and telecommunications networks—has often been extensive. Since the 19th century, regulators in the United States have sought to control entry into specific infrastructural industries, have often regulated prices, and have frequently been highly dogmatic concerning the operation of services (partly for reasons of public safety, but for other reasons as well).

The structures and systems that constitute public infrastructure typically operate at the interface of the public and private sectors. Since individuals and communities derive profoundly important benefits from well-performing public infrastructure, the governance and operation of various components attract a great deal of attention from interest groups. Those interest groups can include companies and workers contributing to direct service provision, and industries and consumers who see their own interests as closely affected by the operations of the infrastructural assets in question. The activities of interest groups who seek to influence public policy relating to various elements of public infrastructure have been the focus of a significant body of scholarship produced by political scientists and economists.[2] Case Study 4.1 explores some of the complications concerning governance of public infrastructure, with a focus on the New York City subways.

case study 4.1 Congestion on the New York City Subways

The New York City subways are becoming increasingly congested, leading to calls for a range of possible solutions, most of which are expensive and would take years to implement.

(David Grossman/Alamy Stock Photo)

Many large cities use commuter rail and subway systems to allow the rapid movement of large numbers of people. In New York City,

as elsewhere, the subway system has been operating for over a hundred years. Although it is part of the fabric of big-city life, it wrestles with congestion problems that continue to grow. Trains and stations are packed at rush hour, creating delays. On one level, these problems highlight the success and popularity of the subway as a means of mass transportation. On another, they highlight the necessity to continuously upgrade infrastructure in the face of expanding consumer demand.

Popular discourse suggests current congestion problems for the New York City subway system derive from limited government commitment to maintaining and upgrading the system. Indeed, politics and the structures that provide funding and oversight of the subway system do complicate matters.

The New York City subway system is governed by the Metropolitan Transportation Authority (MTA). This has not always been the case. Initial system development occurred through various public and private partnerships. However, through asset consolidation efforts, by the mid-20th century the whole system was fully government owned and operated.

In 2015, the MTA committed to spending around $30 billion on new train cars, buses, and a new fare-payment system in the coming years. Money has also been devoted to station improvements and updated signal systems that allow more trains to run. Funding for such improvements is provided by city, state, and federal government sources in addition to issuance of bonds. Given the large amounts of money involved, governance of the MTA is convoluted. This complexity introduces political uncertainty and delays in the release of funds, for changes of government at any level can hinder the ongoing flow of expected funding. Meanwhile, advocates for subway passengers lobby key politicians to resist fare increases that would aid the financing of system improvements.

The recent surge in ridership has pushed the system to its limit. For example, for New Yorkers who rely on the 86th Street subway station on the Upper East Side of Manhattan, the morning commute is a humbling experience. An endless stream of people funnel onto the platforms. Trains arrive with a wall of humanity already blocking the doorways. As a train pulls into the station, riders scan for an opening and, if they can, squeeze in for a suffocating ride downtown. "You can wait four or five subways to get on, and you're just smushed," said one commuter before boarding a train.[3]

Kyle M. Kirschling studied the history of the New York City subway system, focusing on ownership, changing ridership levels, and overall performance.[4] Kirschling contends that problems in system performance—manifested most obviously by congestion—can be credited to public ownership. He notes three issues that reduce the possibility of gaining high returns from ongoing public investments in the system:

1. Wages for MTA workers are significantly higher than those for comparable workers operating in private transportation contexts.
2. Public ownership makes it difficult for sufficient funds to be devoted to system maintenance and upgrades.
3. Those who currently control the system—politicians and government bureaucrats—lack incentives to drive innovation. In contrast, private owners could more readily make management and investment choices that create more benefits for riders and acceptable profits for company owners.

This prescription for system improvements is probably not the most obvious to riders, who just want more trains and better stations. Later in this chapter we explore infrastructure ownership and management issues more closely.

CRITICAL THINKING QUESTIONS

1. What factors make it difficult for the MTA to fund improvements in the New York subway system?
2. What would be some possible benefits and risks of transferring subway system ownership from government to private owners?

WHY GOVERNMENTS GET INVOLVED IN INFRASTRUCTURE

In all countries, governments fund and directly provide many elements of the public infrastructure. In instances of privately owned and operated assets, governments exert considerable control over them. This is as true in highly developed economies as it is in developing ones. Taken in isolation, quite a few elements of public infrastructure could feasibly be privately owned and operated. What rationales exist for government involvement in the provision of public infrastructure? We can consider several. At the same time, we need to acknowledge that once a set of specific institutional arrangements have been put in place to support provision of specific services, making major adjustments to those arrangements becomes difficult.[5]

In the public policy literature, services produced using infrastructural assets are often characterized as public goods. Roads offer a useful example. Roads in specific locations are **public goods** because, once supplied, they are open to consumption by anyone who wants to use them, with no possibility of exclusion. This nonexcludability feature of public goods—like roads—means that funding them except through government actions is virtually impossible. The assumption is that people will **free-ride**—that is, avoid contributing to provision and maintenance of the roads, while receiving benefits paid for by the contributions of others. Each resident might ask, "Why should I contribute to the building of the roads around here if others will? Once they have funded their construction, I'll be able to use them all for free anyway."

Of course, when everyone thinks this way, no one would be "foolish" enough to fund road construction. With no apparent demand being revealed, no (private) supply would be forthcoming. The upshot is that infrastructural items like roads, when they are deemed public goods, are typically funded by governments.

There is something about this roads-as-public-goods example, however, that does not ring true. That is, if there were straightforward ways of excluding people from using roads in a community, they would go from being public goods to being private goods. Individuals wanting to use them would be required to pay a fee. A speculator, predicting that people will have an interest in using roads, could then build roads that are excludable and charge people entry fees to use them. At this point, roads would become the same, for example, as movie theaters. And no one has ever proposed that movie theaters should be supplied and operated by the government. In fact, in the United States, some of the earliest roads and rudimentary road networks were privately owned and operated by companies granted charters to do so by respective state governments.

The early days of road provision in the newly emerging American society enjoyed two features that would soon fade away. First, there were few roads. Second, there were few road users. So establishing barriers to entry onto the roads and imposing **user fees**—charges for the use of a product or service—were both straightforward activities. Presumably, things became more difficult to manage when more roads were developed—with many more ways to access them—and as user numbers increased. At some point, in the absence of low-cost ways to monitor usage and charge user fees, it would have made sense to treat roads as nonexcludable public goods. Then, too, governments in specific jurisdictions would have found it preferable to raise revenues through tax systems and then develop roads and road networks that everybody was free to use.

Actually, it was not the inherent qualities of roads themselves that made them public goods but rather the difficulty of finding low-cost, fair mechanisms for collecting user fees. The same problem continues to plague governments today. However, gasoline taxes help to ensure that some of the costs of using public roads are put back onto those who use them. The more you use the roads, the more gasoline you use, and the more tax you pay toward road maintenance. Of course, today's low gasoline prices—and the enhanced efficiency of car engines—create additional revenue problems. Still, direct user fees or taxes do not comprise the sole source of funding for these public assets.

In regard to local public goods, it appears that many elements of public infrastructure are potentially excludable, and local governments can readily assign user fees. Examples include water supply, drainage, and sewage systems. In each case, service providers can charge for individual use of the service. As metering technology has become more sophisticated, it has become possible for some degree of charging based on usage levels. With these systems, exclusion is possible, although it might sometimes be difficult and undesirable. (For reasons of public sanitation, local governments tend not to want to "turn off" access to sewage and drainage systems—or make use of such systems optional to property owners.) Upon purchasing properties, owners essentially register as liable for payment of various property taxes and fees that cover provision of these kinds of services. The difficulty and undesirability of excluding these services make it appropriate to treat them as public goods.

FUNDING INFRASTRUCTURE

So far, we have considered why governments usually play a central role in the funding and provision of roads and water supply, drainage, and sewage systems. Where individual access to services can be denied and where service usage can be measured through meters, the public goods argument for government involvement in service provision no longer applies. Nonetheless, in many countries, government entities have often provided electricity, gas, and telephone services, even as they have charged consumers for the amount of service being used. Why not have private companies supply all of these services?

Another rationale to justify government provision of infrastructural assets is that they are **natural monopolies**. This term refers to services that cost a lot to establish and that become economically feasible only when large numbers of people use them, and where competitive supply appears either wasteful or unworkable. Indeed, quite a few examples now exist of infrastructural industries operating under private ownership that were initially established, owned, and operated by governments. For instance, during the first half of the 20th century, when massive expansion occurred in the provision of electricity, it was common practice for governments worldwide to be heavily involved in the construction of electric power generation and distribution systems.

In contrast to private entities, governments have tended to be better able to raise the funds needed to support massive projects of this kind. They have also had the coordination capability and know-how required to plan and manage such work. Because governments have run these systems, they have also avoided a common problem associated with natural monopolies: they can safeguard electricity consumers from exposure to **monopoly pricing**. When natural monopolies are privately controlled, there is a risk that pricing practices that exploit consumers to the benefit of shareholders will be imposed. As technical knowledge has increased and innovation has occurred in the management of electricity, gas, and telephone systems, governments have found ways to introduce a degree of competition into provision of these services. Although many governments still tend to have interests in some aspects of these systems, the move toward a degree of private ownership accompanied by close government regulation has been common.

REGULATING INFRASTRUCTURE

When new technologies and systems have become sufficiently large and stable to be thought of as part of the everyday infrastructure, governments have often acted to promote stability in their supply. Such well-intentioned regulation has had mixed consequences. The railroad systems created in the United States in the 19th century present a good example. These systems were mostly developed and managed by private companies, although those companies were frequent recipients of special land rights and financial subsidies granted by state and federal government. Once the systems were in place, governments moved to protect them from competition that could potentially make specific routes uneconomic to run. It turns out, of course, that such regulatory moves restricting competition in the railroads also greatly served the interests of the established companies.

The development of stable road networks and the emergence of the freight-trucking industry in the first three decades of the 20th century were perceived as a threat to the railroads. As a result, the trucking industry became subject to **heavy-handed regulation**. Such regulation determined route structures, fees to be charged, and aspects of service provision, along with prescribing appropriate safety measures. Like the prior regulation of the railroads, trucking regulations of this kind remained in place until well into the 1970s.[6]

In the lead-up to a period of significant **deregulation** during the late 1970s and 1980s, critics of government regulation of infrastructural industries often argued that regulation protected existing industries and reduced the incentives for those regulated industries to continuously engage in system-enhancing innovations.[7] Evidence now provides ample support for these early arguments.[8] Admittedly, in the case of airlines, current services leave many passengers disgruntled. Some have even called for a return to greater regulation. However, brief reflection suggests that passengers now receive many benefits that they did not receive in the past. For example, they now have many more choices that allow them to make trade-offs between their ticket price and the service level they receive.

Today, governments continue to play central roles in the oversight and control of most areas of public infrastructure provision. It remains commonplace for governments to own and operate many major assets. In all countries around the world, governments tend to fund and manage roads, bridges, tunnels, and mass transit systems. Ports and airports are often government assets, although some privatization has occurred. Further, many governments have established **state-owned enterprises** to run infrastructural assets. These government entities are organized to emulate for-profit businesses. Once established, state-owned enterprises can be fully privatized through a one-time sale, or progressively privatized through the periodic sale of shares.

Many governments around the world still maintain major financial interests in "national carrier" airlines—even while those airlines operate in competition with others held in private hands. It is increasingly common for state-owned enterprises to manage water supply systems and elements of electricity systems and oil pipelines. It is also common for private companies to own and operate a lot of aspects of public infrastructure, but with close regulatory oversight from governments. This is a well-used approach in the provision of railroads, airlines, electricity supply, all aspects of telecommunications, and television and cable systems.

What matters here is that a range of models now exist for owning, governing, and managing public infrastructure. Further, given this diversity of models, plenty of evidence is available that can guide policy makers in assessing how best to promote good performance of public infrastructure within their jurisdictions. As is always the case, policy makers are never influenced by efficiency considerations alone. Yet, even if they were, they would probably apply different models to different elements of their overall portfolio of public infrastructural assets.

Although all such assets generate a degree of public value, some remain closer to being public goods than to being private goods. The balance of public- and private-good attributes in any given asset will largely structure discussions of ownership, governance, and management. At the same time, **technological change** can serve, over time, to tip that public-private balance. For example, changes in information technology during recent decades have seen governments experimenting with the use of tolls on specific public roads. Travel on those roads has shifted in nature from being a public right to something closer to a private good.

STIMULATING ECONOMIC DEVELOPMENT

Another aspect of public infrastructure deserves mention in this discussion of why and how governments get involved: governments frequently use the construction of new major infrastructure projects as a tool to reduce the harm of economic downturns and recessions. When governments fund the building of new roads, ports, pipelines, power plants, and so on, they create new employment opportunities for people who otherwise might have been unemployed. This injection of money into the economy can have what are known as **multiplier effects**—that is, those new opportunities for earning wages also create new opportunities for other businesses in the economy, as the wage earners go shopping.

Indeed, governments have historically funded many big infrastructure projects when the broader economy has been doing poorly. Governments can borrow to do so. In the best scenarios, the investments in new infrastructure hold the promise of paying for themselves many times over, in terms of promoting better social and economic outcomes in the future, not just short term (see Case Study 4.2).

case study 4.2 The Levees Protecting New Orleans

Since its founding in 1718, New Orleans has been a city of strategic significance. Its location near the mouth of the Mississippi River ensured its rapid development into a center for trade. Subsequently, its economy has remained closely linked to trade and seafaring. Today, it is a hub for ship-building, a major U.S. naval base, a location for oil and gas refining and storage, and a tourism magnet. Like another strategic seaport, the Dutch city of Amsterdam, New Orleans is low-lying, with an average elevation below sea level.

New Orleans was originally protected only by natural levees—embankments created along the banks of the Mississippi River by sediments deposited as the river level rose and fell. However, artificial levees were soon needed to protect the city from flooding. A long-standing trade-off has been made between the city's strategic location and the risks of flooding.

In the 20th century, the U.S. Army Corps of Engineers built a series of canals, floodgates, and levees to protect New Orleans and the surrounding area. The federal government funded this work. The levees protecting New Orleans are a classic public good. Once created, the levees provided flood protection for the city that all residents enjoyed. That protection was freely available to everyone in the city and no one could be excluded from it.

The arrival of Hurricane Katrina in August 2005 tested the levees to their limit. They failed, with catastrophic effects. Over 80 percent of New Orleans was flooded. Waters rose as high as seven feet, and the flooding remained for weeks. More than 1,200 people died within the city—the total death toll across the southern states exceeded 1,800. Critics consider inadequate design and construction of the existing levees as the cause of the disaster.

In the aftermath of Katrina, the levees were rebuilt and strengthened. The federal government contributed $71 billion to reconstruction efforts in and around New Orleans, and over $14 billion of this was devoted to rebuilding the levees.

Although much of New Orleans is again thriving, debate continues about how safe the city is from future flooding. The levees protecting New Orleans have been built to a standard expected to protect the city from hurricanes of a magnitude observed once in 100 years. Katrina was of a magnitude expected once in 200 years. To protect the city against more severe weather events could cost anywhere from $50 billion to $100 billion.[9] How much should be spent to protect the city?

Katrina caused total damages of $148 billion in New Orleans and beyond. Suppose the damage to New Orleans of a 100-year hurricane totaled $100 billion. In any given year, the expected cost of such an event would then be $1 billion (that is, $100 billion divided by 100). Given this, the $14 billion to rebuild the levees would pay for itself in 14 years (that is, $14 billion divided by $1 billion can be spread across 14 years). The rebuilt levees are expected to have a life span of 50 years.

The Army Corps of Engineers conducts extensive cost-benefit analyses to guide its levee building and maintenance programs. Its staffers also have a common saying: "There are only two kinds of levees, those that have failed and those that will fail."[10] The simple calculation just presented suggests that the benefits of the rebuilt levees far outweigh their costs.

CRITICAL THINKING QUESTIONS

1. Beyond protecting the city from future flooding, what other benefits might federal government funding for rebuilding the levees have brought New Orleans?
2. If the federal government had not funded the rebuilding of the levees, what viable alternative actions might protect the city from flooding?

CONTEMPORARY POLICY ISSUES

In the United States, as well as in many other countries around the world, there currently exist several important policy design issues concerning public infrastructure. Here we consider three:

- Improving priority setting through better use of available information,
- Securing funding and aligning incentives so that decision makers allocate scarce funds efficiently, and
- Aligning incentives to avoid throwing money at **white elephants**— infrastructural assets of limited public value.

SETTING PRIORITIES

A common complaint in many economically advanced nations is that much of the current public infrastructure has been poorly maintained and is in need of replacement. Salient examples of infrastructure failure have resulted in calls for drastic changes in how decisions are made concerning the targets of infrastructure funding.[11]

For future funding success, two points are clear:

1. Existing infrastructure has been acquired through many decades of public investments. Attention must be given to ensuring that those investments continue to generate public value. This goal suggests that routine maintenance work on existing assets should be accorded high priority in infrastructural spending.
2. New infrastructure will continue to be necessary. In particular, expectations about economic growth and the growth of world trade indicate a need for expansion in strategic areas, such as the ongoing enhancement of airports, ports, and highways that support high levels of international trade.

In most countries, established trade routes run through a small number of strategic transport centers. Planning to avoid future congestion in these centers is vital, because as congestion grows it will serve to limit overall economic growth. Therefore, priority should be given to new infrastructure projects that will improve the efficiency of the strategic transport centers. Of course, other areas of infrastructure, such as inner-city transportation (as exemplified in Case Study 4.1), are also important.

SECURING FUNDING

Ongoing maintenance and expansion of the public infrastructure are predicated on the availability of sufficient funds, yet many governments currently find themselves facing tight **fiscal constraints**. When funding is tight, there is an understandable tendency for political leaders to narrow their perspective and focus on how to effectively manage short- to medium-term government finances. This emphasis causes problems for infrastructure planning and financing, because most major infrastructure projects take years to construct.

A frequent present-day suggestion is that governments around the world should make better use of **public-private partnerships** when it comes to planning, financing, and managing elements of public infrastructure.[12] From a government perspective, being attractive as a partner in infrastructure management and development requires demonstrating credible commitments to supporting projects. Private investors tend to be risk averse and are especially wary of committing funds to projects where future financing and construction trajectories are unclear. In the coming decades, governments everywhere will often be in a degree of competition with each other to attract international investors and partner with them on the funding, development, and management of infrastructural projects. Given that approaching reality, having good infrastructure funding mechanisms in place must be a high priority.

Historically, the United States has relied on a series of federal **trust funds** to subsidize the construction and maintenance of infrastructural projects. Trust funds designated for specific purposes keep them safe from politicians who would like to divert those funds elsewhere. Often, similar trust arrangements have been established at the state level. In the future, the U.S. government must make careful efforts to ensure that these trusts continue to receive adequate streams of income; such efforts might demand changing the ways that governments obtain funding for them. Making greater use of user fees that match payment levels to actual service use would be one important option.

ALIGNING INCENTIVES

Even well-designed systems for prioritizing project funding can go awry if there is poor incentives alignment between those who distribute the funds and those who actually manage infrastructure development. A long-standing complaint in the United States has been that methods of allocating funding have created **perverse incentives**, primarily for political gain.[13] For example, there has been a tendency to fund most new asset construction at the expense of funding ongoing maintenance of assets already in place. This is a serious issue because far more public value can be realized from maintaining a heavily used bridge in a metropolitan area than funding a new stretch of highway in a relatively remote location.

The policy challenge is to find effective mechanisms ensuring that funds go to projects that are most needed rather than to projects that are pursued for political expedience. Highway funding in the United States has often been the focus of special interest bidding by members of Congress, commonly termed **pork-barrel politics**.[14] As many politicians rely on such tactics to aid their reelection, it is difficult to eliminate these practices from public expenditure processes. It becomes easier to reduce this kind of game playing, however, when politicians take part in nonpartisan efforts to clarify broad expenditure priorities.

INFRASTRUCTURE IN A FEDERAL SYSTEM OF GOVERNMENT

America's federal system often complicates efforts to secure and distribute funding for building and maintaining infrastructure. Two major problems exist:

1. Governments at all levels face financial stress and are continually under pressure to reduce spending. Since infrastructure projects tend to be expensive, elected decision makers often put off committing funds to them.
2. The federal government in Washington, DC, can rarely make infrastructure decisions without engaging closely with state and local governments. As a result, funding and development of infrastructure can be especially sensitive to obstructionist politics.

Federalism also creates coordination problems in some areas of infrastructure development and management. Public transportation systems in large metropolitan areas often do not provide streamlined services for patrons precisely because of problems with governance. The case of public transport in the San Francisco Bay Area is instructive. There, more than 20 service operators offer services across nine separate counties and over a hundred municipalities. Each operator has its own fare structures and system of timetables. Although some coordination across operators has occurred in places like New York and Boston, no such coordination has occurred in the Bay Area. And although its population has continued to expand, placing greater strain on roads and highways in the region, growth in public transport use has been limited.

In her reflection on how the United States could improve its infrastructure, Rosabeth Moss Kanter has suggested that regional leadership is vital. "In a nation that can't force action from the center and doesn't believe in it anyway, regional coalitions are essential to our democracy and one of our best hopes for getting things done."[15] She points to instances where local leadership appears to have driven improvements in transportation systems. Nonetheless, local problems can fester for lengthy periods in federal systems, with no guarantee that political conditions will drive needed changes.

PUBLIC INFRASTRUCTURE AND THE INVESTMENT PERSPECTIVE

Creating public infrastructure requires resources, effort, and time. If a context exists where borrowing is not possible, whenever decisions are made to build new infrastructure an implicit decision is also made to defer some level of current consumption and leisure. In this view, creating public infrastructure is a classic form of public investment. Decision makers defer some level of today's consumption in the hope that the new infrastructure will yield future gains outweighing present sacrifices. Of course, in advanced democratic nations with well-functioning financial markets, governments often issue bonds or take out loans to fund new infrastructure projects. This step allows them to build infrastructure without immediate sacrifices and pay off the costs while enjoying the benefits. Indeed, in an ideal situation, the new infrastructure would generate a sufficiently strong stream of benefits over a sufficiently long period of time that an objective assessment would indicate that it more than paid for itself.

As with all large investments, choosing to fund and construct new additions to the public infrastructure calls for careful planning and a significant degree of vision. Political leaders need to find ways to convince others that adding new infrastructure will yield long-term benefits. There are many stories of cities where the lack of an effective public transit system or the constant deferral of construction of a new airport has produced congestion problems. Those problems not only add to the daily drudgery of commuters; they can also place a serious brake on longer-term economic development.

As cities develop, even in the absence of needed infrastructure, housing and other forms of land use often crowd out the very spaces that would otherwise be prime sites to locate transportation corridors or build a new airport. Understandably, residents of those areas can become powerful lobbyists for limiting growth, adding to the complexity of subsequent infrastructural planning. In such instances, although a strictly economic cost-benefit analysis might indicate the merits of the new infrastructure, the political cost-benefit calculus may look very different. Political harmony and the prospect of reelection typically win out over the ambitions of political leaders to "build the bridge to the future."

Fortunately, visionary leaders who are also masterful politicians continue to appear at times, and their contributions can have long-lasting impact. For example, the creation of the Interstate Highway System in the United States was championed by President Dwight D. Eisenhower (who served in office from 1953 to 1961). Funding and construction were authorized by the Federal-Aid Highway Act of 1956 and subsequent legislation. The cost of construction, which continued for several decades, is now estimated to have totaled around $450 billion in current dollars. Without a doubt, this was nevertheless a visionary investment in public infrastructure.

Economists have shown a reasonable level of interest in estimating the returns to society of investments in public infrastructure. They have taken two broad analytical approaches:

- In the first approach, economists apply **macroeconomic analysis**—that is, using aggregate statistics, they model the contribution of public infrastructure to overall economic outcomes. For example, they have taken some steps to assess the contribution that the creation of the Interstate Highway System has had on overall economic performance.
- In the second approach, economists apply **microeconomic analysis**, focusing on specific infrastructural assets—or sometimes on classes of assets—and estimate their ROI. For example, a study might involve estimating the construction and maintenance costs of a bridge over its expected life cycle, and then weighing these against estimated benefits. As an extension, those estimated costs and benefits could be compared with those of repairing or expanding an existing bridge. Such studies can be part of the planning work before the bridge is built, or they can take place some years after the bridge has been built and in service.

Here we discuss the relevance of both approaches to assessing the merits of public infrastructure investments.

MACROECONOMIC ANALYSIS

Economists in the United States did a lot of work in the late 1980s and early 1990s to advance the macroeconomic analysis of public infrastructure and its contribution to society.[16] This involved exploring the effects of all infrastructure spending on overall economic performance. David Aschauer produced a set of influential articles arguing that public infrastructure should be recognized as a factor in private sector production.[17] As such, it should be included along with labor and equipment—termed **private capital**—in economic models of firm- or industry-level production functions. Unfortunately, the economic conversation that occurred during this time got hijacked by disputes over the validity of different approaches to the statistical modeling work.

Put simply, a question arose that could not be easily answered: Do public investments in infrastructure *cause* strong economic performance, or is public investment in infrastructure a *consequence* of strong economic performance? When efforts have been made to address the causality issue, estimates have suggested that public investments in infrastructure make a powerful contribution to overall economic output.[18]

Some estimates have indicated that for every public dollar spent on infrastructure, private sector revenues increase by over 30 cents. Since the private sector is far larger than the public sector, this finding suggests a very high social ROI. Surveying available evidence at the time, David Aschauer concluded that "the evidence is clear: there is a strong causal relationship between public capital investment and both productivity and output."[19]

The macroeconomic analyses linking infrastructural investments to broader economic productivity in the United States influenced a range of subsequent studies. In one stream, economists applied this basic framework to assessing the macroeconomic impacts of infrastructural investments in other countries. For example, well-regarded studies considered this relationship in India, South Africa, and Sweden.[20] In all of these cases, compelling evidence suggested that investments in public infrastructure, as measured during a specific period of time, resulted in strong economic benefits over subsequent time.

A common theme in all of these studies is that public provision of well-performing infrastructure serves to reduce the costs of doing business and, hence, adds to the overall productivity of private firms. Typically these studies do not capture the benefits that flow directly to private citizens from provision of public infrastructure, as such benefits are hard to measure and aggregate. This shortcoming has led analysts to agree in general that studies of this kind most likely underestimate the overall social gains to be had from providing high-quality public infrastructure.

MICROECONOMIC ANALYSIS

In the United States, more recent studies of the impact of public infrastructure on broader economic performance have tended to involve microeconomic analysis. In contrast to macroeconomic analysis and its consideration of overall economic outcomes, microeconomic analysis tends to focus on specific assets and their contributions. Such analysis often employs cost-benefit analysis (as introduced in Chapter 3), which allows for the calculation of returns on investments. In a classic contribution of this kind, John G. Fernald estimated the impact of the Interstate Highway System on productivity growth in selected industries from 1953 to

1989.[21] Fernald found that the highest productivity increases occurred in industries where transportation was a critical factor of production. Fernald predicted that the Interstate Highway System could generate returns on average of up to 18 percent.[22]

The investment perspective can also be applied to estimating the monetary benefits to society of investing in a specific asset, such as a new bridge, highway, electricity plant, or airport. In all such cases, the estimation approach involves using cost-benefit analysis. When the benefits are found to outweigh the costs associated with an investment, the investment can be judged worthwhile. A number of challenges are associated with conducting this kind of analysis prior to construction. All of these regard how to take account of uncertainties and how to accurately estimate streams of both costs and benefits, which, for infrastructural assets, will likely flow for many years.

Effective methods have been developed to improve estimation accuracy.[23] For example, consideration of the **life cycle of public infrastructural assets** is important. This involves estimating the longevity of an asset and considering how adequate, routine maintenance can ensure that it continues to perform as expected for many years. Paying appropriate attention to asset life cycles can have major consequences with respect to costs, cost-containment, and how long the asset lasts. Waheed Uddin and his colleagues provide a useful overview of the life cycle cost streams for infrastructural assets.[24] Initially, there is likely to be a high construction cost. Once built and commissioned, the asset is likely to generate annual maintenance costs. Although very low to begin with, these are likely to rise as the asset ages. Therefore, at a given time in the future, a major rehabilitation no doubt will be required, and this could cost an amount equivalent to, say, half of the initial construction cost. Following rehabilitation, the annual maintenance costs are again likely to be very low but to rise steadily as the asset ages.

This cycle of slowly rising annual maintenance costs, punctuated by large rehabilitation outlays, can be expected to continue. However, sometime in the future, it is likely that the cost of another round of rehabilitation will be little different from the cost of completely replacing the asset. At that point, the asset should be abandoned and a replacement built. Of course, with continuous technological improvement, the new asset will no doubt be considerably more technologically advanced than the old one and thus will offer additional advantages.

POLITICAL CONSIDERATIONS

The foregoing discussion has offered a broad introduction to the theory of public infrastructure asset management. In practice, things do not always go as rational planners might expect. As noted, politicians often face powerful incentives to privilege the construction of new public infrastructure over funding routine maintenance and rehabilitation work on existing assets. Matching fund systems, as used extensively by the U.S. federal government, serve to reinforce the preferences of state and local politicians to privilege the construction of shiny new assets over the routine maintenance of those already in place.

KEY INSIGHTS FROM THE INVESTMENT PERSPECTIVE

The investment perspective offers two key insights into policy design and the management of public infrastructure.

1. When visionary leadership is combined with adequate planning, the construction of new assets should significantly raise the quality of life in a given jurisdiction. Benefits can flow both in narrow economic terms and in broader social terms.

2. When a well-implemented life cycle approach is taken to asset management, specific assets can keep contributing public value for long periods of time. However, if asset management is inadequate, overall maintenance costs might escalate over time, and the assets may not last as long as they would have with regular, appropriate maintenance (see Case Study 4.3).

As we shall see next, other considerations concerning the management of infrastructural assets can also have a material bearing on the overall public value generated by public infrastructure.

case study 4.3 Maintaining the Williamsburg Bridge

Sometimes infrastructural assets, once completed, do not receive appropriate routine maintenance. The Williamsburg Bridge spanning the East River in New York was in use for more than 70 years before a full maintenance inspection was completed. Subsequent inspections revealed problems requiring urgent, expensive remedial action.

(Mykhailo Shcherbyna/Alamy Stock Photo)

In his analysis of problems with infrastructure funding in the United States, Barry B. LePatner offered a large amount of evidence concerning poor maintenance of existing assets.[25] One of his cases concerned the Williamsburg Bridge that crosses the East River in New York, joining Brooklyn and Manhattan. Opened in 1903, the bridge cost $24 million at the time, equivalent to $630 million in current dollars.[26] It is well known that the bridge went for decades without appropriate maintenance work being performed. The first complete inspection of the bridge was not performed until 1979—76 years after it was commissioned!

When the Williamsburg Bridge Technical Advisory Committee was formed in the late 1980s to assess whether the bridge should be repaired or replaced, it found that the cost of replacing the bridge's approach structures and rehabilitating the main and side spans, towers, and cables would come to $760 million, compared with the $1.5 billion estimated to construct a new bridge. In 1992, Samuel Schwartz, then deputy commissioner and chief engineer of the New York Department of Transportation, calculated that if New York had spent $3.5 million annually for 89 years (totaling $312 million), the bridge could have been properly maintained and its steel might last more than 200 years. Over those past 89 years, instead of spending $312 million on maintenance, the city probably spent closer to just $31 million. Thus, the $760 million the city eventually spent to rehabilitate the bridge represented a waste of $479 million.[27]

CRITICAL THINKING QUESTIONS

1. What are some other examples in which governments deferred routine maintenance for public infrastructure?
2. What conditions could encourage owners of infrastructural assets to adequately maintain them?

IMPROVING INFRASTRUCTURE PERFORMANCE THROUGH OWNERSHIP CHANGES

The various assets that together comprise public infrastructure tend to have one common feature: they cost a lot to build. As a result, politicians, policy advisors, and many other stakeholders worry about how well these assets contribute to improving social outcomes. A range of issues come into play. For at least half a century, many economists have suggested that how governments choose to fund and control specific assets can have a significant bearing on the public value those assets generate.

Although economists do not all speak with one voice, it is fair to say that most take the view that markets impose strong disciplines on private firms to operate efficiently. Further, economists often claim that similar disciplines are largely absent for public organizations, or for organizations that are subject to significant government regulation of their activities.

The deregulation and privatization movement that began in the United States in the 1970s and rapidly spread to many other countries were driven by a desire to improve the efficiency of large enterprises under heavy government control, even if their ownership had remained in private hands.[28] Those large enterprises often contributed directly to the provision of well-functioning public infrastructure.

They included airlines, railroad companies, electricity suppliers, telephone companies, and many other organizations delivering or maintaining local public services, such as roads, ports, airports, and water supply and sewage systems.

The deregulation and privatization movement created many situations in which different forms of ownership and control of infrastructural assets existed across different jurisdictions. These provided new opportunities for evidence-based, comparative assessment of how different systems of ownership and control affected the performance of infrastructural assets.

A big question for people interested in public policy could now be tackled directly. That is, under what circumstances will private ownership of assets and competition in supply of goods and services generate better economic outcomes than would government ownership and control? Most of the time, the answers supplied to date have indicated how various details in policy design and local economic conditions influence outcomes.[29] Yet the preponderance of evidence suggests that well-designed and managed efforts to transfer ownership and control of publicly owned infrastructural assets into private hands can yield a range of efficiency gains.[30]

CHANGING OWNERSHIP OF ELECTRICITY ASSETS

In the United States, the federal and state governments played major roles in the development of systems of electricity generation and distribution. Those systems started to emerge in the late 1880s, but efforts to significantly enhance the scale of generation and distribution occurred most notably in the early decades of the 20th century. The era of dam building, for example, was epitomized by the completion of the federally funded Hoover Dam in 1936 and the activities of the federally owned Tennessee Valley Authority in the 1930s. As well as adding materially to the infrastructure of the country and laying the foundations for rapid economic development, these infrastructural projects employed legions of workers who otherwise would have been unemployed during the Great Depression (see Chapter 8).

As a result of these initiatives, the generation and distribution of electricity in the United States tended to be controlled by public utility companies. Some of them were independent companies; others were government owned. However, all had their origins in financial arrangements that often rested heavily on provision of government subsidies. Further, their daily operations were subject to significant government regulation. Fear that these companies would use their regional monopoly status to extract profits from consumers led to frequent and detailed rate-setting inquiries. Governments actively established and maintained the terms under which these companies operated. Starting in the 1970s and running through the 1980s, many state governments started to introduce regulatory practices intended to give these utilities more flexibility in their operations. The idea was to provide incentives for electricity firms to improve the efficiency of their operations.

Going a step further, in the 1990s state governments began moving seriously toward deregulating the electricity industry and allowing more market-like arrangements to emerge regarding supply of services to consumers and the ownership of generation and distribution systems. This change was not driven purely by market ideology. During the previous century, a huge amount of technical knowledge had been amassed concerning effective ways to operate electricity systems. That knowledge established the basis upon which various innovations were introduced in the industry. Among those innovations, it became easier for systems designers to see how they could establish and maintain reliable electricity supply for consumers while encouraging competition in some elements of supply. Although transmission systems tended to remain in the control of single owners, competition among electricity plants became feasible, as did competition among companies selling electricity to consumers.

ASSESSING THE EFFECTS OF OWNERSHIP CHANGE

Various teams of economists have investigated the impact of regulatory restructuring on the efficiency of electricity generation in the United States. In one study, Kira R. Fabrizio and colleagues studied the comparative efficiency of fossil-fueled generation plants operating under different regulatory and ownership regimes.[31] These authors found that changes in the regulatory environment led to significant declines in input use at plants owned by independent electric utilities. In the deregulated contexts, employment levels at each plant declined by around 3 percent and nonfuel expenses declined by around 9 percent, relative to plants in which the regulatory regime had not changed. This evidence suggests that a regulatory change alone could improve the operating efficiency of these plants. However, further analysis indicated that the efficiency gains were much higher in plants owned by private electric utilities compared with cooperatively owned and public plants, typically owned by municipal governments or the federal government.

As the authors explain, deregulation generally altered the competitive environment only for private investor-owned utilities within a state. The typically smaller publicly and cooperatively owned utilities were largely protected from competition in these legislative changes.[32] The authors found that, in the deregulated contexts, employment levels and nonfuel expenses at private electric utility plants dropped relative to both measures in the cooperatively owned and public plants.

These findings confirm that ownership and control arrangements can have major implications for the efficiency of electricity plants. When regulations were eased, all plants became more efficient, but the plants under private ownership returned the greatest efficiency gains. Case Study 4.4 explores the impact of ownership changes on efficiency in nuclear power plants.

case study 4.4 Improving Nuclear Power Plant Performance

The majority of nuclear power plants in the United States are located in the northeastern or midwestern states. The plant shown here is Exelon Nuclear's Limerick Generating Station, located on the shores of the Schuylkill River in Pennsylvania

(STAN HONDA/AFP/Getty Images)

Catherine D. Wolfram and Lucas W. Davis explored the impacts of deregulation and consolidation in a major subset of the electricity generation industry—nuclear power plants. For several decades after their establishment, all nuclear power reactors in the United States were owned by regulated utilities. Few utilities owned more than one or two reactors. Being subject to regulation of their pricing arrangements, the revenues of these plants were largely disconnected from their operating performance.[33]

The authors report that, beginning in the late 1990s, electricity markets in many states were deregulated, and 48 of the nation's 103 nuclear power reactors were sold to independent power producers. These divestitures led to substantial market consolidation. As of 2012, one-third of all nuclear reactors in the United States were under the control of three companies. Davis and

Wolfram found that deregulation and consolidation led to increased operating performance of nuclear power plants. This improvement was achieved primarily through reductions in the frequency and duration of reactor outages. Policy Investment Checklist 4.1 summarizes the findings of this study.

Davis and Wolfram's study of electricity production at nuclear power plants offers powerful evidence of how performance changed when new market conditions created incentives for owners to make efficiency gains. In 2010, U.S. nuclear reactors produced 800 billion kilowatt-hours of electricity annually, comprising about 20 percent of all electricity generation in the country. Davis and Wolfram estimated that deregulation and consolidation of these plants led to an increase in electricity production from these plants exceeding 40 billion kilowatt-hours annually. This performance improvement, estimated at around 10 percent per year, resulted in almost enough new power to meet the electricity demand for all the households in New England.[34] The revenue gains alone were estimated to be over $2.5 billion per year. All of these advances came from making better use of existing assets. No new generating capacity was added.

An interesting technical observation made by Davis and Wolfram is that because nuclear power plants do not use conventional fuels, they operate at very low **marginal cost**—that is, the cost of generating an additional unit of output. This technique is different from that of, say, coal-fueled plants, where producing more output means buying and burning more coal. As a result, nuclear power plants primarily

POLICY INVESTMENT CHECKLIST 4.1

Analyzing Changes in the Control of Nuclear Power Plants

1. Focus on Existing Policies and Programs	Once owned and operated as public utilities, following deregulation, 48 of the 103 nuclear power reactors in the United States were sold to private companies. The effects of this privatization suggest lessons for privatization of other forms of public infrastructure.
2. Gather Policy Evidence	A study of electricity generation contained complete records of monthly generation from 1970 to 2009 for all nuclear power reactors operating in the United States. The study compared generation levels between the 48 plants that were privatized and the 55 that remained publicly owned and operated.
3. Measure Desired Effects	The key question was: Did the deregulation and sale of nuclear power reactors lead to improved operating efficiency? The answer was "yes." On average, the privatized reactors generated 10% more electricity per year than those that remained publicly owned and operated.
4. Assess Costs and Benefits	*Costs:* Running costs for privatized reactors increased due to greater power generation occurring in them. Labor and fuel costs did not change. The overall maximum cost associated with privatization was estimated to be a one-time equipment upgrade cost of $450 million.
	Benefits: In total, the privatized reactors were estimated to have had an increase in their operating performance of 40 billion kilowatt-hours annually, an increase worth $2.5 billion per year. In the first year of private operation, the privatized nuclear reactors would have produced a return of over $500 for every dollar spent on improving operating capacity.
5. Offer Robust Advice	Note three things: 1. Selling the reactors would have yielded a financial benefit to the local governments that sold them. This was not included in the benefits noted here. 2. Greater generation of power from the nuclear reactors reduced reliance on coal-fired power plants. The estimated social benefit from reduced carbon dioxide emissions was $700 million annually. 3. Reactor safety matters—problems could have catastrophic effects. Emergency shutdown records show privatized nuclear reactors were safer than those that remained publicly owned and operated.

provide "baseload" generation into power grids—they continuously pump a basic level of power into the system around the clock.

These efficiency gains were achieved primarily by reducing the amount of time taken annually to shut down and maintain each reactor. By reducing the number of days a year when reactors were not operating, the power plant owners could supply more power and generate more revenue. In turn, less demand was created for alternative plants, such as coal- or natural-gas-burning plants, to operate at higher levels to compensate for power loss when reactors were not operating. Davis and Wolfram estimated that the improved efficiency of the nuclear power plants had resulted by 2010 in a decrease of 35 million metric tons of carbon dioxide emissions in the United States. This is more carbon abatement than was achieved by all the wind and solar generation in the United States combined during that same year. As the authors observed, "deregulation is not usually envisioned as a means for achieving environmental goals."[35]

This case study highlights how changes in regulation and ownership have led to significant improvements in the efficiency of U.S. nuclear power plants. Policy analysts have found that changes in the regulation of power generation have generally promoted efficiency gains without compromising plant safety.[36] Government efforts to reduce regulation and create opportunities for power generators to compete in the sale of electricity have had two major effects:

- First, government efforts have forced plants to assure that their generators are more efficient in their operations. These include making better use of human resources as well as taking more care to ensure that the physical plants are maintained and operated in ways that improve overall output levels.

- Second, plant ownership has been consolidated. Of course, regulators must remain vigilant to avoid monopoly ownership in the industry. That said, a positive outcome of consolidation is that the most efficient firms survive. Further, as the stronger performers buy up the assets of the weaker ones, they tend to spread innovative management practices that result in overall efficiency gains.

In the case of the nuclear power plants, as noted by Davis and Wolfram, managerial innovations have had important spillovers for society as a whole. More electricity has been generated at lower cost, and greater efficiency has resulted in less use of fossil fuel plants, which generate undesirable carbon emissions.

This case also highlights how improvements in public policy design can significantly improve the returns that society gains from original investments in infrastructural assets. It underscores that smart policy concerning infrastructure involves much more than assessing the merits of a new construction project. Well-designed policies can ensure that existing infrastructural assets perform at optimal levels over their whole life course. That insight, transformed into practice, could lead to improvements in contemporary management of many other aspects of public infrastructure.

CRITICAL THINKING QUESTIONS

1. This case study has highlighted some positive effects of privatizing infrastructural assets. What negative effects might occur?
2. Under what circumstances could it be efficient for a private company to reduce their efforts to maintain their infrastructural assets?
3. What are some other areas of infrastructure where ownership changes could produce efficiency gains for society?

INFRASTRUCTURE AND THE PROMOTION OF CIVIL RIGHTS

Public policy choices concerning infrastructure provision and maintenance often hold major implications for civil rights. Historically, transportation and mobility have played a big part in struggles for civil rights and equal opportunity in the United States. Until changes occurred in the 1960s, African Americans living in southern states faced restrictions in accessing public transport. Their communities also tended to have fewer public amenities than those populated by whites.

When people live in places that are poorly serviced, without good roads and public transport, their ability to participate in society is significantly reduced. Poor people are often forced to live in communities and suburbs that are long distances from the places offering the best opportunities for paid work. Difficulties in getting to work can keep individuals and families in conditions of poverty, with limited hope for a better future.

In metropolitan areas today, easy access to public transportation is highly valued. As urban living has grown more appealing to professionals wishing to avoid long commutes, housing near public transit or within short driving distances to major sources of employment has risen enormously in price. Low-income people are often priced out of these convenient residential locations. Moving further toward the edge of metropolitan areas, poor people become more reliant on either owning their own cars or using limited public transport options. Even when rents in the suburbs are lower than in gentrified parts of the inner core, the added expense of a car or hours lost commuting lower the quality of life.

A study of New York City residents found that those earning less than $35,000 per year were over 10 times more likely to have to commute over an hour each way to work than were those earning more than $75,000. The same study found that black New Yorkers had commute times on average 25 percent longer than those of their white counterparts.

These observations present a starting place for thinking about the extensive connections that exist between provision of public infrastructure and the promotion of civil rights. Differences not only fall along racial lines. People with disabilities, those with health problems, and the elderly can all be affected—positively or negatively—by the quality of public infrastructure.

LESSONS FOR PUBLIC POLICY

Providing public infrastructure typically requires investing large amounts of money in specific assets. When governments adequately plan for these assets and effective funding systems are in place, they can generate public value for a long time. Yet a number of public policy issues arise concerning the management of these assets. First, politicians face electoral incentives to be seen advocating for and delivering new, exciting things to their constituents. The political rewards are far lower for doing the unseen work of ensuring that adequate funds are available to cover routine maintenance work. Second, intergovernmental funding arrangements can also serve to privilege the development of new infrastructure over the adequate maintenance of existing assets. Third, issues of governance can have important implications for the value that society derives from specific assets.

We can draw six important lessons for public policy from these issues:

- Well-planned and carefully guided investments in public infrastructure can contribute significantly to local, regional, and national development. Good infrastructure also serves to improve the quality of human lives—allowing us to live free of disease, to communicate freely with one another, and to have freedom of movement. At its best, public infrastructure operates as a platform, facilitating all kinds of human flourishing.
- Foresight matters. Public infrastructure is expensive to build. Most of the time, the building of new infrastructural assets requires time, commitment, and focused energy. When public leaders do not pay adequate attention to the maintenance and ongoing development of public infrastructure, they effectively close off future economic and social opportunities for citizens.
- The growth of the world economy will depend crucially on infrastructure policy. The quality and performance of national transportation and communication systems—including roads, ports, and airports—facilitate international trade. Increasingly, nations that want to compete effectively in the world economy must pay careful attention to establishing and maintaining high-quality public infrastructure.
- Governments almost always need to be involved in the financing and development of major public infrastructural assets. Governments tend to be better able than other entities in society to efficiently coordinate the purchase and use of property and resources in the interests of producing new public assets. Further, governments tend to have more ability to raise revenue than private entities. Because they have the option of imposing taxes, they can generally secure loans from investors at significantly lower interest rates than other entities. In contrast to governments, private investors are inherently averse to funding activities where high levels of uncertainty surround when returns on investment will flow, and how large those returns will be.
- Initial forms of ownership and control need not be maintained over the life of an asset. Governments often fund, build, and operate infrastructure; once specific infrastructural assets have been established and considerable knowledge is available concerning their performance (including their financial performance), public value can be associated with government asset sales. At a minimum, such sales can create new sources of funds for governments

to allocate elsewhere—including into the regular maintenance and/or upgrading of existing assets and development of new public infrastructure.

- The ownership and control of infrastructural assets can have major implications for their operating performance. As a general rule, firms subject to market competition face stronger incentives to perform efficiently than do firms protected by government regulations and government ownership. Where there is evidence that deregulation and/or asset sales could lead to performance improvements, it is appropriate for such policy changes to occur. When changes in asset management lead to improvements in their performance, citizens can benefit in a range of ways. For example, they may end up paying less (either directly or through their taxes) for services, and service quality and reliability may improve. Other positive results can include service innovations.

Political considerations often make it difficult for public infrastructure to be managed in ways that deliver high public value. In addition, effective management of infrastructural assets is predicated on the availability of adequate information and professional analysts who can use that information to inform decision making. Such conditions are not always present, especially in jurisdictions where public funds are spread thinly. In the future, those who control infrastructural assets could follow two strategies:

- In the short term, they could look for incremental ways to improve the efficiency of the assets already in place. Fairly straightforward management innovations often can improve the performance of infrastructural assets.
- In the longer term, priority should be placed on ensuring that new assets are procured in cost-effective ways, and that suitable provision is made from the outset for sound asset maintenance over the predicted life cycles of those assets.

CHAPTER SUMMARY

This chapter has presented a general framework for thinking about public infrastructure and the public value we collectively derive from it. By effectively managing existing public infrastructure and funding appropriate expansion efforts, governments can continuously increase economic and social outcomes to the benefit of everyone.

When public infrastructure is working well, we can forget how important it is to our daily lives, and to the good functioning of society and the economy. Sewage systems, clean water supply, electricity, roads, and other transport systems are foundations of our survival in mass societies. Fortunately, they tend to be highly reliable. When problems arise, however, they can escalate fast.

We have considered why it is necessary for government to take the lead in providing and maintaining the various assets that make up the public infrastructure. We now also know, however, that governments can get a lot of things right yet still make mistakes in how they manage infrastructural assets. In the United States, as in other advanced democracies, visionary investments during the 20th century transformed the environment in which we now live. They laid the foundations for incredible levels of technological advance. As new technologies are developed, our shared expectations of public infrastructure will inevitably evolve further.

Current predictions are that the size of the world economy will double within the next 15 to 20 years.[37] For countries to participate fully in that growth, major upgrading will be required in various components of the public infrastructure. It is vital that public policy specialists and advisors appreciate why specific infrastructural assets tend to be supplied in specific ways. Having a sense of the historical development of infrastructural systems can help here. For example, such knowledge can produce an appreciation for how changes in ownership and control of specific assets can be structured to yield positive outcomes, and how negative outcomes might be avoided.

CONNECTIONS TO OTHER CHAPTERS

Public infrastructure provides the foundations upon which a well-functioning society operates. Like defense and homeland security (Chapter 5), it creates a stable environment for individuals, families, social organizations, and businesses to pursue broader goals beyond immediate survival. Public infrastructure enables effective pursuit of other areas of social activity, such as public schooling (Chapter 6) and health care (Chapter 7). Indeed, as was noted in the discussion of infrastructure and the promotion of civil rights, well-developed and appropriately allocated infrastructure can contribute to poverty alleviation (Chapter 8). Science funding (Chapter 10) is also relevant to the development of public infrastructure. For example, as scientific knowledge has expanded, societies have found increasingly effective and sustainable ways both to produce and to consume energy. Application of findings from basic science will continue to play a pivotal role in the development of effective, environmentally sustainable infrastructure. Of course, many connections exist between the provision of public infrastructure and environmental protection (Chapter 11). Trade-offs often must be made between protecting the environment and developing the infrastructure needed to support a modern economy.

KEY TERMS

Public infrastructure	User fees
Regulation	Natural monopolies
Public goods	Monopoly pricing
Free-ride	Heavy-handed regulation

Deregulation
State-owned enterprises
Technological change
Multiplier effects
White elephants
Fiscal constraints
Public-private partnerships
Trust funds

Perverse incentives
Pork-barrel politics
Macroeconomic analysis
Private capital
Microeconomic analysis
Life cycle of public infrastructure
Marginal cost

SUGGESTIONS FOR FURTHER READING

Delmon, Jeffrey. *Public-Private Partnership Projects in Infrastructure: An Essential Guide for Policy Makers.* New York: Cambridge University Press, 2011. See especially Chapter 1, "Introduction" and Chapter 7, "Specific Characteristics of PPP in Different Sectors."

Grigg, Neil S. *Infrastructure Finance: The Business of Infrastructure for a Sustainable Future.* Hoboken, NJ: John Wiley & Sons, 2010. See especially Chapter 1, "An Introduction to Infrastructure Finance" and Part 1, "Infrastructure Sectors and Investments."

LePatner, Barry B. *Too Big to Fall: America's Failing Infrastructure and the Way Forward.* New York: Foster Publishing, 2010. See especially Chapter 2, "Following the Money: Road and Bridge Funding and the Maintenance Deficit."

Megginson, William L., and Jeffrey M. Netter. "From State to Market: A Survey of Empirical Studies of Privatization." *Journal of Economic Literature* 39 (June 2001): 321–89.

OECD. *Strategic Transport Infrastructure Needs to 2030.* Paris: OECD Publishing, 2012.

Uddin, Waheed, W. Ronald Hudson, and Ralph Haas. *Public Infrastructure Asset Management,* 2nd ed. New York: McGraw-Hill Higher Education, 2013. See especially Chapter 1, "The Big Picture" and Chapter 2, "Framework for Infrastructure Asset Management."

Winston, Clifford. *Last Exit: Privatization and Deregulation of the U.S. Transportation System.* Washington, DC: Brookings Institution, 2010. See especially Chapter 1, "Back to the Future to Improve U.S. Transportation" and Chapter 9, "Privatization Experiments."

WEBSITES

- The American Society of Civil Engineers, "Report Card for America's Infrastructure," depicts the condition and performance of the nation's infrastructure in the familiar form of a school report card. Local ASCE experts have prepared State and Regional Infrastructure Report Cards following the methodology of the national Report Card to raise awareness about local infrastructure needs. www.infrastructurereportcard.org

- In 2014, President Obama announced a government-wide initiative to increase infrastructure investment and economic growth by engaging with state and local governments and private sector investors to encourage collaboration and expand the market for public-private partnerships and put federal credit programs to greater use. The Department of Transportation has subsequently highlighted progress of the Build America Investment Initiative. www.dot.gov/buildamerica
- The Council of Foreign Relations has launched a series, "Road to Nowhere: Federal Transportation Infrastructure Policy," which provides a critical assessment of federal transportation policy. www.cfr.org/roadtonowhere

FOR DISCUSSION

1. In many countries around the world, governments have been the primary funders of major infrastructural investments. Although the federal and state governments in the United States have funded many infrastructure projects, initial development of new infrastructure has often been performed by private companies. What are some of the major benefits of government funding of infrastructure development and maintenance? When might private companies do better than governments? Why?

2. Looking to the future, many people are calling for infrastructural developments that promote greater economic efficiency and that avoid damaging the environment. Using the categories *transportation, electricity generation,* and *waste management,* develop answers to the following questions: What could be done to make some current infrastructure operate more efficiently? What could be done to make that infrastructure more environmentally friendly? What challenges would stand in the way of making changes along the lines identified in your responses to the first two questions?

3. Returning home from a visit to Asia, Thomas L. Friedman described the United States as "a place that once thought of itself as modern but has had one too many face-lifts and simply can't hide the wrinkles anymore."[38] Is aging infrastructure necessarily a cause for concern? Beyond the wrinkles, are there more serious things to worry about?

CHAPTER 5

DEFENSE AND HOMELAND SECURITY

Peace is essential for individuals, families, and societies to live well and prosper. Peace does not mean the absence of threats. But it does mean having the capabilities to rapidly identify any threats and defuse them. Like many other countries, the United States emerged through conflict. "Life, liberty and the pursuit of happiness," deemed inalienable rights in the Declaration of Independence (1776), were the guiding principles of those who fought the British in the drawn-out War of Independence (1775–1783). Lessons from that war strongly informed the founding of the nation and the contents of the U.S. Constitution (1789). Throughout U.S. history, the will to use military force to achieve and maintain freedom has always coexisted with the desire for peace and prosperity.

The United States emerged as a world superpower during the last century. Despite the significant military capabilities of other nations, the United States is without doubt the world's only current superpower. Superpower status has served American interests well. It has created conditions allowing the economy to continuously expand and the United States to engage in mutually beneficial trade with many nations around the globe. On a day-to-day basis, Americans can feel reassured that their country's borders are secure, that it is unlikely to be attacked by another nation.

Over recent decades the United States has experienced deadly attacks within the homeland inspired by international terrorist groups. It has also experienced homegrown terrorism, often at the hands of individuals who once trained and served in U.S. defense forces. These actions have challenged the notion that U.S. citizens are safe at home from acts of war. Further, the Second Amendment to the Constitution, allowing people to bear arms in self-defense, has often resulted in devastating violence by malcontents using legally purchased military-style assault weapons in seemingly ordinary places.

Facing page: The *Gerald R. Ford* entered service in the U.S. Navy in 2016. The ship cost over $13 billion to build, making it the most expensive ship in history and the U.S. military's most costly single asset to date.

(U.S. Navy Combat Camera photo by Mass Communication Specialist 2nd Class Ridge Leoni/Released)

This chapter explores public policy issues relating to defense and homeland security. Given the importance of securing peace, significant amounts of government funding are required to keep military forces and other elements of the U.S. security apparatus in place. Pressures on government budgets create worries about the sustainability of this system. The emergence of new threats, such as international terrorism, have raised questions about the appropriateness of current defense configurations. Such concerns mean that policy makers can usually approach defense and homeland security—and their many component parts—by treating public policies about them as investments.

This chapter introduces you to:

- The goals of defense and homeland security policy
- The reasons why defense and homeland security are major expenditure priorities for government
- Traditional defense policy approaches
- The new importance of homeland security
- The influence of federalism on the effectiveness of homeland security initiatives
- Connections between militarism, state gun laws, and public safety
- An investment perspective on defense procurement
- The cost-effectiveness of homeland security initiatives
- Defense, homeland security, and the promotion of civil rights
- Public policy lessons emerging from this review of defense and homeland security

AN INTRODUCTION TO DEFENSE AND HOMELAND SECURITY

The United States has awesome military capability, superior to that of any other nation, and greater than any other force through history.[1] Currently, the country devotes around 3 percent of its Gross Domestic Product (GDP) to funding the defense forces. This translates into annual budget commitments of approximately $600 billion, approved by the U.S. Congress and the president. The U.S. Department of Defense (DoD) employs more than three million people in operational and support roles. Around 450,000 of these people are stationed outside the United States. This number reflects the many military alliances the United States has forged with other countries, many of which host permanent U.S. military bases. The figures mentioned here do not include the budget and staffing for the Department of Homeland Security (DHS)—another significant enterprise, with an annual budget of around $60 billion and more than 240,000 employees.

The U.S. defense establishment is headed by the president, who is the constitutionally designated commander-in-chief of the military. The president, in consultation with the secretary of defense and the National Security Council, determines the nation's security needs. Defense policy is developed at this level and is coordinated through the Office of the Secretary of Defense. Operationally, the defense establishment comprises the Army, Navy, Air Force, and Marine Corps. The leaders of these entities comprise the Joint Chiefs of Staff. The Office of the Chairman of the Joint Chiefs of Staff provides military advice to the president, the National Security Council, and the secretary of defense. The military entities themselves are grouped under unified commanders. Five commanders have geographical responsibilities around the globe. These geographical commands are supported by the Strategic Command, the Special Operations Command, and the Transportation Command.

The DHS was formed to integrate activities and share information among 22 previously established federal departments and agencies. These include the Coast Guard, the National Guard and Reserve, the Federal Emergency Management Agency (FEMA), U.S. Citizenship and Immigration Services, and the Transportation Security Administration. The broader purpose of Homeland Security is to provide coordinated counterterrorism and security management; provide border security; and ensure disaster preparedness, response, and recovery.

Effective configuration and management of both defense and homeland security are vital for maintaining the peace. At a minimum, this requirement means securing the borders of the United States and ensuring that people and groups inside those borders respect the rule of law. To maintain this security, U.S. forces must be active globally. This objective is essential for reducing threats to Americans and for creating good conditions for the conduct of international trade, through which not only Americans but also many other people around the world prosper.

Although defense planners can predict and manage some threats to peace, the dynamic nature of today's world politics adds much uncertainty to the broader context in which Americans engage. Planners need to continuously acquire high-quality intelligence about potential enemy forces and deploy their own forces appropriately. Uncertainty has intensified because of the presence of unstable states and the rise of insurgent groups such as al-Qaeda and the Islamic State. In response, the U.S. military needs to constantly evolve its strategies and its configurations of fighting equipment, even as it maintains forces necessary to counter and preempt well-known threats. The threat of cyberterrorism is likely to become more prominent in the years ahead. This will require new thinking about the protection of U.S. assets at home and abroad.

case study 5.1 Managing Aversion Behavior: Public Perceptions of Danger and Safety

We do many things in our lives because we believe them to be safe and in our best interests. When we learn of danger, we naturally tend to keep out of harm's way. In doing so, however, we sometimes make things worse. (In Chapter 1, we discussed the World Bank's concern over limiting **aversion behavior** after an outbreak of Ebola—for example, staying home from work to avoid harm, even when no such harm actually exists.) Since people often act on their feelings, it is important that their perceptions are appropriately aligned with the reality of the risks they face. Effective systems of defense and homeland security should promote such an alignment.

The deadly attacks of September 11, 2001, left many Americans feeling unsafe. They then engaged in various aversion behaviors. For example, a lot of people chose to drive long distances rather than flying. Unfortunately, this aversion behavior placed people in greater danger than if they had flown: statistically, flying is safer than driving. Analyzing this irony, Gerd Gigerenzer started from the assumption that people tend to avoid highly noticeable situations in which many people may be killed at one point in time, rather than situations in which the same number may be killed, but the deaths are distributed over a longer period of time.[2] Gigerenzer called low-probability, high-consequence events **dread risks**. The crash of four planes in the terrorist attacks of 9/11 is a case of a dread risk. Gigerenzer tested this claim: if (a) Americans reduced their air travel as a consequence of the September 11 tragedy and (b) a proportion of those who reduced their flying instead drove

(rather than staying home or taking a train), then (c) an increase in traffic fatalities would have resulted.

During the months of October, November, and December 2001, U.S. commercial airline travel usage decreased by 20 percent, 17 percent, and 12 percent respectively, compared with the same months in 2000. In those same months, there was around a 3 percent increase in vehicle miles driven, and much of that increase occurred on rural interstate highways, evidence consistent with Gigerenzer's claim. Further, fatal car accidents increased during these same months. Using statistical analysis, Gigerenzer claimed that a total of 350 more traffic fatalities occurred throughout the United States during those last three months of 2001 than would have occurred if 9/11 had not happened.

The 9/11 attacks caused the immediate death of 2,977 innocent victims. Of these victims, 266 were passengers and crew on the four hijacked aircraft. The unusual increase in traffic fatalities during the following months produced further unnecessary tragedy. In Gigerenzer's words, "The number of Americans who lost their lives on the road by avoiding the risk of flying was higher than the total number of passengers killed on the four fatal flights."[3]

This evidence highlights the psychological importance of defense and homeland security initiatives. Following 9/11, people likely engaged in many other aversion behaviors that would be harder to observe systematically than switching their travel habits. Yet some of those harder-to-see aversion behaviors still would have had negative impacts on family life and broader

Strong defense and homeland security are essential for making citizens feel safe from harm. When they experience peace and feel confident about the future, people can devote themselves to all those activities that comprise a thriving, vibrant economy and society. Attaining and maintaining peace is costly. Yet those costs are always far less than the costs of war. Indeed, maintaining the peace also reduces the hidden costs associated with fear of war. Case Study 5.1 provides an example of how public fears can disrupt everyday behavior and lead people to make choices that do not necessarily enhance their safety.

THE PUBLIC PROBLEM: PROTECTING AMERICAN INTERESTS

Very little economic and social development could occur in the absence of some guarantees of protection from external harm. It is the government's responsibility to provide citizens with the dual public goods of safety from external threat and peaceful coexistence. It is difficult to conceive that security for whole societies can be provided through decentralized processes. An individual citizen could wait for others to pay for protection, from which that individual would then benefit. After all, it is difficult to supply defense to one group of citizens without supplying it—as an externality—to everyone else. However, since everyone can see this logic, everyone would choose to be **free riders**—leaving it to someone else to pay the bill. With no apparent demand for defense services, no private companies would form to deliver it.

Given such an equilibrium position, nobody would pay for defense and no one would supply it. This explains why governments everywhere are authorized by society to raise taxes and take actions to protect national borders and keep the peace among citizens. Of course, once a government has claimed this role and has collected tax revenues, it is possible for it to contract some defense or security services to private entities. Such arrangements have occurred through history. Further, it is common for individual citizens, organizations, and corporations to use private security firms to enhance the protection of their properties and themselves. However, in recent years, there has been much debate regarding the reliance that the DoD places on private corporations—often termed **private contractors**—to support the provision of defense. The existence of these secondary security services does not negate the fundamental need for government to manage the payment for and delivery of defense and homeland security.

Since World War II, U.S. military activities in the world have become vast. That vastness seems at odds with a simple argument that governments establish defense and security forces to protect their borders and keep the peace among their citizens. To understand the vastness of U.S. military activities, we need to think in terms of **American world interests**. These are the interests that the U.S. government, acting for its citizens, cares most deeply about and works hardest to protect. In a competitive, threatening world, peaceful existence comes at the cost of having suitable security in place. Sometimes, in the midst of debates about American foreign policy, about when war is appropriate, and about the size of the defense budget, it is easy for people to lose sight of American interests in the world and how they should be advanced and protected.

In 2000, representatives of several groups interested in foreign affairs formed the Commission on America's National Interests.[4] The Commission was supported by the Belfer Center for Science and International Affairs at Harvard University and the RAND Corporation. It was motivated by the contention that "in the absence of American global leadership, citizens will find their fortunes, their values, and indeed their lives threatened as surely as they ever have been."

Graham Allison and Robert Blackwill wrote the Commission's final report. Both men had decades of knowledge of American foreign policy. The report presented a hierarchy of American national interests and cut through many of the debates concerning what America should do in the world. The Commission proposed (p. 6) that vital U.S. national interests are to:

1. Prevent, deter, and reduce the threat of nuclear, biological, and chemical weapons attacks on the United States or its military forces abroad;
2. Ensure the survival of U.S. allies and their active cooperation with the United States in shaping an international system in which we can thrive;
3. Prevent the emergence of hostile major powers or failed states on U.S. borders;

4. Ensure the viability and stability of major global systems (trade, financial markets, supplies of energy, and the environment); and

5. Establish productive relations, consistent with American national interests, with nations that could become strategic adversaries, China and Russia.

The Commission's list of extremely important interests included reducing the threat of nuclear war; reducing the proliferation of weapons of mass destruction; preventing, managing, and—if possible at reasonable cost—ending major conflicts in important geographic regions; preventing massive, uncontrolled immigration across U.S. borders; suppressing terrorism (especially state-sponsored terrorism); and preventing genocide.

One indicator of the gravity of defense and security concerns to U.S. citizens is how often they have elected presidents with military service records. Most American presidents have served in some capacity. Over a quarter of them previously served as generals in the armed forces. Dwight D. Eisenhower, president from 1953 to 1961, is the most recent president to have previously served as a military general. He was a five-star general in the U.S. Army during World War II and served as Supreme Commander of the Allied Expeditionary Forces in Europe. Over subsequent decades, several of Eisenhower's public speeches have become touchstones for reminding people of America's interests.

Early in his term in office, Eisenhower delivered a speech titled "The Chance for Peace." In it he suggested that since World War II, "the way chosen by the United States was plainly marked by a few clear precepts, which govern its conduct in world affairs." Eisenhower listed those precepts as follows:

1. No people on earth can be held, as a people, to be an enemy, for all humanity shares the common hunger for peace and fellowship and justice.

2. No nation's security and well-being can be lastingly achieved in isolation but only in effective cooperation with fellow nations.

3. Any nation's right to a form of government and an economic system of its own choosing is inalienable.

4. Any nation's attempt to dictate to other nations their form of government is indefensible.

5. A nation's hope of lasting peace cannot be firmly based upon any race in armaments but rather upon just relations and honest understanding with all other nations.

Much of Eisenhower's speech was devoted to contrasting America's way in the world with that of the Soviet Union. He noted his fear of nuclear war and said that the Soviet Union's desire for influence in the world left no alternative but "a life of perpetual fear and tension; a burden of arms draining the wealth and the labor of all peoples; a wasting of strength that defies the American system or the Soviet system or any system to achieve true abundance and happiness for the people of this earth." For Eisenhower, the **Cold War** buildup of military force necessitated by Soviet ambition came with enormous **opportunity costs**. He made this point explicitly: "The cost of one modern heavy bomber is this: a modern brick school in more than 30 cities. It is two electric power plants, each serving a town of 60,000 population. It is two fine, fully equipped hospitals. It is some 50 miles of concrete highway."

Speaking nearly eight years later, in 1961, in his farewell address, President Eisenhower again expressed his concerns about the need for enormous defense spending and the risks it brought with it. Yet he saw no alternative: "A vital element in keeping the peace is our military establishment. Our arms must be mighty, ready for instant action, so that no potential aggressor may be tempted to risk his own destruction." In a comment that many since have viewed as prescient, Eisenhower stated: "In the councils of governments, we must guard against the acquisition of unwarranted influence, whether sought or unsought, by the military-industrial complex. The potential for the disastrous rise of misplaced power exists and will persist." Further, Eisenhower appreciated that actions taken by one generation could harm the future prospects of future generations. His comments in this regard have been subsequently evoked, especially in light of the growing federal government debt and the annual interest payments it necessitates: "We cannot mortgage the material assets of our grandchildren without risking the loss also of their political and spiritual heritage. We want democracy to survive for all generations to come, not to become the insolvent phantom of tomorrow."

As we reflect upon American interests, three points become clear. First, democracy and freedom are paramount American values. They give rise to the pursuit of broader interests in the world, such as efforts to maintain and expand global capitalism. Second, the United States can strongly shape the evolution of the world order. However, there are limits to its influence. When powers with apparently malign intent take actions to promote their interests, the only sensible response from the United States involves redoubling defense of its interests. During the Cold War, this resulted in continuous increases in defense spending, which eroded the capacity of the U.S. government to pursue important domestic policy initiatives. Last, America's stance in the world will always be shaped by domestic political considerations.

Presidents and congressional leaders develop U.S. defense and foreign policy with reference both to the actions of other nations and to the domestic situation. This dichotomy has been construed as a **two-level game**.[5] Often, the nation must confront trade-offs between the pursuit of interests internationally and the pursuit of domestic policy initiatives. We pursue the matter of defense spending via In Focus 5.1, which gives an overview of the U.S. defense budget.

in focus 5.1

THE UNITED STATES DEFENSE BUDGET IN CONTEXT

There are many ways for us to understand U.S. commitments to maintaining a strong military. Here, we consider those commitments in three contexts: international comparison, historical trends, and the contemporary annual budgets of the U.S. government.

The United States spends more on defense than any other country in the world. Annual defense spending exceeds that of the next seven biggest spenders combined. Figure 5.1 portrays U.S. defense spending in 2015 with that of other countries. Two aspects are especially important. First, the United States has much more capability than other countries to maintain and continuously improve its military. Second, because of the size and capability of its military, the United States assumes a default position as the leader in defending the interests of all countries with which it shares military alliances.

Many military analysts currently view China as an emerging threat to world peace, and as a contender with the United States for military superiority. Reviewing the spending information in Figure 5.1, we could infer that China has a long way to go on that front. However, since the Chinese economy is based on lower cost structures (including lower average wages), China's military is rapidly approaching a level of sophistication and capability that makes it a strong contender with the United States, especially in its Asia-Pacific sphere of influence.[6]

FIGURE 5.1 U.S. Defense Spending Compared with That of Other Countries, 2015

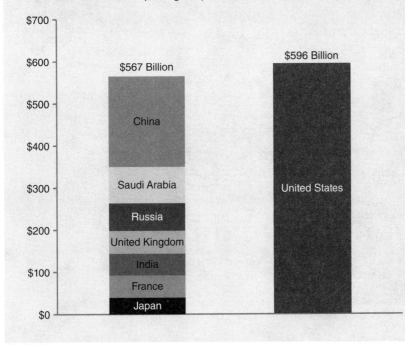

Source: Peter G. Peterson Foundation chart compiling evidence from the Stockholm International Peace Research Institute's SIPRI Military Expenditure Database, April 2016.

Note: Figures are for spending in 2015, all converted, using market exchange rates, from local currencies to U.S. dollars.

Over the decades, the United States has made significant adjustments to its annual defense spending. It has increased during times of war and decreased during times when threats have been perceived as lower. Figure 5.2 shows the trend in U.S. defense expenditures since 1940. Historically, the U.S. government devoted the greatest ever amount of its spending to defense during World War II. At that time, defense spending accounted for over 80 percent of the annual budget of the U.S. government. Since then, there has been a continual decline in the percentage of the annual budget devoted to defense. Currently, it is around 14 percent. This translates into around 3 percent of U.S. GDP being devoted to the military, down from over 30 percent during World War II.

A focus on defense spending as a percentage of either GDP or the U.S. government budget suggests a long-term decline in commitments to the defense forces. However, that view misses a more vital consideration. During the years shown in Figure 5.2, the U.S. economy has experienced more or less continuous expansion, as shown by the top trend line, which traces growth in absolute GDP—that is, GDP measured in constant dollars. As the U.S. economy has expanded, and government spending has expanded, more resources have been devoted in absolute terms to the funding of defense. This is shown in the trend line tracing DoD spending, as that spending has tripled in absolute terms since the late 1940s. A growing economy allows the government to devote more money

FIGURE 5.2 United States Defense Spending as a Percentage of GDP, Federal Spending, and Overall (Fiscal Years 1940–2017)

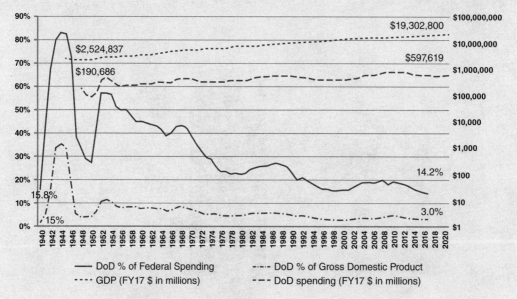

Source: Peter G. Peterson Foundation chart (2016, Figure 60, p. 70) compiling evidence from Table 7-7 of the Fiscal Year 2017 Greenbook produced by the Office of the Secretary of Defense. Note: Right axis is logarithmic.

to defense even as the overall ratio of commitments to defense are declining. With a growing economy, an annual government commitment to defense spending equivalent to around 3 percent of GDP can allow defense forces to continuously improve, as long as that defense spending is wisely managed.

The annual budget of the U.S. government is divided into three expenditure categories. The first is **debt servicing**—the interest the United States pays on money borrowed to cover differences between government revenue and spending. As long as deficits continue, the debt will grow, and so will the need to devote more of each annual budget to debt servicing. Currently, debt servicing accounts for more than 10 percent of the annual U.S. government budget.

The second category is **mandatory spending,** money that must be paid through entitlement programs such as Social Security and Medicare. Mandatory spending comprises around two-thirds of the annual budget. Many programs that comprise mandatory spending have eligibility rules; Congress does not decide each year whether to increase or decrease the budgets for these programs.

The third category is **discretionary spending**, where defense spending falls. This is the spending over which the president and Congress have most control in the budget process. Discretionary spending can be increased or reduced in any given year. Defense spending accounts for more than half of the U.S. government's annual discretionary spending. Along with defense spending, discretionary spending includes contributions to various federal initiatives, including education, health, science funding, and environmental protection. Discretionary spending is the only component of the U.S. government budget for which big adjustments can be made from year to year. For military planners, this aspect is often troubling, as the discretionary nature of defense funding makes it vulnerable to seemingly arbitrary cutbacks.

Many commentators on U.S. politics and policy have voiced concerns about the current configuration of the overall U.S. government budget. The Coalition for Fiscal and National Security has warned that the current configuration of the government's budget is not sustainable and spells major problems ahead for defense spending—and the protection of American interests.[7]

TRADITIONAL APPROACHES TO DEFENSE POLICY

The United States attained its current superpower status slowly and reluctantly. In seeking victory over hostile forces, U.S. defense planners capitalized on advances in aircraft technology and drove innovations in weapons systems. The United States also did much over the past century to advance its interests in the world through the nonmilitary pursuit of security. This has involved building alliances in strategic parts of the world, in addition to contributing generous support to rebuild war-torn economies. Although the United States has long been a military superpower, that status has often been incidental. It has emerged primarily through pragmatic engagement in world affairs, not through an overarching desire for empire or world domination.

THE QUEST FOR MILITARY SUPERIORITY

In a classic study of "the American way of war," military historian Russell Weigley said that, over centuries, the United States has shown a preference for seeking total victory, usually through unleashing sufficient firepower to annihilate an opposition and force unconditional surrender.[8] Certainly during the 20th century the United States, by adopting new technology, developed increasingly sophisticated approaches to gain military superiority. Support for Weigley's contention is provided by the practice during World War II of strategic bombing of enemy targets. Rather than supporting allied soldiers at the front line, aircraft attacked the resources supporting enemy soldiers. American bombing raids targeted munitions factories, power stations, and the centers of political power. In Europe, toward the end of the war, raids on Germany disabled enemy capabilities. In the Pacific, extensive bombing raids on Japan destroyed all industry supporting the war effort. Dropping the atomic bombs on Hiroshima and Nagasaki represented a further step on a continuum of relentless attack.

Weigley's portrayal of American war craft could be extended to explain the development of nuclear and conventional weapon-system capabilities during the Cold War to maintain military superiority over the Soviet Union. Even today, the relative commitment to military spending portrayed in Figure 5.1 suggests a strong desire to maintain military superiority in the world. Yet Weigley's portrayal misses a fundamental aspect of how America fights: its ability to unleash massive firepower has often been restrained. Restraint has strategic value. For example, while the United States has had nuclear capabilities for decades, it has chosen not to use them. In showing restraint, America has kept regional conflicts contained, rather than escalating them to major wars. In the process, civilian casualties have been limited, as have casualties to U.S. soldiers.

America's long quest for military superiority initially focused on specific enemies—Germany, Japan, and the Soviet Union. Recently, the quest has been more general. In Focus 5.2 provides an overview of the proliferation of nuclear weapons since the end of World War II. It also offers further evidence of the quest for military superiority.

THE NONMILITARY PURSUIT OF SECURITY

The United States has long enjoyed unparalleled military capability. The country has also gone to great lengths to build security alliances with other countries. Today, the United States has military alliances around the globe and a clear military presence in many countries. However, efforts to achieve a stable, peaceful world while simultaneously advancing American interests have frequently been pursued through nonmilitary initiatives.

in focus 5.2

THE NUCLEAR AGE AND NUCLEAR PROLIFERATION

World War II ended in August 1945 with Japanese surrender, precipitated by U.S. forces dropping atomic bombs on Hiroshima and then Nagasaki. When the Japanese were told that Tokyo would be next, surrender came swiftly. Estimates suggest that the atomic bombing of Hiroshima killed 90,000 to 146,000 people; the bombing of Nagasaki 39,000 to 80,000. So ended the deadliest military conflict in history, and so began the nuclear age.

In years following World War II, the United States greatly expanded its ability to produce nuclear weapons. Meanwhile, aided by spies passing on crucial bomb-building information, the Soviet Union rushed to establish its own nuclear capabilities. In 1949, the Soviet Union conducted its first successful nuclear bomb test. As nuclear programs were advanced by both sides, the power of bombs quickly grew. The bombs dropped on Hiroshima and Nagasaki created 15- and 21-kiloton blasts, respectively. In 1960, the Soviets exploded a test bomb creating a 50,000-kiloton blast. Its mushroom cloud was 40 miles high; its fireball was so massive it would have produced third-degree burns on people located 60 miles from the test site. Such a bomb, if exploded in a major city, would instantaneously kill millions and cause enormous physical devastation.[9]

While the United States and the Soviet Union proceeded with developing nuclear weapons, successful nuclear tests were conducted by the United Kingdom in 1952, France in 1960, and China in 1964. For all, these tests marked the start of efforts to establish inventories of nuclear weapons. To limit their spread, the United States and other like-minded states negotiated the nuclear Nonproliferation Treaty (NPT) in 1968 and the Comprehensive Nuclear Test Ban Treaty (CTBT) in 1996.

India, Israel, and Pakistan never signed the NPT and possess nuclear arsenals. Iraq initiated a secret nuclear program under Saddam Hussein before the 1991 Persian Gulf War. North Korea withdrew from the NPT in 2003 and has since tested nuclear bombs. Iran and Libya have pursued nuclear activities in violation of the treaty's terms. Syria is suspected of having done the same.[10]

Although the number of nuclear-armed states has grown over the decades since 1945, the number of nuclear weapons in place is much lower now than it was during the height of the Cold War, when the United States and the Soviet Union were racing each other to attain nuclear superiority. Beginning in the 1960s, the two countries signed various treaties designed to limit the accumulation of nuclear weapons. A series of Strategic Arms Reductions Talks (START) were launched in the 1980s that have led to significant reductions in nuclear weapons.

The world's nuclear-armed states now possess a combined total of roughly 15,500 nuclear warheads. Of these, more than 90 percent belong to Russia and the United States. Approximately 10,000 warheads are in military services, with the rest awaiting dismantlement. Figure 5.3 shows countries possessing warheads, and the estimated total in each. The figures for 2016 represent a reduction compared with those of the 1960s, when estimates suggested that more than 30,000 nuclear warheads existed.

Speaking in Prague in 2009, President Barack Obama observed: "In a strange turn of history, the threat of global nuclear war has gone down, but the risk of a nuclear attack has gone up. . . . The technology to build a bomb has spread. Terrorists are determined to buy, build or steal one."

In this speech, Obama announced a new international effort to secure vulnerable nuclear material around the world. Today, many political leaders and commentators consider nuclear weapons falling into the hands of terrorists as the greatest security threat facing the world.[11]

FIGURE 5.3   2016 Estimated Global Nuclear Warhead Inventories

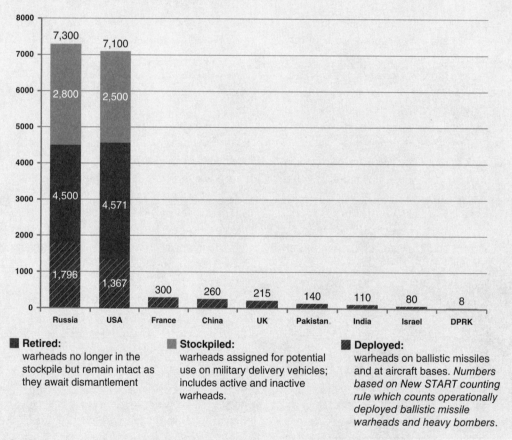

■ Retired:
warheads no longer in the stockpile but remain intact as they await dismantlement

■ Stockpiled:
warheads assigned for potential use on military delivery vehicles; includes active and inactive warheads.

▨ Deployed:
warheads on ballistic missiles and at aircraft bases. *Numbers based on New START counting rule which counts operationally deployed ballistic missile warheads and heavy bombers.*

Source: The Arms Control Association, "Nuclear Weapons: Who Has What at a Glance." Published on Arms Control Association website at https://www.armscontrol.org, p. 3. Figures collated by the Arms Control Association based on data from Hans M. Kristensen and Robert S. Norris; U.S. Department of State. Updated November 3, 2016.

The classic example of American nonmilitary pursuit of security is the Marshall Plan.[12] This plan, named after General George Marshall, was enacted in 1948 to support the reconstruction of European nations after the devastation of World War II. During the subsequent four years, the United States gave the equivalent in 2016 dollars of $120 billion in aid. The largest amounts of support went to the United Kingdom, France, and West Germany. Aid was offered to the Soviet Union and other countries in Eastern Europe; however, that aid was declined. As well as supporting allies in becoming strong economies, the goal of the plan was to reduce the risk that demoralized groups would lose faith in their governments and turn to communism. Under the leadership of General Douglas A. MacArthur, similar efforts helped rebuild the Japanese economy and establish a democratic society. Over subsequent decades, the United States has continued to take a range of nonmilitary actions around the world to support allied countries and expand American economic interests.

THE EMERGENCE OF AN INCIDENTAL SUPERPOWER

Writing of U.S. foreign policy, Derek S. Reveron and his co-authors termed the United States "an incidental superpower."[13] The term usefully encapsulates key aspects of how the nation has acted in the world over the past 150 years. Throughout, the strong desire has been to protect the homeland and avoid empire building. At the same time, there has been continuous acknowledgment of America's interests in the world and how these can be advanced through alliances with other nations that operate according to the precepts of democracy and capitalism. The nation's superpower status is "incidental" because it emerged through pragmatic engagement in the world, not pursuit of a master plan. Further, although the United States has amassed extraordinary military strength, it never did this for gratuitous, empire-building purposes. Rather, it pursued military superiority in the face of clear aggression on the part of other powers. This characterization of the United States and its relationship to the world helps us make sense of contemporary public policy debates regarding defense and homeland security.

THE IMPORTANCE OF HOMELAND SECURITY

The attacks of September 11, 2001, showed everyone what many people in the DoD and the U.S. intelligence community had known for some time: that major damage can be inflicted on Americans and American interests by determined terrorist groups that, by every measure, lack the weapons and sophisticated infrastructure of the U.S. defense forces. The attacks motivated a multinational "coalition of the willing" to wage conventional war on Afghanistan and Iraq. Those military

On September 11, 2001, the al-Qaeda international terrorist group implemented a carefully coordinated plan to hijack four commercial airliners on U.S. domestic flights and use them to attack buildings symbolizing American power. The twin towers of the World Trade Center in New York City suffered catastrophic damage, leading to their collapse and the death of 2,606 people.

(Robert J. Fisch/Public Domain)

maneuvers were designed to break suspected links between the ruling regimes in those countries and al-Qaeda and affiliated movements. The attacks also motivated efforts to improve domestic identification of terrorist activity and coordinate governmental response to large-scale disasters. Here, we discuss the creation of the Department of Homeland Security and evidence of its effectiveness in reducing terrorist threats.

COORDINATION INITIATIVES AND INFORMATION SHARING

Prior to 9/11, the United States addressed threats to the homeland through separate governmental functions: national defense, law enforcement, and emergency management. After the attacks, evidence emerged that various government entities had acquired relevant knowledge of suspicious behaviors prior to the attacks. However, no entity had an overview of the situation, or indeed had amassed the various pieces of information that might have allowed for a preemptive "joining of the dots." This was considered a major failing on the part of the intelligence community and law enforcement more generally. In response, on October 8, 2001, President George W. Bush created the Office of Homeland Security, intended to improve coordination among federal agencies to ensure that something like 9/11 would not happen again. Although the president held a disdain for large bureaucracy, the limits of the office and the politics of the situation soon led to renewed calls for the creation of a cabinet-level agency. The Bush administration worked with Congress to create it. The enacting legislation was approved in November 2002 and the DHS started operating in March 2003. Its primary role is to coordinate counterterrorism and security management. It is also expected to provide border security and to ensure disaster preparedness, response, and recovery.

Since its establishment, the DHS has undergone various restructurings to improve its effectiveness and efficiency. While the department includes many of the U.S. government's homeland security functions, several of these remain in their original executive branch agencies and departments. Examples include the Departments of Justice, State, Defense, and Transportation.

Meanwhile, not all of the missions of the DHS directly relate to "homeland security." For example, the Coast Guard's environmental and recreational boating safety missions—while important—do not really relate to homeland security. Debates have occurred from time to time about whether FEMA and its relief and recovery missions belong in the department.[14] For our purposes, the crucial question is whether all of this reorganization has produced higher levels of protection for the American people.

DETECTING TERRORIST PLOTS

One way to assess the effectiveness of homeland security involves analyzing success in stopping—or foiling—terrorist plots. Analysis by Kevin J. Strom and colleagues involved collating all information regarding 150 terrorist plots against the United States from 1995 to 2012.[15] The authors defined terrorism as an intentional act of violence by a nonstate actor. The act had to be designed to convey some message to a larger audience than the immediate victims. It had to be planned to occur outside the context of legitimate warfare. The authors excluded attacks due to mental illness (which included a number of mass shootings that occurred within the period) and "ordinary" hate crimes focused strictly on the victims. The plots had to be against U.S. targets, on U.S. soil outside a war zone. Plots against U.S. embassies and military bases abroad were included. The plots had to be intended to cause casualties or catastrophic damage to infrastructure, and had to have reached a reasonable level of maturity—for example, logistical preparations were underway when they were detected.

Strom and his colleagues found that motivations for these 150 plots fell into four main categories: (1) al-Qaeda and affiliated movements; (2) U.S. residents inspired by al-Qaeda and affiliated movements; (3) militia/anti-government movements; and (4) white supremacists. Quite a few plots did not fall into any such categories—including anti-abortion and anti-Muslim plots. Table 5.1 lists the seven largest plots (in terms of their deadliness). Of these, five were led or inspired by al-Qaeda. The other two were led by U.S. citizens professing strong

TABLE 5.1 The Seven Largest of 150 Terrorist Plots Against the United States, 1995–2012

PLOT (YEAR)	DESCRIPTION	CASUALTIES
Attempted Christmas Day bombing of NW 253 (2009)	Failed al-Qaeda plot: a passenger on an international flight from Amsterdam to Detroit tried to set off plastic explosives sewn to his underwear. The plot was foiled by fellow passengers.	290 potential deaths
Fort Hood shootings (2009)	Inspired by al-Qaeda, Nidal Hasan, a U.S. Army major and psychiatrist, opened fire on people at a U.S. Army base.	13 killed
Attempted "shoe bombing" of AA 63 (2001)	Inspired by al-Qaeda, an Islamic fundamentalist from the United Kingdom plotted to set off plastic explosives concealed in his shoes on an international flight from Paris to Miami. The plot was foiled by fellow passengers.	197 potential deaths
9/11 attacks (2001)	Al-Qaeda hijacking and crashing of four airliners: two hit the World Trade Center, one hit the Pentagon, and one intended to target the U.S. Congress.	2,977 killed
Columbine High School shootings (1999)	Shooting and attempted bombing by two high school students, Eric Harris and Dylan Klebold, was intended to rival the Oklahoma City bombing of 1995 (see hereafter). The attack was planned as a terrorist bombing but failed. The attackers committed suicide at the scene.	15 killed (including the perpetrators)
Bombings of Kenya and Tanzania U.S. embassies (1998)	Al-Qaeda used synchronized truck bomb explosions to destroy American facilities.	224 killed
Oklahoma City bombing (1995)	Truck bombing of the Alfred P. Murrah Federal Building in downtown Oklahoma City—carried out by Timothy McVeigh, a U.S. Army veteran of the Gulf War, and Terry Nichols—was revenge for earlier U.S. government action against heavily armed separatist groups at Ruby Ridge, ID, in 1992 and Waco, TX, in 1993.	168 killed

Sources: Plots, years, and casualties from Kevin J. Strom, John S. Hollywood, and Mark Pope, Terrorist Plots against the United States *(RAND Homeland Security and Defense Center, 2015), Table 2. Plot descriptions added by the author.*

anti-government sentiments. Overall, Strom and his colleagues found that al-Qaeda and affiliated movements motivated almost 40 percent of the plots. Just as significantly, militia/anti-government and white supremacist movements inspired around another 40 percent of the plots, with a range of loyalties and obsessions motivating the remainder.

This analysis of terrorist plots revealed that, overall, the United States was more successful at detecting and foiling terrorist plots in the years since 9/11 than it was from 1995 to 2001, when around 32 percent of plots were foiled. Following the 9/11 attacks, from 2002 through 2012, 81 percent of plots were foiled. Of all the foiled plots, more than 80 percent were thwarted as a result of observations by law enforcement officials or by the general public.

In five of the seven plots listed in Table 5.1, authorities had received clues but had subsequently dropped them. This is a serious concern. A primary motivation for establishing the DHS was the perceived need for government organizations to improve their information sharing and "joining the dots" to identify and foil plots. It has turned out that plots are more likely to be foiled through perceptive observation by local policing units and members of the public. This finding suggests the importance of ongoing provision of processes and training that help policing units be effective in counterterrorism. Further, members of the public in all communities need to feel sufficiently comfortable with authorities to report potential terrorist-related activities. That these measures have occurred suggests that the intentions behind creating the DHS were sound. Beyond integrating federal agencies, counterterrorism can be bolstered through cross-jurisdictional cooperation, stretching down to the level of local policing and public support.

FEDERALISM AND HOMELAND SECURITY

Although the DHS takes a nationwide approach to counterterrorism, border security, and disaster preparedness, the effectiveness of its activities is influenced by state and local law enforcement entities, such as state troopers and local police departments. This has been starkly illustrated in the aftermath of natural disasters, such as Hurricanes Katrina (2005) and Sandy (2012). It is generally agreed that the federal response to Hurricane Katrina was too slow, which partly had to do with protocols operating at the time concerning coordination between FEMA and state governments. In contrast, a lot of learning took place between 2005 and 2012. As a result, the federal government worked with state and local governments both to prepare for Sandy's landfall and to prepare for disaster recovery. A question arises: Has this improvement in cooperation and coordination regarding natural disasters been mirrored in how different levels of government engage in counterterrorism efforts?

In the aftermath of 9/11, many states created their own homeland security offices and most have developed specific homeland security plans. With assistance from the DHS, many states and large metropolitan areas also established **Fusion Centers**, which gather and share information relating to suspected terrorist plots.

The Bureau of Justice Assistance (BJA) provides another example of cooperation and capacity building sponsored by the U.S. government. This bureau's mission is to support state and local governments in preventing crime and violence. Since 1996, the BJA has offered the State and Local Anti-Terrorism Training (SLATT) program. SLATT provides specialized terrorism/extremism awareness training and helps participants improve their skills in investigation and prevention of terrorist activities. Over the decades during which it has been operating, this program has trained more than 140,000 practitioners working at the state and local level. It has been judged beneficial for how it improves the awareness of local personnel concerning detection of terrorist threats and responses to them. An evaluation of the program suggests that its major benefits come through raising awareness of terrorist behavior, increasing the use local entities make of resources provided by the Bureau's website, and creating networking opportunities for personnel from diverse jurisdictions.[16]

Ultimately, the more uniform the counterterrorism activities occurring at the state and local levels, the more likely it is that plots will fail, and incidents will be managed in ways that minimize danger to innocent citizens. Many actions taken at the sub-national level can contribute to broader homeland security efforts.

Given the frequency with which homeland security is threatened by heavily armed individuals and groups, Case Study 5.2 explores connections between everyday militarism, state gun laws, and public safety. The U.S. Constitution gives

case study 5.2 Militarism, State Gun Laws, and Public Safety

The Second Amendment to the United States Constitution reads, "A well-regulated Militia, being necessary to the security of a free State, the right of the people to keep and bear Arms, shall not be infringed." This language has created enormous debate concerning the amendment's intended scope. Meanwhile, handguns and semiautomatic and automatic rifles have grown more sophisticated and powerful over the years. Every year, many innocent people in the United States die because powerful weapons have been used irresponsibly. Despite the concerns voiced, especially when mass shootings occur, restricting the purchase of guns has proven politically difficult. Although ready access to guns may make some people feel secure, it can make many others feel unsafe.

Gun violence, with its roots in militarism, exacts a terrible toll. In 2014, over 32,000 people in the United States were killed as a result of injuries from firearms. What difference might tighter gun laws make? In 1995, Connecticut implemented a handgun permit-to-purchase law. This law strengthened background check requirements for handguns sold by private sellers and licensed firearm dealers. It required completion of an approved handgun safety course of at least eight hours, and it increased the minimum legal age for handgun purchase from 18 to 21 years. A study of what subsequently happened in Connecticut offers compelling evidence that tighter gun laws can reduce homicides involving guns.

Kara E. Rudolph and her colleagues compared Connecticut's homicide rates after the 1995 law's implementation to rates that might have been expected had the law not been implemented.[17] To develop the **counterfactual case**, the researchers used longitudinal data from a combination of comparison states, where gun control remained much the same as Connecticut's prior to 1995. Using this research approach, Rudolph estimated that the Connecticut law change led to a 40 percent reduction in the state's firearm homicide rates over the decade from 1996 to 2005. This reduction is equivalent to almost 300 fewer firearm homicides in the state during those years. By contrast, there was no evidence for a reduction in nonfirearm homicides in the state over the same period.

Other studies have observed a strong relationship between the permissiveness of state gun controls and annual death rates due to firearm use.[18] Table 5.2 ranks states using the Brady Campaign's State Scorecard for 2015.[19] California has the most restrictive gun laws (and is ranked number 1), while Arizona has the least restrictive laws (and is ranked number 50). The Scorecard ranks states on a number of indicators, including the use of various background checks for people buying guns, laws concerning when guns may be carried, and laws concerning the practices of gun dealers.[20]

Table 5.2 also reports the recorded deaths in each state due to injury by firearms in 2014 (shown as the rate per 100,000 state population).[21] The average rate of gun deaths across all states in 2014 was 12.3. However, as the table makes clear, for those states ranked from 1– to 10 on the Brady Campaign's State Scorecard, the average rate was 6.7, a 46 percent reduction on the average across all states. The average rate of gun deaths for those states ranked from 40 to 50 on the Scorecard was 15.9, 29 percent higher than the average for all states and 237 percent higher than the average for the top 10 states on the Scorecard. Thus, on average, states with restrictive gun laws experience fewer gun deaths each year than those with more permissive laws.[22]

CRITICAL THINKING QUESTIONS

1. The constitutional right to bear arms was established to enhance public security against external threats. In what sense have security conditions changed in the United States since the 1788 ratification of the U.S. Constitution?
2. With respect to prevailing security concerns, what differences among states might explain differences in their gun laws?

TABLE 5.2 Restrictiveness of State Gun Laws and Deaths Due to Injury by Firearms in 2014

	BRADY SCORE[a]	RECORDED DEATHS[b]
AVERAGE FOR ALL STATES:		12.3
California	1	7.7
Connecticut	2	5.3
Massachusetts	3	3.0
New Jersey	4	5.4
New York	5	4.2
Hawaii	6	3.6
Maryland	7	11.9
Rhode Island	8	4.7
Delaware	9	12.1
Illinois	10	9.5
AVERAGE FOR STATES RANKED 1–10:		6.7
Washington	11	9.8
Pennsylvania	12	11.4
Colorado	13	12.6
Minnesota	14	7.4
Iowa	15	7.8
Wisconsin	16	10.4
Nebraska	17	8.9
Michigan	18	11.7
Oregon	19	11.4
North Carolina	20	12.5
Texas	21	11.7
North Dakota	22	12.8
Ohio	23	11.9
New Hampshire	24	8.9
Utah	25	12.8
South Dakota	26	11.1
Missouri	27	18.1
Tennessee	28	16.0
Kansas	29	11.4

	BRADY SCORE[a]	RECORDED DEATHS[b]
Indiana	30	12.7
West Virginia	31	14.0
South Carolina	32	17.3
Vermont	33	9.6
Oklahoma	34	18.0
Georgia	35	14.1
Alabama	36	19.6
New Mexico	37	18.6
Idaho	38	14.7
Mississippi	39	19.6
Maine	40	9.8
Nevada	41	14.9
Florida	42	12.0
Kentucky	43	15.2
Virginia	44	10.9
Arkansas	45	13.8
Montana	46	19.2
Louisiana	47	20.4
Wyoming	48	19.6
Alaska	49	19.6
Arizona	50	13.8
AVERAGE FOR STATES RANKED 41–50:		15.9

Sources: Brady Campaign and Centers for Disease Control and Prevention resources.

[a]Brady Campaign state scorecard rankings on restrictiveness of gun laws, 2014; 1 = most restrictive, 50 = least restrictive.
[b]Deaths due to injury by firearms, 2014, per 100,000 state population.

people the right "to bear arms." Some states make it relatively easy to exercise that right and buy guns; others impose a broad range of restrictions. The danger that heavily armed individuals present to those around them poses a classic public policy dilemma. Although gun laws can never fully protect innocent people from those bearing arms with malicious intent, it appears that state restrictions on the purchase of firearms translate into lower rates of shooting deaths in those states. In that sense, state gun laws represent a factor in homeland security—and, potentially, in foiling terrorism involving firearms. Although significant controversy surrounds the matter, state legislatures have it in their power to improve public safety by regulating gun sales.

CONTEMPORARY POLICY ISSUES

At any given time, policy makers in Washington, DC, are confronted with a variety of issues relating to the protection of American interests, the strength and effectiveness of the defense forces, and the maintenance of homeland security. The need to prioritize the issues on which they will focus is constant; often, they must confront difficult trade-offs. Here, we will distill the plethora of contemporary policy issues by discussing just four. These concern needing to stay strong amid the changing nature of warfare, promoting nuclear disarmament, tackling inefficiencies in the DoD, and clarifying priorities in homeland security. In a sense, all four of these issues are contemporary as well as timeless. Cloaked in different language, all of them have posed challenges in the past, and they are likely to continue to do so in the future.

STAYING STRONG AMID THE CHANGING NATURE OF WARFARE

The nature of warfare is in constant flux. To protect American interests, U.S. defense forces must therefore continually enhance their capability. They need to be prepared to respond rapidly to threats. They need to have the capacity both to neutralize such threats and to play the long game of achieving stable, peaceful relations with countries around the world. Coming out of the experiences of World War II

The Pentagon is the headquarters of the U.S. Department of Defense, located in Arlington, Virginia, across the Potomac River from Washington, DC. The building has become a symbol of America's massive military establishment.

(DoD photo by Master Sgt. Ken Hammond, U.S. Air Force)

and the Cold War, successive presidents, Congresses, and leaders of the DoD have held a consistent view on what U.S. defense forces should be able to do. That is, they should "have the ability to engage and decisively defeat one major opponent and simultaneously have the wherewithal to do the same with another to preclude opportunistic exploitation by any competitor."[23] This is sometimes called the "two major wars" requirement.

There are two parts to staying strong. The first is to ensure that the forces maintain a technological edge over potential enemies. Increasingly this means having the ability to effectively acquire relevant information, appropriately analyze it, and act decisively on it. Although firepower of all kinds is important, knowing where and how to deploy it is vital. Further, in the world of cyberattacks, it becomes crucial to national interests that defense forces and related agencies stay well ahead of all others in their ability to preempt, effectively respond to, and foil any enemy actions in cyberspace. The second part to staying strong is to have a clear sense of strategic priorities, the reason why clarity and agreement about American interests must always be a major priority for defense leaders.

Of course, staying strong militarily depends upon the U.S. government's having adequate revenues to fund continuous improvements in military capability and capacity. Within the defense forces themselves, efficient management of scarce resources is essential. However, beyond that mandate, military strength is ultimately dependent on economic strength. For the United States to remain militarily strong, the country must also remain an economic powerhouse. Indeed, that economic strength has been vital to the attainment of military superiority. Aside from allowing more resources to flow to the military, it has also allowed defense planners to draw on scientific research and technological advances to keep the fighting forces second to none.

PROMOTING NUCLEAR DISARMAMENT

Since the United States first developed nuclear weapons, both their number and the number of states owning them have proliferated. Beginning in the 1960s, the United States and the Soviet Union have sporadically cooperated to reduce their arsenals. Today, were nuclear war to break out between any two of the nations of China, Russia, or the United States, the laws of mutually assured destruction—that is, wide-scale harm—would prevail. The consequences would most likely be far more devastating than those for Hiroshima and Nagasaki in August 1945. Grounds exist for believing the world could become a safer, more peaceful place if multilateral steps could be taken to scale back current stockpiles of nuclear weapons. Such actions should reduce the likelihood that nuclear weapons will fall into the hands of leaders of rogue states such as North Korea or nonstate terrorist groups such as al-Qaeda and the Islamic State.

Of course, the suggestion that states work toward nuclear disarmament is controversial. Leaders in the United States, like leaders elsewhere, are unlikely to want to threaten their military superiority relative to potential enemies. The only basis upon which this could be done would involve high levels of trust. However, international trust is frequently in short supply—that is the reason why countries build strong defense systems in the first place.

In 2016, an historic vote in the United Nations approved a landmark resolution to launch negotiations aimed at outlawing nuclear weapons.[24] Although the resolution gained strong international support, unsurprisingly it was not supported by any nuclear powers, including the United States, or by allied nations that host nuclear weapons. Realistically, full nuclear disarmament could take decades; nonetheless, supporters of this resolution see glimmers of hope. Member of the European Union have agreed to participate constructively in the UN-led negotiations. In addition, previous international efforts to outlaw specific weapons have met with success. Biological and chemical weapons, antipersonnel landmines, and cluster munitions are now explicitly prohibited under international law. At various times in the past, such prohibitions would have seemed very unlikely.

Efforts to promote nuclear disarmament remind us that military superiority is just part of what keeps a nation protected in the world. Diplomatic actions and forms of cooperation intended to build strong trade partnerships can do much to promote the peaceful coexistence of nations.

TACKLING INEFFICIENCIES IN THE DEPARTMENT OF DEFENSE

Many politicians and commentators have long suspected that the U.S. Department of Defense, despite its awesome military capabilities, contains many pockets of wasteful spending and general inefficiency. News reports surface regularly to fuel these suspicions. A recent investigation suggests, first, that this issue remains relevant, and, second, that any efforts to tackle it will meet with strong resistance.

The DoD has a Defense Business Board, composed of outside business experts who advise the department. In 2014, the Board commissioned a report on how the DoD could save by emulating some of the efficiency-enhancing business processes of large U.S. corporations. The report did not consider the day-to-day activities of the military forces. Rather, it explored how improvements in property management, supply chain management, and procurement of equipment could be made in the "back office" administrative activities of the DoD. The report claimed that the department could save $125 billion over a five-year period by emulating best practices of relevant industries. It noted how such savings could be converted to "warfare currency" and used to support actual military activities. For example, the aforementioned savings could fully support deployments of 10 Navy carrier strike groups, each comprising one aircraft carrier, the aircraft on it, an attack submarine, and five other fighting ships.

When this report was made public, senior DoD figures moved to distance themselves from it and mark as "classified" the financial evidence used to generate the savings estimates.[25] Nonetheless, the detailed analysis in the report and careful recommendations for emulation of more efficient business systems suggest that room exists for efficiency gains. We can expect investigations along these lines to continue.

CLARIFYING PRIORITIES IN HOMELAND SECURITY

The DHS was established in haste, partly to address legitimate coordination concerns and partly to respond quickly to political pressures in the aftermath of 9/11. In the years since 2003, some branches of the department have worked together on counterterrorism initiatives. Others, especially the FEMA, have sought to improve federal preparedness for and responsiveness to disasters, natural or otherwise. Two problems remain. First, although the department is large in scope, many other government entities contribute to homeland security. Thus, the cluster of operations housed within the department is somewhat arbitrary—an arrangement that can dilute the total focus on homeland security.[26] Second, insufficient attention has been paid to how elements of homeland security should be prioritized. There is a tendency for attention in the department to lurch between crises. As evidence has emerged of weaknesses in the department, leaders have acted swiftly to address them. The result is that little effort has been devoted to more strategic planning.[27] Evidence presented below in the discussion of the investment perspective suggests that there are serious problems of focus and efficiency in the department. Given the fundamental importance of protecting citizens and maintaining the peace, we should expect to see continuing efforts to improve the effectiveness of homeland security initiatives.

DEFENSE, HOMELAND SECURITY, AND THE INVESTMENT PERSPECTIVE

Earlier we discussed the budget commitments required to maintain current configurations of U.S. defense and homeland security. Beginning during World War II, the country has made systematic efforts to assess the economic rationality of pursuing specific military actions. The branch of applied statistics called operations research emerged directly from those efforts. A lengthy history exists of cost-benefit analysis applied to military contexts.[28] The RAND Corporation, based in Santa Monica, has been a central player in the development of economic modeling to guide procurement of defense equipment and to improve project management of large asset-building programs.[29] Only in recent years, however, have scholars consolidated methods for assessing the merits of defense and homeland security investments.[30] As concerns grow about management of U.S. government debt, policy analysts should give more scrutiny to the value of expenditures on defense and homeland security. Here we will discuss applications of the investment perspective to defense and homeland security.

THE INVESTMENT PERSPECTIVE AND DEFENSE PROCUREMENT

The traditional approach to determining return on investment (ROI) from a policy or program involves dividing the sum of all monetized benefits by the sum of all costs. If the product is greater than 1, the ROI is deemed positive (see Chapter 3). This approach requires that we can plausibly assign monetary values to the benefits of a policy or program. In the realm of defense and homeland security, this is difficult to do. From the perspective of the perfectly rational planner, it would be desirable to assess the ROI of a nation that is going to war. Operation Desert Storm, the Gulf War of 1991, resulted in the retreat of the Iraqi Army and the liberation of Kuwait. Whether in this instance the benefits to the United States of its going to war outweighed the costs will never be definitively determined, and this is the case for many military exercises. Aside from the complexity of decisions associated with going to war, information vital for making investment decisions is typically not available in this area of government spending, since it is classified as secret.

The difficulties in developing overall assessments of the merits of military exercises have led to development and application of **cost-effectiveness analysis**. In this approach, analysts are able to compare the costs of an asset or an action as well as performance. They can then calculate what asset or action produces the best ratio of performance to cost. For example, military planners might have the goal of permanently disabling an enemy stronghold. With that clear goal in mind, they can then explore the feasibility and costs of alternative strategies for goal attainment. Inevitably, this approach involves exploring a range of trade-offs.

Case Study 5.3 presents an application of cost-effectiveness analysis where effectiveness is judged by the degree to which a program can reduce the estimated likelihood of terrorists hijacking passenger planes. Without addressing the bigger question of ROI, military decision making routinely involves much rationality. A clear example of this occurs in **military procurement**—the purchasing of equipment for use by the forces.

An exemplary case of rational planning in military procurement concerns the use of cost-effectiveness analysis to determine whether the U.S. Air Force should continue using the C-17 Globemaster aircraft for various transportation purposes.[31] During the early 1990s, the DoD explored the feasibility of using several alternative aircraft to form the backbone of its transportation fleet. To do so, it set forth airlift requirements and estimated the effectiveness of each alternative aircraft model in meeting those requirements. It then determined the total cost of ownership of each alternative aircraft fleet, over multiple years. Next, to facilitate decision making, it laid out the cost and effectiveness information. Additional analysis tested the sensitivity of the study conclusions to various costing and aircraft performance assumptions. Procurement decisions are typically handled in this way.

An ongoing concern regarding defense procurement is **cost overruns**.[32] These happen when the DoD makes an agreement with a military contractor to supply equipment at a certain price by a certain date. Subsequent to the contract's being agreed upon, the contractor advises that costs will be higher than they originally stated. At this point, continuation of the procurement is in jeopardy. Many controversies have resulted from cost overruns—and for good reason. If contractors routinely underestimate program costs for chosen projects so they can win defense contracts, it is possible that more cost-effective options were mistakenly passed over during the original procurement decisions. Although there is inevitably some uncertainty around the development of new equipment, cost overruns undermine good investment decisions.[33]

THE INVESTMENT PERSPECTIVE AND HOMELAND SECURITY

Homeland security initiatives include many activities that take place out of public view. Political scrutiny of those activities tends to happen only when they have clearly failed. The work of the Transportation Security Administration (TSA) offers a case in point. This branch of the DHS has a broad mandate that includes ensuring the security of ports and of trucking companies. Given that trucks often carry hazardous materials and have been used in terrorist incidents, maintaining security in their operations is an important task. Nonetheless, this aspect of the TSA's work draws little attention. In contrast, the actions of TSA officers involved in passenger screening at airports have gained a lot of scrutiny. Over two million passengers are screened each day; all travelers see TSA employees and have stories about going through security.

After 9/11, all passenger screening activities at airports were placed under the control of the TSA, and employees of private security companies were replaced by federal government employees. Subsequently, various covert testing measures, performed by different federal government entities, have been continuously applied to ensure that screeners are detecting passengers who could pose a security threat.[34] Given the covert nature of these tests, overall system performance measures are not readily available. However, these screening procedures have elicited critical questions, mainly because they are so time consuming for passengers. Questions include: Do screening systems really detect dangerous passengers? Do the costs of screening outweigh the benefits? What unintended consequences might arise from current screening practices?

Recently, efforts have been made to answer each of these questions. First, in 2015, evidence emerged from one of the covert testing programs. In this program, testers made 70 covert attempts to pass through screening with items that would-be terrorists could use to hijack or bomb a plane. During 67 of those attempts, the testers went through screening without detection—a suggested failure rate of 95 percent.[35] Such results do not engender confidence in the screening system.

Second, a simple response to the cost-benefit question would be that because there have been no repeats of 9/11-style terrorism since the start of more intensive passenger screening, the benefits of the system outweigh the costs. The difficulty with such reasoning is that it will justify any level of cost. Economists exploring this response have observed that wasted passenger time is a huge cost to passengers, but it is not a cost to the government.[36] Although it is right to want highly effective screening, we should not let that desire justify the shifting of massive costs onto individuals. Getting people through screening quickly should be a top priority, but for many years it has not been.

Third, terrorists tend to target areas where they can inflict maximum injury. When terrorist target airports, they target the most crowded places, such as ticketing counters. By creating long lines of passengers delayed while waiting for screening, expert analysis suggests that the TSA is unintentionally placing people in danger.[37]

This discussion of passenger screening suggests that more can be done to create effective systems of homeland security. Case Study 5.3 explores this point further, with consideration of approaches to reduce the risk of terrorists hijacking planes. An overall conclusion is that well-established policy approaches are not necessarily the most desirable, in terms of both their cost and their effectiveness. However, change from the status quo can be difficult to achieve.

case study 5.3 Improving Commercial Passenger Airliner Security

The events of 9/11 prompted the U.S. government, along with other governments around the world, to immediately introduce more measures to improve security in airports and on commercial aircraft. The Transportation Security Agency, a branch of the DHS, is responsible for maintaining aviation security. To this end, it manages several "layers" of security intended to deter and apprehend terrorists before they board commercial passenger flights. Pre-boarding security measures include intelligence sharing with other agencies, maintenance of "no-fly" lists of people deemed too threatening to fly, vetting of airport and aircraft crews, passenger screening, and the use of bomb appraisal officers. In-flight security measures include installation of secondary barriers to restrict access to hardened cockpit doors, and use of the Federal Air Marshal

Service (in which armed personnel routinely travel in planes near the cockpit) and the Federal Flight Deck Officer Program (in which civilian air crew are trained to carry and use weapons to secure the cockpit). Mark G. Stewart and John Mueller studied the effectiveness of various aviation security measures, and the discussion that follows draws on their work.[38]

Cost-benefit analysis can be used to compare the monetary value of different airline security strategies intended to save lives. We would begin by determining the annual running costs of a program. The installation of physical secondary barriers to restrict access to hardened cockpit doors in all U.S. aircraft was estimated to cost $13.5 million per year. The Federal Air Marshal Service was estimated to cost $1.2 billion per year. The Federal Flight

Deck Officer Program was estimated to cost $22 million per year. These costs are judged reasonable if they reduce the likelihood of a terrorist hijacking a plane. Using a break-even cost-benefit analysis, we would then calculate the minimum probability of an otherwise successful attack that would be required for the benefit of each security measure to equal its cost. For example, we might ask: How frequently would an attack have to be foiled as a result of this program to make it worthwhile in strictly financial terms? To answer this question, we need to calculate the value of the lives and property saved by foiling a terrorist incident. This is controversial because it means placing a value on human lives.

Stewart and Mueller used evidence from analyses of the costs associated with 9/11 and other estimates of the benefits of avoiding terrorist attacks. They suggested that $50 billion is a reasonable estimate of the costs of an attack using a single aircraft. Next, the authors worked through available evidence to determine the probability that each of these programs would reduce the likelihood of a terrorist attack. Suppose that on any given flight terrorists attempted to gain control of the cockpit. The authors suggested that physical secondary barriers on cockpit doors would reduce the likelihood of success by 75 percent. In contrast, the Federal Flight Deck Officer Program would likely have 10 percent success of foiling the attack. And, since air marshals are not present on every plane, use of that program would likely have just a 1 percent chance of successfully foiling the attack.

Using this information, Stewart and Mueller concluded that use of cockpit door barriers would prove financially worthwhile even if an otherwise successful attack occurred only once in 200 years. In contrast, the Federal Flight Deck Officer Program would be financially worthwhile if an otherwise successful attack occurred once every 50 years. Last, the Federal Air Marshal Service would prove financially worthwhile only if we expected more than two 9/11-style attacks per year. The authors performed a range of alternative analyses—deemed sensitivity analyses—to develop different scenarios where these various aviation security strategies would make sense. They concluded that it is difficult to justify the ongoing costs of the Federal Air Marshal Service. Many other more effective security measures could be put in place if this program were abandoned. This conclusion reminds us that all policy actions—including those that save lives—create opportunity costs. Devoting resources to one course of action always precludes us from taking others.

Policy Investment Checklist 5.1 summarizes the findings of Stewart and Mueller's study of terrorism risks and alternative approaches to improving aviation security. For simplicity, the checklist highlights only differences between the Federal Air Marshal Service and the Federal Flight Deck Officer Program.

CRITICAL THINKING QUESTIONS

1. What might explain the retention of the Federal Air Marshal Service, even though questions have arisen about its value compared with that of other security measures?
2. The Federal Flight Deck Officer Program requires air crew to use weapons to secure the cockpit. What security concerns might arise from greater reliance on this approach to foiling a terrorist attack?

Analyzing Commercial Passenger Airliner Security

1. Focus on Existing Policies and Programs	The U.S. Transportation Security Administration supports a variety of programs operating in airports and on aircraft to reduce the risk of in-flight terrorist activity. Considered here are two in-flight security programs. One deploys armed federal air marshals to sit near the front of the plane on select flights. The second—the Federal Flight Deck Officers Program—allows pilots and crew members who volunteer for the program to carry firearms to defend the flight deck.
2. Gather Policy Evidence	The study calculated the costs and benefits of the two security programs designed to reduce the likelihood of a direct replication of the 9/11 terrorist attacks. The authors performed these by assessing terror threat risk reduction, expected losses, and actual security costs in the context of the full set of the Transportation Security Administration's aviation security layers.
3. Measure Desired Effects	The desired effect is reduced risk of in-flight terrorist attacks. Aviation security programs are judged to be effective if they significantly reduce the risk of terrorist activity. By focusing on risk reduction, meaningful comparisons can be made between various security programs, even when they differ significantly in design and scope.
4. Assess Costs and Benefits	**Costs:** The estimated annual cost of the Air Marshal Service is $1.2 billion. The estimated annual cost of the Federal Flight Deck Officers Program is $22 million. **Benefits:** Benefits are assessed as the monetary value associated with reducing the risk of a 9/11-style attack. A reasonable estimate of the losses from one plane to be used in such an attack is $50 billion. The best estimate is that the Air Marshalls Service reduces the risk of an attack by 1%. The best estimate is that the Federal Flight Deck Officers Program reduces the risk of an attack by 10%. **Return on Investment:** The probability of a 9/11-style attack would need to exceed 240% (more than two attacks a year) to justify the $1.2 billion annual Air Marshal Service cost. In contrast, the probability would need to exceed just 2% (equivalent to more than one attack every 50 years) to justify the $22 million cost of the Federal Flight Deck Officers Program.
5. Offer Robust Advice	This analysis suggests there would be value in reducing the use of the Air Marshal Service and expanding the Federal Flight Deck Officer Program. The analysis is based on various assumptions about terror risks and security program effectiveness. However, it allows for comparison across many different programs using the common metrics of risk reduction, program costs, and benefits of averted tragedy. It opens the way for policy makers to discuss multiple program options and to choose a mixture that yields the best risk reduction within a fixed security budget.

DEFENSE, HOMELAND SECURITY, AND THE PROMOTION OF CIVIL RIGHTS

It is difficult to promote civil rights in the midst of mayhem and conflict. Aside from allowing economic and social development, the conditions of peace create opportunities for advancing civil rights. If we view the goal of peace in this way, effective defense and homeland security produce conditions in which civil rights can flourish. The United States has a proud tradition of respecting the rights of individuals. This has motivated many efforts since the nation's founding to advance civil rights both at home and abroad.

Against that backdrop, many Americans were sickened when evidence came to light in 2004 of abuse of Iraqi prisoners in Abu Ghraib Prison at the hands of U.S. Army personnel on the outskirts of Baghdad. Images circulated showing prisoners being subjected to humiliating and painful acts. Secretary of Defense Donald Rumsfeld testified on the matter before the Senate and House Armed Services Committees. There he stated: "These events occurred on my watch . . . as Secretary of Defense, I am accountable for them and I take full responsibility. . . . There are other photos—many other photos—that depict incidents of physical violence towards prisoners, acts that can only be described as blatantly sadistic, cruel, and inhuman."[39] Further reports confirmed that during the presidency of George W. Bush, forms of torture were used to extract information from suspected enemy combatants.

These actions were taken in full understanding that they violated international conventions. They also violated established U.S. military norms of appropriate treatment of prisoners. Often, these actions deliberately took place in secret facilities in other countries to circumvent opposition, sidestep legal processes, and avoid international scrutiny.

It is easy to forget the heightened emotions unleashed in the aftermath of the al-Qaeda attacks on the United States on September 11, 2001. Many Americans rightly felt fear, anger, and hatred because of what happened. They wanted reassurance that similar attacks would not occur. In that climate, leaders at the highest level allowed treatment of enemy prisoners—or suspected terrorists—that was harsher than what conventions allowed.

During his 2016 election campaign, President Donald Trump was quoted as saying he would allow waterboarding and other unspecified practices he called "a hell of a lot worse."[40] However, given a general distaste for torture among the American population and the spotlight that has been shone on such practices recently, efforts to perform such torture in the future will be difficult.[41] Perpetrators will face the likelihood of prosecution.[42]

The day-to-day actions of the vast majority of personnel delivering defense and homeland security protect civil rights. Revelations of the secretive torture of prisoners on behalf of the United States has damaged the nation's reputation regarding how it treats its enemies. Condoning torture undermines American values. Trust is lost. Short-term gains, if they even exist, are far outweighed by the costs of violating the nation's basic values.

Actions taken by governments in the belief that they will strengthen national defense and homeland security need always to be chosen after taking into account a range of considerations beyond those that relate solely and directly to apprehending individuals with malicious intentions. Even as those posing legitimate threats must be foiled, such efforts must be pursued in a fashion that—as far as possible— safeguards the freedoms, civil rights, and human dignity of all people, of all nations.

LESSONS FOR PUBLIC POLICY

As a collective entity, American citizens enjoy peaceful, prosperous lives. That peace and prosperity is built on vigilant defense of the homeland and protection of American interests in the world. To remain vigilant, the United States has established a powerful military capability, global in its reach. The nation has also continuously ensured that it holds military superiority relative to all potential enemies. Gaining that superiority has been costly. Over many decades, the United States has made huge financial commitments to its military. Inevitably, those commitments have meant other public goals have received fewer resources than they might have. That statement is not to criticize past spending choices. It simply observes that every form of spending has opportunity costs in the form of purchases that otherwise could have been made. We can draw four public policy lessons from the foregoing discussion:

- Strong systems of defense and homeland security allow nations to build strong, thriving societies and economies. Ultimately, the relationship is symbiotic: to keep strong and effective defense and homeland security, nations need to stay economically powerful, too. In this respect, while the U.S. economy is generally strong, the projected growth of U.S. government debt poses a threat to national security. As debt rises, fewer funds will be available for government programs. Spending on defense and homeland security makes up over half of current discretionary expenditures in the national budget. Therefore, it is more exposed to cuts than to spending on welfare- and health-related entitlement programs.
- Clarity over America's vital interests can ensure resources devoted to defense policy are used well. Although the American military has awesome capability, it is not endless. In a world full of hostile forces and frequent outbreaks of regional violence and war, presidents and members of Congress must be able to assess the merits of engaging in any form of military intervention. Recent experiences in the Middle East remind us that wars rarely end swiftly and cleanly.

- Historically, the United States has been a reluctant participant in wars. It has not sought to create an empire. Continuous changes in its global context have forced the United States to keep adjusting how it engages with other nations. Despite its military might, the United States has not had the luxury of seeing the emergence of a stable, peaceful, cooperative world. Notions of what it means to attain military superiority have been constantly confounded. Technological improvements must be ongoing to maintain superiority. It is difficult to maintain a large, sophisticated, and agile military, but that is what the context calls for.
- Capability in defense and homeland security can be eroded by poor resource management. Both the DoD and the DHS could improve their systems supporting frontline staff. Much room also exist for elimination of policies and programs known to be less effective than alternatives.

CHAPTER SUMMARY

In this chapter, we have explored major public policy issues concerning defense and homeland security. Expenditures on defense and homeland security are fundamental for securing national borders and allowing citizens to build and maintain a flourishing society and strong economy. The emergence of new threats, such as international terrorism and single terrorist actors, have put new pressures on U.S. security systems, leading to major changes in the management of defense and homeland security.

After reviewing American interests, we discussed traditional approaches to defense policy. The quest for military superiority remains as strong today as it was during World War II, but the nature of warfare has changed greatly since. This change has placed continuous pressures on defense forces and requires ongoing efforts to improve the quality and effectiveness of weapons systems. In recent decades, homeland security has attained increased importance, as international terrorist groups and homegrown terrorists have sought to harm American citizens. These changes have called for greater coordination of efforts among national-level security initiatives and state and local policing practices.

The chapter has carefully considered how the investment perspective on public policies can inform decisions on defense and homeland security. Applying this perspective can guide choices regarding purchasing military weapons systems, managing military logistics, and delivering homeland security measures. Looking ahead, with defense budgets being squeezed and constant demands being placed on government budgets from the federal to the local level, it is likely that policy developers and public managers will become more cost conscious than ever before. In that context, treating public policies as investments is essential.

There is now room for efficiency gains in many areas of defense and homeland security. Those gains could likely be achieved without compromising security. Indeed, greater application of investment thinking could improve system effectiveness and simultaneously ensure that every dollar is well spent.

CONNECTIONS TO OTHER CHAPTERS

When citizens feel unsafe, they naturally act to protect themselves and those around them. Efforts devoted to watching for threats and ensuring self-protection deplete energy given to other aspects of our lives together. This chapter has emphasized peace as a prerequisite for social and economic flourishing. Effective systems of defense and homeland security are foundational for any society. Defense and homeland security share common features with public infrastructure (Chapter 4). Without any of them, all aspects of a successful and peaceful society can quickly fall apart. In fact, homeland security plans place a central focus on strategies to protect infrastructural assets and restore their functionality following acts of war or other disasters. This chapter has also emphasized the crucial contribution state and local police forces make to identifying home-grown terrorist plots and working to foil them—highlighting a connection between homeland security and criminal justice (Chapter 9).

Since World War II, the U.S. DoD has made extensive use of scientific knowledge (Chapter 10). The successful development of atomic bombs showed that thriving scientific communities, built around excellent universities and national laboratories, could support the attainment of military superiority. The link between science and defense remains strong. In the future, that link will be the key to military superiority in the world, cybersecurity, and continuous improvements in homeland security.

KEY TERMS

Aversion behavior	Debt servicing
Dread risks	Mandatory spending
Free riders	Discretionary spending
Private contractors	Fusion Centers
American world interests	Counterfactual case
Cold War	Cost-effectiveness analysis
Opportunity costs	Military procurement
Two-level game	Cost overruns

SUGGESTIONS FOR FURTHER READING

Bullock, Jane A., George D. Haddow, and Damon P. Coppola. *Introduction to Homeland Security,* 5th ed. Waltham, MA: Butterworth-Heinemann, 2016. A comprehensive introduction to this area of public policy.

Cavelty, Myriam Dunn, and Thierry Balzacq, eds. *Routledge Handbook of Security Studies,* 2nd ed. New York: Routledge, 2016. This volume contains chapters on a range of issues concerning national security.

Melese, Francois, Anke Richter, and Binyam Solomon, eds. *Military Cost-Benefit Analysis: Theory and Practice.* London: Routledge, 2015. This is an excellent compendium of cases where cost-benefit analysis has been applied to assess the value of a range of defense-related spending decisions. Insights from these studies are of relevance well beyond defense spending.

Reveron, Derek S., Nikolas K. Gvosdev, and Mackubin Thomas Owens. *US Foreign Policy and Defense Strategy: The Evolution of an Incidental Superpower.* Washington, DC: Georgetown University Press, 2015. A very good explanation of the evolution of U.S. foreign policy.

Sapolsky, Harvey M., Eugene Gholz, and Caitlin Talmadge. *US Defense Politics: The Origins of Security Policy,* 3rd ed. New York: Routledge, 2017. A thorough overview of defense policy as it has developed in the United States.

WEBSITES

- The Brookings Institution is a public policy organization whose mission is to conduct in-depth research that leads to new ideas for solving problems facing society at the local, national, and global levels. Its defense and security experts cover many relevant topics. https://www.brookings.edu/topic/defense-security/
- The Council on Foreign Relations is a nonpartisan think tank whose mission is to improve understanding of the world and the foreign policy choices facing the United States and other countries. Its website provides useful resources for keeping informed on defense and the broader security environment. http://www.cfr.org/
- The Heritage Foundation is a think tank whose mission is to promote conservative public policies based on the principles of free enterprise, limited government, individual freedom, traditional American values, and a strong national defense. It has several centers devoted to research on national security and foreign policy. http://www.heritage.org/issues/national-security-and-defense

FOR DISCUSSION

1. Looking at the global context, what three developments might you construe as posing threats to vital American interests? What interests are under threat? What military and nonmilitary actions could the United States take to reduce those threats?

2. Commentators often voice concern about the lack of budget discipline shown by presidents and the U.S. Congress. How is budgetary discipline relevant to the nation's defense and security? Suppose you could influence budget choices over the next decade. What advice would you give?

3. If you could influence policy settings to strengthen homeland security, what would be your top suggestions for improvements? How might efforts to attain more effective homeland security support efforts to keep the United States strong in the world?

CHAPTER 6

PUBLIC SCHOOLING

This chapter considers the role of government in education and reviews key issues in the provision of public schooling. Today, most countries of the world have highly organized systems of public education, save for those with the poorest populations, those that are highly fragmented, and those that have limited experience with centralized government. Public schooling has long been understood as a vital element of civilized society. The disciplined training of young people is considered necessary for creating orderly, peaceful, productive societies. Training according to a **curriculum**—an agreed-upon system for introducing knowledge—has been viewed as essential preparation for young people to enter professions. As such, public schooling has been recognized as a fundamental building block of social and economic advancement, both for individuals and whole communities. Democratic government—of the people, by the people, for the people—is predicated on the existence of an engaged and literate populace.

The quality of education that public schools provide is well understood as crucial to preparing young people for productive and socially engaged lives. How quality is defined and measured can create controversy. Education is also understood as a major **social intervention** that, when delivered effectively, can assist children from less privileged backgrounds to attain levels of economic and social success that were beyond the reach of their parents. This observation has driven many efforts to attain more equitable distribution of public funding for schools in the United States and elsewhere. Indeed, access to high-quality public schooling for all children has been viewed as an essential element in the pursuit of civil rights.

This chapter introduces you to:

- Why governments take responsibility for schooling, even with the existence of private school systems
- Traditional approaches to public schooling in the United States

Facing page: Bright yellow school buses are a classic example of the many features of public schooling in the United States that appear to change little from school district to school district and from state to state. But underlying the common features, big differences exist in the demographics, finances, teacher quality, and educational outcomes across the more than 98,000 public schools currently operating in the country.

(AP Photo/Ted S. Warren)

- Why education has risen on the policy agendas of governments everywhere
- How students in American public schools perform compared with students of the same age in other countries
- How charter schools have prompted educational improvements in traditional public schools
- The influence of federalism on the control of public schools and how recent presidents have worked to raise the quality of public schooling
- How treating public policies as investments can be applied to aspects of public schooling
- The historically important connection between access to quality public schooling and the pursuit of civil rights
- Lessons for public policy emerging from this review of public schooling.

AN INTRODUCTION TO PUBLIC SCHOOLING

Mark Twain, author of the classic American novel *The Adventures of Tom Sawyer* (1876), and its sequel, *Adventures of Huckleberry Finn* (1885), once declared: "I have never let my schooling interfere with my education." The comment nicely captures the inevitable tension that exists between the shaping of young minds through the discipline of institutionalized public schooling, and the acquisition of knowledge through curiosity, experience, and self-reflection. The comment also reminds us that all forms of institutionalized learning—even those judged to be highly effective—face limitations. Looking across the trajectory of our lives, whatever formal training we might acquire serves only as a scaffold to support our ongoing, individuated education and personal growth.

It is up to us to make the most of the schooling we receive. Sometimes this goal can mean deliberately rejecting practices or habits of mind developed years ago that no longer seem helpful to us. In this sense, Twain's comment is not so much a complaint about the inadequacies of schooling as an institution as it is an appreciation of how learning and growth continue through life. This interpretation is consistent with a view Twain expressed elsewhere, when he noted that any society scrimping on schooling would wind up building jails.[1]

Various forms of private education have been in existence since the dawn of civilization in ancient Mesopotamia. In contrast, public schooling, where all children falling in specific age ranges must attend organized classes and follow prescribed forms of instruction, dates back to the relatively recent mid-19th century.

That is when public schooling in the Western world became recognized as an important social institution.

Today, more than ever before, provision of high-quality public schooling for all children and young people is considered vital for maintaining good societies, and for ensuring the economic competitiveness of communities, states, and countries in the globalizing world. Governments everywhere now care greatly about the performance of public schools. Whenever they devote significant funds to education budgets, governments seek to hold schools accountable for student learning. This is an area of government spending that both political leaders and educators explicitly view as an investment in the future.

Governments want their investments to yield good returns. For that reason, in the past few decades the United States has witnessed plenty of government efforts to reform systems of public schooling—and these have generated much controversy. At the same time, technological changes have led many people to question the merits of public school systems originally established to prepare young people for a variety of repetitive processing jobs. Ongoing advances in information technology, the growing need for people to contribute through jobs involving team engagement in complex problem solving, and the necessity for continuous process innovation will keep the pressure on public schooling to stay relevant. Given these goals, we can expect debates on the nature and purpose of public schooling to rage for the foreseeable future. Case Study 6.1 focuses on the claim that U.S. schools should focus more on encouraging the creativity of students than on rote learning.

case study 6.1 Encouraging Students to Be Creative Thinkers

What should schools teach? How should they go about doing it? Questions of this kind have been asked since ancient times and have provoked intense intellectual discussions. With the development of schools as major institutions in society, such questions carry huge weight. Most governments around the world now routinely engage in high-level curriculum reviews led by educators and public officials of the highest standing. How schools should be organized and who should control them have become issues of great interest to political leaders. Increasingly, the economic health of countries, states, and cities strongly depends on the education of their citizens. Economic advancement in the United States is now understood to stem from the abilities of the **creative class.** People falling into this loose category are those who have benefitted from high-quality schooling as well as university education and who contribute to the creation of new products and services of high value to consumers both at home and abroad.[2] Indeed, as low-skilled manufacturing and service jobs are being lost to computers, robots, or low-wage economies elsewhere in the world, the pressures are growing for schools to equip many more students than ever before as **knowledge workers**: people who primarily think for a living, rather than engage in repetitive or manual tasks.

Some people suggest it is imperative that young people graduate from high school exhibiting high levels of competency in reading, writing, mathematics, and scientific thinking. Others see these skills as worthwhile only to the extent that young people are creative thinkers who can effectively deploy them to address unique and interesting problems and challenges.

Education intellectual Ken Robinson has been a central figure in recent discussions over what schools should teach and how they should do it. Robinson's motivating belief is that every person has a special set of talents. When people come to recognize those talents and apply them productively, they find themselves in their "element." Given Robinson's premise, the fundamental purpose of schooling should be to guide children and young people so that they are able to fully develop their innate talents.[3] By doing so, schools would assist all people in achieving their full potential as human beings. In turn, Robinson argues that school systems organized toward that goal would generate the best social outcomes.

Given the current emphasis on creativity as the key to knowledge generation, Robinson's ideas, including those in his book *Creative Schools,* have been highly influential.[4] Significantly, Robinson's ideas do not negate the importance of core skills. However, they do pose a strong challenge to advocates who believe that systems of public schooling in countries like the United States should incorporate more of the "old school" approaches to teaching and learning that have apparently led other countries to perform better on international standardized tests of student academic attainment. (See Focus Box 6.1, "Student Performance in the United States—A Comparative Assessment.")

The Boston Arts Academy, established in 1998 through the amalgamation of several Boston public schools, offers an example of a school emphasizing creativity. As a school of choice, the Academy has more students seeking to enroll than available spaces. The school selects students on their exhibited creativity—not on their academic records. Many of the enrollees come from underprivileged backgrounds. Along with developing students' strengths, the school supports them to ensure they improve their performance on state-required standardized tests and those required for university entrance. Importantly, by building the curriculum around students' creativity, the Academy has been able to encourage students to perform at higher levels in all areas.[5]

CRITICAL THINKING QUESTIONS

1. Looking back to your earlier school years, what specific aspects very positively affected your learning and your desire to learn more?
2. When might standardized testing of school students support their development as creative thinkers? Under what conditions might it stifle creativity?

TRADITIONAL FUNCTIONS OF SCHOOLING

Schools, whether public or private, serve four fundamental functions for society.[6]

1. Schools provide care for children, which is vital for allowing parents to devote time to activities other than childrearing.
2. Schools help children learn vital social skills and become effective at managing relationships with others.
3. Schools introduce children to the predominant culture of their society, a crucial goal in highly multicultural societies. Yet such enculturation efforts also can generate considerable controversy.
4. Schools serve to sort children and young people based on their abilities. In the process, they also help prepare young people for higher education and workforce participation.

We will now consider each of these traditional functions of schooling more closely.

CARING FOR CHILDREN

When schools admit children, they free up time for parents to participate in the paid workforce or in other valued nonparenting activities. From a purely economic perspective, a social gain in time can occur when children from multiple households are brought together and cared for in circumstances where the child-to-adult ratio is higher than would be the case in any single household. It is socially efficient to designate in this fashion a small group of people to serve—for regular periods—in the place of parents.

SOCIALIZING CHILDREN

A big part of schooling involves equipping children to be socially engaged, to be able to communicate and work effectively with other children and with adults beyond those in their immediate family and social circles. In this sense, schools do a lot to prime children for productive and satisfying adult lives. Of course, major debates often arise concerning how schools should engage in this function. How should schools manage interactions between boys and girls? Should schools provide sex education? What kind of moral teaching is appropriate in schools? These questions, and many others, emerge whenever we discuss the socialization function of schooling.

PROVIDING ENCULTURATION FOR CHILDREN

Schools perform an **enculturation** function. This involves reinforcing predominant cultural norms, some of which may be new to children whose families have recently immigrated. Often, introducing and reinforcing of cultural norms are accomplished implicitly rather than explicitly. Parents and other adults in society place great weight on the transmission of certain values, areas of knowledge, ways of thinking and acting, and skills understood as essential components of shared cultural traditions. By ensuring that children are trained by people exhibiting desired values, knowledge, skills, and dispositions, schools can perform this function in ways that would be impossible to replicate within individual households.

We might think of a narrow slice of prevailing cultural dispositions as the "skill set" ensuring that children and young people have the aptitude to perform well in higher education and in the workplace. In multicultural societies, there can be major disagreements concerning the extent to which schools should serve to shape and encourage certain cultural practices. As the United States becomes increasingly multicultural, we can expect to see more debate around issues of this kind. They include issues of dress codes, language use, and religious tolerance.

SORTING CHILDREN AND PREPARING THEM FOR THE WORKFORCE

Schools inevitably perform a sorting function. People expect schools to identify the talents and strengths of individual children and work with those children to enhance their capabilities. As children pass through their school years, institutions of higher learning, employers, and parents all expect schools to effectively differentiate children according to their demonstrated talents and capabilities. This is sometimes called **credentialing**. Through it, schools help resolve complex challenges concerning how to rapidly interpret and summarize individual abilities. Examinations offer one method of credentialing. In the absence of schools performing this function, many other social organizations would have to continuously employ their own methods of sorting people. Efficiency gains take place when schools perform this function well.

WHY GOVERNMENTS GET INVOLVED IN SCHOOLING

Effective private schools existed long before public schooling systems were developed. Indeed, the public schools that subsequently emerged were largely modeled on private schools. In most countries today, private schools continue to operate in parallel with public schools. Yet it is curious to note, in contemporary societies, how much public schools have come to be treated as central institutions. In all places where governments have chosen to fund public schooling, separate systems of public and private schooling have emerged, usually with the public overshadowing the private.

Clearly, since private schooling has long existed, it is reasonable to talk of a private market in schooling. Private demand for schooling can be met by private supply. What, then, is the basis for government funding and delivery of public schooling? We suggest three rationales.

1. Governments fund and deliver public schooling because the education of each individual has positive benefits not just for that individual but for society as a whole.
2. Governments fund and deliver public schooling as a mechanism for advancing social justice, recognizing that education is a vital means by which children might receive opportunities that their parents did not receive.
3. Governments fund and deliver public schooling to promote consistency in the quality of the educational opportunities young people experience.

We will now examine these rationales more closely.

PROMOTING POSITIVE EXTERNALITIES

The strongest rationale for the development and maintenance of public schools is that schooling generates spillover effects, commonly termed as **positive externalities**. That is, when a young person receives an education, that education is beneficial both to the individual and to society as a whole. The more educated the people around us are, the better off we all are. Recognizing this precept, starting in the late 1800s, governments began to require all children to receive at least some basic level of **compulsory education**. Thus, all children within certain age ranges were required to attend school, unless compelling reasons could be given by their parents or guardians for them not to do so. Since without financial support, only the wealthiest families could afford to educate their children in private schools, a basis emerged for government to offer financial support for schooling.

ADVANCING SOCIAL JUSTICE

Without government support for schooling, many children would miss out. Further, society would forfeit the positive benefits that come from having an educated citizenry. Indeed, promotion of social justice has served as an important rationale for government support for children to attend schools. However, this goal still does not explain why government would both fund and deliver schooling.

PROMOTING CONSISTENT EDUCATIONAL PRACTICES

The creation of systems of public schools appears to have been associated with government compulsion that all children must attend school. By both funding and delivering public schooling, governments could gain control over what happened in classrooms. For example, they could specify the qualifications to be held by those appointed as teachers and prescribe the content of the lessons—the curriculum.

In the United States, Horace Mann (1796–1859) worked to create a statewide system of professional teachers in Massachusetts, where he served for a time as the secretary for education. Mann modeled this system on European examples of the day and the Prussian notion of the "common school." Common schools were established and regulated in ways that ensured all children received instruction in much the same content, regardless of where they lived.[7] During the second half of the 19th century, many other states followed Mann's lead. By the start of the 20th century, a majority of children across the United States were required to attend public schools for a specified number of years. What we now think of as the institution of public schooling has its organizational basis in the pursuit of universal education and the desire, often times political, to control both its content and its delivery.

TRADITIONAL POLICY APPROACHES

The set of public policies that have enabled the creation and maintenance of public schools as social institutions has been motivated by efforts to raise levels of education in the populace, to promote social equity by making school attendance compulsory, and to control the form and content of schooling through public ownership and control of schools as organizations.

STATE AND LOCAL GOVERNMENT AUTHORITY

In the United States, constitutional responsibility for the provision of public schooling has always resided at the state level. Traditionally, states delegated responsibility for funding and administration of schools to local school districts. Those local districts rapidly became powerful political entities, controlling the content and delivery of public schooling. The result is a highly fragmented system of public schools, where local financial resources and values have heavily influenced the form and content of local public schooling. Funding for public schools has been supported primarily through local **property taxes**, which households pay annually in proportion to the value of the property. As a result, public schools in wealthy districts can acquire a lot of local tax income while imposing relatively low taxes. In contrast, property tax rates must be higher in poorer communities for local public schools to obtain funds equivalent to those obtained in wealthy districts. This funding discrepancy has generated significant disparities across cities, states, and the nation as a whole in the quality of the public schooling children receive.

Since wealthy neighborhoods in the United States have been able to fund local schools more easily than poor neighborhoods, beginning in the 1960s lawsuits filed against states on behalf of poor school districts have led to a requirement that states contribute greater amounts of funding to public schooling.[8] As states have become more involved in funding public schools, they inevitably have called for more **accountability** from school districts. As a result, local school districts have had to document to their states how they have used state funds and what educational outcomes these have produced.

Meanwhile, the role of the U.S. government in public schooling has been quite limited throughout the nation's history. Major political control over schooling lies with the states. One obvious indicator is that the U.S. Department of Education only began operating in 1980. Today, the federal government's role in public schooling continues to be limited, primarily involving the provision of funds to improve children's readiness for school through, for example, Head Start programs and the provision of free lunches. However, the government has increasingly made funding available to raise the quality of the schooling that children living in poor neighborhoods receive.

The system of funding for public schools in the United States is generally regarded as inequitable when compared with the funding approaches of other wealthy countries (e.g., other members of the Organisation for Economic Co-operation and Development [OECD]). For the latter, it is more common for public schools funding to come predominantly from the nation, state, or provincial level rather than the local. Almost everywhere, however, government support for schooling involves both the funding and the delivery of schooling—what we call public schooling.

PUBLIC SUPPORT FOR PRIVATE SCHOOLS

Many countries provide subsidies to private schools in recognition that all of society gains from the education of a child, whether or not the child is in a public or a private school. However, no cases exist where schooling is fully (or even mostly) provided and controlled by private entities, with governments providing subsidies to families so that their children can attend. This is important to note because since the 1950s, the notion of encouraging predominantly private-sector ownership and control of schools has been advocated at length by proponents of limited government. Given that the model of private schools has existed for much longer than that of public schools, it is somewhat surprising that innovation in the governance of public schooling has not been more widespread.

In general, governments everywhere have taken a great interest in the education of children and young people. Because U.S. politicians and citizens have long understood the strategic role that education plays in shaping a jurisdiction's social and economic futures, responsibility for controlling and funding schools has been kept in the public sector.

CONTEMPORARY POLICY ISSUES

Among the many policy issues concerning contemporary public schooling in the United States, several stand out. Here we discuss the ongoing debates about the political control of schools, religion in schools, and academic performance. We also discuss new accountability systems for schools, the rise of school choice and charter schools, efforts to improve teacher quality, and efforts to use information technology effectively to support learning.

POLITICAL CONTROL OF PUBLIC SCHOOLING

The institution of public schooling in the United States and in most other countries of the world carries the legacy of what came to be termed **the one best system**.[9] The Progressive political movement of the late 19th and early 20th centuries strongly advocated that schools and other public organizations exemplify "neutral competence." In the face of early political corruption, in which administrators and teachers in big-city school systems gained and maintained their jobs based on their support for local political "machines," the reformist Progressive movement sought fundamental change.[10] That change theoretically would shield school administrators and the teaching profession from political influence. In practice, school boards became powerful buffers between the world of politics and the world of the schoolhouse.

As the professionalization of school administration and teaching proceeded, the institution of public schooling gained more autonomy from meddlesome politicians. Political control became more confined to big issues, such as the annual budget, the setting of broad parameters for the curriculum, and ways to measure school performance. For the most part, these arrangements hold today. Where changes have been proposed and pursued, they have served either to make incremental adjustments within this bigger institutional structure, or to encourage emergence of alternative systems around its edges.

RELIGION AND PUBLIC SCHOOLS

Public schooling in the United States, as in many other countries, often triggers major political battles. An on-going battle concerns the place of religion in schools. Given the constitutional edict of separation of church and state, public schools are mostly **strictly secular schools** in their practices and their curricular content. However, this position of neutrality on religious matters has been hard to sustain recently in the face of strong pressures from fundamentalist Christian groups. Battles have been fought in several states over the teaching of evolution in schools. Here, Christian groups have strongly lobbied for science instruction to balance discussion of evolution with discussion of creation and intelligent design. Systematic study of teaching practices in this regard has found that individual biology teachers tend to decide for themselves how to address this controversy, even in the face of clear policy guidelines.[11]

The ability of individual teachers, schools, and teachers unions' to undermine efforts to control and reform public schools has been cause for significant controversy on a number of fronts.[12] Indeed, the extent of this issue has led to the claim that public policies do not change schools; rather, schools change public policies.[13] The power of teachers' unions and the traditional education establishment has motivated many efforts to wrest back control of public schooling in the United States. This frustration over the tendency for public schooling to be apparently immune to reform has driven efforts to introduce school choice through giving families **vouchers** so that their children can attend private schools at public cost. Attempts to impose stronger accountability systems on schools have been similarly motivated. In this case, the move toward greater curricular uniformity—such as adoption of the Common Core curriculum in many states—and more consistent application of standardized testing has been intended to keep teachers, schools, and school districts focused on motivating children to achieve specified outcomes. However, as we will discuss in the "New Accountability Systems for Schools" section, debates about the Common Core and state standardized testing are set to continue.

STUDENT ACADEMIC PERFORMANCE

Funding public schools is expensive, yet the nurturing, training, and developing of children into capable young adults is well understood as fundamental to continuous economic and social advancement. Without doubt, the most important education policy challenge facing most jurisdictions today is to ensure that public schools add high value to students, making the best use of scarce resources in the process. In the United States, politicians from the president to state governors to mayors have appreciated the significant contribution that public schools make. Still, for decades there has been a continuous conversation about the performance of public schools and how that performance might be improved.

In 1983, President Ronald Reagan launched a report prepared by the National Commission on Excellence in Education, titled *A Nation at Risk*. The opening lines of the report, among other things, stated:

> The educational foundations of our society are presently being eroded
> by a rising tide of mediocrity that threatens our very future as a Nation
> and a people. What was unimaginable a generation ago has begun to
> occur—others are matching and surpassing our educational attainments. If an unfriendly foreign power had attempted to impose on
> America the mediocre educational performance that exists today, we
> might well have viewed it as an act of war. As it stands, we have allowed
> this to happen to ourselves.[14]

A Nation at Risk signaled the start of a broad movement, which continues today, focused on improving the performance of public schools across the United States. After several decades, the consensus among educational experts and commentators is that very little has improved. Now, however, we have much better evidence about the comparative performance of students in American public schools. Thus, next, we explore what data tell us about the academic performance of a representative sample of 15-year-olds in the United States compared with representative samples of 15-year-olds in other countries (see In Focus 6.1).

in focus 6.1

STUDENT PERFORMANCE IN THE UNITED STATES—A COMPARATIVE ASSESSMENT

In 1997, the OECD, a Paris-based think tank funded by its wealthy nation-members, launched its Programme for International Student Assessment (PISA). PISA evaluates education systems worldwide every three years by assessing the competency of 15-year-olds in reading, mathematics, and science. Students take two-hour paper-based tests; they also answer a background questionnaire that seeks information about them, their home life, and their school and learning experiences. To date over 70 countries and economies have participated in PISA. In 2015, the most recent year for which results are currently available, the focus of PISA was on science.

Table 6.1 reports 2015 PISA results for a select group of countries. As well as allowing us to compare the ranking of student performance by subject across countries, Table 6.1 also contains information on the proportions of students who either performed poorly or excelled in all three subjects. This information offers insights into the degree of equity across student outcomes in any given country, and how that differs between countries. In the United States, 13.6 percent of students who took the test were deemed low achievers in all three subjects, while 13.3 percent were deemed top performers in at least one subject. In comparison, in Canada, 5.9 percent

of students who took test were deemed low achievers in all three subjects, while 22.7 percent were deemed top performers in at least one subject. In Mexico, a much poorer country, 33.8 percent of students who took the test were deemed low achievers in all three subjects, while 0.6 percent were deemed top performers in at least one. This illustrates the different educational outcomes across North America.

Since data collection began in 1997, there have been minimal changes in the trend data that the OECD has gathered on student performance in the United States. For the most part, average U.S. student performance has been about the same as average student performance across the OECD member countries, taken as a group. In discussing the 2015 PISA results for the United States, the OECD noted that although the United States spends more per student than do most countries, this does not translate into better performance. The serious concern for the United States is that there are now quite a few education systems worldwide that are consistently obtaining better results in PISA ratings. Note in Table 6.1, for example, how much more impressive the student results are in Finland, Japan, South Korea, and Singapore compared with the United States.

TABLE 6.1 Cross-Country Comparison of Performance by 15-Year-Old Students in the Programme for International Student Assessment (PISA), 2015

COUNTRY	SUBJECT AREA				
	AVERAGE 2015 PISA SCORE			SCIENCE, READING AND MATHEMATICS	
	MATHEMATICS	READING	SCIENCE	% OF TOP PERFORMERS IN AT LEAST 1 SUBJECT	% OF LOW ACHIEVERS IN ALL 3 SUBJECTS
OECD Average	490	493	493	15.3	13.0
United States	**470**	**497**	**496**	**13.3**	**13.6**
United Kingdom	492	498	509	16.9	10.1
Switzerland	521	492	506	22.2	10.1
Sweden	494	500	493	16.7	11.4
Singapore	564	535	556	39.1	4.8
Russia	494	495	487	13.0	7.7
Norway	502	513	498	17.6	8.9
New Zealand	495	509	513	20.5	10.6
Mexico	408	423	416	0.6	33.8
South Korea	524	517	516	25.6	7.7
Japan	532	516	538	25.8	5.6
Israel	470	479	467	13.9	20.2
Indonesia	386	397	403	0.8	42.3
Germany	506	509	509	19.2	9.8
France	493	499	495	18.4	14.8

TABLE 6.1 continued

COUNTRY	SUBJECT AREA				
Finland	544	526	531	21.4	6.3
Denmark	511	500	502	14.9	7.5
China	531	494	518	27.7	10.9
Canada	516	527	528	22.7	5.9
Brazil	377	407	401	2.2	44.1
Australia	494	503	510	18.4	11.1

Note: All information in this table is derived from page 5 of the OECD's *PISA 2015 Results in Focus* (Paris: OECD, 2016).

NEW ACCOUNTABILITY SYSTEMS FOR SCHOOLS

Because many American states have experimented with school reforms over recent decades, there is some agreement about what kinds of interventions can promote student achievement. To make public schools more accountable for their performance, states have introduced more formal, rigorous student-testing systems. The intention has been to use evidence of student performance to indicate where average student performance is acceptable and where it is not. According to Eric Hanushek and Margaret Raymond, the introduction of rigorous accountability systems at the state level has led to some improvements in student outcomes.[15] A common concern is that these rigorous testing systems provide incentives for schools to "teach to the tests." When this happens, schools give less attention to promoting all-round education, and more to ensuring students perform well and, hence, make the school appear to be doing a good job. Note that the problem here is not with testing itself, but with how certain schools seek to game the system. Testing and data bring with them many positive things in terms of opening up possibilities for discussing what schools are doing well and where improvements are needed. The challenge for the future is to adopt ways of using student data, especially data that continuously track and compare student performance, to rapidly identify how students are performing in the classroom, and to adjust teaching practices and student learning plans accordingly.[16] This is an area where information technology, combined with good insights about effective pedagogical practice, could make a major difference to schooling outcomes, for individual students, and society as a whole.

SCHOOL CHOICE AND CHARTER SCHOOLS

As states have moved to tighten school accountability, many have also made efforts to create public **schools of choice**, such as charter schools. The theory behind the introduction of **charter schools**, which are publicly funded, is that they have more autonomy to develop and shape the content and delivery of classroom activities to match the learning needs of their students.[17] As schools of choice, charter schools can remain financially viable only if they attract and maintain a healthy number of students. Thus, they are required to be more accountable to families while being held to traditional forms of accountability by the state government (or, in some cases, local school districts).

Many stakeholders expected the introduction of charter schools to promote greater innovation in public schooling. By creating a degree of competition between charter schools and traditional public schools, policy makers anticipated that all public schools would become more focused on promoting better student outcomes. On this score, the evidence to date has been mixed. In many ways, charter schools have served to relieve pressure for choice within public school systems. They have tended not to promote broader system change or across-the-board improvement in student performance.[18] Advocates of greater competition in public schooling delivery would suggest that this outcome stems from strict limitations that most states have imposed on the number of charter schools that can develop, and the limited incentives created in school systems for development of new schools. Some notable innovations in charter schools have started to improve practices within traditional public schools. These are highlighted in Case Study 6.2.

IMPROVING TEACHER QUALITY

In the United States, as in other countries, the teaching profession tends not to be held in high esteem throughout society. This point was noted in *A Nation at Risk* back in 1983. Although some critiques of the current public school system argue that teachers' unions have been a powerful brake upon reform efforts, there is a danger in placing too much blame on the teachers themselves. Indeed, solid evidence suggests that nations where students perform well on international standardized tests also have traditions of respect for the teaching profession. For example, those who train as teachers in countries like Finland and South Korea are drawn from among the best-performing high school students. Significant efforts are also made to give these teachers appropriate and rigorous training before they embark on their professional careers.

case study 6.2 Charter Schools and Improvement in Teaching Practice

Charter schools are publicly funded schools that enjoy a high degree of autonomy from traditional school district systems of control and accountability. The first charter schools opened in Minnesota in 1992. Although states grant their independence, charter schools are given no guaranteed student base. They survive on their ability to attract and retain a viable student population.

Since their inception, charter schools were expected to be more innovative than traditional public schools. It was also expected that competition from these schools would pressure traditional public schools to improve their practices. Evidence suggests that charter schools have been more open to innovation than traditional public schools. Often this has involved taking a disparate set of practices developed in traditional public schools and combining them to create a more innovative kind of schooling. The extent to which innovative practices in charter schools have filtered back to traditional public schools has remained a difficult question to answer.[19]

Uncommon Schools is a nonprofit network of over 40 public charter schools operating in New York, New Jersey, and Massachusetts.[20] Enrollments at network schools currently exceed 12,000. The schools aspire to work effectively with families in low-income communities to prepare their children for college and college graduation. Uncommon Schools won the 2013 Broad Prize for Public Charter Schools for demonstrating "the most outstanding overall student performance and improvement in the nation

State-level authorization of charter schools has opened the way for new forms of school management and classroom teaching. Many pay close attention to the quality of the interactions of teachers and students, with the goal of accelerating student progress. At this charter school in New Orleans, Louisiana, the principal spends most of her time out of her office mentoring teachers and staff and engaging with the children.

*(Photo by Melanie Stetson Freeman/*The Christian Science Monitor *via Getty Images)*

in recent years while reducing achievement gaps for low income students and students of color."[21]

An unusual amount of knowledge has been shared about Uncommon Schools as the result of the books written on exceptional teaching by Doug Lemov, a former charter school principal, and a managing director of Uncommon Schools who leads its Teach Like a Champion team. Lemov has made a science out of using educational data to identify top-performing teachers and then studying and codifying their instructional methods. The approach worked as follows. Lemov reviewed school-level results on standardized state tests, like the New York State Assessment Sixth-Grade Math results. For each school, he recorded the percentage of students deemed proficient on the standardized test. Next, he ranked those same schools based on their recorded student poverty rate (judged by the percentage of children eligible to participate in the federally funded free-lunch program) and then graphed these two indicators.

As expected in data like these, there was a strong negative relationship between student poverty rates and student proficiency on standardized state tests. The higher the percentage of students in poverty in a given school, the lower the expected percentage of students deemed proficient. However, Lemov's interest lay in schools that recorded high levels of proficiency despite having high levels of student poverty. A handful broke the trend. Lemov asked: What are teachers doing differently in those schools? Specifically, how did they approach teaching, lesson planning, and relationship management with students and their families?

Lemov's question led him to visit schools, talk with principals and teachers, and—most importantly—codify the specific, concrete, actionable classroom practices of teachers who attained such outstanding results with their students. He developed a set of teaching techniques that he then systematically trained teachers in Uncommon Schools to utilize. Those schools have been generating significant improvements in student outcomes compared to what all the typical social indicators would lead us to predict.

Lemov developed his set of teaching techniques into a book, *Teach Like a Champion,* first published in 2012. It has been estimated that one-quarter of the teacher population in the United States subsequently read the book or were exposed to techniques in it. That is almost 800,000 teachers, across all types of schools—public, independent, private, urban, suburban, and rural. The book has been highly influential in many countries around the world, including Brazil, India, and China.[22]

Without a doubt, Doug Lemov's innovations, as facilitated by the charter school movement, have strongly influenced teaching practices well beyond the Uncommon Schools where they began. Lemov has used evidence-based techniques to deploy resources—teachers, students, classrooms—in a fashion that yields high returns on investments, whereas others continue to use the equivalent resources and obtain limited results. Thus, his approach is highly consistent with the investment perspective of this book. There are vital lessons for public policy to be drawn from this story.

CRITICAL THINKING QUESTIONS

1. Many of the practices of good teaching were developed in traditional public schools. However, it was someone working in a charter school who decided to study and codify good practice. What motivated Lemov?
2. What are some other areas of school practices where it would be good for school leaders to learn from the best of what others are doing? How could they do that?

In reviewing the evidence on the comparative performance of public school systems, Michael Barber and Mona Mourshed concluded that the quality of a public school system can never be better than the quality of the teachers within it.[23] Improving the quality of the teaching workforce, which also involves promoting better school leadership, represents an important policy challenge.

MAKING EFFECTIVE USE OF INFORMATION TECHNOLOGY

An ongoing challenge for policy makers concerns how to harness developments in information technology to improve student learning outcomes. In recent years, the efforts of Salman Khan to establish the Khan Academy have met with a lot of favorable interest.[24] In Khan's view, students should be able to learn lessons individually by reviewing online materials, such as "how to" videos. Students should then spend classroom time working together on challenges, while teachers carefully monitor their efforts. Information technology can greatly assist with this. As a result, teachers become better able to rapidly identify the success and failure of both students and teaching practices, and take appropriate actions to help students develop their potential. This is but one example of ways that innovations from outside the traditional public school system can help to transform it for the better.

President Donald Trump and Education Secretary Betsy DeVos have pledged to promote greater school choice. This could mean more public funds being devoted to vouchers allowing families to send their children to private schools. Here, President Trump and Secretary DeVos are pictured visiting St. Andrew Catholic School in Orlando. The president praised the school for the example it provided of a parochial school working with disadvantaged children.

(Official White House Photo by Shealah Craighead)

We must always be aware, however, that institutional arrangements that have existed for a long time are difficult to change.[25] Given this reality, creating opportunities for greater school innovation, through granting schools more autonomy, can be important. Nonetheless, that autonomy must always be tethered by efforts to keep individual schools tied to the broader system, so that performance monitoring occurs. No public value can be gained from schools that become isolated and engage in ineffective teaching practices. Likewise, opportunities are lost when isolated schools hit upon and pursue highly effective practices that go unnoticed by other schools that could benefit from adapting them.

PUBLIC SCHOOLS IN A FEDERAL SYSTEM

In the United States, as in many other countries, the knowledge and skills utilized by highly educated professionals are increasingly driving economic growth. Thus, the quality of education occurring at all levels, from pre-K through postgraduate, has become more vital than ever to national interests. Reflecting this growing awareness, all recent U.S. presidents have taken a strong interest in raising the quality of education occurring in public schools—with mixed results.

In 1965, President Lyndon Johnson laid the way for subsequent presidents when he championed, and then signed into law, the Elementary and Secondary Education Act (ESEA). The act was motivated by the goal of reducing poverty and widening access to educational opportunity. ESEA offered new grants to districts serving low-income students, federal grants for text and library books, special-education centers, and scholarships for low-income college students. It also provided federal grants to state educational agencies to improve the quality of elementary and secondary education.

President George W. Bush was the first to chart a radically new course for federal spending on public schools. By signing into law the reauthorized ESEA as the **No Child Left Behind** (NCLB) Act, Bush gained congressional support for his education agenda. Most notably, this led to the use of standardized state-level testing to assess the performance of individual schools in improving student test scores. Schools deemed to be underperforming were placed at risk of losing their portion of federal funding and their student base. Under the act, students at public schools deemed to be underperforming could be given vouchers to attend private schools.

NCLB transformed the U.S. government's role in public schooling from a benign funder and cheerleader to a close scrutinizer of performance.

Implementation of the law allowed the federal government to have far more influence on what happened in schools than at any previous time in the nation's history. Assessments of NCLB generally agree that the act significantly increased the pressure on public schools to improve students' standardized test performance. However, in the years since President Bush left office, the federal scrutiny of performance has been significantly reduced in a growing number of states.

President Obama also strongly influenced public schooling in the United States, although to a lesser degree than his predecessor. While keeping much of the apparatus of NCLB in place, in 2010 Obama introduced a novel competition intended to drive quality improvements led by state governments, called **Race to the Top**. The Obama administration established several rounds of competitions among states for federal education funding. To be in contention for the most lucrative rewards, states had to achieve high scores against a specified set of criteria concerning their educational policy settings and outcomes. Although a few states refused to enter the competition, others made concerted efforts to win the promised federal funding. Toward this end, for example, some state legislatures rapidly passed laws allowing more charter schools to open in their states. Others developed rapid workarounds to establish systems for better recording and analyzing student test-score data so that individual student progress could be tracked over time.

Race to the Top demonstrated that the federal government—through use of incentives—could rapidly address policy logjams at the state level. The strategy set a precedent for how the federal government might promote state-level innovations across many areas of public policy well beyond public schooling.

PUBLIC SCHOOLS AND THE INVESTMENT PERSPECTIVE

From the outset, governments treated the creation of public school systems as investments. In every jurisdiction that has a say over education, policy makers face choices about whether children should be compelled to attend school, how long they should attend, and the quality of the schooling experience. Since the late 1950s, economists have made a concerted effort to measure the returns that individuals and societies get from investing in public schooling. This body of scholarship falls under the broader title of the study of **human capital**. Just as economists have been interested to know how investments in various kinds of equipment—termed **physical capital**—serve to advance the economic fortunes of firms, so they have been keen to understand how schooling might improve the economic fortunes of the individual. The research has also explored links between educational investments in individuals and broader social outcomes.

STUDIES AT THE COUNTRY LEVEL

The preponderance of evidence strongly suggests that public schooling is a sound financial investment. Summarizing evidence from multiple studies using data from over 80 countries, George Psacharopoulos and Harry Anthony Patrinos conclude that "overall, the average rate of return to another year of schooling is 10%."[26] Any investment consistently yielding this rate of return would be judged a success. For individuals, the lifetime benefits for an education are huge. Various estimates indicate that the greatest returns, both to the individual and to society, come from investment in the primary years of schooling. Those years provide a strong base for what is to come. Secondary schooling also generates good returns for the educated individual and for society. Beyond these advantages, it appears that attendance at postsecondary education yields large individual benefits but more limited societal benefits. Here, again, context greatly matters.

In countries where economic development is increasingly dependent upon innovation, creativity, and knowledge production, the returns on higher education appear large both for individuals and for society as a whole.[27] It is important to note, however, that even economists who have devoted years to the study of returns on education recognize the limits of their data and analytical methods. In their review of the international evidence on returns to investment in education, Psacharopoulos and Patrinos observed, "It would be preferable if we could cite for each country only estimates incorporating the most rigorous methodology . . . That would give us less than a few countries."[28]

In a summary of the state of knowledge on **the economics of education**, Theodore Breton proposed that public schooling has several effects that serve to raise national income in countries with market economies.[29] According to Breton, schooling has a direct effect on the income received through life by the educated worker. It also has three indirect effects:

1. Schooling of the individual indirectly raises the productivity of other workers. Intuitively, we know that having educated people around us tends to make it easier for us to do our work.
2. Schooling of the individual indirectly raises the productivity of physical capital. Again, we know this. Tools are only effective when people know how to use them. (Automobiles, personal computers, and so on can only be productive when people know how to use them effectively.)
3. As countries grow more prosperous and citizens come to appreciate the value of good systems of public schooling, they create a demand for public schools to become even better.

Breton concludes that "all countries with high levels of human capital provide free, obligatory public schooling or public funds for private schooling through the secondary level. The historic evidence indicates that if poor countries wish to grow, they must provide this financial support for primary and secondary schooling."[30]

Economists recognize that the evidence base they have to work with is often less than ideal. The current state of knowledge suggests two things. First, countries can improve their economic prospects by ensuring that as many children as possible are given the opportunity to attend school. Second, the quality of the schooling matters.

STUDIES OF SPECIFIC POLICY ACTIONS

Ultimately, individuals contribute to society through a combination of cognitive skills (i.e., thinking skills) and noncognitive skills (i.e., social skills). Recent economic research suggests that the quality of the schooling children receive has major consequences for both their individual quality of life and for the broader economic development of their country.[31] Case Study 6.3 explores the effects of class size on student achievement. In discussing research of this kind, we should realize that the economic focus has been on estimating the financial returns on investment in education, as realized by the educated individual on the one hand, and the broader society on the other.

Most economists freely acknowledge the limits of their analysis. They appreciate the full range of contributions of public schooling to the quality of an individual life and to the well-being and cultural advancement of the whole society. These contributions would be measured if it were straightforward to do so. In practice, even estimation of purely economic returns of education can be difficult. Much of the literature on the economics of education has been devoted to discussing the positives and negatives associated with using different variables to capture specific concepts.

case study 6.3 Class Size and Student Achievement

Are small classes in schools more conducive to effective teaching and learning than larger classes? Intuitively, most people think small classes are better. Over the years, governments around the world have spent large amounts of money on reducing class sizes.

In California, a concerted effort to reduce class sizes for students in the early years of school began in the mid-1990s. The results of the 1994 National Assessment of Educational Progress, released in 1995, showed California's fourth graders placing last in reading among the 39 states that participated in the assessment program. Reducing class sizes was proposed as a proven approach to improving student achievement. California Senate Bill 1777, passed in July 1996, provided school districts with $650 per student for each K-3 classroom with 20 or fewer students, if they first reduced all first-grade classes in the school, followed by all second-grade classes, and finally either kindergarten or third-grade classes. The policy came to cost the state an additional $1.6 billion per year in education spending. It was popular with teachers, parents, and school administrators. However, many school districts faced with funding shortfalls from 2008 onward began slipping back to having larger class sizes. Today, they are among the highest in the nation.

Among sources of evidence used to guide policy making in California, the Tennessee Student/Teacher Achievement Ratio (STAR) experiment was highly influential. Project STAR was a longitudinal class-size study that ran for four years. It was funded by the Tennessee state government and conducted by the state's department of education. The study concentrated on manipulating class sizes during kindergarten and the early elementary grades. During the study, over 7,000 students in 79 schools were randomly assigned to one of three classroom situations: small class (13–17 students per teacher), regular class (22–25 students per teacher), or a regular class with a full-time teacher's aide. Students remained in their assigned classroom type from kindergarten through the end of third grade. (Of course, not all students remained in the study for four years, due to family mobility across school districts, which is common.)

Analysis of test performance conducted as part of the study showed that smaller class sizes resulted in higher achievement than that reached by either of the regular-sized classes. Follow-up research focusing on Nashville-Davidson County found that students who attended small classes earned consistently better grades by the end of the 1994–1995 school year (when Project STAR students would have been juniors in high school). The students who had been in small classes also outscored their peers in English, mathematics, and science. In addition, the evidence from the experiment suggested that small class sizes were especially conducive to improved learning on the part of children from minority racial groups and children living in areas with low socioeconomic status.[32]

The results of Project STAR have been subjected to a large amount of subsequent analysis. Policy Investment Checklist 6.1 provides an assessment of the STAR experiment, treating it as a policy investment. The evidence referred to in the checklist is derived primarily from a careful review by Alan B. Krueger.[33] Krueger developed a cost-benefit analysis of the impact of reducing class size. He began by noting that, theoretically, a drop in class size reduces the likelihood of classroom disruptions simply because there are fewer students to be disruptive. With fewer disruptions, teachers of smaller classes are able to spend more time meeting the learning needs of all students.

Based on the Project STAR evidence, Krueger concluded that even subtle changes in student achievement resulting from a drop in class size from 22 to 15 students in the first four years of primary school would yield long-term returns of between $2.30 and $2.60 for every dollar spent. The estimation was made using evidence tying student achievement data to life-time income streams. Krueger appropriately qualified his findings; still, they do suggest that well-implemented program changes in schools can lead to significant results for individuals and societies.

Other researchers have argued that Project STAR was flawed because teachers in the small classes—knowing that their actions were being closely observed—faced strong incentives to change their teaching practices to take advantage of the more intimate teaching conditions. Using a quasi-experimental research design, Caroline M. Hoxby leveled a powerful critique against the argument that class size matters to student achievement.[34] Hoxby, working with

POLICY INVESTMENT CHECKLIST 6.1

Analyzing the Reduction of School Class Size

1. Focus on Existing Policies and Programs	In the mid-1990s California engaged in an expensive effort to reduce class size. Evaluation results have suggested the effort did not produced expected results. Results from the Tennessee Student/Teacher Achievement Ratio (STAR) experiment have been carefully studied. Useful lessons can be drawn from both the California and the Tennessee experiments.
2. Gather Policy Evidence	The Tennessee STAR experiment was designed and conducted in a fashion that met the randomized controlled trial "gold standard" in evidence-based policy development. It generated a lot of data to support subsequent analysis of its effects.
3. Measure Desired Effects	Students who participated in small classes during the STAR experiment were subsequently found to earn consistently better grades in English, mathematics, and science than their peers who were assigned to larger classes. The average improvement was around 8%, compared with that of their peers. Small classes appear to have been especially helpful for minority students' learning. However, some analysts challenge the results and whether broader conclusions can be drawn from them. On average, students in the experiment experienced small classes for a period of 2.3 years.
4. Assess Costs and Benefits	To achieve the desired effect of this program, estimates suggest a total of between $7,000 and $8,000 was spent per student who experienced small classes for 2.3 years, compared with those who did not. The estimated benefit from being in smaller classes those 2.3 years for each student was calculated as marginal improvements in lifetime earnings. Different modeling assumptions produced different results, with an average improvement of around $18,300 over the lifetime. This figure indicates an estimated return on investment of between $2.30 and $2.60 for every dollar spent on reducing class size in the STAR experiment.
5. Offer Robust Advice	Estimating returns on investment for reducing class sizes requires making a lot of assumptions. Different assumptions yield different results. Consequently, disagreement remains over the impact of changes in class size. Recent efforts to compare a variety of education policies for the effects on student outcomes suggest that the money spent to reduce class sizes could be better spent on other things, such as improving the quality of teachers, both through better initial training and ongoing professional development.

evidence from Connecticut, studied cases where teachers and students had unexpectedly been assigned to unusually small classes due purely to demographic factors. For example, if a school in a given year had a kindergarten cohort of 26 and the district's maximum kindergarten class size was 25, then there would be two kindergarten classes of 13 each in that year.

Hoxby compared the subsequent test scores of students who, in elementary school, had been randomly assigned to small classes with those who had been assigned to regular-sized classes. Hoxby found no evidence of achievement differences between those children who had participated in small classes and those who had not.

When might changes in class size matter? In Hoxby's view, teachers experience small class sizes in natural settings repeatedly, but not every year. Teachers do not receive training to take advantage of smaller class sizes. She argued that reduction in class size should be combined with instruction for teachers that helps them modify their teaching techniques to take advantage of the more intimate teaching settings. Although teachers who participated in Project STAR were not given instruction on how to work differently with small classes, it is possible that they adjusted their practices of their own volition.

A careful evaluation study commissioned by the state of California traced the impacts of the Class Size Reduction (CSR) policy across every school year from 1996–1997 to 2000–2001. In its final report, the evaluation team drew four conclusions:

1. Implementation of CSR occurred rapidly, although it lagged in schools serving minority and low-income students.
2. The analyses of the relationship of CSR to student achievement were inconclusive.
3. CSR was associated with declines in teacher qualifications and more inequitable distribution of credentialed teachers. These were due to the new demand for teachers that the policy created. As such, the obvious dip in teacher quality might well have swamped any positive effects of the reduction in class sizes.
4. Students in reduced-size third-grade classes received more individual attention, but similar instruction and curriculum.[35]

Overall, it is estimated that California spent more than $25 billion on CSR. Yet it had no clear impact on student achievement—the original rationale for the policy change. That $25 billion could have been better spent on alternative educational initiatives that very likely could have raised student achievement and improved the morale of teachers and parents.

CRITICAL THINKING QUESTIONS

1. When might small group learning be most beneficial for students? When might group size be less important to learning?
2. Think back on your own schooling. What factors were most vital to helping you engage in your education?

OPTIONS FOR IMPROVING SCHOOL PERFORMANCE

As the evidence and analyses reviewed here indicate, the debate on class size is far from settled. The emerging story is that, compared with a range of other influences, variations in class size have a relatively small effect on student achievement. John Hattie came to this conclusion by reviewing meta-analyses based on about 300,000 research studies relating to student outcomes.[36] According to Hattie, various practices employed by teachers and schools have been shown to have more significant effects on student achievement than reductions in class size. For example, students tend to achieve more when they receive effective instructions and feedback from teachers. Likewise, efforts to increase family involvement in schooling, to reduce student disruptions, and to promote good study skills can do a lot to promote student achievement. (These observations inform the comments in the "Offer Robust Advice" row of Policy Investment Checklist 6.1.) Hattie's review suggests societies would receive high returns on their investments in schooling if they worked at continuously improving the quality of their teachers. Indeed, the suggestion is that governments should trade off smaller class sizes for higher-quality teachers.

Suppose a school system had 1 teacher for every 20 students. By changing this ratio to 1 teacher for every 24 students, the system could reduce the number of teachers employed by 20 percent. The school systems could then use the significant amount of money saved through having to pay fewer salaries in ways that would improve teacher quality. The possibilities could include raising annual expenditures on the professional development of teachers. Based on Hattie's findings, there would be considerable value in giving teachers new tools for working well with students and families, and for appropriately managing disruptive students.

Ideas along these lines have started to gain attention in the United States.[37] However, evidence from New Zealand suggests any policy maker contemplating this notion could be in for a fight. In 2012, the New Zealand government was forced to abandon a plan to trade off smaller class sizes for higher-quality teachers. The proposal upset teachers and parents and resulted in a political mess. The country's top education bureaucrat resigned a few months later.

PUBLIC SCHOOLING AND THE PURSUIT OF CIVIL RIGHTS

Education has long been understood as central to personal development and to an individual's ability to participate fully in the social, economic, political, and cultural activities of a community and a nation. For that reason, equal access for all children to quality public schooling has also long been viewed as a fundamental civil right. In the United States, the Supreme Court case known as *Brown v. Board of Education* (1954) enshrined every child's right to quality public education in the nation's public conscience and ongoing political narrative.

During the time of the Civil War, public schooling everywhere in the United States was rudimentary in nature. For African Americans living in the South, there was no access to public education. In the decades that followed, the nature of public schooling and the structures supporting it grew in sophistication. But those developments were not evenly spread. Indeed, in many states, African American children were excluded from attending public schools. When efforts were made to address educational disparities across the races—and the injustices those disparities created—a common approach involved establishing separate public schools for white children and black children. This racial segregation of public schooling was defended as allowing "separate but equal" treatment. The phrase **separate but equal** was enshrined in law through the U.S. Supreme Court case known as *Plessy v. Ferguson* (1896), which concerned access to public transport.

Following World War II, groups of citizens supporting racial equality began to seriously challenge the legitimacy of public schooling systems in selective states that perpetuated racial segregation. The Supreme Court's ruling in *Brown v. Board of Education* in favor of the plaintiffs and against the Board of Education of Topeka, Kansas, was a turning point. It established a strong legal precedent for the elimination of racial segregation across public schools throughout the United States.

Delivering the opinion of the Supreme Court in *Brown*, Chief Justice Earl Warren famously stated, "We conclude that, in the field of public education, the doctrine of 'separate but equal' has no place. Separate educational facilities are inherently unequal. Therefore, we hold that the plaintiffs and others similarly situated for whom the actions have been brought are, by reason of the segregation complained of, deprived of the equal protection of the laws guaranteed by the Fourteenth Amendment."

Desegregation of public schooling in the United States did not immediately follow from the *Brown* ruling. During the next decade, many racial clashes occurred as those seeking to promote civil rights fought those continuing to perpetuate racial discrimination in public schooling. Among the numerous incidents were the following.

In Alabama, Governor George Wallace, elected in 1962 on a segregationist platform, promised in his inaugural address in 1963, "Segregation now! Segregation tomorrow! Segregation forever!" He subsequently moved to stop African Americans enrolling in traditionally white educational institutions, including public schools and the University of Alabama. President John F. Kennedy used his federal powers to direct Alabama National Guard troops to enforce desegregation. Martin Luther King Jr. referred directly to George Wallace's actions in his "I Have a Dream" speech of August 1963: "I have a dream that one day down in Alabama, with its vicious racists, with its governor having his lips dripping with the words of interposition and nullification, that one day right down in Alabama little black boys and black girls will be able to join hands with little white boys and white girls as sisters and brothers."

The civil rights struggle concerning equal access to quality public schooling continues today. Although legal segregation of public schools is a thing of the past, significant numbers of African American and other minority children in the United States grow up in school districts with limited financial resources. As discussed in the "State and Local Government Authority" section, differences in local property values ensure that public schools in wealthy, predominantly white suburbs operate on significantly higher property tax revenues than do schools in poorer, predominantly minority neighborhoods and suburbs. State and federal government efforts have been designed to address the most extreme forms of disadvantage. Nonetheless, widespread disparities remain in the quality of education that children experience across public schools in the United States.

THE FUTURE OF PUBLIC SCHOOLING

Compulsory attendance through many years of public schooling represents a shared rite of passage for children and young people in most countries of the world. Careful economic analyses of the returns on education expenditures to the individual and society as a whole consistently show it is an investment that yields strong positive returns. Therefore, powerful reasons exist for governments to accord high priority to funding public schools.

All the social and individual benefits of compelling all children and young people to attend years of public schooling cannot be, and should never be, measured solely in financial terms. Although a handful of people might look back on their years of schooling as misery, many others appreciate the myriad ways public schooling—and, often, specific teachers—opened opportunities for them that subsequently enriched their lives socially, culturally, intellectually, physically, and spiritually.

The institution of public schooling is powerfully embedded in most societies. Although forces for innovation are likely to keep pressure on this institution to change, the core functions of schooling should remain stable into the foreseeable future. Of course, technology is continuously changing how we relate to each other, how we define meaningful work, and how we engage in that work. Thus, calls must continuously be made for schools to change, too. Nevertheless, the fundamental functions of education are unlikely to change anytime soon. We will still look to schools to care for children outside the home, to promote their social engagement, to expose them to those things we value about our common cultures and traditions, and to sort and prepare them for the adult world of work and parenting.

Today, governments everywhere understand the importance of having and maintaining well-educated citizens within their jurisdictions. Thus, governments for the past few decades have been on a relentless quest to ensure that their public school systems are capable of generating consistently good outcomes, as measured by such things as student performance on standardized tests. The pursuit of this outcome has been manifest in a range of experiments in the control and delivery of public schooling.

Creating opportunities for greater autonomy and continuous innovation have been important themes in reform efforts. However, holding schools accountable for results has also been recognized as important. In the years ahead, we can expect to see these trends continue. We should also expect that governments will pay much more careful attention to how to grow and maintain cohorts of excellent teachers. It is well understood that the quality of public school systems cannot exceed the quality of the teachers within them. Still, this reality begs the question of how to manage teacher–student interactions most effectively, and how ongoing developments in information technology serve to challenge established understandings of the nature of public schooling.

LESSONS FOR PUBLIC POLICY

Public policies that promote the development of individuals, families, broader organizations, and society as a whole represent important social investments. In this regard, public schools serve a vital purpose. The evidence is clear. Well-functioning systems of public schooling can contribute significantly to economic development, which itself opens many possibilities for the creation and maintenance of great societies. From the preceding discussion, we can draw several lessons for the practice of policy and program design.

- Without public funding, many families would be unable to afford to send their children to school. Given the major funding commitments associated with sending all children to school, it is reasonable for governments to seek to control the organization and management of public schooling. Systems of well-run public schools, accountable to governments and open to community concerns, can do a lot to promote good economic and social outcomes.
- The evidence is clear that public schooling represents a sound investment, from which both the educated individual and all of society gains. However, care must be taken to ensure that schools add high value to students. This can be done through regularly conducting standardized texts. Efforts should be made to track and compare individual student performance across the years. Such approaches create opportunities for necessary remedial actions. The goal should be to assist all children to get the most out of their years in school, hence increasing the returns on the investments being made.
- Good teachers are the most important element of school systems. Care should be taken to attract highly talented people into the teaching profession and to retain them. Further, continuous professional development can allow teachers to keep building their skills, and to adjust their teaching practices to take advantage of developments in information technology and other new aspects of education.
- Encouragement of a degree of innovation within public school systems offers a lot of value. The charter school movement in the United States has allowed entities like Uncommon Schools to flourish and contribute vital insights for how schools everywhere can improve student outcomes. In that case, the innovations involved systematically studying the actions of teachers who were able to encourage children from disadvantaged backgrounds to perform at a high level in school. The key to the innovation was systematically extracting usable knowledge from already existing evidence.
- There is a tendency for policy interventions, like public schooling, to become taken-for-granted social institutions. There are a lot of positive aspects to this approach. However, efforts must be made to reduce the risk of institutional inertia. Encouraging school leaders to innovate in their practices and to continuously discuss their practices with peers is important for reducing the possibility that certain schools or school districts will become pockets of backwardness. The right balance must be struck between promoting accountability, providing

incentives for good performance, allowing appropriate levels of autonomy in school decision making, and encouraging innovation in school practices. It is also likely that the balance will need adjustment over time.

From the policy reformer perspective, we might ask two questions. First, what changes would have an immediate and positive impact on the public schools? Second, what changes should be pursued, even though their positive effects are likely to show up a decade or more into the future?

Based on contemporary evidence, a good quick fix for public school systems is to routinely assess student performance. When this takes place, opportunities arise to analyze and interpret individual and group trends over time. These steps can lead to productive discussions about interventions that might improve the learning of specific students on the one hand, and improve the practices of specific teachers on the other.

For the longer-term impact, a sound policy approach should focus on raising the quality of the teaching profession. Teachers who are bright, engaged, and creative are essential for promoting high-quality learning environments. When such teachers are given opportunities to work together and contribute to the design of their working environments, and when they are encouraged to connect their work in the classroom to the broader goals of public schooling, benefits flow to students, communities, and society as a whole.

CHAPTER SUMMARY

This chapter has explored key issues in public schooling. Although private schools continue to exist, and it would theoretically be possible to achieve good educational outcomes in a society through government funding of private schools, everywhere in the world education of the young principally remains the domain of publicly funded and operated schools. The reasons are complex. They involve beliefs about the function of schools, the importance of compelling all young people to obtain an education, and the desire for political leaders to influence what gets taught in schools and the quality of the classroom experience. In the United States, access for all children to quality schooling—no matter their race or social standing—has long represented a fundamental issue in civil rights, as it does today.

This chapter has emphasized government efforts to promote high standards across all public schools in the contemporary United States. Although public schooling remains the constitutional responsibility of state governments, funding and control continue to be delegated to the local level. However, as politicians, business leaders, and concerned citizens have come to recognize the fundamental link between the quality of a nation's schooling and its economic competitiveness and political standing in the world, governors and presidents have felt pressure to drive educational improvements. What occurs in classrooms across America today has been shaped significantly by the belief that regular, high-stakes standardized testing will keep the academic pressure on schools, teachers, and students.

The question of what works in schools and classrooms to promote educational excellence has motivated much contemporary debate concerning education policy and public schooling. On the one hand, there has been a drive to allow schools more autonomy in their practices. On the other, there has been a drive for greater control. In the midst of these competing forces, educationalists have engaged in a range of experiments to test the merits of various educational practices. Discussion in this chapter focused on two elements—efforts to improve the quality of teachers in classrooms, and efforts to determine the impact of class size on learning.

When public funds are invested in reducing class sizes, it is possible that the change will have limited impacts, especially when that change leads to an influx of less-qualified teachers. No matter the results, reducing class sizes is an expensive undertaking. This raises questions as to whether other policy options—such as professional development of teachers—could produce better results with the equivalent amount of spending. Such questions should evolve in interesting ways given rapid changes in the use of information technology by both teachers and students.

The notion of treating public policies as investments should be highly useful in future discussions about effective approaches to public schooling. Indeed, the investment perspective leads us to explicitly consider and estimate the social and economic value that might be realized from deploying scarce educational funds in different ways. Questions concerning "what works" in public schooling will always be with us. And they should—as long as progress occurs. Careful analysis of evidence holds the promise of settling a range of old debates while guiding the direction of new ones.

CONNECTIONS TO OTHER CHAPTERS

At its best, public schooling provides individuals with powerful scaffolding to support their participation in society and the continuous expansion of their personal development. Exposure to good public schooling can set people on trajectories whereby they are likely to voluntarily participate in further training, have productive and continuous engagement in the paid workforce, enjoy mutually beneficial interactions with others, maintain good health, and attain happiness and fulfillment.

A good education can assist people to escape social disadvantage and poverty (Chapter 8). In addition, efforts to promote quality education across a society can contribute to better public health outcomes (Chapter 7). Often, a major reason why people end up living lives of crime is that they missed out on receiving appropriate and effective schooling. In this way, there is a connection between the organization of public schooling and criminal justice outcomes (Chapter 9). On a more positive note, effective public schooling can lay the foundation for well-trained young people to attain university degrees and, ultimately, for some of them to contribute to the advancement of scientific knowledge and technological innovation (Chapter 10). In turn, such contributions can support the attainment of many improvements in our lives together, and often in the lives of all people around the world.

KEY TERMS

Curriculum

Social intervention

The creative class

Knowledge workers

Enculturation

Credentialing

Positive externalities

Compulsory education

Property taxes

Accountability

The one best system

Strictly secular schools

Vouchers

Schools of choice

Charter schools

No Child Left Behind

Race to the Top

Human capital

Physical capital

The economics of education

Separate but equal

SUGGESTIONS FOR FURTHER READING

Barber, Michael, and Mona Mourshed. *How the World's Best-Performing School Systems Come Out on Top*. London: McKinsey and Company, 2007. An excellent analysis of the features of good school systems.

Chubb, John E., and Terry M. Moe. *Politics, Markets, and America's Schools*. Washington, DC: Brookings Institution, 1990. A classic, evidence-based argument for greater reliance on school choice and public funding of children to attend private schools.

Hanushek, Eric A., and Ludger Woessmann. "The Role of Cognitive Skills in Economic Development," *Journal of Economic Literature* 46, no. 3 (2008): 607–668. An important exploration of how educated citizens contribute to economic growth.

Khan, Salman. *The One World Schoolhouse: Education Reimagined*. New York: Twelve, 2012. A reflection of how technological developments can enhance how teachers and students work together.

Manna, Paul, and Patrick McGuinn, eds. *Education Governance for the Twenty-First Century: Overcoming the Structural Barriers to School Reform*. Washington, DC: Brookings Institution Press, 2013. A collection of essays reviewing contemporary school governance arrangements and fruitful areas for reform.

Robinson, Ken, and Lou Aronica. *Creative Schools*. New York: Penguin, 2016. A rich and provocative exploration of how schools can encourage the full flourishing of children's talents and potential.

Tyack, David, and Larry Cubin. *Tinkering toward Utopia: A Century of Public School Reform*. Cambridge, MA: Harvard University Press, 1995. An excellent explanation of why it is so difficult to achieve change within large, embedded public school systems.

WEBSITES

- The Institute of Education Sciences has launched the What Works Clearing-house (WWC) as a resource for informed education decision making. WWC identifies studies that provide credible and reliable evidence of the effectiveness of a given practice, program, or policy, and disseminates summary information and free reports on the WWC website. www.ies.ed.gov/ncee/wwc/
- The U.S. Department of Education has launched the Nation's Report Card to inform the public about the academic achievement of elementary and secondary students in the United States. Report cards communicate the findings of the National Assessment of Educational Progress, a continuing and nationally representative measure of achievement in various subjects over time. www.nationsreportcard.gov
- The Brookings Institution states that "the economic and political well-being of any society requires a well-educated citizenry. Brookings' work extends beyond K-12 to include preschool interventions, higher education, and the challenges of education in developing countries." www.brookings.edu/topic/education

FOR DISCUSSION

1. Schools are sometimes criticized for not being sufficiently innovative in their practices and, hence, for not meeting the educational needs of current students. (a) Together, make a list of innovative things that schools could do to improve the educational experiences of students. (b) Next, consider what schools would need to do to accommodate these innovations. (c) Finally, discuss possible sources of resistance to each innovation and how such resistance could be overcome.

2. Responsibility for the funding and governance of public schools in the United States has historically been delegated to local school districts. What forces tend to support ongoing local control of public schools? What forces tend to promote more central control of schools, for example, by state governments?

3. In 1997, the OECD launched its Program for International Student Assessment (PISA). It evaluates education systems worldwide every three years by assessing the competencies of 15-year-olds in reading, mathematics, and science. To date over 70 countries and economies have participated in PISA. How do you think results from international assessments like this get to influence debates about public schooling? Can you think of cases where contemporary politicians have used international standing to influence education debates?

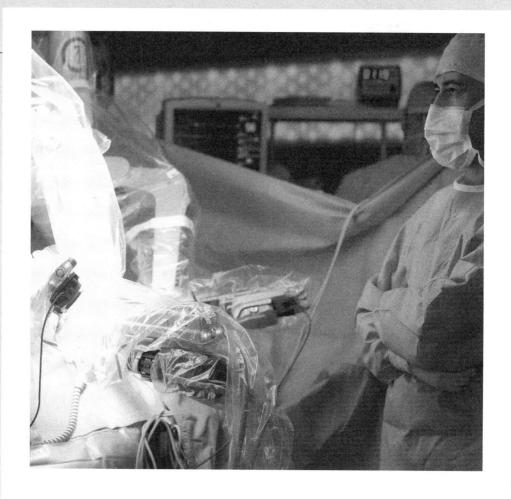

CHAPTER 7

HEALTH CARE

OVERVIEW

Many countries around the world have established systems of health care provision, funded primarily by governments, where health and hospital services are also mostly managed and delivered by government organizations. In the United States, governments have always been involved in establishing healthy living environments. However, for many decades individual health care was treated as a matter for the private sphere. Individuals or their employers purchased health insurance. Health care services were provided by private entities, operating as either for-profit businesses or not-for-profit organizations. That nexus of relationships continues to define much of the structure of health care provision in the United States today. This chapter considers the role of government in health care and reviews key issues in the provision of health insurance and medical services.

During the 20th century, the federal government in the United States came to play an increasingly important role in providing health insurance for groups considered to be in high need of a social safety net. Today, the United States operates a unique blend of public and private health care provision. This system is vast and expensive. For many, it offers outstanding health care. For many others, the system is far from perfect. Health care funding and questions of who should be eligible for government assistance provoke heated political debates.

This chapter introduces you to:

- The reasons why governments have an interest in health care and often take major responsibility for funding and delivering health care services
- International perspectives on health care spending and outcomes

Facing page: Doctors use the da Vinci surgical system to perform minimally invasive surgery. Medical procedures assisted by high technology allow hospitals in the United States to offer state-of-the-art heath care. However, such procedures are expensive. Cost issues continue to raise ongoing concerns about health care affordability and equality of access to quality services.

(Master Video/Shutterstock.com)

- Criteria for assessing the advantages and disadvantages of single- and multi-payer health insurance systems—both in the United States and elsewhere
- Traditional approaches to arranging the funding and delivery of health care in the United States
- Features and impacts of Medicare, Medicaid, and the Affordable Care Act (ACA)
- The important role of federalism in the development of health policies
- Application of the investment perspective to various areas of preventive health care
- Health care and the promotion of civil rights
- Lessons for public policy emerging from this review of health care

AN INTRODUCTION TO HEALTH CARE

Enjoying good health is central to the quality of our lives. Healthy people are better able to participate in important social activities, such as studying, working, raising children, getting involved in the community, and caring for others. As medical knowledge has advanced, the life expectancy of humans has grown. In the United States, average life expectancies grew during the past century by over 30 years. This finding also holds true in many other wealthy countries. People who maintain a healthy diet, get regular exercise, and are able to seek prompt medical treatment when health problems arise are well placed to live long, productive lives.

Governments have long taken actions to improve the environments we live in, striving to keep them healthy. Whenever they have done so, however, they have typically met with significant opposition from various interest groups benefiting from the status quo. Case Study 7.1 explores one way that contemporary governments have been going further than ever before to create healthy environments. Here, we see how some governments have imposed taxes on sugary drinks in an effort to promote healthier consumption choices and reduce the growing problem of obesity.

case study 7.1 Using Taxes to Reduce Sugar Consumption

When people consume sugary foods, they place a lot of energy in their bodies that they cannot easily expend. Their bodies store portions of surplus energy as fat. As their bodies grow larger, it becomes harder for their metabolism to process energy intake. As a result, people who are overweight can readily gain more weight and find it increasingly difficult to lose it. Physicians, dieticians, and other health experts believe that a strong relationship exists between high levels of sugar consumption, weight gain, and obesity.

Obesity is considered a health problem for several reasons. Most importantly, when people carry a lot of weight, they face higher risks of developing heart problems, diabetes, and other debilitating conditions. In many countries, obesity is becoming more common, especially among children. A major concern about childhood obesity is that it is a strong predictor of obesity in adulthood. Figure 7.1 presents a map of the United States identifying differences in rates of obesity among adults by state.

Health activists, including physicians and dieticians, often treat obesity as a public policy issue. Central to this view is the claim that the health problems associated with obesity impose costs not just on those who are obese but on society as a whole. These costs come in the

FIGURE 7.1   U.S. Adult Obesity Rates Mapped by State, 2014

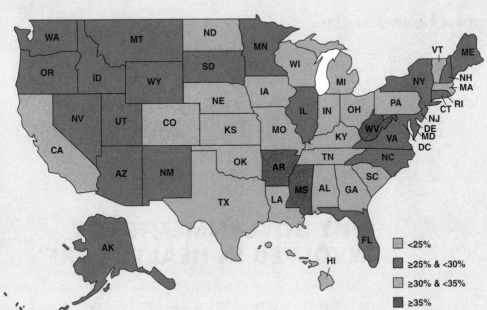

<25%

≥25% & <30%

≥30% & <35%

≥35%

Source: The State of Obesity: Better Policies for a Healthier America, 2015 *(Washington, DC: Trust for America's Health/ Robert Wood Johnson Foundation), p. 9.*

form of higher health care spending, a reason why economists describe obesity as an individual health condition that generates **negative externalities**—unwanted outcomes for others.

Governments have used a number of public policy tools to address negative externalities. These include information provision, regulation, and imposition of taxes. In the case of obesity, the focus has been on foods that contribute most to causing it, and sugar is a major culprit.

Recent years have seen international efforts to introduce taxes on sugar or sugary drinks.[1] For example, since 2015, the city government of Berkeley, California, has imposed a tax on sugary drinks, with the goal of encouraging suppliers to sell drinks with lower sugar content to local stores.[2] Imposing such taxes has created controversy, with manufacturers of sugary drinks leading the opposition.[3]

Revenues raised from the Berkeley tax contribute to funding all city programs. However, in line with the investment perspective on public policies, a portion of the revenue raised by the tax is devoted to actions designed to further reduce consumption of sugar in the city. For example, a local government committee works with neighborhoods to help reduce sugar consumption among all people, and especially among children.

In Berkeley, health activists have noted a phenomenon common to many places: unhealthy food choices and obesity are more prevalent in poor neighborhoods and within some racial groups than in others. For this reason, they have suggested there is an important civil rights element to the tax on soda drinks and the educational and outreach programs that revenues from this tax are helping to fund.

CRITICAL THINKING QUESTIONS

1. Opponents of taxes on sugar or sugary drinks believe such taxes are a symptom of government overreach to control people's consumption choices. What do you think?
2. What other policy approaches, beyond taxing sugar or sugary items, could support the goal of reducing obesity in a population?

WHY GOVERNMENTS GET INVOLVED IN HEALTH CARE

What role should government play in the funding and delivery of health care? In many countries, the popular view is that access to basic health care is a human right. This has led to the development of well-subsidized systems of public health. It is common for governments both to fund health care and to deliver services. That is the case, for example, in the United Kingdom, where the National Health Service has been operating since 1948. Canada also has a well-established system of national health insurance. We also frequently find hybrid systems of health care funding and provision. In such cases, publicly funded and provided health care services run alongside privately funded and provided health care services.

In the United States, around 18 percent of the country's Gross Domestic Product (GDP) is spent on health care. Many other countries also spend large amounts of money on health care. However, a surprising number of other countries currently enjoy higher average life expectancies for their populations than America does, and they devote a much smaller proportion of their GDP to health care (see Table 7.1). The apparently unending increases in health care spending in the United States and the reality that many citizens continue to lack access to basic health care have sounded alarm bells and fueled major political battles. The public policy debates over the ACA and its repeal emerge from differences in material interests and philosophical differences concerning the role of government in society.

Four factors make health care a matter of public concern: the public nature of disease, the complex nature of health and medical issues, the affordability of health care, and the incentives health care consumers and producers face. These factors help explain why health policy is a major concern of governments everywhere, and why historically most governments have been closely involved in funding and delivering at least some elements of health care. Here, we discuss each factor in turn.

PREVENTING THE SPREAD OF DISEASE

When we seek to stay healthy, we benefit ourselves and those around us. However, many threats to individual health loom as something more than a series of individual concerns. The health of neighbors, work colleagues, classmates, friends, and family members can have important individual health and nonhealth impacts. These **spillover effects**—termed by economists as negative and **positive externalities**—suggest that health care should be a concern of society as a whole, and thus of governments.

Historically, local governments have taken care to promote good public health. Measures include provision of clean water systems and ensuring safe disposal of human waste and garbage that, if not treated appropriately, could rapidly foster life-threatening diseases. Good public health has also been promoted through **immunization programs**, ensuring that children and adults are inoculated against diseases that have previously ravaged human societies, such as typhoid, tuberculosis, polio, and measles. Sanitation services and immunization against diseases represent classic examples of **public goods**. That is to say, they are goods that—in the absence of government supply—would likely not be supplied in sufficient quantities to make them effective. Further, if governments did not create strong and predictable demand for these services, supply could be either haphazard or nonexistent. Thus, in practice, governments often provide as well as fund these services.

The U.S. Centers for Disease Control and Prevention (CDC) is the national public health institute responsible for reducing the risks of diseases emerging and spreading across the United States. Case Study 1.1 highlighted the CDC's contributions to fighting Ebola. More recently, the CDC has been working to avoid the spread of the Zika virus.

MANAGING COMPLEXITY

Throughout our history, we humans have exerted vast effort to understand the physiology of the human body, revealing the nature of disease and isolating factors that contribute to good and bad health. It is essential, however, to distinguish people with sound and appropriate medical knowledge from those who lack it. Priority has long been placed on finding ways to protect ignorant and vulnerable people—including children—from falling victim to the practices of people engaged in unsound medicine. Governments have often performed a funding and a regulatory role in this regard. The need for trained physicians led to the development of hospital- and university-based medical schools. It also has led to the creation of **credentialing systems** to certify individuals are suitably trained to practice medicine.

Governments have also long been involved in funding efforts to advance scientific knowledge relating to health, disease, and medicine. In this respect, knowledge development has been considered a vital public good, one that can benefit all members of society. Indeed, the advancement of knowledge concerning health, disease, and medicine has been of vast benefit. The spillover effects have spread both from generation to generation and around the world. In this sense, the reduction of ignorance has been, and continues to be, an investment yielding enormous positive returns. (We will explore this topic in greater depth in Chapter 10 on science funding.)

MAKING HEALTH CARE AFFORDABLE

Concerns about **social equity** represent another reason why governments get involved in health care. Obtaining high-quality, cutting-edge medical treatment is frequently something that only the richest people in society are able to access. **Insurance schemes** and other systems of **pooling resources** to support those in need have been created to improve access to health care for people who otherwise could not afford it.

Affordability issues have ensured that health care has been a matter of public concern for a long time. During the 20th century, many governments around the world created systems to fund—and often deliver—health care services to growing proportions of the population. Affordability issues remain central to public discussions of health care. Arguments about the appropriate role of government in the funding and delivery of health services are likely to continue for a long time. In recent U.S. history, those arguments have been politically divisive, a matter we will return to several times throughout this chapter.

ALIGNING INCENTIVES

Although discussions of health care often involve comparisons between market-like provision of services and provision by government, much of what we think of as health care does not lend itself to distribution through highly decentralized systems of supply and demand. Kenneth J. Arrow skillfully made this point in a classic article on the economics of medical care.[4] Arrow noted that individuals typically face a lot of uncertainty about their need for medical treatment. When they actually need it, they can face several kinds of costs. First, there is usually a significant likelihood that they will not be able to function fully. This potential for reduction or even loss of income-earning ability can have implications not only for the individual but also for family members. Thus, both the cost of falling ill itself and the cost of medical care are concerning. Most individuals therefore would like to insure against these potential losses.

When insurance is provided, issues of **incentives alignment** emerge. Consider the people who seek to be insured. There is a concern that those people who expect to need care in the near future will be the ones most eager to sign up for insurance. There is also concern that once covered, some individuals—encouraged by their doctors—will seek additional medical interventions that they would not have sought in the absence of insurance.

Now consider those firms selling health insurance. They face incentives to avoid making payouts. Thus, they may place various restrictions on those who sign up for insurance—for example, limits on the kinds of care that are covered. Insurers may also require **copayments**—that is some financial contributions by the individual receiving treatment. Copayment requirements sometimes come in the form of **deductibles**, a specified amount of payment the patient makes before insurance reimburses them the remaining medical costs. Further, those selling health insurance might have restrictions as to who can buy insurance from them; most frequent is the refusal of coverage for a preexisting condition. Insurers want to avoid situations where they provide insurance to large numbers of people who are likely to incur significant immediate health care costs. These basic observations about demand for health care, the desirability of health insurance, and the calculations of those selling insurance go a long way toward explaining why health policy is a major concern for governments around the world.

INTERNATIONAL PERSPECTIVES ON HEALTH CARE PROVISION: EXPENDITURES AND OUTCOMES

Before we focus specifically on the United States, let us take an international look at the complexities of health care. Analysis of health care spending across many countries indicates an important relationship: generally speaking, the more money a country spends per person per year on health care, the higher the life expectancy at birth of people living in that country. However, there are limits to this simple relationship. Among generally more wealthy countries, those spending the highest amounts do not necessarily enjoy the greatest life expectancy.[5]

Table 7.1 provides an international comparison, as of 2015, of six indicators of health expenditures, life expectancies, and **nonmedical determinants of health**. These indicators show major differences in the resources that countries devote to health care, as measured both in terms of health expenditures as a share of GDP and as annual expenditures per person. Major differences across countries also exist in terms of life expectancy at birth. For example, in 2015, the expected life span for a person born in South Africa was 57.6 years, nearly three decades less than the life expectancy for a person born at the same time in Switzerland.

Table 7.1 also reveals major differences across countries in three nonmedical determinants of health: the prevalence of adult obesity, average annual adult consumption of alcohol, and the percentage of adults who regularly smoke.

EXPENDITURES AND LIFE EXPECTANCIES

The United States devotes more of its resources to health care than any other country in the world. In 2015, health expenditure as a share of GDP was 16.9 percent in the United States, compared with an average of 9.0 percent for all members of the Organisation for Economic Co-operation and Development (OECD), a think tank composed of 35 wealthy countries. Yet, for all this spending, the United States does not enjoy the world's best health outcomes.

In terms of life expectancy, many other countries perform better than America. Switzerland holds the highest life expectancy, at 83.3 years, more than four years greater than that of the United States. Although Switzerland is a high spender on health care, devoting 11.5 percent of GDP to it in 2015, annual expenditure per person is 36 percent lower than annual expenditure per person in the United States. Even on the North American continent, cross-country differences are stark. Compared with Canada the United States paid more than twice as much per person on health care in 2015. Despite this expenditure, average life expectancy in Canada was 81.5 years, 2.7 years longer than in the United States.

NONMEDICAL DETERMINANTS OF HEALTH

We will find the six indicators presented in Table 7.1 useful to refer to throughout the remainder of this chapter. For example, toward the chapter's end we will discuss **wellness programs** in the United States—programs designed to encourage children and adults to make healthy lifestyle choices and to engage in regular exercise. Although Table 7.1 indicates that rates of obesity among U.S. adults are among the highest in the world, average alcohol consumption and the proportion of adults who regularly smoke are less than in many other countries.

TABLE 7.1 International Comparison of Health Expenditures, Life Expectancies, and Nonmedical Determinants of Health, 2015

COUNTRY	HEALTH EXPENDITURE (% OF GDP)	HEALTH EXPENDITURE PER CAPITA (U.S. $)	LIFE EXPECTANCY, YEARS[a]	ADULT OBESITY (% OF POP.)	ADULT ALCOHOL CONSUMPTION[b]	% OF ADULT POPULATION SMOKING DAILY
United States	16.9	$9,451	78.8	36.5	8.9	12.9
OECD average	9.0	$3,814	80.6	17.6	9.0	19.3
Australia	9.3	$4,420	82.4	28.3	9.7	13.0
Austria	10.4	$5,016	81.6	12.4	12.3	24.3
Brazil	6.2	$1,020	74.5	15.8	7.3	8.7
Canada	10.1	$4,608	81.5	25.4	8.0	14.0
Chile	7.7	$1,728	79.0	25.1	7.9	29.8
China	5.6	$731	75.8	2.9	5.8	25.5
Czech Rep.	7.5	$2,464	78.9	21.0	11.9	22.3
Denmark	10.6	$4,943	80.8	13.4	9.4	17.0
Finland	9.6	$3,984	81.3	16.6	8.8	15.4
France	11.0	$4,407	82.8	12.9	11.5	22.4
Germany	11.1	$5,267	81.2	14.7	10.9	20.9
Greece	8.2	$2,245	81.5	17.3	7.5	27.3
India	4.7	$267	68.0	2.1	2.6	12.6
Indonesia	2.8	$302	68.9	2.4	0.1	37.9
Ireland	9.4	$5,131	81.4	23.0	11.0	24.0
Israel	7.4	$2,533	82.2	15.7	2.6	17.1
Italy	9.1	$3,272	83.2	10.0	7.6	19.7
Japan	11.2	$4,150	83.7	4.1	7.1	19.6
Korea	7.2	$2,488	82.2	4.3	9.0	20.0

TABLE 7.1 continued

COUNTRY	HEALTH EXPENDITURE (% OF GDP)	HEALTH EXPENDITURE PER CAPITA (U.S. $)	LIFE EXPECTANCY, YEARS[a]	ADULT OBESITY (% OF POP.)	ADULT ALCOHOL CONSUMPTION[b]	% OF ADULT POPULATION SMOKING DAILY
Mexico	5.8	$1,052	74.8	32.4	5.5	8.9
Netherlands	10.8	$5,343	81.8	11.4	8.4	19.1
New Zealand	9.4	$3,590	81.6	28.4	9.1	15.5
Norway	9.9	$6,567	82.2	10.0	6.1	13.0
Russian Fed.	5.9	$1,369	70.9	16.0	13.8	22.0
South Africa	8.8	$1,146	57.6	16.0	8.1	19.8
Spain	9.0	$3,153	83.3	16.6	9.3	23.0
Sweden	11.1	$5,228	82.3	11.0	7.2	11.9
Switzerland	11.5	$6,935	83.3	8.1	9.5	20.4
United Kingdom	9.8	$4,003	81.4	24.8	9.4	19.0

Source: *OECD Health at a Glance* (2016), Tables 1.1.1, 2.5.1, 2.6.1, 2.7.1, 7.1.1, and 7.2.1.

Note: "Adult" = 15 years and older.

[a]For those born in 2015. [b]Annual liters per capita.

HEALTH DIFFERENCES WITHIN THE UNITED STATES

Country-level indicators can mask important variations within national populations. This is the case for the United States. Evidence from the local level shows major disparities in health status. Some subpopulations enjoy levels of health and well-being that place them among the most privileged people on Earth. Others do far worse.[6]

A 2016 study focusing on U.S. counties revealed differences in life expectancies of more than 15 years.[7] Geographically, the lowest life expectancies were in counties in Appalachia and the Deep South, extending across northern Texas. Counties with the highest life expectancies tended to be in the northern plains and along the Pacific coast and the eastern seaboard. A number of western counties with large Native American populations exhibited low life expectancies. Meanwhile, clusters of counties with high life expectancies were observed in Colorado, Minnesota, Utah, California, Washington, and Florida.[8] We discuss population health disparities further in the section of this chapter on U.S. health care and civil rights.

FUNDING HEALTH CARE: COMPARING SINGLE- AND MULTI-PAYER SYSTEMS

Before turning attention fully to health care in the United States, it is useful for us to consider a major difference among nations in regard to single- versus multi-payer health insurance systems.

Table 7.2 uses five criteria to assess points of difference across national health insurance systems. In **single-payer systems**, governments use the general tax system to fund health insurance for the whole population. Because all citizens are automatically covered by the system, there is no concern that only those people who expect to need medical procedures will opt in. By contrast, in **multi-payer systems**, insurance companies have often sought to manage their risk of making significant payouts by seeking to screen whom and what they cover. These differences alone can explain major variations in the administrative costs associated with single- versus multi-payer systems. It also happens that even when individuals are covered by insurance companies, they sometimes need to find additional funding to cover medical procedures that are not covered in their health insurance policies.

The United States has developed a multi-payer system, where the federal government and state governments are important payers. In contrast, many other countries—including the United Kingdom, Canada, and Australia—have developed essentially single-payer systems. However, in most single-payer systems, opportunities exist for those who desire to purchase private health insurance to do so. This has allowed for the relief of some of the cost pressure in large public health systems. Debate over health care policy has been intense in the United States; however, heated debate has occurred in many other countries. All systems—single- or multi-payer—face cost pressures. Concerns about access to services, opportunities to benefit from the latest technology, and fairness are common everywhere. That said, one factor that makes health care so expensive in the United States is that many health specialists receive significantly higher incomes relative to health specialists with the same expertise practicing in other countries.[9]

TABLE 7.2 Comparing Single- versus Multi-Payer Health Insurance Systems

CRITERIA	SINGLE-PAYER	MULTI-PAYER
1. Revenue Collection It is desirable for revenue collection covering health insurance to be efficient, equitable, and administratively simple.	Governments raise general taxes and some proportion is allocated to the funding of health insurance. Efficiency, equity, and administrative simplicity in revenue-raising mirror those of the general tax system.	Premiums are paid by various entities—employers, individuals, and government. Equity among rich and poor is harder to achieve. But when tax revenues are limited, governments can enlarge health insurance revenues from other sources, such as wealthier groups purchasing private health insurance.
2. Overall Cost Control From a national perspective, it is desirable to avoid excessive spending on health care, so that scarce resources can be allocated elsewhere.	Governments can use annual budget processes and the rationing of services to control overall system cost. But these can create major political controversy.	Because payments are made by many entities, overall cost control in the system is harder to achieve.
3. Risk Pooling When many people with a wide range of health conditions are covered by the same insurance plan, the plan itself becomes more financially sustainable.	All citizens are covered by the one insurance system, creating a large risk pool. There is no need to screen members as to their risk factors, although screening people for medical procedures must continue to avoid unnecessary use of services.	With many smaller insurance systems, each insurer seeks to avoid attracting people who will subsequently require expensive medical procedures. Patient advocates may challenge perceived unfair treatment. Administrative costs are generally higher as a result.
4. Purchasing Services Health insurers purchase services for their beneficiaries. Large insurers can exert more control over prices than smaller ones.	Power lies with the payer, and this allows for more control over prices, including the prices beneficiaries pay for prescription drugs.	With many payers, it is hard for any to exert strong power in negotiating prices. For example, prescription drug prices may be higher than in a single-payer system. But, with more payers, more scope exists for innovations in the set of insurance schemes offered to beneficiaries.
5. Social Cohesion It is desirable for provision of health insurance to preserve and/or enhance social cohesion.	With all citizens covered by the same insurance system, a degree of social cohesion may exist. But wealthy people may feel unduly constrained, and opt out from the system and hold private health insurance.	Social cohesion may be strained when poor people believe they receive worse treatment than wealthy people. However, when people can exercise choice over their insurance plans, they often feel more positive in general about the system.

Source: The content of this table is based on discussion in the following article, which is highly informative but does not include any table of the kind presented here: Peter Hussey and Gerard F. Anderson. "A Comparison of Single- and Multi-payer Health Insurance Systems and Options for Reform," Health Policy 66, no. 3 (2003): 215–28.

TRADITIONAL POLICY APPROACHES IN THE UNITED STATES

In the United States, health care has always been treated as a matter to be addressed primarily in the marketplace. On the supply side, hospital and other health care services have been managed as private or not-for-profit entities. On the demand side, payment of health care expenses has been arranged through private insurance systems. Frequently, health insurance for an individual and his or her family members has come as an employment benefit. (This is still largely the case, even with implementation of government programs subsidizing the cost of health insurance.)

THE HISTORICAL BACKDROP

Historically, because of political opposition, government involvement in the system has been limited. However, the government has long provided subsidies to support the training of medical personnel. Government regulations have determined who can practice medicine. Governments have largely funded medical research. The missing component has been government assistance to allow its citizens wide access to health care services. Those who have not received health benefits through employment and who have lacked disposable income to purchase their own health insurance have had to go without.

From early in the 20th century, concerned health care professionals, philanthropists, politicians, and citizens worked constantly to secure access to health care services for those who could not afford them. They saw government subsidization of services, or direct government service provision, as ways to promote affordability. These efforts mostly resulted in limited changes. Mark Peterson has documented the history of presidential efforts to secure greater access to health care for the American people.[10] He has noted that, despite the efforts of Presidents Roosevelt, Truman, and Clinton, a mix of interest-group and ideological pressures have continuously served to inhibit fundamental changes. William Weissert and Carol Weissert have systematically laid out how different interest groups and institutions of government have tended to weigh in on health care policy issues.[11]

KEY MOMENTS IN HEALTH CARE POLICY DEVELOPMENT

There have been two key moments in U.S. health care policy development. The first occurred in 1965, under the presidency of Lyndon Johnson, with the introduction of Medicare and Medicaid. The second occurred in 2010, with the signing of the Affordable Care Act (often referred to as Obamacare). In both moments, those who promoted these policies and their associated programs had been seeking more comprehensive access to health care than what eventuated.

The most important thing for us to observe about these watershed moments is that, in both cases, they took the predominantly private, market-driven provision of health care in the United States as a given. They did not challenge that approach because the interests and institutional arrangements supporting them were powerful and strongly resistant to change. Instead, they created means by which access to health care could be extended—through government subsidies—to selected groups who would otherwise miss out.

Medicare is a federal program that provides health insurance coverage to people who have disabilities, are diagnosed with certain medical conditions, or are 65 years or older. **Medicaid**, which is funded jointly by federal and state governments, provides health care coverage to low-income people who meet specific eligibility requirements. In Focus 7.1 offers an explanation of the features and impacts of Medicare and Medicaid.

in focus 7.1

FEATURES AND IMPACTS OF MEDICARE AND MEDICAID

Medicare and Medicaid were both established in 1965 via amendments to the Social Security Act. They were centerpieces of President Lyndon Johnson's Great Society initiative, which introduced various measures to address poverty and racial injustice. Both programs have subsequently been expanded through the actions of multiple presidents, both Democratic and Republican.

Medicare

Medicare was established as an **entitlement program** (a government program guaranteeing access to some benefit by members of a specific group and based on established rights or by legislation) specifically to provide health insurance to all people 65 and older.[12] People in this age group remain the primary beneficiaries of the program, although it has been expanded to provide insurance for younger people with permanent disabilities or several specific, highly debilitating diseases. Since its introduction, Medicare has been credited with significantly improving the health status of people over 65.

- As of 2015, more than 57 million people were covered by Medicare.
- Total Medicare costs, funded entirely by the federal government, amounted to $540 billion in 2015. They accounted for 15 percent of the total federal budget.

Medicaid

Medicaid is an entitlement program that provides health insurance for low-income people. Most Medicaid beneficiaries lack access to private insurance and many have significant health care needs.[13] Medicaid is also the primary source of long-term care coverage in the United

States. Funding is provided primarily by the federal government but is disbursed by the states, and states contribute to the program's costs.

Over the decades, Medicaid has expanded to cover a broad low-income population. Beneficiaries include pregnant women, children, some parents in both working and jobless families, and children and adults with various physical and mental health conditions and disabilities. Medicaid also covers millions of people with chronic conditions and disabilities who have been excluded from private insurance or cannot afford it, or for whom private insurance coverage is inadequate. The Affordable Care Act (see In Focus 7.2)

greatly expanded the reach of Medicaid, making it broadly a program for people under age 65 with income at or below 133 percent of the federal poverty level. However, provider shortages and low provider participation in Medicaid, especially among specialists, are ongoing concerns.

- As of 2015, over 62 million people were covered by Medicaid.
- Total Medicaid costs, shared between federal and state governments, amounted to $552 billion in 2015. The federal component amounted to $334 billion, accounting for 9 percent of the total federal budget.

The **Affordable Care Act** of 2010 was designed to expand access to health insurance by making it mandatory that all Americans have membership in health insurance schemes and by subsidizing the cost of that membership. The act also contained a range of provisions intended to reduce future costs to the government of health care coverage. An In Focus section later in this chapter sets out key features and impacts of the ACA.

CONTEMPORARY POLICY ISSUES

The passage, implementation, and ongoing debate concerning the legacies of the ACA have dominated the contemporary scene concerning health care in the United States.

EXPANDING HEALTH INSURANCE COVERAGE

President Obama signed the Patient Protection and Affordable Care Act into law in 2010. At the signing ceremony, President Obama observed: "The bill I'm signing will set in motion reforms that generations of Americans have fought for and marched for and hungered to see. . . . With all the punditry, all of the lobbying, all of the game-playing that passes for governing in Washington, it's been easy at times to doubt our ability to do such a big thing, such a complicated thing; to wonder if there are limits to what we, as a people, can still achieve. . . . But today, we are affirming that essential truth—a truth every generation is called to rediscover for itself—that we are not a nation that scales back its aspirations."

The ACA, the most important public policy to have emerged from Barack Obama's presidency, was generally viewed from the outset as imperfect. Many Democratic Party supporters and lawmakers would have preferred a new health care law giving government a larger role in funding services. Many Republican Party supporters and lawmakers would have preferred to see government play a very limited role in funding health care.

Some Republicans viewed the ACA as a move toward **socialization of health care**, one that raised the possibility that the government would play a much more significant role in people's lives than had been the case in the past. They especially disliked the requirement of the law that citizens must have some form of health insurance coverage or face fines. Because of these fundamental disagreements with the law, many Republican politicians have done what they can to undermine it. For example, Republican governors resisted the provision of the law that states establish health insurance markets. As a consequence, the U.S. government was obliged to establish those markets. Figure 7.2 indicates states whose governors resisted the ACA expansion of Medicaid.

Although the political disputes continue, citizens who were previously uninsured or struggling to cover health insurance premiums embraced the opportunities the ACA created. Subscription to health insurance schemes offered through the state insurance markets has been strong. Further, the ACA has created dynamics in the health care system prompting providers to pursue cost-saving innovations. Although the ACA is viewed as imperfect, the high degree of disagreement over the role of government in health care has long made significant policy change all but impossible. Despite its imperfections and subsequent efforts to unravel it, the ACA as a policy intervention will continue to dominate the evolution of health care policy and practice for the foreseeable future.

FIGURE 7.2 State Medicaid Expansion Decisions

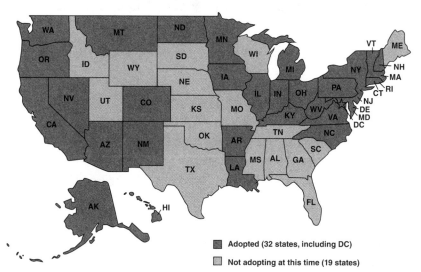

Source: "Status of State Action on the Medicaid Expansion Decision," Kaiser Family Foundation State Health Facts, updated March 14, 2016.

Adopted (32 states, including DC)

Not adopting at this time (19 states)

FEATURES AND IMPACTS OF THE AFFORDABLE CARE ACT OF 2010

The ACA was structured to address gaps and limitations in the existing health insurance system. Rather than introduce changes subsuming established ways of doing things, the act built on many features of the existing public-private system of health insurance.[14]

Key Features

- The ACA launched insurance market reforms that created coverage and affordability standards and allowed for community rating of providers. It required expansion of dependent coverage to the age of 26 and the elimination of lifetime limits on the dollar value of coverage.
- It required all U.S. citizens and legal residents to have qualifying health insurance. Those without coverage pay a tax penalty.
- It established a national high-risk pool to provide health coverage to individuals with preexisting medical conditions and who had been uninsured for at least six months.
- It created state exchanges as marketplaces for low- to moderate-income individuals and small businesses to compare and purchase private insurance meeting specified coverage and cost standards.
- It provided premium subsidies for individuals to purchase private insurance in an exchange.

- Medicaid was broadly expanded in states agreeing to do so (see Figure 7.2). It allowed all individuals under 65 with incomes up to 133 percent of the federal poverty line to be covered by Medicaid.
- Employers with 50 or more full-time employees that did not offer coverage were required to pay a fee of $2,000 per employee, excluding the first 30 employees. Employers with over 200 employees were required to automatically enroll employees into plans offered by the employer. Employees could opt out of coverage.
- The act established a range of measures to prevent illness and promote wellness.

President Barack Obama signed the Patient Protection and Affordable Care Act into law on March 23, 2010, surrounded by others who had worked extensively to promote health care reform as well as family members of citizens who stood to benefit from the reforms.

Impacts

- Coverage options available through the ACA allowed many uninsured Americans to gain coverage. A survey by the Kaiser Family Foundation indicated 11.5 million otherwise uninsured adults gained coverage through marketplaces as of early 2017.[15]
- The uninsured rate dropped most noticeably in states that embraced the ACA's expansion of Medicaid. Among states adopting the expansion, the uninsured rate dropped from 18.4 percent in 2013 to 14.1 percent in 2014. In states not adopting the Medicaid expansion, the uninsured rate dropped from 22.7 percent in 2013 to 20.2 percent in 2014.
- As of early 2017, the Congressional Budget Office predicted that repeal of key provisions of the ACA would result in an immediate loss of health insurance coverage for 18 million people. This number would rise with further reductions in the coverage of Medicaid.[16]

A STABLE, EVOLVING SYSTEM

The complex multiple-payer, multiple-provider system of health care funding and provision in the United States has been in place a long time. Changes to the system will continue, but they will be incremental. Indeed, although the ACA made health insurance coverage possible for many more people than in the past, the act itself did not usher in major changes in the governance or organization of health care services. In that sense, the ACA represented a form of incremental policy making, even though it was characterized as far more dramatic—especially by those who opposed it and have worked to repeal it.[17]

For decades, policy discussions in the United States concerning health care have focused on three issues: costs, coverage, and quality of care. These issues are likely to remain the focus of policy discussions in the years ahead.

HIGH COSTS

The cost of health care is what makes it a major public policy issue. If everyone could afford to pay for medical services and prescription drugs when they need them, there would be little controversy. Presently, those costs make **self-insurance**—saving to cover possible health care eventualities—prohibitively expensive for most people. Thus, there is a tradition that people pool their resources and purchase health insurance. The tying of health benefits to employment has been a defining characteristic of the United States labor market, and the majority of citizens receive health insurance—or at least part of their health insurance—through their employment status, or that of family members. Provision of such health insurance is expensive, because health care costs are expensive. Now, when people are unemployed, too sick to work, or too old to work, government assistance is available to allow them access to health care. But, again, because of the high costs of health care, the costs to the government of programs like Medicare, Medicaid, and the ACA are of major concern.

Many people predict that America's total cost of health care will increase in the coming years as the population ages. This cost will affect governments, businesses, and individuals. Therefore, pressure to contain costs within the health care system will continue. This is likely to have implications for many service providers, including medical professionals, who currently tend to enjoy much higher relative wages in the United States than in other countries.[18]

COVERAGE GAPS

Although the ACA has ensured that millions of Americans now have health insurance coverage where they lacked it in the past, issues of coverage remain:

1. Because of complicated **eligibility rules**, and differences in the number of health insurance providers listed on various state health insurance exchanges, some people remain unable to afford health insurance.
2. Different health insurance schemes offer distinctly different levels of coverage. As a result, many people who have health insurance can still expect to pay out of pocket for many kinds of medical expenses, including prescription drugs. Some of those drugs are hugely expensive, especially when they first enter the market.
3. Major differences exist across the states in terms of accessibility of health services for those who rely on Medicare and Medicaid for this purpose. To the extent that governments and insurance providers cannot impose sufficient pressure on health care providers to contain costs, coverage will inevitably be an issue. With finite resources, those who fund health care services will necessarily need to limit who gets coverage and how comprehensive or scant that coverage will be.

QUALITY OF CARE

At the high end, the quality of care for hospital patients in the United States is considered excellent. Of course, quality care is expensive. Quality of care is uneven across the United States, however, and this inequality has affected overall health statistics (see Table 7.1). As cost pressures continue in the system—posing problems for various funders—it is likely that questions concerning the quality of care and the adequacy of system outcomes will receive close, ongoing scrutiny.

HEALTH CARE AND FEDERAL SYSTEMS OF GOVERNMENT

In the United States, as elsewhere, provision of services that ensure a healthy living environment have historically been provided mainly by local governments. These governments have supported the development of appropriate infrastructural services (water supply, wastewater and sewage disposal). Sometimes city and county governments have also funded local hospital services.

The U.S. federal government has played a major role in funding health research, through the National Institutes of Health (NIH). As noted, through the work of the CDC, the federal government has also taken the lead over many decades in protecting people from major diseases. Increasingly, it has also led the way in expanding access to health care services for disadvantaged groups, through major programs such as Medicare and Medicaid.

At the state level, governments have promoted health care by subsidizing medical schools, through the hospitals associated with them, and through various social insurance schemes. Often state insurance schemes have supplemented federal funds.

An advantage of U.S. federalism is that it has allowed states to adopt policy innovations regarding the provision of health care to citizens. When they are perceived to be effective and desirable, such innovations can be emulated elsewhere in the federal system. Effective policy innovations often spread from state to state, but diffusion from states to the federal level can also occur. For example, efforts in Massachusetts to ensure that all residents of the state held health insurance provided the basic blueprint for provisions in the ACA.

In 2006, Massachusetts adopted a comprehensive health reform package with the intention of providing almost universal health insurance coverage for all state residents. The reforms included actions that changed the use of federal Medicaid funds distributed to the state. Those actions were allowed under a waiver program initially launched by the federal government in 1997 to support an expansion in coverage under Medicaid.[19]

A year after implementing the reform, Massachusetts experienced an unprecedented drop in the number of uninsured. Indeed, the state continues to have the lowest rate of uninsured residents in the country. In 2015, the overall percentage of all people in the United States without health insurance stood at 9 percent. In Massachusetts, the percentage of residents without health insurance was 4 percent.[20] The Massachusetts Health Reform had several features that made it an attractive model for the ACA.[21]

- From the outset, the reform enjoyed broad support from employers, providers, insurers, and citizens.
- It involved insurance market reforms that created coverage and affordability standards and allowed for community rating of providers. The state also merged the individual and small-group markets into a single **risk**

pool—the group of insured people who collectively stand at risk of needing medical treatment. (This action reduced the common "small risk pool" problem of the multi-payer system and the administrative costs involved in addressing it.)

- It created the Connector, a marketplace for individuals and small businesses to compare and purchase private insurance that meets specified coverage and cost standards.
- Medicaid was expanded to cover more children, while eligibility levels for adults, pregnant women, and long-term unemployed remained unchanged.
- Individuals were required to have health insurance or face a financial penalty.
- Employers with 11 or more employees were required to provide insurance or pay a specified "Fair Share" contribution per employee.

The Massachusetts Health Reform did more than provide a model for the architects of the ACA. Because it was well underway by 2008, it had generated evidence of its workability and desirable impacts. Those promoting health reforms at the national level then used this evidence.

In Case Study 7.2 we further explore how federalism accommodates differences in the ways jurisdictions respond to health issues. We also return to the topic of federalism and health care later in this chapter, in the discussion of health care and the promotion of civil rights. Contemporary state-level choices regarding the expansion of Medicaid have opened the possibility of large disparities across states in their numbers of uninsured citizens.

case study 7.2 State and Local Efforts to Reduce Cigarette Smoking

Cigarette smoking is the leading cause of preventable death in the United States. The CDC reports that smoking is responsible for about one in five deaths annually. On average, smokers die 10 years earlier than nonsmokers. More than 480,000 people die per year in the United States from diseases caused by smoking. Meanwhile, more than 16 million Americans are living with diseases caused by smoking. So for every person who dies each year because of smoking,

more than 30 others are living with a serious smoking-related illness.

The costs associated with smoking-related illnesses are huge. It is estimated that, in 2012, nearly $170 billion was spent on direct medical care for adults who fell ill through smoking. The U.S. Department of Health and Human Services reported in 2014 that more than $156 billion is lost to the economy through smoking-related premature deaths and deaths from exposure to secondhand smoke.[22]

TABLE 7.3   Changes in Percentage of Adult Population Smoking Daily, 1980–2011

YEAR	UNITED STATES	CANADA	UNITED KINGDOM
1980	33.2	33.5	39.0
1990	25.5	28.2	30.0
2000	18.2	23.1	27.0
2011	14.8	15.7	19.6

Amid this bad news, there are signs of hope. First, smoking rates in the United States have been steadily decreasing over the past few decades. Table 7.3 reports changes in the percentage of the adult population smoking daily, from 1980 to 2011, for the United States. For comparison, changes in Canada and the United Kingdom are also included in the table.[23] From 1980 to 2011, the United States saw a 55 percent reduction in the share of the adult population smoking.

The major reason smoking has declined appears to be greater willingness on the part of governments to impose **excise taxes** on cigarette sales. These are taxes that apply to nonessential items with the intention of discouraging their purchase. Numerous studies have observed that cigarette consumption decreases when the price of cigarettes increases.[24] Excise taxes have this effect.

In the United States, the federal government, all state governments, and many local governments place excise taxes on cigarettes. At the state level, the size of this tax differs dramatically. A common observation is that these state taxes tend to be lower on average in states where tobacco is a major agricultural product. Note in Table 7.4 the strong relationship between the level of the state excise tax and adult smoking habits.

Table 7.4 indicates state cigarette tax rates and the percent of adults reporting that they currently smoke for selected states. (As the state level data for adult smoking may include adults who smoke less than daily, the average rate across all states is 19.0 percent, 4.2 percent higher than the 14.8 percent national figure for adults smoking daily reported in Table 7.3.) The table also indicates states that are major tobacco producers.[25]

Of the 13 states listed in Table 7.4, 7 impose taxes above $2.50 per 20-pack of cigarettes. Six impose taxes of less than 50 cents per pack. Note two trends:

1. Cigarette use is lower in states with relatively high excise taxes, compared to those with relatively low excise taxes.
2. None of the states with high excise taxes is a major tobacco producer. In contrast,

three of the six states listed as having low excise taxes are major tobacco producers.

Potent as they are, taxes are just one of several policy instruments available for governments seeking to discourage smoking. In the United States, beginning in the 1970s, both local and state governments began experimenting with other policy approaches. These included restrictions on smoking in government buildings, restaurants, and bars. Many private corporations have joined the efforts. Efforts have also been made to curb youth access to cigarettes.

Political scientists Charles R. Shipan and Craig Volden studied the impacts of antismoking policies in U.S. cities on antismoking policies adopted by state governments.[26] They found that policies often bubble up from city governments to state governments. However, the nature of state politics is critical to this relationship. Local-to-state diffusion of antismoking policies was more likely to occur in states where strong health advocates were present. Policy changes were less likely in tobacco-producing states and states with powerful tobacco lobbyists.

TABLE 7.4 Comparing State Taxes on Cigarettes and Cigarette Use, 2013

STATE	STATE CIGARETTE EXCISE TAX[a]	% OF ADULTS REPORTING CURRENT CIGARETTE USE	MAJOR TOBACCO-PRODUCING STATE[b]
States with Relatively High Excise Tax on Cigarettes			
Connecticut	3.40	15.5	0
Hawaii	3.20	13.3	0
Massachusetts	2.51	16.6	0
New York	4.35	16.6	0
Rhode Island	3.50	17.4	0
Vermont	2.62	16.6	0
Washington	3.03	16.1	0
STATES WITH RELATIVELY LOW EXCISE TAX ON CIGARETTES			
Alabama	0.43	21.5	0
Georgia	0.37	18.8	1
Missouri	0.17	22.1	0
North Carolina	0.45	20.3	1
North Dakota	0.44	21.2	0
Virginia	0.30	19.0	1

Note: Evidence in this table collated by the author from data produced by the Centers for Disease Control and Prevention and the Tax Foundation.

[a]Dollars per 20-pack. [b]1 = yes, 0 = no.

CRITICAL THINKING QUESTIONS

1. What policy tools, beyond taxes, can discourage people from smoking?
2. Beyond the example of cigarette taxes and the influence of the tobacco industry, what are some other areas of health-related policy where major interest groups influence policy choices?

HEALTH CARE AND THE INVESTMENT PERSPECTIVE

The investment perspective on public policy proposes that well-chosen actions in the present can generate a stream of positive benefits in the future. The perspective makes a lot of sense in the field of health care, where investment thinking has guided many public policy decisions. Evidence suggests that more consistent and disciplined application of this perspective could yield significantly improved health outcomes at a national level. It could also result in major savings in health care spending.

The challenge to the investment perspective is that reductions in health care costs would be realized many years after the original investments were made. But people tend to discount the future and live, instead, for today.[27] One response involves helping people extend their time horizons. Another is adjusting the opportunities people face in the present, so that the choices they make today align with good outcomes in the years to come.

LONG-TERM BENEFITS OF HEALTH CARE SPENDING

In an in-depth study, Bryan Luce and his colleagues analyzed the return on investment (ROI) of health care in the United States from 1980 to 2000.[28] The authors used three distinctive approaches to explore ROI. First, they calculated that each additional dollar spent on overall health care services produced health gains valued at $1.55 to $1.94. Second, for every additional dollar spent by Medicare, the return on health gains associated with treatment for heart attack, stroke, diabetes, and breast cancer were $1.10, $1.49, $1.55, and $4.80, respectively. Last, the ROI for specific treatment innovations ranged from $1.12 to $38.00 for every additional dollar spent. The authors concluded that the value of improved health in the U.S. population in 2000 versus that in 1980 significantly outweighed additional health care expenditures in 2000 versus those in 1980.

Kevin M. Murphy and Robert H. Topel have offered further powerful evidence of the value of health and longevity to society as a whole.[29] Their chosen method involved calculating the social gains from people living longer and from progress against various diseases. These authors suggested that over the 20th century, cumulative gains in life expectancy were worth over $1.2 million per person for both men and women. By living longer, we are able to generate more income. We also have more years to enjoy life, and to bring comfort and joy to others—although these things are harder to measure.

Murphy and Topel further calculated that between 1970 and 2000, increased longevity added about $3.2 trillion per year to the national wealth of the United States, a previously uncounted value equal to about half of average annual GDP over the period. They suggested that reduced mortality from heart disease alone increased the value of life by about $1.5 trillion per year since 1970. Last, they predicted that potential gains from future innovations in health care would be large. For instance, a modest 1 percent reduction in cancer mortality would be worth nearly $500 billion to the economy as a whole.

The NIH is an important example of the investment perspective being applied to health care. For well over a century, the U.S. government has funded medical research to promote better health outcomes. Today, the NIH has an annual budget of over $30 billion, which supports medical research performed at more than 2,500 universities and university hospitals across the country, as well as at the 25 NIH institutes and centers located in Bethesda, Maryland. It is the largest funder of medical research in the world and a powerhouse for promoting advances in medical science and population health research.[30]

Knowledge generated through NIH sponsorship has served to reduce disability, heart disease, and various forms of cancer, and to prolong life in general. This knowledge has directly benefited citizens of the United States and, through the diffusion of medical and health care innovations, people in many other countries around the world.

GETTING BETTER OUTCOMES AT LOWER COST

The investment perspective underlies recent work by a range of medical and health researchers who have been exploring the potential to reduce current system costs. The motivating question becomes: If other health care systems are getting better results for less, could health care providers in the United States do better?

Three recent studies illustrate how researchers are answering this question. First, Karen Joynt and her colleagues studied high-cost Medicare patients, exploring the possibility that some acute care costs might be avoidable.[31] They found that more than 70 percent of the approximately $92 billion in acute care costs in the Medicare population in 2010 were spent on just 10 percent of patients. This 10 percent comprised the high-cost cohort of interest to the researchers. Heart disease, strokes, cancer, and orthopedic conditions were among the most frequently noted reasons that these patients presented at hospital. By reviewing their records, the researchers concluded that relatively few opportunities existed for preventing acute care spending on this group, once the patients were in the hospital system.

Joynt and her colleagues noted that preventive care measures would likely lead to less demand for acute care services in the long term. That view is consistent with evidence found in a series of studies of Medicare patients produced by J. Michael McWilliams and colleagues.[32] They found that, upon reaching the age of eligibility for Medicare, many people experienced improved health outcomes because they could now access a range of preventive services. From this evidence, we might conclude that early preventive measures are the best-known way to reduce current acute care costs.

A second study on how to achieve better use of resources currently in the system focused on patients not following prescribed treatment regimes. David Cutler and Wendy Everett reported that as many as half of all patients do not adhere faithfully to their prescription medication regimens.[33] As a result, more than $100 billion is spent each year on avoidable hospitalizations. They suggest that the reasons for nonadherence are complex, but addressing even some of the problem would reduce a major source of waste in the present system.

The third study of interest explored reducing medical expenditures through administrative reforms. Based on a literature review, James Mongan, Timothy Ferris, and Thomas Lee concluded that major cost savings could be achieved through payment reform.[34] Hospitals are typically paid for performing specific procedures, as are the medical specialists working in them. As a result, they may use multiple procedures where careful prioritization and fewer procedures might produce similar health outcomes. Mongan and his colleagues also proposed that effort go into developing more efficient medical-record management systems and other ways of reducing general administrative waste.

Another example of the investment perspective in health care concerns the growing popularity of workplace wellness programs. The nature and impact of these programs are the focus of Case Study 7.3.

case study 7.3 Workplace Wellness Programs

The Affordable Care Act of 2010, despite a huge political battle, significantly expanded medical insurance coverage for many low- and middle-income Americans. The ACA was also noteworthy for boosting disease prevention and public health services in the United States.

The Prevention and Public Health Fund allocated $15 billion over 10 years to reduce the prevalence in society of avoidable diseases, such as diabetes, lung cancer, and sexually transmitted diseases. In addition, under the act, insurers were required to provide effective preventive interventions without cost sharing. The act also created new incentives for employers to reduce health insurance premiums through the use of workplace wellness programs. These provisions of the ACA were introduced to spur greater use of services to promote good health among adults and children. Harold A. Pollack described this as "a major policy change that commands attention."[35] Here we discuss workplace wellness programs and treat them as a policy investment.

The places people spend a lot of time together are perfect for promoting good habits of healthy eating, regular exercise, abstinence from smoking, and so on. Schools and workplaces represent prime locations of this kind. Wellness programs have been operating in such contexts for decades, but the provisions of the ACA have brought them more attention. They have also prompted greater scrutiny of their health impacts and economic benefits.

In recent years, Google has often topped *Fortune* magazine's list of the "100 Best Companies to Work For." The company's workplace wellness programs comprise an important cluster in its portfolio of employee benefits. Those benefits include making full fitness facilities available, holding regular fitness classes, and ensuring that healthy food choices are available throughout the day. Google's overarching company philosophy is that healthier people work harder, are happier, help others, and are more efficient. This perspective—that caring for employees

Companies are increasingly creating opportunities for employees to engage in various health and well-being programs, either by creating in-house facilities and programs or by subsidizing attendance at open-to-market programs. When programs are well organized and people form the discipline of regular participation in them, they can support improved health outcomes, which has both immediate and long-term benefits.

(dpa picture alliance/Alamy Stock Photo)

can have broader organizational pay-offs—is well established, and is now pursued by many organizations.

Given that public funds are set aside to promote workplace wellness programs, the fundamental public policy questions are: What impacts do these programs have on health and well-being? What are the costs and benefits associated with these programs? Policy Investment Checklist 7.1 sums up the treatment of workplace wellness programs as a policy investment.[36]

Unfortunately, however, most wellness programs have not been evaluated. Of those that have been, only a minority have employed randomized control trials, or similar research designs that allow confident assessment of program effects. Katherine Baicker, David Cutler, and Zirui Song have conducted a careful analysis of workplace wellness programs and their effects.[37] The research involved a meta-analysis of previous studies of wellness programs. When selecting studies to include in their analysis, they chose only those where the programs of interest had a well-defined intervention and a well-defined treatment and comparison group, even if the comparison group were not strictly randomly assigned. Taking this approach, they ended up analyzing 36 studies. Almost all had been implemented in large firms employing over 1,000 workers. A range of industries were represented. Participation was usually voluntary.

Among the programs that were studied, 80 percent started with a health risk assessment for each participant. Such assessments are commonly used along with tests of blood pressure, cholesterol, and body mass index. These initial assessments provide each employee with information on risk factors that motivate participation. Provision of self-help

case study 7.3 continued

Analyzing Workplace Wellness Programs

1. Focus on Existing Policies and Programs	More than 60% of Americans get their health insurance coverage through an employment-based plan. Employers receive incentives to reduce health care costs and, therefore, to reduce the health insurance premiums they pay. They can accomplish these goals by encouraging healthy behaviors in their employees. Workplace wellness programs tend to be most common in organizations with large workforces.
2. Gather Policy Evidence	A significant meta-analysis noted that in 2006, 19% of U.S. companies with ≥500 reported offering wellness programs. In 2008, 77% of large manufacturing firms reported that they offer formal health and wellness programs. Many such programs have been evaluated. A number have been run as experiments, with pre- and post-trial testing, and use of control groups. The results reported here come from a meta-analysis of 36 studies of wellness programs operating in U.S. workplaces. Of these, 22 assessed differences in health care costs, 22 assessed differences in absenteeism, and 8 assessed both. Nine of the 36 studies randomly assigned employees to the program and control groups.
3. Measure Desired Effects	Two desired effects were considered: 1. Did those employees who participated in a workplace wellness program accrue lower health care costs compared with nonparticipating employees in the same organization? 2. Did participants in a workplace wellness program take fewer days away from work (i.e., on sick leave) compared with nonparticipating employees? The evidence suggested the answer was "yes" to both questions.
4. Assess Costs and Benefits	Simple estimates using reported figures suggest that the average cost per employee per year of the 36 wellness programs was $210, with an average benefit per employee per year of $326. These estimates yield a return on investment of $1.55 for every dollar spent. However, costs, benefits, program duration, and program size differed significantly across workplaces, and the authors of the meta-analysis accounted for these differences. They estimated the average drop in medical costs to be $3.27 for every dollar spent on wellness programs, and the average drop in absentee day costs to be $2.73 for every dollar spent.
5. Offer Robust Advice	Almost all the programs in the meta-analysis were established by large organizations. It is likely those organizations expected the programs to generate desirable outcomes. Thus: 1. We should be cautious in generalizing from the findings; the positive returns on investment estimated here might not be realized across all workplaces investing in wellness programs. 2. This analysis was based on evidence from studies that ran for 1 to 6 years (average duration = 2.5 years). Typically, we could expect the costs of wellness programs to be incurred up front, whereas the benefits might accumulate gradually. Actual returns on investment from such programs could be higher than has been indicated here.

education materials occurred in 42 percent of the programs studied; individual counseling in 39 percent; classes, seminars, and group activities in 36 percent; and added incentives for participation were used in 31 percent. The programs included in the study tended to focus on obesity and smoking, the two top causes of preventable death in the United States. More than 60 percent of the programs explicitly focused on weight loss and fitness. Half focused on smoking, often in conjunction with obesity. Indeed, multiple risk factors were covered in 75 percent of the programs. Beyond obesity and smoking, common risk factors given attention were stress, back care, nutrition, alcohol consumption, and blood pressure.

Of the 36 studies Baicker and her colleagues analyzed, 22 tested for the effects of workplace wellness programs on employee health care costs, 22 focused on employee absenteeism, and 8 examined both. The studies ran over various time periods ranging from one to six years. The authors estimated the ROI for each program. Focusing first on reduced health care costs per employee per year, the authors estimated that for each dollar spent on the workplace wellness programs, on average $3.37 was saved. With respect to reductions in absenteeism, the authors estimated that for each program dollar spent, on average $2.73 was saved through reduction in absenteeism.

It is notable that Baicker and her colleagues found positive ROI for these programs, even over the relatively short time horizons involved. This suggests that longer term, the ROI could be even higher. The authors inferred that these programs were likely to have other benefits as well. Although they did not quantify them, those benefits might include improved quality of life for the individuals concerned, reduced staff turnover, and lower costs for public programs such as disability insurance and Medicare.

CRITICAL THINKING QUESTIONS

1. What features would you find in an ideal workplace wellness program?
2. What other wellness programs could be modeled on those that have already been introduced in workplaces?

HEALTH CARE AND THE PROMOTION OF CIVIL RIGHTS

Martin Luther King Jr. once said, "Of all the forms of inequality, injustice in health care is the most shocking and inhumane."[38] Access to health care is often viewed as a civil rights issue because it is closely tied to many other aspects of social and economic justice. For example, lack of access to quality and affordable health care can be financially devastating for people experiencing a medical emergency and for their families. Likewise, lack of access to health care means serious medical problems can prevent people from engaging in paid work. For these reasons, access to health care is considered a basic human right in many countries.

The ACA was intended to expand access for individuals living in the United States to buy health insurance. One measure to support this involved expanding Medicaid provision by states, so that all citizens living at or below 133 percent of the federal poverty level would be eligible for health care through Medicaid. As noted, Medicaid is funded by the federal government, but administration is delegated to the states. Under the terms of the ACA, the federal government would pay states 100 percent of Medicaid costs for people with incomes up to 133 percent of the federal poverty level through 2017, after which yearly reimbursement levels would decline and remain fixed at 90 percent from 2020. This expansion was expected to greatly increase health insurance coverage among citizens in states currently not holding health insurance.

A 2013 Supreme Court ruling confirmed that individual states could decide for themselves whether or not to support and fund another key component of the act—Medicaid expansion. As of 2016, 32 states, including the District of Columbia, had adopted the Medicaid expansion, 19 had not.

The refusal of 19 states to adopt the Medicaid expansion is curious. Why would any state choose to do that? After all, states have been offered a federally funded program that would provide major benefits to millions of their citizens, contribute billions of dollars to their economies, and help support their health care providers.

Charles Barrilleaux and Carlisle Rainey have used sophisticated quantitative methods to isolate the factors driving why some states have refused to adopt Medicaid expansion. They argue that the states that refused Medicaid expansion actually display more need for it, as judged by the proportion of citizens in their states who were currently uninsured. These authors also noted the politics at play. In their assessment, all states with Democratic governors supported expansion, whereas some Republican governors supported expansion and some opposed it. Most telling is that all the states that opposed expansion had Republican governors. From this evidence, the authors concluded that the politics surrounding Medicaid expansion had been highly partisan. Republican governors tended to resist the expansion, because the ACA was introduced by a Democratic president.

Paul Krugman, a Nobel Prize–winning economist and *New York Times* columnist, explored this matter from the civil rights perspective. In his view, the refusal to expand Medicaid in selective states was evidence of deep racism, which he characterizes as "slavery's long shadow."[39] Krugman admitted such a claim "brings angry denials from many conservatives." Still, his assessment did lead many to wonder whether unexpressed racism continues to influence public policy choices.

To explore this concerning issue, the author of this text noted the states that, as of September 2015, had either expanded or refused to expand Medicaid in line with provisions of the ACA.[40] (Figure 7.2 presents the evidence in a map of the United States.) For all 50 states, he also noted the percentage of the population identified as African American in the latest census.[41] The author then noted states that permitted slavery up to the end of the Civil War. On average, the populations of states that adopted the Medicaid expansion were 8.5 percent African American. In contrast, the populations of states that refused to adopt the expansion were 15.1 percent African American. Among states that never permitted slavery, 76 percent had adopted Medicaid expansion. In contrast, just 31 percent (5 of 16) of states that permitted slavery at the time of the Civil War had adopted Medicaid expansion. These results confirm that states refusing to expand Medicaid had proportionately more African Americans in their populations. They also confirm that former slave states had been considerably more reluctant than others to expand Medicare.

All states recently had a choice to address historic inequalities and perceived injustice in health care. In each case, governors and legislators probably generated reasoned narratives to support their positions. Still, intentionally or not, they passed up a significant opportunity to advance civil rights for their poorest citizens, many of whom are African American. Reflecting on this situation, Paul Krugman observed, "Every once in a while you hear a chorus of voices declaring that race is no longer a problem in America. That's wishful thinking."

THE FUTURE OF HEALTH CARE

For some people, the whole system of health care delivery and funding in the United States looms like a giant train wreck. For others, it is a system that has achieved unparalleled success. Over the past century, it has generated a continuous stream of technologies and practices that promote better health outcomes. At the same time, politicians have found ways to cajole private health care providers and insurance companies to change their practices in ways that increase affordability to average citizens. Further, major government programs have been established and incrementally adjusted to ensure that some of the poorest in society are able to access at least a minimum level of care. In the years ahead, two major health care trends are likely to keep developing in the United States and elsewhere. These both concern the use of information technology.

INFORMATION TECHNOLOGY AND THE PATIENT

Through the Internet, health professionals and ordinary citizens now share access to vast amounts of information on health conditions and their management. This equality of access to medical information is changing relations among doctors, other clinicians, and patients. Patients are increasingly able to ascertain their health care options, given their symptoms. If they are unsure, they can tap social media to hear what others facing similar circumstances have done. Of course, it is important that they tap credible information sources.

In addition to those sources, **bio-sensitive wearable technologies** that monitor basic physiological processes open major possibilities for changing traditional expert–patient relations. Information retrieved from these devices can feed into databases allowing instantaneous checking of an individual's key health metrics. Health care organizations can use such information to identify when specific interventions may be necessary. They can remotely check that patients are taking medications as required—and to issue alerts if they have missed doses. Thus, medical expertise need not be physically located in the same communities (or states, or nations) as the patients seeking help. Meanwhile, closer to home, pharmacies and other health care facilities are also easing the ability for people to undertake tests of biological measures, such as blood glucose or cholesterol levels. The range of such tests is rapidly expanding, and prices are coming down.

Assessing the health care impacts of advances in information technology, Tim Usherwood, a professor of general practice at the University of Sydney, has observed, "Physical infrastructure for emergency management, surgical intervention and care of the very sick will still be needed. But information technology's ability to collapse time and space will increasingly alter how health care is accessed and delivered in the community, enabling the right care every time, and at the patient's convenience."[42]

INFORMATION TECHNOLOGY AND HOSPITAL SYSTEMS

Huge scope exists for using information technology to revolutionize the administration of hospital systems. Jonathan Bush is founder and CEO of athenahealth, a public company that provides cloud-based billing and records software to doctors and hospitals. Bush is also the author of *Where Does It Hurt? An Entrepreneur's Guide to Fixing Health Care.*[43] Bush stated, "The biggest problem with health care is not how expensive it is—it's how inhumane it is." His widely cited quote means that the expenses associated with much health care—especially hospitalization—create formidable barriers for poor people in the United States to receive high-quality care. His solution to the problem is to give more power to patients as consumers of health care.

It is beyond dispute that information technology is opening opportunities for the radical reform of old, expensive ways of managing hospital systems and charging for services. In the process, it is likely hospital administrators will explore new ways of dividing up specialist expertise and use of equipment so that savings can be made. Such savings could be passed back to patients as lowered health insurance premiums, or could allow more care to be covered for the same premium. A variety of procedures once the exclusive domain of medical specialists could be delivered with more cost-effectiveness by medical intermediaries who do not require the same specialist knowledge. This is an argument for reserving use of expensive specialists to perform only those tasks that require specialist skills, while allocating more straightforward elements of procedures to others. Such reforms are more likely to result from competition and innovation in elements of medical service provision than from changes in public policy.

LESSONS FOR PUBLIC POLICY

Access to good health care can be transformative for societies, both improving people's quality of life and prolonging lives—yet, delivering good quality health care is expensive. The continuously rising cost of health care, as a proportion of GDP, has led to calls for fundamental changes in how health care systems are managed. Several lessons for public policy come from observing trends in health care and the roles that governments play in its funding and delivery.

- Market competition among health service providers in the United States has driven ongoing technological advances. Medical care in the United States is recognized as world leading, and many hospitals and clinics have specialist teams known for their efforts to expand the frontiers of good medical practice.
- Major advances in medical and health-related research must be supported by government sources. The U.S. government, through the National Institutes of Health, has taken a leading role in promoting medical research. That research has often laid the foundation for technology transfer and commercialization efforts. Since all people stand to gain—eventually—from advances in health care knowledge, it makes sense that the underlying science should be publicly funded.
- The United States is not alone in having experienced many fraught debates over directions for health care funding. No country anywhere has a perfect system in place for funding health care. Many governments worry about its growing costs, and many have tried various reform efforts over recent decades. The health care case offers an example of **path dependency**. That is, once a system of health care funding is in place, and specific interest groups have identified stakes in that system, any efforts to deviate from that path will meet with powerful resistance.
- As long as pressures remain on governments in the United States to promote greater affordability of services, the country's system of health care will remain under pressure to deliver better health outcomes for a greater number of people at lower costs. Such pressures, and the competitive dynamics at the heart of the system, create good conditions for promoting continuous innovation in the health care sector.
- Looking to the long term, innovation should be encouraged at every step in the huge systems of health care that now exist in the United States, as it should be for other nations.
- The investment perspective on public policy is indeed applicable to health care. That all of us can expect to live longer and in better health than our forebears is testament to the vast gains that have come from previous investments in health research and the development of health care systems.

Much scope exists for improving the administration of various facets of the health care system. The top short-term priority should be to reduce the costs of health care, while avoiding actions that would compromise health outcomes. Paralleling these goals, further efforts should be made to maintain strong funding for basic medical and related sciences. Such scientific work is fundamental for saving lives and enhancing the quality of life for everyone, including generations to come.

CHAPTER SUMMARY

This chapter has explored public policy issues in health care. When most citizens in a nation are able to live long, healthy lives, everyone benefits. Healthy people can contribute to family life, enrich their communities, and support themselves and others through paid work. Wealthy nations tend to devote more of their GDP to health care than do poorer nations. With wealth, societies gain more appreciation for human capability and the importance of keeping people healthy and socially engaged.

The chapter has shown that the United States has developed a unique public-private model of health care funding. It relies on private health insurance systems and on private or not-for-profit organizations to provide health and hospital services. Over time, the role played by government in funding health care in the United States has expanded. Medicare and Medicaid are the fundamental programs through which the federal government, aided by state governments, provides insurance coverage to those who otherwise would not receive it.

The Affordable Care Act expanded Medicaid, made a range of regulatory changes, and established state health insurance exchanges to extend health coverage to those who previously could not access any kind of insurance. Because the ACA extended the reach of government, many opponents have criticized it as an example of overbearing government encroaching on individual freedoms and market processes.

In this chapter we have also considered how U.S. federalism has allowed local and state governments to contribute to the design of policies extending access to health care and promoting improved health outcomes. Massachusetts was a crucial policy innovator in extending health insurance coverage to all residents and created a blueprint for key features of the ACA. Thus, many state governments have been vital partners of the federal government in the recent expansion of Medicaid.

Meanwhile, supporters of the expansion of insurance coverage, and other provisions of the ACA, welcomed it for the way it extended health and financial security to millions of people. Indeed, measures introduced in the ACA—including the expansion of Medicaid to cover more people on low incomes—can be viewed as contributing to the advancement of civil rights.

Health care provision in the United States has been continuously shaped by the innovations of private entities. Scientific knowledge concerning ways to maintain human health has frequently informed the development of those innovations; looking ahead, we should expect many more.

Health care lends itself to the approach of treating public policies as investments. Preventive care and wellness programs show how relatively small amounts of current spending can avert costly future interventions. With politicians, providers of medical services, insurance companies, and citizens focused on the costs of health care, we can expect to see the prominence of investment thinking in health policy discussions grow.

CONNECTIONS TO OTHER CHAPTERS

Governments can play an important role in helping as many people as possible achieve and maintain good health. In this sense, public policies relating to health care parallel public policies that contribute to the development and maintenance of physical infrastructure (Chapter 4). There are also important connections between environmental protection and the maintenance of safe and healthy living conditions in which communities can thrive (Chapter 11).

For individuals, enjoying good health opens many possibilities. Healthy children are better able than others to participate fully in schooling and develop the skills and knowledge to become effectively contributing members of society (Chapter 6). When people suffer from poor health, it is harder for them to engage in society. This limitation can reduce their ability to prepare themselves for paid work, enter the workforce, and maintain stable employment. Important connections exist between health care and the alleviation of poverty (Chapter 8).

Last, scientific and technical advances have proven fundamental to enhancing the quality of health care and making it more affordable. Connections also exist between this discussion of health care and our discussion of science funding (Chapter 10).

KEY TERMS

Negative externalities

Spillover effects

Positive externalities

Immunization programs

Public goods

Credentialing systems

Social equity

Pooling resources

Incentives alignment

Copayments

Deductibles

Nonmedical determinants

Wellness programs

Single-payer systems

Multi-payer systems

Medicare

Medicaid

Entitlement program

Affordable Care Act

Socialization of health care

Self-insurance

Eligibility rules

Excise taxes

Bio-sensitive wearable technologies

Risk pool

Path dependency

SUGGESTIONS FOR FURTHER READING

Gusmano, Michael K., and Sara Allin. "Health Care for Older Persons in England and the United States: A Contrast of Systems and Values." *Journal of Health Politics, Policy and Law* 36, no. 1 (2011): 89–118. A useful comparative treatment of health systems and their outcomes.

Haeder, Simon F. "Beyond Path Dependence: Explaining Healthcare Reform and Its Consequences." *Policy Studies Journal* 40, no. S1 (2012): 65–86. A good discussion of how specific ways of providing access to health care tend to shape and limit future policy options.

Mongan, James J., Timothy G. Ferris, and Thomas H. Lee (2008). "Options for Slowing the Growth of Health Care Costs." *New England Journal of Medicine* 358, no. 14 (April 3, 2008)): 1509–14. A very good survey of ways to reduce costs in health care—a vital issue.

Vladeck, Bruce C., and Thomas Rice. "Market Failure and the Failure of Discourse: Facing Up to the Power of Sellers." *Health Affairs* 28, no. 5 (2009): 1305–15. Application of basic economic thinking to explore market power in the U.S. health care system.

Weissert, William G., and Carol S. Weissert. *Governing Health: The Politics of Health Policy,* 4th ed. Baltimore, MD: Johns Hopkins University Press, 2012. An excellent overview of the policies and politics that influence health care delivery in the United States.

WEBSITES

- The U.S. Department of Health and Human Services is the U.S. government's principal agency for protecting the health of all Americans and providing essential human services. Its "Open Government" program provides access to health information and health datasets generated or held by the U.S. government. This is a one-stop resource for data into new applications, services, and insights that can help improve health. www.healthdata.gov

- The National Institutes for Health are the U.S. medical agency, supporting scientific studies that turn discovery into health. www.nih.gov

- The Henry J. Kaiser Family Foundation offers an extensive array of documents and data sources relating to contemporary health care issues in the United States. http://kff.org/

- Trust for America's Health is a nonprofit, nonpartisan organization dedicated to saving lives by protecting the health of every community and working to make disease prevention a national priority. www.healthyamericans.org

FOR DISCUSSION

1. The United States has long led the world in medical research. When debates about the affordability of health care have occurred there, those favoring a free market approach have always made the claim that the market-like nature of much health care funding is essential to the pursuit of highest-quality health care practices. What is the link between the health care market and continuous advancement in medical technology?

2. The affordability of health care to low- and middle-income Americans remains an ongoing concern. Health policy researchers have made many suggestions for reducing costs and waste in various parts of this complex, privately and publicly funded system of health care delivery. One common view is that savings made in some parts of the system could be used to promote affordability in others. (a) Where are some good places to look for savings in the current system? (b) What system features could inhibit the reallocation of savings to promoting greater affordability for low- and middle-income groups? (c) Where might reallocation be achieved most easily?

3. The World Health Organization regularly reports health statistics by country (see, for example, its *World Health Statistics 2016*), as does the OECD (see *Health at a Glance: OECD Statistics, 2016*). These statistics show that high-income countries tend to spend higher proportions of their GDP on health care than do middle- and low-income countries. Further, life expectancies are significantly higher in high-income countries than in low-income countries. What explanations would you give for the observation that high-income countries spend even higher proportions of their GDP on health care than do other countries?

CHAPTER 8

POVERTY ALLEVIATION

The United States is one of the richest countries in the world. Most Americans live well; nevertheless, many do not. Official U.S. Census Bureau statistics reveal that, at any given time, at least 1 in 10 Americans lives in poverty. In 2016, more than 45 million Americans were in poverty; of those, 15 million, or around one in five, were children. When people are in poverty, they often feel hungry. They tend to eat cheap, unhealthy food. Other necessities of life become hard to acquire. People in poverty often have a meager set of clothes, lack safe and healthy housing, and find it difficult to access health care. Children in impoverished households can suffer great hardship.

Through history, poverty as a social phenomenon has spurred considerable charity work and political organizing by better-off people seeking to help those in need. The development of modern welfare states has either stemmed from or built on systems of charity developed by church groups and private philanthropists. Today, many countries have government programs operating alongside traditional forms of voluntary charity. When individuals lack resources to look after themselves properly, some form of direct financial assistance can be highly beneficial. However, hardship and need can arise on multiple fronts. Because of this wide range, access to affordable housing, health care, and other services can also help alleviate poverty.

Since government programs to assist the poor usually involve transferring money from those who are better off, they often breed resentment. For centuries, notions have existed about who comprise "the deserving poor," compared with those deemed "undeserving." In the United States, the attributes of individual freedom, self-reliance, and self-improvement represent bedrock social values. Consequently, public sentiments have always been ambivalent toward the development of a welfare state. Government assistance to the poor has tended to be carefully targeted and grudgingly given. Nevertheless, during the

Facing page: Volunteers at the Glide Memorial United Methodist Church in San Francisco prepare meals for local people experiencing homelessness and poverty.

(AP Photo/Julie Jacobson)

20th century, the federal government came to play an increasingly important role in funding and coordinating poverty alleviation programs. These have been—and continue to be—delivered in partnership with state and local governments. The work of charities also remains essential for helping the poor. In the sections that follow, we will discuss the development of poverty alleviation efforts in the United States and contemporary policy issues. In doing so, we will explore how we might view such efforts as investments.

This chapter introduces you to:

- Alternative definitions of poverty
- Patterns of poverty in the United States
- Common causes of poverty
- The reasons why governments have an interest in poverty alleviation and have established major programs to assist those in need
- Traditional government approaches to poverty alleviation in the United States
- Features of key poverty-alleviation programs
- The important role of federalism in coordinating government responses to poverty
- Contemporary policy issues relating to poverty
- Application of the investment perspective to poverty alleviation
- Poverty alleviation and the promotion of civil rights
- Lessons for public policy emerging from this review of poverty alleviation

DEFINITIONS OF POVERTY

What does it mean to be poor? Although most people can give a general answer, precise definitions can be elusive. Among those who study poverty, a collective view has emerged that poverty is best understood in two distinctive ways. The first is absolute poverty; the second is relative poverty. Each definition has several possible variants. Here, we begin by exploring the meaning of each term and the relationship between the two. This approach leads into a discussion of the psychology of poverty. We then review the official definition of poverty in the United States.

Fortunately, poverty is rarely a permanent feature of people's lives. In the United States, as in other wealthy countries, many adults experience short-term periods of poverty due to changes in their paid employment status, or in that of those they depend on for support. In a special research project, the U.S. Census

Bureau estimated that during the four-year period from 2009 to 2012, 34.5 percent of the U.S. population had at least one spell of poverty lasting two or more months. Chronic poverty over the same four-year period was relatively uncommon. From 2009 to 2012, 2.7 percent of the population lived in poverty through all 48 months.[1] Historically, many people who have experienced poverty as children have been able to escape it in adulthood. For people with conditions that make it difficult to work, however, the threat of long-term poverty is greater.

ABSOLUTE POVERTY VERSUS RELATIVE POVERTY

Many people experience poverty in groups—for example, as a family or household. The existence of poverty in a household is usually determined by comparing total household income with the number of adults and children within it. Assumptions are made concerning the needs of adults and children and how income is distributed among individuals in the household. Judgments can then be made, with the use of a poverty line, as to whether a household is experiencing poverty. A **poverty line** is a dollar figure deemed by experts in nutrition and household budgeting to be sufficient to support at least a subsistence level of living for a certain period of time. For example, in 2015, the World Bank declared that many people in the world were living on less than $2 per day. The figure of $2 per day represents a poverty line. It could equally be represented by the figure of $14 per week or $730 per year.

For a household composed of a single adult, it is easy to determine if that adult is living above or below the poverty line. Determinations become more complicated when households have multiple members, when some adults have incomes and others do not, and when children are present. Generally, when governments or international agencies seek to make determinations about what members of a population are living in poverty, they apply different poverty lines to different households based on their composition. As the number of people living in a household increases, so too does the associated dollar figure comprising the poverty line. Taking the World Bank figure just noted, the poverty line for a household comprising two adults would equal $4 per day.

When people experience **absolute poverty**, they are deemed unable to meet basic needs for living—that is, they lack sufficient food to maintain good health, and they may have difficultly accessing safe drinking water. In addition, absolute poverty often connotes a lack of sanitary living conditions—for example, access to proper toilets and facilities for regular bathing or showering. Housing is also usually marginal and limited for those in absolute poverty. They may need to shelter in the outdoors, or in makeshift accommodations. People in absolute poverty often seek shelter or temporary accommodation from others, which usually means sharing crowded spaces.

Scholars of poverty distinguish between absolute and relative poverty. The concept of **relative poverty** captures the understanding that people living in economically advanced societies might experience significant hardship even though their circumstances do not place them in absolute poverty. Peter Townsend (2016) offers a useful definition of relative poverty: "People may be said to be deprived if they do not have, at all, or sufficiently, the conditions of life—that is the diets, amenities, standards of services—which allow them to play the roles, participate in the relationships and follow the customary behavior which is expected of them by virtue of their membership in society."[2] This definition is helpful for a discussion of poverty in wealthy countries.

To participate fully in a sophisticated market economy, all of us require significant personal resources. From the perspective of developing economies where people live on $2 a day, the vast majority of people in the United States live well. However, it is clear that access to food, clean water, minimal clothing, and basic shelter is not sufficient to allow satisfactory economic and social engagement. When we think of poverty as a relative concept, our estimates of an appropriate poverty line tend to rise dramatically. In 1993, the U.S. General Social Survey asked the following question: "People who have income below a certain level can be considered poor. That level is called the 'poverty line.' What amount of weekly income would you use as a poverty line for a family of four (husband, wife, and two children) in this community?" Updated to reflect 2016 dollars, the answers ranged from around $40 per week (less than $2 per person per day) to $2,500 per week (closer to $90 per person per day). The average response was about $570, or a little over $20 per person per day.[3] The wide range of these responses reveals notions of poverty are subjective. Our judgments are shaped by our own lives and the resources we can access.

THE PSYCHOLOGY OF POVERTY

Thinking of poverty in relative terms reminds us that people tend to evaluate their own circumstances through comparison with those around them. Thus, poverty often affects people's sense of self and can be demoralizing and stressful.[4] Sendhil Mullainathan and Eldar Shafir apply insights from cognitive psychology and behavioral economics to understand human decision making. They have sought to understand the impact of poverty on how people process information and make day-to-day decisions. In their view, poverty drives people to focus intently on their immediate financial problems in a way that restricts the attention they pay to other important matters. They call this limited focus the "bandwidth tax." For people in economic stress, such a mindset restricts their ability to reflect more broadly on their current circumstances and how they might get beyond them. Indeed, the myopia created by poverty can lead people in such circumstances to make poor choices, some of which can contribute to keeping them in poverty. Mullainathan and Shafir suggest:

> If you want to understand the poor, imagine yourself with your mind elsewhere. You did not sleep much the night before. You find it hard to think clearly. Self-control feels like a challenge. You are distracted and easily perturbed. And this happens every day. On top of the other material challenges poverty brings, it also brings a mental one.[5]

Mullainathan and Shafir suggest that this insight is important for public policy designers seeking to reduce poverty. We will shortly begin discussing such matters. For now, let us consider the possibility that some public policies designed to move people out of poverty might have unintended and unhelpful consequences because of the additional stress they induce.

THE OFFICIAL DEFINITION OF POVERTY IN THE UNITED STATES

For administrative purposes, poverty is often defined purely in monetary terms. The U.S. Census Bureau uses a set of poverty lines or **money income thresholds** that vary by family size and composition to determine who is in poverty. If a family's total income is less than the family's threshold, that family and every individual in it is considered in poverty. The poverty thresholds used today were originally derived in 1963–1964, by combining U.S. Department of Agriculture food budgets designed for families under economic stress with data about what portion of their incomes families spend on food. A judgment was made that families require three times the amount they spend on food in order to live above the poverty line. The thresholds established through that exercise have been revised ever since, to take account of annual changes in the **Consumer Price Index**—that is, the average percentage change from year to year in the cost of purchasing a standard set of consumption items. Table 8.1 presents the U.S. Census Bureau's poverty thresholds for 2015. The threshold for a single adult aged 18 to 64 was $12,331; for a family comprising two adults and two children it was $24,036.

Suppose a family has four members, two adults and two children. As noted, their threshold income in 2015 was officially defined as $24,036. If the two adults made $25,000 between them, this amount would be deemed the total family income. Since that income is above the $24,036 threshold, this family was considered not to be in poverty.

The official definition of poverty in the United States combines notions of absolute poverty and relative poverty. It is consistent with use of absolute poverty measures because the money income thresholds are applied consistently across household groups and across geographical locations. Yet it is also consistent with relative poverty measures because the money income thresholds were designed with specific reference to the cost of living in the United States.

It is instructive to compare the official income thresholds with median household incomes in the United States. In 2015, the Census Bureau declared the median household income to be $56,516.[6] Its poverty thresholds for most forms of household composition fall well below the median level of household income. Even for a large family comprising two adults and six children, the official poverty threshold in 2015 was $38,999—around 70 percent of the nation's median household income. It is equivalent to about $13 per day per person, or $90 per person per week. In Focus 8.1 further explores the nature of poverty in the United States.

TABLE 8.1 U.S. Census Bureau Poverty Thresholds for 2015 by Size of Family and Number of Related Children under 18 Years

SIZE OF FAMILY UNIT	WEIGHTED AVERAGE POVERTY THRESHOLDS	RELATED CHILDREN UNDER 18 YEARS								
		0	1	2	3	4	5	6	7	≥8
One person (unrelated individual)	12,082									
Under 65 years	12,331	12,331									
65 years and over	11,367	11,367									
Two people	15,391										
Householder under 65 years	15,952	15,871	16,337								
Householder 65 years and over	14,342	14,326	16,275								
Three people	18,871	18,540	19,078	19,096							
Four people	24,257	24,447	24,847	24,036	24,120						
Five people	28,741	29,482	29,911	28,995	28,286	27,853					
Six people	32,542	33,909	34,044	33,342	32,670	31,670	31,078				
Seven people	36,998	39,017	39,260	38,421	37,835	36,745	35,473	34,077			
Eight people	41,029	43,637	44,023	43,230	42,536	41,551	40,300	38,999	38,668		
Nine people or more	49,177	52,493	52,747	52,046	51,457	50,490	49,159	47,956	47,658	45,822

Source: U.S. Census Bureau, "Poverty Thresholds by Size of Family and Number of Children," 2016, http://www.census.gov/data/tables/time-series/demo/income-poverty/historical-poverty-thresholds.html.

Note: All figures are in U.S. dollars.

in focus 8.1

PATTERNS OF POVERTY IN THE UNITED STATES

The U.S. Census Bureau produces annual reports comparing recent poverty figures with earlier ones. The Census Bureau statistics shown in Figure 8.1 indicate poverty rates over time.[7]

The official poverty rate in the United States in 2015 was 13.5 percent. That figure was slightly lower than the official poverty rate for the years since 2008 when the U.S. economy was in recession. The general pattern for the official poverty rate is that it declined dramatically in the 1960s and reached its lowest levels during the 1970s. In the early 1980s, the rate moved closer to 15 percent. Since then, it has moved within the band lying between 10 and 15 percent. Whenever there is recession, the poverty rate increases. Figure 8.1, showing the poverty rate has never gone below 10 percent, replicates the Census Bureau's record of changes in the official poverty rate. Figure 8.1 also indicates periods between 1959 and 2015 when the U.S. economy was in recession. Significantly, there was a rise in the poverty rate during every recession, indicating the importance of overall economic performance for affecting employment opportunities for individuals and—by extension—their risk of falling into poverty.

When statisticians break the population down by demographic groups, different poverty rates are revealed. For example, separating people by age offers one set of insights. During the 1960s, the poverty rate was relatively high among the elderly, those aged 65 and older. A valid explanation would appear to be that untreated health problems kept many with limited alternate sources of income from participating in paid work. However, due to important public policy changes, it started declining. By the mid-1970s, the poverty rate for this group had dropped below that of children and young people (those under age 18). Since then, poverty among the young has always been higher than poverty among the elderly. Figure 8.2 replicates the Census Bureau's record of changes in the official poverty rate for these groups. It also shows that, historically, the group with the lowest poverty rate has been working-age adults, those

FIGURE 8.1 Poverty Rate in the United States (as Percentage of the Full Population), 1959–2015

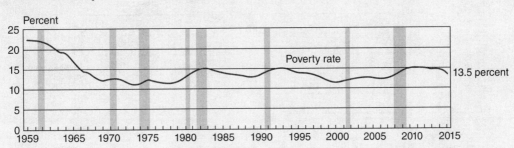

Source: Bernadette D. Procter, Jessica L. Semega, and Melissa A. Kollar, Income and Poverty in the United States: 2015 (Washington, DC: U.S. Census Bureau, September 13, 2016), Fig. 4, p. 12. Shaded bands indicate recessions.

aged 18 to 64. However, the poverty rate among this group has trended upward since around 2000, when it started to be higher than that of those aged 65 and older.

Stark differences in poverty rates appear when people are grouped by characteristics like gender, race, and ethnicity. In 2015, among those aged 65 and older, the female poverty rate was 10.3 percent compared with the male rate of 7.0 percent. In the same year, for those aged 18 to 64 years, the female poverty rate was 14.2 percent compared with the male rate of 10.5 percent. There was hardly any difference along gender lines for children and young people, for whom the overall poverty rate in 2015 was 19.7 percent. However, in 2015, among all age groups, the poverty rate for non-Hispanic whites was 10.1 percent. This compares with rates of 24.1 percent for blacks, 21.4 percent for Hispanics, and 11.4 percent for Asians.

Other between-group differences in poverty rates are significant. Here, we briefly consider differences with respect to immigration status, educational status, and whether a person has a disability. In 2015, 86.5 percent of the U.S. population was native born, compared with 13.5 percent foreign born. Among the native-born population, the poverty rate was 13.1 percent, compared with 16.6 percent for those who were foreign born. Among the foreign born, differences in poverty rates were stark between those who have become naturalized U.S. citizens (11.2 percent) and those who have not (21.3 percent).

With respect to educational attainment, in 2015 the poverty rate among those with at least a bachelor's degree was 4.5 percent. For those with a high school diploma but with no college the rate was 12.9 percent. For those without a high school diploma it was 26.3 percent. Physical and mental disability also affects the

FIGURE 8.2 Poverty Rate in the United States by Age Group, 1959–2015

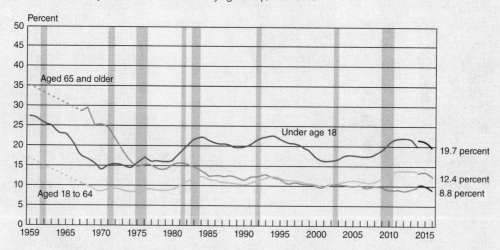

Source: Bernadette D. Procter, Jessica L. Semega, and Melissa A. Kollar, Income and Poverty in the United States: 2015 (Washington, DC: U.S. Census Bureau, September 13, 2016), Fig. 5, p. 14. Shaded bands indicate recessions.

Note: The data for 2013 and beyond are based on redesigned income questions, hence the discontinuities at 2013. Data for people aged 18 to 64 and aged 65 and older are not available from 1960 to 1965, hence the dotted lines.

likelihood that people will live in poverty. For those aged 18 to 64, in 2015 the poverty rate for those with a disability was 28.5 percent compared with 11.0 percent for those without.

Given that states differ with respect to racial and ethnic composition, we should expect variations in state poverty rates. The map in Figure 8.3 shows a snapshot of the 2015 poverty rate by state. Southern states tend to have higher poverty rates than other states, especially when compared with states in the Midwest. Beyond these differences in state poverty rates, other patterns exist in the geography of poverty. There is a strong tendency in the United States—as in other developed countries—for people living in the same suburb to share broadly similar income levels. Consequently, more diversity in poverty rates is revealed in county-level data.

FIGURE 8.3   Poverty Rate by State (as Percentages of Full State Populations), 2015

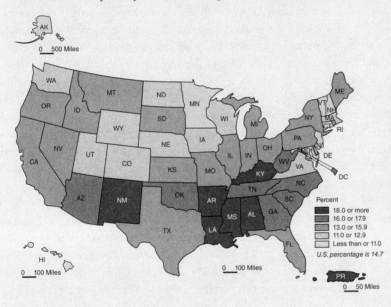

Source: U.S. Census Bureau, 2016, http://www.census.gov/ library/visualizations/2016/ comm/cb16-158_poverty_ map.html.

COMMON CAUSES OF POVERTY

We have already seen that individual characteristics—like youth or old age, or living with a disability—can increase people's risk of experiencing poverty. We have also seen that poverty rates usually rise during economic recessions. These factors suggest that there are both individual and broader, or structural, reasons why people might fall into poverty. We can identify **structural causes of poverty** by asking: Could an adult who fell into poverty because of this cause have realistically done anything to avoid the outcome? If our answer is "no," the cause was most likely structural. That said, poverty often has **individual causes**, where something about an individual's capabilities or personal choices contributed to his or her poverty.

In a discussion of individual causes, "blaming the victim" frequently takes place. Certainly, there are times when their life choices have led people—and their children—into poverty. But blaming the victim is not a useful way to explain why people are in poverty and what they and we can do about it. Unfortunately, however, the language of blame and the concept of the "culture of poverty" have influence, and they have often shaped policy making.

ECONOMIC CONDITIONS

People are more likely to experience poverty when they live in places with poor economic conditions. Those conditions can occur because of several factors. First, industries that once employed many local residents have gone into decline or actually disappeared. For example, workers have often lost employment when automobile manufacturing plants have closed. Likewise, the end of coal-mining activities has left local workers with specific skills unable to find suitable alternate employment. These local conditions can be the result of both the decision making of specific firms or broader changes. A given firm might decide that its operations in one location are no longer viable compared with those elsewhere—either somewhere in the same country, or overseas. And sometimes whole industries go through **economic transformations**. For example, use of robots in manufacturing can reduce the number and type of jobs across an industry, and the effects might be global in scope. Historically, widespread economic transformations have dramatically affected working populations. During all such transformations, some workers are able to make suitable adjustments and avoid poverty, while others either cannot or will not.

Second, poverty rates rise during **economic recessions.** Recessions occur when the whole economy temporarily slows and annual changes in Gross Domestic Product switch from positive (say, 2% to 3%) to zero or negative (say, –2% or –3%) for two consecutive fiscal quarters. The causes of recessions are complicated. National governments have the ability to manage the broader economy—the macro economy—through their taxation and spending decisions, their control of government debt levels, and their influence on the circulation of money in the economy. State and local governments have less ability to control their overall economic conditions, because only the national government can control monetary policy. Further, many state constitutions limit the capacity for their governments to go into debt to fund current activities—a strategy that may allow them to stimulate their local economies during a downturn.

Third, sometimes local, state, and national economies are hit by **exogenous shocks**—unanticipated events that can have immediate and devastating effects and often plunge people into periods of poverty. The terrorist attacks of September 2001 had an immediate and negative impact upon the economy of New York City and more broadly that of the United States. Those who lost loved ones in the attacks often suffered a range of hardships, including poverty. The attacks also led to declines in the tourism sector of the economy, which had negative spillover effects on low-wage workers. Likewise, adverse weather events like Hurricane Katrina in 2005, which caused widespread devastation in New Orleans and the Gulf States, and Hurricane Sandy in 2012, which affected the mid-Atlantic states, can drive large numbers of people in the affected regions into short-term poverty.

IMMIGRATION

There are many reasons why people emigrate from one country to another. People with high skills developed in one country might shift voluntarily to another where those skills attract higher remuneration. In such cases, immigration produces major financial gains for those prepared to take a risk and move. However, there are times when people emigrate involuntarily because of difficulties in their homeland. For centuries, wars, persecution of ethnic minorities, and economic transformations have been responsible for many people moving between countries. Frequently, when people make such moves, they suffer temporary hardship and find themselves in poverty. We noted earlier that U.S. poverty rates tend to be higher among immigrants compared with native-born people. However, the evidence that poverty rates are lower among naturalized citizens also suggests that immigrants are often on an upward financial trajectory and their living conditions improve over time.

Recent turmoil in the Middle East and Africa has resulted in a refugee crisis. Many refugees from Syria have sought safety and new lives for themselves in Europe. Some have settled further afield, including in the United States. In the process, despite having held lucrative jobs in their homeland, they can go through lengthy employment in low-paid jobs or unemployment where they relocate, leaving them vulnerable to falling into poverty. It can also be difficult for some immigrants to assimilate to a new country when they come from places with a different common language and different cultural traditions.

Politicians, reflecting the concerns of voters, often worry that an influx of immigrants may harm the economic circumstances of local citizens. Whether those worries are well-founded in any specific case is an empirical question. Nonetheless, when immigration is not carefully managed, the risks of such outcomes increase. In the short term, greater numbers of unskilled workers in an economy will inevitably increase competition for jobs. In such circumstances, employers will probably pay low wages, confident that people will still want to work for them. The overall effect can be more people living either in poverty or in fear of it.

LACK OF EDUCATION AND TRAINING

Earlier, we noted stark differences in poverty rates based on people's level of educational attainment. In the United States, as in other wealthy countries, those who did not complete high school are more likely to be in poverty than those who did. Those with university degrees are least at risk. Getting an educational qualification is a powerful way for people to avoid falling into poverty for two reasons. First, with education, people acquire general knowledge and skills that allow them to bring value to any employment situation. Second, educational attainment is a strong marker of an individual's capacity to learn. Thus, people with a sound education are generally better able to switch from one sector to another and quickly build the sector-specific skills and knowledge they need to thrive in a new work environment.

A major challenge in advanced economies, like that of the United States, is that people increasingly need to display strong communication and analytical skills to gain entry to paid work. The days when strength mattered more than verbal or thinking skills are long gone. It is now becoming much harder for people who have not completed high school to thrive in the job market.[8]

Although lack of education might seem an individual cause of poverty, various structural forces beyond people's control can shape their chances of gaining a good education in the first place. For example, when people have experienced poverty as children, they often have not been able to make the most of the public schooling opportunities open to them. Further, variation in public school funding often means children growing up in poverty in the United States face a double deficit. Because of limited funds, the public schools they attend frequently lack the teaching talent and resources to help them thrive through their school years, attain a higher education, and subsequently break out of poverty in adulthood.

HEALTH PROBLEMS AND PHYSICAL AND MENTAL DISABILITIES

Health problems can have two effects that place individuals at greater risk of falling into poverty. First, when people suffer severe health problems, they usually need to take time off work. If they lack provisions for paid sick days, they can lose income. Second, treatment of health problems often requires patients to cover some of the costs themselves. Health insurance coverage still does not protect everyone. Indeed, even those with health insurance often face a range of out-of-pocket expenses, including the costs of prescription drugs. Such health-associated costs can plunge individuals and families into poverty.

Earlier, we noted that poverty rates are significantly higher among those who live with a physical or mental disability than among those who do not. As with chronic health problems, disabilities can seriously impair people's ability to participate in the paid workforce. Whenever people have difficulty working, they face the prospect of receiving lower incomes and, hence, living closer to the poverty line. As people age, many become frail; their risk of experiencing poor health and disabilities grows. Lacking savings, a pension, family support, or government assistance, elderly people can fall into poverty with little prospect of escaping it—an explanation of why elderly people have tended historically to face poverty at higher rates than people aged 18 to 64.

FAMILY CIRCUMSTANCES

Family circumstances also affect a person's likelihood of living in poverty. First, responsibilities for care can make it hard for families to make ends meet. If there are dependents in a household, pressure on those who are able-bodied can lead them to make difficult trade-offs between their participation in paid work and their domestic care responsibilities. The birth of a new baby, caring for an elderly relative, and assisting other family members through difficulties represent just some of the factors that can strain family finances.

Second, family location can lead to poverty. People often live in places where good and suitable jobs are hard to find, yet moving can be a challenge. Learning where better jobs might be is not easy, especially for people who lack adequate education. Even when people know that they would face better circumstances elsewhere, family ties or lower accommodation costs might keep them in their current location. Last, transport complexities and costs can reduce earning potential. Many people live far from the places where they would find the most desirable jobs. Getting to work can prove difficult and moving might bring higher housing costs. Family circumstances of this sort help explain why people do not simply go where the jobs are.

EMPLOYMENT DISCRIMINATION

Employment discrimination occurs when people are not offered employment or given opportunities for promotion based on specific aspects of their identity, such as their race or gender. Increasingly, laws in the United States and elsewhere prohibit employment discrimination, such as the Equal Pay Act (1963) and the Civil Rights Act (1964). Nonetheless, African Americans have faced extensive employment discrimination in the United States, and thus as a group have experienced higher levels of poverty compared with people of other races and ethnicities. Likewise, women have historically faced many forms of employment discrimination. It has been difficult for women to break into specific occupation categories such as science or engineering because these have been identified—explicitly or implicitly—as jobs for men only. It is easy to see how forms of employment discrimination have forced individuals and groups of people to work in certain occupations that are relatively low paid, come with fewer benefits, and offer less job security. Many people in these circumstances thus fall into poverty. Later in this chapter, we discuss further poverty alleviation and the promotion of civil rights.

The Americans with Disabilities Act of 1990 prohibits discrimination in employment for people with disabilities. The need for this landmark legislation confirms that many people with disabilities have historically faced discrimination in the workplace. One of the pernicious aspects of discrimination is that it can lead people to self-select away from pursuing specific employment opportunities; they do not seek them because they have been demoralized in the past. While the link between employment discrimination and people living in poverty is rarely direct, group-level comparison of outcomes reveals groups who have historically faced discrimination in society continue to be overrepresented among those living in poverty.

THE PROBLEM OF A "CULTURE OF POVERTY"

To a greater extent than is often acknowledged, our career aspirations, our connections to paid work, and our interest in work are socially mediated. It matters whom we spend our time with. The view that there is a culture of poverty has commonly been aired in debates about the merits of government or private assistance to people with little or no income. To those who believe that a culture of poverty exists, many people in poverty are there because they have made bad life choices. Further, those life choices have been reinforced by the culture in which they exist on a day-to-day basis. Even with the best of intentions, people who are surrounded by others living in poverty often find it extremely difficult to change the thought patterns and daily behaviors that contribute to their being in those circumstances.

Fortunately, studies do indeed show that many people are able to turn their lives around, remove themselves from cultures of poverty, and live more fulfilling lives.[9] Typically such changes arise when outsiders with resources and a strong desire to make a difference are in easy reach. For example, well-led schools or summer programs can sometimes be catalysts for change in the lives of young people. Case Study 8.1 offers an insight into how challenging circumstances can inhibit individual efforts to get out of poverty, even when they display good intentions to do so.

case study 8.1 Good Intentions, Challenging Circumstances, and Poverty

When disasters happen, people in economically weak positions often face worse challenges than others. Hurricane Katrina caused havoc in 2005. Afterward, many people in the poor neighborhoods of New Orleans were displaced from their homes and unable to keep working because their workplaces had also been destroyed or disrupted. During an investigation of the disaster, researchers from both the Federal Reserve Board and the Brookings Institution came to understand that a lot more than rebuilding damaged infrastructure would be required to help those who were worst affected to return to their former ways of life. Their investigations led to the development of a series of case studies exploring common features of communities throughout the United States that had experienced concentrated poverty. Across the cases, recurrent causes of poverty included lack of local economic opportunities combined with limited education and training among area residents.[10]

Following the *Deepwater Horizon* oil spill in the Gulf of Mexico in 2010, researcher Laura Olson produced a social impact assessment.[11] (Case Study 11.1 provides further discussion of this oil spill and its effects.) In it, Olson presented a case study of a single fisherman and the problems he confronted at the time. The case is instructive for illustrating how structural conditions and individual characteristics can interact in ways that make poverty hard to escape.

In Olson's account, the fisherman lived on the Louisiana coast, fishing, shrimping, and crabbing in the local waters. In the early 2000s he owned and operated four fishing boats, managed crews, had good business connections, and had acquired modest housing for himself and his family, despite the fact that he could neither read nor write.

When Hurricane Katrina struck in 2005, the fisherman lost almost everything he owned—the two trailer homes that were his living quarters, several of his boats, a vehicle, and a huge assortment of fishing equipment. He eventually got access to a temporary trailer home provided on loan by the Federal Emergency Management Agency (FEMA), and also found a way to start fishing again.

After the *Deepwater Horizon* disaster of 2010, state and federal authorities closed down fishing areas off the Louisiana coast for a number of months because of contamination. BP, the owner of the oil well, somewhat reluctantly but under government pressure made provisions to compensate local fishermen for their losses. Being unable to read and write, the fisherman in Olson's story had great difficulty completing the necessary forms to prove he was eligible for a payout. When he eventually received some funds from BP, the amount was minuscule compared with his prior earnings. The fisherman found the pressures overwhelming. Olson suggested that "[his] ability to cope was like a thin thread that Katrina had worn down and the hardships and uncertainties of the spill had caused to snap" (p. 16).

As a result of the diminished state of his business after Katrina and then the challenges created by the oil spill, the fisherman had very little money to survive day to day. He shared custody of his three school-age children with his estranged wife. He tried to put whatever money he had into supporting them. Just as his former fishing activities were curtailed, the fisherman also found that FEMA was seeking to repossess his temporary housing because his use had exceeded the available time limit. Olson's story ends with the fisherman still struggling to regain his once successful livelihood.

This case study highlights several important points. First, the fisherman had once been able to develop a viable business, purchase a home, and raise a family, despite his poor education. His life would likely have continued to go well. However, he was subjected to two serious shocks over which nobody had any control. Second, when disaster affected his business and destroyed his home, his lack of knowledge, skills, and contacts to the broader community made it hard for him to access the support that he needed and that was available. Third, throughout these episodes, the fisherman maintained strong commitments to rebuilding his business and supporting his children. What made all of this difficult was the lack of any kind of financial cushion. He was close to being trapped in a situation of poverty, despite his best intentions and efforts.

CRITICAL THINKING QUESTIONS

1. The disasters described in this case affected many people. How might those with better education have more readily overcome the challenges the fisherman faced?

2. As you consider your community, what life events or individual choices could cause a person to slip from relative material comfort into a lengthy period of living in poverty?

WHY GOVERNMENTS GET INVOLVED IN POVERTY ALLEVIATION

Private individuals, groups, and charitable organizations have worked for centuries to alleviate poverty both in their local neighborhoods and in the wider world. Even today, although governments and international organizations like the World Bank and the United Nations do much to address poverty, the contributions of charities remain vital. When we consider poverty in wealthy countries, it is instructive to explore why governments get involved. Why not leave poverty alleviation to well-organized charities, faith-based groups, and private philanthropists? Those who have studied the history of poverty and poverty alleviation in the United States offer two answers. First, as systematic evidence regarding the numbers of people in poverty and where they were located began to be collected in the early 20th century, it became clear that a patchwork of charities could not possibly address the scale of poverty found across the country. Second, although charities unquestionably do a lot of good work, they each tend to target their provision of assistance to specific groups of people in need. With the best intentions, multiple charities can still ignore some pockets of poverty. Over the decades, gaps in private responses to poverty have resulted in many calls for governments to offer programmatic relief.[12]

We discussed the various goals of public policy in Chapter 1. In one way or another, most of them help to explain why governments get involved in poverty alleviation. Here, we consider the goals of maintaining public order, promoting social equity and human flourishing, and supporting economic growth. Of course, the reasons for government programs differ across countries. The broader philosophies or values that underpin civil society inevitably shape a government's view of poverty and the appropriateness of different responses. The values of individual freedom, self-reliance, and self-improvement have influenced the development of poverty alleviation efforts in the United States. They have permitted development of a policy-making tradition, however, that has sometimes incorporated harsh distinctions between the "deserving" and the "undeserving" poor.

MAINTAINING PUBLIC ORDER

At some level, all governments have engaged in poverty alleviation efforts to maintain public order. Sometimes the focus has been on encouraging individuals to display a good work ethic. Sometimes the focus has been broader. When large numbers of people have been affected by economic recession, governments have taken measures to address poverty partly to avoid political activities that could call into question the prevailing economic order.

The **Poor Relief Act of 1601**, adopted by the British Parliament, established a system for addressing poverty at the local, or parish, level. Each parish was expected to provide assistance to people who could not support themselves and who had no family members (parents or children) who could assist them. The distinction between the "deserving" and "undeserving" poor was codified through this law and the local practices it encouraged. Anyone who was deemed capable of working was "undeserving" of assistance. Such individuals were required either to live and work in "poor houses" or to move on to other parishes. The provisions of this English poor law and subsequent revisions of it strongly influenced the treatment of the poor in the United States, right into the 20th century. For instance, throughout the 19th century, any voluntary idleness was regarded as a vice. In this old regime, unemployed men were often assigned to a master as indentured servants, punished for vagrancy and forced out of town, or put in jail. By taking this hard line, local and state governments across the United States were able to inculcate the basic assumption that if people were not prepared to work, then they could not expect to eat. Even when more humane public policies have been established in the United States and elsewhere, they have nonetheless been intended to promote order and desirable habits among the poor. While seeking to reduce suffering, policy makers have keenly sought to avoid encouraging idleness or ways of living that are at odds with prevailing morality.

President Franklin D. Roosevelt's **New Deal** policies, introduced in the 1930s to alleviate the devastating results of the 1929 stock market crash, laid the foundation for the welfare system that exists to this day in the United States. Those policies were motivated in large part to ward off challenges to the prevailing economic orthodoxy. In the grand scheme of things, most policy makers have viewed creating public policies that provide some relief to the poor as a modest price to pay for maintaining consensus on the merits of the capitalist system. The degree and nature of assistance given to the poor remains a source of considerable debate in the United States and elsewhere.

PROMOTING SOCIAL EQUITY AND HUMAN FLOURISHING

Policies to alleviate poverty have sometimes been motivated by a desire to promote greater social equity. Although people seem to have an instinctive desire to work hard and improve their lot, most are also driven by a sense of altruism. Many people do not like to see others needlessly suffer. To that extent, they will often support policy measures intended to relieve suffering and promote a degree of social equity.

Related to the concern for social equity is the desire to promote human flourishing. Human talent tends to be distributed evenly across populations—although people born into families with sufficient resources are better able than others to cultivate those talents. From a societal perspective, it makes sense to alleviate poverty—especially in circumstances where doing so might create opportunities for individuals to fully realize their human capabilities.[13] Policies consistent with this view have often been designed to reduce poverty in families. The intention has been to break generations of poverty and to support children to develop their talents. In the process, more cohorts of young people can build capabilities that both increase their chances of escaping poverty in adulthood and allow them to contribute to the longer-term economic development of their society.

SUPPORTING ECONOMIC GROWTH

Public policy advocates of **Keynesian economics**—named after John Maynard Keynes—support increased government spending as a way to boost economic activity in times of recession, even if this causes governments to go into temporary debt. Such spending releases more money into society; as individuals spend that money, the whole economy can experience economic growth. Over a period of years, this growth may produce sufficient increases in tax revenues to offset the initial burst of additional spending. For example, government assistance to unemployed workers—through benefit payments or wages paid by employment schemes—serves both to alleviate poverty and to support economic growth. This approach was first used in the United States as a way to get out of the Great Depression of the 1930s. It was again used most recently by many governments around the world—including the U.S. government—to increase domestic economic activity during the global financial crisis of 2007–2008.

Programs that help unemployed people—especially young people—to find and remain in paid employment can both alleviate poverty and support longer-term economic growth. Currently, many political leaders around the world are concerned that aging populations will place significant demands on government budgets in the years ahead. To avert debt problems, such leaders appreciate the importance of increasing the population of people in paid employment. Through their tax payments, these people will help governments fund the costs of caring for the elderly. This is a vital way in which poverty alleviation can also support economic growth.

TRADITIONAL POLICY APPROACHES TO POVERTY ALLEVIATION

Support for public schooling, subsidizing health care, housing assistance, assurance that people can easily get from where they live to where there is paid work, and providing income assistance can all do much to reduce poverty in society. Indeed, successive governments in the United States have made significant provisions of every kind. Since other chapters of this book review public schooling, health funding, and public infrastructure, the following sections of this chapter will focus on policies that offer direct financial assistance, tax credits, subsidies, or support for finding paid work.

LEGACIES OF THE NEW DEAL

Efforts to establish a coherent set of poverty alleviation policies began in the United States during the 1930s. President Franklin D. Roosevelt assumed office in 1933, in the midst of the Great Depression. Determined to address the economic problems of the time, he spearheaded the creation of various public assistance programs collectively termed the New Deal. The Federal Emergency Relief Administration put cash into empty pockets through direct dollar payments and the funding of work schemes. The Civil Works Administration did likewise by employing people on public construction projects. By early 1934, almost a quarter of the U.S. population was benefiting from this kind of relief—an indicator of the magnitude of the crisis.

These programs were, however, short lived. Roosevelt himself said at the start of 1935 that "to dole out relief in this way is to administer a narcotic, a subtle destroyer of the human spirit." He expressed a strong desire for the federal government to "quit this business of relief."[14] As these direct relief programs were rolled back, others were established that have continued ever since. These include the creation of the Social Security fund, supported by contributions from employers and employees; and cash payments for relief of families, which came to be called Aid to Families with Dependent Children (AFDC). Further legacies included federal housing subsidies and the introduction of a minimum wage law.

The Tennessee Valley Authority created work for many in the 1930s as it embarked upon an ambitious dam-building project.

THE WAR ON POVERTY

In the mid-1960s, President Lyndon Johnson led the next big public policy push to alleviate poverty in the United States, as part of his Great Society program. Declaring a "War on Poverty," Johnson introduced the Medicare program, which provides universal health care coverage to people over age 65, and the Medicaid program, which—with matching contributions from state governments—provides health care coverage to poor people. Social Security payments to the elderly from Social Security were also increased during the Johnson administration.

By the end of the 1960s, the key elements of the U.S. system of government-led poverty alleviation were in place. Nonetheless, they generated controversy. Beginning in the 1970s, the design and scope of poverty alleviation measures were hotly debated. In a classic argument, Charles Murray claimed that public policy settings in the United States had added to the problem by breeding generations of people who were dependent on government "handouts." To bolster this claim, Murray pointed to the significant increase during the 1970s in the number of households where multiple generations of unmarried mothers were raising children without a man in sight, supported by AFDC rather than resident, working fathers.[15] Reflecting on the efforts initiated by President Johnson, President Ronald Reagan is reported to have quipped, "We fought a war on poverty, and poverty won."[16] Criticisms of these programs led, among other things, to a focus on ways to redesign AFDC.

AN EMPHASIS ON PERSONAL RESPONSIBILITY

When President Bill Clinton assumed office in 1993, he vowed to "change welfare as we know it." Indeed he did so, but only through a process that involved a high degree of give and take with his political opponents in Congress. In 1996,

President Bill Clinton and First Lady Hillary Clinton discuss Social Security with visitors to the Oval Office in 1995.

Clinton signed into law the Personal Responsibility and Work Opportunity Reconciliation Act. Among other things, this law renamed AFDC as Temporary Assistance to Needy Families (TANF)—with an emphasis on "temporary." TANF was designed to provide assistance in a way that would allow children to be cared for in their own homes or in the homes of relatives. It aimed to prevent or reduce out-of-wedlock pregnancies and encourage the formation and maintenance of two-parent families. It also placed stringent time limits and work requirements on those receiving welfare payments. Simultaneously, it opened up opportunities for states to experiment more easily with how welfare payments were disbursed to those in need.

We will discuss the design of welfare-to-work programs hereafter. Such programs represent the main legacy of the emphasis on personal responsibility that came back with a vengeance in debates over welfare in the 1980s and 1990s and are reoccurring presently.

SOCIAL INSURANCE VERSUS MEANS-TESTED CASH TRANSFERS

Although the details of poverty alleviation programs in the United States are complex, they fall into two categories. **Social insurance programs** rely on contributions from those people who will ultimately be eligible to receive benefits. Social Security is the most significant example (see In Focus 8.2 for details about Social Security). In a variation on social insurance, some programs cover any people who fall within a given category; for example, Medicare benefits people who are 65 or older.

Means-tested cash transfers make assistance available to people as long as they can demonstrate that they both fall within specific categories and are sufficiently needy to be eligible for assistance. TANF is such a program. The U.S. government sets the broad eligibility requirements for assistance. Each state determines the details of the means-testing and disbursement rules, and their governmental budgetary processes define the overall funds available for payment through means-tested cash transfers. In contrast to social insurance, the transfers do not require any prior contributions by those eligible to receive them.

in focus 8.2

THE FINANCIAL STRUCTURE OF SOCIAL SECURITY

Since its founding in 1939, the U.S. Social Security Fund has earned a reputation as the country's most successful poverty alleviation program. In 2015, it provided benefit payments to about 60 million people—43 million retired workers and their dependents, 6 million survivors of deceased workers, and 11 million disabled workers and their dependents.

Meanwhile, in the same year, an estimated 169 million people made contributions to the fund. Total expenditures in 2015 were $897 billion. Total revenue was $920 billion, consisting of $827 billion in contributions and $93 billion in interest earnings.[17] Unlike their criticism of other poverty alleviation programs, many policy makers view Social Security positively because it pays benefits only to those who have contributed to it, or to their immediate family. Social Security has prevented many people from falling into poverty due to disability, old age, or the death of a person they have relied upon for household income.

Social Security is modeled on other insurance schemes.[18] The essence of insurance schemes is that when people face the possibility of a loss, they can protect themselves against the consequences by banding together with others facing the same risk. Each member of the group contributes an amount of money related to the average likelihood that the loss will occur. Each member is protected from a large possible loss by making a smaller but certain contribution. As with other insurance schemes, workers trade periodic payments for protection against the risk of a particular, defined loss. In the case of Social Security, the risk is the loss of wages for specific reasons.

Social Security contributions are based on wages only up to a maximum, because only those wages are insured against loss. That maximum is periodically raised. Those contributions form the basis for calculating benefits. It is a foundational requirement of Social Security that the contributions it receives are placed in trusts. Those trusts can place their surplus funds only in safe investments—in practice, always the purchase of U.S. government bonds.

Although the financial structure of Social Security has been successful to date, it is distinctive from other insurance schemes in ways that threaten its **actuarial integrity**. Insurance schemes are deemed actuarially sound when the contributions made to them over time are sufficient to cover all future benefit payouts (sometimes called *future liabilities*). That integrity is achieved by managing annual contributions and specifying future payouts (by assuming that certain events will occur in the lives of those holding the insurance).

Debate over Social Security has arisen concerning both the levels of the annual contributions individuals make and the levels of the payments that are made from them. Poverty rates fell among the elderly in the United States from the 1960s onward because the payments from Social Security were increased during the 1960s and 1970s. In their 2016 annual report, however, the trustees of the Social Security fund expressed concerns about the fund's future solvency. Without timely legislative changes to increase contribution levels and reduce payment levels, funds could become seriously depleted in the coming decades.

Those currently contributing to Social Security face no guarantee that any future payments they receive will be sufficient to keep them out of poverty. They face no guarantees about the levels of contributions they will be required to make from here into the future. Thus, this program, which has achieved so much success in the past, might well stumble in the future, in terms of effectively keeping past contributors above the poverty line in their old age, or avoiding other challenges such as political resistance from younger generations who figure they are unlikely ever to benefit from the program.

FEDERALISM AND POVERTY ALLEVIATION

Although discussion of poverty alleviation in the United States tends to focus on laws made in Washington, DC, many of the policy choices that influence poverty rates occur at the state and local levels. For example, policies that affect the quality of public infrastructure and public schooling are heavily influenced by state legislative choices, as are policies toward subsidized housing. Here we will briefly discuss the role of state and local governments in providing public housing. We will then consider the potential for state-level variations in poverty alleviation initiatives to influence the residential mobility of the poor.

In the late 19th and early 20th centuries, charitable groups in the United States lobbied governments to address the quality of the housing where many poor people lived. The crisis of inadequate accommodation was considered most acute in the nation's large cities. Overcrowded conditions led to the spread of serious diseases. As part of the New Deal, the U.S. Congress passed the Housing Act of 1937, which provided for federal subsidies of local public housing. Since then, federal and state governments have been active in subsidizing local housing developments. In the 1950s, local governments engaged in widespread slum clearance initiatives, which resulted in the construction of many housing projects. They offered much-needed low-cost housing to poor people in cities. However, some of these developments, given their defects, subsequently became hotbeds of crime and unemployment—a result that led to subsequent redevelopment initiatives.

New York City public housing blocks form the backdrop to the beach at Coney Island and its iconic amusement park. Commonly referred to as "projects" or "developments," such blocks scattered across the city provide essential low-cost housing for those who might otherwise face poverty. Starting in recent decades, high-rise structures of this kind have been removed in favor of low-rise buildings, intended to reduce stigmas and concerns about concentration of crime.

As of 2014, the U.S. government was providing housing subsidies worth around $50 billion.[19] That amount covered subsidies for developers of low-rent private housing complexes, transfers to cover some of the costs of public housing, and vouchers assisting low-income householders to live in private rental properties. Often, public housing is provided by city governments, with additional support from state governments. For example, the New York City Housing Authority owns and operates over 300 developments across the city, providing subsidized housing for more than 400,000 New Yorkers. Despite continuing complaints that many people cannot find satisfactory homes, for the most part this federal system of supporting housing for low-income households has been highly successful.[20]

Following welfare reforms of the 1980s and 1990s that ultimately saw AFDC become TANF, states gained more autonomy from the federal government in how they disbursed financial assistance to poor families. At the time, federalism scholars speculated that these changes would lead some states to become "welfare magnets." The suggestion was that poor people would relocate to states with relatively generous systems of welfare support.[21] In turn, this action would prompt states "to race to the bottom"—that is, to reduce their welfare support in an effort to discourage poor people from exploiting payment systems. Subsequent research has shown that few state legislatures ever actively pursued policies to reduce welfare support.[22] That said, states have kept tight control over welfare spending.[23] Meanwhile, greater state discretion in the disbursement of federal funds has triggered various welfare experiments. We discuss variations in welfare-to-work programs hereafter.

CONTEMPORARY POLICY ISSUES

Poverty and efforts to address it will continue to provoke public policy discussions in the coming years. Here we discuss three areas of concern: the challenges faced by the president and Congress in reducing the federal budget deficit, the changing expectations of what constitute necessary job skills in the contemporary economy, and the ongoing need to make work pay.

GOVERNMENT BUDGET STRESS

The U.S. government currently carries a staggering amount of debt. In 1997, that debt stood at approximately $5 trillion. In contrast, just two decades later, that debt had more than quadrupled to approximately $20 trillion. Whenever a government spends more in a given year than it collects in taxes and other revenues, it operates on a **budget deficit**. Those deficits add to the nation's debt. The government is required to pay interest on that debt. The result is budget stress, for which presidents and members of Congress—no matter what party they represent—must find ways to curb government spending. When governments experience budget stress and many organized groups are fighting to maintain established government programs, the economically and politically weakest groups are invariably the biggest losers.

Government budget stress spells bad news for people in poverty or, indeed, for any who are living on low incomes, and makes it difficult for various long-standing poverty alleviation programs to maintain current payment levels. In the coming years, we can expect to see major budget battles and many attempts to shift spending on poverty alleviation to state or local governments.

JOB SKILLS IN A KNOWLEDGE ECONOMY

Like other advanced economies, the United States has gone through major industrial transformations over the past 50 years. In that time, computers and robots have greatly assisted in the automation of activities that once employed vast numbers of people. Figure 8.4 depicts U.S. manufacturing output and employment during recent decades. The top line-plot shows that the inflation-adjusted output of the manufacturing sector was as high in 2015 as it had ever been. However, the bottom line-plot shows that, as output was rising, manufacturing employment dropped by more than six million jobs. The lines tell a story of increasing productivity in manufacturing. At the same time, the series of gray bars shows the steadily declining number of workers required to generate $1 million of manufacturing output during the time period. In 1980, it took 24.9 jobs to generate $1 million in manufacturing output; in 2015, it took just 6.4 jobs.[24]

The emerging knowledge economy is one that places highest value on thinking and communication skills. Within this economy, there is unquestionably ongoing demand for workers holding lesser skills. While manufacturing jobs may be declining, there will always be a need for people to perform an array of service jobs. Even so, what it means to be literate these days is quite different—and more

FIGURE 8.4   U.S. Manufacturing-Sector Output and Employment, 1980–2015

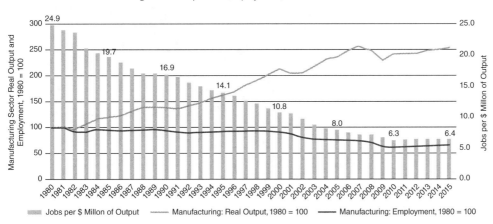

Source: Mark Muro and Sifan Liu, "Why Trump's Factory Job Promises Won't Pan Out—in One Chart," The Avenue (blog), Brookings Institution, November 21, 2016, https://www.brookings.edu/blog/the-avenue/2016/11/21/why-trumps-factory-job-promises-wont-pan-out-in-one-chart/. Dollar amounts have been inflation-adjusted to 2016 amounts.

sophisticated—from what it meant to be literate in earlier decades. Most workers are now expected not only to be able to read and write but also to be technology literate. Their ability to access and make effective use of relevant information is critical to succeeding in their work. The premium on education and sector-specific skills has never been higher. For people with limited capabilities and skills, entry to the labor market has become increasingly difficult. All these changes open the possibility that low-skilled people will become even more economically and socially marginalized.

MAKING WORK PAY

There will always be disagreement about what governments can do to assist the poor. Yet it is generally agreed that paid employment should be the primary way for capable, working-age adults to avoid poverty. The corollary is that paid work should produce a living wage. Barbara Ehrenreich offers compelling insights in *Nickel and Dimed* (2001) into the hardscrabble nature of life in low-wage America. Federal and state governments have used two approaches to improve the take-home pay of those on lower wages. The first is the **Earned Income Tax Credit**. Introduced in the 1970s, this credit reduces the amount of federal income tax those on low wages must pay. The credit level is adjusted for the number of dependents in a household. It has also been increased during recessions, such as the global financial crisis of 2007–2008.

A second approach to making work pay involves setting a **minimum hourly wage**. Many countries have made this provision. It was first introduced in the United States, amid much controversy, during the New Deal era of the 1930s, and has been periodically increased. Many states have chosen over the years to set their own

The emerging knowledge economy is exemplified by the growing use of computer-operated machines to replace traditional blue collar jobs. Here, robots have replaced human workers on an automobile assembly line.

(Cultura Creative [RF]/Alamy Stock Photo).

minimum wage rates above the federal rate. In 2016, the federal minimum wage was $7.25 per hour. However, both New York and California are on a path to increasing, over several years, their minimum hourly wage to $15.00. In the 2016 elections, voters in Arizona, Colorado, Maine, and Washington all supported increases in their minimum wages, also to be phased in over several years. They join many other states that now have minimum wages above the federally mandated level.

When we look to the future, it is likely that considerable debate will continue regarding effective strategies for making work pay. Although using multiple policy approaches holds appeal, one frequent concern is that beneficiaries of government assistance can face **high effective marginal tax rates**. That is, as their wages increase and they no longer become eligible for benefits like the Earned Income Tax Credit or housing vouchers, the withdrawal of benefits becomes equivalent to facing a higher rate of tax. This raises concerns about how to maintain incentives for poor people to work hard and increase their wages.

Indeed, uncoordinated withdrawal of various forms of assistance to the poor could potentially create **poverty traps**. These arise when people who are poor decide that engaging in increasing amounts of paid work is less attractive than remaining eligible for government assistance. Making work pay calls for careful policy design and ongoing monitoring of how different policies affect labor-market participation.

POVERTY ALLEVIATION AND THE INVESTMENT PERSPECTIVE

In his 1964 State of the Union Address, President Lyndon Johnson observed, "Unfortunately, many Americans live on the outskirts of hope—some because of their poverty, some because of their color, and all too many because of both. Our task is to help replace their despair with opportunity." In the sentences following these, Johnson announced his administration's War on Poverty. Johnson strongly believed that, as a wealthy nation, the United States should increase opportunities for everyone living in it. He also recognized that public policies designed to tackle poverty and its root causes represent investments. As he put it, "One thousand dollars invested in salvaging an unemployable youth today can return $40,000 or more in his lifetime."

The essence of the investment approach to poverty alleviation involves helping people enter and remain in the paid workforce. When such support exists, those who have received support can realize two important outcomes. First, they face the prospect of more active participation in society—earning a steady income, working with others, and establishing and maintaining a financially viable household. Second, they can switch from being on a path to welfare dependency to supporting themselves and paying taxes. Both outcomes are highly desirable from a societal perspective.

Funds to provide job training to young people were offered as part of the War on Poverty. In subsequent decades, various job-training programs have been funded through a range of federal and state government agencies. Such funding has declined because of perceptions that it is ineffective; however, careful scrutiny suggests otherwise. Harry J. Holzer has concluded that "modest expenditures usually produce modest positive impacts."[25] Recent investigations of these programs—which have sometimes been termed explicitly as workforce investments—support the conclusion that they yield positive results for participants, when compared with results for control groups.[26]

In the spirit of promoting more consistent application of an investment perspective toward poverty alleviation programs, David L. Weimer and Aidan R. Vining edited a volume of studies in 2009 titled *Investing in the Disadvantaged*.[27] The project, supported by the John D. and Catherine T. MacArthur Foundation, brought together a range of studies. These included assessments of the returns on investment of educational programs, health care programs, initiatives in the criminal justice space, and programs encouraging welfare recipients to return to the workforce. The overall picture emerging here is that careful efforts to work with people facing disadvantage can turn their lives around. However, program intentions and details matter. In the future, more care needs to be taken in designing poverty alleviation programs if they are to generate long-term social benefits. Significantly, this can often mean spending money to support individuals who historically would have been given little consideration by both government agencies and private charities.

Here, we will consider two ways that the investment perspective is being applied with respect to poverty alleviation. First, In Focus 8.3 shows how New Zealand's government has used extensive data analysis to guide how it supports young people at risk of requiring long-term government assistance. Second, Case Study 8.2 explores how the investment perspective has been applied to U.S. welfare-to-work programs. In general, some programs have been more successful than others.

in focus 8.3

FROM DATA ANALYSIS TO TARGETED INTERVENTIONS IN NEW ZEALAND

Since 2011, the government of New Zealand has embarked on an investment approach to improving how it works with citizens at risk of falling into poverty. Beginning from the view that welfare expenditures create major funding liabilities for governments, it made an effort to model those liabilities using **actuarial analysis** of individual behaviors and the costs of those behaviors to government.[28] The analytical approach follows how insurance companies calculate the financial risks of individual policy holders. Such information provides guidance for setting the terms of individual insurance coverage. The New Zealand government has sought to use long-term liability modeling to guide the support it provides to different client groups. This investment approach was prompted by the desire to avoid a future where annual welfare payments for elderly people and those of working age on long-term benefits would overwhelm tax revenues and create serious budget deficits.

Table 8.2 shows how New Zealand's data analysis has allowed it to predict the future liabilities associated with clients displaying specific risk factors.[29]

The evidence in Table 8.2 offers a compelling case for government efforts to adopt a targeted approach to working with young people. When young people display multiple risk factors, they become more likely to face unemployment and then engage in criminal activity. When young women display multiple risk factors, they are also more likely to become teenage mothers. Through isolating these risk factors and engaging in early interventions, the government can support those at most risk, keeping them in school or finding alternative ways of preparing them for employment. It can also offer forms of financial support that encourage participation in the paid workforce. The responsible welfare agency in New Zealand now continuously tracks how movement of individuals from welfare programs has reduced the government's future financial liability, in terms of anticipated future welfare payments.

TABLE 8.2 Risk Factors and Estimated Costs of At-Risk Young People in New Zealand

Four Risk Factors for Children aged 0–14 (and % Where Factor Observed)
Documented evidence of abuse or neglect (8%)
Being mostly supported by a benefit since birth (15%)
Having a parent with a prison or community sentence (17%)
Having a mother who did not graduate from high school (10%)

Justice System and Welfare Program Costs of At-Risk Children by Age 35			
CHILDREN AGED 0–14 YEARS AND OBSERVED RISK FACTORS	CHILDREN IN EACH RISK SET		EXPECTED COST PER PERSON BY AGE 35 ($)
	COUNT	%	
0	602,577	69	23,500
1	149,229	17	70,150
2	77,820	9	121,500
3	35,712	4	166,000
4	7,842	1	193,700

Note: Figures in this table are based on New Zealand Treasury calculations made in 2016 using data from 2013. Dollar figures have been converted from 2016 New Zealand dollars to 2016 U.S. dollars by the author (assuming 1 NZD = 0.71 USD).

case study 8.2 Welfare-to-Work Programs

When the Temporary Assistance to Needy Families program was authorized in 1996, it supported the notion that those who receive welfare benefits should also undertake some paid work or be engaged in training that would increase their ability to secure paid employment. Prior to the introduction of this program, which replaced Aid to Families with Dependent Children, waivers had been made available to states to experiment with **welfare-to-work programs**. As a result, a variety of such programs were in operation at the start of the 1990s. Many more were in operation by the end of the decade. Today, welfare-to-work programs are a fixture of the U.S. welfare landscape.

Welfare-to-work programs are highly consistent with treating public policies as investments. They can help participants achieve steady employment and attain financial independence. They can also reduce longer-term welfare spending, as people switch their status from welfare recipients to taxpayers. However, program design matters. First, programs might be devised with the primary goal of reducing short-term government welfare costs. In such programs, the emphasis is on moving people directly into paid work, so that benefit payments can be avoided. Second, the primary goal of programs might be to effectively equip participants for entry into paid work. These programs might be more tolerant of training for participants, if the expectation is that this will lead to a good work placement.

It is important that we notice the trade-off between the two outcomes for these programs. One places government cost savings over benefits to the participant. The other places good employment outcomes for the participant over short-term government cost savings. When designing welfare-to-work programs, some policy developers have attempted to balance these competing outcomes. Clearly, it is undesirable to have a program that encourages participants to remain in what looks like endless job training. It is equally undesirable to have a program that encourages participants to take a series of poorly matched, unsatisfactory job opportunities that neither build workforce skills nor establish a track record of stable employment.

Many comprehensive studies of the effects of welfare-to-work programs have now been conducted. The best of these conform to the gold standard of program evaluation, with random assignment of recipients into the experimental or control groups, and careful assessment of before and after conditions. A major synthesis report on the costs and benefits of such programs, produced in 2009 by David Greenberg, Victoria Deitch, and Gayle Hamilton, brought together findings from 28 welfare-to-work programs that were run in 11 U.S. states and two Canadian provinces and involved more than 100,000 research subjects.[30] The report's findings remain the strongest and most comprehensive to date on the topic. Policy Investment Checklist 8.1 summarizes those findings.

The study assessed six variations on welfare to work, summarized as follows:

1. Earning supplement programs provide individuals with financial incentives intended to encourage work. They are an efficient mechanism for transferring income to low-income families because participants gain more than a dollar for every dollar the government spends.

2. Mandatory mixed-initial-activity programs require individuals to participate first either in an education or training activity or in a job search activity. These can generate positive returns on investment for the government and can be financially beneficial to the participant.

3. Mandatory job-search-first programs require individuals to look for jobs immediately or be assigned to other activities if they do not find work. These programs are less expensive to the government than mandatory mixed-initial-activity programs. However, they are unlikely to increase participants' incomes.

4. Mandatory work experience programs assign individuals to unpaid jobs. This step usually happens after a period of unsuccessful job search. These programs are not costly to the government and can be beneficial to participants because they give them job skills.

5. Mandatory education-first programs require individuals to participate in some general education courses prior to job search. They do not produce a good return on investment because they are costly to the government and do little to increase participants' incomes.

6. Time-limited-mix programs require individuals to participate in employment-oriented activities. These provide financial incentives for work and limit the amount of time individuals remain eligible for welfare benefits. Although there is some evidence that these can benefit participants, they are usually costly to governments.

These findings strongly indicate that welfare-to-work programs can generate positive returns on public investments. However, once again, the details of program design matter. Further, Greenberg and his colleagues found that, during the 1990s, as increasing numbers of people requesting welfare were being enrolled in welfare-to-work programs, conditions in their study control groups were changing. Thus, the potential gains of the experimental programs might have been underestimated, simply because more people outside the studied experiments were now receiving similar treatment. Evidence produced by the synthesis report has laid the foundation for improved program design, as well as improving future evaluations of the returns on investment of such programs.

CRITICAL THINKING QUESTIONS

1. People in poverty have often been characterized as either "deserving" or "undeserving" of assistance. How might taking an investment perspective on poverty alleviation change how we think about those characterizations?

2. If you were required to design a welfare-to-work program that could be defended in debates about reducing future government spending, what kind of program would you propose?

case study 8.2 continued

Analyzing Welfare-to-Work Programs

1. Focus on Existing Policies and Programs	Since the 1980s, federal and state policy makers have reshaped the U.S. system of cash welfare assistance for low-income families. Numerous welfare-to-work programs have been introduced. Of these, many have been evaluated, with assessments made of their overall value. A synthesis of evaluation findings offers insights on which programs work best in terms of (1) helping people stay in paid work and (2) reducing ongoing welfare costs.
2. Gather Policy Evidence	Researchers evaluating welfare-to-work programs in the United States have often adopted the "gold standard" of using randomized controlled trials. The evidence here draws from a synthesis of 28 cost-benefit studies based on random assignment of clients either to the programs or to control groups. The programs studied were introduced in 11 states and two Canadian provinces in the 1980s and 1990s, before passage of the 1996 welfare reform law, which saw many more such programs implemented.
3. Measure Desired Effects	Welfare-to-work programs can have different objectives: 1. Some focus on increasing participant income. 2. Some focus on reducing welfare costs. 3. Some seek to balance participant and government gains. The synthesis allowed conclusions to be drawn about what program design elements are best suited to achieving each program objective. Program effects were uniformly judged after each had been running for five years.
4. Assess Costs and Benefits	1. Among programs focused on increasing participant income, those that offered an earnings supplement made participants better off on average by over $5,000 compared with peers in control groups. Such programs also tended to produce breakeven results for governments. 2. Among programs focused on reducing welfare costs, those that mandated job-search-first saved governments around $2,000 per participant compared with spending on those in the control groups. However, participants tended to be worse off than those in the control group by $600. 3. Among programs seeking to balance participant and government gains, the most successful were those that mandated involvement in mixed initial activities, such as training in job skills and support in job search. Such programs made participants better off on average by over $800 compared with peers in the control groups. They tended to produce breakeven results for governments. Overall, when their objectives were clear, programs tended to produce positive returns on investment.
5. Offer Robust Advice	There are many types of welfare-to-work programs. Governments must clarify their objectives—it is hard to make participants better off while simultaneously reducing government spending, at least within a five-year period. The synthesis of evidence found big differences in return on investment within program type (earnings supplement, mandatory job-search first, mandatory mixed initial activities). Attention to design is vital for increasing program success.

POVERTY ALLEVIATION AND THE PROMOTION OF CIVIL RIGHTS

During the 1960s, strong calls were made for expansion of civil rights in the United States. Movement leaders saw a direct link between poverty alleviation and the promotion of civil rights. In documenting the development of government policies to alleviate poverty, James T. Patterson observed, "The civil rights movement quickened the sense of inequality and relative deprivation that affected all low-income people, whether black or white. No explanation of the welfare explosion can slight its significance."[31]

In launching the Children's Defense Fund (CDF) in 1973, Marian Wright Edelman saw herself as continuing her struggle for the advancement of civil rights in the United States. Over the ensuing decades, the CDF has led the way in advocating to improve the situation of children in the United States. Civil rights are advanced when children have enhanced opportunities to grow into healthy, well-educated, and well-socialized adults. Unfortunately, many are currently held back because of the pernicious effects of poverty.

In 2015, the CDF released a report entitled *Ending Child Poverty Now*. The report noted the statistic that one in five children in the United States lives in poverty, and noted that the proportion is higher for black children and children in households headed by single mothers. The report observed that poverty hurts children, even though children played no part in creating the circumstances in which they find themselves. In her foreword to the report, Marian Wright Edelman stated, "America's poor children did not ask to be born; did not choose their parents, country, state, neighborhood, race, color, or faith. In fact, had they been born in 33 other industrialized countries they would be less likely to be poor."[32]

Why should child poverty be considered such a serious matter? In its report, the CDF offers several reasons. Poverty has been shown to slow brain development in infants and expose children to high levels of stress. When allowed to continue, these factors can disrupt the development of social competence and reduce children's ability to succeed in school. In turn, when children struggle socially and in school, they face greater likelihood of entering adulthood with low educational attainment. This can lead to lives punctuated by unstable employment, periods of poverty, and greater risk of involvement in the criminal justice system. All these factors clearly suggest that child poverty inhibits human flourishing. They also suggest that society as a whole misses out on many contributions that people damaged through childhood poverty otherwise could have made. The report called for political leaders and policy makers to adopt an investment perspective and take a series of actions to reduce child poverty.

Child poverty is a pressing civil rights issue in itself. Yet, as long as large numbers of children grow up in poverty, it is likely that various forms of social inequality in the United States will increase. Consequently, many other civil rights issues experienced more acutely by adults will remain unresolved. These include forms of workplace discrimination, social exclusion, and bias in the criminal justice system.

LESSONS FOR PUBLIC POLICY

This survey of poverty and poverty alleviation suggests several lessons for public policy. Among these, one of the most important is that moralizing about poverty and the character of those in poverty is often misplaced. Serious consequences would result if governments were to align their poverty alleviation policies with the voices of those who tend to blame the victims. The Great Depression and the more recent global financial crisis have shown why. In both cases, structural economic problems arose that no individuals—including many well-placed political leaders—had it within their powers to avert. Those structural problems called for structural responses. The closer we look at poverty, the more we come to see that individual choices tend not to be the only, or the most important, explanations for why people experience it. The lessons for public policy set forth here build on that insight.

- People who experience poverty tend to have limited supports in their lives. Adults who are most at risk of poverty tend to have lower education than others and to be in low-paying jobs. Given these preexisting conditions, when an economic shock occurs, these people are more exposed to harm than are those with a higher education. They also may find it much more difficult than others to turn things around and return to a more stable situation.
- All government poverty-alleviation programs tend to exist alongside a range of charitable activities. However, because they tend to lack the scale of governments, charitable efforts alone are rarely sufficient to effectively address poverty.
- Government actions can be highly effective in reducing poverty. The record in the United States during the past century is highly positive in this regard. For example, during that time, poverty among older people has gone from being commonplace to rare. Similarly, other groups—including single mothers with dependent children—are generally better off today than at earlier points in the nation's history.
- Whether or not government is effective in addressing poverty among specific groups is highly dependent upon the political will of citizens and their representatives. In the United States, poverty alleviation programs that exhibit a high degree of self-help are generally given more support than those that can be easily characterized as a "handout." This observation has important implications for the designs of public policies. It helps explain why Aid to

Families with Dependent Children received extensive criticism while Temporary Assistance of Needy Families has received bipartisan support for over two decades.

- Well-designed poverty alleviation efforts can serve as investments. They can help vulnerable individuals turn their lives around and become productive, contributing members of society. Evidence for this view has been provided over recent decades by well-designed welfare-to-work programs.
- Given the complex reasons why people fall into poverty, it is helpful for policy designers to think carefully about how the choices they make could inadvertently serve to increase poverty in specific population groups. For example, good public transport systems can make a huge difference to the lives of low-income people, easing their ability to get themselves to paid employment.

Poverty alleviation will remain a significant public policy issue into the future. People now live longer on average than ever before. Future governments will need to find ways to subsidize the incomes of many elderly people whose retirement savings have been insufficient to keep them out of poverty. The only feasible way to do this is to ensure that sufficient numbers of working-age people are both financially independent and paying taxes.

Looking to the future, governments everywhere need to think hard about how to assist young people in entering the paid workforce and how to ensure that all those of working age participate in paid work to the extent that they can. The days when societies could allow people of working age to languish in unemployment are gone. We need smart public policies that allow all people to become and remain productive and socially engaged. By working toward that goal, societies will create the conditions whereby they can show compassion to those who are truly disadvantaged and give them the best possible support.

CHAPTER SUMMARY

Poverty is a big issue in the lives of many people, and not just those who live in poorer nations. Poverty rates are significant in the United States, varying among population groups by age, geographical location, and level of education. During the 19th and early 20th centuries, many countries with advanced economies developed extensive welfare states. Paralleling those efforts, the United States developed a range of policies to alleviate poverty, particularly during the 1930s New Deal era and the 1960s Great Society era. Yet there has always been reluctance in the United States to develop systems whereby cash assistance to the needy is funded out of general taxes. The strong commitment to individual responsibility has ensured that all poverty alleviation programs for adults tend to encourage active participation in the paid workforce, wherever feasible.

The Social Security system, originating in the 1930s, has attained a high level of popularity because it works on a system of contributions, like an insurance scheme. Likewise, Temporary Assistance for Needy Families, which replaced Aid to Families with Dependent Children, has enjoyed bipartisan support due to its provisions that all those who receive it engage either in paid employment or in workforce training.

Several times in this chapter we have encountered the categorization of people in poverty as either "deserving" or "undeserving" of assistance. These categories, which date back for centuries, emerged when poverty alleviation efforts lay almost entirely in the hands of private charities. Generally, people who were considered able to work but nonetheless unemployed were deemed "undeserving." Meanwhile, those who were elderly or affected by serious illnesses or work-based injuries were considered "deserving" of assistance. Unfortunately, this crude classification system has continued.

Our discussion highlighted the merits of approaching poverty alleviation as an investment. This perspective presents a serious challenge to the old deservedness dichotomy. When a government helps an individual find and settle into well-suited paid work, the chances are high that the individual will go on to live a life with limited future calls on government assistance. This observation justifies spending significant sums on that initial support, because the returns on such an investment are expected to be high.

Efforts to promote civil rights can also do a lot to alleviate poverty, because poverty is often most prevalent among those individuals and groups who have been most marginalized in society. Such marginalization can have many sources, including various forms of discrimination. In our exploration of the link between poverty alleviation and the promotion of civil rights, we focused on the importance of seeking to alleviate child poverty. Last, we discussed the important federalism dimension to the provision of welfare assistance in the United States, noting especially the success of intergovernmental cooperation to provide affordable housing.

CONNECTIONS TO OTHER CHAPTERS

The chances that a person will fall into poverty can be driven by structural and individual factors. Public policies can work to influence both. In the best scenarios, good policy choices can reduce the likelihood of people experiencing poverty. Emphasized here are policies intended to increase people's incomes through the receipt of cash transfers, engagement in the paid workforce, or some combination of both. People with education past high school are less likely to experience poverty than those with only a high school education or less. This finding underscores the importance of public schooling (Chapter 6) as a mechanism for helping people develop skills and go on to lead independent, fulfilling lives.

When people suffer ill health or face medical emergencies, they and their families can be at greater risk of poverty. Policies affecting the provision and accessibility of health care can bear materially on poverty rates. The Great Society programs of the 1960s introduced important government support for health care coverage in the United States; elsewhere we have discussed those and more recent developments in health care policy (Chapter 7).

Difficulties finding employment and the experience of poverty can sometimes lead people to live outside the law. Links exist between poverty and crime (Chapter 9). Last, when governments provide sound infrastructure, including accessible public transport, people who are poor can experience more material comfort at home and more readily commute to work. Public infrastructure (Chapter 4) is obviously relevant to the alleviation of poverty.

KEY TERMS

Poverty line
Absolute poverty
Relative poverty
Money income thresholds
Consumer Price Index
Structural causes of poverty
Individual causes of poverty
Economic transformations
Economic recessions
Exogenous shocks
The Poor Relief Act of 1601
The New Deal

Keynesian economics
Social insurance programs
Means-tested cash transfers
Actuarial integrity
Budget deficits
Earned Income Tax Credit
Minimum hourly wage
High effective marginal tax rates
Poverty traps
Actuarial analysis
Welfare-to-work programs

SUGGESTIONS FOR FURTHER READING

Abramsky, Sasha. *The American Way of Poverty: How the Other Half Still Lives.* New York: Nation Books, 2013. This is a very good introduction to contemporary issues in poverty, and how people live with it in contemporary U.S. society.

Cancian, Maria, and Sheldon Danziger, eds. *Changing Poverty, Changing Policies.* New York: Russell Sage Foundation, 2009. This is a very useful set of essays on key elements of poverty.

Ehrenreich, Barbara. *Nickel and Dimed: On (Not) Getting By in America.* New York: Picador, 2001. This is an excellent inside look at what it takes to get by on minimum wages. See especially Ehrenreich's evaluation of her experiences, presented as a summary chapter.

Iceland, John. *Poverty in America: A Handbook.* Berkeley: University of California Press, 2012. A very readable introduction to issues in the study of poverty.

Patterson, James T. *America's Struggle against Poverty in the Twentieth Century.* Cambridge, MA: Harvard University Press, 2000. See especially the early chapters on the development of systems of relief for the poor.

Weimer, David L., and Aidan R. Vining, eds. *Investing in the Disadvantaged: Assessing the Benefits and Costs of Social Programs.* Washington, DC: Georgetown University Press, 2009. This book offers an excellent collection of essays on policies to support the poor and how the effectiveness of such policies is best evaluated.

WEBSITES

- The Children's Defense Fund advocates for children, the most highly represented group among those currently in poverty in the United States. The website offers a range of resources and suggestions for resources elsewhere on the web. http://www.childrensdefense.org/

- MDRC is a research organization committed to finding solutions to difficult social problems—from reducing poverty to bolstering economic self-sufficiency. The organization works to test new policy-relevant ideas and communicate what has been learned to policy makers and practitioners. http://www.mdrc.org/

- The National Poverty Center at the Gerald R. Ford School of Public Policy, University of Michigan, conducts and promotes multidisciplinary, policy-relevant research and seeks to inform public discussion on the causes and consequences of poverty. http://poverty.umich.edu/

FOR DISCUSSION

1. Direct cash transfers and temporary work programs introduced in the 1930s rapidly relieved suffering among almost a quarter of the American population. These programs show that when conditions are catastrophic and strong political will is present, government efforts to alleviate poverty can be highly effective. Why do we nevertheless still see high levels of poverty, especially among children, in today's United States?

2. Throughout the history of poverty alleviation efforts in the United States, much discussion has focused on separating the "deserving" from the "undeserving" poor. Suppose you were to make a list of people in poverty and why they are in poverty. As you look at the list, how easy or difficult would you find it to decide who is "deserving" and who is "undeserving" of support?

3. The investment perspective on poverty alleviation asserts that effectively targeted support to individuals can help them gain paid work, stay in employment, and therefore contribute more fully in society. But some people may never be able to participate in paid work. How should governments treat those who simply cannot support themselves and live independently?

CHAPTER 9

CRIMINAL JUSTICE

Well-functioning justice systems are essential to the development and maintenance of peaceful, productive societies. Just as collectivities of people look to governments to protect them from actual or potential external adversaries, so they look to governments to create domestic order. It would be a problem for social order if more than one system of justice existed in a given jurisdiction. Under such circumstances, different sets of laws would apply to different sets of people, creating high levels of social disjuncture.

Viewed in this way, the provision and administration of laws, as a function, must be performed by one entity—and that entity is government. Citizens cede **natural monopoly power** to the government to establish and maintain a system of justice—that is, they give governments, and governments alone, the power to arrest people, to imprison them, or to otherwise punish them. Governments gain an implicit monopoly on force in return for the promise that they will keep the peace and allow all law-abiding citizens to live freely and pursue those things that bring them happiness.

This chapter explores criminal justice and its administration in the United States. Consideration is given to the currently high rates of incarceration at the federal and state levels and their impacts. The proportion of African Americans in prison in the United States is far higher than that of whites and Hispanics. This difference has led to consideration of the factors driving people to commit crimes and become imprisoned. Over recent years, efforts have been made to address the large size of the U.S. prison population. Such efforts have included sentencing reforms and efforts to explore why people fall into lives of crime and how they can avoid this path.

The notion of treating public policies as investments may seem at odds with many practices in the realm of criminal justice. Indeed, it is hard to imagine some especially violent people ever being able to contribute effectively in society. However, policy experiments—primarily in other countries—are demonstrating that working in

Facing page: In the United States, each state has its own system of laws and courts. Most matters of law are managed at the state level, with complex cases being heard in state supreme courts, such as the Supreme Court in Iowa City, Iowa, whose building is shown here.

different ways with criminals can place them on track to leading good lives and avoiding future imprisonment. The chapter gives these positive developments considerable emphasis.

This chapter introduces you to:

- The essential role that systems of criminal justice play in shaping social interactions, preserving peace, and allowing disputes to be peacefully resolved
- How the United States compares with the rest of the world in terms of its current prison population
- Traditional approaches to criminal justice in the United States
- Alternative conceptions of the purpose of prisons and how these can lead to differences in the practices of prison guards and probation officers
- How federalism has produced many differences in the ways individual American states define criminal behavior and punish those who break the law
- How definitions of criminal behavior evolve
- The costs associated with imprisonment
- The use of the death penalty
- How treating public policies as investments can be applied to aspects of criminal justice
- Criminal justice and the pursuit of civil rights, with an emphasis on differences in contemporary incarceration rates among blacks, whites, and Hispanics
- Lessons for public policy emerging from this review of criminal justice

AN INTRODUCTION TO CRIMINAL JUSTICE

To support the pursuit of justice, all governments must establish and maintain appropriate systems of lawmaking and legal interpretation. In such systems, the judiciary has the function of reviewing evidence surrounding specific cases and deciding in what sense and to what extent parties may have violated established law.

Much of the work of the judiciary revolves around settlement of disputes where criminal proceedings are unnecessary. This is the realm of such sub-branches of the system as constitutional law, commercial law, personal injury law, and family law. In all instances, independent judges preside over independent courts. Their role is to review relevant evidence and reach considered judgments on specific cases where parties are in dispute. Backed up by the appropriate laws and relevant policing authorities, judges, upon reaching their decisions, direct parties to take specific actions deemed appropriate for ensuring that justice is done.

When criminal behavior has been alleged, defendants enter the criminal justice system. The task for the judiciary is to determine if wrongdoing occurred and, if so, what form of punishment is appropriate, given the covering law. In the United States, as in all other countries, those found guilty of a crime face punishment. This takes them into the world of corrections—where serving time in prison is one of several possible punishments.

Administration of criminal justice is a significant public policy issue. No society can function effectively without a sound legal system that is supported by institutions that ensure widespread respect for the law and adherence to it. Yet its significance cannot suggest that crime and punishment should assume a central role in popular culture. Nor does it suggest that vast amounts of public funding should be spent on prisons.

THE U.S. PRISON POPULATION
IN COMPARATIVE PERSPECTIVE

At present in the United States, more than two million people are in prison—more than in any other country in the world. Table 9.1 presents comparative figures for total prison population and prisoners per 100,000 of the national population across a selection of countries. By any measure, the incarceration rate for the United States is extraordinarily high. At 698 prisoners per 100,000 of the population, the rate is nearly five times the rate for the world as a whole, more than six times the rate for Canada, and more than three times the rate for Mexico. China, a nation often portrayed in the popular media as having an oppressive state, has 119 prisoners per 100,00 of the population. Its rate is higher than that for many nations in Europe, yet it is almost six times smaller than the U.S. rate.

The direct and indirect costs to U.S. society of this high rate of imprisonment are huge. When public funds are spent on the building and management of prisons, they are diverted from more productive uses. In the name of public safety and retribution, lives are wasted. They are wasted in the form of prisoners languishing in confinement, doing nothing to acquire skills that could truly transform their lives. They are wasted in the form of prison officers engaging in lives of utter boredom punctuated by occasional moments of violence, on the part of both prisoners and prison officers. And they are wasted in the even more banal forms of administration and service delivery that make prisons workable. At the same time, so much of this waste has been normalized that most of us think uncritically of prisons as fundamental institutions in society.

The prisons of today are more secure and make greater use of surveillance technology than did prisons of the past. Yet all of them have the stink of the Dark Ages about them. The thought that we could realize much better social outcomes than we experience at present is the primary motivation of this chapter. Improvements could undoubtedly be made in the administration of criminal justice. In the short term, those improvements might not produce significant cost savings; in the longer term, they could. At the same time, they would undoubtedly improve the quality of life for many people. The key is to find sets of early interventions that can divert a person from a future path of crime and punishment onto a path of self-reliance and social conformity.[1] Some of those interventions fall outside the scope of criminal justice and into the realm of schooling and welfare reform. Nonetheless, there are different and more effective ways of administering criminal justice than some of the approaches now in use. Even small changes along those lines could have positive social benefits. More significant changes will take many decades before they yield major social improvements. Case Study 9.1 regarding prisoner abuse indicates that much is needed to improve upon current administration of criminal justice.

TABLE 9.1   International Comparison of Prison Populations, 2015

COUNTRY	PRISON POPULATION[a]	PRISON POPULATION RATE[b]	COUNTRY	PRISON POPULATION[a]	PRISON POPULATION RATE[b]
United States	2,217,000	698	**World**	10,357,134	144
Australia	35,949	151	Italy	52,434	86
Austria	8,188	95	Japan	60,486	48
Belgium	11,769	105	Korea	50,800	101
Brazil	607,731	301	Luxembourg	631	112
Canada	37,864	106	Mexico	255,138	212
Chile	44,238	247	Netherlands	11,603	69
China	1,657,812	119	New Zealand	8,906	194
Czech Rep.	20,628	195	Norway	3,710	71
Denmark	3,481	61	Poland	72,609	191
Estonia	2,830	216	Portugal	14,238	138
Finland	3,105	57	Russian Federation	642,470	445
France	60,896	95	Singapore	12,596	227
Germany	63,628	78	Slovak Republic	9,991	184
Greece	11,798	109	Slovenia	11,511	73
Hungary	18,424	187	South Africa	159,241	292
Iceland	147	45	Spain	63,025	136
India	418,536	33	Sweden	5,400	55
Indonesia	161,692	64	Switzerland	6,923	84
Ireland	3,733	80	Turkey	172,562	220
Israel	20,245	256	United Kingdom	85,843	148

Data Source: Roy Walmsley, "World Prison Population List," 11th ed. Essex, UK: International Centre for Prison Studies, February 2, 2015.

Note: This list of countries is shorter than the list contained in the "World Prison Population List" and from where the world average figures have been drawn.

[a]Total number in penal institutions, including pretrial detainees. [b]Per 100,000 of national population.

case study 9.1 Prisoner Abuse in New York's Attica Correctional Facility

In 2015, three prison guards from Attica Correctional Facility in upstate New York pleaded guilty to state charges stemming from the beating of a 29-year-old inmate. Their guilty pleas came on the eve of their criminal trial in Federal District Court in Buffalo on assault charges. Each could have been sentenced to as many as 25 years in prison.

Through the plea bargain they lost their jobs at Attica but avoided the possibility of prison time. This was the first case ever in which New York State prison guards faced criminal indictments for nonsexual assault on an inmate.

The case was publicized in detail by the *New York Times*.[2] Indeed, the guilty pleas were submitted the day after an article appeared in that newspaper, naming the officers involved. The guards—like all the guards at Attica at the time—were white. The inmate was African American.

The beating took place one evening in August 2011. Prisoners in C Block that night were noisy. When a guard shouted for them to be quiet, an inmate retorted for the guard to be quiet himself. (The actual language used by both guard and inmate was crude.) Following the exchange, inmates were ordered to their cells. Half an hour later, three officers came to the cell of an inmate they—apparently incorrectly—surmised had voiced the earlier retort. The inmate was ordered to strip for a search. He was then led to a darkened dayroom for what he was told would be a urine test.

Once in the dayroom, the three guards attacked the naked inmate with batons and kicks, striking him more than 50 times. After several minutes, during which the inmate screamed for

Attica Correctional Facility in upstate New York has long been considered one of the most repressive and brutal prisons in the state.

(Dan Farrell/New York Daily News via Getty Images)

his life and many other inmates heard the thuds of wood on flesh, he was left with cracked ribs and two broken legs. The guards then handcuffed him and pushed him down a staircase. This mistreatment led to a broken shoulder. At the bottom of the stairs, a guard finally smashed the inmate's face against a wall, damaging an eye.

After the beating, the three prison guards who did it sought to have the inmate placed in solitary confinement. However, his injuries were such that he required medical treatment. The extensive wounds suffered by the inmate led to him being hospitalized in Buffalo. At this point, the guards could no longer control the narrative and contrive to hide what they had done. The union representing them nonetheless took various actions to support and protect them, including raising legal funds.

The *New York Times* article on this beating suggests it was far from an isolated case. Indeed, some of the guards at the prison had histories of engaging in brutal behaviors that had led to civil cases being brought against them. One had previously been named in at least 24 federal civil rights lawsuits filed by inmates.

Many incidents of prison guard brutality toward prisoners in facilities across the United States have been documented. New York's prisons are not alone in harboring such incidents.

Given the U.S. Supreme Court decision of *Porter v. Nussle* (2002),[3] requiring that inmates alleging abusive treatment must exhaust administrative remedies in the prison facility before bringing an action in district court, suspicions exist that much more brutality occurs than is ever officially reported.[4] Meanwhile, stories of rape and other forms of sexual violence perpetrated on prisoners by fellow inmates and by guards led the U.S. Congress to pass the Prison Rape Elimination Act of 2003. Evidence suggests such abuse continues to occur.[5]

Repression and abuse of prisoners are of major concern, from the perspectives of human rights and of promoting the good society. Prisoners who have been systematically victimized, humiliated, isolated at length from meaningful contact with others, and subjected to brutal beatings or sexual attacks return to society broken and angry.

CRITICAL THINKING QUESTIONS

1. Why might prison guards engage in brutality toward prisoners?
2. What changes would be required to minimize all forms of brutality in prisons?

THE PUBLIC PROBLEM

The social contract tradition in political theory has provided extensive discussions of the rights that citizens confer to their governments in return for protection and social order. The contributions of John Locke and Jean-Jacques Rousseau heavily informed the drafting of the U.S. Constitution as well as the constitutions of the early states. In federal systems of government, like that of the United States, careful efforts must be made to ensure appropriate coordination of the national system of justice and of those operating at the state level. Indeed, coordination also must occur within states, to ensure that systems of justice in cities, counties, and other within-state jurisdictions do not conflict with or contradict the broader governing laws. Given this need for one system of govern-ment to ensure social order, it follows that the administration of criminal justice must be conducted solely by governments. In practice, although many different individuals and entities contribute to the operation of criminal justice systems, ultimate responsibility for the effectiveness and outcomes of the system lies with the government.

ESTABLISHING AND MAINTAINING SOCIAL ORDER

Systems of criminal justice function to establish and maintain orderly societies. To this end, they administer sanctions on those who break the law. They use punishments both to deter people from engaging in crime and to ensure that those who do wrong pay for what they did. Of course, to promote a good society, it is important that those who engage in crime not only pay for what they did but desist from committing fur-ther crime. A perennial challenge for society concerns how to balance the need for deterrence and punishment of serious crime against the need for offenders to be reha-bilitated. **Rehabilitation** is the process that involves preparing convicted offenders to live peacefully and productively in society after they have received their punishment.

Questions of human nature arise here. Some people hold the view that crimi-nal justice exists entirely to ensure the safety and well-being of law-abiding citizens. In this view, those who commit serious crime should face serious punishment and be removed from society for as long as possible. The humanity of the offender is often given limited consideration. A contrasting view acknowledges the wrongdo-ing of the offender and the need for punishment. However, it also recognizes that the offender has the capacity to be transformed into a law-abiding and productive member of society. In this view, a significant role of criminal justice is to work with offenders to allow them to make the most of their lives after they have paid for their offenses. Since the differences of view here are driven by differences in values, moral conundrums arise.

BALANCING PUNISHMENT AND REHABILITATION

Different views on the balance to be struck between punishment and rehabil-itation lie at the heart of the public policy disputes concerning criminal justice. Those disputes are likely to continue for a long time. Nonetheless, evidence can play a vital role in shifting the terms of public disputes. The investment perspective on public policy promotes greater use of evidence in making and administering public policy. As such, the view taken here is that placing too much weight on the punishment of offenders has shown itself to be extremely costly and socially destructive. In contrast, better long-term social outcomes can be attained when criminal justice is used both to punish and to rehabilitate offenders.

TRADITIONAL POLICY APPROACHES

Through history, governments in all jurisdictions and countries have assumed the paramount role in administering criminal justice. Various systems of punishment have evolved and many cruel and unusual forms of punishment have been practiced over the centuries. Frequently, forms of **corporal punishment**, such as floggings, have been used, and public administration of punishment has served both to humiliate criminals and to instruct the citizenry. Publicizing the punishment of wrongdoers was frequently considered a deterrent to crime. Even today, public floggings and executions are performed in countries where respect for human rights is limited. There has also often been a powerful desire to remove prisoners to the outer reaches of society—to place them where they could do no harm. That very desire motivated the **transportation of convicts** from Britain to its colonies. Convicts were transported from Britain to colonial North America from around 1620 through 1780, when the practice was curtailed because of the War of Independence (1775–1783).[6]

EARLY FORMS OF PUNISHMENT IN THE UNITED STATES

Early approaches to criminal justice in the American settlements were heavily influenced by ideas and practices devised in Britain. The initial criminal codes made provision for fines, floggings, banishment, public confinement and display in cages or stocks, various forms of servitude, and the death sentence. Placing convicts in jail cells was used mainly as a transitional step before the administration of a punishment. **Imprisonment** as a form of punishment in itself emerged only in the early 1800s. For a long period afterward, imprisonment was treated as one of several possible punishments for wrongdoing. The relative lack of strong governmental systems in the United States—especially in the southern states—allowed **vigilante justice** to thrive. For example, David Garland has documented many instances of public torture and lynching being undertaken by mobs while the formal authorities looked on. In his view, the continuation of the death penalty in contemporary society is a carefully crafted remnant of those times: a civilized, nonviolent counterpart of those past excesses, "overlaid with ambivalence, anxiety, and embarrassment."[7]

FROM CORPORAL PUNISHMENT TO LENGTHY PRISON TERMS

It was only in the 20th century that imprisonment came to fully replace various forms of corporal punishment as the primary way that society made offenders pay for their crimes. Within the basic model of the prison, different views on the purpose of confinement have prevailed at different times. The **Pennsylvania system** was predicated on the view that prisoners could be rehabilitated to live peacefully in society. The preferred means of treatment involved solitary confinement. In contrast, the **New York system** that evolved in New York State emphasized the need for punishment. The model required prisoners to engage in daily hard labor, which was performed in a communal setting.

The New York system came to prevail across the United States, as it was considerably less expensive than the Pennsylvania system. Meanwhile, in the southern states, criminal justice again developed differently. Most significantly, in the wake of the Civil War (1861–1865), states created **chain gangs** of prisoners that were deployed to construct roads and railroads. The **convict lease** system was also introduced in many southern states. In this system, the state leased prisoners to large companies as a form of cheap labor, working in both industrial and agricultural settings. The conditions experienced by prisoners were frequently extremely cruel. However, this practice continued well into the 20th century.[8]

ESTABLISHING HUMANE PRISONS

Against this backdrop, the development of the modern state and federal prison systems, where prisoner labor cannot be exploited and the cruelest punishments have ceased, is a positive advance from the past. The segregation of prisoners based on their age, gender, and the severity of their crimes has also served to reduce the risks that imprisonment poses to offenders. The rise of **community sentencing**, which involves serving out a term of punishment through community work, or early release from prison for good behavior—termed **parole**—can also be seen as a positive advance from the past. Even so, the debate over punishment versus rehabilitation of offenders continues. Efforts by politicians "to get tough on crime" over recent decades have tended to make prison life harder, to have limited the use of community sentencing, and to have reduced the extent to which prisons assist offenders in building the skills and resilience needed to integrate, upon their release, back into society and lead crime-free lives (see Case Study 9.2).

case study 9.2 Preparing Prisoners for Effective Release and Social Integration

Imprisoning criminals is costly. A 2010 estimate placed the average annual cost in the United States of holding one prisoner at over $30,000.[9] Viewing expenditures on prisons as a major drain on society, governments around the world have begun exploring options for reducing their prison populations. Of these approaches, one involves working to reduce the likelihood that prisoners, upon their release, will reoffend and return to prison.

Returning to crime is termed **recidivism**. Recidivism rates are difficult to measure and compare because of differences in the definitions being used and the amount of time after release from prison being considered. A U.S. study based on 30 states explored what happened over the next five years to a cohort of inmates released in 2005.[10] It examined their experience of parole—that is, their early release from prison before their sentence was completed. It also explored their experience of **probation**, where they are closely monitored and required to report to local probation officers on a regular basis. (Note that probation can sometimes be imposed on a convicted criminal as a way of avoiding serving time in prison.) Three years after release, almost half the released inmates had gone back to prison for either a parole or probation violation or an arrest for a new offense. Within five years, fully three-quarters of those released in 2005 had been arrested for a new crime.

Are there actions that would reduce reoffending and reimprisonment? A review of recidivism rates worldwide suggests that some countries are better than others at preparing inmates for effective release and social integration.[11] For example, in comparing cohorts of prisoners released between 2005 and 2011 in the United States, Norway, and Singapore, reconviction rates after two years appear to have been 25 percent lower in Singapore and 44 percent lower in Norway compared with those in the United States. Indeed, across 18 countries, Norway and Singapore performed best on keeping recidivism rates low. Even so, one in five released prisoners in Norway had been reconvicted within two years. This rate suggests that helping inmates break away from a life of crime is a challenge everywhere.

Both Norway and Singapore have prison systems that place a strong emphasis on rehabilitating prisoners through education, job training, and various forms of therapy. They have not always done so. Until the late 1990s, these countries ran prison systems that had many similarities with those in the United States and elsewhere. Norway has subsequently placed emphasis on working with prisoners to help them prepare for productive, socially engaged lives upon their release from prison. Singapore has done the same, while consciously working to make the broader society more hospitable to ex-convicts.

In Norway, strong efforts are made to ensure that everyone, upon release from prison, will have housing, employment, income, and—as needed—access to education, health care, and addiction treatment.[12] Aside from the obvious limits on freedom, prisoners in Norway are encouraged to live lives that resemble life outside prison. This approach ensures that their time behind bars is used effectively to improve their self-development. They are encouraged to take responsibility for the crimes they committed and for how they will live in and contribute to broader society in the future.

In Singapore, a fundamental shift has occurred over the past two decades in its system of criminal justice.[13] Today, prisons are not simply places established to promote security and safety. They are also places that support the rehabilitation and reintegration of offenders into society. Prison guards in Singapore now think of themselves as "captains of lives." In making this shift, the Singapore Prison Service came to understand that rehabilitation would be more effective if inmates had the support of their families. Many efforts have been made to ensure that inmates stay in close contact with family members while doing their time.

Other efforts in Singapore have focused on changing how people in society view inmates and treat them upon release. For example, in a partnership project between the government and the community that began in 2004, the Yellow Ribbon Fund was created to support interactions among prisoners, ex-prisoners, and the broader society. Opportunities were established for citizens to visit prisons and engage with convicts—events have included annual art and poetry competitions for prisoners. Major efforts have also been made to encourage companies to hire ex-convicts for paid employment.

These actions go a long way to explaining why Singapore's recidivism rate dropped by 40 percent between 1998 and 2009. More importantly, these actions have allowed many convicts to turn their lives around and, upon release, fully participate in paid work and pursue active social lives.

CRITICAL THINKING QUESTIONS

1. What factors do you think are most likely to lead a released prisoner to commit new crimes?
2. If you were to differentiate prisoners based on the crimes they have committed, which ones would you focus on to promote effective rehabilitation into society?

CRIMINAL JUSTICE IN A FEDERAL SYSTEM

As noted, criminal justice is administered in the United States through separate systems operating at the local, county, state, and federal levels. This feature of federalism opens many possibilities for variation in the definition of criminal behavior and how those convicted of breaking the law are treated. At times, those seeking legal reforms find the system frustrating. For example, President Obama expressed a desire for greater efforts across the country to control the purchase and use of firearms. However, the U.S. Constitution grants most power to the individual states on this matter. Likewise, President Obama voiced concerned over the high levels of incarceration found in the United States. Although he was able to make some administrative adjustments to reduce the length of sentences served in the federal prison system, his influence proved limited.

The autonomy of the states to establish and maintain their systems of criminal justice has also opened many opportunities for those seeking legal reform. As in other policy areas, considerable room exists for states to experiment in their approaches to criminal justice. Experiments deemed worthwhile and effective can diffuse to other states; in some instances, these experiments fail to evoke interest elsewhere.

Issues in federalism and criminal justice continually appear through this chapter. The following section considers the evolving definitions of criminal behavior. Salient examples include contemporary differences across states in their interpretation of appropriate sexual practices and use of recreational drugs. Later in the chapter, we will consider differences across states in incarceration rates, use of the death penalty, and reliance on private companies for the management of prisons. In Chapter 5, "Defense and Homeland Security," we considered differences in state gun laws. We saw that the nature of such laws can greatly affect levels of gun-related deaths. Federalism creates conditions for many comparisons of natural experiments in the organization of criminal justice. These can have many benefits for reformers seeking to identify effective public policy settings in this area.

EVOLVING DEFINITIONS OF CRIMINAL BEHAVIOR

Legal definitions of criminal behavior are continuously evolving. This evolution tends to occur within the legislative process. Over time, behaviors once considered criminal in nature can become legal. Likewise, as awareness of the implications of specific behaviors change, some can be deemed crimes.[14] Within federal systems of government, it often happens that definitions of criminal behavior in one jurisdiction contrast with definitions elsewhere. Across the United States, differences arise both in definitions of criminal activity and in the severity of the punishments given to those found guilty of committing specific crimes.

The practice of prostitution offers an example of behavior that is deemed legal in some jurisdictions and illegal in others. Some critics argue that prostitution is degrading and that it should be discouraged. Others suggest that it will happen no matter what its legal status. Therefore, to protect prostitutes from violence and exploitation and to reduce the spread of sexually transmitted diseases, they argue that legalization is appropriate.

In the United States, prostitution is considered a matter for regulation primarily by state governments. Currently, prostitution is legal only in certain counties in Nevada. From 1980 to 2009, prostitution was also legal in Rhode Island, although throughout that period the state's laws criminalized public solicitation and the running of brothels. In 2009, buying and selling of sex was made illegal in Rhode Island.

Possession and use of marijuana is another practice that has met with distinctive responses among states across the United States. Although it is still considered an illicit drug in many places, states are increasingly making provision for its medical use. State laws are also changing to allow legal sales of marijuana and private consumption.

CONTEMPORARY POLICY ISSUES

Since the 1960s, policy debates about criminal justice have been dominated by social conservatives. Broadly, social conservatives have claimed that little can be done to prevent certain young people from pursuing lives of crime.[15] They have argued that the best way to make society safer is to deter criminal activity through use of strict criminal sanctions. When such deterrence does not work, the conservatives have claimed that criminals should be incapacitated through use of long prison sentences.[16] Criminologists, who have tended to take the view that only broader social justice will reduce crime, have offered few pragmatic policy ideas.

According to Francis T. Cullen and his colleagues, criminologists have rarely engaged in policy-oriented research for fear of being viewed by colleagues as pawns of the state, brokering knowledge to "discipline and punish" the poor.[17] In taking this purist position, criminologists have left an intellectual void in policy making, and conservatives have jumped at the chance to fill it. The result has been an escalation of people passing through the criminal justice system.

Many issues arise in public policy regarding criminal justice. In what follows, we consider four, all of which serve as sites for debate between social conservatives and liberals. The four issues are:

1. the prison population,
2. sentencing reform,
3. the death penalty, and
4. the use of private prisons.

THE PRISON POPULATION

Table 9.2 offers an overview of changes through the decades in the total U.S. prison and jail population, its estimated cost to the nation, and changes in crime rates over time. Between 1960 and 1980, the prison population grew as rates of violent and property crimes grew. In contrast, between 1990 and 2010, these crime rates each declined by over 40 percent, but the number of inmates almost doubled. Indeed, crime rates in 2010 were comparable to those in 1970. Despite this statistic, there were over 11 times as many inmates in U.S. prisons and jails in 2010 as there were in 1970. In constant dollar terms, American taxpayers were funding prisons to the tune of $65 billion more in 2010 than they were in 1970. Yet they were experiencing an equivalent level of public safety.

Incarceration rates, which report the proportion of citizens in prison at any given time, have reached unprecedented levels in the United States, and an appetite for the death penalty has been reawakened. At the same time, conservative politicians have worried about the costs associated with adopting this tough line on crime. This concern has led to an examination of court procedures, with an eye to reducing procedural inefficiencies. It has also led to engagement of private prison services, based on

TABLE 9.2 Changing Prison Population Rates, Prison Expenditures, and Crime Rates in the United States, 1960–2012

YEAR	TOTAL PRISONERS HELD IN THE U.S.[a]	TOTAL PRISON EXPENSES[b]	NATIONAL VIOLENT CRIME RATE[c]	NATIONAL PROPERTY CRIME RATE[c]
1960	212,344	6.64	160.9	1,726.3
1970	198,831	6.22	363.5	3,621.0
1980	503,600	15.76	596.6	5,353.3
1990	1,148,700	35.94	729.6	5,073.1
2000	1,945,400	60.86	506.5	3,618.3
2010	2,279,100	71.30	404.5	2,945.9
2012	2,231,300	69.81	386.9	2,859.2

Sources: Compiled by the author. Prisoner numbers from U.S. Bureau of Justice Statistics; expenses calculated by the author based on Vera Institute of Justice estimated average cost per prisoner in 2010 of $31,286; crime rates from the Federal Bureau of Investigation, Uniform Crime Reporting Statistics.

[a]In prisons and jails. [b]In billions of U.S. dollars, estimated, 2010. [c]Reported incidents per 100,000 population.

the view that private sector managers will be more adept than their public sector counterparts at introducing efficiencies into prison operations. Only in the past decade have we begun to see more balanced discussions emerging around criminal justice and how to most effectively address high prison rates while avoiding a rise in crime rates.

The contemporary scene in the United States has been termed the **carceral state**.[18] In this view, the continuity between the past and the present is acknowledged. That is to say, it has long been recognized that issues of law and order have been central to the development of government at the local, state, and federal levels in the United States, as elsewhere. Political elites in the United States have often promoted punitive approaches to maintaining law and order. Maintenance of a well-behaved, orderly adult population has ensured continuous supply of disciplined labor in various workplaces. It has also reduced the risk of challenge to unequal distribution of wealth in society.

What is new about developments since the 1970s is the growth of incarceration rates, the significantly higher likelihood of nonwhites ending up in prison, and the uneven impacts of **felon disenfranchisement** on voting behavior. Apparent declines in voter turnout can be blamed in part to the practice of prohibiting people on probation, in prison, and on parole from voting.[19] It is common practice in many states to deny voting rights for life to anyone who has served time in prison.

Another aspect of the carceral state is that it takes people out of the labor force, not just for the duration for their time in prison but often for life. Bruce Western has argued that because of their involvement in the penal system, young black men hardly benefited from the economic boom of the 1990s.[20] Those who spent time in prison had much lower wages and employment rates than did similar men without criminal records. The losses from mass incarceration spread further. Western estimated that by the end of the 1990s, 1 out of 10 young black children had a father in prison. This phenomenon has helped perpetuate the cycle of broken families, poverty, and crime. In the carceral state, prison becomes all-pervasive. Indeed, for many communities in the United States today, prison has come to shape the experience of young people—especially young men—far more than other formative institutions, such as schools, universities, or the military.

SENTENCING REFORM

Sentencing is a central aspect of criminal justice. The "get tough" approach to criminal justice has fueled the rise in prison populations in the United States since the 1970s. For example, the **truth-in-sentencing** movement led to more convicted offenders being sent to prison for longer periods of time. Some states have eliminated parole. These changes have satisfied those who see criminal justice as primarily about punishment and deterrence from crime. However, the changes have placed a significant strain on state budgets. Table 9.3 reports state prison populations and incarceration rates in 2013. Incarceration rates differ significantly from state to state. Louisiana had the highest rate, with 1,420 people in prison for every 100,000 people in the state population. In contrast, Maine had the lowest incarceration rate, at 320 per 100,000 population. Table 9.3 also lists average annual cost per inmate for 40 states. The average cost per inmate across these states in 2010 was $31,286.[21] But costs differ significantly across the states, running from $14,603 per inmate in Kentucky to over $60,000 in the state of New York.

When states cannot afford to keep putting people in prison, but the state laws call for truth in sentencing, few options for relieving pressure exist other than to make changes to sentencing practices. The result has been the birth of efforts to provide judges with risk assessment tools that can guide their sentencing practices. Under this approach, analysts use historical evidence to estimate the factors that tend to be associated with the recidivism of nonviolent offenders. They then use this evidence to construct guidelines or worksheets that judges refer to when selecting a sentence. The approach, which is also termed **actuarial sentencing**, combines knowledge of each offender, the nature of the crime or crimes being punished, and the offender's prior conviction record to suggest a sentence that will be effective and not unnecessarily lengthy.[22]

There is debate about the merits of sentencing guidelines that adopt a risk-based approach. They can lead to reduced imprisonment of nonviolent offenders, and more focused efforts to work with offenders in ways that can reduce their

TABLE 9.3 State Prison Populations, Incarceration Rates, and Average Annual Cost Per Inmate

STATE	PRISON POPULATION[a]	INCARCERATION RATE[b]	AVERAGE ANNUAL COST/INMATE[c]
Alabama	46,000	1,230	$17,285
Alaska	5,100	940	—
Arizona	55,200	1,090	$24,805
Arkansas	22,800	1,010	$24,391
California	218,800	750	$47,421
Colorado	32,100	790	$30,374
Connecticut	17,600	620	$50,262
Delaware	7,000	960	$32,967
Florida	154,500	990	$20,553
Georgia	91,600	1,220	$21,039
Hawaii	5,600	510	—
Idaho	10,200	860	$19,545
Illinois	69,300	700	$32,268
Indiana	45,400	910	$14,823
Iowa	12,700	530	$32,925
Kansas	16,600	760	$18,207
Kentucky	32,100	950	$14,603
Louisiana	50,100	1,420	$17,486
Maine	3,800	350	$46,404
Maryland	32,700	710	$38,383
Massachusetts	21,400	400	—
Michigan	60,200	790	$28,117
Minnesota	15,700	380	$41,364
Mississippi	28,800	1,270	—
Missouri	44,500	950	$22,350
Montana	6,000	760	$30,227
Nebraska	8,500	600	$35,950
Nevada	19,900	930	$20,656
New Hampshire	4,800	460	$34,080
New Jersey	37,600	540	$54,865
New Mexico	15,500	980	—

STATE	PRISON POPULATION[a]	INCARCERATION RATE[b]	AVERAGE ANNUAL COST/INMATE[c]
New York	81,400	530	$60,076
North Carolina	55,300	730	$29,965
North Dakota	2,700	470	$39,271
Ohio	69,800	780	$25,814
Oklahoma	37,900	1,300	$18,467
Oregon	22,900	740	—
Pennsylvania	85,500	850	$42,339
Rhode Island	3,400	400	$49,133
South Carolina	32,600	800	—
South Dakota	5,300	820	—
Tennessee	48,100	960	—
Texas	221,800	1,130	$21,390
Utah	12,500	620	$29,349
Vermont	2,100	410	$49,502
Virginia	58,800	910	$25,129
Washington	29,700	550	$46,897
West Virginia	9,700	660	$26,498
Wisconsin	34,800	780	$37,994
Wyoming	3,800	840	—

Sources: Prison population and incarceration rates reported by U.S. Department of Justice, 2014. Average annual cost per inmate calculated and reported by Vera Institute of Justice, 2012.

[a]Total number in penal institutions, including pretrial detainees, 2013. [b]Per 100,000 of state population, 2013. [c]Estimate, 2010.

likelihood of reoffending.[23] However, the approach has not caught on, partly due to issues of data quality and partly due to concerns about the ethics of imposing different sentences on different people for committing the same crime.[24]

THE DEATH PENALTY

Use of the death penalty is a perennial source of heated debate. It was a far more common practice in earlier centuries than it is today. Currently, fewer than 25 countries around the world support the death penalty. Countries that most frequently use it are China, Iran, Pakistan, and Saudi Arabia.

In the United States, the death penalty has always been unevenly applied. In 1972, the United States Supreme Court ruled all existing capital statutes unconstitutional. However, the death penalty was reintroduced via another Supreme Court ruling in 1976. Table 9.4 details recent use of the death penalty. The federal government and 31 states now hold around 3,000 inmates under sentence of death. Alabama, California, Florida, and Texas hold more than half of the inmates on death row. The Federal Bureau of Prisons held 61 prisoners under sentence of death in 2015. In 2014, 35 executions were carried out in seven states and none were conducted by the federal government. The preferred method of execution is by lethal injection, although electrocution, lethal gas, hanging, and firing squad are also retained as methods of execution across the states.

Table 9.5 lists the 19 states that do not currently have the death penalty, and the year of abolition for each. Among states where the death penalty is available as

TABLE 9.4 Jurisdictions with the Death Penalty

U.S. JURISDICTION	PRISONERS EXECUTED IN 2014	PRISONERS EXECUTED 1977–2014	PRISONERS ON DEATH ROW, APRIL 1, 2015
Federal Government	0	3	61
States with the death penalty (31)			
Alabama	0	56	201
Arizona	1	37	124
Arkansas	0	27	35
California	0	13	746
Colorado	0	1	3
Delaware	0	16	17
Florida	8	89	401
Georgia	2	55	85
Idaho	0	3	11
Indiana	0	20	14
Kansas	0	0	9
Kentucky	0	3	34
Louisiana	0	28	85
Mississippi	0	21	48
Missouri	10	80	33
Montana	0	3	2
Nevada	0	12	78
New Hampshire	0	0	1
North Carolina	0	43	157
Ohio	1	53	145
Oklahoma	3	111	48

U.S. JURISDICTION	PRISONERS EXECUTED IN 2014	PRISONERS EXECUTED 1977–2014	PRISONERS ON DEATH ROW, APRIL 1, 2015
Oregon	0	2	36
Pennsylvania	0	3	184
South Carolina	0	43	44
South Dakota	0	3	3
Tennessee	0	6	73
Texas	10	528	271
Utah	0	7	9
Virginia	0	110	8
Washington	0	5	9
Wyoming	0	1	1
Totals	**35**	**1,382**	**2,976**

Data Sources: Death Penalty Information Center (2015); U.S. Department of Justice (2014).

TABLE 9.5   Jurisdictions without the Death Penalty

STATES WITHOUT THE DEATH PENALTY (19)	YEAR DEATH PENALTY WAS ABOLISHED
Alaska	1957
Connecticut	2012
Hawaii	1957
Illinois	2011
Iowa	1965
Maine	1887
Maryland	2013
Massachusetts	1984
Michigan	1846
Minnesota	1911
Nebraska	2015
New Jersey	2007
New Mexico	2009
New York	2007
North Dakota	1973
Rhode Island	1984
Vermont	1964
West Virginia	1965
Wisconsin	1853
Other Jurisdiction	
District of Columbia	1981

Source: Death Penalty Information Center (2015).

a sentence, application varies from state to state. Some states use it extremely rarely. There are differences, too, between the sentencing of offenders and the likelihood that the sentence will be carried out. Executing offenders costs more than imprisoning them for life. One calculation has determined that California spent $4 billion on the death penalty from 1977 to 2002.[25] Over those 25 years, the state conducted 13 executions. Death penalty trials in California are 20 times more expensive than trials seeking a sentence of life in prison without parole. This figure is consistent with figures reported in other states.

PRIVATE PRISONS

Throughout history, private actors have been closely involved in the administration of criminal justice, both in the United States and elsewhere.[26] In the early days of prison administration, some states allowed private individuals and firms to build, manage, and handle the day-to-day operations of some prisons. For a time, Louisiana leased the entire operation of the prisons to private enterprises, and made a profit from doing so.[27]

Over the past few decades, private companies have once again come to play a significant role in the delivery of prison services in the United States. Many policy makers have desired to create self-sufficient or even profitable prisons. Questions about the morality of private companies administering key elements of criminal justice deserve close scrutiny.[28] At the same time, it is noteworthy that management of the most difficult offenders and administration of the death penalty has always been seen as a necessary role of the state. In 2013, of the 1,574,741 prisoners held in custody by the federal government or state governments, 133,044—just under 8.5 percent— were held in private prisons. Many states have no inmates in private prisons.

In the broader view, the debate about use of private corporations to manage prisons is a relatively minor aspect. Much more significant are the social consequences of placing large numbers of offenders in prison. Questions about the relative efficiency gains of using some combination of public and private service delivery are secondary. In the end, it might well be that some forms of private service delivery are better and more efficient, although this has been difficult to verify due to problems of comparability and effective research design.[29] For now, our attention should be fixed on the overall cost of current criminal justice policy settings and the direct and indirect costs they impose on society.

CRIMINAL JUSTICE AND THE INVESTMENT PERSPECTIVE

High incarceration rates and the significant costs associated with keeping offenders in prison create funding dilemmas for governments. Those high incarceration rates have been driven by policy choices. Politicians wanting to deter would-be offenders, to punish those who have committed crimes, and to keep them off the streets for lengthy periods often do not count the costs of doing so.[30] Although few politicians want to be viewed as anything other than "tough on crime," the costs of criminal justice have led to new discussions about possible alternatives to building more prisons. Developing an evidence base to inform sound public policy in this area is difficult. However, efforts in this direction have started, as we note in this discussion of Washington State's experience with the investment perspective.

THE INVESTMENT PERSPECTIVE IN THE STATE OF WASHINGTON

The best policy work adopting an investment perspective on criminal justice has been produced by Steve Aos and his colleagues at the Washington State Institute for Public Policy (WSIPP). In 2005, long-term forecasts indicated that the state of Washington would need to construct two new prisons by 2020 and possibly another by 2030. At the time, a typical new prison housing 2,000 prisoners cost about $250 million to build and $45 million per year to operate. (The adult prison incarceration rate in the state of Washington tripled between 1970 and 2000. However, that incarceration rate was well below the average incarceration rate for the United States as a whole.)

The 2005 Washington Legislature directed the WSIPP to investigate whether it was possible to reduce the future need for prisons in the state, save money for taxpayers, and contribute to lower crime rates. In response, Aos and his colleagues drew upon existing evidence to identify "portfolios" of policy choices that would replace "lower rate-of-return investments with strategies that produce higher rates of return on the taxpayers' dollar."[31]

In developing their response, the authors began by asking: What strategies work to reduce crime? To answer this question, they took a careful, evidence-based approach, working only with findings from previous evaluations that included a nontreatment or treatment-as-usual comparison group well matched to the program group. Next, the authors asked: What are the benefits and costs of each program? Once they had determined if anything works to lower crime outcomes, they sought to know whether the amount of crime reduction in each case justified the program's expenditures. Having generated this evidence, the authors then pursued answers to a third question: How would alternative portfolios of evidence-based and economically sound options affect future prison construction, criminal justice costs, and crime rates? Overall, the study reviewed the findings of 571 comparison-group evaluations of adult corrections, juvenile corrections, and prevention programs. For those programs with statistically significant reductions in recidivism rates, the authors then conducted cost-benefit analyses. They calculated program benefits of reductions in crime both for taxpayers and for crime victims.

The WSIPP study concluded that making greater use of a range of programs for adult and juvenile offenders could significantly reduce the cost of criminal justice in the state. Aos and his colleagues concluded that Washington could avoid a significant amount of future prison construction, save considerable public funds, and slightly lower crime rates by making the proposed changes. Since all of the programs discussed in the report were already in place and known to be effective elsewhere, they were not hugely controversial.

Options for adult offenders included better drug treatment in prison and community corrections, cognitive-behavioral treatment in prisons and community corrections, and education in prison, including vocational education. Options for juvenile offenders included forms of family therapy, aggression replacement training, and efforts to assist juveniles on drugs. Based upon the WSIPP's findings, the 2007 legislature allocated $44 million in the biennial budget for the expanded use of evidence-based programs. Investments were made in juvenile and adult criminal justice programs, as well as in prevention programs.

THE JUSTICE REINVESTMENT MOVEMENT

The search for effective ways to reduce crime without expanding the prison population has given rise to the **justice reinvestment** movement. The term "justice reinvestment" was coined by Susan Tucker and Eric Cadora in a policy paper published by the Open Society Institute in 2003. The paper has prompted subsequent discussions and actions intended to reduce the money spent on prisons and to use the savings to build safer, more sustainable communities.[32] The original discussion of justice reinvestment started with the observation that the people populating state prisons tend to be drawn disproportionately from specific neighborhoods. Tucker and Cadora wrote of "million dollar blocks," where the incarceration rates of those who resided there were up to 25 times higher than average incarceration rates. Figure 9.1 presents an example of this mapping exercise.

By mapping incarceration data and matching it with other relevant data, Tucker and Cadora were able to demonstrate the devastating effects that incarceration was having on specific neighborhoods. They proposed that resources be focused on high-incarceration neighborhoods, to strengthen them so they would be less likely to generate offenders and better able to support law-abiding reintegration of offenders upon their release.[33]

Subsequent development of the justice reinvestment concept has led to the development of a "systems analysis" method containing the following four steps.

1. Determine the number of prisoners coming from specific communities and how much is being spent annually to keep those offenders in prison.
2. Provide policy makers with options to reduce prisoner expenditures and simultaneously increase public safety in those communities.
3. Quantify savings and suggest appropriate ways to reinvest those savings in select high-stakes communities.
4. Measure the impact of the policy change and enhance accountability for the results.

FIGURE 9.1 Prison Expenditure and Million Dollar Blocks. Shown here is one such map produced for New York City. Of the more than two million people in jails and prisons in the United States, a disproportionate number come from a few neighborhoods in the country's biggest cities. In some areas, the concentration is so dense that states are spending in excess of a million dollars a year to incarcerate the residents of single city blocks. Using data from the criminal justice system, the Spatial Information Design Lab and the Justice Mapping Center created maps of these "million dollar blocks."

Prison expenditures by block group in millions of dollars, 2003

(Prison expenditures by census block in New York City, 2003. Image Courtesy Center for Spatial Research, Columbia University produced in 2006 as part of Architecture and Justice.)

State legislatures have shown a considerable amount of interest in justice reinvention. It holds appeal across the political spectrum. Reducing mass incarceration is an idea that appeals to the political left; reducing the costs of government is an idea that appeals to the political right. As a result, justice reinvention has received a reasonable level of bipartisan support.[34] State-level policy work on justice reinvestment has been promoted and supported by the Council of State Governments, the Pew Center on the States, the Public Welfare Foundation, the Urban Institute, and the Bureau of Justice Assistance. For example, the Justice Center at the Council of State Governments has been monitoring developments and has devised a series of lessons for those seeking to further promote justice reinvestment. The Justice Center's lessons are consistent with the four-step systems analysis just noted. However, they also emphasize the importance of engaging diverse constituencies in any initiatives and the importance of strengthening community supervision.[35]

Although still in its infancy, the justice reinvestment movement has resulted in cost savings for a number of jurisdictions.[36] More significantly, it has heralded the greater use of evidence to guide criminal justice policy choices.[37] The emphasis on carefully distinguishing among offenders based upon their likely danger to society has reduced the number of offenders being sent to prison. It has also increased the use of parole as a means of reducing the time offenders spend in prison.

Tucker and Cadora's initial proposal, that savings from prison costs be reinvested into strengthening specific communities with historically high crime rates, has not been uniformly followed. However, efforts to work more closely with offenders in the community—rather than sending them to prison and keeping them there for lengthy periods—is a positive step. As evidence of success in this area builds, it is likely that more serious attention will be given to ways of preventing people from embarking on lives of crime.

JUSTICE REINVESTMENT IN MICHIGAN

Among states that have so far experimented with justice reinvestment, Michigan has received wide acclaim. Historically, the state has been a big spender on prisons, having been in an exclusive club of states spending more on prisons than on higher education. From 2006 to 2009, however, Michigan achieved a 12 percent decline in its prison population.[38] Consequently, the decision taken to close three prisons in the state resulted in annual savings of well over $100 million. The strategy for reducing Michigan's prison population has been in place for some time and was developed to ensure that crime rates will not increase as a consequence.

In 2002, supported by a strong legislative coalition and the judiciary, the state governor repealed almost all of the state's mandatory minimum drug laws—which had been among the toughest in the nation. These were replaced with drug **sentencing guidelines** that gave judges greater discretion. This change had the immediate result of reducing the number of people in prison on drug offenses. The numbers have been dropping every year. Michigan had a history of denying parole to prisoners, which was another factor driving high prison rates. Addressing this issue was a challenge, because members of the state parole board needed to be convinced that early release of prisoners would not result in reoffending.

Starting in 2005, Michigan made efforts to provide more systematic evidence to members of the parole board regarding prisoners and predictions of their likelihood to reoffend. These led to an increase in parole approvals. At the same time, the state worked more closely with parole officers to reduce the likelihood of offenders returning to prisons on the basis of technical parole violations. This led to a decline in reincarcerations, beginning in 2007. Last, the reduction in prison numbers was supported by changes in the sentencing guidelines judges used. Use of graduated sanctions and services that respond to the level of risk and need have improved outcomes for people sentenced to probation, reducing the chances they would be imprisoned while on probation (see Case Study 9.3)

case study 9.3 Improving Probation and Parole Supervision

Imprisoning offenders is expensive. Beyond this aspect, emerging evidence suggests that, when compared with serving community-based sentences, serving time in prison tends to increase the chances that individuals become career criminals.[39] Further, by taking convicts out of society for lengthy periods, prisons reduce the chances that—upon release—convicts will adapt to normal life and become productive, positively engaged citizens. Incarceration creates significant disruptions with respect to housing, employment, parenting, education, and other aspects of daily living. Readjustment into society can be highly stressful for released prisoners. Most prison systems do little to facilitate a smooth transition from prison back to the community.[40]

From a public policy perspective, value lies in reducing the initial entry of offenders into prisons, and in reducing the likelihood that offenders who have served time in prison will reoffend

and return there. Efforts have been made in recent years along these lines. In all instances, the focus has been on probation and parole agencies, and how changes in their practices might improve offender outcomes.

Faye Taxman has played a central role in translating evidence into practice regarding community supervision of offenders.[41] The approach she has proposed has come to be known as the **"Risk-Need-Responsivity" model.** It has five parts:

1. A standardized risk and needs assessment is conducted to determine what approach might work best for supervising an offender on probation or parole.
2. The offender is matched to appropriate community services and interventions.
3. Treatment programs are used that emphasize cognitive-behavioral programming. Officers are required to use cognitive restructuring strategies with offenders.

4. Compliance issues are addressed through the swift and certain use of administrative sanctions and rewards.

5. Last, significant efforts are made to create positive working relationships between officers and offenders to facilitate changes in the thoughts and actions of the offender.

In adopting this evidence-based approach to community supervision, considerable effort is required to change the practices of probation and parole officers. For example, in a context where officers have been conditioned to fixate on technical violations of the conditions of probation or parole, more interactions between officers and offenders can have the unintended consequence of increasing admissions or returns to prison. A graduated sanctions approach can reduce the likelihood of this outcome, especially when the offender is clear about the sanctions and rewards they will receive for specific types of behavior.

Growing evidence supports the value of improving interactions between community-based corrections officers and offenders. Policy Investment Checklist 9.1 draws upon the results of studies in Australia and Canada to assess the professional development of **probation officers** as a policy investment.[42]

Probation officers work with convicted offenders serving community sentences or released prisoners who are on parole or probation. The evidence shows that professional development of probation officers can positively influence the behavior of offenders and ex-offenders. It is more difficult to assess the return on investment for this approach. However, cost-benefit analyses performed by the WSIPP suggest that the return on investment

from equivalent programs is approximately $100 for every dollar spent.[43] That estimate may actually underplay the value of such professional development of probation officers. The effectiveness of the programs can vary. Poorly managed approaches seem to change the knowledge of probation officers but not their actual practices. Knowing-doing gaps need to be addressed.

Using evidence of interactions between probation officers and offenders, Guy Bourgon and Leticia Gutierrez conducted a direct test of the Risk-Need-Responsivity model in three Canadian provinces.[44] Probation officers involved in the study were divided into experimental and control groups. All were required to attend a half-day presentation reviewing the Risk-Need-Responsivity model and its application. However, the probation officers in the experimental group were then required to undergo three days of further training, known as the Strategic Training Initiative in Community Supervision. A key emphasis of the training was to provide officers with a comprehensive and practical cognitive-behavioral model of change. In addition, the training provided the opportunity for officers to learn and practice cognitive as well as other intervention skills and techniques that engage offenders in cognitive restructuring and prosocial change.

The one-on-one interactions between officers and multiple offenders were recorded over a period of six months. Evidence was also collected on the subsequent recidivism rates of all the offenders with whom the officers in the study interacted. Two important findings emerged:

1. There was nothing new about the Risk-Need-Responsivity model. During the previous 10 years, all jurisdictions with

Analyzing Professional Development of Probation Officers

1. Focus on Existing Policies and Programs	Offenders are often placed on probation having served time in prison or as an alternative to imprisonment. They live in the community but must regularly meet with a probation officer. Managing offenders in this way saves on prison costs. However, there is a risk of reoffending. Studies conducted in Australia and Canada have explored whether the interactions between probation officers and offenders can reduce the likelihood of recidivism. These studies have focused on the professional development of probation officers.
2. Gather Policy Evidence	The Australian and Canadian studies both used experimental designs. In each case, the experimental group consisted of experienced probation officers who were given additional training in how to work with ex-offenders, and the control group comprised experienced probation officers who did not receive the additional training. Neither study randomly assigned officers to the training. However, the Australian study used larger numbers and employed random sampling of offender records from across probation officers who had received the further training and those who had not.
3. Measure Desired Effects	Both the Australian and Canadian studies showed clear decline in recidivism rates among offenders matched with probation officers who had received the additional professional development compared with offenders matched with those who had not received additional training. The differences were substantively and statistically significant. In Canada, the difference was 12.7% recidivism within 1 year versus 31.0%. In Australia, it was 23% recidivism after a year versus 49%.
4. Assess Costs and Benefits	Neither the Australian nor the Canadian studies assessed costs and benefits. However, the costs of these programs all involved providing additional professional development to currently employed probation officers. The training in both instances lasted for 3–5 days. It is likely that replacement officers would need to be employed while people received training. The benefits would be more difficult to assess. However, they relate to reducing criminal offenses and reducing the risk of offenders going to prison. The likelihood of generating a positive return on investment is high.
5. Offer Robust Advice	The evidence from these two studies conducted in different countries at different times is compelling. Improving the training of probation officers can increase their ability to work effectively with offenders. In turn, this can reduce the likelihood of reoffending. In separate analyses, the Washington State Institute for Public Policy verified the positive impact of programs to improve engagements between parole officers and offenders and calculated a rate of return from those programs of approximately $100 for every dollar spent.

probation officers taking part in this study had made efforts to incorporate the model into their correctional services. However, the study revealed that officers in the control group—who did not receive the specific training associated with this experiment— rarely used cognitive intervention techniques. Bourgon and Gutierrez contended that although officers believed they had the skills to employ such techniques, they in fact did not.

Bourgon and Gutierrez's review of officers' routine training showed that the majority of training focuses on other aspects of the job (such as legal matters, use of the computer system, policies, and risk assessment) rather than on practical knowledge and development of cognitive intervention techniques.

2. The authors found that officers who received the three days of training in techniques of cognitive-behavioral change had a significant impact on the actions of the offenders they worked with. The one-year recidivism rate of 12.7 percent for offenders with whom officers employed cognitive techniques was significantly lower than the 31.0 percent one-year recidivism rate of the offenders with whom the officers did not employ cognitive techniques.[45]

An earlier study conducted in Australia by Christopher Trotter employed a similar experimental design combined with extensive training of probation officers.[46] In this case, officers in the experimental group received five days of training focusing on prosocial modeling and reinforcement techniques. They also had to engage in ongoing seminars about the approach. An example of prosocial reinforcement, as recorded in officer file notes, might be: "Informed the [offender] that because he had kept the last three appointments and had found work I would only need to see him every month from now on" or "Told [the offender] how good it was that he was beginning to think about the harm that he had caused to the child he assaulted." The idea of the officer being a prosocial model included being punctual and reliable, polite and friendly, and honest and open; understanding the offender's point of view; and

expressing views about the value of social pursuits such as mixing with noncriminal friends, good family relations, and working.[47] The effect of the training was captured through subsequent analysis and comparison of file notes contained in officers' records of their interactions with offenders. The file notes were coded to generate an index that could be correlated with offender recidivism rates. Recidivism was measured both one year and four years after the intervention. The use of the prosocial approach had significant effects. After one year, the recidivism rate for offenders who worked with officers trained in prosocial techniques was 23 percent compared with 47 percent for offenders whose officers had not been trained. After four years, the recidivism rate for offenders who worked with trained officers was 49 percent compared with 73 percent for offenders whose officers had not been trained.

Both studies reported here indicate recidivism continued among offenders, even when they were assigned to probation officers who had received training in practices expected to promote better outcomes. A heartening conclusion to draw here, however, is that relatively short amounts of intensive training (3–5 days) can have positive effects on relations between officers and offenders—and can cause recidivism rates to drop significantly.

These research results suggest that systematically improving the training of probation officers could dramatically improve outcomes of community corrections. At their best, efforts to work effectively with offenders in the community hold the potential of delivering better social outcomes than incarceration, and at much less cost. This approach to administering criminal justice is not a panacea.

There will always be some segment of criminals in society who are violent and erratic and who, in the public interest, must be confined to prison. For such people, there is little likelihood that community sentencing will ever work. They have complex problems that, to be addressed, would call for careful, secure, long-term treatment. Meanwhile, for offenders who are not violent and who have been judged to be amenable to positive behavioral changes, enhanced community sentencing and support make a lot of sense.

To increase the effectiveness of community supervision, investments must be made in the initial training and ongoing professional development of probation and parole officers. Evidence also suggests that officers are better able to make positive differences in the behavior of offenders when they are not burdened with heavy caseloads.[48] Given these findings, improving community supervision and the outcomes it generates calls for deployment of more—and better-trained—professionals than is typically the case right now.

CRITICAL THINKING QUESTIONS

1. What are the main potential benefits of improving how probation officers interact with convicted criminals?
2. Why might various citizens and interest groups resist the application of the investment perspective to criminal justice?

CRIMINAL JUSTICE AND THE PURSUIT OF CIVIL RIGHTS

Criminal justice policies often evoke heated discussions concerning civil rights. Prison population statistics collected by the U.S. Department of Justice offer an insight into why.[49] Table 9.6 reports the racial composition of the U.S. population compared with the racial composition of men in U.S. prisons. Black males are significantly overrepresented in the prison population, compared with the representation of blacks in the whole population. To a lesser extent, Hispanic men are also overrepresented in the prison population, whereas white men are significantly underrepresented.

Table 9.7 reports imprisonment rates in the United States in 2014, by race, sex, and selected age ranges. Almost 3 percent of black males in the United States of all ages were imprisoned in 2014. This number compares to just over 1 percent of Hispanic males and 0.5 percent of white males. Black females were imprisoned at more than twice the rate for white females.

Black males had higher imprisonment rates across all age groups than all other races. For males ages 18 to 19—the age range with the greatest differences in imprisonment rates between whites and blacks—black males were over 10 times

TABLE 9.6 U.S. Population and Male Prison Population Percentages by Race

RACIAL GROUP	U.S. POPULATION %, 2015	U.S. MALE PRISON %, 2014
Black	13.3	37.0
Hispanic	17.6	22.0
White	61.6	32.0
Other	7.5	9.0

Sources: Table compiled by author based on U.S. Census Data, 2015, and evidence in E. Ann Carson, *Prisoners in 2014* (Washington, DC: U.S. Department of Justice, September 2015), 14.

TABLE 9.7 U.S. Imprisonment Rates by Demographic Characteristics

PRISONER GROUPS BY RACE, SEX, AND AGE RANGE	INMATES PER 100,000 OF THE POPULATION, 2014	POPULATION PERCENTAGE
Black males, all ages	2,724	2.8
Hispanic males, all ages	1,091	1.1
White males, all ages	465	0.5
Black females, all ages	109	1.1
Hispanic females, all ages	64	0.6
White females, all ages	53	0.5
Black males, ages 18–19	1,072	1.1
White males, ages 18–19	102	0.1
Black females, ages 18–19	32	0.03
White females, ages 18–19	8	0.007

Source: E. Ann Carson, *Prisoners in 2014* (Washington, DC: U.S. Department of Justice, September 2015), Table 10.

more likely to be imprisoned than white males. The difference between black and white female inmates in the same age range was smaller but still substantial. Black females ages 18 to 19 were four times more likely to be imprisoned than white females in that age range.

In seeking to understand the origins of these huge racial disparities across U.S. prisons, researchers have begun focusing intensely on what happens to young people before they become incarcerated criminals. This focus led to the coining of new terms during the 1990s: "the prison track" and the "school-to-prison pipeline."

Discipline practices in schools can have big impacts on student performance and the likelihood that students will gain a good education and get on track to steady employment. In a careful analysis of school discipline, Russell J. Skiba and his colleagues found that black elementary school students were twice as likely to be referred to the school office for problem behavior as their white peers. At the middle school level, this statistic increased such that black students were almost four times as likely as white students to be referred to the school office. These researchers also found that African American and Hispanic children were more likely than their white peers to receive expulsions or out-of-school suspensions for the same or similar problems.[50]

When children are expelled or suspended from school, the result tends to be heightened academic failure. Children who have spent time out of school are more likely to have to retake grades, drop out of school completely, become teen parents, and engage in delinquent behavior. Indeed, one study found that school suspension is a top predictor for those students who become incarcerated by ninth grade.[51]

These dispiriting findings have led civil rights activists and researchers to begin working together to find effective ways to begin dismantling the school-to-prison pipeline. Approaches have included working with schools to introduce discipline policies that reduce reliance on suspension and expulsion. Efforts have also been made to reduce the extent to which schools involve police in classroom or on-campus misdemeanors.[52] Even so, there are often broader social forces at play, such as poverty, broken families, and problems of community violence that influence what happens in schools. These are not readily addressed, even when schools and community groups act with the best of intentions.

EVOLVING PRACTICES IN CRIMINAL JUSTICE

Some barbaric forms of punishment were employed in the United States until the early 20th century. Most were inherited from Britain and typically were viewed as more humane than practices of earlier centuries. The system of criminal justice operating in the United States today continues to harbor gruesome elements. Indeed, many things about the system should change. Were those changes made, it is likely that all of society would benefit. Nevertheless, there has been significant progress over the past hundred years in how offenders are treated in the United States. That progress should offer hope to those who seek further reform.

Systems of criminal justice are essential to the development and preservation of peaceful, prosperous societies. Federal and state governments must take charge and become the arbiters of what constitutes prosocial or antisocial behavior. Part of their role is to deter people from breaking the law. As such, crimes must be appropriately punished. However, even the most evil criminals are human beings and are therefore deserving of respectful treatment. When a society treats its criminals inhumanely, the rights of all people risk being eroded. That risk needs to be minimized. Further, consideration also needs to be given to the future role that any offender might play in society. The most positive outcome of any sentence would be that the offender pays for the crime, feels remorse, commits to becoming a law-abiding citizen, and then continues through life as a decent and productive citizen. In reality, some offenders are clearly so damaged and so difficult to deal with that this outcome is highly unlikely.

Going forward, the public policy challenge has several elements, but the main ones are as follows. Strategies must be developed to identify young people at risk of entering lives of crime. Actions should then be taken to guide them away from antisocial activities and toward being good and self-supporting citizens. When people are found guilty of committing criminal offenses, their sentences should be administered in ways that evoke remorse but that also create opportunities for the offenders to be transformed. Community sentencing is less likely to be highly disruptive of the offenders' lives, making it easier for them to become law-abiding, good citizens.

LESSONS FOR PUBLIC POLICY

Since the 1970s, the United States has come to be an international outlier because of its high incarceration rates. Increasing numbers of prison inmates were not driven by crime rates, which have stayed fairly stable throughout the period. The changing incarceration rates were driven by the appetites of lawmakers to get tough on crime. Of late, those appetites have begun to abate somewhat, mainly because of the realization that building and maintaining prisons are costly exercises. Placing offenders in prisons is highly disruptive to their lives and not always the most appropriate form of punishment. For many reasons, high incarceration rates are not sustainable; further, sustainable alternatives are available.[53]

Policy makers have often gone on their tough-on-crime crusades in complete ignorance of what factors drive crime, what the recidivism rates and risks are, and how their choices will affect the need for more prisons.[54] Given these issues, the realization of the opportunity costs associated with high incarceration rates has had a somewhat sobering effect. Several lessons for policy and program design come from observing trends in criminal justice over the past few decades.

- Citizens and lawmakers in the United States have exhibited a strong appetite for getting tough on crime. Although offenders must be punished for their crimes, approaches to sentencing have often been based on emotion rather than on clear thinking. Good criminal justice systems consider both what constitutes suitable punishment and what can be done to effectively rehabilitate offenders.

- Over recent years, significant effort has been made to develop sentencing guidelines that make effective use of available information regarding the most appropriate form of sentencing to use, given the offenses committed and the known characteristics of the offenders. This risk-assessment approach could be employed more frequently, especially for nonviolent offenders. The use of actuarial sentencing—which takes a more comprehensive approach to the measurement and management of risks—is in its infancy. A concern is that some inevitable slippage could occur between population-based predictions and individual-level motivations. Nonetheless, the general approach promises to bring a more knowledge-driven and cost-effective approach to the administration of criminal justice.
- Efforts have been made to carefully evaluate the effectiveness of different programs for working with offenders. These usually focus on the extent to which specific programs reduce recidivism. When combined with cost-benefit analysis, such evaluations can provide sound guidance for policy development. This kind of analytical work lies at the heart of justice reinvestment efforts.
- Whenever an individual enters a life of crime, this creates significant, ongoing costs. In light of this, early efforts to identify and assist young people at risk of becoming offenders can have long-term payoffs both for those young people and society. In this chapter, we have noted how forms of community sentencing can be used for prosocial ends. The justice reinvention movement suggests that the focus should move to even earlier points in people's lives. Good experiences in early childhood education and schooling can reduce the risk of young people becoming criminals.

In the short term, a range of actions could be taken to transform criminal justice into a more effective aspect of public policy. These involve working with offenders in the community, and working with the communities that generate offenders in the first place. Actions now being taken are increasingly based upon careful analysis of what works. This trend should continue. In the longer term, efforts need to go into eliminating some of the most problematic features of the criminal justice system. Ongoing use of the death penalty, lengthy prison terms, and inhumane treatment of prisoners are inappropriate practices for any country committed to the advancement of human rights. Changing these negative aspects would make the United States a better society.

CHAPTER SUMMARY

This chapter has explored key issues in criminal justice. A well-functioning society is possible only when those with a tendency to commit crime are impeded from doing so. In the contemporary United States, criminal behavior is harshly treated, as is made clear from the extremely high number of people who are imprisoned by the federal and state governments, compared with numbers elsewhere in the world. The United States also remains among a minority of countries around the world that use the death penalty.

A range of issues concerning crime and punishment have been discussed. The topic lends itself to investigation both in terms of differences across states and in terms of civil rights. As such, consideration has been given to differences in incarceration rates across states, differences in the costs of imprisonment, approaches to sentencing reform, and differences in the use of private prisons.

The chapter focused throughout on exploring alternate ways of working with prisoners and those on probation to reduce the likelihood that they will commit crimes in the future. Although it may seem odd to approach criminal justice policies as investments, doing so offers a new way of thinking about crime and punishment. When people commit crimes, of course they should be punished. Yet consideration must be given to the potential for turning people from leading lives of crime into living as productive citizens. Although various countries around the world are making efforts along these lines, the results are not overwhelming. No country anywhere has found ways to avoid the use of prisons. At the same time, it is clear that lives *can* be changed. In the process, significant amounts of money, otherwise spent on prisons, can be freed up for more productive uses. Given how much money is now spent on criminal justice, this is an approach that deserves more attention, especially by the United States, given its huge incarceration rates.

CONNECTIONS TO OTHER CHAPTERS

Both Tucker and Cadora's mapping initiative and moves to project justice reinvestment have highlighted the significance of local contexts for generating young people who fall into lives of crime. There are important connections between crime and poverty (Chapter 8). The notion of the school-to-prison pipeline also reminds us that when young people have behavioral difficulties in school, they can quickly fall out of the education system and into the criminal justice system. Schools cannot do everything people would like them to do, in terms of helping young people get on track to leading productive, socially engaged lives. But they can do some things. Performing well in school—and being encouraged by outstanding teachers—can help young people avoid falling into bad ways (Chapter 6). Indeed, in many ways, what happens in schools offers the best hope for helping young people break free from social disadvantage and the pressures that lead some to lives of crime.

KEY TERMS

Natural monopoly power

Rehabilitation

Corporal punishment

Transportation of convicts

Imprisonment

Vigilante justice

Pennsylvania system

New York system

Chain gangs

Convict lease

Community sentencing

Parole

Recidivism

Probation

Incarceration rates

Carceral state

Felon disenfranchisement

Truth in sentencing

Actuarial sentencing

Justice reinvestment

Sentencing guidelines

"Risk-Need-Responsivity" model

Probation officers

SUGGESTIONS FOR FURTHER READING

Clear, Todd R. "A Private-Sector, Incentives-Based Model for Justice Reinvestment," *Criminology and Public Policy* 10, no. 3 (2011): 585–608. This is a good introduction to justice reinvestment and its goals.

Garland, David. "The Peculiar Forms of American Capital Punishment," *Social Research* 74, no. 2 (2007): 435–64. This is a useful historical analysis of the use of capital punishment.

Gottschalk, Marie. "Hiding in Plain Sight: American Politics and the Carceral State," *Annual Review of Political Science* 11 (2008): 235–60. This is an excellent analysis of the central role that prisons play in the lives of many Americans.

Schneider, Anne Larason. "Public-Private Partnerships in the U.S. Prison System," *American Behavioral Scientist* 43, no. 1 (1999): 192–208. This is a good introduction to key issues concerning the use of private prisons.

Sung, Hung-En. "Democracy and Criminal Justice in Cross-National Perspective: From Crime Control to Due Process," *The Annals of the American Academy of Political and Social Science* 605 (2006): 311–37. A good discussion for putting the U.S. system of criminal justice in an international context.

Western, Bruce. (2006). *Punishment and Inequality in America.* New York: Russell Sage Foundation, 2006. A thorough analysis of the links between social class, race, and imprisonment in the United States.

WEBSITES

- The Council of State Governments Justice Center is a national nonprofit organization that serves policy makers at the local, state, and federal levels from all branches of government. Staff members provide practical, nonpartisan advice and evidence-based, consensus-driven strategies to increase public safety and strengthen communities. www.csgjusticecenter.org

- The Bureau of Justice Statistics is the primary source for criminal justice statistics in the United States. Its aim is to collect, analyze, publish, and disseminate information on crime, criminal offenders, victims of crime, and the operation of justice systems at all levels of government. www.bjs.gov

- The Washington State Institute for Public Policy aims to carry out practical, nonpartisan research—at legislative direction—on issues of importance to Washington State. The goal is to provide Washington policy makers and budget writers with a list of well-researched public policies that can lead to better statewide outcomes coupled with a more efficient use of taxpayer dollars, especially in the realm of criminal justice. With the assistance of the Pew Charitable Trusts and the MacArthur Foundation, this approach has spread to other states. www.wsipp.wa.gov/BenefitCost

FOR DISCUSSION

1. Suppose your state legislature has expressed interest in exploring ways to reduce state prison costs. One issue to be considered is the length of sentences for some prisoners. Within the past year, an incident occurred where a lone gunman killed four people and injured 10 others in a shooting at a popular bar. If you were charged with leading a legislative task force to consider sentencing reform in your state, what issues would you see as most important to explore? How would you seek to manage conflicting views about reducing inmate numbers and the need for appropriate punishment of people who commit multiple murders and other serious crimes?

2. In a discussion of crime and public policy, John J. DiIulio claimed that there are some instances where violent juvenile offenders are simply beyond help. "Let us, therefore, do what we can to deter them by means of strict criminal sanctions, and, where deterrence fails, to incapacitate them. Let the government Leviathan lock them up and, where prudence dictates, throw away the key."[55] In what sense is this observation consistent with notions of the good society?

3. Public-private partnerships and other forms of collaboration between governments and nongovernment entities are now commonplace. Such partnerships in the U.S. prison system have existed for a very long time. However, some people feel uneasy about private companies profiting from prison management. What are the main points of disagreement in this area of public policy?

4. The justice reinvestment movement proposes a means of reducing high incarceration rates and strengthening communities that have been primary generators of young people destined for lives of crime and imprisonment. In his short article, "Lessons for Justice Reinvestment from Restorative Justice and the Justice Model Experience," Shadd Maruna offers some useful insights concerning the longer-term sustainability of this movement.[56] With reference to Maruna's argument, discuss the strengths and weaknesses of the justice reinvestment model.

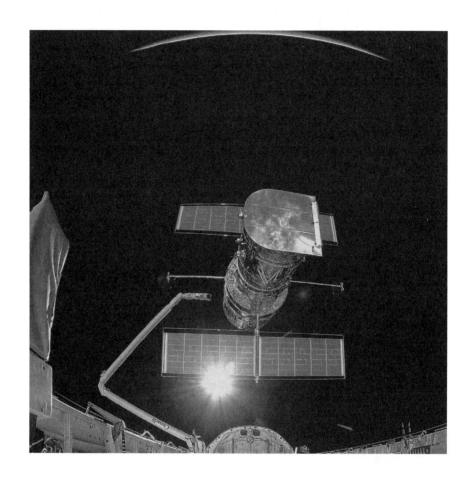

CHAPTER 10

SCIENCE FUNDING

This chapter explores the commitments that governments in the United States have made, and continue to make, to science funding. How we live is due largely to the cumulative impacts of continuous advancement in human knowledge and its practical application. Many things we now take for granted are products of scientific and technological innovation, and the combination of innovations. Our conceptions of time, our food supply, electricity, health systems, public schooling, the structures we live in, systems of transport, communication systems—all of these beneficial things have emerged as products of human intellect and skill.

Human intellect and skill have operated collectively. They have been passed along, expanded, altered, and codified in various ways from generation to generation. Public policies—the results of collective decision making—influence the processes of knowledge creation, dissemination, and application. The choices societies make can significantly influence their own well-being and that of future generations.

The focus on science funding here is deliberately narrow. However, the bigger story concerns the ongoing construction of knowledge economies, and the role that governments play in their creation. Consideration of science funding leads us to explore the intersections between the advancement of knowledge and technological development. It also leads us to reflect on the function of universities, as sites both for knowledge advancement through research and for knowledge transfer through teaching and training.

This chapter introduces you to:

- The reasons why governments fund scientific research
- Federalism's influence on science funding decisions
- Traditional approaches to funding science

Facing page: The Hubble Space Telescope that orbits the Earth was launched in 1990 via the Space Shuttle *Discovery*. The Hubble Telescope can produce extremely high-resolution images outside the distortion of Earth's atmosphere. Information produced by the Hubble has led to scientific breakthroughs, including accurate determination of the rate of expansion of the universe.

(NASA/Public Domain)

325

- Contemporary policy issues including the funding of big science projects, the challenges of short-term thinking, and the promotion of scientific talent
- The application of the investment perspective to science funding
- The ways in which scientific knowledge has been transformed into applied technology
- Connections between science funding and the pursuit of civil rights
- Lessons for public policy emerging from this review of science funding

AN INTRODUCTION TO SCIENCE FUNDING

Science funding is often considered something worth pursuing only if money remains after funding a range of other, more pressing government priorities. There have been exceptions to this view—mostly during wartime—when the United States has perceived itself to be in a battle for supremacy and has considered the application of scientific knowledge as the key to success.

The investment perspective on public policy suggests an approach different from that of merely allocating budgets in pursuit of immediate priorities. The greatest challenge to that change is clear. As any seasoned scientist will warn, most scientific inquiry takes a long time to generate useful results. Further, new knowledge frequently emerges in ways that can be difficult to predict. For those who believe that all government spending should yield fast and tangible results, funding science is a farce. In contrast, when supporters take a longer view, the evidence is clear that societies prepared to strongly support scientific research realize many benefits. Those benefits—when we view them broadly—significantly outweigh the original costs.

The life of Apple founder Steve Jobs offers a fascinating metaphor for the process of scientific inquiry and where it leads. Nobody would ever challenge Jobs's intellect, creativity, and impact. Yet although his life had periods of incredible focus, it also had periods where end goals did not crystallize. Indeed, some of the most important inputs into specific projects were not originally undertaken with a specific goal in mind, let alone the goal to which they ultimately contributed. In the broader world of scientific research, this pathway is not unusual. Reflecting on his life, Jobs said: "You can't connect the dots looking forward; you can only connect them looking backward. So you have to trust that the dots will somehow connect in your future."[1] This precept is as true for the collective enterprise of scientific research as it is for the life of any individual.

WHY GOVERNMENTS GET INVOLVED IN SCIENCE FUNDING

Looking into the past, we can clearly see how a lot of careful scientific research has contributed to advances in human knowledge and, ultimately, improvements in the human condition. This reality suggests that science funding *is* important. Supporters consider investing in science as a way to reduce information problems. Curious investigators might wonder about the nature of specific phenomena and seek to explain those phenomena. Often, they might seek to identify causal relationships. At other times, pressing problems such as disease might lead scientists to work at building knowledge that they can ultimately deploy to fight the illness. Efforts to understand heart disease and various forms of cancer offer salient examples. And, as scientific work generates new knowledge, it also creates new opportunities for economic development.

There is no perfect correlation between efforts to advance the frontiers of science and efforts to promote economic development. Nonetheless, it is easy to see how advances in medical science have opened up new markets in provision of, for example, medical services and pharmaceuticals. Likewise, advances in physics have opened up spaces for major developments in the generation and distribution of electricity and—following from this—advances in information technology. Huge public value can indeed be the result of funding science.

SCIENTIFIC RESEARCH AS A PUBLIC GOOD

Scientific research is a classic **public good**. In the absence of government funding, almost all scientific work would be funded by (wealthy) individuals and firms only if that work were anticipated to generate knowledge of direct interest to the funders. If funding were only private, given the idiosyncrasies of those prepared to purchase scientific research, there would be little supply of it. Few people would train to be scientists if they believed their chances of employment depended mainly upon the whims of a few specific investors.

PURE AND APPLIED SCIENCE

Science is usually divided into two broad types. **Pure** or **basic scientific research** is curiosity driven and is not intended to solve any immediate problem. **Applied scientific research** is problem driven and usually involves taking existing knowledge and using it to answer specific questions. Applied science is recognized as highly relevant and useful; hence, it more easily attracts funding than does pure or basic science. However, the line dividing basic and applied science is never clear.[2] Sometimes, problems that originally appear to involve application of existing knowledge end up creating opportunities for pure research. For example, efforts to improve agricultural methods and productivity have supported the contemporary development of interest in genetic modification of plant species. That work has stimulated a lot of pure research across multiple scientific disciplines.

The pressing challenge for basic scientists is to attract funding. Few people see the merits in funding science that may not have any immediate and useful payoffs. Therefore, funding basic science most often involves an act of faith. Nonetheless, over the longer term, basic science in a broad array of disciplines has advanced human knowledge to the greater benefit of everyone, as we will discuss.

SCIENCE FUNDING

For centuries—and certainly for all the years since European settlement of North America—science funding has been provided from two main sources: the coffers of private universities and direct government support. Today, the U.S. government provides funding for science in a range of direct and indirect ways, as do state governments. Governments tend to commit to science by funding either universities or government research laboratories. Whether public or private, universities that fund science do so mainly by transferring financial support from their teaching income. The fees students pay to attend universities serve at least partly to pay the wages of people who engage in some combination of research and teaching.

Scientific research can proceed on the basis of private support, but this manner of funding is less common. Historically, there have been instances of wealthy people with an interest or belief in science serving as patrons to scientists. Yet, even in those cases, the patrons have usually had fixed views about the kind of science they are prepared to support.

It is also the case that some private companies support scientific research. Bell Laboratories offers a famous example (see Case Study 10.1).[3]

case study 10.1 Bell Laboratories and Private Science Funding

This historic laboratory originated in the late 19th century as the Volta Laboratory and Bureau created by Alexander Graham Bell. Bell Laboratories was established in the 1920s and remains in operation today as Nokia Bell Laboratories, owned by the Finnish company Nokia. From the outset, the organization served as the research and development arm of the American Telephone and Telegraph Company (AT&T). The primary work of Bell Labs involved providing technical support to the telephone system. The company also did contract research for the U.S. government. Bell Labs nonetheless also engaged in some basic scientific research. Although this was never its core business, it attracted a lot of renowned scientists to the labs. Indeed, scientists at Bell Labs have been the recipients of the Nobel Prize on eight occasions.

Scientists employed there also won other prestigious prizes. They were recognized for, among other things, developing the transistor and the laser, advancing computer technology, and generating insights into the nature of matter and the behavior of atoms.

Despite this long tradition of outstanding scientific research, Bell Labs always operated primarily to advance the position and the profits of its parent companies. Today, although Nokia Bell Labs continues to operate, its support for basic or pure scientific research has ceased. The progressive move away from funding basic science toward funding research with immediate applications seems to have begun during the 1980s, coinciding with the period when AT&T lost its monopoly status and the company and its subsidiaries were forced to operate in a more competitive environment.[4]

An implication of the Bell Labs example is that private support for basic research is an exception because it calls upon exceptional profit-making capability. A current example, Google.org, the foundation associated with Google, is funding efforts to develop specific technologies, and some of those efforts require basic scientific research. However, the support is targeted toward projects that have clear synergies with Google's core capabilities of making use of massive amounts of information—again, a profit-making success.

CRITICAL THINKING QUESTIONS

1. Under what circumstances might private funding of science generate broad, public-good outcomes?
2. Why does public funding of science make sense, even when private funding is available?

The Google Driverless Car has been developed through private research funding from the company Google, Inc. Historically, private research funding tends to occur only when the funders can see an obvious commercial benefit from the research findings. Google usually funds research projects that make use of big data—the company's area of competitive strength.

(AP Photo/Tony Avelar, File)

ACTIONS TO GUIDE GOOD FUNDING CHOICES

The U.S. government funds scientific research, as do the governments of most developed countries, because it is expected to benefit society in the long term (see the following section). By doing so, it is able to create opportunities for scientists to engage in projects that are not expected to generate knowledge with immediate social payoffs. Historically, it has taken a range of actions to reduce the risk that this use of taxpayer money will represent a poor investment:

1. The people whose scientific research is publicly supported are carefully screened. Only scientists with a record of productivity and who have been judged highly qualified by their peers receive permanent positions in universities or government laboratories.
2. When funding is permanent, it tends to be tied to other activities beyond research. Most significantly, scientists in universities are appointed as professors who are generally expected both to conduct original research and to perform some teaching.
3. Funding for scientific research tends to be finite and is linked to specific projects. It is rare that major projects are funded for more than a few years at a time.

Scientists involved in research must keep proving the value of their work—usually as judged by the quality and quantity of the research articles they publish. Those who do not sustain a coherent record of scientific productivity find it difficult to attract ongoing funding. As a result, the system of science funding is strongly biased toward supporting researchers who are talented at identifying interesting and relevant research questions, seeing significance where others might not, and reporting their work in ways that clearly demonstrate the advance of common wisdom within the specific field. Training of new scientists is supported in a similar fashion. Most often, funding for research projects includes support for graduate students and postdoctoral fellows. This approach to science funding remains predicated predominately on faith, although many efforts are made to reduce the risk that large amounts of money will be wasted.

SCIENCE FUNDING IN FEDERAL SYSTEMS OF GOVERNMENT

Everyone can benefit from significant scientific breakthroughs. Indeed, such a finding can positively influence people's lives for many generations. Astronomy and the development of navigation systems guided by the position of stars in the night sky, or celestial navigation, offers one such example. Today, most navigation is guided by satellite navigation receivers, or the Global Positioning System (GPS).

Given that scientific research often requires significant investments, the governments of individual jurisdictions might decide to leave the funding of science to others. However, the dynamics established in this manner create a poor overall outcome. If everyone chooses to leave funding of science to others, the risk emerges that no science funding will occur at all. This aspect of collective action is often called the **free rider problem**. If we can free-ride on the efforts of others, no incentive exists for us to provide a desired good—in this case, science funding.

In the United States, most funding of science research is provided by the U.S. government. This approach to funding overcomes the free rider problem that could arise if funding were left to the states. However, states do continue to provide a degree of funding for science, primarily through their support for public universities. The explanation for some residual level of state funding is clear. If a state can create a powerful local scientific community, the chances increase that discoveries within that community will generate local spillover benefits, and all citizens of a state could gain from those benefits. The University of California system offers a good example of how a state has contributed to the funding of local scientific work. Over the past century, its various campuses have been credited with generating many benefits for residents of California, including mitigation of risks to agriculture development and many medical advances, such as those involving organ transplantation.[5]

Other states, seeing the benefits California has derived from its system of high-quality public universities, have likewise made efforts to establish and fund strong local science communities based around public universities. For example, North Carolina funded initial investments in the Research Triangle Park in the decades following World War II. These investments led to federal research laboratories being located in the area.[6] Today, Research Triangle Park contains the highest concentration of people with PhDs within the United States. Local efforts to fund science sometimes yield significant payoffs, but they can take decades to be realized. Hence, it is most common that the bulk of science funding in federal systems of government comes from national governments, rather than state or local governments.

TRADITIONAL POLICY APPROACHES

The development of a strong and vibrant scientific research tradition in the United States is largely due to funding streams originating in Washington, DC. In the early years of the Union, science was poorly funded. Universities and colleges, of which there were few, were established primarily by churches for the purpose of training clergy. Until well into the 20th century, U.S. universities were not effectively prepared for supporting scientific research. Even the teaching of science, let alone scientific research, was limited through most of the 19th century. As a consequence, it was common then for young Americans with scientific ambitions to head for Europe, where German universities were particularly admired as strong centers for scientific research and training.

EXAMPLES OF PRIVATE RESEARCH UNIVERSITIES

Johns Hopkins University, founded in Baltimore in 1876, was the first university in the United States that deliberately followed the European tradition in according high status to the conduct of scientific research by its professors. At his inauguration, the university's first president, Daniel Coit Gilman, said the aim of Johns Hopkins was "the encouragement of research . . . and the advancement of individual scholars, who by their excellence will advance the sciences they pursue, and the society where they dwell."[7] The approach taken at Johns Hopkins subsequently influenced practices at Harvard University and Yale University. Leaders of other universities then used the model of Harvard, in particular, to support their arguments for how their own universities should be organized.

The founding of the University of Chicago in 1890 confirmed the place of research in the emerging American universities. The founding president, William Rainey Harper, emphasized that the University of Chicago was to be foremost a place for advancing research and the training of graduate students for research careers. From the outset, the work of giving instruction was deemed secondary to the primary mission of serving as a research university.[8]

THE CREATION OF LAND GRANTS

The highly practical and independent mindset of Americans in the first century of the Union sometimes actually impeded the development of scientific communities. For a time, a view prevailed that little practical use lay in science education. It was only when major engineering projects began to take off in the United States in the mid-1800s that serious demand developed for better science education. For example, construction of the railroads (especially feats like the cutting of the Central Pacific railroad through the Sierra Nevada mountain range) and the building of city electrical grids necessitated the training of cadres of engineers with appropriate technical knowledge.

The federal government greatly advanced opportunities for teaching science in universities—and subsequent conduct of scientific research within them—through passage of the Morrill Act of 1862. This act provided for land grants to be made from the federal government to every state for the purpose of funding the creation of universities. Revenues from the lands were used to establish universities committed to advancing agricultural and mechanical arts. As those universities developed, more emphasis was given to science in their curricula. The land grant universities—including the University of California–Berkeley,

Cornell University, the Massachusetts Institute of Technology (MIT), Michigan State University, the University of Minnesota, and the University of Wisconsin–Madison—have long served as important sites for the advancement of scientific research and training.

SPECIFIC FEDERAL SCIENCE PROJECTS

The federal government also advanced scientific research through the funding of specific science programs. The U.S. Geological Survey represented the first of several government agencies that did much to advance aspects of pure scientific research while ostensibly funding highly practical projects, such as mapping the territory of the expanding country. Beginning in the late 19th century, a range of government agencies began to fund scientific research through designated portions of their annual budgets. After World War I, the U.S. government began seriously investing in scientific research to support national security. During World War II, centralized sites such as Ernest O. Lawrence's laboratory at the University of California–Berkeley allowed large numbers of scientists to work together on achieving defined goals. Following World War II, many such concentrations of scientific talent were transformed into national laboratories, owned by the U.S. Department of Energy and managed under contract. Examples include the Brookhaven National Laboratory at Upton, New York, and the Oak Ridge National Laboratory at Oak Ridge, Tennessee.

DEFENSE AND SCIENCE FUNDING

The federal government's practice of looking to scientists to support weapons development and advances in technical infrastructure to improve combat capabilities was established during World War I. The acceleration of this practice during World War II proved decisive in embedding the view that scientific advance was essential to national security and American supremacy in the world. Because scientists in the United States had long looked with envy toward the organization of scientific research in German universities, where many had trained, on the eve of America's entry into World War II the science community forcefully argued the need for the U.S. government to develop a nuclear weapon.

From 1941 through to 1945, the Manhattan Project operated across multiple sites—Columbia University, the University of Chicago, and the University of California–Berkeley among them, as well as federal lands designated for use by the army. Los Alamos, in the desert of New Mexico, became the center of nuclear weapon development, and it was here that the first nuclear bomb was tested in July 1945. Following the American bombing of Hiroshima on August 6, 1945, and Nagasaki on August 9, 1945, the Japanese surrendered. The central role of scientific knowledge in attaining military superiority was no longer questioned. Many of these laboratories' subsequent contributions have had highly positive social effects, including the development of nuclear energy for electrical power generation and of new technologies that have been applied to national challenges affecting the environment, industrial operations, and forensics.

Daniel J. Kevles notes that during World War II, federal science funding increased from $48 million to $500 million per year.[9] The federal government contribution to science funding shifted from less than 20 percent of total public and private expenditures on science to over 80 percent. Most of the shift was funneled through commitment to military projects, the Manhattan Project being the most costly of all.

CREATING SCIENCE FUNDING INSTITUTIONS

Although many individuals made notable contributions to the development of scientific infrastructure in the United States, Vannevar Bush is typically credited with establishing the trajectory for science funding in the immediate post–World War II period. His ideas had powerful influence at the time and continue to resonate through the way they shaped the institutions of public science funding. An accomplished academic and electrical engineer, Bush began his administrative career as dean of MIT's School of Engineering during the 1930s. In 1938, he moved to Washington in an administrative capacity and soon rose to head the federal Office of Scientific Research and Development, a post he held throughout World War II. This office was central to the funding of the Manhattan Project.

In 1944, Bush—at the request of President Roosevelt—developed a report reflecting on the significant role that science had played in the war effort and how insights from this period could be applied to the funding of science during peacetime. Bush delivered his report in 1945 to Roosevelt's successor, President Truman. The report, *Science: The Endless Frontier,* made the case for the federal government to become the permanent patron of science funding in the United States. Many decades later, this report continues to be acknowledged as the basis for current science funding arrangements, in which the federal government plays the strongest role.[10]

In *Science: The Endless Frontier*, Bush proposed three guiding principles for science funding.

1. Research grants should be made directly to universities, establishing what is known today as the system of **competitive extramural funding**. The system ensured that federal funding would flow beyond government agencies, institutes, and laboratories to universities, where it could be used both to fund specific projects and to support the training of graduate students.

2. Nonpartisan experts should be relied upon to select the projects to be funded; recipient institutions would organize how the scientific work would be performed and administered, and there should be no political interference in the conduct of the research.

3. All extramural science funding should be channeled through one institution, and science funding should be arranged in a fashion that would ensure predictable and stable resources over time.

In the years following Bush's report, Congress and the president moved to establish the **National Science Foundation** and to consolidate the **National Institutes of Health** into the basic forms they take today. However, other government agencies continued to direct and fund specific science projects through their own budgets. In addition, no effort was made to secure science funding in a fashion that would protect it from changing political views on the kinds of commitments that the federal government should make to it.

CONTEMPORARY POLICY ISSUES

Contemporary science funding in the United States is dominated by the federal government's contributions and commitments. Although more restricted funding comes from state governments, the private sector, private benefactors, and a degree of cross-subsidization from university tuition fees, the federal government is the largest financial backer of the nation's scientific activities. Much of this funding is channeled to university-based researchers through competitive allocation systems. The most significant are those administered by the National Institutes of Health and the National Science Foundation. Additional funding for university-based researchers is available through other agencies, such as the Department of Defense and the Department of Energy.

As well as funding university-based research, the federal government provides direct support to a diverse and extensive set of federal research projects and facilities. Highly important examples include the National Aeronautics and Space Administration (NASA), which was responsible for the Apollo program (1963–1972), Skylab (1973–1979), the space shuttle program (1981–2011), and the United States's contributions to the International Space Station. NASA continues to conduct a range of high-profile, high-cost space exploration projects. Numerous smaller examples of federal science facilities exist in the form of federal laboratories, such as the Brookhaven National Laboratory on Long Island, New York. Like other federal laboratories, Brookhaven began life in the post–World War II period as a nuclear research facility. Today, while continuing to support nuclear and high-energy physics research, the laboratory also facilitates environmental research, research in the neurosciences, and structural biology.

THE EXPANSION OF PUBLIC UNIVERSITIES

From a global perspective, there is little doubt that the university system in the United States and the country's science funding model are the envy of many other nations. Although many of the building blocks of the system were established by the 1930s, this system is very much a product of the post–World War II period, and especially the Cold War between the United States and the Soviet Union that continued until the end of the 1980s.

The surprise Soviet launch of the tiny, unmanned *Sputnik* satellite on October 4, 1957, had an immediate bracing effect. As Homer A. Neal and his colleagues relate, "More than any other event in the U.S. history, the *Sputnik* crisis focused the attention of the American people and policymakers on the importance of creating government policies in support of science and of education, with the aim of maintaining U.S. scientific, technological, and military superiority over the rest of the world."[11] Among other things, the extraordinary expansion of public university systems during the 1960s, such as the University of California and the State University of New York, can be explained in large part by the consensus view that scientific research held the key for the United States to maintain military superiority in the world.

THE LINEAR MODEL OF SCIENCE

We should note two important aspects about contemporary science funding. First, the system today is very much a product of the view that excellent scientific work is vital to promoting valued economic, social, and geopolitical outcomes. Second, there is growing concern that science funding could be managed much more effectively than has been the case in the past.

Vannevar Bush is credited with popularizing the **linear model of science** and ensuring that it became the basis for funding models in the United States. In this model, all research starts with a curiosity-driven scientist who is engaged in pure or basic scientific research for no reason other than to understand something that is presently not well understood or explained. Some of the results of this curiosity-driven work then inform applied scientific research, which addresses specific and known problems. From here, researchers conduct development work that may then lead to commercialization of the results, and the taking to market of new products.

There is a fundamental irony in the popularity of the linear model in discourse about science funding. In the early 19th century, the initial efforts to gain government support for pure or basic scientific research in the United States were strongly talked down by pragmatists, who could see little use for it.[12] Donald E. Stokes carefully explored this irony (see In Focus 10.1).[13] According to Stokes, throughout much of the history of the United States—including the second half of the 20th century—the linear model was used to justify science funding when the broader rationale for such funding has been more pragmatic: to win wars.

in focus 10.1

QUESTIONING THE PURE BASIC RESEARCH MODEL: THE STOKES CONCEPT

Writing in the late 1990s, public policy scholar Donald E. Stokes contended that much scientific research in the United States had been funded and conducted with clear end uses in mind. In the process, quests for fundamental understanding were necessary. Stokes proposed that "pure basic research" is not driven by considerations of use but is driven by a quest for fundamental understanding. He argued that the Danish physicist and Nobel Prize winner Niels Bohr (1885–1962) was an archetype of the "pure basic research" scientist, because his focus on the structure of the atom was entirely driven by curiosity. He proposed that "pure applied research" is driven by consideration of use and not by a quest for fundamental understanding.

Stokes argued that the American inventor Thomas Edison (1847–1931), who developed a cheap and effective light bulb, exemplified the "pure applied research" scientist. Stokes then proposed that "use-inspired basic research" is driven by consideration of use but also embodies a quest for fundamental understanding. He suggested that the French chemist and microbiologist Louis Pasteur (1822–1895) embodied this approach. Much of Pasteur's work was motivated by finding ways to prevent the entry of destructive microorganisms into the human body. Among other things, Pasteur pioneered vaccination against diseases and the process that came to be known as the pasteurization of milk. In his book *Pasteur's Quadrant* (1997), Stokes contended that the relationship between science and its application in technology is much more complex and dynamic than is implied by the earlier linear model.

Stokes championed a conception of science that muddies the lines and causal directions between use-inspired research and the attainment of fundamental understandings. In his view, that conception better captured what had long been happening in American science. Further, it presented a defensible basis upon which to construct a new compact between government and science funding.

Although the linear model of the relationship between pure or basic scientific research and technological development continues to inform a lot of thinking around science funding, there appears to be greater acceptance today of the ways that curiosity and utility can be equally valid and mutually stimulating as motivations for scientific research. There is also far more appreciation now for how applied research endeavors have prompted exploration of significant basic science problems during the history of scientific practice in the United States. This approach matters for how science funding is understood, justified, and debated. In short, the view that excellent science can emerge from attending to practical problems—such as the pursuit of continuous technological, economic, and military superiority—presents a strong and historically proven justification for giving high priority to science funding.

THE BIG SCIENCE MODEL

The second aspect of contemporary U.S. science policy is that federal science funding is now being scrutinized in ways that were uncommon in the past. With tightened fiscal conditions at the federal level, questions have been raised concerning whether programs and projects might be more effectively managed. In the immediate post-*Sputnik* era, the U.S. government made many commitments to funding scientific projects. It was during this time that Alvin Weinberg coined the term "big science" to describe expensive and expansive projects that served to organize the work of many scientists around pursuit of common goals.[14]

The Apollo program is an example of the **big science model**—one that generated a range of outcomes deemed to be successes. More recently, the Human Genome Project served to motivate and energize the activities of scientists across a range of disciplines—and it continues to do so (see Case Study 10.2). At the same time, big science projects can create major political and financial risks. These can come in the form of budget overruns and after-the-fact inquiries into the merits of specific funding decisions. Indeed, critics have viewed some of those commitments as—at the least—misguided.

case study 10.2 The Human Genome Project

The **human genome** is the complete set of genetic information for humans. The International Human Genome Sequencing Consortium published the first draft of the human genome in 2001. Mapping the sequence of the human genome represented the largest single undertaking in the history of biological science. It stands as a fundamental scientific achievement. Scientists are using the knowledge of genome structure and the data resulting from the **Human Genome Project (HGP)** as the foundation for advancements in medicine and science. Goals include preventing, diagnosing, and treating human disease.

The economic impacts generated by sequencing the human genome are large and widespread. Between 1988 and 2012, the human genome sequencing projects, associated research, and industry activity—directly and indirectly—generated an estimated economic impact of $965 billion, personal income exceeding $293 billion, and more than 4.3 million job-years of employment (see Table 10.1).

U.S. government investment in the genomic revolution has contributed to a total economic output of nearly $1 trillion. If we consider only HGP funding as the initial financial input, these genomic activities are estimated to have yielded a return on investment (ROI) equal to $178 for every dollar invested. Consideration of all federal investment in HGP-related genomics activities through 2012 still yields an ROI of $65 for every dollar invested.

As the sequencing information from the HGP was posted publically on a daily basis to the World Wide Web, the data could immediately be put to use advancing application of knowledge across a broad range of scientific disciplines and applied fields. Revealing the human genome sequence had a direct impact on biomedical science. It also had a transformational effect on the identification of mechanisms of disease and diagnoses of genetic diseases and disorders. Further, having the full human sequence has served to advance additional human biomedical applications in other areas of research and development such as gene therapy, vaccine development, regenerative medicine and stem cell therapy, and the refined matching of organs and tissue between donors and patients.

With the first full draft of the human sequence in hand, new areas of biomedical science have opened. For example, **pharmacogenomics** and **companion diagnostics** are being used to identify appropriate drugs based on patient genomic profiling and to refine their dosing. All such developments hold the promise of revolutionizing medical practice in the coming decades.

TABLE 10.1 Cumulative Economic Impact of Human Genome Sequencing, 1988–2012

	FEDERAL INVESTMENT	EMPLOYMENT (JOB YEARS)	PERSONAL INCOME	TAX REVENUES	ECONOMIC OUTPUT
Total Impact	$5.4	4.3 million	$293	$54.8	$965

Source: Battelle data analysis and estimations; IMPLAN U.S. Economic Impact Models, The Impact of Genomics on the U.S. Economy, Battelle Technology Partnership Practice for United for Medical Research, 2013.

Note: Dollar figures in billions, 2012.

CRITICAL THINKING QUESTIONS

1. What conditions are needed to support complex scientific explorations that advance through the work of multiple teams over many years?
2. What are some other areas of big science where a range of payoffs are likely to appear in the future?

A famous example regards the initial funding and then abandonment of the Department of Energy's Superconducting Super Collider project. The original intention was to build a facility that would support a variety of physics experiments in a manner that could not be supported by existing equipment in the United States or Europe. The original budget estimates anticipated that the facility would cost $4.4 billion to commission. However, as work began on the project, budget figures changed, and estimates of the completion costs became far higher than the original figures. This increase led to debate in Congress, with voices being raised that funding for this project would make it impossible to fund other worthy projects, such as the International Space Station. After more than $2 billion were spent on digging about 15 miles of tunnels deep underground near Fort Worth, Texas, Congress pulled funding on the project.

As a result, considerably more care has gone into ensuring that big science projects are appropriately budgeted and that they enjoy broad stakeholder support before they are initiated. The fate of the Superconducting Super Collider also tells us something about a shift that started to happen in the 1990s, whereby interest and appetite for government funding of big projects shifted somewhat from the past focus on physical science toward human science.

THE CHALLENGE OF SHORT-TERM THINKING

Plenty of evidence reveals the everyday benefits we derive from technological developments informed by scientific research. Even cursory considerations of the role science plays in supporting the quality of contemporary life show that contributions have come from a range of disciplines and fields of research. Despite this knowledge, science funding has rarely been given top priority by political leaders. As we have discussed, exceptions have occurred during times of war or when the United States has perceived a threat from a credible rival—such as the former Soviet Union.

Many scientists now feel frustrated by fiscal constraints, especially the automatic spending cuts set to continue within the U.S. federal government from 2013 onward. For example, critics have claimed that these across-the-board cutbacks in federal spending have put the brakes on important medical research funded by the National Institutes of Health. Since it is likely that the federal government will face tough choices in seeking to attain and keep a sound financial position during the coming years, issues of this kind will remain for some time. Amid the clamor and shouting of lobbyists in Washington, DC and in state capitals, those advocating on the part of science are finding it even harder than usual to be heard.[15]

Matters that voters and politicians perceive as more important and urgent than science and the training of future scientists will always be funded ahead of them. Both parties tend to worry more about issues like national security, income support, and access to health care—all only peripherally related to science and research. In light of this reality, scientists, university officials, and other advocates will constantly need to find effective ways to demonstrate why science funding matters. On that score, recent efforts to promote human stem cell research show how advocates have successfully linked funding of this science to the promise of major medical advances that will address the effects of currently debilitating diseases.[16] Advocates of human stem cell research have found ways of presenting it as important and urgent, and thus worthy of significant financial support from both the federal and state governments.[17]

THE PIPELINE OF SCIENTIFIC TALENT

It is easy to attract young people into careers in fields that are perceived as growing and that offer well-remunerated jobs. Although the prospects for doing well in some scientific disciplines remain strong, supporters increasingly acknowledge that scientific careers may well be financially unrewarding, if not precarious. In many science disciplines today, tenure-track academic positions in universities are scarce; even where they exist, those holding them face strong pressures to seek external funding to support their research.

It is now a common requisite for those pursuing academic science careers to undertake at least two postdoctoral fellowships before they become eligible for tenure-track positions. Such a mandate can mean the prospect of relatively low and potentially tenuous income streams for budding scientists well into their late thirties. It therefore seems rational for people to choose careers in other fields that are equally intellectually challenging but that offer more immediate and secure financial rewards. Those who might have become gifted physicists end up instead as partners in hedge funds. The broader dynamics at play can lead to the choking of young talent in academic disciplines. Viewed broadly, and from a longer-term perspective, this trend can have far-reaching consequences.[18]

COMMERCIAL APPLICATION OF SCIENTIFIC KNOWLEDGE

The translation of scientific findings into usable knowledge represents another key policy issue relating to science funding. The funding of science projects associated with the pursuit of military superiority during the 20th century has been credited for the massive economic development around Route 128 in Massachusetts and Silicon Valley in California.[19] The lessons of this period were not lost on actors in other regions of the United States.

During the 1960s and 1970s, concern began to emerge that the potential for scientific knowledge to be translated into commercial technologies was not being effectively harnessed. At that time, the federal government held the intellectual property on any federally funded research. Critics expressed the view that a transfer of intellectual property rights could prompt considerably more translation of science findings into usable technologies. This concern led to the adoption of the **Bayh–Dole Act,** or the **Patent and Trademark Law Amendments Act of 1980**. Under the Bayh–Dole Act, universities, small businesses, and nonprofit institutions were allowed to maintain ownership of inventions derived from federally funded science projects conducted on site. This act has had important consequences.

Since passage of the Bayh–Dole Act in 1980, universities in the United States have greatly expanded their patenting and licensing activities. Analysts observing this change have credited it with having stimulated significant economic growth.[20] Others have proposed that considerably more opportunities exist for promoting research-based innovation in the United States, as long as the policy settings are carefully designed.[21] Richard L. Florida has been at the forefront of efforts to explain and promote the ways that university-based scientific inquiry, and the broader culture of technology, talent, and tolerance that surrounds universities, can serve to generate strong local, state, and national economic development.[22] Many opportunities appear to exist for deliberately strengthening the nexus between science funding and economic growth.

SCIENCE FUNDING AND THE INVESTMENT PERSPECTIVE

The investment perspective on public policy urges that we pay close attention to how much money governments spend on specific areas of activity and assess the degree to which that money is money well spent. We can use a variety of approaches to estimate the impact of policy actions on valued public outcomes.

If we systematically observe the impacts of these policy actions and find them to be positive, we can perform further calculations to assess the return on the public investment. The investment perspective is attractive because it accords with common sense. In many instances in our own lives, we intuitively weigh up the costs and benefits associated with taking specific courses of action. Governments often strive to make good investments. However, the information they need to inform sound decision making can be surprisingly difficult to uncover. Simultaneously, other considerations crop up for decision makers—many of which are political—and these may result in intuitions such that specific policy actions will override the desire to engage in more considered, deliberate decision making. Given that the premise of scientific inquiry is to improve human understanding and human judgment, we might expect that science funding would be supported by a well-established infrastructure facilitating good decision making about what investments to make. Surprisingly, this is not the case—either in the United States or elsewhere.

THE APPEAL OF RATIONAL FUNDING DECISIONS

In the opening pages of *The Science of Science Policy: A Handbook*, Kay Husbands Fealing and her colleagues observed:

> Science policy debates are typically dominated not by a thoughtful, evidence-based analysis of the likely merits of different investments but by advocates for particular scientific fields or missions. Policy decisions

are strongly influenced by past practice or data trends that may be out of date or have limited relevance to the current situation. In the absence of a deeper understanding of the changing framework in which innovation occurs, policymakers do not have the capacity to predict how best to make and manage investments to exploit the most promising and important opportunities.[23]

Words of critics and malcontents? Hardly. Husbands Fealing and her fellow contributors to the handbook came from the mainstream academic community and institutions of science funding in the federal government. Even for those who benefited greatly from the ascendance of science funding in the United States from the 1950s onward, there was considerable unease with the way that those funding decisions were actually made.

Those with close interests in science funding, and who have long participated in science administration or studied this area of public policy, agree on a basic point: they accept the obvious truth that science funding has had an enormous impact on innovation, economic growth, and social well-being. Yet, in their various ways, they also worry that of the approximately $150 billion spent annually on science by the U.S. federal government, some proportion of it—and nobody knows how much—might be getting spent on projects that are hopelessly irrelevant.

THE QUEST TO ASSESS RETURN ON INVESTMENT

It is difficult to accurately assess the ROIs made in specific science projects. However, efforts along these lines are advancing, as well as efforts to assess the return on broader portfolios of investments in science and technology. For example, in 2000, during one of the recurring periods when funding for the National Institutes of Health was under threat of being seriously cut, Senator Connie Mack (R–FL) circulated a report entitled *The Benefits of Medical Research and the Role of the NIH*. Although we cannot view the document as a formal analysis of ROI, it effectively summarizes the range and magnitude of impacts that can be attributed to scientific research the NIH has supported over the decades.[24]

In their handbook on the science of science policy, Husbands Fealing and her colleagues highlight a range of more micro-level analytical approaches that can be used to assess the merits of science funding. In the years ahead, we are likely to see a greater development of work along these lines. Often it will involve careful tracing exercises. For example, in a series of significant publications, Lynne Zucker and Michael Darby and their various colleagues showed how collaboration of star scientists—as measured by citations of their research articles—in the activities of biotechnology firms can greatly enhance the growth of those firms.[25] Case Study 10.3 describes some useful new efforts to measure the tangible output of science funding.

case study 10.3 From Scientific Knowledge to Technological Innovation

A recurring concern in science funding is that taxpayer dollars might be devoted to projects that yield no significant public benefits. However, governments have initiated various policies to reduce this risk. With respect to judging what projects to fund, assessment of lead investigators most commonly informs the selection process. Funding tends to follow researchers judged by peers either to have produced a strong record of good work or the capability of doing so in the future. Governments have also made efforts to promote broader application of research findings.[26] The intention here has been to promote greater use of scientific knowledge that may otherwise accumulate in universities and be reported in research journals but not generate any broader public benefits.

As a consequence of the Bayh–Dole Act 1980, some universities have become especially effective at promoting technology transfer—MIT and Stanford University are stand-out cases. Many other universities have found it difficult to cover the annual costs of their technology transfer offices. The reasons are complex, and they involve the costs of proving a concept, seeking a patent, and gaining investor interest.[27]

In 1983, Pennsylvania established a state-funded program called **Ben Franklin Technology Partners**. The program is of high relevance to all involved in science funding. Set up as an investment entity, the Technology Partners selected and invested in start-up companies that its board judged to have potential to become economically successful through translating specific scientific findings into readily commercialized technologies. By design, the Technology Partners worked closely with universities in Pennsylvania. Most funded projects had a university partner component. The program also had representatives of universities on its board, which otherwise consisted of representatives of industry in the state. As such, both people with business acumen and academic researchers informed the investment decisions with solid credentials as productive scientists.

Throughout its existence, those at the Ben Franklin Technology Partners and others have made careful efforts to rigorously evaluate the impact of the program. They have compared employee numbers and average employee wages between firms supported by the Technology Partners and a sample of appropriately matched firms that did not receive program support. In the absence of other comprehensive studies assessing the ROI in science, the evaluations of this program offer valuable lessons. Policy Investment Checklist 10.1 summarizes how the investment perspective applies to the case of the Ben Franklin Technology Partners Program.

An evaluation of the program was published in 2009 by the Economy League of Greater Philadelphia.[28] The evaluation compared the performance of the Technology Partners' clients directly to a control group of similar companies that did not receive the Technology Partners' assistance. This approach allowed program impacts to be isolated from other factors affecting company performance, including firm size, industry trends, and general economic conditions in Pennsylvania. Among other things, the study found that the presence of the Technology Partners boosted the Pennsylvania economy by approximately $9 billion from 2002 through

Analyzing the Ben Franklin Technology Partners Program

1. Focus on Existing Policies and Programs	Pennsylvania's Ben Franklin Technology Partners Program is similar to programs that have been established elsewhere to promote technology transfer from universities to industry. We focus on this program because it has been thoroughly evaluated over a period of decades.
2. Gather Policy Evidence	Studies of the Ben Franklin Technology Partners Program have consistently compared employee numbers and average employee wages between firms supported by the Partners Program and appropriately matched firms that have not received support from the Program.
3. Measure Desired Effects	The desired effect of the Ben Franklin Technology Partners Program was improvement in economic outcomes for the state. The key question was: Did this program make a noticeable difference to economic outcomes? The measured answer was a strong "Yes."
4. Assess Costs and Benefits	To achieve the desired effect of this program, in the period from 2002–2006 the State of Pennsylvania invested $140 million in the Technology Partners Program. However, the Program was estimated to have generated $517 million in additional state tax revenue for a return of $3.50 for every $1.00 invested.
5. Offer Robust Advice	In the case of the Technology Partners Program, outside experts conducted several evaluations over several decades. Each studied different sets of firms in different time periods but found similar results. These analyses suggest that the policy indeed produced sound returns on the investment.

2006 (see Policy Investment Checklist 10.1). During that period, the state government received more than $517 million in additional tax revenues as a direct result of the Technology Partners' activities with specific firms. This sum represents an ROI of approximately $3.50 for every dollar of the $140 million that the state invested in the Technology Partners during the period. Figure 10.1 presents the estimated benefits of the program during the period from 2002 through 2006. A subsequent assessment produced in 2013 confirmed this rate of return using more recent evidence.[29]

Client impacts have rippled throughout the Pennsylvania economy, contributing to higher Gross State Product and additional statewide employment. From 2007 through 2011, Technology Partners generated 7,485 jobs in client firms and an additional 12,715 jobs beyond those client firms—a total of 20,200 jobs in the Commonwealth that otherwise would not have existed. Further, since 1989, Technology Partners has generated 51,000 more jobs in client firms, and 89,000 additional jobs as a result of increased purchasing and investment by client firms,

FIGURE 10.1   Estimated Economic Benefits of the Benjamin Franklin Technologies Partners Program on Pennsylvania's Gross State Product, 2002–2006

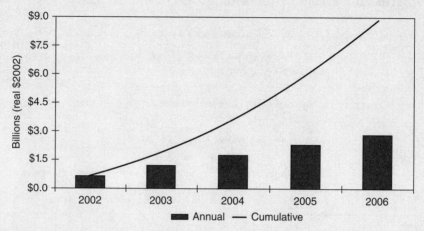

Source: Economy League of Greater Philadelphia, A Continuing Record of Achievement: The Economic Impact of Ben Franklin Technology Partners 2002–2006 *(2009).*

yielding a total of 140,000 new jobs attributable to their work.[30]

Although this study concerns a specific state program, it offers an excellent example of how systematic analytical work can isolate the benefits of promoting the application of scientific knowledge in the development of technological innovations. Over the years since its founding, leaders of Ben Franklin Technology Partners have amassed and made effective use of large amounts of information concerning how technology companies might be successfully launched and developed in Pennsylvania. As such, they have shown that, through careful management, it is possible to consistently improve the potential of technology firms to exploit scientific knowledge for commercial success. Although they focus on the transfer of university-generated scientific knowledge, evaluations of this program show how ROI might be measured more generally in the area of science funding.

CRITICAL THINKING QUESTIONS

1. How did the Technologies Partners Program reduce the risk of making poor investment decisions?
2. Beyond partnership strategies, what are some other ways that governments could encourage greater commercial application of scientific knowledge?

SCIENCE FUNDING AND THE PURSUIT OF CIVIL RIGHTS

In the United States, science funding has had a range of impacts on the advancement of civil rights. Admittedly, those impacts have been less obvious than the impacts of poverty alleviation efforts and public schooling, but they have been no less significant. Here, we consider two impacts. The first is cultural and involves the emergence of role models for young people—especially for minorities and women. The second is economic and involves how scientific and technological advances have reduced the costs of transportation and communication, making them available to a far higher proportion of the population than was ever the case in the past. NASA provides an excellent example of all of these goals.

Scientific activities such as NASA's ongoing space programs present high-profile opportunities to celebrate human achievement. Over the past century, African Americans, women, and other historically marginalized groups have attained many successes in university settings, as well as in the broader scientific community. They have been instrumental in changing perceptions of who can contribute to the advancement of human knowledge and scientific discovery. As part of its education program, NASA has produced an African American Astronaut Fact Sheet.[31] Such catalogues of achievement expand our sense of possibility. They allow all people—including African Americans and women—to appreciate that scientific activities are not the sole domain of people heralding from generations of privilege. Such salient lessons are especially helpful for encouraging children to imagine themselves as someday contributing at a similar level, no matter who they are or what their current circumstances. In contrast, closed scientific communities, operating with limited funding, tend to be less capable than the American scientific community of encouraging diversity among their members and celebrating that diversity as a marker of national success.

Over the past century, scientific and technological advances have reduced the costs of transportation and communication. In so doing, various transport options and modes of electronic communication have become available to a far higher proportion of the population than was ever the case in the past. These advances have made it easier for people who might otherwise have been marginalized to participate in society. We often look to increased access to quality educational opportunities, or political actions, as principal drivers of improved civil rights. Yet many incremental changes that improve our day-to-day lives also serve to advance civil rights and broaden social inclusiveness.

Technological innovations have continuously changed our sense of possibility with respect to movement and communication. They have also had profound impacts on educational experiences and political advocacy efforts. The Khan Academy—with its many YouTube lessons—offers an example of how technological innovation is revolutionizing our sense of how learning might happen in

This crew portrait of the December 2006 flight of the Space Shuttle *Discovery* makes clear that diversity among crew members has broken down stereotypes concerning who can become space scientists.

(NASA/Public Domain)

classrooms (see further discussion of the Khan Academy in Chapter 6).[32] In the process, it is reducing differences between the educational experiences open to children in elite schools and those in less privileged situations. It is contributing to the advancement of civil rights.

Likewise, communication technology is changing political advocacy efforts. Recent actions across the United States to protest local police brutality have been facilitated by the use of smartphones, social media, and the many ways people now have to make video recordings of events. Here we see that advances in information technology create opportunities for new discussions of police practices that once could be hidden from broad public display. Having been exposed, those practices have ignited important new discussions of civil rights, their protection, and their violation.[33]

LESSONS FOR PUBLIC POLICY

Government funding for science is often treated as a luxury—something that should not be prioritized over more pressing areas of social need. Yet, viewed over a period of decades, it is clear that the generation of scientific knowledge can yield huge social benefits. In the United States, perhaps more than anywhere else, the strengthening of the scientific community during the course of the 20th century contributed greatly to the nation's wealth. Translation of new scientific knowledge and procedures into new technologies served to transform many aspects of everyday life. The benefits flowed not only to citizens of the United States but also to many people around the world.

- In the United States, science funding has always been treated as an important form of investment. There have been times when a pragmatic focus on present spending priorities and a lack of appreciation for the full value of scientific research have obscured the long view and slowed pursuit of the endless frontier. Scientists themselves have undoubtedly sometimes lacked the kind of savvy political advocacy needed to ensure any policy areas gain and secure powerful, ongoing political support.
- Many national governments around the world have observed the economic success achieved by the United States during the 20th century and have attributed that success to the commitment to science funding. Consequently, they have begun to make significant investments in science themselves, with the intention of creating their own powerful science communities. To the extent that scientists in those emerging communities around the globe maintain contact with scientists in the United States, it is possible that many benefits will flow in all directions.
- AnnaLee Saxenian has presented this positive perspective in her study of how scientists who trained and worked in the United States subsequently returned to their homelands to strengthen the science communities there.[34] Most significantly, Saxenian's story emphasizes the ways that these "new Argonauts" both contributed locally and took actions that created enduring commercial ties to the United States.
- The constant worry is that as these global science communities expand and become more self-confident, they may see less need to maintain ties with scientists and entrepreneurs in the United States.
- As long as scientists and technology entrepreneurs in the United States cultivate and maintain a global perspective, they will undoubtedly continue to generate wealth at home and in new settings elsewhere.
- More efforts could—and should—be made to carefully measure the economic and social impacts of government-funded science projects. The better governments get at assessing the benefits of science projects, the better able they will become at prioritizing scarce funding in this area.

THE FUTURE FOR SCIENCE FUNDING

During the 20th century, the United States became a recognized superpower—dominant in the world economically and militarily. This rise in international status had many causes. Yet there is no denying that a profound sense of curiosity and possibility provided the foundation for the massive industrialization of the country starting in the mid-19th century. Throughout those years of industrial development and growing technological sophistication, leading figures in politics and business came both to appreciate and to embrace the contributions that scientific investigation could make to broader economic and social progress.

The United States has long benefited from the foresight of industrialists-turned-philanthropists, such as Andrew Carnegie (1835–1919), John D. Rockefeller (1839–1937), and Leland Stanford (1824–1893). Their various early actions helped set the country on a course where scientific work would be well supported, initially from private sources, yet with federal government funding playing an ever-increasing and prominent role. The 20th century saw promotion of scientific research as fundamental to the pursuit of military, technological, and economic supremacy. The systems of science funding in place today were established in the aftermath of World War II, and they have continued to serve the country well.

The image of pure scientists, protected from worldly cares, and funded to toil in laboratories on curiosity-driven projects, has rarely been accepted in the fast-paced, pragmatic culture that epitomizes so much about the United States. It is no surprise, then, to find that the enterprise of science and the university system more generally have benefited most when clear links have been drawn between the urgent concerns of the nation and the potential contributions of science.

Looking to the future, the pathway for science funding in the United States seems reasonably clear. It will be characterized in a number of ways.

- First, science funding will be pragmatic. Politicians and the public who elect them want assurance that science funding will generate valued benefits. To that extent, science projects linked to advances in health care, information technology, national defense, and environmental sustainability will be more likely to receive funding than those contributing to equally worthy but less pragmatic goals.
- Second, it will explicitly be treated as an investment. To the extent that they ever really existed in the United States, the days of significant funding for pure or basic scientific research as an end in itself are all but over. We already are seeing considerable efforts to find reliable and readily applied measures of the actual and anticipated contributions that funding of science makes to the public good.
- Third, it will be focused on maintaining economic supremacy. Efforts over recent decades to explicitly link scientific endeavor, technological innovation, and taking valued products and services to market have generated many benefits.

Although it may be true that, as Steve Jobs said, you can't connect the dots looking forward, a lot of people have figured out smart strategies of prediction. As such, we should expect to see most science funding targeted—in myriad mutually supportive, often unexpected, ways—to the interaction of use-inspired science with the pursuit of fundamental understanding. If, indeed, science funding is characterized in these ways in the decades ahead, science will maintain a high status in U.S. society. Pursuit of the endless frontier will remain exciting, esteemed, and significant.

CHAPTER SUMMARY

This chapter has provided an overview of science funding and the public policy issues associated with it. Although funding for scientific research has historically come from a range of sources, governments continue to be the major funders. Further, because there is a tendency for some jurisdictions to rely upon others to fund scientific work, the resolution of this problem in federal systems of government is that national governments become the predominant funders of science, as is the case in the United States.

Throughout the chapter, we have considered how the scientific community developed in the United States and how science came to be seen as having high value for the country. The contributions of science to the war effort during World War II—especially in the form of the Manhattan Project—had a fundamental impact on political views toward public funding of science.

We have also discussed the contemporary scene in science funding. The system today is very much a product of the view that excellent scientific work is vital to promoting valued economic, social, and geopolitical outcomes. However, there is growing concern that science funding could be managed much more effectively than has been the case in the past. Toward that end, the investment perspective is helping policy makers assess where science funding has been yielding strong ROI. Strong evidence of this kind should greatly improve the case for enhanced funding of scientific projects in the future.

CONNECTIONS TO OTHER CHAPTERS

The development of a strong scientific community is predicated to a significant degree on the prior education of young people. As such, the discussion of public schooling (Chapter 6) is highly relevant to our discussion here of science funding and its impacts. Science also contributes directly to many developments in medicine and the promotion of public health; the discussion in this chapter therefore also has several connections with our discussion of health care (Chapter 7). Finally, as issues in environmental protection continue to emerge, we will look to the scientific community to advise us on how to live sustainably in our communities. A variety of connections exist between the discussion in this chapter and the discussion of environmental protection (Chapter 11).

KEY TERMS

Public good

Pure or basic scientific research

Applied scientific research

Free rider problem

Competitive extramural funding

National Science Foundation

National Institutes of Health

Linear model of science

Big science model

Human genome

Human Genome Project (HGP)

Pharmacogenomics

Companion diagnostics

Bayh–Dole Act, or the Patent and Trademark Law Amendments Act of 1980

Benjamin Franklin Technology Partners

SUGGESTIONS FOR FURTHER READING

Branscomb, Lewis M. "From Science Policy to Research Policy," Chapter 5 in *Investing in Innovation: Creating a Research and Innovation Policy That Works,* Lewis M. Branscomb and James H. Keller, eds. (1999). Cambridge, MA: MIT Press, pp. 112–39. This chapter explores the broadening of science funding in the United States since the 1960s.

Bush, Vannevar. *Science, The Endless Frontier: A Report to the President on a Program for Postwar Scientific Research* (1945). Washington, DC: reprinted by National Science Foundation, 1960. This book offers a highly influential, landmark statement on the appropriate role of government funding in the promotion of scientific research.

Neal, Homer A., Tobin L. Smith, and Jennifer B. McCormick. *Beyond Sputnik: U.S. Science Policy in the Twenty-First Century.* Ann Arbor: University of Michigan Press, 2008. See especially the chapters in Section 1, "Overview of U.S. Science Policy," which provide an excellent introduction to contemporary science policy in the United States.

Kevles, Daniel J. *The Physicists: The History of a Scientific Community in Modern America,* expanded ed. Cambridge, MA: Harvard University Press, 1995. See especially Chapter 5, "Research and Reform," and Chapter 21, "The Bomb and Postwar Research Policy." The latter chapter provides a fascinating history of the significance of the development of the nuclear bomb for the subsequent growth of funding for science research in the United States.

Stokes, Donald E. *Pasteur's Quadrant: Basic Science and Technological Innovation.* Washington, DC: Brookings Institution Press, 1997. See especially Chapter 4, "Renewing the Compact between Science and Government." This chapter explores how governments can improve how they support scientific research and the process of technological innovation.

WEBSITES

- The National Science Foundation keeps close track of research around the United States and the world, maintaining constant contact with the research community to identify ever-moving horizons of inquiry, monitoring which areas are most likely to result in progress, and choosing the most promising people to conduct the research. www.nsf.gov.
- STAR METRICS is a federal and research institution collaboration to create a repository of data and tools that will be useful to assess the impact of federal R&D investments. This project is led by the National Institutes of Health and the National Science Foundation. www.starmetrics.nih.gov.
- Research America aims to increase public and policy-maker awareness of the health and economic benefits of medical research and build a strong base of citizen support for more research and innovation. www.researchamerica.org.

FOR DISCUSSION

1. A continuing debate in the United States has concerned how much support should be given to funding "pure" or "basic" scientific research. Although the debate has often been heated, there is a growing sense that the separation of "pure" or "basic" science from "applied" or "problem-driven" science is artificial. What does it mean to do "pure" scientific research? Why does "pure" science matter?

2. Supporters often claim that a strong commitment to science funding during the 20th century created the basis for significant wealth generation in the United States. What are some examples that demonstrate this apparent link between science funding and wealth generation?

3. The development of North Carolina's Research Triangle Park was prompted by a conscious desire to replicate the success of California's Silicon Valley. What major building blocks are necessary for policy designers to establish a strong scientific community within a specific geographical location? What factors might support or undermine efforts to replicate the success of Silicon Valley?

4. Science funding is often claimed to be an investment in the future. Indeed, that is the basic argument of this chapter. However, the suspicion remains that a lot of science funding is wasteful. What actions might policy designers take to increase the odds that science funding will yield strong returns, while avoiding the temptation to micromanage scientific work?

CHAPTER 11

ENVIRONMENTAL
PROTECTION

This chapter explores the use of public policies to protect the environment. How well we live depends greatly on the quality of our natural environment, but the demands of human progress have damaged that environment. World-wide efforts to extract and exploit natural resources, expand agricultural production, generate electricity, and build great cities have often brought people into conflict with the environment.

The complex issues associated with environmental protection have generated many controversies. At a conceptual level, most of these issues involve two kinds of conflict: those between individual and collective preferences, and those between current and future preferences. This chapter argues that sound efforts to protect the environment work like investments. In complex societies, government actions represent the most feasible means of reconciling these conflicts.

This chapter introduces you to:

- The reasons governments create public policies to protect the environment
- Traditional policy approaches to protect the environment
- Public opinion on trade-offs between environmental protection and economic growth
- Environmental protection in a federal system of government
- The contemporary scene concerning environmental protection
- Contemporary policy issues
- Application of the investment perspective to environmental protection
- Actions being taken to increase use of renewable electricity generation
- Environmental justice and the promotion of civil rights
- Lessons for public policy emerging from this review of environmental protection

Facing page: "Earthrise" is the name given to this photograph of the Earth taken by astronaut William Anders on December 24, 1968, during the Apollo 8 mission to orbit the Moon. The image shows Earth as a small, blue globe. Command Module Pilot Jim Lovell commented from the spacecraft: "The vast loneliness is awe-inspiring and it makes you realize just what you have back there on Earth." The U.S. nature photographer Galen Rowell has described the image as "the most influential environmental photograph ever taken."

AN INTRODUCTION TO ENVIRONMENTAL PROTECTION

Human progress often puts us in conflict with the natural environment. Yet, paradoxically, only through that progress have we been able to achieve our present awareness of the trade-offs that exist between our drive for economic and social progress and environmental protection. The notion that everyone in the world creates a **carbon footprint**—the amount of carbon dioxide or other carbon compounds released into the atmosphere by the activities of individuals, companies, or countries—reflects sophisticated conceptual thinking.[1]

At present, many of us contribute to the production of unsustainable levels of carbon emissions. This is a system-level problem rather than an individual-level one. System configurations within individual countries make it difficult for individuals to change their practices. Moreover, many people, communities, and businesses have strong interests in maintaining the status quo. Thus, even if the present situation is unsustainable from an environmental perspective, those strong vested interests pose barriers to change. Nevertheless, our awareness that we are leaving an unsustainable carbon footprint is itself cause for optimism. The better able we are to see the connections between collective human actions and environmental impacts, the closer we will move toward sustainable development.

A lot of evidence suggests that excessive emissions of **greenhouse gases** are contributing to **global warming**, the gradual increase in the overall temperature of the Earth's atmosphere.[2] (The main greenhouse gases are carbon dioxide and sulfur dioxide. As their presence in the Earth's atmosphere increases, they serve to trap heat near the Earth's surface, leading to higher global temperatures.) If the average atmospheric temperature of the planet rises by just two degrees, the process of climate change theoretically will be irreversible. Predictions are that the changes in sea levels and weather patterns brought by climate change will significantly threaten human life and the lives of many other animal and plant species.[3] We are witnessing heightened extinction rates among animal species; because of rising sea levels, some low-lying islands in the Pacific Ocean have already been lost, and others are in danger of disappearing. The prospect of further destruction has motivated calls for major changes in how we interact with our environment. Worldwide climate change is the fundamental environmental issue of our time. However, as we shall see later in the chapter, other major environmental protection issues arise in more localized contexts. They too are receiving close attention from citizens and their governments. In Case Study 11.1 we consider how a major oil spill affected local communities across several states.

case study 11.1 Extraction Industries and Environmental Damage

Modern economies the world over rely on **extraction industries**—those that use natural resources from the earth such as oil, coal, gas, and iron ore. As societies, we highly value the products derived from these industries. Yet we also place high value on protecting the environment. Other industries—including agriculture, aquaculture, and fishing—rely on clean water, soil, and air as inputs into their production processes. When extraction industries damage the environment, they can also harm adjacent ecological, economic, and social systems.

In April 2010, the BP oil company's Macondo well blew out in mile-deep water in the Gulf of Mexico. The blowout caused an explosion on the *Deepwater Horizon* drilling rig. Eleven workers were killed. More were injured. The blowout caused one of the worst environmental disasters in American history. Over a three-month period, 170 million gallons of oil gushed from the broken well into the Gulf. The blowout was caused by failure to follow established drilling procedures.

Motivated by a desire to avoid unnecessary revenue losses, oil companies take care to avoid costly equipment failures. In addition, the creation and management of oil wells are subject to extensive government regulation designed to protect the environment. Regulation of equipment standards, well management, and safety practices represent public policy investments.

The oil spill from the *Deepwater Horizon* disaster caused vast ecological damage to the United States. Fish stocks, marine mammals (such as dolphins), shellfish (such as oysters), and bird life were all significantly affected. Across Alabama, Louisiana, Florida, Mississippi, and Texas, beaches and wetlands sustained damage as oil washed ashore. The spill gravely affected both local fishing and tourism industries.[4]

It took five years for BP's financial liability to be determined. In 2015, BP reached an agreement to settle all federal and state claims arising from the spill. This included a payment of $5.5 billion under the Clean Water Act, $7.1 billion to the U.S. government and the five Gulf states for damages to natural resources, $4.9 billion to settle economic and other claims made by the five states, and up to $1 billion to 400 local governments. Beyond these payments, BP had already paid more than $24 billion in damages and medical claims to individuals and businesses. Overall, the disaster cost BP more than $53 billion. However, the actual costs to the environment and coastal communities were likely much higher.[5]

If there are any positives here, we might say that the penalties paid by BP for its environmental damage served as a warning to other companies everywhere that participate in extraction industries. The disaster prompted many efforts globally to reduce the risk of similar disasters occurring. It also facilitated learning about how best to manage ecological damage caused by oil spills.

CRITICAL THINKING QUESTIONS

1. Extraction industries must maintain operations while lowering the risk of environmental damage. What are some other examples of extraction industries creating risks of environmental damage?
2. What are some things governments might do to lower the risk of damage to the environment from industrial activities?

WHY GOVERNMENTS GET INVOLVED IN ENVIRONMENTAL PROTECTION

Environmental damage is often portrayed as a **negative externality**. That is, damage occurs as a spillover effect of other activities, but the cost of that damage is not reflected in the costs of those activities causing it. Protecting the environment is a classic example of an effort requiring coordinated, collective action.

Consider an example. A coal-fired electricity plant generates and sells electricity to consumers. However, burning coal generates carbon dioxide, sulfur dioxide, and other fine **particulate matter**—that is, a mixture of solid and liquid particles suspended in the air. If no restrictions or taxes are imposed on the electricity plant for releasing pollutants, the negative externality goes unchecked. The price of the power sold by the power company to consumers does not reflect the full social cost of the power generation, because it does not incorporate the cost of the pollution.

None of these consequences would be a problem if people lived upwind of the electricity plant and few such coal-fired electricity plants existed. However, when people live downwind of such plants, they can experience health problems. Further, as the number of coal-fired electricity plants increases, their smoke can have detrimental effects on the atmosphere. Coal-fired electricity plants are considered a major source of greenhouse gases. In aggregate, the presence of many such plants releasing smoke into the atmosphere is now known to have major negative health and climate consequences.[6] Case Study 11.2 discusses contemporary air pollution problems in China.

THE TRAGEDY OF THE COMMONS

When public policies encourage people to act in ways that are consistent with protecting the environment, those public policies represent important investments. They constrain current freedoms and impose current costs on individuals in ways that avoid future, collective catastrophes. The underlying logic of this claim was laid out by the ecologist Garrett Hardin in an essay from 1968, "**The Tragedy of the Commons.**"[7] Earlier economists had given considerable attention to problems associated with **public goods**, their provision, and their management.[8] Hardin described all naturally occurring public goods as **the commons**—land or resources belonging to or affecting the whole of a community. He also noted that our attitudes toward the commons change as more and more of us crowd in upon them. Hardin's lasting contribution was to emphasize the implications of the general argument for the management of natural resources in the presence of continuous population growth.

Consider Hardin's case about people who graze their herds of cattle on a pasture that is open to everyone. Each person will seek to increase the size of his or her herd grazing on the pasture. All goes well until the pasture reaches its **carrying capacity**—that is, so many cattle are feeding on the pasture that it cannot rejuvenate. For each individual, however, the incentive always exists to add a further head of cattle to the herd. The individual benefits of overgrazing always exceed the costs. Hardin described the problem and the dynamics it creates as follows:

> Adding together the component partial utilities, the rational herdsman concludes that the only sensible course for him to pursue is to add another animal to his herd. And another; and another. . . . But this is the conclusion reached by each and every rational herdsman sharing a commons. Therein is the tragedy. Each man is locked into a system that compels him to increase his herd without limit—in a world that is limited. Ruin is the destination towards which all men rush, each pursuing his own best interest in a society that believes in the freedom of the commons. Freedom in a commons brings ruin to all.[9]

GLOBAL WARMING AS A TRAGEDY OF THE COMMONS

We can use the same narrative structure that Hardin employed in the previous quotation to tell a story about the contemporary scene, carbon emissions, and global warming. In this case, the Earth's atmosphere is the commons. We might restate Hardin as follows:

> Adding together individual gains, the rational leaders of each country conclude that the only sensible course of action for that country is to keep pursuing economic development, which typically necessitates ever-increasing carbon emissions from power plants and various modes of public and private transportation. All countries want to enjoy the fruits of economic development and prosperity. More and more countries, using the same technology, pursue these goals. This behavior is entirely rational on the part of the leaders of each country. Therein is the tragedy. Each country is locked into a system that compels it to increase its carbon

emissions without limit—in a world where the atmosphere's capacity for carrying those emissions is limited.

We might say global warming is the destination toward which all countries rush, pursuing their own best interests in a world where each country jealously guards its freedom to do so. Since for centuries a few large, wealthy countries have been free to pursue economic development and prosperity in this manner, why should others relinquish that freedom? But freedom for all to pollute the atmosphere brings global warming and its costly consequences for everyone.

The continuous increase of carbon emissions poses a major threat to our planet. Fortunately, past public and private actions have effectively addressed other problems of the commons. To avoid future catastrophe due to global warming, however, we must find feasible technical solutions and forge sufficiently binding international political commitments. The challenges are huge, as Case Study 11.2 makes clear.

case study 11.2 Beijing's Health-Threatening Air Pollution Problems

When smog levels in Beijing climb above World Health Organization recommendations, the Chinese government issues Red Alert warnings and closes schools in the city. Those who venture outside wear protective face masks to avoid inhaling polluted air.

(REUTERS/Damir Sago)

Around the world, the economic growth of countries is typically supported by the development of electricity-generating capacity and increased use of motor vehicles. Because coal-fired power plants are common in these countries, economic development tends to be accompanied by increases in atmospheric pollution. Such is the case in China, where rapid economic advancement has led to unsafe levels of smog in many cities.

The **Air Quality Index** (AQI) is a universal measure of atmospheric pollution levels. It has been applied to monitor air quality in many locations. (A real-time visual map has been developed to compare air pollution levels in multiple locations around the world.[10]) Across the United States, the AQI for any region tends to be well below 100 at any given time. By contrast, in Beijing and other Chinese cities, the AQI can often go above 200 and has been known to top 500. Residents of the industrialized regions of modern China live with unhealthy levels of air pollution. Now Red Alert warnings are given in Beijing when the AQI is expected to exceed 200. When the warnings are issued, schools are shut down, transport restrictions are put in place, and residents are encouraged to stay indoors.[11]

Children and elderly people are most susceptible to health problems resulting from inhaling high levels of particulate matter. It is common to find higher levels of asthma and other respiratory diseases, heart problems, and lung cancer among populations living with highly polluted air.[12] The same sources of particulate matter also contribute to production of greenhouse gases.

Jinglei Gao and colleagues have explored efforts to improve air quality in China. They weighed costs and benefits associated with public policies intended to improve air quality.[13]

Estimated costs included reducing emissions from vehicles and also from factories, thus eliminating small coal-fired boilers and outdated production processes. Estimated benefits included better outcomes in population health and agricultural production. Gao and his colleagues tested several scenarios and concluded that mitigating serious air pollution in China would cost the equivalent of $18 billion in U.S. dollars but the benefits would exceed $112 billion. The estimated return on investment would be better than $6 for every dollar spent on improving air quality. The authors noted that efforts in this direction have already begun, especially around Beijing. Still, there is a very long way to go.

CRITICAL THINKING QUESTIONS

1. How do Beijing's air pollution problems illustrate the tragedy of the commons?
2. What strategies could help developing countries grow economically without suffering serious problems of air pollution in their cities?

PUBLIC POLICY RESPONSES TO THE TRAGEDY OF THE COMMONS

The tragedy of the commons is the product of negative externalities that become more acute as a specific commons becomes overcrowded. However, throughout history governments have addressed a lot of commons problems—including those of grazing lands. Four approaches are discussed here.

1. Privatizing Common Resources   As soon as herders receive private property rights, they face powerful incentives to avoid overgrazing on their lands. In the privatized scenario, each herder determines the optimal carrying capacity of his or her parcel of land and manages cattle numbers accordingly. Mismanagement—in the form of either under- or overuse—leads to lower returns on the investment in the land. Here, the role for government is to assign initial property rights and establish legal processes that ensure enforcement of property rights and their transfer among consenting parties.

Effectively designed and implemented, such privatization and market-making actions by governments avoid the tragedy of the commons. That said, the transition from commons to private property can impose high losses on those who do not obtain private rights in the new regime.[14] However, variations on privatization of the commons have promoted sustainable management of natural resources and reduced practices that degrade the environment.

2. Creating Quota Systems   Officials frequently use a range of privatizing approaches to ensure maintenance of sustainable fishing stocks in various demarcated areas (e.g., rivers, lakes, and specific areas of the open seas). People who want to fish must usually purchase **seasonal permits** that give them limited rights to fish. These specify the fishing practices that are legal and those that are not. In New Zealand, for example, the commons of the fishery in the seas around the country is managed through the **Independent Transferable Quotas** system. The system has received considerable international acclaim. Transfer of quotas, which is closely policed and is supported by a range of regulations and prohibitions, has essentially privatized access to the fisheries. It avoids the tragedy of the commons while allowing many people to continue to build livelihoods around fishing—and even more people to enjoy sustainable consumption of this continuously renewing and healthy resource.[15]

3. Creating Pollution Permits   Distribution of **tradable rights to pollute** is another privatization model that avoids the fate of the degraded commons. In this approach, individual polluters receive permits to release a certain amount of pollution. Under this **cap-and-trade system**,[16] a first action involves determining the total amount of pollution that can be released without contributing to environmental degradation. The determined amount then becomes the basis for setting a total emissions cap. The cap is typically fixed for a lengthy period of time; however, it can be adjusted. Once the cap is in place, emissions permits grant permit holders the right to release specific amounts of pollution.

If individual polluters do not use all of their permitted allocation, they can sell the unused portion to other polluters—the trade component of cap and trade. If the amount of pollution allowed to be released—the cap—is reduced over time, the price of permits is expected to rise. Heavy polluters who do not change their practices will therefore face higher costs for their polluting behavior. This system provides an incentive for polluters to reduce the amount they pollute and search for ways to produce goods or services using new processes that do not create pollution. For example, under such a system, electricity companies would face incentives to reduce their production of carbon and find clean means of generating electricity, such as building wind farms (discussed in Case Study 11.4).

4. Regulating and Encouraging Innovation   As well as assigning property rights, governments can take other actions to avoid the tragedy of the commons.

These include placing restrictions or regulations on the actions of individuals and firms and encouraging innovations that lead to more effective use of scarce resources.

TRADITIONAL POLICY APPROACHES TO ENVIRONMENTAL PROTECTION

Over the past two centuries, conservation of highly valued wilderness areas and spaces of natural beauty represented the most consistent form of state and federal government policies for environmental protection in the United States.

NATURE CONSERVANCY

The Antiquities Act of 1906, signed into law by President Theodore Roosevelt, made provision for systematic demarcation of wilderness areas and especially beautiful natural areas. The law has frequently been invoked by presidents ever since. When the federal government established the National Park Service in 1916, government efforts to manage these sites were increased. During the 1950s and 1960s new emphasis was placed on giving the public better access to the national parks. These federal initiatives were mirrored at the state and local levels by many efforts to protect areas of natural beauty and create opportunities for their public enjoyment.

This long-standing commitment to conserving wilderness areas is a triumphant exemplar of how good public policies can serve as investments. In this case, environmental protection efforts have ensured preservation of lands, forests, and waters. The actions of forebears have left important legacies for subsequent generations and modeled good practice.

ENVIRONMENTAL REGULATION

Public recognition of the negative effects of human development on the environment grew in the United States as the human population boomed and industrialization became more extensive. Early in the 20th century, some efforts were made to curb pollution in urban areas and to protect drinking water. In most instances, the federal government delegated regulatory responsibilities to states and localities. The first major thrust for national-level, comprehensive legislative actions to protect the environment emerged with the environmental movement of the 1960s. Public sentiment toward industry changed at this time.

Rachel Carson's book *Silent Spring,* published in 1962, raised popular awareness of the damage to wildlife—and the threat to the human food chain—resulting from extensive agricultural use of pesticides such as DDT. A further catalyst for action arose in 1969 when the heavily polluted Cuyahoga River caught fire in Cleveland, Ohio. At times during the 20th century, the river was one of the most polluted waterways in the United States. The fire, and a major article in *Time* magazine, helped spur an avalanche of water pollution control activities, resulting in the Great Lakes Water Quality Agreement and the Ohio Environmental Protection Agency (OEPA), and the creation of the federal Environmental Protection Agency (EPA), discussed in the next section. The fate of the river became symbolic of the negative effects of industrialization.

EXTENDING THE ROLE OF GOVERNMENT

Capturing the public mood for change, Congress, with President Richard Nixon's support, engaged in a flurry of legislative action in the late 1960s and early 1970s. Landmark legislation from this period included the National Environmental Policy Act of 1969, the Clean Air Act Amendments of 1970, the Federal Water Pollution Control Act Amendments of 1972, and the Federal Environmental Pesticide Control Act of 1972.

The U.S. **Environmental Protection Agency (EPA)**, established by President Nixon, began operations in 1971. It became the federal government's primary organization for monitoring pollution levels and the actions of regulated industries. The agency also took responsibility for producing detailed environmental impact statements concerning federal government actions, a requirement of the National Environmental Policy Act of 1969.

In its early years, the EPA earned a reputation for supporting **command and control** regulation of environmental pollution. The agency took an adversarial stance toward industry, stating explicitly what practices could or could not be engaged in, and specifying in detail the procedures to be followed to reduce pollution to acceptable levels. Although such an approach is sometimes necessary, it can also create economic inefficiencies and promote animosity between regulators and those they regulate. These flaws led to calls for change, both from regulated businesses and from scholars, especially economists.

Business backlash toward the EPA resulted in major efforts to roll back environmental regulations during the presidency of Ronald Reagan (1981–1989). Although these efforts had some effect on the administrative practices of the time, they did not result in longer-term relaxation of government commitments to environmental protection. Indeed, these Reagan-era practices fueled a popular backlash of its own, which resulted in greater public commitment to environmental protection during the late 1980s and the 1990s.[17]

USING INCENTIVES TO PROMOTE ENVIRONMENTAL PROTECTION

Scholars who called for less environmental regulation included Charles L. Schultze, director of the Bureau of the Budget during President Lyndon Johnson's Great Society agenda and chair of the Council of Economic Advisers during President Carter's administration. In his book *The Public Use of Private Interests* (1978),

Schultze supported use of regulatory practices that placed less reliance on telling businesses what to do. Instead, Schultze proposed that governments set clear environmental goals and provide powerful incentives for industries to adapt to achieve them.[18]

Meanwhile, in *Going by the Book: The Problem of Regulatory Unreasonableness* (1982), Eugene Bardach and Robert A. Kagan called for regulators to take a more conciliatory and cooperative stance toward regulated industries.[19] The ideas put forward by Schultze, Bardach, Kagan, and others subsequently influenced policy design. That influence is still apparent today, where much greater use is being made of cooperative ecosystem management, and incentives for industries to promote improved environmental outcomes.

ENVIRONMENTAL PROTECTION AND U.S. PUBLIC OPINION

Public opinion significantly affects the policy choices governments make.[20] In the United States, public opinion on environmental issues started being canvassed in the late 1960s. Since the 1980s, the Gallup organization has consistently used the same two questions to assess how members of the American public weigh economic concerns versus environmental concerns. Figure 11.1 reproduces the main findings, which show that, for the most part, a majority of the public tends to agree with the statement that "Protection of the environment should be given priority, even at the risk of curbing economic growth," compared with the statement that "Economic growth should be given priority, even if the environment suffers to some extent."

Studying these data, pollster Art Swift has noted two things.[21] First, beginning near the start of the global financial crisis (2007–2008), increasing proportions of the public prioritized economic growth over the environment. Second, immediately after the BP *Deepwater Horizon* oil spill in 2010, the public briefly indicated

FIGURE 11.1   Gallup Public Opinion Survey Findings over Time

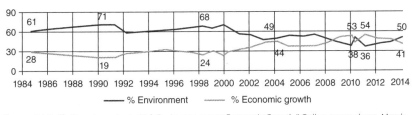

Prioritizing Environmental Protection vs. Economic Growth, 1984–2014

With which one of these statements about the environment and the economy do you most agree—protection of the environment should be given priority, even at the risk of curbing economic growth (or) economic growth should be given priority, even if the environment suffers to some extent?

Source: Art Swift, "Americans Again Pick Environment over Economic Growth," Gallup press release, March 14, 2014. http://www.gallup.com/poll/168017/americans-again-pick-environment-economic-growth.aspx.

higher support for prioritizing protection of the environment over economic growth. (See Case Study 11.1 earlier in this chapter).

From 1984 to 2014, a majority of respondents to the Gallup survey who identified with the Democratic Party always agreed that "protection of the environment should be given priority, even at the risk of curbing economic growth." In contrast, respondents who identified with the Republican Party were much more likely to agree that "economic growth should be given priority, even if the environment suffers to some extent."

Differences in opinion do not fall solely along partisan lines. Intergenerational differences also emerged in the survey results. For example, in 2014, 60 percent of survey respondents aged 18 to 29 supported environmental protection. In contrast, in the same 2014 survey, just 39 percent of respondents aged 65 and over agreed that protection of the environment should be given priority (see Table 11.1).

We can draw several conclusions from the evidence on factors shaping U.S. public opinion on environmental protection.

1. Support for environmental protection seems contingent on favorable economic conditions.
2. Public opinion may react to changes in the condition of the natural environment, such as dramatic events like the BP *Deepwater Horizon* disaster.
3. Some changes in opinion may result from a desire to see changes in government policy choices. Specifically, when government policy moves in one direction, the public may move in the opposite direction to restrain government's movement. Some analysts have viewed growth in pro-environmental attitudes during the 1980s as a reaction against the Reagan administration's opposition to environmental regulation.[22]

TABLE 11.1   Gallup Public Opinion Survey Results on Intergenerational Differences

With which one of these statements about the environment and the economy do you most agree—protection of the environment should be given priority, even at the risk of curbing economic growth (or) economic growth should be given priority even if the environment suffers to some extent?

	% ENVIRONMENT	% ECONOMIC GROWTH
18–29	60	30
30–49	52	41
50–64	49	41
65+	39	50

Source: Art Swift, "Americans Again Pick Environment over Economic Growth." Gallup press release, March 14, 2015. http://www.gallup.com/poll/168017/americans-again-pick-environment-economic-growth.aspx.

ENVIRONMENTAL PROTECTION IN FEDERAL SYSTEMS OF GOVERNMENT

Federalism facilitates variation in how sub-national governments address policy problems. States and localities can serve as natural laboratories for the creation and implementation of new policy approaches. Since people in neighboring jurisdictions keep close watch on what is happening around them, effective policies developed in one state often gain rapid attention and support in other, nearby states. As information technology and transportation systems have advanced, knowledge of practices in pioneering states now spreads faster than ever before. Networks of policy professionals now serve as key conduits for the spread of policy ideas. Old state-to-state diffusion patterns have begun to break down. Spaces have opened up for much more cross-jurisdictional sharing and discussion of policy ideas than in the past.

In terms of specific, effective initiatives to promote environmental protection, state-level politicians in the United States have made the most impressive contributions over the past two decades. States have done much to build up their capacity for administering environmental regulations, in large part because the federal government has often delegated enforcement responsibilities to the states. In many instances, states have developed their own environmental protection authorities, with structures replicating those of the EPA. Thus, states have amassed the technical and administrative capabilities to effectively govern environmental protection.[23] We should also note that there has been a lot of variance in the attitudes of state-level politicians concerning the importance of promoting environmental protection.

Citizen ballots in many states have produced some high-profile cases of environmental protection agencies taking their cues on environmental protection from strong popular mandates. For example, in California, Proposition 65 (formally titled "The Safe Drinking Water and Toxic Enforcement Act of 1986") is a state law passed by direct voter initiative. Its goals are to protect drinking water sources from toxic substances that may cause cancer and birth defects and to reduce or eliminate exposure to those chemicals. Proposition 65 is administered by the state's Environmental Protection Agency. The law prohibits businesses from knowingly discharging listed substances into drinking water sources, or onto land where the substances can pass into drinking water sources. It also prohibits businesses from knowingly exposing individuals to listed substances without providing a clear and reasonable warning.

As a result of policy initiatives of this kind, states have promoted cooperation among stakeholders in protecting local ecosystems and curbing various forms of pollution. In addition, some ambitious initiatives have promoted cooperation across states in reducing atmospheric pollution. Of course, there are huge differences in geography, industries, environmental issues, political preferences, and administrative capabilities across the 50 states. Consequently, for every state in which policy entrepreneurs have promoted specific environmental protection measures, other states have proven to be laggards in addressing major pollution problems.[24] Nevertheless, the states represent exciting laboratories for environmental protection policy in the United States.[25] We are likely to see continued state leadership in this policy area, even as the commitments to environmental protection at the national level wax and wane.

THE POLITICS OF ENVIRONMENTAL PROTECTION

Over the past few decades, in the United States, as elsewhere, government policies to protect the environment have almost always been construed by opponents as antibusiness. Since electricity production using fossil fuels, motor vehicle use, and some forms of manufacturing contribute the most to atmospheric pollution, any efforts to curb such pollution inevitably have adverse effects on many businesses. Business interests, being concentrated and readily able to engage in collective action, tend to mount powerful political opposition to any proposals that would constrain their practices and harm their financial performance.[26] These dynamics have limited the actions of political leaders seeking to reduce atmospheric pollution. The same dynamics have made it difficult for politicians to pursue a range of other policy actions that would protect the environment, such as restricting water pollution, mining activities, and so on.

In recent decades, environmental protection battles in the United States have mostly taken a partisan tone. Republican presidents and members of Congress have sought to limit the actions of the EPA and have done what they can to block other initiatives aimed at environmental protection. Many Republican politicians have denied that human actions are contributing to the growth of greenhouse gases and the risk of global warming. Meanwhile, members of the Democratic Party have been more open to actions that would promote environmental protection. However, they have been constrained by fear of losing business support and by the efforts of Congressional Republicans to block such initiatives.

The presidency of George W. Bush (2001–2009) was characterized by a determined effort to roll back previous regulatory efforts to protect the environment. In contrast, Bill Clinton's presidency (1993–2001) was characterized by an ambitious agenda for environmental protection. Among other things, new provisions accommodated federal support for the development of renewable sources of electricity generation. Nonetheless, the Clinton agenda was ultimately limited by congressional resistance.

Both Clinton and Bush used **executive orders**—that is, rules or orders issued by the president to an executive branch of the government and having the force of law—to pursue environmental policy objectives. Both presidents used their positions to greatly expand federal conservation efforts. Clinton protected large tracts of national forest from future logging. In the process, he preserved more public land than any president since Theodore Roosevelt. George W. Bush protected huge areas of ocean around American Samoa from future fishing, drilling, or mineral extraction.[27]

in focus 11.1

THE CONFERENCE OF PARTIES IN PARIS (2015) AND ITS AFTERMATH

In November 2015, representatives of more than 180 countries producing more than 90 percent of global emissions met in Paris to develop a common framework for addressing climate change. During this **Conference of Parties** (COP21), delegates sought to commit all countries to put forward their best efforts for reducing climate change. In 2017, President Trump promised to withdraw the United States from the commitments it made to the Paris Agreement.

The Paris Agreement marked the latest step in the evolution of the United Nations' climate change regime, which originated in 1992 with the adoption of the Framework Convention. In the years that have followed, the regime has evolved in different directions. The 1997 Kyoto Protocol took a more "top-down" but highly differentiated approach, establishing negotiated, binding emissions targets for developed countries, and no new commitments for developing countries.

With the 2009 Copenhagen Accord and 2010 Cancun Agreements, parties established a parallel "bottom-up" framework, with countries undertaking national pledges for 2020 that represented political rather than legal commitments. This approach attracted much wider participation, including—for the first time—specific mitigation pledges by developing countries. However, pledges of these countries fell far short of the reductions needed to meet the goal set in Copenhagen and Cancun of keeping average warming below two degrees Celsius in excess of pre-industrial levels.

The Paris Agreement blended bottom-up flexibility, to achieve broad participation, with top-down rules, to promote accountability and ambition. Three elements make up the overall "Paris Outcome":

1. The Paris Agreement: This enduring, legally binding treaty on climate action contains emission reduction commitments from 187 countries starting in 2020. The Paris Agreement became official when 55 countries covering 55 percent of global emissions agreed to it.

2. COP Decision: The COP agreed to a set of decisions with immediate effect to accelerate climate action and to prepare for the implementation of the Paris Agreement once it becomes official.

3. Paris Action Agenda: Alongside the formal agreements, countries, regions, cities, investors, and companies made a large number of commitments for additional action to reduce emissions and increase resilience. The measures included establishing a $100 billion climate finance fund for developing countries by 2020, with a commitment to further finance in the future.

Like his predecessors, President Barack Obama felt the constraints of Congress on his political leadership with respect to environmental policy. Even so, he laid out an ambitious program of efforts for his second term in office, most of which concerned reducing atmospheric pollution and promoting international cooperation in the fight to prevent global warming. An important example included raising the corporate average fuel efficiency (CAFE) standard for automobiles, a move designed to make a significant long-run dent in the levels of carbon emitted into the atmosphere in the United States. Upon succeeding him in office, President Donald Trump sought to undo many of the environmental protection initiatives introduced by President Obama.

CONTEMPORARY POLICY ISSUES

Many policy issues arise in the area of environmental protection. Rather than discuss them by substantive area (i.e., air, land, and water), here we consider three issues that cut across all substantive areas: the measurement of environmental impacts, the selection of policy instruments, and the promotion of environmental protection.

MEASURING ENVIRONMENTAL IMPACTS

Measurement issues are important in the pursuit of environmental protection. The saying "you manage what you measure" is relevant. Indeed, most stories about advocacy for policies to protect the environment begin when people observe patterns, document them, and devise ways of measuring salient variables. For example, observed death of vegetation and decline of fish stocks in a river might lead to an examination of causes. What relationships might exist between changing natural conditions and these observed outcomes? How might runoff from bordering farms or discharges from nearby towns be affecting life in the river?

Good measurement is essential to good policy making. In a review of policy impacts in the United States since the first Earth Day in 1970, Myrick Freeman III documented the results of cost-benefit analyses of a range of initiatives to improve environmental outcomes.[28] He made constant reference to measurement and estimation challenges. He noted that "all benefit-cost analyses have uncertainties and omissions." Natural scientists complain that economists do not give sufficient attention to the valuation of policy effects on whole ecological systems or on biodiversity. Modeling relationships and impacts is extremely difficult to do in such instances, yet that is a prerequisite for rigorous and defensible estimation of policy costs and benefits.

In a major contribution to measuring environmental policy impacts, Nicholas Z. Muller and his colleagues developed a framework to include environmental externalities in a system of national accounts for the United States.[29] These authors estimated the air pollution damages for each industry in the country. They did not take account of other kinds of pollution—for example, water pollution, soil pollution, or noise and visual pollution.

In this study, Muller and his colleagues connected emissions of sulfur dioxide, nitrogen oxide, fine particulate matter, and several other forms of air pollution to the physical and economic consequences of these discharges on society. The effects factored in their calculations included human health, decreased timber and agricultural yields, reduced visibility, accelerated depreciation of materials, and reductions in recreational services. For the electric power generation sector, they also included damages from carbon dioxide emissions. The authors concluded that, among other things, oil- and coal-fired power plants, solid waste combustion, livestock production, truck transportation, and sewage treatment produce air pollution damages larger than their overall value added to society.

SELECTING AND IMPLEMENTING POLICY INSTRUMENTS

After decades of policy debate and development of policy interventions, policy makers wishing to promote environmental protection now have access to a lot of evidence about the efficacy of different policy instruments under different conditions, and their associated administrative costs. A well-founded criticism of heavy-handed government practices, and their directive approach, is that they stifle experimentation and human ingenuity and, hence, the evolution of more efficient and effective ways of addressing specific problems.[30]

In weighing up the use of alternative policy instruments, policy makers need to take account of, among other things, mechanism design costs, monitoring costs, and enforcement costs. Traditional approaches to pollution abatement used directive approaches. Under this approach, the government actually tells polluters what equipment to use to address the problem at hand. Although economists contend that such approaches are not as efficient as incentives-based alternatives, there are instances where they are useful. Sheila M. Olmstead has noted that efforts to remove contaminants from drinking water are best addressed through imposition of directive approaches. In this case, tolerance of deviations from established standards could have catastrophic population-health implications.[31] The existence of high lead levels in the water supply to Flint, Michigan—as discovered in 2015—offers a compelling and tragic example. Clearly, there are times when strong standards should be set. Setting them can ease monitoring costs, because no room is left for variation—contamination levels are deemed either acceptable or not acceptable. Period. Likewise, requiring double hulls be a mandatory feature of all large, ocean-going oil tankers reduces the risk of unintended oil spills in a fashion that keeps monitoring costs low.

Evidence is now accumulating about a range of ways in which incentive-based, market-like arrangements have effectively reduced pollution problems and managed common pool resources. Imposing taxes on polluters is a straightforward way to internalize externalities. For example, taxes on gasoline and diesel sales increase the cost of polluting for those engaging in it. Imposing the tax on the purchase of the polluting fuel, rather than on the pollution itself, eliminates significant monitoring and enforcement costs. In the United States, both the imposition of taxes on fuel consumption and the setting of new-auto fuel-efficiency standards have led manufacturers to reduce atmospheric pollution from motor vehicles.

With more experiments in use of incentives to reduce various forms of pollution, evidence is now emerging that should be useful to policy designers in the future. However, some questions arise about the interaction effects that can occur with the simultaneous use of multiple policy instruments to address one problem.[32] Other questions concern interactions between policies set at the federal level and those set at the state levels.[33] These matters deserve careful attention. However, in a world where perfect solutions are rarely attainable and may not be politically feasible, a "mix and match" approach to the use of policy instruments appears to make sense. A lot of room exists for more careful exploration of the effectiveness of different policy instruments for the pursuit of environmental protection in varying contexts.

PROMOTING ENVIRONMENTAL PROTECTION

Avoiding the tragedy of the commons usually requires a central authority to arrange and enforce a form of social contract. But what if the central authority that has the means to act lacks the political will to do so? Elinor Ostrom suggested that alternative possibilities exist, and that they are highly relevant to management of environmental commons, including the Earth's atmosphere. Ostrom argues that many local efforts to combat global warming could have positive effects. This approach she called **polycentricity**—that is, coordination via many localized efforts.[34]

In the polycentric governance model, the recipe for securing good outcomes requires giving the individuals involved in collective action clear evidence of how changed practices will work to their own benefit. As an example, Ostrom suggested that citizens who insulate their homes and therefore use less energy to heat them should be sold on the benefits of insulation based on savings in their household budget, rather than on the infinitely small contribution their actions would make to avoiding global warming. "As more information is provided about these small-scale, but cumulatively additive benefits, one can expect further efforts to be undertaken that cumulatively and significantly reduce [greenhouse gas] emissions."[35]

The polycentric logic Ostrom proposed emphasizes the need to motivate local initiatives, even when higher-level rules have been made. In any system, enforcement is always easier (and hence, cheaper) when individuals see the personal benefit in following them and are confident that others are also playing by the rules.

The policy implication that follows from Ostrom's claim is that, wherever possible, incentives should promote local collective action that is consistent with higher-level pursuit of environmental protection. Indeed, over the past few decades, political leaders have developed ways to cooperatively engage citizens as well as larger stakeholder groups in environmental protection efforts.[36] When local initiatives encourage a common goal, opportunities arise for innovation, learning, adaptation, sharing best practices, and building trust.

As increasing numbers of people take actions to reduce atmospheric pollution, the likelihood increases that moral suasion will be effective for motivating the same actions in others. Given this support, would-be political leaders at the city, state, or national level may find it personally uncomfortable—and, eventually, politically foolish—to run on electoral platforms that go against the practices and beliefs embedded in local communities. From a policy design perspective, this observation suggests that coordinated local activities could truly lead to eventual good global outcomes. And this result does not require that everyone who is doing the right thing locally actually needs to think globally.

Although concern about global warming often dominates contemporary media discussions about environmental protection, many other environmental issues generate political controversy. One example is **fracking**, which involves pumping large amounts of water, sand, and chemicals underground to split open rocks to allow oil and gas to flow (see Case Study 11.3). This process has allowed mining companies to develop unconventional sources of oil and gas, especially in areas such as Ohio and Oklahoma, with their large underground shale deposits. Improved technology has allowed energy companies to access huge stores of natural gas. Currently, fracking is taking place in over 30 states. Indeed, almost half of the current production of crude oil and over half of the natural gas production in the United States involves fracking.[37] However, many are raising questions about the lack of safeguards to ensure that fracking is done in ways that avoid harm. Again, official discussion should involve what policy instruments might both enable fracking and ensure environmental protection.

case study 11.3 Controversy Surrounding Fracking to Release Oil and Natural Gas

Fracking has driven a natural gas boom that began in the early years of the 21st century. As U.S. natural gas production has risen, it has decreased the price of natural gas, a benefit to millions of Americans. In addition, fracking is credited with having greatly reduced U.S. reliance on imported oil and gas. And since natural gas does not produce carbon emissions, it is a good substitute energy source for coal.

Against this positive backdrop, fracking has generated controversy both in the United States and abroad. Common complaints include that it can contaminate drinking water and harm air quality near drill sites, and that these environmental effects can cause health problems for nearby residents. Expert evidence suggests that such risks and others increase when fracking is poorly managed and is conducted near

Activists in Pennsylvania oppose fracking in their state. Fracking operations have drawn significant protest across the United States because of perceived risks of environmental damage and population health risks.

(Sipa via AP Images)

populated areas.[38] Citizens have sought to ban fracking through ballot initiatives in several state elections.

In 2015, President Obama introduced a regulation requiring all companies engaging in fracking to reveal the chemicals they use in the process. In a highly publicized 2014 decision, New York State Governor Andrew Cuomo banned fracking in the Empire State. Cuomo said he made his decision because of concern over the lack of evidence about the population health risks. Critics have claimed that the decision was all about politics, and that it came at a time when natural gas prices in the United States were falling because of high rates of supply.[39]

The evidence base on the environmental and human health risks of fracking is incomplete. Advisors to Governor Cuomo provided a highly detailed review of the evidence.[40] For the most part, the review concluded that the appropriate evidence base needed to judge health risks would involve collecting data over a period of years, and then comparing future population health conditions of interest with baseline conditions. An even more detailed study on the environmental costs and benefits of fracking has been produced by Robert B. Jackson of the Woods Institute for the Environment and Stanford University, and his colleagues. Through a systematic evidence review, they concluded that effective management of the oil and gas extraction processes can effectively address the risks associated with fracking.[41]

Fracking is a technology that, when managed effectively, can generate many benefits at limited cost. However, when managed poorly, it can introduce serious risks of environmental damage and human health problems. The investment approach to public policy urges careful review of evidence before policy decisions are taken. Presently, fracking activities appear to generate more benefits than costs when they follow suitable technical and environmental standards, in locations where the risks to humans are well known and minimal.

CRITICAL THINKING QUESTIONS

1. What classic trade-offs are exhibited in the debate about the merits of fracking?
2. Given the introduction of new technologies that have potentially harmful effects for the environment and for the public, what actions can citizens take to mitigate the risks of harm?

ENVIRONMENTAL PROTECTION AND THE INVESTMENT PERSPECTIVE

In the past, when governments acted to protect the environment, they rarely treated the new public policies as investments. Myrick Freeman III has observed, "Broadly speaking, the goals of environmental policy can be based either on a balancing of benefits and costs (economic efficiency) or on some other goal, such as safety, protection of human health, protection of ecosystems or the achievement of technically feasible levels of emissions control."[42] Freeman also recalled that the U.S. Congress explicitly rejected the economic approach to goal setting when it established the first two major environmental laws of the 1970s—the **Clean Air Act** and the **Federal Water Pollution Control Act**. That rejection indicates how—from the outset—many public policies in pursuit of environmental protection have implicitly pitted that effort against the pursuit of economic gain.

Given that so much environmental damage has been caused by economic development, clear grounds exist for advocates of environmental protection to snub economic thinking. But the times are changing. Over the decades since the environmental movement started, economic ideas about how to effectively pursue environmental protection have gained far greater prominence in policy discourse and have started to influence policy design. Here, we consider several examples that illustrate how the investment perspective can advance the design and assessment of environmental protection efforts.

INVESTING TO REDUCE ACID RAIN

Acid rain is rainfall made sufficiently acidic by atmospheric pollution that it causes environmental harm, typically to lakes and forests. It has been recognized since the 1970s as a source of environmental degradation in the United States, especially to its northeastern lakes. Coal-burning power plants have been identified as culprits in producing high levels of sulfur dioxide and nitrogen oxide in the atmosphere. These pollutants harm environments downwind of the power plants. In response to the problems associated with acid rain, Title IV of the Clean Air Amendments Act of 1990 established the **Acid Rain Program**. The U.S. Congress passed Title IV to reduce sulfur dioxide and nitrogen oxide emissions from coal-fired power plants.

The provisions in the Acid Rain Program concerning emissions of sulfur dioxide signaled a departure from previous regulatory practices. A cap-and-trade scheme, it established a cap on overall emissions and allowed trading of emissions allowances between power plants. It created flexibility for the regulated entities to identify for themselves the lowest-cost approach to reducing total emissions of sulfur dioxide.

According to a cost-benefit analysis produced by Lauraine G. Chestnut and David M. Mills, the U.S. Acid Rain Program has been highly successful.[43]

Since 1990, there have been significant advances in the science of establishing causal links between pollutants and their environmental and human health effects. As economists have gained the ability to more accurately measure and monetize the impacts of pollution from sulfur dioxide and nitrogen oxide, the benefits of limiting such pollution have become clearer. Efforts to curb acid rain represent a public policy investment that has yielded extensive benefits.

To comply with the Acid Rain Program, power plants switched to burning low-sulfur coals and installed chimney scrubbers to control sulfur dioxide emissions. These actions also reduced mercury emissions and the emission of fine particulate matter, both significant environmental and human health hazards. Chestnut and Mills estimated that the costs to power plants of introducing changes in their emissions practices amounted to $3 billion in 2010.[44]

Meanwhile, Chestnut and Mills estimated that the annual social benefits of reducing sulfur dioxide and nitrogen oxide emissions amounted to $122 billion in 2010. The program benefits were categorized to include benefits to human health, freshwater lakes and streams, coastal estuaries, forests, and in terms of human visual enjoyment of a less polluted environment. The authors also noted other potential benefits to the built environment.

The estimated 40-to-1 annual return on investment from this policy (i.e., $122 billion divided by $3 billion) indicates the major gains that can come from concerted efforts to protect the environment. It is especially noteworthy that, following adoption of the policy, subsequent evidence has indicated that initial estimates concerning the costs of this policy were too high and many human health benefits had been either underestimated or ignored. The evidence emerging from assessments of the Acid Rain Program confirms it as a policy success.

INVESTING TOGETHER TO REDUCE HARMFUL EMISSIONS

Although the language of investment does not explicitly appear in discussions of the Acid Rain Program, subsequent policy work has adopted such language. Political leaders around the world are increasingly recognizing the massive environmental, economic, and social damages that could be wrought by uncurbed global warming. But can they act together to change things?

Taken together, the nine northeastern states of the United States were estimated in 2010 to be the world's 10th biggest producer of carbon dioxide emissions. (As noted, such emissions are now recognized as a major contributor to the greenhouse gas effects that can promote global warming.) In 2003, New York's then-governor, George Pataki, requested that other governors of northeastern states join with him to help the region lead the United States in efforts to fight global climate change. After a prolonged set of negotiations involving governments, industry, and nonprofit organizations, they established the

Regional Greenhouse Gas Initiative (RGGI), the country's first cap-and-trade pollution reduction program intended to address climate change.

The initiative, which boasts the participation of all nine northeastern states, launched in 2009 and targets carbon dioxide emissions from electric power plants in the region. Those plants have been estimated to produce around a quarter of the region's carbon dioxide emissions. (Almost half the carbon emissions in the region result from motor vehicles, and the remaining quarter from combined residential, commercial, and industrial use of fossil fuels.)

According to Tony Dutzik and his colleagues, the RGGI has shown promising early signs of effectiveness.[45] For our purposes, it offers a significant example of how policy makers have been treating policies to protect the environment as investments. To comply with the program, power plant owners must purchase emission permits or allowances that match the amount of carbon dioxide they release into the atmosphere. Four times per year the allowances are sold at auction on behalf of the states, and revenues from their sale are returned to the states. As part of the agreement, at least one quarter of the revenues returned to each state are required to benefit consumers or support strategic energy initiatives.

In practice, most of the auction revenues returned to the states have been used to assist energy consumers and to fund investments in greater energy efficiency or the development of clean, renewable energy sources. Examples of clean energy programs that have received investments from RGGI include energy audits and energy efficiency improvements for small businesses and homeowners, grants to homeowners and businesses seeking to install solar panels or wind turbines (see Case Study 11.4), direct assistance to industry to improve energy efficiency in factories, and rebates to consumers on energy-efficient appliances.

The RGGI has shown that market-based approaches to reducing global warming pollution can work effectively. Dutzik and his colleagues have noted that the RGGI provides "a platform that could be expanded to other jurisdictions and sectors of the economy or emulated by other states and regions." These authors further note:

> As the Northeast continues to invest in more efficient homes, offices, and factories over time, the region will become better able to ramp down its dependence on dirty sources of energy without risk to the economy. At the same time, the region will develop a growing legion of businesses with expertise in delivering cleaner energy products and services, expanding access to those products and services and reducing costs—leaving the region better to reduce emissions further....[46]

The state of Connecticut, an RGGI member, has been leading the way in the United States with another policy approach that explicitly brings an investment perspective to promotion of clean energy generation and environmental protection. In 2011, Connecticut's General Assembly established the

Clean Energy Finance and Investment Authority (CEFIA). Its mandate is to support the governor's and legislature's energy strategy to deliver cleaner, cheaper, and more reliable sources of energy while creating jobs and supporting economic development. The intention behind CEFIA is to move the state's clean energy programs away from reliance on grants, rebates, and other subsidies from various government entities, including the federal government.

CEFIA operates as a clean energy investment bank that leverages public money by attracting private-sector funds and expertise. It then issues loans to developers to help them fund clean energy generation projects across the state. Supporters have heralded the model as worthy of emulation by other jurisdictions seeking to harness private-sector resources in pursuit of environmental protection.[47]

If we look ahead, it seems entirely possible that new financial entities like CEFIA could establish self-sustaining revolving funds to support continuous development of clean energy sources. Such entities would play a useful role in promoting clean energy innovation, by supporting the development of technologies to a point where they are deemed promising enough to attract backing from private investors.[48] We see here a clear example of how the investment perspective on public policy is shaping contemporary approaches to environmental protection.

case study 11.4 Renewable Electricity Generation

Roscoe Wind Farm in Texas is one of the largest in the world. Although wind farms can produce a significant amount of electricity, there are some limitations to their effectiveness. For example, because of fluctuations in wind strengths, their efficiency in generating electricity differs throughout the day. As a result, they usually need to be combined with more reliable sources of energy.

(SuperStock/Alamy Stock Photo)

Since 1992, the U.S. government has offered the Federal Renewable Electricity Production Tax Credit (PTC). Initiated under Bill Clinton's presidency, this subsidy program provides an incentive for energy companies to produce electricity from sources that do not generate atmospheric pollution. The tax credit offers different levels of incentive for different generation systems. For example, wind-powered generating systems attract a higher subsidy than do hydroelectric systems. The greater the amount of electricity generated in each of the renewable power stations, the greater the amount of subsidy the generating companies receive in the form of the tax credit. As designed, the tax credit offers identical incentives to electricity generators across the country to build and run power stations that utilize renewable power sources. From an environmental protection perspective, this is an attractive and effective policy.

Kyle Siler-Evans and colleagues analyzed regional variations in the benefits of wind and solar generation in the United States.[49] The study extended the scope of cost-benefit analyses of alternative systems of electricity generation. It explicitly took account of cost savings in terms of health, environmental, and climate effects associated with switching away from coal-fired electricity to use of solar- and wind-powered electricity. Through their analysis of regional differences in electricity

systems, Siler-Evans and his colleagues offered insights into policy design. Specifically, their analysis suggested that governments can realize better returns—in terms of various benefits—by introducing region-based incentives into policies designed to promote greater investment in renewable electricity generation. Policy Investment Checklist 11.1 summarizes how the investment perspective applies to the case of the PTC for renewable electricity generation.

Kyle Siler-Evans and colleagues created a data set containing information about the effectiveness of a specific model of wind turbine

Analyzing the U.S. Government's Production Tax Credit

1. Focus on Existing Policies and Programs	The Production Tax Credit (PTC) provides incentives for electricity producers to develop wind farms. It encourages less reliance on burning fossil fuels (especially coal) for electricity generation. Studying its effects can offer lessons for the use of similar incentive-based policies intended to promote environmental protection.
2. Gather Policy Evidence	A study of electricity generation from 2009–2011 incorporated evidence on the production of electricity across a range of sites. These included coal-fired and gas-fired plants as well as wind farms and solar power-generation systems. The evidence allowed for comparisons across generation systems.
3. Measure Desired Effects	The desired effect of the PTC was to reduce reliance on fossil fuels for electricity generation. The key question was: Did this program make a noticeable difference to pollution levels caused by burning fossil fuels? The answer was "yes," but system management mattered, too.
4. Assess Costs and Benefits	The costs of the PTC were calculated, as were the social benefits from wind farms. The PTC was estimated to produce $1.60 for every $1.00 invested—a decent return. However, returns on investment differed by region. The return on subsidies to wind farms in Ohio was seven times higher than the return on subsidies to wind farms in California.
5. Offer Robust Advice	This study suggests that the greatest benefits of the PTC are realized in locations that have historically been most dependent on coal-fired electricity. However, wind farms typically do not operate so efficiently in these regions because of prevailing weather conditions. Good policy choices would take account of these trade-offs.

in 33,000 locations across the United States, and about the effectiveness of a specific model of solar panel in 900 locations. They also collected data on the generating capacity and emissions of more than 1,400 coal- and gas-fired power stations located across the country. These data captured every hour of generation from 2009 through 2011. In addition, the authors estimated that the social costs (health, environmental, and climate) of carbon dioxide emissions were around $20 per ton. Armed with this information, they were able to calculate the return on investment on the PTC as it applied to generation from wind farms. (At present, the PTC does not cover solar power generation.)

Crucially, the authors took account of the different ways that regional electricity systems (or grids) make use of different kinds of generating plants at different times of the day. For example, coal plants are mostly active during the day. Natural gas plants, in contrast, tend to be more active during the night. (Coal plants release far greater levels of carbon dioxide and sulfur dioxide than do natural gas plants.) This part of their study allowed them to note that major regional differences exist in the use of electricity plants using fossil fuels. California's use of fossil fuels for electricity generation, for example, primarily involves natural gas plants; thus, the state generates fewer damaging emissions than other states that rely mostly on coal plants.

The authors calculated that the return on investment of the PTC has been positive—the social benefits from existing wind farms alone are estimated to be 60 percent higher than the

cost of the subsidy.[50] However, their analysis suggested that the return on subsidies of wind farms in Ohio were over seven times higher than the return on subsidies in California. Indeed, electricity from wind farms in Ohio tends to be a substitute for electricity generated from coal plants, whereas electricity from wind farms in California tends to be a substitute for the cleaner-burning natural gas plants that predominate in that state. They found similar regional disparities across the country, suggesting that smarter, region-based targeting of incentives could lead to achievement of better health, environmental, and climate benefits from efforts to promote renewable electricity generation.

The study by Siler-Evans and colleagues offers insights into the general relevance of public policy for environmental protection. For our purposes, three insights stand out:

1. Viewing a situation purely from the perspective of energy generation levels can lead to a very different judgment about the right mix of generating systems compared with a judgment that has also taken account of negative externalities. From a strictly energy-generating perspective, coal-fired plants are almost always more desirable than wind farms, no matter where their location. However, wind farms might be preferable to coal-fired plants when judgment includes negative externalities.

2. Because there are major regional differences in the net benefits to be realized from switching to renewable energy sources, it makes sense to encourage renewable generation in locations where the net benefits will be

highest. This approach calls for a different policy design from one where all forms of renewable energy generation attract a financial incentive from government, regardless of location.

3. Finally, it is important to think about energy generation in marginal—or incremental—terms. Those who care mostly about energy production and less about environmental impact will typically consider coal-fired electricity plants as more effective. In contrast, those who care more about protecting the environment and less about energy production will typically advocate for the merits of generating electricity from renewable sources. The world of policy making calls for effective balancing of these competing considerations.

CRITICAL THINKING QUESTIONS

1. How could businesses and households, as consumers of electricity, reduce the pollution caused by coal-fired electricity plants?
2. How could governments help electricity generation companies further reduce their reliance on coal-fired electricity plants?

In Case Study 11.4 we can see that, from an environmental protection perspective, building more electricity plants that utilize renewable sources would be desirable in midwestern and northeastern states of the United States. However, at current levels of technology development, it is unrealistic to believe that a complete switch to renewable sources would be feasible anytime soon. Using an approach to energy planning that balances a broad range of costs and benefits would likely take several directions:

1. There would be more efforts to reduce the pollution emitted from coal power plants, while they continue to operate.
2. There would be more efforts to commission renewable energy plants that are highly efficient in energy production.
3. There would be more efforts to reduce the amount of electricity used by businesses and households.

Extensive technological innovation would surely assist all such efforts. This goal suggests the need for more incentives to drive practical transition to energy production and usage that supports economic development while promoting environmental protection.

ENVIRONMENTAL PROTECTION AND THE PROMOTION OF CIVIL RIGHTS

Exploring how environmental protection—or the lack of it—can generate biased outcomes that favor some groups at the expense of others represents a vital contemporary chapter in the struggle for civil rights. Case Study 11.5 details the history of the Louisiana Army Ammunition Plant, long a toxic wasteland affecting the health of those living in the area.

case study 11.5 Environmental Justice and Civil Rights

Charles M. Blow is a *New York Times* Opinion page columnist. In a 2015 column, Blow described the sorry state of the abandoned Louisiana Army Ammunition Plant, near the small town of Minden.[51] Blow noted that Minden's population is primarily African American and relatively poor—55 percent of the residents are black, the median household income is less than 60 percent of the U.S. median household income, and 24 percent of the residents are poor.

Abandoned long ago, the Louisiana Army Ammunition Plant became a toxic wasteland. Among other things, "for more than 40 years, untreated explosives-laden wastewater from industrial operations was collected in concrete sumps" and "emptied into 16 one-acre pink water lagoons."[52] The EPA found the lagoons had contaminated the area's groundwater.

After manufacturing ceased at the site, the U.S. Army employed a contractor to "demilitarize" the ammunition still there. The contractor, now bankrupt, did so from 2010 to 2012, when an explosion "sent a mushroom cloud 7,000 feet high and broke windows" in houses up to a mile away. Thousands of tons of propellant had been stored in nearly a hundred bunkers onsite, the state police found. The EPA finally announced, after months of interagency disputes, that they would burn the remaining 15 million pounds of munitions onsite over 12 months in open "burn trays"—an obsolete process banned overseas.

Blow asked, "How was this allowed to come to such a pass in the first place? How could this plant have been allowed to contaminate the groundwater for 40 years? How could the explosives have been left at the site in the first place? How is it that there doesn't seem to be the money or the will to more safely remove them? Can we imagine anyone, with a straight face, proposing to openly burn millions of pounds of explosives near Manhattan or Seattle?

"I have skin in this game," he concluded. "My family would fall in the shadow of the plume. But everyone should be outraged about this practice. Of all the measures of equality we deserve, the right to feel assured and safe when you draw a breath should be paramount."

In telling this story, Blow highlighted the concept of **environmental racism**. This term emerged during the 1970s to describe the tendency for environmentally hazardous or degraded environments, such as toxic waste dumps or abandoned industrial sites, to be located near low-income or minority communities. Robert D. Bullard gave close attention to this practice in his book *Dumping in Dixie: Race, Class, and Environmental Quality*, first published in 1994.[53] Subsequent scholarship has broadened from the notion of environmental racism to explore the broader issue of **environmental justice**. Environmental justice studies document the unequal impacts of environmental pollution on different social classes and racial or ethnic groups. Hundreds of studies now confirm that, in general, ethnic minorities, indigenous people, people of color, and low-income communities face more exposure than other groups to air, water, and soil pollution from military, industrial, and general business activities.[54]

Blow's story of environmental threats to a small town in Louisiana illustrates the main point of scholarship in this area—that is, to use careful evidence-based research to expose instances of injustice, highlight hypocrisy, and force greater attention to upholding the civil rights of all people. When poor minority people are exposed to greater environmental threats than other groups, additional forms of disadvantage are perpetuated upon them. Most significantly, these threats can lead to health risks. In turn, poor health can affect the ability of children to participate effectively in schools and of adults to participate effectively in the workforce. These are fundamental forms of disadvantage.

Identification of such environmental injustices is likely to become an even more significant area of social science research and public policy discussion in the years ahead.

CRITICAL THINKING QUESTIONS

1. What are some recent examples of how environmental degradation has more greatly affected the lives of poor people compared with those who are financially comfortable?
2. What analytical approaches could policy analysts use routinely to test claims that specific instances of environmental degradation have harmed some communities more than others?

LESSONS FOR PUBLIC POLICY

Many countries wrestle with the challenges that arise when economic development and population growth spur degradation of the natural environment. That degradation can come in many forms, but all of them tend to approximate either over-exploitation of shared resources or pollution that causes lasting damage to land, water, or air—and to human beings. Often, when environmental protection efforts occur, they result in pitched battles between those seeking change and those who benefit economically from the status quo.

Environmentalists versus entrenched business interests—this is often the typical story. It is the reason why, for example, critics of discourse about reduction of atmospheric pollution construe it as a series of fights: government against the automobile industry, government against the oil industry, or government against the operators of coal-fired electricity plants.

Although environmental protection is a complex area of public policy, a review of achievements over the past half century suggests some salient lessons for future policy development.

- Foresight matters. The United States has achieved successful preservation of large tracts of land and water through invocation of the Antiquities Act of 1906. When governments take control of specific areas or resources, they also gain the ability to effectively manage their preservation and development. The biggest environmental battles have arisen where property rights have been underspecified. As knowledge has grown concerning our environment and how human actions can affect it for good or ill, the potential for foresight has increased. Foresight can be manifest in many ways beyond controlling specific areas of land and water. Restrictive provision of fishing licenses and double-hulling of oil tankers are just two instances where foresight can shape policies that contribute to good environmental outcomes.

- People and industries adapt to the conditions they face. It would be virtually impossible for politicians to impose restrictive covenants in established neighborhoods or industrial areas. But the situation changes dramatically when they give people choices about opting into specific locations and the rules and restrictions that come with these choices. Evan McKenzie has carefully documented the rise of common-interest housing developments, where homeowners are willing to cede a range of individual rights to live in orderly communities where they—and everyone around them—fully appreciate and respect what it means to be a good neighbor.[55] The owners of business parks often establish equivalent restrictions when opening space to clients. These examples suggest that environmental protection can be successful in many localized settings if those opting into specific plans understand from the outset the restrictions under which they must live.

- Incentives can spur innovation. Although there will remain instances where command-and-control approaches to pollution control make sense, plenty of evidence now demonstrates the feasibility of market-based approaches to environmental protection. Tax-based and tradable permit–based mechanisms, which change the preferences and practices of both consumers and producers, result in better environmental outcomes. Most significantly, market-like incentives encourage innovation, as consumers seek to reduce the prices they pay for goods and services and as producers seek to profit from efficiencies in their manufacturing processes. Many possibilities exist for innovations that will maintain high living standards while significantly reducing environmental degradation.
- The commonly noted trade-off between environmental protection and economic development is not inevitable. The history of automobile production, maintenance, and repair has included generations of winners and losers. Yet, gains go both to consumers and to the environment when cars become more fuel efficient and clean burning. There will be money to be made well into the future in the design and manufacturing of environmentally friendly cars and trucks. Those manufacturers wedded to old technology and unable to adapt will be swept away by those open to innovation. Likewise, energy producers who can generate and sell electricity without releasing large quantities of carbon dioxide and other pollutants into the atmosphere face a bright future.

Governments everywhere have the potential to improve environmental protection in ways that are acceptable to citizens. Over the past 30 years, the United States and other countries have implemented many new policy approaches to promote environmental protection. Although many challenges remain, the evidence is now clear. When governments take actions to improve environmental outcomes, they often have positive effects on population health. Those actions represent important investments. Good choices made in the present, even when they impose unwelcome restrictions, can contribute to streams of positive outcomes in the future—outcomes that far outweigh the overall costs.

THE FUTURE OF ENVIRONMENTAL PROTECTION

Environmental protection has become a huge and urgent issue worldwide. Unfortunately, many political leaders have found it difficult to gain sufficient popular support to introduce policy changes that would avert environmental desecration. The problems we face occur at all levels—local, national, regional, and global. They concern effective management of land, air, and water, and the human, animal, and plant life they sustain. Human development has wrought some terrible destruction, but incredible things have come of that human development. too. There have been trade-offs. Many have occurred implicitly; some, explicitly.

The challenge is to improve education and human consciousness in ways that facilitate widespread agreement that life as we know it is wondrous and precious. The more that people and politicians accept this philosophy, the more likely they will be to pursue human development that is sustainable and that does not unduly damage the world around them.

CHAPTER SUMMARY

This chapter has explored the use of public policies to protect the environment. The issues associated with environmental protection are complex, generating many controversies and conflicts. Here, the focus has been on two kinds of conflict: those between individual and collective preferences, and those between current and future preferences. Government actions often represent the most feasible way of reconciling these conflicts. We have paid attention here to approaches being taken to address climate change. Differences among America's states are stark in this respect.

Issues around environmental protection often evoke strong emotions, because of a clash of the interests at stake. Public opinion is often divided over whether environmental protection should be pursued to the detriment of economic activity. Some groups almost always prioritize environmental protection; others almost always prioritize economic growth. Public opinion data have revealed that younger people are much more likely to prioritize the environment, whereas older people are much more likely to prioritize economic growth. These generational differences may reflect educational differences and general awareness about the importance of protecting an environment (and, ultimately, ourselves) from harm. However, they might also reflect the differences between younger people who are confident that their incomes will increase with time, and older people who are primarily on fixed incomes and are more vulnerable to changes in the fortunes of the broader economy.

Federalism offers opportunities for different jurisdictions to experiment with public policies that could reduce local emissions of greenhouse gases. Of course, jurisdictional differences are not always benign. The discussion of environmental justice has highlighted that different approaches to managing environmental impacts of industry can have positive effects for some groups and negative effects for others.

Finally, throughout the chapter, the importance of evidence in policy debates has emerged as a theme. Evidence is critical to establishing cap-and-trade emissions schemes. It is critical in debates over the merits and risks of fracking to release oil and gas deposits. It is critical to judging whether specific activities represent forms of environmental injustice. Careful use of evidence stands at the heart of the investment perspective on public policy.

CONNECTIONS TO OTHER CHAPTERS

Historically, human advancement has been predicated on exploitation of the environment. That advancement over centuries has involved development of many forms of knowledge, many skills, and all kinds of technology. One of the by-products of these developments is that we now know a lot about the effects of extraction activities on the environment. A very strong link exists between environmental protection efforts and the funding of science (Chapter 10). Further, issues of human health have arisen several times in this discussion of environmental protection. Careful environmental stewardship is vital for reducing the harm that exploitation of our environment can cause us. Thus, numerous connections exist between the content of this chapter and that on health care (Chapter 7). Important connections also exist between the discussion of electricity generation, clean modes of transportation, and our earlier discussion of public infrastructure (Chapter 4).

KEY TERMS

Carbon footprint
Greenhouse gases
Global warming
Extraction industries
Regulation
Negative externality
Particulate matter
The tragedy of the commons
Public goods
The commons
Carrying capacity
Air Quality Index
Seasonal permits
Independent Transferable Quotas
Tradable rights to pollute
Cap and trade

Environmental Protection Agency (EPA)
Command and control
Executive orders
Conference of Parties
Polycentricity
Fracking
Clean Air Act
Federal Water Pollution Control Act
Acid rain
Acid Rain Program
Clean Energy Finance and Investment Authority (CEFIA)
Regional Greenhouse Gas Initiative
Environmental racism
Environmental justice

SUGGESTIONS FOR FURTHER READING

Bennear, Lori Snyder, and Robert N. Stavins. "Second-Best Theory and the Use of Multiple Policy Instruments," *Environmental Resource Economics* 37 (2007): 111–29. A useful overview of policy tools to reduce environmental harm.

Carson, Rachel. *Silent Spring*. New York: Houghton Mifflin, 1962. A classic examination of the effects of human activities on environmental degradation.

Hardin, Garrett. "Tragedy of the Commons," *Science* 162 (1968): 1243–48. A classic contribution to our understanding of how individual incentives create challenging collective action problems.

Kamieniecki, Sheldon, and Michael E. Kraft, eds. *The Oxford Handbook of U.S. Environmental Policy*. New York: Oxford University Press, 2013. A comprehensive set of essays summarizing major research contributions to the study of environmental policy.

Ostrom, Elinor. "Polycentric Systems for Coping with Collective Action and Global Environmental Change," *Global Environmental Change* 20, no. 4 (2010): 550–57. An important statement from this renowned scholar of collective action problems and how they might be resolved.

WEBSITES

- The U.S. Environmental Protection Agency was created for the purpose of protecting human health and the environment by writing and enforcing regulations based on laws passed by Congress. The agency also works with industries and all levels of government in a wide variety of voluntary pollution prevention programs and energy conservation efforts. www.epa.gov
- The Regional Greenhouse Gas Initiative, Inc. (RGGI, Inc.), is a nonprofit corporation created to support development and implementation of the Regional Greenhouse Gas Initiative. RGGI is a cooperative effort among nine U.S. states to reduce greenhouse gas emissions. www.rggi.org
- The Environmental Council of the States (ECOS) is the national nonprofit, nonpartisan association of state and territorial environmental agency leaders. ECOS plays a critical role in facilitating a quality relationship between federal and state agencies and provides for the exchange of ideas, views, and experiences among states and with others. www.ecos.org

FOR DISCUSSION

1. In her book *Silent Spring* (1962), Rachel Carson argued strongly against the widespread use of pesticides in agriculture. She worried that new production methods would contribute to a tragedy of the commons where many species of plant and animal life would be harmed and human life threatened. How is the message of *Silent Spring* relevant now?

2. In the federal system of government, numerous governments at the state and local level make autonomous decisions about public policy issues, including many relating to environmental protection. How can federalism support

environmental protection? How can it undermine key elements of environmental protection?

3. In the early days of efforts to protect the environment in the United States, governments often made use of "command and control" regulations. In a classic book, *The Public Use of Private Interests* (1977), Charles L. Schultze argued that governments should focus less on telling firms what to do and more on getting incentives right so that firms would find it in their own interest to clean up their production processes. What are some examples of the pursuit of environmental protection in which there is public use of private interests?

CHAPTER 12

POLICY LEGACIES

This book has provided a survey of the nature of public policy, the ways in which policies are made, and the major issues associated with public policy in a variety of substantive areas. Coverage has ranged from public infrastructure to defense and homeland security, public schools, health care, and other areas where governments act to make a better world. Throughout these chapters, emphasis has been on the importance of treating public policies as investments. When scarce taxpayer funds are spent on government policies and programs, we need to be assured that the spending is generating high levels of social value. In the past the record on this matter has often been mixed.

Many people worry that current government programs contain areas of waste. Sometimes they view long-standing programs as having resulted in years of wasted funds and wasted opportunities. There is an urgent need for change—toward better public policy analysis that is intellectually well founded and strongly informed by evidence.

Consistent application of the investment perspective on public policy is not the silver bullet that will make everything right in the world of public policy making. However, it can do much to bring about a higher level of rational, evidence-based decision making as to how governments should act to promote the well-being of citizens.

This chapter suggests a change agenda involving greater, more consistent application of the investment perspective. In doing so, it explores why public policy matters, how we can better assess the long-term impacts of policies, and how such an assessment will contribute to investment analysis. The chapter concludes with suggestions regarding the qualities of effective policy analysts. They need to be well versed in technical skills; at the same time, they need to exhibit a range of people skills. In combination, these qualities allow policy analysts

Facing page: Large infrastructure projects serve as reminders of policy legacies. The three-mile-long New NY Bridge was built to span the Hudson River, replacing the Tappan Zee Bridge. The bridge was designed to last at least 100 years and was financed by state and federal government funds. The original Tappan Zee Bridge, constructed in the 1950s, was designed to last only 50 years. Over the decades, this river crossing has come to make a vital contribution to the New York state economy.

(Jim Henderson/Public Domain)

to better interpret the needs of others and communicate clearly their evidence-based judgments concerning how public policy may best meet those needs.

This chapter discusses:

- The promise of public policy
- Key lessons from the Applications chapters of this book
- Policy legacies and how to assess them
- The investment approach and its successes and challenges
- Qualities of effective policy analysts

THE PROMISE OF PUBLIC POLICY

Public policy as a field of activity involves governments doing things on behalf of citizens that they could not do for themselves, either individually or collectively. It makes no sense for a government to coordinate collective action when such action would arise in the absence of government. Collective action is costly—it requires energy, time, and resources. Understood in this way, governments are entities that operate for the primary purpose of addressing challenges placed by society in the "too hard" basket. Public policy involves tackling the difficult stuff. We have seen examples of this goal continually in this book.

When we view public policy as government efforts to address major social challenges, we begin to see why specific policies—and why governments as well—often receive criticism. People ask why governments cannot operate more like private companies. It is a fair question, since many private companies seem to have established strong client-driven cultures. At their best, private companies are service oriented, economically efficient in their operations, and continually striving to innovate and get better at what they do. We rarely hear these attributes being said of government. The "too hard" basket offers one reason why the actions of governments—in the form of public policies—often seem underwhelming. Another reason is democracy itself. Although citizens might agree that specific challenges are too hard to be resolved in the absence of government action, their agreement about this is no guarantee that they will concur as to what problem needs to be addressed or how best to address it.

Economists sometimes talk about the challenges of **optimal resource use**. Success involves achieving maximum gains from minimum necessary inputs. The ideal solution is referred to as being "first best." In simple situations, with no interactions between challenges, first best might be attainable. However, most often, those involved in addressing optimization problems must settle for "second best" or "third best" solutions. If we use the optimization problem as a metaphor for public policy development, we can immediately see that any "first best" solution is unlikely to be attainable. In fact, not only does policy making involve working on challenges that are typically joined up with other challenges, but it is also inherently political. Much time devoted to policy making involves striving to find approaches that improve social outcomes, while simultaneously balancing many other considerations—some practical, some political.

Given these challenges, what is the "promise" of public policy? The promise is that it can make a better world. Indeed, it has, and it continues to do so. Throughout this book, we have seen many examples of how governments have used public policies to improve social conditions. Certainly, we can bemoan that we are a long way from ideal outcomes. Yet we also must marvel at how complex systems of public infrastructure facilitate our health, our social and economic activities, and our engagements with the broader world. Likewise, we must marvel at how public policies have promoted safer lives for citizens, achieved mass education, greatly improved access to health care, and significantly reduced poverty. Progress on these and other fronts—including environmental protection and medical breakthroughs—will often strike people as having been too slow or too superficial. Certainly, there is cause for complaint. Yet nobody could possibly disagree that over the past century, public policy has produced a better world. Today, throughout the world, a large majority of people live better than populations of a century ago. Public policy has played a significant part in that progress—indeed, it would not have been realized in the absence of public policy.

Viewed from the perspective of months and years and election cycles, many arguments can be made for being cynical about government and the promise of public policy. Sometimes policies judged by many to be taking us to a better place get overturned or slowed down. This is an irony of democracy. The task of getting good public policies in place is difficult, as is the task of keeping them in place. Further, much work is always needed to stop poorly conceived public policy ideas from being adopted and implemented.

The day-to-day battles over public policy choices are important. They can also wear people down. Ultimately, we need to ask questions about the bigger picture of society and how specific policy choices are likely to affect social and economic outcomes. Often, public policies have differential impacts on citizens. This is why policy making involves conflict. For my part, as a policy analyst, I am most interested in how we get through the battle in a manner that leaves at least some people better off and even fewer people worse off. Although public policy can encourage social and economic progress, in the short-term some people may be required to relinquish things they value. For example, nobody likes paying taxes. Yet it is only through taxation that public policies of broad social benefit can be funded. A basic resource for those embroiled in political battles over public policy choices involves recognizing the promise of public policy and the truly great social and economic outcomes it can promote.

KEY LESSONS FROM THE APPLICATIONS CHAPTERS

Each Application chapter of this book contains lessons for public policy. These lessons emerge from careful review of specific areas of public policy, such as criminal justice and environmental protection. Although the lessons in each chapter relate closely to the policy focus of the chapter, they often generalize beyond a given area of public policy. Thus, here, we will consider six lessons that capture the most important common themes emerging through the Applications chapters:

- Foresight matters.
- Public perceptions drive policy durability.
- Governance influences service performance.
- Government cannot do everything.
- Policy design can encourage innovation.
- Federalism encourages policy learning.

Anyone involved in the design, development, and implementation of public policies should bear such lessons in mind. We will now discuss each lesson in turn.

FORESIGHT MATTERS

Public policies can have both short-term and long-term consequences. Societies benefit when governments take actions that address both current concerns and those likely to arise in the future. Looking to the future and imagining how public policy choices made today could influence subsequent outcomes is sometimes called **stewardship**. In some countries, policy advisors in government are required to pay attention to stewardship issues—that is, when they give advice to the current government, they must also think ahead to a future time when a different government with different preferences might be in power. Through this process, the advisors are expected to act in the interests of future generations.[1]

Public infrastructure is a clear example of a policy area where foresight matters. When governments build and maintain roads, electricity systems, drinking water supplies, and sewage systems, they raise the quality of everyday life for all their citizens. Since these systems can last for many years, efforts made now can contribute to the quality of life for generations not yet born. This same logic spills over into areas of social policy. For example, when governments pay attention to raising the quality of public schooling, they not only make school more engaging and beneficial for young people. They also create the possibility that in the years ahead cohorts of skilled, knowledgeable, and civically minded individuals will contribute in positive ways to the effective functioning of society and the economy.

It is troubling when governments take actions that seem motivated solely by the intention of meeting the short-term needs of powerful interest groups. In this regard, it seems that public policy in the areas of criminal justice and environmental protection has sometimes lacked foresight. For example, when state legislatures introduced sentencing requirements that put more people in prison for longer times, they often ignored the longer-term budget implications of their decisions. They also appear to have given little thought to the possibility that many prisoners, given long prison terms, lose the dispositions and skills that would allow them, upon release, to become productive, independent, and law-abiding members of society.

PUBLIC PERCEPTIONS DRIVE POLICY DURABILITY

Public policies can have their legitimacy questioned if they do not enjoy broad public support. Continued efforts to repeal the Obama administration's Affordable Care Act illustrate this point. While the act contained positive features that appear to have made health care more available and affordable for millions of people, there was a backlash against the act's mandate for all Americans to purchase some form of health care insurance. That backlash emerged not just because of concerns over the direction of health care funding in the United States, but also because there is a long-held philosophy in the United States that people should enjoy as much freedom of choice as possible.

In the area of public welfare and poverty alleviation, we again find that public perceptions drive policy durability. Social Security is an example of a long-standing public policy that enjoys broad support. One reason for that broad support is that payments to beneficiaries are funded by individual contributions, made during people's years in the paid workforce. In contrast, policies viewed as giving a "handout" have rarely received strong public support in the United States. Indeed, citizens tend to be most comfortable with benefit payments that are tied to engagement in the workforce or to some form of prior service. This view is consistent with the long-held collective one in the United States that people should be independent and take care of themselves. Of course, exceptions have always been made for those who have been deemed "deserving" of assistance due to physical impairments or old age.

Looking to the future, advocates of policy change in any area of public policy would serve their cause well by remembering the power of public perceptions. For example, in the years ahead, efforts will be needed both to reduce the emission of greenhouse gases and to adapt to climate change. Policy approaches compelling people to act in certain ways will run up against opposition from people seeking to preserve freedom of choice. In the broader area of environmental protection, it has long been the case that various incentives-based systems are effective in promoting socially desirable behavioral changes. Policies that reward valued practices and make undesirable practices costly preserve individual freedoms while nudging people to switch from things they used to do. That observation applies across many areas of public policy, including public schooling and health care.

GOVERNANCE INFLUENCES SERVICE PERFORMANCE

In our earlier discussion of the promise of public policy, a dilemma emerged. That is, because some things are too difficult for society—including private companies—to solve, government needs to step in. At the same time, we also know that private companies in competitive environments face strong incentives to meet customer needs, drive down costs, and pursue innovation. It would be beneficial to society if government could somehow harness those private sector practices for the pursuit of broader public goals. It turns out that this objective can be reached. However, it must be reached with care. There is no guarantee that what worked well in one sector of society will necessarily work well in another.

Governance refers to the ownership and control of specific organizations. Chapter 4, on public infrastructure, presented an example of how policy changes allowed for changes in the governance of electricity plants. Initially, when the technology was new, it made sense for governments to fund, build, and operate such plants. However, after several decades, when the technology was stable and more was understood about how electricity markets might work, policy changes introduced the possibility of private ownership and operation of these plants. Evidence suggests that when the plants shifted into private control they started to operate at higher levels of efficiency. The private companies that owned the plants found ways to reduce operating costs. This is a classic example of a governance change leading to an improvement in service performance.

If changing ownership and control of organizations can work in the area of public infrastructure, what are the possibilities that similar changes could produce positive effects in many other areas? That question has driven many contemporary policy reform efforts, across many areas of government activity. Countries that have relied strongly on public provision of health care services—for example, the United Kingdom and Australia—have made efforts to explore opportunities for improved service performance through contracting some specific areas of service to private or not-for-profit companies. Similarly, governments from the national level to the local level in the United States have made a variety of efforts to change the governance of public schools, to see if market-like processes might encourage schools to work harder at securing good outcomes for their students.[2] The introduction of school vouchers and charter schools offer such examples of governance changes. Similarly, the U.S. Department of Defense has a long history of contracting out a range of services to private providers.

Governments everywhere will always face pressures to provide more and better services to citizens while keeping taxes as low as possible. Given these dynamics, we can expect to see many experiments with governance of service provision in the future. This is an area of public policy that is ripe for careful, evidence-based investigations of the conditions under which governance changes produce sustained, beneficial outcomes for citizens.

School classes often appear similar from school to school. However, governance influences performance. Schools may be public or private. Some publicly funded schools may be required to compete for students. School governance arrangements can contribute significantly to differences in desired learning outcomes for children.

(David Grossman/Alamy Stock Photo)

GOVERNMENT CANNOT DO EVERYTHING

Throughout the Applications chapters of this book, we have considered many examples of the broad reach and capabilities of government in society. In discussing the promise of public policy, we have observed that, through such reach and capability, governments have done much over time to improve citizens' quality of life. In light of these successes, people sometimes form the view that governments should always be poised to intervene when new problems arise in society. Yet there are clear limits to what governments are capable of doing through public policy. Often, well-designed policies remain somewhat blunt instruments in terms of how they can support citizens.

Public schooling provides an example. Although schools extend incredible educational opportunities to young people, many parents will tell you that even the best schools have their limits. Families ultimately have more influence on the development and socialization of young people than do the schools those young people attend. Further, even within the schools, parents often need to serve as determined advocates for their children to ensure that they benefit from available opportunities.

Looking elsewhere in society, we see the limits of government programs, even those that work well. For example, even when individuals are able to take advantage of government subsidies for health care services, in many instances those services becomes much easier to access when a private individual with a good education and organizational savvy can assist a person in need to get the care that he or she requires. Programs designed to help individuals train for paid employment likewise provide important services in society. However, clients of those services can benefit when family members or volunteers are able to offer some additional basic support, such as driving clients to and from training, or talking with them about what they are learning and how they can apply it.

Given that government cannot do everything, a big area for further exploration concerns the interface between what governments do and what private companies, not-for-profit agencies, families, and volunteers do. Although specific aspects of the U.S. health care system are often criticized, this also happens to be a system characterized by a range of complex relationships among different forms of service providers—ranging from the for-profit to the voluntary. Cooperation and coordination across providers open a lot of space for services to work effectively for individuals. Nevertheless, service gaps can emerge. The public policy challenge here—as in many other areas—is to consider how government and nongovernment entities can work together to produce the best results for citizens.

POLICY DESIGN CAN ENCOURAGE INNOVATION

When people talk excitedly about places like Silicon Valley, their excitement is spurred by appreciation for the product and service innovations that have emanated from those regions over recent decades. More broadly, when people marvel at market processes—indeed, talk of the miracle of the market—they tend to focus on the capacity for private firms to identify customer needs and respond effectively to them. In the best cases, those firms anticipate our needs before we do. There is a dynamism about the world of businesses that encourages the pursuit of innovation, and all of us benefit from it.

The best kind of public policy serves to promote innovation in society. When governments ensure that good infrastructure is in place and well maintained, when they guarantee peaceful, safe societies, and when they promote the education and health of citizens, they do much to support social and economic dynamism, and the continual innovation that emerges from that.

At the broad level of economic management, citizens look to governments to encourage a strong, vibrant business sector. Many private firms face strong pressures to innovate in their production processes, in the goods and services they produce, and in the ways they manage client relations. A common complaint about government is that too often it lacks this drive toward continuous improvement. Must there be no change? What set of arrangements could lead to innovation and a search for excellence among those organizations delivering public policies? How could public schools be encouraged to get better? How could the military be encouraged to maintain strong systems of defense while reducing the costs of doing so?

Over recent decades, there have been many efforts to encourage innovation in service provision across a range of areas of government activity. In public schooling, the pursuit of innovation has occurred at two levels. First, there have been moves to raise educational standards by the use of state testing systems. These have required schools to reflect on what they do and how they could better assist students with their learning. Second, there have been moves to free schools from constricting regulations and to create a degree of competition among publicly funded schools. The charter schools movement is a classic example. Some evidence suggests that these measures have promoted more innovation in public schools—although not all schools that have been given the opportunity to innovate have done so.

When policy design is used to encourage innovation, several actions need to be taken. It is important that organizations receive incentives to innovate. It is also important that impediments to innovation be reduced. Finally, it can be helpful when mechanisms are put in place to monitor innovative programs and to make the results broadly known. In market settings, plenty of incentives exist for consultants and others to rapidly learn what works well and advise others how to produce similar results. In nonmarket settings, information flow can be more difficult; however, the collection and diffusion of innovative ideas can support local innovations. Several examples of nonprofit organizations that have taken the lead here include the activities of the Ash Center for Democratic Governance and Innovation at the Harvard Kennedy School of Government.[3]

The Apple Corporation, like other businesses located around Silicon Valley, has come to symbolize the dynamism found in the world of business. At their best, businesses pursue innovations from which all of us can benefit. Good policy design should encourage innovation in the delivery of publicly funded services. That is where the continuous enhancement of public value starts.

(REUTERS/Noah Berger)

FEDERALISM ENCOURAGES POLICY LEARNING

The system of federalism in the United States offers outstanding opportunities for policy experimentation, variation, and learning. This insight has emerged in almost every chapter of this book. For example, when a state engages in a policy innovation concerning public schooling, it creates learning opportunities for other states. The same opportunities apply to public infrastructure management, health care, welfare policies, criminal justice, and environmental policies. When states take a variety of approaches to tackling similar problems, they can learn from one another through comparative analysis.

As well as creating conditions that allow for policy innovation, the competitive dynamic associated with federalism gives states strong incentives to make effective and efficient policy choices. Those that do not can find themselves losing ground, in terms of becoming less attractive locations for businesses, college students, and educated, mobile professionals. States can benefit from keeping close track of how well their various policy settings perform compared with those of their neighbors and states elsewhere in the union. These same competitive dynamics and opportunities for learning are apparent at the local government level as well. In short, federalism provides excellent conditions for policy makers in national, state, and local governments to systematically extract usable knowledge from evidence of existing policies and their effects and apply this to policy plans for the future.

ASSESSING POLICY LEGACIES

Public policies are adopted with the purpose of achieving improved social, economic, or environmental outcomes. The key lessons of the Applications chapters offer some insights into conditions that support the creation and maintenance of good public policies. They also offer insights into the interface between government programs and society, and how public policies might evolve through time. In this section, we consider **policy legacies**—the long-term impacts of public policies on society. Assessing policy legacies is vital work. When done well, it provides useful insights that can guide subsequent public policy design work. This book has emphasized the importance of treating public policies as investments. Good investment decisions are always informed by careful assessment of relevant available evidence. Given such care, assessing policy legacies should be a regular, systematic practice. For those who develop public policies, understanding the legacies of past policies represents an important way to learn how policies work, what conditions support good outcomes, why policies sometimes fail, and how mistakes and problems of the past can be avoided. This careful exploration of specific prior public policy efforts is termed **ex-post analysis**. It can serve many purposes, but a highly practical purpose is informing future policy work. The following sections offer some considerations to guide the assessment of policy legacies.

UNDERSTANDING PATH DEPENDENCIES

Public policies are nearly always adopted and implemented in contexts that are already influenced by previous public policies. For example, any efforts to change science funding through the National Science Foundation (NSF) must be informed by how current policy settings serve to create incentives and guide institutional practices. For numerous years, many research universities have depended on the ability of professors and research teams to effectively attract funds from the NSF. Given this reality, changes to eligibility requirements or expectations around institutional matching funds could create significant ripples. Indeed, the ways in which policies have been structured in the past sometimes make it almost impossible to effect anything other than minor changes now. This impasse occurs because interested parties often advocate for the status quo when it is working well for them.

Path dependencies exist whenever how things have been done in the past serves to constrain and guide how things will be done in the future. Naïve politicians sometimes think that, if elected, they will be able to go to the capital and promote "common sense" policy changes that others have been too timid or inept to try. Although the desire to change the world—or to change a specific area of public policy—is often admirable, the cumulated effects of past policy choices can hinder reform. In light of this stumbling block, close exploration of the history of a policy area is likely to reveal useful insights as to why things are the way they are now. Further, this kind of investigation can also offer important clues as to how change might set public policy on a new and improved direction. When path dependencies are understood, space is opened up for exploring how a few small, incremental changes made now could clear the way for other desired policy changes.

MEASURING THE IMPACT OF BOTH OLD AND NEW POLICIES

Throughout this book, we have considered many case studies that treat public policies as investments. All include efforts by researchers to carefully measure policy impacts. Measurement often involves identifying policy costs and comparing them with policy benefits. It is through careful cost-benefit analysis that judgments can be made about the public value achieved as a result of the investment. Carefully measuring the impact of an established or new policy is a core component of assessing policy legacies.

When impacts are measured and costs and benefits are taken into account, space is opened for a broader discussion of the overall merits of a specific public policy. For example, efforts to lower class sizes in California were found to have been highly expensive and to have generated few positive results for children's education. With these facts at hand, it becomes possible to discuss alternative policy choices. What if the funding devoted to that initiative had been devoted to a more effective alternative? Currently, such comparative assessments of policy legacies are in their infancy. Efforts of this kind to carefully measure impacts and compare what was actually achieved with what might have been achieved could significantly improve the quality of information guiding future policy investments.

ASSESSING IMPLICATIONS FOR CIVIL RIGHTS

All public policies tend to have multiple impacts. These frequently affect different groups differently. In each chapter of this book, we have discussed the intersection of public policy and the advancement of civil rights. Efforts to assess policy legacies can play a crucial role in helping us to understand the positive and negative consequences of policy choices for different social groups. Such analytical work can be guided by sophisticated frameworks that have now been developed to assess, among other things, the gendered impacts of public policies, the ways that policies affect various racial and ethnic groups differently, and the implications of specific policies for people with disabilities.

OTHER CONSIDERATIONS

As more consistent efforts are made to assess policy legacies, room is opened for considering a range of policy impacts beyond those discussed in this book. It is always useful to explore the positive and negative policy impacts that were not initially envisioned. These are often called the **unintended consequences**. For example, a program designed to help preschool children negotiate to avoid conflicts in the playroom might have the unintended consequence of reducing instances of family violence at home.

It is also useful for those assessing policy legacies to be alert to the **unintended costs** of policies. Frequently, public policies impose costs on businesses and families that are not accounted for within government budgets. For example, compliance costs arise when households or businesses must show proof of their eligibility for various forms of assistance. The more alert we become to the unintended consequences and costs of established policies, the more we can ensure that future policies do not produce such outcomes.

PUBLIC POLICIES AS INVESTMENTS

Treating public policies as investments involves combining several contributions to policy analysis and public management. The starting place is an interest in enhancing public value. This provides the rationale for exploring lessons to be drawn from policies and programs already in place elsewhere. Then there has to be a commitment to careful specification of desired outcomes and an estimation of the costs of achieving those outcomes in the local context. Policies will work effectively only when they take into account the contexts and the practices of targeted individuals and organizations.

Throughout this book, we have developed and applied a general investment approach to public policy: As policy analysts we should follow the five steps in the Policy Investment Checklist:

1. We should focus on existing policies and programs. This encourages creative adaptation of working programs to local conditions while avoiding the fallacy that an ideal response can be found to a less-than-ideal world.
2. We need to gather relevant evidence of how services of interest have performed to date. Good evaluations are necessary to generate such evidence. The best of these involve randomized controlled trials.
3. We should have a plan in place to measure the desired effect. For example, in the realm of criminal justice, the focus might be on helping prisoners develop the habits of mind and skills required to reenter society as law-abiding individuals able to support themselves financially and contribute to their communities in positive ways.
4. We should be able to assess the costs and benefits of implementing the program locally. With costs and benefits estimated, we can derive the expected return on investment.
5. Last, we should offer robust advice. We must explain how we performed our analysis, what assumptions drive it, and how changes in key assumptions change our results.

SUCCESSES OF THE INVESTMENT PERSPECTIVE

We are the inheritors of many public policy legacies that have had highly positive consequences for social and economic development. Some of these policies have been discussed and highlighted throughout the Applications chapters of this text. Table 12.1 provides a summary of successes of the investment perspective using a general, high-level approach. For example, it should be immediately obvious to all of us that individually and collectively we benefit greatly from public spending on infrastructure and public schooling. There are many public policy successes in these areas that deserve praise. That said, as we begin to look more closely at the provision of public infrastructure and the organization of public schooling, it is clear that not all instances of public spending represent good investments.

TABLE 12.1 Examples of Successful Public Policy Investments

CASE	DESCRIPTION	RELEVANT CHAPTER
Public infrastructure	Water, sewage, electricity, and transportation systems represent crucial investments that improve the quality of our daily lives and facilitate economic activity.	4
Defense and homeland security	By protecting borders, promoting public safety, and creating peaceful communities, defense and homeland security contribute greatly to a vibrant society and economy.	5
Public schooling	Society gains from making funds available for all children to receive primary and secondary schooling.	6
Health care	Public health efforts that reduce the spread of disease, encourage healthy living, and ease access to primary health care contribute to the quality of individual lives, reduce future health care costs, and promote greater labor market participation.	7
Poverty alleviation	Social Security has required individuals in paid work to contribute funds for their future well-being. In so doing, the program has reduced poverty rates among the elderly.	8
Criminal justice	Efforts to limit the time convicted criminals spend in prison and that rehabilitate them to live lawful, productive lives upon release can reduce the costs of criminal justice and promote better social outcomes. This means scarce government resources can be devoted to other, more productive uses.	9
Science funding	Careful allocation of public funds to research can produce significant future benefits—evidence can be found in the results of medical breakthroughs, development of technology, and many practical insights emerging from economic and social research.	10
Environmental protection	Efforts to balance economic activity with care for the environment have been made to ensure sustained human progress while avoiding health risks and "clean up" costs for today's young people and generations to come.	11

With respect to infrastructure, we must worry that scarce public funds devoted to building a new bridge, highway, or airport represents a sound investment. We might not be able to easily compare across all forms of infrastructure spending to convince ourselves that a given investment is wise. However, it should be fairly apparent within a given geographical region where the most pressing needs lie at any given time. Sometimes, political calculations influence infrastructural spending priorities. With sound evidence available of the likely return on investment from different infrastructure projects, the potential is diminished for political expedience to overrule sound investment choices.

With respect to public schooling, evidence suggests that sometimes scarce government funds get spent in ways that generate fewer gains for society than those that could have been realized through different spending choices. For example, statewide efforts to reduce class sizes can be politically expedient because many people—including teachers—believe small classes are better for learning. The logic seems obvious. Yet rarely do debates around class size involve discussions of alternative approaches to attaining desired outcomes. The key question we need to ask is this: What investments can we make in public schooling that are likely to generate the best student achievement outcomes? This question forces us to think of reducing class sizes as being just one among a range of possible options. We can estimate the costs associated with each option. We can also use evidence of what works to guide our review of those options. When this kind of analysis has been performed, a variety of policy options have been found to improve student outcomes to a higher degree and at much lower cost than reducing class sizes. Among those, focusing on the training of teachers and the ways that they interact with students appear to be valuable options. On reflection, a highly skilled teacher with 30 children is likely to add a lot more value than two mediocre teachers with 15 students each.[4]

The investment perspective on public policy leads us to ask questions about the broad allocation of government funds. For example, in the next budget should we devote additional funds to public schools or to prisons? The perspective also encourages questions about the appropriate allocation of funds in specific policy domains. Do we need more teachers and smaller classes? Or do we need to better support the teachers we have now, giving them the skills they need to inspire a love of learning in every child they teach?

CHALLENGES TO THE INVESTMENT PERSPECTIVE

We make investments today with the hope of positive future returns. Under such circumstances, there is always uncertainty about the likelihood that we will realize any estimated return on investment. This is an important limitation of the investment perspective. However, such uncertainty can be reduced. In the cases used throughout this book, the investment approach has been applied to assessing the returns from public policies that have been operating for long periods of time. Such retrospective analysis—or ex-post analysis—is of high value because it offers evidence of actually implemented policies and the amount of value they have returned to society. When we have available a lot of evidence of this kind, we can become more confident that a new investment designed along the lines of these past investments will generate broadly equivalent results. Concerns about the limitation of the investment perspective confirm the importance of assessing policy legacies. We do this to provide evidence that we can use to inform future policy investment decisions.

The investment perspective involves making powerful use of evidence. If a public policy is not generating positive returns to society, little reason exists to keep that policy in place. However, in saying that, we run the risk of appearing to lack compassion. Suppose the goal of a public policy is to ease the final years of life of people with terminal diseases. A hard-headed rationalist might suggest that funding such a policy is a waste of money. Surely we should be spending scarce resources on helping young people become effective, productive citizens rather than assisting people who have no ability to give anything back to society in terms of contributing to families, engaging in the community, and paying taxes.

This example creates a significant challenge to the investment perspective. My response is this. There are good reasons for societies to be both rational and compassionate. Greater application of the investment perspective opens the possibility of avoiding the use of scarce resources on wasteful programs. To the extent that savings occur through application of the investment perspective, society has the capacity to act entirely out of compassion—not rational calculation—to support those who cannot support themselves. There will be debates over when it makes sense to be compassionate and how governments might demonstrate compassion. The investment perspective cannot help us resolve those debates. However, it can reveal the costs of different policies and their likely results. This feature in itself is a highly valuable contribution to collective decision making.

Other challenges suggest a number of limits to the investment perspective:

1. Interest group politics can drive policy debates and crowd out room for discussion of what policy actions would generate positive returns on investment for society.
2. Once government programs have been in place for a few years, they become difficult to remove, even if they are performing poorly. This **institutional inertia** can present a challenge to the investment perspective. It means that sometimes good investment decisions will not be taken because there is no political appetite to mount the changes such decisions would necessitate.
3. There are times when good information on the performance of existing policies and programs simply does not exist. It remains common for many policies and programs to be in place for years without being subjected to evaluations. Even then, some of those evaluations might not include cost-benefit analyses to assess the merits of the investments.

All of these challenges are significant. At the same time, the investment approach to public policy is one that can ultimately be of great benefit to society. It promises to raise the quality of public policy making and, through that, the quality of people's lives. "Investing for a better world" surely should be a mantra for those involved in policy analysis and in policy development.

Next, we will consider the qualities of effective policy analysts. Some of these relate directly to expanding the application of the investment approach. Others focus more on the people skills required of policy analysts.[5] When all these qualities exist consistently, policy analysts and the teams they work with can indeed improve the quality of public policy-making processes.

EFFECTIVE POLICY ANALYSTS

This book has emphasized the important roles good evidence and careful analysis play in the development of public policies that generate positive intended outcomes. For decades, those contributing to the teaching of public policy and policy analysis have proposed that policy analysts make sound use of evidence. In that sense, the argument made here is not novel. What is new is the argument that consistent treatment of public policies as investments will generate outcomes that produce a better world. Given that goal, what qualities should aspiring policy analysts and those already in such roles exhibit?

Here, we will discuss eight important qualities. The list is not exhaustive, nor are the qualities mutually exclusive. However, those who consistently aspire to these qualities will be valued by those they work with.

1. ASPIRE TO CREATE PUBLIC VALUE

Whenever policy analysts are exploring an issue, they should take time to talk with others about the nature of the problem and possible approaches to addressing it. The notion that you, as a policy analyst, aspire to creating public value is appealing. Of course, this goal is contested. Still, by asking questions about public value and how it can be created, you can open space for thinking hard about what outcomes matter most in a specific area of government activity, and how you, as a policy analyst, might most effectively pursue these outcomes.[6]

2. IDENTIFY WHAT WORKS

Increasingly, a lot of evidence has become available concerning the effectiveness—or the disadvantages—of various approaches to addressing public problems. When policy analysts begin working on an issue, it is essential that they determine if they can address the problem, and, if so, what approaches will work best. As people study cases of what has worked or not worked in the past, they often gain insights that can help them better define the problem. For example, it might be the case that a large problem can be broken into smaller parts. Although not all parts of it can be effectively addressed, some could be. Identifying them is the start to making positive change.

3. THINK LIKE SCIENTISTS

Good public policies operate like investments. Resources are devoted to specific policies and the result is measurable improvements in the lives of those affected by them. To make well-informed investments, you will need evidence of what works. Thus, it is useful for you to bring to your work the mindset of scientists. Scientists look at evidence and ask how it was generated. They seek to identify causal relationships between actions and observed results. They often state hypotheses about specific relationships and then use evidence to test those relationships. The method most frequently used by scientists is experimentation, in which a hypothesis is tested through application of an intervention in a select number of cases, and comparison of results between the cases that received the intervention and those that did not. As you have seen throughout this book, many opportunities exist for public policies to be treated as hypotheses and for careful investigation of their impacts to take place. By thinking like a scientist, you can improve the likelihood that your work will ultimately contribute to making the world a better place.

4. BUILD SKILLS IN DATA ANALYSIS

Scientists use evidence to answer questions. Throughout this book, we have encountered many examples of how careful review of evidence can reveal the return on specific policy investments. Thus, it is useful for you, as a policy analyst, to have skills in data analysis. Many times in their work, analysts are called to make use of basic statistical tests. At other times, they are expected to be knowledgeable interpreters of evidence and analysis that others have supplied. For these reasons, it will be helpful for you to have skills in data analysis. At a minimum, you can use these skills to request and better interpret the quantitative work of others. You should become effective at rapidly figuring out what relationships across variables matter in given circumstances and how you might test the strength of those relationships. The use of data analysis is a powerful way of approaching policy problems and the development of alternative ways of addressing them.

5. APPLY DESIGN THINKING

Public policies may be made in capital cities, but they live or die in suburbs and neighborhoods. For decades, policy analysts have been encouraged to think hard about the day-to-day experiences of the clients of government services and those delivering such services. Only through understanding your world can you begin to devise policies that will contribute to improved outcomes. Recently, people developing public policies have begun to adopt the practices of industrial designers as a means of understanding how clients interact with government services.[7] This **design thinking** is a powerful analytical approach that fits neatly with the investment perspective. The investment perspective is based on the assumption that specific interventions will generate valued results. However, the possibility exists that those interventions will work well in some locations and not so well in others.

By applying design thinking, you can begin to devise policies and programs in ways that allow for local variation in implementation, with the goal of raising overall policy effectiveness. Design thinking challenges the notion that smart people in Albany, Sacramento, or Washington, DC, can define policy problems without needing to leave the office. It forces policy analysts to get out of their comfort zones. Yet, when they do this well, many opportunities for policy learning emerge. The discipline of design thinking holds the promise of improving the odds that public policies will produce intended positive effects.

6. PRACTICE POLITICAL ASTUTENESS

Policy analysts are often expected to be politically neutral experts, people who would give much the same advice no matter the political leanings of those whom they are advising. Yet, even as you, as a policy analyst, strive to present your advice in nonpartisan ways, it is vital that you exhibit a high degree of **political astuteness**. This is the ability to effectively interpret the context within which your advice is being developed and the concerns of those you seek to advise.[8] It is important to keep up to date with current politics in your area of interest, know the backgrounds and political preoccupations of those you engage with, and be sensitive to the language you use when presenting evidence and advice. A huge part of gaining influence as a policy analyst and advisor involves winning the trust of those around you. Although you can never control for every contingency that arises, there are many things you can do to eliminate unnecessary points of disagreement between you and others. By thinking hard about this, you improve your ability to make your points clearly and effectively.

The risk of meddling in politics is that you will lose trust. You should leave the explicit political calculations to those who seek election and reelection. But you should take the time to understand their concerns and how you can address them. Political astuteness is an essential skill for allowing policy analysts to observe windows of opportunity for the development of transformative policy proposals.

7. TELL GOOD STORIES

People with good technical skills often think they will gain influence based solely on the quality of their analytical work. This is rarely the case. In policy-making circles, participants often act on the basis of **causal stories**. These are representations of issues and proposals for ways forward that suggest a clear link among what is happening, why it is happening, and how it can be addressed. The investment approach to policy analysis and policy development is founded on careful gathering and examination of evidence. Although people in policy-making circles need to be convinced of the strength and merits of evidence-based policy proposals, they do not have to be bombarded with all the facts that you know. The challenge is to think about the issues that are uppermost in the minds of each audience you address and to speak to those issues directly, in language that is appropriate for the context. Thinking of yourself as a storyteller means that you need to think about the narrative thread that runs through all your statements. Continually returning to the issue of narrative and storytelling will help you to determine what evidence you need to present and how you will present it.[9]

8. PLAY THE LONG GAME

The policy-making process is complex. Shifting politics and circumstances have the effect of imposing elements of chance on all of the outcomes of public policy debates. Even when you have worked diligently to acquire the various technical and people skills needed to offer usable knowledge to decision makers, there are no guarantees that your work will receive a thorough reception. At times, your advice will be heeded. At other times, it will be ignored. Yet, if you keep working at improving the advice you give, you can increase your chances of gaining influence in policy discussions.

Inevitably you will come up against moments in your careers when your efforts will appear to have been wasted. These are the times when it would be easiest to give up. They are also the times when it is most important that you keep trying. The lessons that you learn at these moments can help you succeed in the future.

CHAPTER SUMMARY

This final chapter of the book has explored why public policy matters, how we can better assess the long-term impacts of policies, and how such assessments can contribute to investment analysis. We have also considered the qualities of effective policy analysts. The view expressed throughout the book is that public policy is critically important to the quality of human life. By extension, this means that those who engage in policy development and advising are doing fundamentally important work. Doing this work well requires their being open to exploring evidence on what works. It also requires their developing creative ways of conveying advice to members of the public and to decision makers.

We are all the inheritors of legacies left by others. The change agenda presented here comes as a call for policy analysts to see their work as guiding the making of policy investments. Good investment advice is based on sound interpretation of relevant information. It is tailored to meet the needs of those receiving it. The contention of this chapter—and indeed of this book—is that all of us should care deeply about policy legacies, as they strongly influence our future. There is a lot of work to be done and it is noble work. It is work that, collectively and cumulatively, will contribute to the greatest promise of public policy: making a better world.

KEY TERMS

Optimal resource use
Stewardship
Governance
Policy legacies
Ex-post analysis
Path dependencies

Unintended consequences
Unintended costs
Institutional inertia
Design thinking
Political astuteness
Causal stories

SUGGESTIONS FOR FURTHER READING

Balla, Steven J., Martin Lodge, and Edward C. Page, eds. *The Oxford Handbook of Classics in Public Policy and Administration.* New York: Oxford University Press, 2015. This book reflects on the ongoing influence of a large number of classic contributions to the study of both public policy and public administration.

Mintrom, Michael. *Contemporary Policy Analysis.* New York: Oxford University Press, 2012. This book offers an easily accessible, comprehensive introduction to concepts and analytical strategies used by policy analysts.

Moran, Michael, Martin Rein, and Robert E. Goodin, eds. *The Oxford Handbook of Public Policy.* New York: Oxford University Press, 2008. This book offers a set of literature reviews covering all major aspects of public policy. It is especially strong in discussions of institutional settings, policy-making processes, and policy instruments.

Weimer, David L., and Aidan R. Vining. *Policy Analysis: Concepts and Practice,* 6th ed. Abingdon, Oxfordshire: Routledge, 2015. This book offers a very strong technical introduction to policy analysis and its application.

WEBSITES

- The American Enterprise Institute is a privately funded, conservative think tank located in Washington, DC. Its website offers information relating to many contemporary policy issues www.aei.org
- The Ash Center for Democratic Governance and Innovation at the Harvard Kennedy School of Government has created a comprehensive evidence base concerning public policy innovations. http://ash.harvard.edu/
- The Brookings Institution is a privately funded, centrist think tank located in Washington, DC. Its website offers information relating to many contemporary policy issues. www.brookings.edu
- McKinsey & Company is a global consulting group that provides advice to organizations across many industries, the public sector being one of them. Its website offers commentary and insight on a broad range of topics associated with organizational effectiveness. http://www.mckinsey.com/

- The Organisation for Economic Co-operation and Development is a Paris-based think tank, funded by 35 countries committed to democracy and the market economy. The organization collects a vast array of statistical and substantive policy information from its members. It offers useful information on many policy issues. http://www.oecd.org
- The Pew Charitable Trusts is an organization committed to improving public policy, informing the public, and invigorating civic life. Its website provides background information on a range of contemporary policy issues. http://www.pewtrusts.org/
- The RAND Corporation, like McKinsey, is a global consulting group with a strong interest in public policy. Its website contains information on a broad range of public policy topics. http://www.rand.org/

FOR DISCUSSION

1. Governments are frequently criticized because the public policies they have developed and implemented do not fully address agreed-upon problems, the policies create new problems of their own, or they reflect both of these criticisms. In light of these potential flaws, how might we discuss public policies in ways that acknowledge their limitations, while opening space for reasoned exploration of how improvements could be realized?

2. This book is enthusiastic about how public policy can improve the quality of people's lives. Consider a specific area of public policy of interest to you. In what ways has that public policy positively affected society? Where has it been less successful? Looking to the future, what might be some effective ways to improve people's lives through policy in this area?

3. People interested in public policy can pursue a variety of careers. Those with expertise in public policy often move through different roles during these careers. Consider the careers of several people who are currently contributing to the development or reform of public policy. Focus your discussion on people currently active in public policy making at a specific level of government—for example, local, state, or national. What is their career background? What specific experiences appear to have assisted them most in establishing their capabilities in policy development? What lessons for your own career might you draw from this discussion?

GLOSSARY

The Abecedarian Project provided full-time educational child care and high-quality preschool to children aged zero to five from very disadvantaged backgrounds.

Absolute poverty is where a person is deemed unable to meet basic needs for living—that is, they lack sufficient food to maintain good health and they may have difficulty accessing safe drinking water.

Accountability refers to the obligation of an individual or organization to account for their activities.

Acid Rain Program is a market-based initiative taken by the U.S. Environmental Protection Agency in an effort to reduce overall atmospheric levels of sulfur dioxide and nitrogen oxides, which cause acid rain.

Actuarial integrity refers to the financial reliability of a scheme. For insurance schemes, integrity is achieved through management of annual contributions and specification of future payouts.

Actuarial sentencing refers to the use of historical evidence to estimate the factors that tend to be associated with the recidivism of nonviolent offenders.

Administrative evaluations involve systematic efforts to explore the impacts of policies and associated programs and form judgments about how well they are achieving their intended goals.

Advocacy coalitions, within the context of policy change, are portrayed as collections of people from a variety of positions (e.g., elected and agency officials, interest group leaders, researchers) who share a specific belief system—a set of basic values, causal assumptions, and problem perceptions—and who show a nontrivial degree of coordinated activity over time.

The Affordable Care Act (2010) was designed to expand access to health insurance by making it mandatory that all Americans have membership in health insurance schemes and by subsidizing the cost of that membership.

Agenda setting is a catch-all term that describes how advocates, interest groups, and others concerned about specific public problems work to draw attention to those problems and their proposed policy solutions.

Air Quality Index (AQI) is a universal measure of atmospheric pollution levels.

American world interests are the interests that the U.S. government, acting for its citizens, cares most deeply about and works hard to protect.

Applied scientific research is problem driven and usually involves taking existing knowledge and using it to solve a specific problem.

Aversion behavior is when people disengage or avoid instances for fear of harm.

Bayh–Dole Act refers to a law that allowed universities, small businesses, and nonprofit institutions to maintain ownership of the intellectual property rights associated with inventions derived from federally funded science projects conducted on site.

Ben Franklin Technology Partners is a state-funded investment entity in Pennsylvania. The partners selected and invested in start-up companies that its board judged to have potential to become economically successful through translating specific scientific findings into workable technologies that could be readily commercialized.

Big science model refers to expensive and expansive projects that serve to organize the work of many scientists around the pursuit of common goals.

Bio-sensitive wearable technologies are technologies that monitor basic physiological processes and open major possibilities for changing traditional expert–patient relations.

Budget deficit is whenever a government spends more in a given year than it collects in taxes and other revenues. Cumulative deficits, unmatched by surpluses, generate government debt.

Bureaucracy is the major "doing" part of government. The bureaucracy's main responsibility is to implement public policies and programs. It is often portrayed as a separate branch of government, reporting to the executive.

Cap-and-trade system is a government-mandated, market-based approach to controlling pollution by providing economic incentives for achieving reductions in the emissions of atmospheric pollutants.

Carbon footprint refers to the amount of carbon dioxide or other carbon compounds released into the atmosphere by the activities of individuals, companies, or countries.

Carceral state is a state modeled on the idea of a prison.

Carrying capacity refers to the number of people, animals, or crops that a region can support without environmental degradation.

Causal stories are representations of issues, and proposals for ways forward, that suggest a clear link among what is happening, why it is happening, and how it can be addressed.

Centers for Disease Control and Prevention (CDC) is the U.S. national public health institute that operates within the U.S. Department of Health and Human Services.

Chain gangs are groups of prisoners chained together to perform menial or physically challenging work as a form of punishment.

Charter schools are publicly funded schools that have more autonomy to develop and shape the content and delivery of classroom activities to match the learning needs of their students.

The Chicago Child-Parent Center Study was a longitudinal study that followed the progress of 989 children enrolled in twenty-four preschools in low-income areas of Chicago between 1983 and 1986.

Clean Air Act is a United States federal law designed to control air pollution on a national level.

Clean Energy Finance and Investment Authority (CEFIA) is a clean energy investment bank in Connecticut that leverages public money by attracting private-sector funds and expertise.

Cold War was a state of economic, political, and military tension between the United States and its allies, and the Soviet Union and its client states. It lasted from the end of World War II (1945) until the fall of the Berlin Wall (1989).

Collective action calls for individuals to coordinate their intentions with others and accept that whatever outcomes emerge may differ from those they, individually, would have desired.

Command and control regulation is the direct regulation of an industry or activity by legislation that categorically states what is permitted and what is illegal.

Commons refer to land or resources belonging to or affecting the whole of a community.

Community sentencing involves serving out a term of punishment through community work rather than going to jail or prison.

Companion diagnostics is a diagnostic test used as a companion to a therapeutic drug to determine its applicability to a specific patient.

Competitive extramural funding is a system where research grants are made directly to universities. The system ensures that federal research funding flows beyond government agencies, institutes, and laboratories to universities.

Compulsory education refers to the requirement of all children within certain age ranges to attend school.

Conference of Parties refers to the supreme decision-making body of an international convention. In this context of environmental protection, it refers to the governing body of the United Nations Framework Convention on Climate Change.

Consumer Price Index is the average percentage change from year to year in the cost of purchasing a standard set of consumption items.

Convict lease refers to a system where states leased prisoners to large companies as a form of cheap labor, working in both industrial and agricultural settings.

Copayments refer to financial contributions by the individual receiving treatment.

Corporal punishment is a punishment intended to cause physical pain on a person, such as flogging.

Cost-benefit analysis is a method to assess if the valued effects of a policy or program over a period of time do, in fact, outweigh the costs, making it worth pursuing.

Cost-effectiveness analysis is a form of economic analysis that compares the relative costs and outcomes of different courses of action intended to attain a common result, such as public safety.

Cost overruns involve unexpected costs incurred within a project in excess of budgeted amounts. They arise due to an underestimation of the actual cost during budgeting, and are common in military procurements.

Counterfactual case refers to the conceptual creation of possible alternatives to life events that have already occurred; something that is contrary to what actually happened.

Creative class refers to a loose category of people who have benefited from high-quality schooling as well as university education and who contribute to the creation of new products and services of high value to consumers both at home and abroad.

Credentialing refers to the expectation of schools to effectively differentiate children according to their demonstrated talents and capabilities.

Credentialing systems are used to indicate if individuals are suitably trained to practice particular professions, such as law and medicine.

Curriculum refers to an agreed-upon system for introducing knowledge in schools.

Debt servicing is the interest that a government must pay on money borrowed to cover differences between government revenue and spending.

Deductibles refer to a specified amount of individual payment to be made before insurance will be paid to cover remaining costs.

Deregulation involves reducing the amount of regulation currently in place.

Design thinking is a practice of industrial designers involving close observation of clients and their needs. Design thinking is increasingly being used by public policy analysts and developers to understand how clients interact with government services.

Direct democracy is where eligible voters get to deliberate and vote on each policy issue.

Direct service supply is when government takes responsibility for providing services for public use.

Discount rate is an amount used to determine the value in present dollar terms of an amount of money expected to be spent or received at some future point.

Discretionary spending is a category of the U.S. government's annual budget. This is the spending over which the president and Congress have most control in the budget process.

Dread risks refer to low-probability, high-consequence events, such as 9/11.

Early childhood education is the care and education of children aged from a few months to the age when they enter primary school.

Earned Income Tax Credit is a tax credit that reduces the amount of federal income tax those on low wages must pay. The credit level is adjusted to take account of the number of dependents in a household.

Economic recessions occur when the whole economy temporarily slows and annual changes in Gross Domestic Product (GDP) switch from positive figures to zero or negative figures.

Economic transformations refer to a long-term change in dominant economic activity, such as the use of robots in manufacturing.

Economics of education refers to the relationship that public schooling has on the national income in countries with market economies.

Elite theory posits that American democracy has long been dominated by powerful elites. The theory divides society into the powerful few and the powerless, apathetic masses.

Enculturation refers to the reinforcement of predominant cultural norms.

Entitlement program is a government program guaranteeing access to some benefit by members of a specific group and based on established rights or by legislation.

Environmental justice refers to studies that document the unequal impacts of environmental pollution on different social classes and racial or ethnic groups.

Environmental Protection Agency (EPA) is the U.S. government's primary organization for monitoring pollution levels and the actions of regulated industries. It was established by the Nixon administration.

Environmental racism describes the tendency for environmentally hazardous or degraded environments, such as toxic waste dumps or abandoned industrial sites, to be located near low-income or minority communities.

Ex-post analysis refers to the careful exploration of specific prior public policy efforts, their costs, and impacts.

Excise taxes can be used to influence behavior. Classic examples include taxes on cigarettes and alcohol and fines for traffic infringements or other illegal behavior.

Executive of any government tends to comprise the leading political figure in the jurisdiction and his or her cabinet colleagues.

Executive orders are rules or orders issued by the U.S. president to an executive branch of the government and having the force of law.

Exogenous shocks are unanticipated events that can have immediate and devastating effects and often plunge people into periods of poverty.

Federal Water Pollution Control Act established the basic structure for regulating pollutant discharges into the waters of the United States.

Federalism is a system of government in which multiple governments hold power over specific jurisdictions.

Felon disenfranchisement is the exclusion from voting of people otherwise eligible to vote due to conviction of criminal offense. It is common practice in many American states.

Fiscal constraints refers to the tightening or unavailability of sufficient funds to support current government programs.

Focusing events are sudden events that cause both citizens and policy makers to pay more attention to a public problem and often to press for solutions.

Fracking involves pumping large amounts of water, sand, and chemicals underground to split open rocks, allowing oil and gas to flow.

Free ride refers to a benefit obtained at another's expense or without the usual cost or effort.

Free rider problem refers to a situation where some individuals in a population either consume more than their fair share of a common resource, or pay less than their fair share of its cost.

Fusion Centers are information-sharing centers located across the United States that gather and share information relating to suspected terrorist plots.

Global warming refers to the gradual increase in the overall temperature of the Earth's atmosphere.

Governance refers to the ownership and control of specific organizations.

Greenhouse gases are gases such as carbon dioxide and sulfur dioxide that trap heat near the Earth's surface, leading to overall increases in global temperatures.

Gross Domestic Product (GDP) is an indicator of economic output. Changes in this indicator are often interpreted as a measure of how well governments have performed in contributing to the well-being of their citizens.

Heavy-handed regulation refers to the weight of regulation imposed.

High effective marginal tax rates are applied as people's wages increase and they no longer become eligible for benefits like the Earned Income Tax Credit or housing vouchers. The withdrawal of benefits becomes equivalent to facing a higher rate of tax.

The High/Scope Perry Preschool Study examined the lives of 123 African Americans born in poverty and at high risk of failing in school.

Human capital refers to the returns that individual and societies get from investing in public schooling and education.

Human Development Index is a well-being indicator that combines the measure of GDP per capita with measures of access to education and life expectancy.

Human genome is the complete set of genetic information for humans.

Human Genome Project (HGP) is an international research effort to determine the DNA sequence of the entire human genome.

Immunization programs are healthcare programs ensuring that children and adults are inoculated against diseases that have previously ravished human societies.

Imprisonment refers to the act of putting or confining someone in prison.

Incentives alignment refers to harmonization between parties that could otherwise have competing interests in a transaction. For example, incentives alignment matters between providers, insurers, and consumers of health care.

Incrementalism is the making of policy changes through small steps. It takes complexity and disagreement into account in the policy-making process.

Independent Transferable Quotas are a type of catch-share system, which is a tool some governments use to manage fisheries.

Individual causes refer to poverty experienced by a person due to their own individual capabilities or personal choices.

Institutions are sets of rules that structure how we interact in various social settings. They help groups overcome collective action problems because they guide our behavior in given situations.

Institutional inertia refers to the tendency of institutions to perpetuate established procedures and modes, rather than change.

Insurance schemes involve the pooling of individual contributions, with the aim of improving individual access to benefits that people would otherwise be unable to afford, such as provision of health care.

Intensive Family Preservation Services are short-term, home-based crisis intervention services intended to keep children in their biological home—rather than to move them to foster homes—by improving family functioning.

Interest groups comprise organized efforts of people who share common goals.

Interest rate can be understood as the cost of borrowing money. It is normally expressed in terms of a percentage of the overall loan.

Interests include all the ways that organizations and people believe their well-being can be enhanced or diminished by taking specific actions.

Investment perspective is based on the view that all government programs should be treated as investments whereby current expenditures serve to promote better social outcomes for the future.

Judicial evaluations are based on formal processes, which involve court cases concerning specific government programs and their effects.

Judiciary is the branch of government that interprets legislation and tests its correspondence with the constitution and broader body of established law within a jurisdiction.

Jurisdiction can be a nation, state, city, or school district. It refers to an area with a set of laws under the control of a system of courts or a government entity which are different from neighboring areas.

Justice reinvestment is a data-driven movement that attempts to understand the drivers of crime and redistribute resources to high-risk areas rather than rely on mass incarceration.

Keynesian economics, named after John Maynard Keynes, support an increase in government spending as a way to boost economic activity in times of recession, even if such spending causes governments to go into temporary debt.

Knowledge is awareness or familiarity gained by experience of a fact or situation, or acquired through education.

Knowledge workers are people who primarily think for a living, rather than engage in repetitive or manual tasks.

Legislatures are where public policy is generally formulated, debated, and approved.

Life cycle of public infrastructural assets involves estimating the length of life of an asset and considering how adequate, routine maintenance can ensure that the infrastructure continues to perform for many years.

Linear model of science is a model that suggests that all research starts with a curiosity-driven scientist who engages in pure or basic scientific research for no other reason than to understand something that is presently not well understood or explained.

Lobbyists are those seeking to influence the policy preferences of lawmakers.

Longitudinal studies are observational research methods in which data is gathered for the same subjects repeatedly over a period of time.

Long-term unemployed is typically defined as being without work for more than six months.

Macroeconomic analysis refers to the use of aggregate statistics to model overall economic outcomes.

Mandatory spending is a category of the U.S. government's annual budget. It is money that must be paid through entitlement programs such as Social Security and Medicare.

Marginal cost is the cost of generating an additional unit of output.

Market making in relation to government refers to the creation of policy settings that enhance market performance or establish market-like competition for service providers.

Means-tested cash transfers are a form of poverty alleviation that make assistance available to people as long as they demonstrate that they both fall within specific categories and are sufficiently needy to be eligible for assistance.

Medicaid provides health coverage to low-income people who meet specific eligibility requirements.

Medicare is a federal program that provides health insurance coverage to people who have disabilities, are diagnosed with certain medical conditions, or are aged 65 years or older.

Meta-analysis involves evaluating high-quality studies of the programs of interest and determining the average "effect size" of the programs, found across various studies.

Microeconomic analysis is the study of how actions of individuals or firms affect the economy. Such analysis typically focuses on behavior of consumers and producers in specific markets.

Military procurement refers to the purchasing of equipment for use by military forces.

Minimum hourly wage is a legally mandated price floor on hourly wages, below which nonexempt workers may not be offered or accept a job.

Money income thresholds are measures used to determine poverty relative to family size and composition.

Monopoly pricing is a pricing strategy followed by a seller, who prices a product to maximize his or her profits under the assumption that he or she does not need to worry about competition.

Multi-payer systems enable individuals to choose among competing health insurers for their care.

Multiplier effects refers to the increase in final income arising from any new injection of spending.

National Institutes of Health is an agency of the U.S. Department of Health and Human Services. It is the primary agency of the U.S. government responsible for biomedical and health-related research.

National Science Foundation is a U.S. government agency that supports fundamental research and education in all the nonmedical fields of science and engineering.

Natural monopolies refer to services that cost a lot to establish and that become economically feasible only when large numbers of people use them, and where competitive supply appears either wasteful or unworkable.

Natural monopoly power refers to the power of government to establish and maintain systems, for example in criminal justice. Governments—and governments alone—have the power to arrest people, to imprison them, or to otherwise punish them.

Negative externalities refer to unwanted outcomes for others who played no part in the transaction generating those outcomes.

Net Present Value is the total amount that comes from summing up discounted benefits minus costs over the assumed life of a policy or program.

New Deal refers to policies introduced by President Roosevelt in the 1930s to alleviate the devastating results of the 1929 stock market crash. The New Deal laid the foundation for the welfare state that exists to this day in the United States.

New Deal 25 Plus was a mandatory program in the United Kingdom for longer-term unemployed people who were claiming a Jobseeker's Allowance for 18 or more months.

New Deal for Lone Parents was a voluntary program in the United Kingdom that aimed to help and encourage lone parents to improve their job readiness and employment opportunities and gain independence through working.

New Institutionalism emphasizes the human effort and motivation behind the design and incentives that institutions create to motivate human action.

New York system is a view on the purpose of prison confinement. In contrast to the Pennsylvania system, it emphasized the need for punishment in the form of hard labor.

No Child Left Behind (NCLB) refers to an educational initiative created in by the U.S. Congress in 2001 with bipartisan support and signed into law by President George W. Bush in 2002. The act used financial incentives to significantly increase the pressure on public schools to improve student performance on standardized tests.

Nonmedical determinates of health are those that fall outside the sphere of medical or health care but have shown to affect health outcomes, such as tobacco use and alcohol consumption.

The one best system refers to a new interpretation of the development of America's educational system during the early years of the 20th century.

Opportunity costs represent alternatives given up when a decision is made to pursue a specific course of action.

Optimal resource use involves achieving maximum gains from minimum necessary inputs.

Parole refers to the early release from prison for good behavior.

Particulate matter refers to a mixture of solid and liquid particles suspended in the air.

Patent and Trademark Law Amendments Act of 1980 see: Bayh–Dole Act.

Path dependency refers to the idea that once a system is in place, it is hard to change. One reason path dependency occurs is that specific interest groups with identified stakes in a system will powerfully resist any efforts to deviate from it.

Pennsylvania system refers to a view on the purpose of confinement in prison. It was predicated on the view that prisoners could be rehabilitated to live peacefully in society.

Perverse incentives are a type of negative unintended consequences resulting from a misalignment of incentives.

Pharmacogenomics is the branch of genetics concerned with determining the likely response of an individual to therapeutic drugs.

Physical capital refers to various kinds of equipment that serve to advance the economic fortunes of firms.

Policy adoption is a phase of the policy process in government bodies accept policies for future implementation.

Policy implementation is a complex process of turning policy into practice.

Policy legacies are long-term impacts of public policies on society.

Policy stream refers, in John Kingdon's conceptualization of the policy-making process, to a more or less independent stream, in which communities of policy specialists generate and debate numerous ideas for policy solutions or viable policy alternatives.

Political astuteness is the ability to effectively interpret the context within with your advice is being developed and the concerns of those you seek to advise.

Political evaluations describe a range of primarily impressionistic reactions to specific government programs.

Political stream refers, in John Kingdon's conceptualization of the policy-making process, to a more or less independent stream, composed of things like election results, changes in administrations, changes in the partisan or ideological distribution of legislatures, interest group pressure campaigns, and changes in the public opinion or the national mood.

Polycentricity refers to coordination of action via many localized efforts.

Pooling resources is a mechanism used to improve access to health care for people who could not otherwise afford it.

Poor Relief Act of 1601 was an act of the British Parliament to address poverty at the local, or parish, level.

Pork-barrel politics refers to the appropriation of government spending for localized projects secured solely to bring money and other benefits to a representative's district.

Positive externalities occur when the consumption or production of a good, like individual education, causes benefit to a third party who had no part in the original transaction.

Poverty line is a dollar figure deemed by experts in nutrition and household budgeting to be sufficient to support at least a subsistence level of living for a certain period of time.

Poverty traps arise when people who are poor decide that engaging in increasing amounts of paid work is less attractive than remaining eligible for government assistance.

Private capital is money that does not come from government.

Private contractors are any nongovernment service providers. In the context of public safety, the term refers to private security firms that individual citizens, organizations, and corporations enlist to enhance the protection of their property and themselves.

Probation officers are officials who work with convicted offenders doing community sentencing or released prisoners who are on parole and probation.

Probation refers to the release of an offender from detention, subject to a period of supervised good behavior.

Problem definition refers to the consideration of what the public problem might be.

Problem stream refers, in John Kingdon's conceptualization of the policy-making process, to a more or less independent stream in which efforts are made to draw attention to certain issues and to encourage a public policy response.

Property taxes are annual taxes paid by households and are proportional to the value of the property.

Proximate policy makers include legislators, political executives, appointed bureaucrats, and some party officials—anyone with some decision-making authority.

Public goods are goods that, in the absence of government supply, would likely not be supplied in sufficient quantities to make them effective.

Public infrastructure consists of all the collectively used structures and systems that support human activities.

Public mood is a widely shared emotional state that can serve to condition community and individual support of specific government action.

Public opinion refers to the collective opinion of many people on some issue or problem.

Public policy consists of rules governments enforce and actions they take in society.

Public-private partnerships are contractual arrangements between a public agency and a private sector entity. They can be used to finance, build and operate projects, such as public infrastructure.

Punctuated equilibrium is a theory of the policy process characterized by long periods of stability interrupted by moments of abrupt, significant change.

Pure or basic scientific research is curiosity driven and is not intended to solve any immediate problem.

Quasi-experimental assessments are types of evaluations that aim to determine whether a program or intervention has the intended effect on a study's participants. A quasi-experimental assessment lacks one or more of the design elements that make up a randomized controlled experiment.

Race to the Top refers to an educational strategy introduced by the Obama administration. It established several rounds of competitions among states for federal education funding.

Random assignment is an experimental technique for assigning participants to different groups in an experiment.

Randomized controlled experiment is a study design that randomly assigns similar participants into either an experimental or a control group.

Rational choice strategy suggests a rational linear approach to problem definition, laying out alternative solutions, predicting the consequences, valuing the outcomes, and making a choice.

Recidivism is the tendency of convicted criminals to reoffend.

Recombination relies on the assumption that some elements are similar and others are different from one another. Recombination results when different elements are brought together to lead to social, economic, and technical breakthroughs.

Regional Greenhouse Gas Initiative (RGGI) is the first cap-and-trade pollution reduction program established in the United States to address climate change.

Regression analysis is a statistical method that attempts to determine the strength of the relationship between one dependent variable and at least one independent variable.

Regulation is a government-imposed rule or set of rules defining what is considered appropriate behavior.

Rehabilitation refers to the process that involves preparing convicted offenders to live peacefully and productively in society after they have received their punishment.

Relative poverty captures the understanding that people living in economically advanced society might experience significant hardship even though their circumstances do not place them in absolute poverty.

Representative democracy is where citizens vote periodically for candidates who will represent them in deliberative bodies—such as committees, boards, councils, or legislatures.

Return on investment (ROI) is obtained by dividing the sum of estimated policy benefits by the sum of estimated policy costs.

Risk-Need-Responsivity model is a model used to develop recommendations for how prisoners should be assessed based on the risk they present and what they need, and what kinds of environments they should be placed in to reduce recidivism.

Risk pool refers to the group of insured people who collectively stand at risk of needing medical treatment.

Rule of law is the notion that individuals should submit to rules made by a specific government.

Scarring refers to the negative long-term effects associated with spending too much time away from training or paid employment.

Schools of choice programs provide students with multiple school enrollment opportunities.

Seasonal permits are mechanisms used to ensure maintenance of fishing stocks or other stocks of wildlife subject to hunting and capture for commercial or recreational purposes.

Self-insurance refers to individuals' savings to cover possible health care eventualities or catastrophic events in their lives.

Sensitivity analysis involves running a number of alternative scenarios using different modeling assumptions to test the extent to which the results are robust or, alternatively, how much they are being driven by the choices incorporated into the model.

Sentencing guidelines categorize offenses and identify the sentence required upon conviction. Judges are allowed to increase or decrease sentences or depart from the guidelines, but must clearly state the reasons on the record.

Separate but equal refers to a legal doctrine of racial segregation in American society.

Service delivery is where governments employ the service providers and coordinate the creation and maintenance of the facilities that allow for service delivery.

Single-payer systems are where governments use the general tax system to fund health insurance for the whole population.

Social equity is when certain goods and responsibilities are divided evenly across a society.

Social insurance programs are poverty alleviation programs in the United States that rely on contributions from those people who will ultimately be eligible to receive benefits.

Social intervention is an action that involves the intervention of a government or an organization in social affairs.

Socialization of health care refers to medical and hospital care for all at nominal cost by means of government regulation of health care and subsidies derived from taxation.

The Social Progress Index promotes broader discussion of factors shaping the quality of lives for citizens. It captures, among other things, access to medical care, quality of water supply, personal safety, health and well-being, access to information and communications, access to basic and advanced knowledge, personal rights, and tolerance and inclusion.

Spillover effects are economic events in context that occur because of something else in a seemingly unrelated context.

State-owned enterprises are government entities organized to emulate for-profit businesses.

Statistical modeling is a process in which mathematics and data are used to construct an equation that represents a given real-life phenomenon.

Stewardship involves looking to the future and imagining how public policy choices made today could influence subsequent outcomes.

Strictly secular schools refer to the strict separation between church and state and how that plays out in the education system.

Structural adjustment refers to the change effected in the basic framework of an economy by the impact of policy reforms.

Structural causes of poverty refer to poverty experienced by a person due to major inequalities built into the structure of society.

Subsidy occurs whenever an individual or entity receives cash from the government that is not a payment for service.

Sustainability is the ability to endure indefinitely.

Technical lock-in reduces the potential for innovation to occur within a regulated area of activity.

Technological change describes the change in a set of feasible production possibilities. It has the ability to increase the amount of output an economy can produce, even if the level of inputs remain constant.

Think tanks tend to be nonprofit organizations that gather evidence and make arguments with the intention of influencing the policy-making process.

Tradable rights to pollute is a privatization model that allows individual polluters to receive permits to release a certain amount of pollution.

Tragedy of the Commons is an economic problem in which every individual tries to reap the greatest benefit from a given resource. As the demand for the resource overwhelms the supply, every individual who consumes an additional unit directly harms others who can no longer enjoy the benefits. But nobody faces an incentive to act differently.

Transportation of convicts refers to the relocation of criminals from Britain to colonial North America from around 1620 through to 1780.

Triple-P Positive Parenting Program is a program that helps parents create more affirming relationships with their children and thus improve family life and reduce the risk of violence and instability in their families.

Trust funds are funds that comprise a variety of assets intended to provide benefits to an individual or organization.

Truth-in-sentencing are laws enacted to reduce the possibility of early release from incarceration.

Two-level game refers to the entanglements of domestic and international politics and the trade-offs required in formulating foreign policy.

Unemployment benefit See **unemployment insurance**.

Unemployment insurance refers to a government benefit received by people who have been in full-time employment but who lose their jobs and are required to search for new employment.

Unintended consequences are positive and negative impacts of policies that were not initially intended.

Unintended costs are costs imposed on businesses and families that are not accounted for within government budgets.

User fees are charges for the use of a product or service.

Vigilante justice is when a person who is not a member of law enforcement pursues and punishes persons suspected of lawbreaking.

Vouchers allow individuals or families to expend an amount of government funding in a specified service of their choice. They have been used to allow children who would otherwise attend public schools to attend a limited range of private schools.

Welfare state is where government provides a social safety net for citizens, to avoid them from falling into long-term poverty.

Welfare-to-work programs are poverty alleviation programs that help participants achieve steady employment and attain financial independence.

Wellness programs are programs designed to encourage children and adults to make healthy lifestyle choices and to engage in regular exercise.

White elephants refer to assets that are costly to maintain and produce limited public value.

Windows of opportunity refers to critical times when conditions in all three of John Kingdon's so-called streams favor the joining of problems, solutions, and political momentum.

NOTES

PREFACE

1. Milton Friedman (with Rose D. Friedman), *Capitalism and Freedom* (Chicago: University of Chicago Press, 1962), 15.
2. Madeleine Bunting, "Market Has No Use for the Elderly," *The Guardian Weekly*, October 28, 2011, 28.

CHAPTER 1

1. World Health Organization, *Ebola Situation Report* (Geneva, Switzerland: World Health Organization, March 27, 2015).
2. The World Bank, "Ebola: Economic Impact Already Serious; Could Be 'Catastrophic' Without Swift Response." Press release and accompanying report, September 17, 2014.
3. "Lexington: The Ebola Alarmists: Stoking Panic Will Not Help America Fight Ebola," *The Economist*, October 11, 2014.
4. W. Richard Scott, *Institutions and Organizations: Ideas, Interests & Identities,* 4th ed. (Los Angeles: Sage, 2013) terms these "the three pillars of institutions."
5. See, e.g., James G. March and Johan P. Olsen, *Rediscovering Institutions* (New York: Free Press, 1989); Douglass C. North, *Growth and Structural Change* (New York: Norton, 1981); Douglass C. North, *Institutions, Institutional Change, and Economic Performance* (Cambridge, UK: Cambridge University Press, 1990); and Oliver Williamson, *The Economic Institutions of Capitalism* (New York: Free Press, 1985).
6. See, e.g., Elinor Ostrom, *Governing the Commons: The Evolution of Institutions for Collective Action* (Cambridge, UK, and New York: Cambridge University Press, 1990).
7. See Greg Linden, Jason Dedrick, and Kenneth L. Kraemer, "Innovation and Job Creation in a Global Economy: The Case of Apple's iPod," *Journal of International Commerce and Economics* 3, no. 1 (2011): 223–39.
8. Various studies by economists indicate that cities and regions with relatively high proportions of citizens holding degrees tend to have unusually high-performing economies. The finding holds true both in the United States and elsewhere. See, e.g., Richard L. Florida, *The Rise of the Creative Class* (New York: Basic Books, 2004) and *The Flight of the Creative Class* (New York: Harper Business, 2005).
9. See OECD, *Education at a Glance 2015: OECD Indicators* (OECD Publishing, 2016), Indicators A5 and A6.
10. I updated to 2016 figures as follows: Take median usual weekly earnings (2015 data); adjust with CPI to 2016; multiply by 52; then multiply by 40 as data are for persons aged 25 and over and retirement age is assumed to be 65. See https://www.bls.gov/emp/ep_chart_001.htm.
11. A more detailed review of policy goals is presented in Chapter 4 of Michael Mintrom, *Contemporary Policy Analysis* (New York: Oxford University Press, 2012).
12. Dinah Walker, *Trends in US Military Spending,* Report to Council on Foreign Relations (New York: Council on Foreign Relations, 2014).
13. For a longer discussion of the work of policy analysts, see Chapter 2, "What Policy Analysts Do," in Mintrom, *Contemporary Policy Analysis.*
14. Peter Self, *Econocrats and the Policy Process: The Politics and Philosophy of Cost-Benefit Analysis* (London: Macmillan, 1975).
15. Michael Mintrom and Claire Williams, "Public Policy Debate and the Rise of Policy Analysis," in *Routledge Handbook of Public Policy,* eds. Eduardo Araral Jr. et al. (Oxon: Routledge, 2013), pp. 3–16.

16. Jean Hartley et al., "Public Value and Political Astuteness in the Work of Public Managers: The Art of the Possible," *Public Administration* 93, no. 1 (2015): 195–211.

17. A more lengthy discussion of policy instruments is provided in Chapter 3, "What Governments Do," in Mintrom, *Contemporary Policy Analysis.*

18. Marc Wilson, "Safety Concerns of Startup Airlines." *Journal of Air Transportation World Wide* 2, no. 1 (1997): 1–30.

19. Michael E. Porter, Scott Stern, and Michael Green, "Social Progress Index 2014," *Skoll World Forum on Social Entrepreneurship,* April 8 (London: Skoll Foundation, 2014).

20. Porter et al., 42.

CHAPTER 2

1. Quoted in Robert Pear, "If Only Laws Were Like Sausages," *New York Times,* December 5, 2010, p. WK3.

2. Among the many authors who have previously characterized policy making as a series of stages, there are some differences in the labels placed on each stage. However, there is broad agreement concerning the sequencing of the stages.

3. Paul Pierson, "Increasing Returns, Path Dependence, and the Study of Politics," *American Political Science Review* 94, no. 2 (June 2000): 251–67.

4. John W. Kingdon, *Agendas, Alternatives, and Public Policies,* 2nd ed. (Boston: Longman, 2011), and Deborah Stone, *Policy Paradox: The Art of Political Decision Making* (New York: W.W. Norton & Company, 2012) have both contributed lists of such factors.

5. See James A. Stimson, *Public Opinion in America: Moods, Cycles, and Swings,* 2nd ed. (Boulder, CO: Westview Press, 1999).

6. Paul R. Krugman, *Peddling Prosperity: Economic Sense and Nonsense in the Age of Diminished Expectations* (New York: W.W. Norton, 1995).

7. Kingdon (2011) refers to this as "coupling," pp. 172–79.

8. Michael Fullan, *The New Meaning of Educational Change,* 4th ed. (Teachers College Press, New York, 2007).

9. Steven N. S. Cheung, "Roofs or Stars: The Stated Intents and Actual Effects of a Rents Ordinance," in *Empirical Studies in Institutional Change,* eds. Lee J. Alston, Thrainn Eggertson, and Douglass C. North (New York: Cambridge University Press, 1996), chap. 6.

10. Michael Howlett, M. Ramesh, and Anthony Perl, *Studying Public Policy: Policy Cycles & Policy Subsystems,* 3rd ed. (Don Mills, Ontario: Oxford University Press, 2009).

11. See, e.g., Peter H. Rossi, Mark W. Lipsey, and Howard E. Freeman, *Evaluation: A Systematic Approach,* 7th ed. (Thousand Oaks, CA: Sage, 2003); Carol H. Weiss, *Evaluation: Methods for Studying Programs and Policies,* 2nd ed. (Upper Saddle River, NJ: Prentice Hall, 1998).

12. Kathleen O'Toole, "Economist Says Civil Rights Movement Was Economic Success," Stanford News Service (news release), January 26, 2000, http://news.stanford.edu/pr/00/000126CivilRightsEcon.html.

13. Supreme Court Justice Louis Brandeis, *New York Ice Co. vs. Liebmann,* dissenting opinion, 1932.

14. Jack L. Walker, "The Diffusion of Innovations among the American States," *American Political Science Review* 63, no. 3 (1969): 880–99.

15. See, e.g., Paul A. Sabatier and Hank Jenkins-Smith, eds., *Policy Change and Learning: An Advocacy Coalition Approach* (Boulder, CO: Westview Press, 1993).

16. Thomas R. Dye, *Who's Running America: Institutional Leadership in the United States* (Englewood Cliffs, NJ: Prentice-Hall, 1976). This book has been updated many times; see, e.g., *Who's Running America? The Obama Reign,* 8th ed. (Boulder, CO: Paradigm Publishers, 2014).

17. A decades-long debate followed publication of Charles A. Beard's *Economic Interpretation of the Constitution of the United States* (New York: Macmillan, 1913).

18. See, e.g., Daniel Carpenter (2001). *The Forging of Bureaucratic Autonomy: Networks, Reputations and Policy Innovation in Executive Agencies, 1862–1928.* Princeton, NJ: Princeton University Press.

19. Peter A. Hall and Rosemary C. R. Taylor, "Political Science and the Three New Institutionalisms," *Political Studies* 44, no. 5 (1996): 936–57.

20. James G. March and Johan P. Olsen, *Rediscovering Institutions: The Organizational Basis of Politics* (New York: Free Press, 1989).

21. Charles E. Lindblom, "The Science of 'Muddling Through.'" *Public Administration Review* 19, no. 2 (1959): 79–88. Lindblom's characterization of policy making as "muddling through" drew on Herbert Simon's (1947) ideas about bounded rationality and administrative behavior. See Herbert Simon, *Administrative Behavior: A Study of Decision-Making Processes in Administrative Organization* (New York: Macmillan, 1947).

22. Charles E. Lindblom, *The Policy-Making Process* (Englewood Cliffs, NJ: Prentice Hall, 1968), 93.

23. Aaron B. Wildavsky (1964), *The Politics of the Budgetary Process.* (Boston: Little, Brown, 1964).

24. John W. Kingdon, *Agendas, Alternatives, and Public Policies,* updated 2nd ed. (Boston: Little, Brown, 2011), pp. 87–89.

25. Ibid., 165.

26. Frank R. Baumgartner and Bryan D. Jones, *Agendas and Instability in American Politics* (Chicago: University of Chicago Press, 1993). This book was released in a second edition in 2009.

27. See Paul A. Sabatier, "An Advocacy Coalition Framework of Policy Change and the Role of Policy-Oriented Learning Therein," *Policy Sciences* 21, no. 2 (1988): 129–68. See also Paul A. Sabatier and Hank C. Jenkins-Smith, eds., *Policy Change and Learning: An Advocacy Coalition Approach* (Boulder, CO: Westview Press, 1993); Paul A. Sabatier and Christopher M. Weible, "The Advocacy Coalition Framework: Innovations and Clarifications," in *Theories of the Policy Process,* 2nd ed., Paul A. Sabatier, ed. (Boulder, CO: Westview Press, 2016), 189–217.

28. Paul A. Sabatier, "An Advocacy Coalition Framework of Policy Change and the Role of Policy-Oriented Learning Therein," *Policy Sciences* 21, no. 2 (1988): 139.

CHAPTER 3

1. See Jonathan Boston, *Governing for the Future: Designing Democratic Institutions for a Better Tomorrow* (Bingley, UK: Emerald Group Publishing, 2016). See also Alan Jacobs, *Governing for the Long Term: Democracy and the Politics of Investment* (New York: Cambridge University Press, 2011).

2. Charles E. Lindblom, "The Science of Muddling Through," *Public Administration Review* 19, no. 2 (Spring 1959): 84.

3. Rather, there is a process of what Carol H. Weiss, in *Social Science Research and Decision-Making* (New York: Columbia University Press, 1980), has termed "knowledge creep and decision accretion."

4. Jim Nussle and Peter Orszag, "Let's Play Moneyball," chap. 1 in *Moneyball for Government* (Washington, DC: Results for America, 2014).

5. Ibid., 4.

6. Brian Head, "Three Lenses of Evidence-Based Policy," *Australian Journal of Public Administration* 67, no. 1 (2008): 1–11.

7. Thomas McCraw, *Prophets of Regulation* (Cambridge, MA: Belknap Press of Harvard University Press, 1984).

8. See "Alfred Kahn: Alfred Kahn, Deregulator, Died on December 27th, Aged 93," *The Economist,* January 20, 2011 (obituary published in print edition).

9. Daniel Yergin and Joseph Stanislaw, *The Commanding Heights: The Battle between Government and the Marketplace That Is Remaking the Modern World* (New York: Simon & Schuster, 2002).

10. David Hyman's *Public Finance: A Contemporary Application of Theory to Policy,* 10th ed. (Boston: Cengage Learning, 2010) is an exception, where a chapter is devoted to portraying cost-benefit analysis as a tool for assessing government investments. Patricia Pulliam Phillips and Jack J. Phillips's *Measuring ROI in the Public Sector* (Alexandria, VA: American Society for Training and Development, 2002) offers an interesting contrast to the current set of public finance and public policy textbooks. Phillips and Phillips present a series of case studies that build on the common theme of applying

investment analysis to calculating the benefits of government-sponsored training programs.

11. John W. Kingdon, *Agendas, Alternatives, and Public Policies,* 2nd ed. (Boston: Longman, 2011), 141.

12. Harold Demsetz, "Information and Efficiency: Another Viewpoint," *Journal of Law and Economics* 12, no. 1 (1969): 1–22.

13. See, e.g., William G. Howell et al., *The Education Gap: Vouchers and Urban Schools* (Washington, DC: Brookings Institution Press, 2006).

14. See, e.g., Michael Mintrom, "Building Expert Knowledge," chap. 3 in *People Skills for Policy Analysts* (Washington, DC: Georgetown University Press, 2003).

15. See Nancy Cartwright and Jeremy Hardie, *Evidence-Based Policy: A Practical Guide to Doing It Better* (New York: Oxford University Press, 2012).

16. Gary Banks, "Evidence-Based Policy Making: What Is It? How Do We Get It?" in *Critical Reflections on Australian Public Policy,* ed. John Wanna (Canberra: Australian National University Press, 2010).

17. George Argyrous, "Evidence Based Policy: Principles of Transparency and Accountability," *Australian Journal of Public Administration* 71, no. 4 (2012): 457–68.

18. Specifically, since random assignment cannot be guaranteed in quasi-experimental studies, researchers must incorporate into their modeling work all other plausible explanations for observed differences in valued outcomes between entities that were exposed to the programs and those that were not.

19. John Hattie, *Visible Learning: A Synthesis of Over 800 Meta-analyses Relating to Achievement* (London, UK: Routledge, 2009).

20. The return on investment studies performed by the Washington State Institute for Public Policy indicate widely divergent levels of return on investment for a range of different policies and programs; see Stephanie Lee et al., *Return on Investment: Evidence-Based Options to Improve Statewide Outcomes,* Document No. 12–04–1201 (Olympia: Washington State Institute for Public Policy, 2012). Straightforward advice on conducting cost-benefit analysis is provided in chap. 13 of Michael Minton's *Contemporary Policy Analysis* (New York: Oxford University Press, 2012). The currently most authoritative and comprehensive treatment of cost-benefit analysis is provided by Anthony Boardman et al., *Cost-Benefit Analysis: Concepts and Practice,* 4th ed. (New York: Pearson, 2014).

21. James J. Heckman, "Skill Formation and the Economics of Investing in Disadvantaged Children," *Science* 312, No. 5782 (June 2006): 1900–1902.

22. Lawrence J. Schweinhart et al., *Lifetime Effects: The High/Scope Perry Preschool Study through Age 40* (Ypsilanti, MI: High/Scope Press, 2005).

23. Brenda Bushouse, *Universal Preschool: Policy Change, Stability, and the Pew Charitable Trusts* (Albany, NY: SUNY Press, 2009).

24. Wiji Arulampalam, Paul Gregg, and Mary Gregory, "Unemployment Scarring," *The Economic Journal* 111, no. 475 (November 2001): 577–84.

25. Claudia Thomas, Michaela Benzeval, and Stephen A. Stansfeld, "Employment Traditions and Mental Health: An Analysis from the British Household Panel Survey," *Journal of Epidemiology and Community Health* 59, no. 3 (2005): 243–49.

26. Joanna Abhayaratna and Ralph Lattimore, *Workforce Participation Rates—How Does Australia Compare? Staff Working Paper* (Melbourne, Australia: Productivity Commission, 2006).

27. Richard Hendra et al., *Breaking the Low-Pay, No-Pay Cycle: Final Evidence from the UK Employment Retention and Advancement (ERA) Demonstration,* Research Report No. 765 (London, UK: Department for Work and Pensions, 2011).

28. Ibid., 207–209.

29. Hendra et al., *Breaking the Low Pay, No Pay Cycle.*

30. Paul E. Peterson and Mark C. Rom, *Welfare Magnets: A New Case for a National Standard* (Washington, DC: Brookings Institution, 1990).

31. Peter K. Eisinger, *The Rise of the Entrepreneurial State: State and Local Economic Development Policy in the United States* (Madison: University of Wisconsin Press, 1988).

32. Kirsten Monaco and Jeffrey Cohen, *Ports and Highways Infrastructure Investment and Interstate*

Spatial Spillovers, final report (Long Beach, CA: METRANS, 2006).

33. Paul E. Peterson, *The Price of Federalism* (Washington, DC: Brookings Institution Press, 1995).

34. Madeleine Bunting, "Market Has No Use for the Elderly," *The Guardian Weekly,* October 28, 2011, raised the concern.

35. See Michael Mintrom, "Gender Analysis" and "Race Analysis," respectively chaps. 14 and 15 in *Contemporary Policy Analysis.* (New York: Oxford University Press, 2012).

36. Heckman, "Skill Formation."

37. Jens Ludwig and Deborah A. Phillips, "Long-Term Effects of Head Start on Low-Income Children," *Annals of the New York Academy of Sciences* 1136, no. 1 (2008): 257–68.

38. The mission statement is provided on the institute's website, http://www.wsipp.wa.gov/.

39. Lee et al., *Return on Investment,* p. 3.

40. The following overview of work at WSIPP is informed by discussion in Lee et al., 1–2.

CHAPTER 4

1. See, e.g., Neil S. Grigg, *Infrastructure Finance: The Business of Infrastructure for a Sustainable Future* (Hoboken, NJ: John Wiley & Sons, 2010); Waheed Uddin, W. Ronald Hudson, and Ralph Haas, *Public Infrastructure Asset Management,* 2nd ed. (New York: McGraw-Hill Higher Education, 2013).

2. See, e.g., Frank Baumgartner and Beth L. Leech, *Basic Interests: The Importance of Groups in Politics and in Political Science* (Princeton, NJ: Princeton University Press, 1998); Jeffrey M. Berry and Clyde Wilcox, *The Interest Group Society* (New York: Longman, 2009); Alfred E. Kahn, *The Economics of Regulation: Volume 1—Economic Principles* (New York: John Wiley & Sons, 1970); Alfred E. Kahn, *The Economics of Regulation: Volume 2—Institutional Issues* (New York: John Wiley & Sons, 1971); Roger C. Noll and Bruce M. Owen, *The Political Economy of Deregulation* (Washington, DC: American Enterprise Institute, 1983).

3. See Emma G. Fitzimmons, "Surge in Ridership Pushes New York Subway to Limit," *New York Times,* May 3, 2016, A15.

4. Kyle M. Kirschling, *An Economic Analysis of Rapid Transit in New York, 1870–2010* (New York: thesis completed in the Columbia University School of Architecture, Planning, and Preservation, 2012).

5. Douglass C. North, *Institutions, Institutional Change, and Economic Performance* (Cambridge, England: Cambridge University Press, 1990).

6. Lawrence S. Rothenberg, *Regulation, Organizations, and Politics: Motor Freight Policy at the Interstate Commerce Commission* (Ann Arbor, MI: University of Michigan Press, 1994).

7. Milton Friedman, *Capitalism and Freedom* (Chicago: University of Chicago Press, 1962); Kahn, *The Economics of Regulation: Volume 2.*

8. Peltzman, "The Economic Theory of Regulation after a Decade of Deregulation," *Brookings Papers on Economic Activity. Microeconomics* (1989); Clifford Winston et al., *The Economic Effects of Surface Freight Deregulation* (Washington, DC: Brookings Institution, 1990).

9. See John M. Barry, "Is New Orleans Safe?" *New York Times,* August 2, 2015, SR1.

10. Quoted in Douglas A. Kysar and Thomas O. McGarity, "Did NEPA Drown New Orleans? The Levees, the Blame Game, and the Hazards of Hindsight," *Duke Law Journal* (2006): 179–235.

11. See, e.g., Barry B. LePatner, *Too Big to Fall: America's Failing Infrastructure and the Way Forward* (New York: Foster Publications, 2010).

12. Jeffrey Delmon, *Public-Private Partnership Projects in Infrastructure: An Essential Guide for Policy Makers* (Cambridge, NY: Cambridge University Press, 2011); OECD, *Strategic Transport Infrastructure Needs to 2030* (Paris: OECD Publishing, 2012).

13. Edward Gramlich, "Infrastructure Investment: A Review Essay," *Journal of Economic Literature* 32, no. 3. (1994): 1176–1196; LePatner, *Too Big to Fall.*

14. As explained by Costas Panagopoulos and Joshua Schank in *All Roads Lead to Congress:*

The $300 Billion Fight over Highway Funding (Washington, DC: CQ Press, 2008).

15. Rosabeth Moss Kanter, *Move: Putting America's Infrastructure Back in the Lead* (New York: W.W. Norton, 2015), 269.

16. See Gramlich, "Infrastructure Investment: A Review Essay" (1994).

17. See, e.g., David A. Aschauer, "Is Public Expenditure Productive?" *Journal of Monetary Economics* 23, n. 2 (1989): 177–200.

18. Alicia H. Munnell, "Policy Watch: Infrastructure Investment and Economic Growth," *Journal of Economic Perspectives* 6, no. 4 (1992): 189–98.

19. David A. Aschauer, "Genuine Economic Returns to Infrastructure Investment," *Policy Studies Journal* 21, no. 2 (1993): 380–390. Aschauer went on to suggest that "[a]s long as the returns to infrastructure investment exceed the growth rate of the economy, an increase in public investment—financed through a reduction in either public or private consumption—will tilt national consumption favorably towards the future. If it is true that the United States does not save and invest enough, then one way partly to overcome this deficiency is through appropriate investment in our infrastructure" (p. 389).

20. For India, see Xiaobo Zhang and Shenggen Fan, "How Productive Is Infrastructure? A New Approach and Evidence from Rural India," *American Journal of Agricultural Economics* 86, no. 2 (2004): 492–501; for South Africa, see Johannes W. Fedderke and Aylit T. Romm, "Growth Impact and Determinants of Foreign Direct Investment into South Africa, 1956–2003," *Economic Modelling* 23, no. 5 (2006): 738–60; and for Sweden, see Ernst Berndt and Bengt Hansson, "Measuring the Contribution of Public Infrastructure Capital in Sweden," *Scandinavian Journal of Economics* 94, Supplement: Proceedings of a Symposium on Productivity Concepts and Measurement Problems: Welfare, Quality and Productivity in the Service Industries (1992): S151–68.

21. John G. Fernald, "Roads to Prosperity? Assessing the Link between Public Capital and Productivity," *American Economic Review* 83, no. 3 (1999): 619–38.

22. Fernald's (1999) findings are consistent with earlier estimates produced by the Congressional Budget Office (1988) that indicated overall returns of 15 percent on new urban highways and of 35 percent on highway maintenance programs (see Gramlich, 1994, Table 4). Recent efforts to assess the impacts of other forms of infrastructure on broader economic performance have taken a similar methodological approach as that used by Fernald (1999). For example, Nina Czernich and her colleagues (2011) estimated the effect of broadband infrastructure, which enables high-speed Internet, on economic growth in a set of wealthy countries in the years 1996 to 2007. They found that a 10 percentage point increase in broadband penetration raised annual per capita growth by 0.9 to 1.5 percentage points. That represents an extraordinary return on investment. See Nina Czernich et al., "Broadband Infrastructure and Economic Growth," *The Economic Journal* 121, no. 552 (2011): 505–32.

23. See, e.g., Uddin et al., *Public Infrastructure Asset Management*, chap. 14.

24. Uddin et al., 21.

25. LePatner, *Too Big to Fall*, 41–76.

26. I have standardized all dollar amounts in this case study to 2016 values.

27. LePatner, *Too Big to Fall*, 68. The calculation is: Actual rehabilitation cost in 1992 – Estimated cost of routine maintenance that was not performed over 89 years = Waste, or money that could have been saved by performing the routine maintenance. In numbers (millions), this is $760 – $281 = $479.

28. William L. Megginson and Jeffry M. Netter, "From State to Market: A Survey of Empirical Studies on Privatization," *Journal of Economic Literature* 39, no. 2. (2001): 321–89.

29. Carlo Cambini and Laura Rondi. "Incentive Regulation and Investment: Evidence from European Energy Utilities." *Journal of Regulatory Economics* 38, no. 1 (2010): 1–26; Mark Armstrong and David E. M. Sappington, "Regulation,

Competition, and Liberalization," *Journal of Economic Literature* 44, no. 2 (2006): 325–66.

30. Megginson and Netter, "From State to Market."

31. Kira R. Fabrizio, Nancy L. Rose, and Catherine D. Wolfram, "Do Markets Reduce Costs? Assessing the Impact of Regulatory Restructuring on U.S. Electric Generation Efficiency," *American Economic Review* 97, no. 4 (2007): 1250–77.

32. Fabrizio et al., "Do Markets Reduce Costs?," 1259.

33. Lucas W. Davis and Catherine D. Wolfram, "Deregulation, Consolidation, and Efficiency: Evidence from U.S. Nuclear Power," *American Economic Journal: Applied Economics* 4, no. 4 (2012): 194–225.

34. Ibid., 203.

35. Ibid., 195.

36. Catherine Hausman, "Corporate Incentives and Nuclear Safety." *American Economic Journal: Economic Policy* 6, no. 3 (2014): 178–206.

37. OECD, *Strategic Transport Infrastructure Needs*; Thomas L. Friedman, "A Word from the Wise," *New York Times*, March 2, 2010, A31.

CHAPTER 5

1. See Heritage Foundation, *2017 Index of U.S. Military Strength* (Washington, DC: Heritage Foundation, 2016), http://index.heritage.org/military/2017/.

2. Gerd Gigerenzer, "Out of the Frying Pan into the Fire: Behavioral Reactions to Terrorist Attacks," *Risk Analysis* 26, no. 2 (2006): 347–51.

3. Gigerenzer, p. 347.

4. Graham T. Allison and Robert Blackwill, *America's National Interests* (Cambridge, MA: Commission on America's National Interests, 2000), http://www.belfercenter.org/sites/default/files/legacy/files/amernatinter.pdf.

5. Robert D. Putnam, "Diplomacy and Domestic Politics: The Logic of Two-Level Games," *International Organization* 42, no. 3 (1988): 427–60.

6. David Petraeus and Michael E. O'Hanlon, "America's Awesome Military," Brookings Report (Washington, DC: Brookings Institution, September 30, 2016), https://www.brookings.edu/research/americas-awesome-military.

7. Coalition for Fiscal and National Security, "Strengths at Home and Abroad: Ensuring America's Fiscal and National Security" (Washington, DC: Peter G. Peterson Foundation, May 10, 2016), http://www.pgpf.org/sites/default/files/Strength-at-Home-and-Abroad-Ensuring-Americas-Fiscal-and-National-Security.pdf.

8. Russell Frank Weigley, *The American Way of War: A History of United States Military Strategy and Policy* (Bloomington: Indiana University Press, 1960).

9. Benjamin Starr, "Visualizing the Frightening Power of Nuclear Bombs." *Visual News* (April 24, 2012), https://www.visualnews.com/2012/04/24/visualizing-the-frightening-power-of-nuclear-bombs.

10. See Arms Control Association, "Nuclear Weapons: Who Has What at a Glance," https://www.armscontrol.org, accessed August 4, 2017.

11. See Sam Nunn, "Foreword," *NTI Nuclear Security Index: Building a Framework for Assurance, Accountability, and Action*, 3rd ed. (Washington, DC: Nuclear Threat Initiative, January 2016), 3, http://www.ntiindex.org/wp-content/uploads/2016/03/NTI_2016-Index-Report_MAR-25-2.pdf.

12. See Nicolaus Mills, *Winning the Peace: The Marshall Plan and America's Coming of Age as a Superpower* (Hoboken, NJ: John Wiley & Sons, 2008).

13. Derek S. Reveron, Nikolas K. Gvosdev, and Mackubin Thomas Owens, *US Foreign Policy and Defense Strategy: The Evolution of an Incidental Superpower* (Washington, DC: Georgetown University Press, 2014).

14. William L. Painter, "Select Issues in Homeland Security Policy for the 114th Congress" (Washington, DC: Congressional Research Service, May 19, 2015).

15. Kevin J. Strom, John S. Hollywood, and Mark Pope, *Terrorist Plots against the United States: What We Have Really Faced, and How We Might Best Defend against It*, RAND Homeland Security and Defense Center Working Paper (Santa Monica, CA: RAND Corporation, 2015).

16. Lois M. Davis et al., "Assessment of the State and Local Anti-Terrorism Training (SLATT) Program" (Santa Monica, CA: RAND Corporation, 2016).

17. See Kara E. Rudolph et al., "Association between Connecticut's Permit-to-Purchase Handgun Law and Homicides," *American Journal of Public Health* 105, no. 8 (2015): e49–e54.

18. See Matthew Miller, David Hemenway, and Deborah Azrael, "State-Level Homicide Victimization Rates in the US in Relation to Survey Measures of Household Firearm Ownership, 2001–2003," *Social Science and Medicine* 64, no. 3 (2007): 656–64.

19. The Brady Campaign State Scorecard 2014, published in March 2015. See http://www.crimadvisor.com/data/Brady-State-Scorecard-2014.pdf.

20. The state scores used in the scorecard take account of the annual number of gun deaths in each state, but this is not a major factor in the development of the individual state scores.

21. Kaiser Family Foundation, "Number of Deaths Due to Injury by Firearms per 100,000 Population, 2014," http://kff.org/other/state-indicator/firearms-death-rate-per-100000/.

22. The 2015 Brady Scorecard and the 2014 deaths due to injury by firearms are the latest available at the time of writing. An earlier analysis using the 2014 Brady Scorecard results and 2013 deaths due to injury by firearms produced results highly consistent with those reported here.

23. Heritage Foundation, *2017 Index*, p. 8.

24. International Campaign to Abolish Nuclear Weapons, "UN Votes to Outlaw Nuclear Weapons in 2017, October 27, 2016, http://www.icanw.org/campaign-news/un-votes-to-outlaw-nuclear-weapons-in-2017/.

25. Craig Whitlock and Bob Woodward, "Pentagon Buries Evidence of Bureaucratic Waste," *Washington Post*, December 5, 2016. See the PowerPoint slides associated with a public presentation of the report in January 2015 at http://dbb.defense.gov/Portals/35/Documents/Meetings/2015/2015-01/RD%20Task%20Group%20Final%20Brief_6Feb2015.pdf

26. Peter J. May, Ashley E. Jochim, and Joshua Sapotichne, "Constructing Homeland Security: An Anemic Policy Regime," *Policy Studies Journal* 39, no. 2 (2011): 285–307.

27. See William L. Painter, "Selected Issues in Homeland Security Policy for the 114th Congress" (Washington, DC: Congressional Research Service, May 19, 2015), 66.

28. Keith Hartley, "Defense Economics: Achievements and Challenges," *The Economics of Peace and Security Journal* 2, no. 1 (2007): 45–50.

29. An excellent overview, told through the career of a key defense strategist, is Andrew Krepinevich and Barry Watts, *The Last Warrior: Andrew Marshall and the Shaping of Modern American Defense Strategy* (New York: Basic Books, 2015). See also E. S. Quade, "A History of Cost-Effectiveness" (Santa Monica, CA: The RAND Corporation, 1971), http://www.rand.org/pubs/papers/P4557.html.

30. Francois Melese, Anke Richter, and Binyam Solomon, "Introduction—Military Cost-Benefit Analysis (CBA): Theory and Practice," in *Military Cost-Benefit Analysis: Theory and Practice*, eds. Francois Melese, Anke Richter, and Binyam Solomon (London: Routledge, 2015), chap. 1.

31. W. Greer, "An Application of Military Cost-Benefit Analysis in a Major Defense Acquisition: The C-17 Transport Aircraft," in *Military Cost-Benefit Analysis: Theory and Practice*, eds. Francois Melese, Anke Richter, and Binyam Solomon (London: Routledge, 2015), chap. 15.

32. Leslie Wayne, "Pentagon Struggles with Cost Overruns and Delays," *New York Times*, July 11, 2006, C1.

33. A small body of economic literature has addressed this concern, which takes us into the realm of game theory and contract specification. A foundational contribution is that by Jean-Jacques Laffont and Jean Tirole, *A Theory of Incentives in Procurement and Regulation* (Cambridge, MA: MIT Press, 1993).

34. Jane Bullock, George Haddow, and Damon P. Coppola, *Introduction to Homeland Security*, 5th ed. (Waltham, MA: Butterworth-Heinemann, 2016), 293.

35. Editorial Board, "The Airport Security Sieve," *New York Times*, June 2, 2015, A28.

36. Sendhil Mullainathan and Richard H. Thaler, "Waiting in Line for the Illusion of Security," *New York Times*, May 27, 2016, BU4.

37. Henry H. Willis and Michael A. Brown, "Out of Line: How to Better Protect Airports from Terrorist Attacks," *US News and World Report,* May 2, 2016; see also The RAND blog, http://www.rand.org/blog/2016/05/out-of-line-how-to-better-protect-airports-from-terrorist.html.

38. Mark G. Stewart and John Mueller, "Terrorism Risks and Cost-Benefit Analysis of Aviation Security," *Risk Analysis* 33, no. 5 (2013), pp. 893–908.

39. Donald Rumsfeld testimony before the U.S. Senate Armed Service Committee hearing on the treatment of Iraqi prisoners, May 7, 2004.

40. Eric Fair, "Owning Up to Torture," *New York Times,* March 19, 2016, SR9.

41. Paul Gronke et al., "US Public Opinion on Torture, 2001–2009," *PS: Political Science and Politics* 43, no. 3 (2010), pp. 437–44.

42. Carl Levin and Jay Rockefeller, "The Torture Report Must Be Saved," *New York Times,* December 9, 2016, A23.

CHAPTER 6

1. "Every time you stop a school, you will have to build a jail. What you gain at one end you lose at the other. It's like feeding a dog on his own tail. It won't fatten the dog." Mark Twain, speech, November 23, 1900.

2. Richard Florida, *The Rise of the Creative Class—Revisited: Revised and Expanded* (New York: Basic Books, 2014).

3. Ken Robinson, *Finding Your Element: How to Discover Your Talents and Passions and Transform Your Life* (London: Penguin, 2013).

4. Ken Robinson and Lou Aronica, *Creative Schools: The Grassroots Revolution That's Transforming Education* (London: Penguin, 2016).

5. Ibid., 182–86.

6. Mark Blaug, "Where Are We Now in the Economics of Education?" *Economics of Education Review* 4, no. 1 (1985): 17–28.

7. William Hayes, *Horace Mann's Vision of the Public Schools: Is it Still Relevant?* (Lanham, MD: Rowman & Littlefield Education, 2006).

8. Douglas S. Reed, *On Equal Terms: The Constitutional Politics of Educational Opportunity* (Princeton, NJ: Princeton University Press, 2001).

9. David B. Tyack, *The One Best System: A History of American Urban Education* (Cambridge, MA: Harvard University Press, 1974).

10. Jack H. Knott and Gary J. Miller, *Reforming Bureaucracy: The Politics of Institutional Choice* (Englewood Cliffs, NJ: Prentice-Hall, 1987).

11. See Michael Berkman and Eric Plutzer, *Evolution, Creationism, and the Battle to Control America's Classrooms* (New York: Cambridge University Press, 2010).

12. Terry M. Moe, *Special Interest: Teachers Unions and America's Public Schools* (Washington, DC: Brookings Institution Press, 2011).

13. See Michael G. Fullan, *The New Meaning of Educational Change,* 4th ed. (New York: Teachers College Press, 2016).

14. The National Commission on Excellence in Education, *A Nation at Risk: The Imperative for Educational Reform* (Washington, DC: U.S. Department of Education, 1983), 1.

15. Eric Hanushek and Margaret Raymond, "Does School Accountability Lead to Improved Student Performance?" *Journal of Policy Analysis and Management* 24, no. 2 (2005): 297–327.

16. Helen S. Timperley and Viviane M. Robinson, "Achieving School Improvement through Challenging and Changing Teachers' Schema," *Journal of Educational Change* 2, no. 4 (2001): 281–300.

17. Joe Nathan, *Charter Schools: Creating Hope and Opportunity for American Education.* (San Francisco: Jossey-Bass, 1996); Sandra Vergari, *The Charter School Landscape* (Pittsburgh: University of Pittsburgh Press, 2002).

18. Jack Buckley and Mark Schneider, *Charter Schools: Hope or Hype?* (Princeton, NJ: Princeton University Press, 2007).

19. See Michael Mintrom, "Policy Design for Local Innovation: The Effects of Competition in Public Schooling," *State Politics & Policy Quarterly* 1, n. 4 (2001): 343–63.

20. See Doug Lemov, *Teach Like a Champion 2.0: 62 Techniques That Put Students on the Path To College,* 2nd ed. (San Francisco: Jossey-Bass, 2015).

21. Quoted in Lemov, p. xxxii.

22. Documented in the opening pages of Lemov, 2015.

23. Michael Barber and Mona Mourshed, *How the World's Best Performing School Systems Come Out on Top* (London: McKinsey and Company, 2007).

24. Salman Khan, *The One World Schoolhouse: Education Reimagined* (New York: Grand Central Publishing, 2012).

25. David Tyack and Larry Cuban, *Tinkering toward Utopia: A Century of Public School Reform* (Cambridge, MA: Harvard University Press, 1995).

26. George Psacharopoulos and Harry Anthony Patrinos, "Returns to Investment in Education: A Further Update," *Education Economics* 12, no. 2 (2004): 112.

27. Eric Hanushek and Ludger Woessmann, "The Role of Cognitive Skills in Economic Development," *Journal of Economic Literature* 46, no. 3 (2008): 607–668.

28. Psacharopoulos and Patrinos, p. 117.

29. Theodore Breton, "The Role of Education in Economic Growth: Theory, History, and Current Returns," *Educational Research* 55, no. 2 (2013): 121–38.

30. Ibid., 134.

31. Hanushek and Woessmann, "The Role of Cognitive Skills."

32. Elizabeth Word et al., *The State of Tennessee's Student/Teacher Achievement Ratio (STAR) Project: Technical Report 1985–1990* (Nashville: Tennessee State Department of Education, 1990).

33. Alan B. Krueger, "Economic Considerations and Class Size," *The Economic Journal* 113, no. 485 (2003): F34–F36.

34. Caroline M. Hoxby, "Does Competition among Public Schools Benefit Students and Taxpayers?" *American Economic Review* 90, no. 5 (2000): 1209–38.

35. George W. Bohrnstedt and Brian M. Stecher, *Class Size Reduction in California: Findings from 1999–2001 and 2000–2001* (Sacramento: California Department of Education, 2002).

36. John Hattie, "The Paradox of Reducing Class Size and Improving Learning Outcomes," *International Journal of Educational Research* 43, no. 6 (2005): 387–425.

37. Sara Mosle, "Does Class Size Count?" *New York Times,* May 4, 2013.

CHAPTER 7

1. Matthew Harding and Michael Lovenheim, "The Effect of Prices on Nutrition: Comparing the Impact of Product- and Nutrient-Specific Taxes," Working Paper No. 19781 (Washington, DC: National Bureau of Economic Research, 2014).

2. See "Frequently Asked Questions about Berkeley's Soda Tax," http://www.berkeleyvsbigsoda.com/faq.

3. "Should There Be a Tax on Soda and Other Sugary Drinks?" *Wall Street Journal,* July 12, 2015, https://www.wsj.com/articles/should-there-be-a-tax-on-soda-and-other-sugary-drinks-1436757039.

4. Kenneth J. Arrow, "Uncertainty and the Welfare Economics of Medical Care," *American Economic Review* 53, no. 5 (1963): 941–73.

5. See OECD, *Health at a Glance: OECD Indicators, 2016* (Paris: OECD Publishing, 2016), Table 1.1.2, p. 25.

6. See Steven H. Woolf, and Laudan Aron, eds., *US Health in International Perspective: Shorter Lives, Poorer Health* (Washington, DC: National Academies Press, 2013), especially Box 1-2, "Disparities in Life Expectancy in the United States," pp. 40–41.

7. Raj Chetty et al., "The Association between Income and Life Expectancy in the United States, 2001–2014," *Journal of the American Medical Association* 315, no. 16 (2016): 1750–66.

8. Sandeep C. Kulkarni et al., "Falling Behind: Life Expectancy in US Counties from 2000 to 2007 in an International Context," *Population Health Metrics* 9, no. 1 (2011): 16–27.

9. Miriam J. Laugesen, *Fixing Medical Prices: How Physicians Are Paid* (Cambridge, MA: Harvard University Press, 2016).

10. Mark Peterson, "It was a Different Time: Obama and the Unique Opportunity for Health Care

Reform," *Journal of Health Politics, Policy and Law* 36, no. 3 (2011): 429–36.

11. William G. Weissert and Carol S. Weissert, *Governing Health: The Politics of Health Policy,* 4th ed. (Baltimore, MD: John Hopkins University Press, 2012).

12. This brief summary is based on Kaiser Family Foundation, "A Primer on Medicare: Key Facts about the Medicare Program and the People It Covers," March 2015. See http://kff.org/report-section/a-primer-on-medicare-what-is-medicare/.

13. This brief summary is based on Kaiser Family Foundation, "Medicaid: A Primer," 2013. See http://kff.org/about-kaiser-commission-on-medicaid-and-the-uninsured/.

14. This brief summary draws upon two analyses of the act and its impacts: (1) Jennifer Tolbert, "The Coverage Provisions in the Affordable Care Act: An Update," Kaiser Family Foundation Issue Brief, March 2015, http://kff.org/health-reform/issue-brief/the-coverage-provisions-in-the-affordable-care-act-an-update/; (2) Kaiser Family Foundation, "Summary of the Affordable Care Act," April 23, 2013, http://kff.org/health-reform/fact-sheet/summary-of-the-affordable-care-act/.

15. See http://kff.org/interactive/interactive-maps-estimates-of-enrollment-in-aca-marketplaces-and-medicaid-expansion/.

16. Congressional Budget Office, "How Repealing Portions of the Affordable Care Act Would Affect Health Insurance Coverage and Premiums," January 2017, https://www.cbo.gov/sites/default/files/115th-congress-2017–2018/reports/52371-coverageandpremiums.pdf.

17. Reed Abelson and Margot Sanger-Katz, "Obamacare Isn't in a 'Death Spiral.' (Its Replacement Probably Won't Be Either.)," *New York Times,* March 16, 2017, A12.

18. Miriam J. Laugesen and Sherry A. Glied, "Higher Fees Paid to US Physicians Drive Higher Spending for Physician Services Compared to Other Countries," *Health Affairs* 30, no. 9 (2011): 1647–56.

19. See Sharon K. Long and Karen Stockley, "Sustaining Health Reform in a Recession: An Update on Massachusetts as of Fall 2009," *Health Affairs* 29, no. 6 (2010): 1234–41.

20. Kaiser Family Foundation, "Health Coverage and Uninsured," accessed August 7, 2017, http://kff.org/state-category/health-coverage-uninsured/.

21. Kaiser Family Foundation, "Massachusetts Health Care Reform: Six Years Later," May 2012, http://kff.org/health-costs/issue-brief/massachusetts-health-care-reform-six-years-later/.

22. All information in this paragraph is drawn from the Centers for Disease Control and Prevention "Fast Facts" sheet concerning tobacco consumption. See http://www.cdc.gov/tobacco/data_statistics/fact_sheets/fast_facts/index.htm.

23. The information in the table was collated by the author, based on OECD data. See http://www.oecd-ilibrary.org/social-issues-migration-health/data/oecd-health-statistics/oecd-health-data-non-medical-determinants-of-health_data-00546-en.

24. See Dan E. Peterson et al., "The Effect of State Cigarette Tax Increases on Cigarette Sales, 1955 to 1988," *American Journal of Public Health* 82, no. 1 (1992): 94–96.

25. Data in this table were collated by the author from Centers for Disease Control and Prevention, "Current Cigarette Smoking among Adults in the United States, last updated December 1, 2016, http://www.cdc.gov/tobacco/data_statistics/fact_sheets/adult_data/cig_smoking/. State cigarette excise tax rates in 2013 were obtained from the Tax Foundation, "State Cigarette Excise Taxes, 2009–2013," February 27, 2013, http://taxfoundation.org/article/state-cigarette-excise-tax-rates-2009-2013.

26. Charles R. Shipan and Craig Volden, "Bottom-up Federalism: The Diffusion of Antismoking Policies from US Cities to States," *American Journal of Political Science* 50, no. 4 (2006): 825–43.

27. See Jonathan Boston, *Governing for the Future: Designing Democratic Institutions for a Better Tomorrow* (Bingley, UK: Emerald Group Publishing, 2016).

28. Bryan Luce et al., "The Return on Investment in Health Care: From 1980 to 2000," *Value in Health* 9, no. 3 (2006): 146–156.

29. Kevin M. Murphy and Robert H. Topel, "The Value of Health and Longevity," Working Paper 11405 (Cambridge, MA: National Bureau of Economic Research, 2005).

30. See National Institutes of Health Budget information, https://www.nih.gov/about-nih/what-we-do/budget.

31. Karen Joynt et al., "Contribution of Preventable Acute Care Spending to Total Spending for High-Cost Medicare Patients," *Journal of the American Medical Association* 309, no. 24 (2013): 2572–78.

32. J. Michael McWilliams et al., "Use of Health Services by Previously Uninsured Medicare Beneficiaries," *New England Journal of Medicine* 357, no. 2 (2007): 143–53.

33. David Cutler and Wendy Everett, "Thinking Outside the Pillbox—Medication Adherence as a Priority for Health Care Reform," *New England Journal of Medicine* 362, no. 17 (2010): 1553–1555.

34. James Mongan, Timothy Ferris, and Thomas Lee, "Options for Slowing the Growth of Health Care Costs," *New England Journal of Medicine* 358, no. 14 (2008): 1509–14.

35. Harold A. Pollack, "Prevention and Public Health." *Journal of Health Politics* 36, no. 3 (2011): 518.

36. All the information contained in this table is based on evidence reported by Katherine Baicker, David Cutler, and Zirui Song, "Workplace Wellness Programs Can Generate Savings," *Health Affairs* 29, no. 2 (2010): 304–11.

37. Ibid., 304–311.

38. Martin Luther King Jr., address to the Second National Convention of the Medical Committee for Human Rights, Chicago, March 25, 1966.

39. Paul Krugman, "Slavery's Long Shadow," *New York Times,* June 22, 2015, A19.

40. Kaiser Family Foundation, "Status of State Action on the Medicaid Expansion Decision," http://kff.org/health-reform/state-indicator/state-activity-around-expanding-medicaid-under-the-affordable-care-act/.

41. The U.S. Bureau of the Census website: http://www.census.gov/quickfacts/table/ PST045214/00.

42. Tim Usherwood, "How New Technologies Are Shaking Up Health Care," *The Conversation,* September 2, 2015, see http://theconversation.com/how-new-technologies-are-shaking-up-health-care-42318.

43. Jonathan Bush and Stephen Baker, *Where Does It Hurt? An Entrepreneur's Guide to Fixing Health Care* (New York: Portfolio/Penguin, 2014).

CHAPTER 8

1. Bernadette D. Procter, Jessica L. Semega, and Melissa A. Kollar, *Income and Poverty in the United States: 2015* (Washington, DC: U.S. Census Bureau, 2016).

2. Peter Townsend, *International Analysis of Poverty* (Abingdon-on-Thames: Routledge, 2016), 84.

3. See John Iceland, *Poverty in America: A Handbook* (Berkeley: University of California Press, 2012), 10. The figures reported there were updated to 2016 by the author.

4. For discussions of poverty and stress in families, see Catherine DeCarlo Santiago, Martha E. Wadsworth, and Jessica Stump, "Socioeconomic Status, Neighborhood Disadvantage, and Poverty-Related Stress: Prospective Effects on Psychological Syndromes among Diverse Low-Income Families," *Journal of Economic Psychology* 32, no. 2 (2011): 218–30. See also Karen Seccombe, "Families in Poverty in the 1990s: Trends, Causes, Consequences, and Lessons Learned," *Journal of Marriage and Family* 62, no. 4 (2000): 1094–113.

5. Sendhil Mullainathan and Eldar Shafir, *Scarcity: Why Having Too Little Means So Much* (New York: Times Books, 2013), 161.

6. Note that this estimate is very close to the World Bank's estimate of 2015 U.S. per capita GDP of $56,115 (adjusted for purchasing power parity), reported in Table 1.2.

7. Unless otherwise stated, all data reported here are drawn from Procter et al., *Income and Poverty in the United States: 2015.*

8. See, e.g., Richard Florida, *The Rise of the Creative Class—Revisited: Revised and Expanded* (New York: Basic Books, 2014), and Richard J. Murnane

and Frank Levy, *Teaching the New Basic Skills. Principles for Educating Children to Thrive in a Changing Economy* (New York: Free Press, 1996).

9. Cecily R. Hardaway and Vonnie C. McLoyd. "Escaping Poverty and Securing Middle Class Status: How Race and Socioeconomic Status Shape Mobility Prospects for African Americans during the Transition to Adulthood," *Journal of Youth and Adolescence* 38, no. 2 (2009): 242–56.

10. David Erickson et al., *The Enduring Challenge of Concentrated Poverty in America: Case Studies from Communities across the US* (Washington, DC: Federal Reserve System and the Brookings Institution, 2008).

11. Laura Olson, *The Deepwater Horizon Gulf Oil Spill: Response, Resilience, and Recovery* (Washington, DC: The George Washington University Institute for Crisis, Disaster, and Risk Management, 2010).

12. For further discussion, see John Iceland, *Poverty in America: A Handbook* (Berkeley: University of California Press, 2012); James T. Patterson, *America's Struggle against Poverty in the Twentieth Century* (Cambridge, MA: Harvard University Press, 2000).

13. For further discussion of this point, see Amartya Sen, "Editorial: Human Capital and Human Capability," *World Development* 25, no. 12 (1997): 1959–61.

14. Quoted in Patterson, *America's Struggle against Poverty*, 59.

15. Charles A. Murray, *Losing Ground: American Social Policy, 1950–1980* (New York: Basic Books, 1984).

16. Quoted by Nicholas Lemann, "The Unfinished War," *Atlantic Monthly* 262, no. 6 (1988): 37–56.

17. Board of Trustees, *The 2016 Annual Report of the Board of Trustees of the Federal Old-Age and Survivors Insurance and Federal Disability Insurance Trust Funds* (Washington, DC: U.S. Government Printing Office, 2016).

18. Nancy J. Altman, "Demystifying Social Security Financing and the General Fund," *Poverty and Public Policy* 2, no. 1 (2010): 9–16.

19. See Congressional Budget Office, *Federal Housing Assistance for Low-Income Households* (Washington, DC: Congressional Budget Office, 2015).

20. See Alana Semuels, "The Power of Public Housing," *The Atlantic,* September 15, 2015.

21. Paul E. Peterson and Mark Rom, "American Federalism, Welfare Policy, and Residential Choices," *American Political Science Review* 83, no. 3 (1989): 711–28.

22. See William D. Berry, Richard C. Fording, and Russell L. Hanson, "Reassessing the "Race to the Bottom" in State Welfare Policy," *Journal of Politics* 65, no. 2 (2003): 327–49.

23. Craig Volden, "The Politics of Competitive Federalism: A Race to the Bottom in Welfare Benefits?" *American Journal of Political Science* 46, no. 2 (2002): 352–63.

24. See Mark Muro and Sifan Liu, "Why Trump's Factory Job Promises Won't Pan Out—in One Chart," *The Avenue* (Washington, DC: The Brookings Institution, 2016).

25. Harry J. Holzer, "Workforce Development as an Antipoverty Strategy: What Do We Know? What Should We Do?" in *Changing Poverty, Changing Policies*, Maria Cancian and Sheldon Danziger, eds. (New York: Russell Sage Foundation, 2009), 307.

26. Sheena McConnell et al., *Providing Public Workforce Services to Job Seekers: 15-Month Impact Findings on the WIA Adult and Dislocated Worker Programs* (Washington, DC: Mathematica Policy Research and Social Policy Research Associates, 2016).

27. David L. Weimer and Aidan R. Vining, eds., *Investing in the Disadvantaged: Assessing the Benefits and Costs of Social Policies* (Washington, DC: Georgetown University Press, 2009).

28. For an overview, see Deloitte/New Zealand Institute for Economic Research, *State of the State: New Zealand 2016, Social Investment for Our Future* (Wellington: NZIER, 2016).

29. The evidence reported here comes from the New Zealand Treasury, *Characteristics of Children at Greater Risk of Poor Outcomes as Adults*, Analytical Paper 16/01 (Wellington: The Treasury, 2016).

30. David Greenberg, Victoria Deitch, and Gayle Hamilton, *Welfare-to-Work Program Benefits and Costs: A Synthesis of Research* (Washington, DC: MDRC, 2009).

31. Patterson, *America's Struggle Against Poverty*, 174–75.

32. Children's Defense Fund, *End Child Poverty Now* (Washington DC: Children's Defense Fund, 2015), 3. Accessed at: http://www.childrensdefense.org/library/PovertyReport/EndingChildPovertyNow.html.

CHAPTER 9

1. Francis T. Cullen et al., "Public Support for Early Intervention Programs: Implications for a Progressive Policy Agenda," *Crime & Delinquency* 44, no. 2 (1998): 187–204.

2. See Tom Robbins. "A Brutal Beating Wakes Attica's Ghosts," *New York Times,* March 1, 2015, A1. See also Tom Robbins, "Justice Department Reviewing Inmate Abuse by Attica Guards," *New York Times,* May 18, 2015, A14.

3. *Porter v. Nussle,* 534 U.S. 516, 532 (2002).4. See Andrea Jacobs, "Prison Power Corrupts Absolutely: Exploring the Phenomenon of Prison Guard Brutality and the Need to Develop a System of Accountability," *California Western Law Review* 41 (2004): 277–301.

5. See Nancy Wolff et al., "Sexual Violence inside Prisons: Rates of Victimization," *Journal of Urban Health* 83, no. 5 (2006): 835–48. For more recent evidence, see Ramona R. Rantala, Jessica Rexroat, and Allen J. Beck, "Survey of Sexual Violence in Adult Correctional Facilities, 2009–11—Statistical Tables," *Bureau of Justice Statistics,* January 23, 2014.

6. When it was no longer possible to ship convicts to America, the British began shipping them to Australia.

7. David Garland, "The Peculiar Forms of American Capital Punishment," *Punishment: The US Record* 74, no. 2 (2007): 456.

8. Edward L. Ayers, *Vengeance and Justice: Crime and Punishment in the 19th Century American South* (New York: Oxford University Press, 1984).

9. Christian Henrichson and Ruth Delaney, "The Price of Prisons: What Incarceration Costs Taxpayers" *Federal Sentencing Report* 25 (2012), p. 68. See Figure 4.

10. See Matthew R. Durose, Alexia D. Cooper, and Howard N. Snyder, "Recidivism of Prisoners Released in 30 States in 2005: Patterns from 2005 to 2010" (Washington, DC: Bureau of Justice Statistics, 2014).

11. See Seena Fazel and Achim Wolf. "A Systematic Review of Criminal Recidivism Rates Worldwide: Current Difficulties and Recommendations for Best Practice," *PloS One* 10, no. 6 (2015), e0130390.

12. See Jessica Benko, "The Radical Humaneness of Norway's Halden Prison," *New York Times,* March 29, 2015.

13. See Lena Leong, "The Story of Singapore Prison Service: From Custodians of Prisoners to Captains of Life" (Singapore: Civil Service College, 2010), https://www.cscollege.gov.sg/Knowledge/Pages/The-Story-of-Singapore-Prison-Service-From-Custodians-of-Prisoners-to-Captains-of-Life.aspx.

14. For a range of examples, see Darryl K. Brown, "Democracy and Decriminalization," *Texas Law Review* 86, no. 2 (2007): 223–75.

15. A classic statement along these lines is provided by Robert Martinson, "What Works? Questions and Answers about Prison Reform," *The Public Interest* 35, no. 2 (1974): 22–54. Importantly, Martinson retracted his claim that nothing works in an article published five years later. See Robert Martinson, "New Findings, New Views: A Note of Caution Regarding Sentencing Reform," *Hofstra Law Review* 7 (1978): 243–58.

16. See, e.g., William Bennett, John DiIulio, and John Walters, *Body Count: Moral Poverty and How to Win America's War against Crime and Drugs* (New York: Simon & Schuster, 1996).

17. Cullen et al., "Public Support," 188.

18. Marie Gottschalk, "Hiding in Plain Sight: American Politics and the Carceral State," *Annual Review of Political Science* 11 (2008): 235–60.

19. According to Jeff Manza and Christopher Uggen, *Locked Out: Felon Disenfranchisement and American Democracy* (New York: Oxford University Press, 2006).

20. Bruce Western, *Punishment and Inequality in America* (New York: Russell Sage Foundation, 2006).

21. Henrichson and Delaney, *The Price of Prisons*.

22. Kelly Hannah-Moffat, "Actuarial Sentencing: An 'Unsettled' Proposition," *Justice Quarterly* 30, no. 2 (2013): 270–96; Matthew Kleiman, Brian J. Ostrom, and Fred L. Cheesman, "Using Risk Assessment to Inform Sentencing Decisions for Nonviolent Offenders in Virginia," *Crime & Delinquency* 53, no. 1 (2007): 106–32.

23. Judith Greene and Marc Mauer, *Downscaling Prisons: Lessons from Four States* (Washington, DC: The Sentencing Project, March 1, 2010). See http://www.sentencingproject.org/publications/downscaling-prisons-lessons-from-four-states/.

24. Sonja B. Starr, "Evidence-Based Sentencing and the Scientific Rationalization of Discrimination," *Stanford Law Review* 66 (2014): 803–72.

25. Arthur L. Alarcón and Paula Mitchell, "Executing the Will of the Voters? A Roadmap to Mend or End the California's Legislature's Multi-billion-dollar Death Penalty Debacle," *Loyola of Los Angeles Law Review* 44 (2010): S41.

26. Marie Gottschalk, "The Past, Present, and Future of Mass Incarceration in the United States," *Criminology & Public Policy* 10, no. 3 (2011): 483–504.

27. Anne Larason Schneider, "Public-Private Partnerships in the US Prison System," *American Behavioral Scientist* 43, no. 1 (1999): 192–208.

28. John D. Donahue, *The Privatization Decision: Public Ends, Private Means* (New York: Basic Books, 1989).

29. See Alexander Volokh, "Prison Accountability and Performance Measures," *Emory Law Journal* 63 (2013): 339–416.

30. Shawn D. Bushway, "So Policy Makers Drive Incarceration—Now What?" *Criminology & Public Policy* 10, no. 2 (2011): 327–333; Chris Fox and Kevin Albertson, "Could Economics Solve the Prison Crisis?" *Probation Journal* 57, no. 3 (2010): 263–80.

31. Steve Aos, Marna Miller, and Elizabeth Drake, *Evidence-Based Public Policy Options to Reduce Future Prison Construction, Criminal Justice Costs, and Crime Rates* (Olympia, WA: Washington State Institute for Public Policy, October 2006), 2, http://www.wsipp.wa.gov/ReportFile/952/Wsipp_Evidence-Based-Public-Policy-Options-to-Reduce-Future-Prison-Construction-Criminal-Justice-Costs-and-Crime-Rates_Full-Report.pdf.

32. Susan B. Tucker and Eric Cadora, "Justice Reinvestment—to Invest in Public Safety by Reallocating Justice Dollars to Refinance Education, Housing, Healthcare and Jobs," *Ideas for an Open Society* 3, no. 3 (2003): 1–8.

33. The effects of incarceration on family members and other associates of inmates are given detailed exploration in Saneta deVuono-Powell et al., *Who Pays? The True Cost of Incarceration on Families* (Oakland, CA: Ella Baker Center, Forward Together, Research Action Design, 2015).

34. Todd Clear, "A Private-Sector, Incentives-Based Model for Justice Reinvestment," *Criminology & Public Policy* 10, no. 3 (2011): 585–608.

35. Council of State Governments Justice Center, *Lessons from the States: Reducing Recidivism and Curbing Corrections Costs through Justice Reinvestment* (Washington, DC: Council of State Governments Justice Center, 2013), https://csgjusticecenter.org/wp-content/uploads/2013/04/FINAL_State_Lessons_mbedit.pdf.

36. Ibid.

37. Michael Mintrom and Joannah Luetjens, "Creating Public Value: Tightening Connections between Policy Design and Public Management." *Policy Studies Journal* 45, no. 1 (2017): 170–90.

38. As documented by Green and Mauer, *Downscaling Prisons*.

39. William D. Bales and Alex R. Piquero, "Assessing the Impact of Imprisonment on Recidivism," *Journal of Experimental Criminology* 8, no. 1 (2012): 71–101.

40. Christy A. Visher and Jeremy Travis, "Transitions from Prison to Community: Understanding Individual Pathways," *Annual Review of Sociology* 29 (2003): 89–113.

41. Faye S. Taxman, "Crime Control in the Twenty-First Century: Science-Based Supervision," *Journal of Crime and Justice* 35, no. 2 (2012): 135–44.

42. See, e.g., James Bonta et al., "An Experimental Demonstration of Training Probation Officers in Evidence-Based Community Supervision," *Criminal Justice and Behavior* 38, no. 11 (2011): 1127–1148; and Christopher Trotter, "The Impact of Different Supervision Practices in Community Corrections: Cause for Optimism," *Australian and New Zealand Journal of Criminology* 29, no. 1 (1996): 29–46.

43. See Aos et al. (2006), 9, Exhibit 4, which provides cost and benefit calculations for cognitive-behavioral therapy in prison or the community.

44. Guy Bourgon and Leticia Gutierrez, "The General Responsivity Principle in Community Supervision: The Importance of Probation Officers Using Cognitive Intervention Techniques and Its Influence on Recidivism," *Journal of Crime and Justice* 35, no. 2 (2012): 149–66.

45. See also Bonta et al. (2011).

46. Trotter, "The Impact of Different Supervision."

47. Ibid., 32.

48. Taxman, "Crime Control in the Twenty-First Century."

49. The following information is drawn from E. Ann Carson, *Prisoners in 2014* (Washington, DC: U.S. Department of Justice, Bureau of Justice Statistics, September 17, 2015, NCJ 248955), 15.

50. Russell J. Skiba et al., "Race Is Not Neutral: A National Investigation of African American and Latino Disproportionality in School Discipline," *School Psychology Review* 40, no. 1 (2011): 85–107.

51. Robert Balfanz et al., "High-Poverty Secondary Schools and the Juvenile Justice System: How Neither Helps the Other and How That Could Change," *New Directions for Youth Development* 99 (2003): 71–89.

52. Matt Cregor and Damon Hewitt, "Dismantling the School-to-Prison Pipeline: A Survey from the Field," *Poverty & Race* 20, no. 1 (2011): 5–7.

53. Melissa Hickman Barlow, "Sustainable Justice: 2012 Presidential Address to the Academy of Criminal Justice Sciences," *Justice Quarterly* 30, no. 1 (2012): 1–17.

54. Council of State Governments Justice Center, *Lessons from the States.*

55. John DiIulio, "Help Wanted: Economists, Crime and Public Policy," *The Journal of Economic Perspectives* 10, no. 1 (1996): 3.

56. Shadd Maruna, "Lessons for Justice Reinvestment from Restorative Justice and the Justice Model Experience," *Criminology & Public Policy* 10, no. 3 (2011): 661–69.

CHAPTER 10

1. Steve Jobs, Commencement Address, Stanford University, June 12, 2005. Prepared print version reproduced in *Stanford News,* June 14, 2005. See http://news.stanford.edu/news/2005/june15/jobs-061505.html.

2. Lewis M. Branscomb, "The False Dichotomy: Scientific Creativity and Utility," *Issues in Science and Technology* 16, no. 1 (Fall 1999): 66–72; Donald Stokes, *Pasteur's Quadrant: Basic Science and Technological Innovation* (Washington, DC: The Brookings Institution, 1997).

3. Jon Gertner, *The Idea Factory: Bell Labs and the Great Age of American Innovation* (New York: Penguin, 2012).

4. Steve Coll, *The Deal of the Century: The Breakup of AT&T* (New York: Atheneum, 1986).

5. See Martin Kenney and David Mowery, eds., *Public Universities and Regional Growth: Insights from the University of California* (Stanford, CA: Stanford University Press, 2014).

6. See Michael Ian Luger and Harvey A. Goldstein. *Technology in the Garden: Research Parks and Regional Economic Development* (Chapel Hill: University of North Carolina Press, 1991).

7. Inaugural Address of Daniel Coit Gilman as first president of Johns Hopkins University, February 22, 1876. See http://webapps.jhu.edu/jhuniverse/information_about_hopkins/about_jhu/daniel_coit_gilman/.

8. Daniel J. Kevles, *The Physicists: The History of a Scientific Community in Modern America* (Cambridge, MA: Harvard University Press, 1995), 62.

9. Ibid., 341.

10. Homer A. Neal, Tobin L. Smith, and Jennifer B. McCormick, *Beyond Sputnik: U.S. Science Policy in the Twenty-First Century* (Ann Arbor, MI: University of Michigan Press, 2008).

11. Ibid, 3.

12. Kevles, *The Physicists.*

13. Stokes, *Pasteur's Quadrant.*

14. Alvin Weinberg, "Impact of Large-Scale Science on the United States," *Science* 134 (1961): 161–64.

15. Rachael Lallensack, "Budget Battle Looms for US Science Programmes, *Nature* 549, no.17 (2017), http://www.nature.com/news/budget-battle-looms-for-us-science-programmes-1.22548

16. Michael Mintrom, "Policy Entrepreneurs and Controversial Science: Governing Human Embryonic Stem Cell Research," *Journal of European Public Policy* 20 (2013): 442–57.

17. Ruha Benjamin, *People's Science: Bodies and Rights on the Stem Cell Frontier* (Stanford, CA: Stanford University Press, 2013).

18. Kendall Powell, "The Future of the Postdoc," *Nature* 520 (2015): 144–47, http://www.nature.com/news/the-future-of-the-postdoc-1.17253; Ed Michaels, Helen Handfield-Jones, and Beth Axelrod, *The War for Talent* (Boston, MA: Harvard Business School Press, 2001).

19. AnnaLee Saxenian, *Regional Advantage: Culture and Competition in Silicon Valley and Route 128* (Cambridge, MA: Harvard University Press, 1994).

20. David C. Mowery et al., *Ivory Tower and Industrial Innovation: University-Industry Technology Transfer before and after the Bayh–Dole Act* (Stanford, CA: Stanford University Press, 2004).

21. See, e.g., Lewis M. Branscomb and James H. Keller, *Investing in Innovation: Creating a Research Innovation Policy That Works* (Cambridge, MA: MIT Press, 1998).

22. Richard Florida, *Cities and the Creative Class* (London: Routledge, 2004); Richard Florida, *The Flight of the Creative Class: The New Global Competition for Talent* (New York: HarperCollins, 2005).

23. Kay Husbands Fealing et al., eds. *The Science of Science Policy: A Handbook* (Stanford, CA: Stanford University Press, 2011), 1.

24. See U.S. Joint Economic Committee, *The Benefits of Medical Research and the Role of the NIH* (May 2000). See http://www.faseb.org/Portals/2/LinkClickLinks/nih_research_benefits.pdf.

25. See, e.g., Lynn G. Zucker, Michael R. Darby, and Jeff S. Armstrong, "Commercializing Knowledge: University Science, Knowledge Capture, and Firm Performance in Biotechnology," *Management Science* 48, no. 1 (2002): 138–53.

26. Andrew Gunn and Michael Mintrom, "Education Policy Change in Europe: Academic Research Funding and the Impact Agenda," *European Education: Issues and Studies* 48, no. 4 (2016): 241–57.

27. Michael Mintrom, "Universities in the Knowledge Economy: A Comparative Analysis of Nested Institutions," *Journal of Comparative Policy Analysis* 11 (2009): 327–53.

28. See Economy League of Greater Philadelphia, *A Continuing Record of Achievement: The Economic Impact of Ben Franklin Technology Partners 2002–2006* (2009), http://benfranklin.org/wp-content/uploads/bftp_exec_sum_021309.pdf.

29. Pennsylvania Economy League and KLIOS Consulting, *Achievement in Uncertain Times: The Economic Impact of Ben Franklin Technology Partners, A Continuing Record of Achievement [2007–2011]* (Harrisburg, PA: Pennsylvania Economic League and KLIOS Consulting, 2013). See http://benfranklin.org/wp-content/uploads/BFTP.PEL_exec-summary_Final.pdf.

30. Ibid.

31. See https://www.nasa.gov/pdf/286592main_African_American_Astronauts_FS.pdf.

32. See Salman Khan, *The One World Schoolhouse: Education Reimagined* (New York: Grand Central Publishing, 2012).

33. For example, see "Baltimore: New Smartphone App Sends Police Incident Videos to Lawyers, Police Hand Over Probe into Freddie Gray

Death," *ABC News (Australia)*, April 30, 2017, http://www.abc.net.au/news/2015-05-01/us-smartphone-app-sends-police-incident-videos-to-lawyers/6436064.

34. Saxenian, *The New Argonauts*.

CHAPTER 11

1. Christopher M. Jones and Daniel M. Kammen, "Quantifying Carbon Footprint Reduction Opportunities for U.S. Households and Communities," *Environmental Science & Technology* 45, no. 9 (2011): 4088–95.

2. See Keynyn Brysse et al., "Climate Change Prediction: Erring on the Side of Least Drama?" *Global Environmental Change* 23, no. 1 (2013): 327–37. See also Intergovernmental Panel on Climate Change (IPCC), "Summary for Policymakers" in *Climate Change 2007: The Physical Science Basis. Contribution of Working Group I to the Fourth Assessment Report of the Intergovernmental Panel on Climate Change,* Susan Solomon et al., eds. (United Kingdom: Cambridge University Press, 2007).

3. James Hansen et al., "Assessing 'Dangerous Climate Change': Required Reduction of Carbon Emissions to Protect Young People, Future Generations and Nature," *PLoS ONE,* 8 (2013): e81648.

4. Alexandra Adams, "Summary of Information concerning the Ecological and Economic Impacts of the BP Deepwater Horizon Oil Spill Disaster," Natural Resources Defense Council Issue Paper (IP: 15–04-A), New York, 2015.

5. *The Economist,* "A Costly Mistake," July 2, 2015.

6. Nicholas Z. Muller, Robert Mendelsohn, and William Nordhaus, "Environmental Accounting for Pollution in the United States Economy," *American Economic Review* (2011): 1649–75.

7. Garrett Hardin, "Tragedy of the Commons," *Science* 162 (1968): 1243–48.

8. See, e.g., Mancur Olson, *The Logic of Collective Action: Public Goods and the Theory of Groups* (Cambridge, MA: Harvard University Press, 1965).

9. Hardin, "Tragedy of the Commons," 1244.

10. See AQICN.org.

11. See "Beijing Raises 'Red Alert' Threshold for Air Pollution Warning," *The Guardian,* February 22, 2016.

12. See World Health Organization, *Health Effects of Particulate Matter: Policy Implications for Countries in Eastern Europe, Caucasus and Central Asia* (Copenhagen: World Health Organization, 2013).

13. Gao, J. et al. (2016), "Improving Air Pollution Control Policy in China—A Perspective Based on Cost–Benefit Analysis," *Science of the Total Environment* 543 (2016): 307–14.

14. J. M. Neeson, *Commoners: Common Right, Enclosure, and Social Change in England, 1700–1820* (Cambridge, UK: Cambridge University Press, 1993).

15. Richard G. Newell, James N. Sanchirico, and Suzi Kerr, "Fishing Quota Markets," *Journal of Environmental Economics and Management* 49, no. 3 (2005): 437–62.

16. See, e.g., Sergey Paltsev et al., "Assessment of US GHG Cap-and-Trade Proposals," *Climate Policy* 8, no. 4 (2008): 395–420.

17. This view is stated by Michael E. Kraft and Norman J. Vig, eds., *Environmental Policy: New Directions for the Twenty-First Century* (Washington, DC: CQ Press, 2013).

18. Charles L. Schultze, *The Public Use of Private Interest* (Washington, DC: Brookings Institution Press, 1976).

19. Eugene Bardach and Robert Allen Kagan. *Going by the Book: The Problem of Regulatory Unreasonableness* (Piscataway, NJ: Transaction Publishers, 1982).

20. See, e.g., John W. Kingdon, *Agendas, Alternatives, and Public Policies,* updated 2nd ed. (Boston: Longman, 2011).

21. Art Swift, "Americans Again Pick Environment over Economic Growth" (Gallup Press release, March 14, 2014), http://www.gallup.com/poll/168017/americans-again-pick-environment-economic-growth.aspx.

22. David P. Daniels et al., "Public Opinion on Environmental Policy in the United States," *The Oxford Handbook of U.S. Environmental Policy,*

Sheldon Kamieniecki and Michael E. Kraft, eds. (New York: Oxford University Press, 2013), 461–86.

23. Barry Rabe, "Contested Federalism and American Climate Policy," *Publius* 31, no. 3 (2011): 494–521.

24. Barry Rabe, "Racing to the Top, the Bottom, or the Middle of the Pack? The Evolving State Government Role in Environmental Protection," in *Environmental Policy: New Directions for the Twenty-First Century,* eds. Michael E. Kraft and Norman J. Vig (Washington, DC: CQ Press, 2013), 30–53.

25. Barry Rabe, *Statehouse and Greenhouse: The Emerging Politics of American Climate Policy* (Washington, DC: Brookings, 2004).

26. Jeffrey M. Berry and Clyde Wilcox, *The Interest Group Society,* 5th ed. (New York: Longman, 2009); Charles E. Lindblom, "The Market as Prison," *The Journal of Politics* 44, no. 2 (1982): 324–36.

27. Norman J. Vig, "The American Presidency and Environmental Policy," in *The Oxford Handbook of U.S. Environmental Policy,* Sheldon Kamieniecki and Michael E. Kraft, eds. (New York: Oxford University Press, 2013): 306–28.

28. A. Myrick Freeman III, "Environmental Policy since Earth Day I: What Have We Gained?" *Journal of Economic Perspectives* 16, no. 1 (2002): 125–46.

29. Muller, Mendelsohn, and Nordhaus, "Environmental Accounting for Pollution."

30. This point was made well by Milton Friedman, *Capitalism and Freedom* (Chicago: University of Chicago Press, 1962).

31. Sheila M. Olmstead, "The Role of Market Incentives in Environmental Policy," in *The Oxford Handbook of U.S. Environmental Policy* (2013): 553–81.

32. Lori Snyder Bennear and Robert N. Stavins, "Second-Best Theory and the Use of Multiple Policy Instruments," *Environmental and Resource Economics* 37, no. 1 (2007): 111–29.

33. Lawrence H. Goulder and Robert N. Stavins, "Challenges from State-Federal Interactions in US Climate Change Policy," *American Economic Review* 101, no. 3 (2011): 253–57.

34. Elinor Ostrom, "Polycentric Systems for Coping with Collective Action and Global Environmental Change," *Global Environmental Change* 20 (2010): 550–57.

35. Ibid., 553.

36. See, e.g. Dorothy M. Daley, "Public Participation, Citizen Engagement, and Environmental Decision Making," chap. 22 in *The Oxford Handbook of U.S. Environmental Policy,* Sheldon Kamieniecki and Michael E. Kraft, eds. (New York: Oxford University Press, 2013); Mark Lubell and Brian Segee, "Conflict and Cooperation in Natural Resource Management," in *Environmental Policy,* 8th ed., Norman J. Vig and Michael E. Kraft, eds. (Washington, DC: CQ Press, 2013), 185–205.

37. Marcelo Prince and Carlos A. Tovar, "How Much U.S. Oil and Gas Comes from Fracking?" *Wall Street Journal,* April 1, 2015, http://blogs. wsj.com/corporate-intelligence/2015/04/01/ how-much-u-s-oil-and-gas-comes-from-fracking/.

38. Robert B. Jackson et al., "The Environmental Costs and Benefits of Fracking," *Annual Review of Environment and Resources* 39 (2014): 327–62.

39. Will Oremus, "New York's Fracking Ban Is about Politics, Not Science. And That's Just Fine," *Future Tense: The Citizen's Guide to the Future* (blog), December 17, 2014, http://www. slate.com/blogs/ future_tense/2014/12/17/cuomo_s_new_york_ fracking_ban_the_politics_of_procrastination.html.

40. New York State Department of Health, *A Public Health Review of High Volume Hydraulic Fracturing for Shale Gas Development* (Albany: New York State Department of Health, December 2014), http://media.syracuse.com/news/ other/2014/12/17/NYS%20%20DOH%20 fracking%20health%20report.pdf.

41. Robert B. Jackson et al., "The Environmental Costs and Benefits of Fracking," *Annual Review of Environment and Resources* 39 (2014): 327–62.

42. Freeman, "Environmental Policy," 126.

43. Lauraine G. Chestnut and David M. Mills, "A Fresh Look at the Benefits and Costs of the US Acid Rain Program," *Journal of Environmental Management* 77, no. 3 (2005): 252–66.

44. Chestnut and Mills, "Fresh Look," 252–66.

45. Tony Dutzik, Elizabeth Ridlington, and Rob Sargent, *A Double Success: Tackling Global Warming While Growing the Economy with an Improved Regional Greenhouse Gas Initiative* (New York: Environment New York Research and Policy Center, 2013).

46. Ibid., 16.

47. Ken Berlin et al., *State Clean Energy Finance Banks: New Investment Facilities for Clean Energy Deployment* (Washington, DC: Brookings, 2012).

48. Ibid.

49. Kyle Siler-Evans et al., "Regional Variations in the Health, Environmental, and Climate Benefits of Wind and Solar Generation," *Proceedings of the National Academy of Sciences* 110, no. 29 (2013): 11768–73.

50. Ibid.

51. See Charles M. Blow, "Inequality in the Air We Breathe?" *New York Times,* January 21, 2015, http://www.nytimes.com/2015/01/22/opinion/charles-blow-inequality-in-the-air-we-breathe.html.

52. Ibid.

53. See Robert D. Bullard, *Dumping in Dixie: Race, Class, and Environmental Quality,* 3rd ed. (Boulder, CO: Westview Press, 1994/2000).

54. See Paul Mohai, David Pellow, and J. Timmons Roberts, "Environmental Justice," *Annual Review of Environment and Resources* 34 (2009): 405–430; Rachel Morello-Frosch and Bill M. Jesdale, "Separate and Unequal: Residential Segregation and Estimated Cancer Risks Associated with Ambient Air Toxics in US Metropolitan Areas," *Environmental Health Perspectives* 114, no. 3 (2006): 386–93.

55. Evan McKenzie, *Privatopia: Homeowner Associations and the Rise of Residential Private Government* (New Haven, CT: Yale University Press, 1994); Evan McKenzie, *Beyond Privatopia: Rethinking Residential Private Government* (Washington, DC: Urban Institute Press, 2011).

CHAPTER 12

1. See Jonathan Boston, *Governing for the Future: Designing Democratic Institutions for a Better Tomorrow* (Bingley, UK: Emerald Group Publishing, 2016).

2. Paul Manna and Patrick McGuinn, eds., *Education Governance for the Twenty-First Century: Overcoming the Structural Barriers to School Reform* (Washington, DC: Brookings Institution Press, 2013).

3. The Ash Center has produced many publications on innovation in government. See, for example, Sandford F. Borins, *The Persistence of Innovation in Government* (Washington, DC: The Brookings Institution/Ash Center Series, 2014). The Ash Center's website is http://ash.harvard.edu/.

4. See John Hattie, *Visible Learning: A Synthesis of Over 800 Meta-analyses Relating to Achievement* (New York: Routledge, 2009).

5. For an extended discussion on people skills needed for policy making, see Michael Mintrom, *People Skills for Policy Analysts* (Washington, DC: Georgetown University Press, 2003).

6. Michael Mintrom and Joannah Luetjens, "Creating Public Value: Tightening Connections between Policy Design and Public Management," *Policy Studies Journal* 45, no. 1 (2017): 170–90.

7. Michael Mintrom and Joannah Luetjens, "Design Thinking in Policymaking Processes: Opportunities and Challenges," *Australian Journal of Public Administration* 75, no. 3 (2016): 391–402.

8. Jean Hartley et al., "Public Value and Political Astuteness in the Work of Public Managers: The Art of the Possible," *Public Administration* 93, no. 1 (2015): 195–211.

9. Michael Mintrom, "Writing for Multiple Audiences," chap. 8 in *People Skills for Policy Analysts* (Washington, DC: Georgetown University Press, 2003).

INDEX

Note: page numbers followed by *f* and *t* refer to figures and tables, respectively. Page numbers in *italics* refer to photographs.

A